READER'S DIGEST

READER'S DIGEST

ASK
THE
FAMILY
HANDY-
MAN

Reader's
Digest

The Reader's Digest Association, Inc., Pleasantville, New York

Ask the Family Handyman

STAFF

■ PROJECT

Senior Project Editor
Julie Trelstad

Senior Project Designer
Carol Nehring

Senior Editor
Don Earnest

Associate Editors
Joseph Hurst-Wajsczuk
Elizabeth Wagner

Assistant Editor
Karen Liljedahl

Associate Designers
Jim Cozby
Edward Jacobus
Robert Steimle

Copy Editor
Katherine G. Ness

Indexer
Felice Levy

**Editorial Director,
Do-it-Yourself Books**
David Schiff

**Design Director,
Do-it-Yourself Books**
Sandra Berinstein

**■ READER'S DIGEST
GENERAL BOOKS**

Editor-in-Chief
Christopher Cavanaugh

Art Director
Joan Mazzeo

**■ FAMILY HANDYMAN
MAGAZINE**

Editor
Gary Havens

Executive Editor
Ken Collier

Photo page 272 courtesy the National
Fenestration Rating Council, Inc., Silver
Springs, Maryland

Reader's Digest and the Pegasus logo are
registered trademarks of The Reader's
Digest Association, Inc.

Printed in the United States of America

Second Printing, December 1999.

about this book...

INTRODUCTION

This book is packed with answers to your questions about improving, maintaining, and repairing your home. They are real questions that were sent to the Ask Handyman column of The Family Handyman magazine— a column that has been one of the magazine's most popular feature since its first issue in 1951.

Ask The Family Handyman is organized into two parts. Part One, "Your House Inside" answers questions about walls, ceilings, room painting, wallcoverings, tile, flooring, interior trim, paneling, stairs, interior doors, cabinets, countertops, and built-ins. Part Two, "Your House Outside," provides answers about siding, exterior trim, roofs, gutters, windows, exterior doors, and house painting.

Some of the questions have popped up in The Family Handyman magazine again and again through the years, although the answers change. In the first issue, for example, a reader asked what to do about a squeaky floor. The answer then involved shims and finish nails. Today's answer, (page 54) uses a more recent invention—finish screws which hold better than nails and let you skip the shims.

Other questions do change with the times. Back in 1951, a reader asked how he might convert his old-fashioned raised-panel doors into the "modern flush type." The solution was to glue and nail plywood to both sides. Today, of course, homeowners are more likely to want to upgrade their flush doors to the classic look of raised panels. You'll find out how to do that on page 81.

This book does more than answer specific questions. Special feature boxes throughout provide the background information you need. The features called "How is it Done" provide step-by-step instructions for home projects. Other features called "What Do I Need?" help you gather the tools and materials you need to get the projects done. Still other features present useful new products or provide safety tips.

In compiling and editing Ask the Family Handyman we have focused foremost on providing practical information that will help you the next time your faucet fails or your house needs re-roofing.

We have tried to make the information accessible and fun to read. We hope that for years to come, you'll pull this book off the shelf and Ask the Family Handyman whenever you have a question about maintaining or improving your home.

Library of Congress Cataloging in Publication Data

Ask the Family handyman / Reader's Digest
        p. cm.
        ISBN 0-7621-0142-3
        1. Dwellings—Maintenance and repair Miscellanea, I. Reader's
Digest Association. II. Family handyman.
TH4815.A85   1999
643'.7—dc21   99-24913

Contents

10 YOUR HOUSE INSIDE

12 Drywall
Installing Drywall
Taping Drywall
Repairing Drywall
22 Plaster Walls
Repairing Plaster
Hanging Things on Walls
24 Ceilings
Repairing and Improving
26 Painting
Preparing Walls
Stripping Paint
Selecting and Using Paint
Decorative Techniques
Painting Masonry
Painting Woodwork
Painting Cabinets
Paint Cleanup
38 Wallcoverings
Repairing Wallpaper
Preparing to Paper
Hanging Wallcoverings
Wallpaper Finishing Touches
44 Ceramic Tile
Planning a Tiling Job
Installing Underlayment
Installing Tile
Tile Care and Repair
54 Wood Flooring
Choosing Wood Flooring

Installing Wood Flooring
Repairing Wood Floors
Repairing a Wood Finish
62 Carpeting
Installing Carpeting
Carpet Care and Repair
66 Vinyl and Other Flooring
Installing Vinyl Flooring
Vinyl Care and Repair
Marble, Slate, and Cork
70 Trim
Types of Trim
Repairing Trim
Installing Trim
76 Paneling
Wood Panelling
78 Stairs
Repairing Stairs
80 Interior Doors
Installing Interior Doors
Repairing Interior Doors
Pocket and Folding Doors
88 Cabinets
Installing Cabinets
Renewing Cabinets
Repairing Cabinets
95 Countertops
Repariing Countertops
98 Built-ins
Built-Ins

100 YOUR HOUSE OUTSIDE

102 Siding
Wood Siding
Stucco Siding
Vinyl and Other Siding
Brick Siding
108 Exterior Trim
Trim
110 Roofs
Installing a New Roof
Repairing Asphalt Shingles
Cedar Shingles and Shakes
Metal and Tile Roofs
116 Gutters
Installing and Repairing Gutters
118 Windows
Window Repair

Storm Windows
Replacement Windows
Energy
128 Exterior Doors
Installing Doors
Door Repairs
Security
Garage Doors
140 Housepainting
Selecting Paint and Gear
Surface Preparation
Painting Siding
Painting Brick and Stucco
Painting Doors and Details
Cleaning Up

Contents

150 BUILDING AND REMODELING

152 Foundations
Foundation Repair

156 House Structure
Structure Basics
Bearing Walls
Structural Problems

160 House Framing
Buying Lumber
Nails and Fasteners
Framing Walls
Framing Floors
Framing Ceilings

170 Carpentry
Tape Measures
Measuring and Marking
Nailing Techniques

176 Workshop Tools
Tooling Up for DIY Projects

178 Remodeling
Heavy Lifting
Regulations
Basement
Storage Solutions
Design Considerations
Converting Decks and Porches

192 HOUSE SYSTEMS

194 Plumbing
Small Bath Plumbing
Metal Pipe
Plastic Pipe
Toilet Repair
Installing Toilets
Clogged Pipes
Drains
Faucets
Shower Repairs
Kitchen Sinks
Fixtures
Bathtubs
Water Heaters
Water Heater Repairs

230 Electrical
Circuit Breakers and Fuses
Electrical Grounding
Electrical Safety
Electrical Wiring
Outlets
Ground Fault Circuit
    Interrupters
Switches
Lighting Fixtures
Recessed Lighting
Light Bulbs
Ceiling Fans
Motion Sensors and Doorbells

254 Appliances
Ovens and Stoves
Refrigerators and Freezers
Dishwashers
Washing Machines
Dryers

264 HOME COMFORT

266 Weatherproofing
Types of Insulation
Upgrading Insulation
Insulation Strategies
Air Leaks

276 Heating
Ducts and Heat Pumps
Furnaces and Thermostats
Fireplaces
Chimneys

288 Cooling
Air Conditioners

290 Ventilation
Fans
Vents

294 Air Quality
Indoor Pollution
Fire Prevention

298 Humidity
Condensation, Mildew, and
    Moisture

Contents

302 WORKSHOP

304 Workshop Safety
Safety Gear

306 Tools and Materials
Small Shop Strategies
Wood
Tool Repair
Clamps
Sharpening
Cutting Skills
Table Saws
Routers

Sanders
Drills
Grinders
Glues

328 Repair and Finishing
Finishing Wood
Clear Finishes
Finishing Problems
Furniture Finish Repairs
Furniture Repairs

338 OUTDOOR DO-IT-YOURSELF

340 Paving
Sidewalks
Sidewalk and Patio Repair
Driveway Repair

346 Decks
Care and Repair
Deck Finishes

352 Fences
Installation and Repair
Sheds and Outbuildings

356 Lawn and Garden
Lawns
Mulches
Planting and Pruning Trees
Pest Control

366 Outdoor Equipment
Lawn Mowers
Tool Repair
Grills
Snow Throwers

372 INDEX

Drywall

12 Installing Drywall
16 Taping Drywall
20 Repairing Drywall

Plaster Walls

22 Repairing Plaster
23 Hanging Things on Walls

Ceilings

24 Repairing and Improving

Painting

26 Preparing Walls
28 Stripping Paint
30 Selecting and Using Paint
32 Decorative Techniques
33 Painting Masonry
34 Painting Woodwork
36 Painting Cabinets
37 Paint Cleanup

Wallcoverings

38 Repairing Wallcoverings
39 Preparing to Paper
40 Hanging Wallcoverings
42 Wallpaper Finishing Touches

Ceramic Tile

44 Planning a Tiling Job
46 Installing Underlayment
48 Installing Tile
52 Tile Care and Repair

Wood Flooring

54 Choosing Wood Flooring
56 Installing Wood Flooring
58 Repairing Wood Floors
60 Repairing a Wood Finish

Carpeting

62 Installing Carpeting
64 Carpet Care and Repair

Vinyl and Other Flooring

66 Installing Vinyl Flooring
68 Vinyl Care and Repair
69 Marble, Slate, and Cork

Your
House
Inside

Trim

70   Types of Trim
71   Repairing Trim
72   Installing Trim

Paneling

76   Wood Paneling

Stairs

78   Repairing Stairs

Interior Doors

80   Installing Interior Doors
82   Repairing Interior Doors
86   Pocket and Folding Doors

Cabinets

88   Installing Cabinets
92   Renewing Cabinets
94   Repairing Cabinets

Countertops

95   Repairing Countertops

Built-Ins

98   Built-Ins

INSTALLING DRYWALL

Nails vs. Screws

Q. ***When I see pros hanging drywall, they use screws. I've always used nails. Which is better?***

Either type of fastener will do the job, but thanks to electric screw guns and cordless drills, most pros prefer screws over nails. Unlike the nails, electric drivers quickly drive screws to the correct depth, automatically, without ever damaging the drywall. Screws have greater holding power and can be spaced 8 inches apart along the edges of a panel and 12 inches apart inside the panels (nails need to be spaced every 7 inches). Screws are also easier to remove.

Whether you use screws or nails, proper fastening technique is critical for a good job. Sink the fastener head just far enough below the drywall surface so that you can hide it with joint compound. Be careful not to drive the fastener so deep that it breaks through the facing paper or crushes the gypsum core. Use 1⅜-inch nails and 1⅝-inch screws for both ½-inch and ⅝-inch drywall.

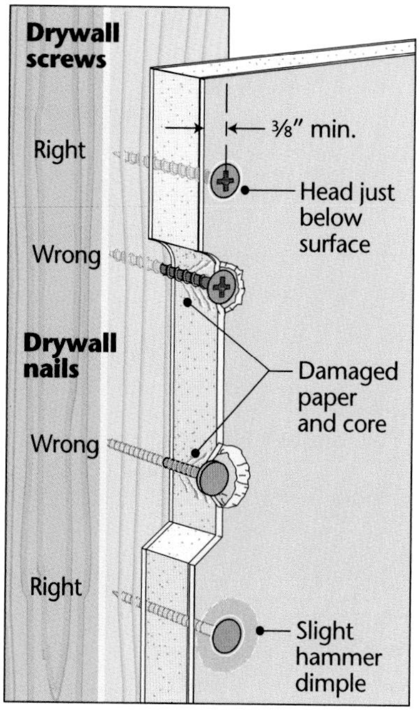
Drywall screws
⅜" min.
Right
Head just below surface
Wrong
Drywall nails
Damaged paper and core
Wrong
Right
Slight hammer dimple

BUYING DRYWALL

Drywall comes in thicknesses ranging from ¼ inch to ⅝ inch; but ½ inch is the most common. A standard sheet measures 4 x 8 feet. Longer sheets—typically 12 feet—reduce the number of seams to tape but are more difficult to maneuver and lift. Fire-resistant drywall is required by code in fire-prone areas, and moisture-resistant drywall, sometimes called greenboard, is needed in high-moisture areas.

To estimate the number of sheets of drywall you'll need for a wall, multiply the wall's width by its height, add 15 percent for waste, then divide by 32 (or 48 for a 12-foot sheet).

COMMON SIZES	USE
¼ in., ⅜ in.	For covering existing walls (¼ in.) and ceilings (⅜ in.); flexes for curved walls. Often a special order.
½ in.	Most common choice for residential walls and ceilings.
½ in. fire-resistant	For garages and other fire-prone areas.
½ in. moisture-resistant	For semi-damp areas, especially under tiles. (Use cement backer board around tubs and showers, p.46.)
⅝ in. regular or fire-resistant	Gives added durability, sound-deadening, and fire protection. Significantly heavier.

Silent Helper

Q. ***Is there some easy way to prop up drywall while I'm attaching it to the ceiling?***

To hold up ceiling panels, you can make a simple support called a deadman or T-brace (see Steps 1 and 2, facing page). It's easy to make with a couple of 2 x 4's. Just measure the distance from the floor to the ceiling joists, and cut a 2 x 4 so that it's 1½ inches shorter than that length. Then cut another 3-foot length of 2 x 4 and nail it flat on the end of the first one. Wedge the deadman under the panel to hold up the drywall.

Drywall Meets Brick

Q. ***I'm installing a low divider wall that abuts a brick wall. How do I finish the edge where the drywall meets the brick?***

Your best bet is to install a metal channel called a J-bead (see Drywall Materials, p.17) along the drywall edge that butts against the brick. The drywall edge fits into the J-bead, creating a crisp line, and the bead's raised edge makes it easy to apply joint compound. Protect the brick with masking tape and paper; joint compound and paint are difficult to remove from masonry.

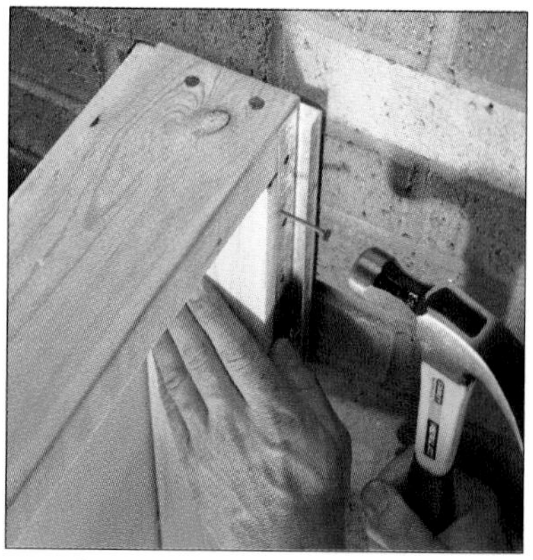

Use J-bead to edge drywall next to brick.

HANGING DRYWALL

Always work from top to bottom when you hang drywall: hang the ceiling panels first, then the walls. Hang the wall panels horizontally, working from the ceiling down. On both the ceiling and the walls, be sure to stagger the panels so that the seams between panels don't line up with the seams in the adjoining row.

Few walls and ceilings are flat and square; measure carefully to make sure each sheet fits. Before putting the first panel in a row against the wall, make sure its free end will fall along the middle of a joist or a stud. If not, trim the wall end of the panel. Always put cut edges against the wall and straight factory edges together to form tight seams. Don't worry about gaps less than ⅜ inch; you can fill them later when taping.

Here are some additional tips:
- Before you start, turn off the power to a room's electrical boxes at the main service panel.
- Drywall is heavy; ask a friend or two to help. For ceiling work, make a T-brace (see Silent Helper, facing page). If you must work alone, consider renting a drywall jack (see Hanging Drywall Alone, p.14).
- To help you position fasteners, mark the ceiling joists' locations on the top plate of the stud wall. Mark the studs' locations on the floor and the ceiling.
- Make a cutout for a ceiling fixture box as you would for a wall box (see Step 5, below).

Note: We used green water-resistant drywall here for photo clarity. It's designed for use in semi-damp areas. Check your local building code for guidance.

1 Starting in a corner of the ceiling, shove the first drywall panel against the wall, prop a T-brace (or helper) under the wall end, and hoist it into place.

2 Fasten the panel to the joists with 1¼-in. drywall screws, spaced 12 in. apart. Along the edges, space screws 8 in. apart and stay ⅜ in. in from the edge.

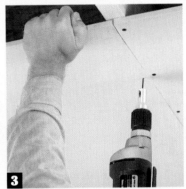

3 Butt the next panel against the first and screw it in place. Continue to the opposite wall. Then complete the other ceiling rows, staggering the seams.

4 Lift the first wall panel against the ceiling. Rest the panel on a few nails for support; then screw it to the studs. Cut out doors and windows later.

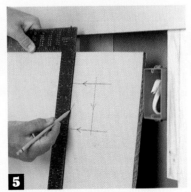

5 Measure and mark electrical box cutouts with a tape measure and square. Drill holes in two opposite corners and cut out the opening with a drywall saw.

6 To position a lower wall panel, lift it against the upper panels with a pry bar and wood block. The remaining gap at the bottom will be hidden by trim.

Drywall

Hanging Drywall Alone

Q. *Is there a better way for a one-man crew to hang drywall, besides having to wrestle with T-braces?*

On those occasions when you're working solo, consider getting a drywall jack from a rental store. This tool is a manually operated lift designed to support and position drywall panels. Its telescoping base means less strain on your back, and its articulated head is particularly useful for hanging cathedral ceilings.

A drywall jack is fairly inexpensive to rent, and if you are working alone, it may well be worth the cost.

CUTTING A DRYWALL SHEET

Few rooms are perfect multiples of 8, 10, or 12 feet, which means that you'll have to cut drywall panels to fit. For a clean look, butt together the factory edges and orient your cuts to inside or outside corners. Don't worry if your cuts aren't perfect; gaps up to ⅜ inch wide can be filled with joint compound.

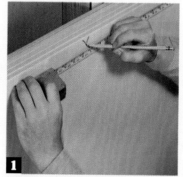

1 Measure the desired length on the face of the panel. Mark the dimensions near the top and bottom edges.

2 Use a chalk line to mark the cut. Hook the line at the bottom, hold it taut against the top, then snap the line.

3 Score the front paper with a utility knife. To deepen the cut, take two or more passes with the knife.

4 Snap the panel from the back; then slice through the back paper. Smooth the cut edge with a rasp, if necessary.

Rust-Stained Corners

Q. *Rust stains have appeared on some of the outside corners of our drywall. What's causing this problem and how can we correct it?*

The stains are most likely caused by corrosion of the metal corner bead, which has led to a brown rust stain bleeding through the surface paint. Moisture condenses on the corner bead because the metal is cooler than the rest of the wall. The moisture combines with the alkaline drywall mud to eat away at the corner bead. Most likely, your walls had been painted with a latex primer and overcoat. Since rust is water soluble, it has bled through to the surface.

One way to control the problem is to provide better ventilation at the source of the high humidity. Use a kitchen vent fan when cooking, especially when boiling water. When showering, use the bath vent fan or open the window.

Before applying another latex topcoat, you'll need to seal the stain. Look for an oil-base or shellac-base primer/sealer/stain killer. These sealers are great for sealing not only water soluble stains, but for sealing knots on wood before painting.

Covering a Curved Wall

Q. *I'd like to build a curved wall. How do I get a sheet of drywall to bend around the framing?*

It depends on how tight the curve's radius is. Half-inch drywall is only flexible enough to bend around a radius of 10 feet or more. If the radius is 4½ to 10 feet, use two layers of ¼-inch drywall. For a tighter curve, you can dampen both sides of the panels to increase flexibility.

To hang the drywall, fasten the board to the first stud. Have a helper bend the panel around the curve as you drive fasteners into each stud. (See Framing a Curved Wall, p. 167.)

If you're using two layers of ¼-inch drywall, completely fasten the first layer and then apply a layer of construction adhesive. Put the second panel on top and screw it only along its edges. Using adhesive reduces the number of screws and all you'll have to tape and finish is the edges.

To make the drywall bend smoothly, place the studs closer together than you normally would. Don't try to pull the panel in place with screws. Have a helper bend it for you.

Avoiding Pipes and Wires

Q. *Considering the hundreds of screws that I'll use to hang my drywall, how can I avoid skewering a pipe or wire?*

Poking through plumbing or electrical lines is not only annoying but also potentially dangerous. The best way to prevent this from happening is to flag the locations of pipes and wires by marking them on the floor before you start. Protect wires within 1¼ inch of the stud face and pipes within 1½ inch with steel plates.

Mark the locations of pipes and wires, and use plates to make them screw-proof.

Fitting Drywall around Doors and Windows

Q. *It takes forever to measure and cut drywall around windows and doors. Is there a better way?*

The fastest and most accurate way to hang drywall around interior doors and other openings is by not using a tape measure at all. Professional hangers panel the entire wall and then cut out any openings. Use a drywall saw to make the cut, and smooth any rough edges with a rasp. Don't worry about wasting material; you can often use the cutouts for the closets. Fewer seams will speed up finishing. Eliminating joints at the corners of doors and windows also lessens the potential for cracks.

Saw out a door for a perfect drywall fit.

Corners Not Square

Q. *I'm having trouble fitting drywall into corners where the walls are not plumb. Is there an easy way to do this?*

Before fitting the last panel of drywall into a corner, make sure the edge of the next-to-last panel is plumb and centered on the stud. Then trim the last panel to fit. Measure the width of the opening at the top and at the bottom. Transfer those dimensions to the drywall, snap a chalk line, and cut the sheet. The piece should fit snugly but not so tightly that you have to force it into place.

Drywall

TAPING DRYWALL

Here's Why You Use Tape

Q. *The joints in my drywall have cracked because I didn't use tape with the drywall compound. How can I repair them?*

Unfortunately, you'll need to redo all the joints. The paper tape not only hides the joints, it adds reinforcement and prevents them from cracking as the house settles.

To fix a joint, first apply a 1/16-inch layer of joint compound to the joint with a 6-inch joint knife. Lay the paper tape on the bed of compound and cover it with a thin layer of compound. When this coat is dry, apply the second coat with a 12-inch joint knife. When the second coat is dry, apply a very thin third coat. Once the third coat has dried, sand it

lightly to eliminate edges and lumps. Remember to wear a dust mask and safety goggles when sanding.

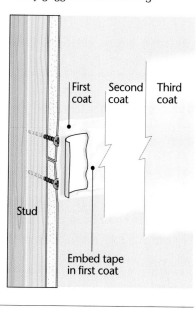

Hiding Butt Joints

Q. *I can't get flat drywall seams when I tape butt joints. How do the pros get them?*

They don't. Fact is, untapered edges at the ends of drywall sheets protrude above the wall surface and are more noticeable than the joints between

the tapered ends. Professional hangers try to avoid butt joints altogether by installing longer sheets that reach from corner to corner.

For situations where a butt joint is unavoidable, you'll need to build up a tiny bulge at the seam and feather it out in both directions. Keep each coat smooth and thin by running one end of a trowel or a 12-inch joint knife on the tape and the other end on the drywall. Expect to apply three or four coats of compound. Once it's dry, sand the compound lightly, concentrating on the edges where it blends into the paper.

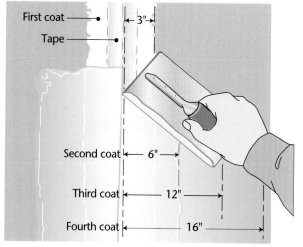

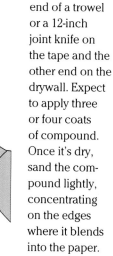

Taping Uneven Joints

Q. *How can I finish a drywall joint when one panel sticks out 1/4 inch more than the other?*

You might be able to avoid this if you hang your drywall horizontally rather than vertically, but here's how to fix the problem. You need to build up the low side of the joint with compound. A setting compound can fill your deep recess without cracking. To hide the joint, smooth the compound over a wide area— at least 10 inches. Setting compound is tough to sand; be sure to feather it out with a trowel before it dries.

To check your progress, lay a straightedge against the joint. Continue building up the low side until there's no visible gap underneath your level. Once you've built up the low side, finish the joint with tape and regular compound.

Gaps at Electrical Boxes

Q. *How do I fix the gaps in drywall around electrical outlets?*

Treat all gaps greater than 3/8 -inch as you would any other drywall joint: apply paper tape and three layers of joint compound.

⚠ Turn off power to an electrical box at the main service panel before working around it.

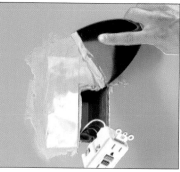

Fix any gaps around electrical outlets with tape and joint compound.

DRYWALL MATERIALS

DRYWALL COMPOUND, called mud in the building trades, comes in a variety of types. Usually you just need a setting type and an all-purpose joint compound. Both should be labeled lightweight, a variety that is not as hard as others but is easier to sand. Setting compound comes as a powder and begins to harden as soon as water is added (look on the bag for hardening times—20, 60, 90 minutes or more). It dries  without shrinking or cracking. Use it when you need the compound to be thicker than 1/8 inch or when you are in a hurry. All-purpose compound is easier to use because it's already mixed and hardens slowly. The downside is that you have to allow a day or so between coats for it to dry.

In addition to these two joint compounds, you'll need a primer to seal the wall prior to painting, or a combination primer-sizing to go under wallcovering.

DRYWALL TAPE. There are two types of drywall tape: paper and fiberglass mesh. Paper tape is simply perforated heavy paper that gets sandwiched between layers of compound to reinforce the joint so that it doesn't crack. A 300-foot roll will suffice for an average-size room. Mesh tape is very easy to use because it's sticky and adheres directly to the joint without a bed of compound. Mesh tape is strong enough to use with any type of compound for small repairs, but for bigger taping jobs it must be covered with setting compound. Unlike paper tape, mesh tape can't be creased to fit tightly in corners. Mesh tape costs more than paper.

CORNER BEAD is usually applied when two drywall panels meet at an outside corner or an archway. But there are types for other situations. The common right-angle corner bead covers most outside corners. Bullnose is a variation of it that gives inside corners, outside corners, and archways slightly rounded edges instead of sharp ones. For sharp corners, even when the walls don't quite meet at a right angle, there's flexible corner bead. J-bead or L-bead wraps the ends of drywall sheets where they meet a wall covered with another material, like brick or paneling. Arch bead is used to cover curved corners, usually those on curved archways.

Left to right: corner bead, bullnose, L-bead, J-bead, and flexible arch.

Taping Inside Corners

Q. *I've gotten the hang of taping outside corners, but I can't get clean-looking inside corners. What am I doing wrong?*

Inside corners are no more difficult to finish than nontapered joints. To tape an inside corner, start by applying a 1/16-inch layer of compound to both sides of the corner with a 6-inch joint knife. Next, crease the paper tape in the center, press it into the corner, and embed it in the compound. To finish the joint, consider investing in a corner trowel so that you can finish both sides at once. You can use a regular 6-inch knife as shown below, as long as you finish one side at a time. Otherwise your knife will dent the soft compound on one side while you smooth the other.

Embed the creased tape in compound.

Finish the corner one side at a time.

Corner-Bead Perfection

Q. *How do I install corner bead on an outside corner?*

Corner bead strengthens and protects the edges of drywall on outside corners and around archways that don't have wood trim. Use a piece of corner bead that will cover the full length of the corner. For example, cover an outside corner on a 10-foot wall with a single section, not two 5-foot pieces.

Fasten the corner bead every 12 inches, creating a shallow depression for drywall compound. When the corner bead is pushed flush against the corner and nailed in place, the outside edge should protrude about ⅛ inch above the surface of the dry-

wall. When two pieces of corner bead meet at the top of a doorway, cut the ends of the beads so that they meet at a 45° angle. Also make sure the ends line up perfectly. If the

Miter the corner bead at the corners. Outside edges should protrude about ⅛ in.

adjoining pieces don't line up, your knife will jump and make a ridge in the joint compound. To cover the beads, apply at least three increasingly wider layers of joint compound.

Corner bead helps guide the knife. Use a wider knife with each coat of compound.

Bubbles in Joint Tape

Q. *What can I do to get rid of bubbles in my drywall tape?*

Bubbles often occur when the layer of compound under the tape in the joint is too thin. They can also happen when the paper face of the drywall underneath has separated from the gypsum core. Cut out any tape bubbles with a knife; then recoat the area with compound.

To remove a bubble, cut out loose tape before applying more compound.

Sanding with Less Mess

Q. *I've heard I can use a moist sponge to sand drywall joints. Is that true, and how do I do it?*

Wet sanding is great for small projects when you want to avoid dust. With a light touch, it's easy to get good results. You can use a kitchen sponge or, better yet, a sponge float used for stucco finishing. For hard-to-reach areas, use a sponge mop. Start by moistening your sponge

Use a damp sponge for dust-free sanding.

in a pail of warm water and moving it across a section about 3 feet long. Work the area until it's smooth, then continue down the joint. Rub over any high spots until a little compound collects on the sponge. Rinse the sponge frequently. If the joint softens too much and smears, let it dry and go over it again later.

SAFETY CHECK

Buckets Can Kill Kids

The 5-gallon buckets that drywall compound and paint come in are very handy, but don't leave them around with liquid in them—small children can drown in them. According to the Consumer Product Safety Commission, children under 2 years old cannot right themselves after they fall in. Curious pets are also at risk. If you're using 5-gallon buckets that are filled with liquid, make sure you keep the covers tightly snapped on.

Sanding Is a Crucial Step

Q. *I've applied three coats of drywall compound and my walls still aren't smooth. Should I sand?*

While expert knife work can eliminate most additional smoothing, some sanding is unavoidable. Sanding drywall is tedious, but the results—seamless joints and smooth walls—make the job worthwhile. The trick is to sand as little as possible. Sand joints and patches over fasteners lightly, stopping every so often to run your hand over the area to check for smoothness.

To keep drywall dust from getting everywhere, cover doorways and anything left in the room, including heating ducts, with plastic sheeting. Put an old fan (dust is tough on the motor) in the window to suck dust out of the room. Always wear goggles and a dust mask when sanding, to protect your eyes and lungs.

If you notice small gouges that you missed with the compound, mark them with a pencil and fill them in later. Oversanding can make the drywall facing and paper tape fuzzy. Light fuzz can be covered with paint, but bad scuffs will show through. Smooth over them with a very thin coat of compound.

A mesh sanding screen cuts through compound quickly, but in most areas, you can use regular 100-grit sandpaper. Use a swivel-headed pole sander to reach high walls and ceilings. Use a foam sanding block to smooth out inside corners.

Realize that heavy-texture paints or thick wallpaper can hide minor imperfections. However, glossy paint will highlight mistakes, so the finish must be perfect. If you find flaws after priming, spread a thin layer of compound and follow up with a light sanding. Seal the patch with a second coat of primer.

Using a
Dustless
Sander

DUSTLESS SANDERS, which are basically sanding blocks with a vacuum hookup, can capture most of the drywall dust and keep you and your room dust-free. However, dustless sanders aren't perfect. With some systems the vacuum causes the sanding block to grab onto the wall, creating extra scratches. In this case, you'll need to start with a coarse paper and then resand with a finer-grit paper. Double-sanding this way takes twice as long as sanding by hand (but you will save time on cleanup). Also, until you get the hang of power-sanding, it's easy to oversand and ruin your taping job.

Remember to wear a dust mask and goggles whenever you sand.

Drywall

Busted Outside Corner

Q. *Racing to fix a leak, I slammed my toolbox into a beaded drywall corner. How should I fix it?*

Fixing a busted corner is not as difficult as you might think. And all it will cost you is a few hours spread over a couple of days. You'll need a putty knife, a 6-inch joint knife, a hammer, a ¾-inch-diameter bolt, a nail set, some ring-shank drywall nails, and joint compound. It's best to use setting compound (see Drywall Materials, p.17), which is harder to sand but dries faster and shrinks less.

First use the hammer and the flat end of the bolt to straighten and smooth the worst side of the damaged corner. Secure the flattened section of corner bead with three or four ring-shank drywall nails to keep it from moving.

Next pry off any loose joint compound with a putty knife. Remove any compound that comes off easily; otherwise, it will just flake off when you apply new compound.

Drill pilot holes before nailing the other side of the corner bead in order to avoid cracking any more compound on the corner. Use a nail set to drive the nails flush so you don't accidentally damage the wall.

With the corner bead securely in place, fill and smooth both sides of the busted corner with joint compound. If you fill one side first and let it dry before doing the other, you'll have a firm corner edge to use as a guide when filling the other side. Three coats of compound will create the neatest corner. Don't overwork the compound—too much back-and-forth action might pull it out. Once the compound is dry, sand out less-than-perfect knife work and feather the edges.

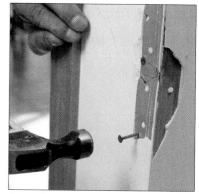

Secure loose bead with ring-shank nails.

Apply compound to one side at a time.

Bad Drywall Joint

Q. *One of the drywall joints in my wall looks terrible. There is a crack down the middle and one side is lower than the other. Help!*

First repair the crack. The tape covering the seam has probably ripped and pulled away from the wall, causing the crack. To fix it, cut the tape 2 inches beyond the crack in both directions and scrape it off.

Next push on the seam to make sure that both drywall panels are securely attached to the stud. If one is loose, reattach it with drywall screws. Scratch off any loose joint compound and vacuum out the dust.

If one panel is more than ⅛ inch lower than the other, you need to build up the lower side before taping the joint. Apply setting compound with a 12-inch joint knife to fill the gap. When both panels are flush, re-tape the joint. Be careful not to let the new tape overlap the old tape.

To finish the joint, feather the edges with a sanding block. Vacuum any dust; then apply a coat of primer and a top coat of paint.

To fix a joint, you will need to replace torn tape.

Nails Keep Popping

Q. *I had my roof redone, and now I have nails (some rusting) popping through my drywall ceiling. What happened? How can I fix the pops and keep them from reappearing?*

Your drywall may have gotten wet during reroofing. But nail pops also occur when framing shrinks, or even from heavy foot traffic. Old nails without ring shanks work loose easily.

To repair a popped nail, drive a drywall screw about 1½ inches away from the nail, sinking the screw head slightly (see Nails vs. Screws, p.12). Then pull out the popped nail. Don't drive it back in or it may re-emerge. Patch the nail hole and the screw dimple with joint compound. Seal rust spots with a shellac-base primer before repainting.

Cracks in Drywall Panels

Q. *My drywall has some cracks—not in the joints but in the drywall panels. Can they be easily fixed?*

As houses naturally shift and settle, drywall tends to crack around the corners of windows and doorways. The best way to make a lasting repair is to treat these cracks as you would a joint. To do this you'll need a utility knife, setting and regular joint compound, a 6-inch joint knife, and paper drywall tape.

Start by cutting along both sides of the crack to create a V-shaped groove in the drywall. The groove removes any bulge and provides a place for the compound to grip. Fill the groove with setting compound (it dries faster and cracks less), let it dry, and sand it smooth. Next spread a thin layer of regular com-

Cut a V-shaped groove along the crack.

pound and embed paper tape in it. Finish this joint with an additional two or three coats of compound. Let the final coat dry; then lightly sand out the edges of the patch.

Finish the cut with tape and compound.

how is it done?

FIXING A HOLE IN DRYWALL

The fastest way to patch a hole in drywall (or plaster) is to use a drywall plug. A plug is simply a piece of drywall cut to the hole size with its facing paper left a little larger. This extra paper along the edges keeps the drywall from falling through the hole and provides an edge on which you can apply joint compound. With practice, you can finish a plug repair in a few hours.

To make the repair, first square up the damaged area of the wall (Step 1). Next cut a piece of drywall that is 3 inches longer and wider than the hole. Working from the back of your patch, score a line 1½ inches in from each edge. Snap these borders and peel off the plaster core, leaving the face paper on the front. Apply joint compound to the paper edges and press the plug into the hole. As you smooth out the plug against the wall, press hard enough to push the plug flush to the wall, but not so hard that all the compound starts to ooze out from under the paper. Allow the first coat to dry; then apply two additional finishing coats of compound. For faster repairs, try using a setting-type compound and a hair dryer to speed up the drying time.

To inspect your work, hold a lamp against the wall to cast light across the patch. Minor scratches and bumps will stand out. Sand out any scratches or apply additional compound as necessary.

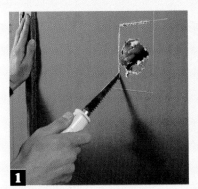

1 *Cut a rectangular hole around the damaged area with a drywall saw.*

2 *Apply joint compound to the plug's paper edges and press it in the hole.*

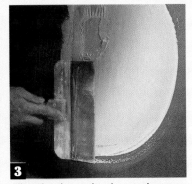

3 *Allow the plug to dry; then apply two additional coats of joint compound.*

Plaster Walls

REPAIRING PLASTER

Plaster-to-Drywall Joints

Q. *How can I make a joint between plaster and drywall unnoticeable?*

Make sure that the plaster is solid, with no major irregularities. Then carefully cut it back to the center of a stud. Bevel the edge slightly for 2 inches to allow for tape and compound. Next attach the drywall.

(Most plaster walls are ⅜-inch thick, but you may have to shim the drywall to make it even with plaster.) Finish the joint with tape and joint compound as you would drywall. First dampen the plaster edge with a spray bottle so that it won't draw moisture from the compound too quickly. For best results, skim-coat the whole wall (see Making Walls Smooth, p.26).

Fixing Plaster around Trim

Q. *Our house needs new trim, but the plaster under the old trim is falling off. Can it be repaired?*

Removing old trim and loose plaster can get messy, but if you score the wall with a utility knife, the plaster will tend to break along the scored lines. Remove the trim and the plaster, then build up the area with a setting-type compound (see Drywall Materials, p.17). Apply the compound with a trowel to about ⅛ inch below the finished surface. Finish with several thin coats of lightweight joint compound. Prime and paint the wall before installing the trim.

To repair a large section of plaster, use a drywall patch (see Plaster-to-Drywall Joints, above).

Plaster Won't Hold Screws

Q. *The screws on my heat registers have broken the plaster and lath. Now there's nothing to anchor the screws to. What can I do?*

Replace the broken plaster with a piece of plywood. To do this, chip out a 3-inch-wide strip of plaster going to the nearest stud. Make sure the area is rectangular. Cut a piece of plywood (⅜ inch is usually the best thickness) to fit, and attach it to the stud with drywall screws. Apply joint compound and paper tape on top of the plywood patch, and smooth it to match your wall.

A plywood patch provides a more solid screw support than crumbling plaster.

Flaky Basement Walls

Q. *A blistered, chalky residue has worked through our painted basement walls. We want to paint the walls and finish the basement. What should we do?*

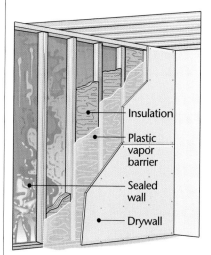

The blistered residue you describe is common on basement walls. Moisture from outside works its way through the foundation into the plaster and forms a chalky residue called efflorescence.

Before you do any more work in your basement, look for any misdirected rainwater from downspouts or an inadequate slope in the ground next to the house that may cause water to run toward the basement.

The best solution for a crumbling basement wall is to seal the foundation, then build a separate interior wall and cover it with drywall. First clear away any loose plaster and efflorescence with a wire brush and coat the wall with a sealer. When this is dry, build a stud wall with a treated wood bottom plate (see Framing Walls, p.166). Install fiberglass batts or rigid panel insulation between the studs. Staple a plastic vapor retarder over the frame before hanging the drywall.

HANGING THINGS ON WALLS

Hanging a Mirror

Q. *What's the best way to hang a frameless mirror?*

The key is to use mounting clips. Better ones are padded and have a slotted screw hole so that the top clips can be slid up to install the mirror, then lowered to hold it in place.

Install the bottom clips first. Use a carpenter's level to draw a line for the clip screws (about an inch above the desired bottom). About 4 inches in from each corner, screw the clips into the wall studs. Next draw a line and install the top two clips so that they'll hold the mirror when lowered. If additional support is needed, use mirror mastic to affix the mirror back to the wall.

To install the bottom clips, draw a level line as a guide for placing the clip screws.

At the top, mount the clips so that they grab the mirror's edge when lowered.

how is it done?

INSTALLING HOLLOW-WALL FASTENERS

In an ideal world, every nail would hit a stud. In reality, wall fasteners are essential more often than not for hanging towel racks, pictures, and shelf supports.

To select the right fastener, first check the thickness of your wall. Some expanding fasteners won't work in walls thicker or thinner than they were designed for. Next, check the length and size of the screw. Most walls can accommodate any length of screw. With hollow-core doors, make sure the screw won't poke through. Screw sizes also affects the anchor mechanism. To be safe, buy fasteners that include screws.

For the fastener to work, drill a hole to the size specified on the package. Position the hole carefully; most fasteners can't be shifted once they're inserted.

Be aware that fasteners can't be used for everything. For safety, heavy items like cabinets, stair rails, and bookshelves should be screwed directly into studs.

Tap a plastic anchor in place so its face ring is flush; then insert the screw. Expanding anchors provide a two-way bite. Supports loads up to 20 lb.

Close the spring-loaded wings and insert the toggle bolt into a drilled hole. The wings flip open in the cavity to anchor the screw. Supports 30 lb.

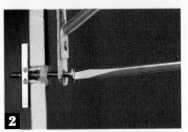

Insert the toggler, pull the support flange tight against the wall with the break-away handle, then insert the screw. Supports 50 lb.

Ceilings

Attaching to Concrete

Q. *I have a concrete ceiling covered with crumbling plaster. I want to cover it with drywall, but how do I attach it?*

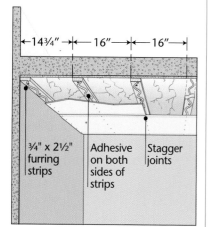

The best way to attach drywall to concrete is to first install 1 x 3 furring strips. You want to position the strips so that the sheets of drywall end on the center of a strip—except along the walls, where the drywall and furring abut the wall. To do this, reduce the first space by half the width of your furring (1¼ inches). Continue to snap chalk lines every 16 inches.

To attach a furring strip, use self-tapping concrete screws and construction adhesive. First apply a ⅜-inch bead of construction adhesive to the backside of the strip and stick the strip in place so that it aligns with the chalk line. Once the strips are in place, install screws every 12 inches. To do this, drill pilot holes through the strip, then switch to a masonry bit to drill into the concrete. Be prepared to do some shimming to level out the old surface.

Once the adhesive is dry, run a second bead of adhesive on the face of the strips, then attach ⅜-inch drywall to the strips using 1-inch screws (see p.13 for additional installation tips).

Cracked Plaster Ceiling

Q. *My plaster ceiling is cracking in several places. Can I fix it without having to recoat the entire ceiling?*

As long as it is not crumbling, you can screw loose or cracked plaster back onto the wood lath behind it by using a gadget called a plaster washer. Attach a washer with a drywall screw about every 4 inches in all directions, starting at the outer edge of the loose area and working toward the center. Once the plaster is firmly reattached, hide the washers with several coats of drywall compound; then sand and paint.

If your entire ceiling is loose or if there are lots of soft spots, you're better off replacing or covering the ceiling with ⅜-inch drywall.

Small Cracks in Texture

Q. *There are some small cracks in my drywall ceiling, which is spray-textured. Can I repair them without scraping away the texture?*

When your ceiling has cracks, you should first try to find out what's causing them. Most likely the house has settled or the wood ceiling joists have shrunk a little. But it's best to

Use a mini-roller to texture small patches.

Fixing Damaged Texture

Q. *I have textured ceilings that are flaking, stained, and missing some texture. Is there a quick fix?*

Begin by first removing any loose or marred texture with a putty knife and priming water stains with a stain sealer. Next, mix some perlite beads (available at home centers) into your joint compound. Spread the mixture onto a textured roller and roll it onto the ceiling. You can apply a second coat if the patch needs more texture to match. Once the patch dries, paint the entire ceiling. Texture patches are also available in spray cans, but they are somewhat hard to control.

If you make a mistake, scrape off the material and start again. If the damaged area is larger than 2 square feet or if there are several damaged spots, consider hiring a pro to retexture the entire ceiling. You can also do this job yourself (as described in Spray-Texture a Ceiling, p.25).

have it checked by a home inspector to rule out a structural problem.

Once you're sure the problem is not structural, buy a tube of white latex caulk and cut a small opening in the end of the nozzle. Squeeze just enough caulk to fill the crack. Immediately dab the caulk (it dries fast) with a damp sponge until it blends with the surrounding ceiling texture. Then paint the ceiling if necessary.

SPRAY-TEXTURE A CEILING

Spray texture is great for hiding unsightly drywall seams, patches, cracks, and other imperfections. It also adds some soundproofing to the room. The spray texture commonly used is similar to joint compound with small beads of plastic mixed in. The texture goes on gray, turns white as it dries, and takes 3 or 4 hours to dry. A 40-pound bag will cover about 200 square feet. Thinned joint compound can also be sprayed on. Once it's applied, you can knock down the peaks with a knife to produce a flatter "orange peel" effect.

The equipment you need to spray-texture a ceiling—spray gun, a hopper (to hold the texture), air hose, and compressor—is available at most rental stores.

Be careful not to strain your back and shoulders. When fully loaded with texture, a hopper can weigh 20 to 25 pounds. Use both hands to steady the gun and hopper.

1 Mix the texture with water with a hand mixing tool until it looks like runny oatmeal. Let it set for 15 to 20 minutes.

2 Texturing is messy. Use plastic sheeting to protect the walls, floor, and yourself. A hat and goggles are a must.

3 Extend the spray onto the plastic sheeting to be sure that you evenly cover the edges and corners with texture.

Removing Ceiling Texture

Q. *How do I remove old ceiling texture to get a smooth finish?*

Test a small area first: Spray the area with water, wait an hour for it to soften, then try scraping it smooth. If water doesn't work, try rubbing alcohol. If the alcohol works, you can use a commercial texture stripper. To use the stripper, simply roll it on, let it work for a few hours, then scrape it off. If alcohol doesn't work, consider calling in a pro or covering the ceiling with drywall (see facing page).

Be warned: Once the texture is removed, you'll have to finish the joints and repair any damage that the texture previously covered up.

Roll on a chemical stripper if the texture is made or covered with latex paint.

To convert a wallpaper scraper to a texture remover, simply reverse the blade.

SAFETY CHECK

Think Before You Scrape

Pre-1978 textured ceilings may contain asbestos and should not be sanded or scraped. A safer solution would be to cover the old ceiling with drywall.

Painting

PREPARING WALLS

Cleaning the Walls

Q. *How do I get rid of the yellowish tar film left on our walls by the previous owners, who smoked? I want to repaint the walls.*

You're right in wanting to clean the walls, because paint won't stick to a dirty surface. Use a nonsudsing cleanser (you can get phosphate-free types). Mix 1 ounce of cleanser into each gallon of water. Scrub the walls with a sponge until the residue vanishes. Finish by wiping the walls with clean water. Wait until the walls are completely dry before you prime and paint them.

Ceiling Streaks

Q. *My rough-textured ceilings have dusty-looking streaks along the joists and around the perimeter. Repainting doesn't make them go away. Is there anything I can do?*

The streaks are caused by poor or uneven insulation along the ceiling joists. Insufficient insulation can allow condensation to form on the ceiling, directly below the joists. Dust then settles along these moist strips, causing streaks. The solution is to distribute the insulation more evenly.

To improve the insulation along the joists, lay more insulation across

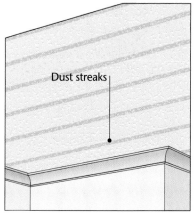

them at a right angle to the existing batts. For the easiest installation, use unfaced batts. Faced batts should be slashed every few inches to prevent trapped moisture and subsequent rot.

Making Walls Smooth

Q. *Some walls in my house have sand finishes. Others have peeled-away paint with edges that show through every coat of paint I apply. How can I get smooth walls for wallpaper or paint?*

To smooth a sand finish, you'll need to skim-coat the wall—that is, apply a thin coat of joint compound over the entire surface. It takes a practiced

Cover up sand texture and other wall defects by skim coating with thin coats of lightweight all-purpose joint compound.

hand to get a smooth surface. Large surfaces are best done by a professional. If the texture is not too rough, or if you plan to hang wallpaper, you can do the skim coating yourself. (An alternative is to cover the wall with lining paper; see facing page).

Begin by removing the highest spots. Use a sanding block or scrape with a broad knife held perpendicular to the wall. Vacuum the wall thoroughly, then spread several coats of all-purpose lightweight joint compound over the entire surface. Avoid the setting type; use a compound that is easy to sand. Make several thin applications, feathering them out at the trim. For a fast first coat, try thinning the compound slightly with water and applying it with a roller. Then remove the excess compound (everything above the tops of the sand grains) with your broad knife.

Knowing when to quit working on the surface is one of the keys to skim coating. Concentrate on filling low spots on the surface and don't worry about thin ridges left by the knife—you can sand or scrape them off.

Use a sanding block to smooth the surface, or to make sanding less tedious, use a universal pole sander with 80-grit drywall sandpaper. The pole has a rubber-faced pad and a swiveling head that holds sandpaper flat on the wall regardless of the angle of the pole. It also lets you make longer strokes.

Priming and sizing are the crucial next steps: A primer seals the wall and should be applied before painting or wallpapering. Sizing prepares the surface for the wallpaper. Omit the step and you'll have trouble: The wallpaper could either pull off your skim coat or bond permanently with the wall. If you're wallpapering, you can use separate primer and sizing or find a combination product.

For walls where the old paint edges show through, sand and feather out the edges to make them less noticeable. Or smooth the rough areas with drywall joint compound or spackling compound. Use a wide putty knife to fill in the area; let it dry and sand it smooth.

Alligator Cracks

Q. *The paint on my walls is splitting, with very fine cracks all over. This happens every time the walls are painted. How can I prevent this?*

What you see is called alligatoring, and it is probably caused by a bad original base coat. Scrape off any peeling paint. Then spread a thin coat of joint compound over the entire wall and sand it lightly. The compound will smooth the wall and provide a good base for a new coat of primer and paint.

Peeling Paint

Q. *The paint on the walls in my 80-year-old home keeps peeling off. What can I do? Can I wallpaper over peeling paint?*

It's possible that a substance called calcimine (a mixture of glue, whiting, and water) was used as a whitewash on your walls when the house was first built. Calcimine makes a very poor base for modern paints, and not even wallpaper will cover the peeling paint very well.

First, check the paint to see if it contains lead (see Safety Check, right). If it does, follow the procedures recommended by the EPA. If it doesn't, remove as much of the peeling paint as you can. Make sure to use drop cloths and wear a dust mask. Finish by sanding the wall smooth using a universal pole sander.

Use drywall joint compound or spackling putty to fill nicks in the walls. Test a fast-drying latex primer or an oil-base primer on a small area, followed by the paint you want to use. If the finish holds with the primer, prime the whole room or wall with it before repainting.

Painting over Paper

Q. *Do I have to remove wallpaper before painting a wall? Isn't it easier just to paint over it?*

Years ago you could not paint over wallpaper and expect to get good results. Today, however, it's a different story. As long as the wallpaper adheres tightly to the wall, you can paint over it. Just be sure to prime the wall first with a non-water-base primer. (A water-base primer may cause the wallpaper paste to dissolve, loosening the covering.)

The one drawback to painting over wallpaper is that the seams between the wallpaper strips are likely to show through the paint. If you have the time, you can use a decorative painting technique such as rag- or sponge-painting (see Decorating Techniques, p.32) to obscure the seams.

Lining Paper

Q. *The plaster walls in our living room are cracked and patched and covered with old paint. Must we sand the walls before painting them, or is there an easier way?*

An alternative to sanding that you may find easier is to hang lining paper. Often applied horizontally, this patternless wallcovering doesn't need to be matched. It creates a smooth surface that can be painted or wallpapered. Three types of lining paper are available. For walls with minor to moderate imperfections, use canvas lining paper: For sandy surfaces or rough walls, polyester lining paper—which comes in several weights—is the best choice. Fiberglass lining paper, available in light- and heavy-duty versions, may be used for smooth and rough walls. Of the three types, fiberglass is the most difficult to hang.

Hiding Rust Stains

Q. *Every so often the upstairs tub leaks, causing rust stains on the ceiling. How can I keep these stains from showing through?*

First get the leaks under control or no paint job will last. Then apply a stain-blocking sealer-primer that contains shellac to keep the rust from bleeding through your paint.

To determine if the ceiling is dry, put your hand flat against the area that had the leak. If the stained area feels cooler than the surrounding ceiling, it still needs time to dry completely before you apply the sealer. When it is dry, sand the area with 100-grit sandpaper and paint it with two coats of the stain-blocking primer. Finish the job with a coat of latex paint.

Painting

Stripper vs. Heat Gun

Q. *Which is better for stripping wood trim—a chemical stripper or a heat gun?*

Chemical stripping is usually the best method to use if you intend to stain and varnish the wood. It's also a good choice if the original finish was a varnish. If the original finish was paint, you could be in for a big job that might not be worth the effort. It's often difficult to completely strip paint from the pores, cracks, and joints in wood. For the best results, you have to take the woodwork down and strip it piece by piece.

Even if you intend to repaint, chemical strippers often still work better than heat guns. With heat, it's easy to burn the wood while stripping intricate areas. Chemical strippers are better for preserving fine woodwork details because they lift paint from curves and other hard-to-scrape areas, rather than melting it off. But be careful. Elaborate trim in Victorian-style homes is often made

of plaster, which will be ruined by a chemical stripper if you mistake it for wood. Also, chemical strippers contain hazardous components, so you need good ventilation and protective gear. Wear heavy rubber gloves, goggles, and a respirator whenever you work with these substances.

Stripping paint with a heat gun is usually faster and less messy than chemical stripping if you want to remove lots of paint layers. It's also a good choice if you intend to repaint. While a heat gun is harsher on details than chemical strippers, you can fill nicks and gouges with wood putty, then sand them smooth. A fresh coat of paint will hide whatever remains of most blemishes.

Don't strip paint that contains lead (see Safety Check, p. 27). The heat can vaporize the lead. Vaporized lead can be inhaled, making it dangerous. Keep a bucket of water nearby in case the heat gun starts a fire. Avoid pointing a heat gun toward a window because the heat can break the glass.

With a chemical stripper, work on a horizontal surface in a well-ventilated area.

With a heat gun, you can quickly peel paint to assess the wood underneath.

To strip trim in place, tape off the walls with masking tape and newspaper. Tape off the floor with masking tape, plastic, and replaceable layers of newspaper.

Stripping Woodwork

Q. *How can I remove paint from wood trim with a chemical stripper without harming the floors or walls?*

It's virtually impossible to completely protect floors and walls from chemical paint remover unless you take down the woodwork and strip it elsewhere. If possible, remove the woodwork and lay it flat in a well-ventilated place (like a garage). This will make the job safer for you and easier to clean up. If you can't remove the woodwork and need to strip it on site, tape off the walls and floor with masking tape, plastic, and newspaper. Roll up and replace the

newspaper as the sludge accumulates. Expect to recaulk and repaint around the edges.

Apply the stripper thickly enough to cover all the paint. If you give it plenty of time to work, the paint should come right off. Use a putty knife to remove sludge from flat surfaces. A cotton swab or toothpick can be used to clean out carved details. Lightly scrub the wood with soapy water to remove loose paint, varnish, stain, and stripper. Wipe away remaining sludge with a damp sponge rinsed in clear water. Dry the wood with a clean cloth. Sand with 120-grit sandpaper to remove any raised grain and to clean the surface.

CHOOSING A CHEMICAL PAINT REMOVER

There are four basic types of chemical paint removers. Choose one according to how fast you want to work, how comfortable you are using hazardous chemicals, and the amount of paint you have to strip.

FAST-ACTING STRIPPERS containing toxic methylene chloride are effective on most coatings and are popular among professionals. Wear an organic vapor respirator when you use them and ventilate the area well.

WATER-BASE STRIPPERS take up to 24 hours to work. They're a little safer than fast-acting strippers, but their long-term health effects are still being tested. Many irritate the skin, and some require respirators.

CAUSTIC STRIPPERS are also slower-acting but use high alkalinity to remove paint. They don't generally release harmful fumes, but they'll irritate and burn your skin if not immediately washed off. Caustic strippers remove thick layers of paint but require a neutralizer (vinegar rinse) before refinishing. Don't use a caustic stripper on veneered surfaces or hardwoods.

STRONG SOLVENTS such as acetone, toluene, and methanol remove thin layers of paint but evaporate quickly and can leave a sticky mess behind. They are commonly sold as refinishers for varnished wood, to partially remove and clean the finish. Safe use requires good ventilation and a respirator.

SAFETY CHECK

Tips for Safe Stripping

Read ingredients and warning labels before you buy stripper.
■ Avoid using stripper in a basement; the fumes are difficult to blow out, even with a fan.
■ If you have to use stripper indoors, turn off the furnace; chemical vapors can corrode the heat exchanger.
■ Paint sold before 1978 may contain hazardous lead. Your local health department has information about lead paint.
■ Use an organic vapor respirator with fresh cartridges to avoid inhaling toxic fumes.
■ Use rubber or neoprene gloves, not latex or vinyl. Wear long sleeves and wash your hands often.
■ Strippers don't work well in extreme heat or cold; for best results, use them where the temperature is around 70° F.
■ Dispose of newspapers for trash collection after the sludge from the stripper has dried.

Removing Paint from Tile

Q. *My ceramic bathroom tiles are painted. How can I remove the paint without damaging the tile?*

The approach that is least likely to damage the tile is to carefully scrape the paint off with a razor scraping tool. If there is more tile than you want to scrape, try using a water-base paint stripper (not methylene chloride-base), but do a test in an inconspicuous corner first.

Be aware that the tile underneath may not be in great shape; perhaps that's why it was painted in the first place. If the tile was sanded or etched before the paint was applied, the damage is irreparable.

Even if the tiles look good, you will still need to scrape out and replace the old grout. Considering the time and expense involved in this procedure, it may actually be more practical to remove the old tile and replace it with brand-new tile.

Getting Paint Out of Nooks and Crannies

Q. *How can I remove the paint out of all the crevices and corners?*

Most strippers won't lift all the paint with just one application. Deeper buildups in corners and edges almost always require a second coat of stripper. Tools that can help include brushes, cotton swabs, dental picks, and old screwdrivers. Use steel wool only with solvent-base strippers; water-base strippers cause the steel wool to rust.

Be creative when it comes to finding tools to dig stubborn paint out of deep crevices. Try old spoons and dental picks.

Painting

SELECTING AND USING PAINT

Exterior Paint Indoors

Q. *I have leftover exterior paint that I don't want to go to waste. Can I use it inside the house?*

You can use exterior paint indoors, but it might not roll on as easily as interior paint, nor will the color be as rich. Interior paint has more pigment, or color, than exterior paint. Interior paints are also available in a wider selection of colors. Though it's OK to use exterior paint indoors, you should *never* use interior paint outdoors. Interior paint lacks the weather resistance and durability necessary for outdoor use.

One Shade Off

Q. *When I paint a room, the area I cut in with a brush around door and window trim dries lighter than the areas I roll. What can I do about this?*

You might be applying a thicker coat with the roller than with the brush. To avoid this, use a 2- or 2½-inch latex brush with exploded-tip slanted bristles, which leave a fine, soft line. Apply two coats about 1½ inches wide around the trim and the door and window frames. Then use a roller with a ⅜-inch nap to roll as close to the trim as you can.

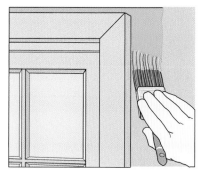

Roll the paint onto the walls so the the film thickness matches the brushed coat. Use minimal pressure with the roller. (Pressing hard makes the coat thinner.) Make sure you stir your paint often. If the pigment settles to the bottom, it can cause variations in the paint's shade.

Spray-Painting Walls

Q. *I plan to paint my interior walls with a sprayer. How is it different from using a roller or brush?*

Before using a paint sprayer, make sure you have good ventilation. This is critical because paint fumes can build up in an enclosed area and be ignited by a spark or a flame. Wear a respirator that has been approved by the National Institute for Occupational Safety and Health. Also wear a hat, old clothes, and wrap-around goggles to protect your eyes. Carefully cover floors and trim to avoid getting paint where you don't want it. To minimize overspray, practice on scrap pieces of cardboard or wood to get used to the feel of the sprayer before you begin on your walls.

Overlap each pass slightly, but not too much, or you'll get too much paint on the wall. Keep your body parallel to the surface you're painting and try not to move your arm in an arcing motion. Remember to bend your wrist and keep the sprayer at a right angle to the wall. To avoid spots or runs where your start and stop, start moving your arm before you pull the trigger.

For outside corners, stand 6 to 8 inches away from the edge and use a back-and-forth motion as you did on the flat wall. On inside corners, turn the spray gun 90 degrees so that the spray pattern is horizontal, and move the gun vertically in the corner.

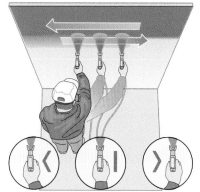

On a flat surface, bend your wrist as you move your arm to apply paint evenly. Slightly overlap each pass—as you would with a lawn mower when you cut grass.

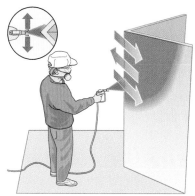

On an outside corner, stand directly facing the edge. Move the spray gun back and forth, bending your wrist as you move to ensure complete, even coverage.

Face an inside corner and turn the gun, or adjust the spray nozzle; so that the spray pattern is applied horizontally. Then move the gun vertically to spray.

Quality Latex Paint

Q. *Oil-base paint is no longer sold where I live because of laws banning substances with high VOC content. Can I get a latex paint that goes on more like oil paint?*

In the past, oil-base paints outperformed latex paints on several fronts: They went on smoother and thicker, they covered better, and they did not leave brush marks. The trouble was that oil-base paints contained high levels of volatile organic compounds (VOC's), which are now strictly regulated in most states because of their negative effect on the ozone layer. Fortunately, in the 20 years since the Federal Clean Air Act began regulating VOC's and other pollutants, paint manufacturers have developed improved latex paints. Today, with the addition of thickeners, surfactants, resins, and other additives, a better-quality latex paint performs as well as or better than oil-base paint, without the solvents that contribute to air pollution.

If you want top-quality results from a latex paint, you have to buy top-quality paint with the better resins, thickeners, and additives.

CHOOSING A PAINT SPRAYER

There are three types of paint sprayers available to buy or rent, each with its own advantages.

AIRLESS SPRAYERS are powered by either gasoline or electricity. Most have a hose (or draw tube) that you place in the paint container; some have their own paint container. Paint is drawn into the tube, then pushed through a supply hose to the spray gun under very high pressure. The paint is then atomized—reduced to a fine spray—by being pushed through the gun's tip at pressures ranging from 1,200 to 3,000 pounds per square inch (psi). This sprayer efficiently covers a large area in a short time. Use an airless sprayer to paint the exterior of your house.

The portable electric airless sprayer is the least expensive of all sprayers and works well for painting shutters, fences, decks, and iron railings. It will hold only about 1 quart of paint, though some have separate tanks or tubes that can be extended into a larger container.

CONVENTIONAL AIR SPRAYERS, often called cup-and-gun sprayers because the spray gun and paint reservoir cup are one unit, are mostly used in production line work. Most rental stores don't stock them.

HIGH-VOLUME LOW-PRESSURE (HVLP) SPRAYERS are very popular because they use under 10 psi to spray the paint. The lower pressure means greater control with less overspray. An HVLP sprayer looks like a conventional sprayer; it uses a one-piece spray gun and paint reservoir cup. HVLP sprayers are portable and affordable, and you can adjust the spray patterns from ½ inch to 12 inches wide. HVLP sprayers run on a 15-amp electrical circuit and work with most types of paint.

 Caution: Paint sprayers force paint out at high pressure; you can cause serious injury by actually injecting paint into your flesh. Never point a sprayer at anyone or anything other than the surface you wish to paint.

A conventional sprayer is mostly for pros.

A portable electric airless sprayer is a good choice for small projects.

An HVLP sprayer allows for greater control.

Painting

DECORATIVE TECHNIQUES

Getting the Right Mix

Q. *When sponge painting or rag-rolling, what's the secret of getting the right consistency?*

Use water to thin latex paint for sponging or ragging. From left to right: too runny, just right, too thick.

A good mix for latex paint is about 1 part water to 8 parts paint for sponging, and 1 part water to 4 parts paint for ragging. This ratio will vary from paint to paint. Generally, the higher the quality of the paint, the more it needs to be thinned. Thinning paints gives them a softer look and makes the texture of the rag and sponge more evident. The paint should cling to the wall without running down in drips. Also, use a damp—not wet—sponge or rag to dab the paint on.

Clean, Sharp Stenciling

Q. *When I do stenciling, I never get nice sharp lines. How do I stop the paint from getting under the stencil and causing fuzzy edges?*

The three keys to good stenciling are using the proper brush, not loading the brush with too much paint, and keeping the stencil in place. Use a stencil brush with flat, blunt bristles. Dip the stencil brush in the paint and blot the excess on a rag until the brush is almost dry. Then dab the paint on instead of brushing it.

To keep the stencil in place, use repositionable adhesive from an art supply store. Spray the adhesive on the back of the stencil and press it in place. The adhesive lets you peel off and reuse the stencil without damaging the stencil or the wall.

SPONGE-AND-RAG PAINTING

Sponging combined with ragging produces an attractive, subtle effect. All you need is a paint roller, two or three paint trays, natural (not square cellulose) sponges, and lint-free cheesecloth. Use latex paint, which dries quickly between applications of color and cleans up with water. First, select a midrange color that you would like to see as dominant. Then select a lighter and a darker version of it and one or two accent colors.

To use a sponge, wet it, wring it out, lightly dab it in paint, and rub off the excess before lightly dabbing the paint on the wall. To rag, dampen a baseball-size wad of cheesecloth, then dab it in paint. Use a stiff-bristle brush to cover any hard-to-reach areas.

1 Roll on a base coat of the darkest shade of the main color. When dry, sponge on the lightest shade in a dappled pattern, using a twisting and patting motion.

2 After the light shade dries, sponge on the first accent color and let it dry. Then use a balled-up rag to dab on the second accent color.

3 When the accent color dries, use a rag to dab the midrange shade of the main color over most of the wall, letting the other colors peek through.

PAINTING MASONRY

Painting Ceramic Tile

Q. *The ceramic tile in my bathroom is in good condition, but the color is very outdated. Can I paint it?*

Many people are surprised to learn that you can paint ceramic tile.

First clean off any mildew or soap residue; then prime the tile with a primer-sealer specially formulated to adhere to ceramic and other hard-to-stick-to surfaces. Some formulas can bond without any additional sanding, etching, or deglossing. A primer-sealer provides an anchor for the top coat to grip. For best results, the top coat should be a high-gloss alkyd—latex paint won't stick to ceramic tile.

Painting a Basement Floor

Q. *My basement floor is covered with a glossy oil-base enamel. I want to repaint it, but nothing will stick to it. What can I do?*

Oil-base enamels are glossy, which causes an adhesion problem. Try roughening the surface with 80-grit sandpaper on a universal sanding pole (a pivot-headed pole normally used for sanding drywall).

Another solution is to use a water-soluble nonflammable paint stripper on the floor. But make sure that there is good ventilation if you use this method. Avoid flammable stripping compounds because they might be ignited by a pilot light. The stripper should etch the paint enough to let the new paint bond to the old surface.

how is it done? STAINING CONCRETE

One way to get a good-looking concrete floor is to stain it. First, clean the floor with trisodium phosphate or a similar cleanser. Next etch the floor with muriatic or phosphoric acid so that it will accept stain. Be sure to wear rubber gloves and full-wrap goggles when working with acid. *Always add acid to water, not water to acid.*

If you need more than 1 gallon of stain, mix it all in one large container for uniform color. Apply it with a ¼- to ½-inch-nap roller. Use a synthetic brush to cut in along walls. Don't thin stain with water or apply it when it's above 90° or below 50° F. Wait 24 hours to see if you need a second coat. When staining outdoors, make sure it's not going to rain for a couple of days.

1 *Wash the floor with trisodium phosphate. Then wet it with a hose. Sprinkle on muriatic acid; scrub it in with a stiff-bristle floor brush for a minute or so.*

2 *Let the acid foam and etch the surface for 20 min. Then triple-rinse it with a hose. If an area didn't foam, clean it well with degreaser and etch it again.*

3 *After the floor dries thoroughly, roll on stain in 3 x 3-ft. sections with a short-nap roller. Wait 24 hr. before using the surface, 72 hr. before driving on it.*

Painting

PAINTING WOODWORK

Nice Neat Trim

Q. *How do I paint wood details neatly, without getting paint where I don't want it?*

With the right technique and materials, you can produce straight, neat edges along windows, doors, and

Press painter's tape firmly in place along trim with a putty knife or your thumbnail.

moldings. Use an angled brush with natural bristles for alkyd paint or synthetic bristles for latex. Don't skimp on brushes—paint doesn't stick as well to cheap ones. Good-quality paint will cling better to the surface.

Paint trim last, after the walls and ceilings. Create a clean edge by

Slip a paint edger between the carpet and the baseboard to minimize mess.

removing old caulk and sanding uneven wood edges. Press painter's masking tape in place with a putty knife to prevent paint from seeping beneath it. Remove the tape before the paint is completely dry. Use a metal paint edger between the carpet and the baseboard to protect the carpet. Never work out of a full gallon can. Pour your paint into a small container and work from that. Don't wipe your brush against the inside of the paint container—this removes too much paint. Lightly slap the brush against the inside of the container to remove excess paint.

Windows can be difficult to paint, especially those divided into small panes. Start at the center and work outward to the frame and trim. Let the paint flow $\frac{1}{16}$ inch onto the glass to protect the seal between the glass and the putty or wood.

The best tool is patience—you can't rush a good trim job.

Finishing a Crackled Door

Q. *I just stripped the paint off my old oak door and found that the surface is covered with tiny cracks. Can I fill the cracks and get a no-sheen finish on the door?*

You don't need to fill in the surface cracks, which are caused by dryness. Filling the cracks with putty or wood filler will only make them more noticeable when the door is finished. If you finish the door promptly, there should be no more cracking. The best way to get a no-sheen look is with an oil finish. For an exterior door, use the same kind of transparent penetrating finish that is sold for finishing wood siding and wood garage doors. You can also use varnish, allow it to dry; then rub it out with a very fine steel wool dipped in soapy water to dull the sheen.

Painting Paneling

Q. *The paneling in our family room is dark and unattractive. Can I paint it?*

Yes, you can paint paneling. First you need to clean it with soap and water and let it dry. Fill any holes with patching compound. Then sand the paneling to smooth the patches and to give the primer a good surface to stick to. Surface preparation is key to this job. Brush away the dust from sanding and wipe the surface with a damp cloth. If the paneling is knotty pine, use a primer-sealer that contains shellac so the knots don't bleed through. Apply an alkyd or latex primer over the paneling and let it dry completely before painting the top coat. When the first coat is dry, apply a second coat.

Avoiding Brush Marks

Q. *How can I paint woodwork without getting brush marks?*

Brush marks occur when paint dries before it has had a chance to flow out properly. The key to preventing this problem is to use a slow-drying top-quality paint. Look for paint with a drying time of about 24 hours. Whenever possible, paint on a horizontal surface. Remove doors, for example, and lay them flat for painting. For woodwork, always brush in the direction of the grain. This will make any brush marks less noticeable. If your first coat of paint isn't covering completely, don't try to make the coat thicker. Most paint jobs require at least two coats. Let the paint dry and then coat again. In avoiding brush marks, it's also important to use good-quality brushes.

Door Edge Colors

Q. *What colors do I paint the edges of a door when one side matches one room and the other matches the adjoining room?*

Paint the edges the same color as the room they typically face. When the door is open at a right angle, the edge with hinges will face into one room—paint that edge to match that room. The other edge will face into the room the door opens into—paint that edge to match that room.

Yellow edge

Blue edge

Pickling Wood

Q. *How do I get a whitewash-like effect on new wood trim?*

To get this two-tone effect, known as pickling, first apply a coat of whatever color wood stain you want on the trim, wiping it on with a sponge.

Let the stain dry; then apply a light coat of white paint over the stain and wipe away the excess while the paint is wet. This will leave paint in the wood grain. Finish with a non-yellowing varnish. You can also achieve this effect by rubbing paste wood filler on the wood instead of white paint.

Refinishing Stair Rails

Q. *How do I paint the intricate handrails on my interior staircase?*

First prepare the surface by caulking any cracks and holes and sanding rough areas. Use painter's tape and plastic to cover everything you don't want painted, such as the landing, steps, and wall. Then apply an interior primer. If the banister is closer than 5 inches to the wall, use a 2- or 2½-inch slant-edge brush. Otherwise you'll save time by using a paint mitt. After the primer has dried, apply one or two coats of paint the same way.

To give yourself time, use a relatively slow-drying primer and paint— an alkyd enamel or a latex paint with an additive that slows drying time. Also select a semigloss or high-gloss paint for greater washability and durability. Make sure there is good ventilation, and take your time.

Reviving a Natural Finish

Q. *The varnished woodwork in my home looks dull. How can I give it a little more life?*

If your woodwork is in good condition and just needs some brightening, you can revive it by cleaning it and applying new varnish. You'll need two or three sanding sponges of fine to medium grit, a gallon of mineral spirits, all-cotton rags, a tack cloth, brushes, and varnish. Protect the floor and surrounding area with plastic drop cloths.

To start, dip a medium-grit sanding sponge into mineral spirits and clean and scuff the finish; repeat with a fine grit. You want to remove the top layer of finish but not to scrub so hard that you remove the stain. Mineral spirits are toxic; follow all label warnings carefully. Wipe the surface with a clean rag dipped in spirits; let it dry.

After the surface dries fully, spot-stain any areas where the finish has worn through. If you need to mix stains to get a good color match, make sure they are the same type (mix oil stain with oil stain, for example). Also fill any holes with

matching-colored wood putty before you varnish. Using a 1½- or 2-inch natural-bristle brush, apply a coat of oil-base varnish and let it dry. Then lightly sand, and wipe the wood with a clean tack cloth before applying a second coat.

Scrub with sanding sponges dipped in mineral spirits to remove old finish.

Spot-stain areas where the finish is worn through before applying new varnish.

Painting

PAINTING CABINETS

Preparing Cabinets

Q. *I'm thinking of painting my wooden kitchen cabinets. What does the preparation involve?*

If your solid wood or veneered plywood cabinets are in good shape, they can be painted quite easily.

Use a sanding sponge to get into corners and curves. Sand lightly, just enough to roughen the surface so the paint will stick.

First remove the doors and drawers and take off the knobs, pulls, and hinges. Wash each surface to be painted with trisodium phosphate (TSP) to remove all grease and dirt. Then sand with 100-grit paper. Just dull the gloss; don't remove any old finish unless it's loose or peeling. A sanding sponge helps in corners and along edges. Vacuum the dust; then remove any residue with a tack cloth. (If you don't, you'll end up with dust specks in your paint finish.)

To finish the job, sand between the primer and split coat (see Choosing Cabinet Paint, right), and between the split coat and the finish coat, with 220-grit sandpaper. Vacuum and wipe with a tack cloth after each sanding. If you need to apply a second finish coat, you don't have to sand; just use the tack cloth to remove dust before you paint.

Painting Metal Cabinets

Q. *I have some old metal kitchen cabinets that I've sanded down to bare metal. What's the best method for painting them?*

You'll get the best results with electrostatic spray-painting. Electrostatic painting requires a special power pack to give the metal surface a negative charge. The negative charge attracts the sprayed paint, resulting in less overspray. To find a company that does this, look in the Yellow Pages under Painting Contractors. Most jobs can be done in the home without removing the cabinets. An epoxy-base paint is best—it's tough and will last for years. The cost is usually moderate, considering the result. There's an additional charge to paint the insides of the cabinets. Appliances can also be painted to match.

Painting Veneer

Q. *My kitchen cabinets are particleboard with a thin veneer. Will the finish accept paint?*

Not all particleboard veneers can be painted. If you're not sure what the veneer is, test a small inconspicuous area. First use trisodium phosphate (or a substitute) to remove dirt and grease. Then sand the area with 180-grit paper. If there's no dust, it is a hard melamine or plastic laminate coating, which won't take paint well. If it gets gummy, it is vinyl film, which also won't take paint.

If the area sands out easily and leaves a residue of dust, it's probably wood veneer. To be sure, brush oil-base primer on the area and let it dry for a day. If the paint doesn't scrape off easily, you're in luck. If it does, forget about painting the cabinets.

Choosing Cabinet Paint

Q. *What kind of paint should I use on my wood cabinets?*

First prime with an oil-base undercoat made especially for enamels. Then mix and apply a split coat—a 50:50 mixture of the primer and the final finish paint. The third coat is the finish color. For durability and easy cleaning, use oil-base enamel for the finish coat. If you want a less shiny finish, use a satin enamel. If the finish coat doesn't cover well, wait for it to dry, then apply a second coat.

For the best results, paint cabinet doors on a horizontal surface. Wear a respirator to protect against paint fumes.

Additives for Better Flow

Q. *A friend said to use a paint additive for my cabinets for a smoother finish. Would it make a difference?*

Paint additives can help the paint go on more easily and smooth out better, especially if you're brushing on the paint. There's less drag on the brush when you use an additive, and it doesn't affect the durability of the paint. You can buy an additive in a paint store. Follow directions, and mix it into the paint thoroughly.

PAINT CLEANUP

Cleaning Brushes

Q. *I forgot to clean my brushes after varnishing and painting. Now they're as hard as rocks. Is there a way to salvage them?*

You're not the first person, and definitely not the last, to make that mistake. Fortunately, you can buy a powdered solvent at your local hardware store that will break down the hardened paint and varnish and soften the bristles overnight.

Read the instructions carefully, because some solvents are not recommended for natural-bristle brushes and won't remove hardened polyurethane or vinyl.

After soaking the bristles in the solvent, put on rubber gloves and brush out the old residue with a stiff, nylon scrub brush. Then rinse the bristles in warm, soapy water. To store the brush, wrap it in its original sleeve or in a piece of brown kraft paper to shape it until it's dry.

Flex and separate bristles in a bucket of warm, soapy water.

If you've lost the cardboard sleeve it came in, wrap the brush in brown kraft paper.

Discarding Leftover Paint

Here are some ways to safely dispose of leftover paint:

■ If the paint is latex, remove the lid and let the paint dry out. Be sure you do this in an area away from children and animals. Once the paint's completely dry, your garbage collector should be willing to take it. Leave the lid off so the collector knows the paint is dry.

■ If the paint is oil-base, it is flammable and considered a hazardous waste, and must be disposed of accordingly. Many communities have designated hazardous waste collection sites and days. If yours does not, contact your local environmental control agency for advice. Never pour oil-base paints down the drain or onto the ground.

■ Paint thinners, turpentine, mineral spirits, and other solvents used with paints should be disposed of in the same manner as oil-base paints.

Disposing of Toxic Rags

Q. *How do you safely dispose of rags soaked in combustible liquids?*

Rags soaked in linseed oil or solvents—such as mineral spirits or denatured alcohol—should be spread out flat to dry or hung on a clothesline in a well-ventilated area away from children, pets, and flames. Once they've dried, you can throw them out with your other garbage.

Dispose of rags soaked with paint remover the same way, as long as the paint stripped was not lead-base. If it was, call your local health department for instructions on how to safely dispose of them.

Cleaning Rollers

Q. *Is it worth the effort to clean and save paint rollers? Or should I just buy cheap disposable ones?*

Cheap rollers don't perform as well as more expensive ones. You'll be better off buying good rollers and cleaning them. To clean a roller of latex paint, scrape off the excess. Dunk the roller in warm water and work the nap along the entire roller with your hand. Spin it into an empty bucket, rinse in clean warm water, then spin again. You can buy an inexpensive spinning device at many paint stores. Loosely wrap the roller in plastic wrap and stand it on end.

Scrape off excess paint with a special paint cleaning tool. Some paint scrapers and stirring sticks have similar notches.

Wallpaper

REPAIRING WALLPAPER

Fixing a Hole

Q. *I have discovered a hole in the wallpaper in my hallway. Is there a way to fix this?*

Yes, there is a way to cover that hole, but fixing a hole in wallpaper requires a small leftover piece of the same paper. If you didn't save any, you might be able to get some from the dealer, who sold the wallpaper to you originally.

To fix the hole, center the scrap piece over the hole and line up the pattern so it matches the pattern on the wall exactly. Then lightly tape it to the wall with masking tape.

Using a straightedge and utility knife, carefully cut a rectangular area slightly larger than the hole. Press just hard enough to cut through both layers of wallpaper. Remove the patch and the damaged paper behind it. Now you will have a rectangular hole and a patch that fits it exactly. Apply wallpaper paste to the patch and press it in place to transfer the paste to the wall. Remove the patch, and when the paste becomes tacky, put the patch back in place and smooth it with a damp sponge.

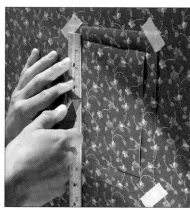

Tape a scrap piece over the damaged part and cut out a rectangular area, cutting through both layers of paper.

Apply paste to patch, put patch on wall to transfer paste, then remove. When paste gets tacky, smooth patch back on.

Cleaning Off Dirt

Q. *I'd like to clean my wallpaper, but I'm afraid of ruining it. Can you give me some tips?*

Most modern wallcoverings can be washed with mild soap and water. Start at the bottom and work your way up. If you start at the top, dirty water will flow down the wallcovering and leave streaks that are difficult to remove. Never use powdered cleanser. Nonwashable wallcovering can be cleaned with cleaning dough, which works like a big eraser. If you're unsure if your wallcovering is washable, ask the dealer who sold it to you or call the manufacturer.

Deflating Bubbles

Q. *How can I get rid of a bubble in my wallpaper?*

First use a glue injector to inject wallpaper seam adhesive into the middle of the bubble. Use a seam roller to spread the adhesive toward the edges of the bubble. Then drive excess adhesive back toward the center and out the needle hole. Wipe off the squeezed-out adhesive with a damp sponge, and flatten the needle hole with the roller.

Apply seam adhesive along the edge of the curled seam, press it back down, and remove any excess with a damp sponge.

Repairing Curling Seams

Q. *Some seams in our wallpaper are starting to curl. How can I restick them in place for good?*

Loose seams can be reglued with special seam adhesive. Apply the adhesive along the edge of the curled seam, then flatten it with a wallpaper seam roller. Remove any excess adhesive with a damp sponge. If the seams are badly curled, you may need to hold them flat with thumbtacks or easy-release masking tape to give the adhesive time to set.

To flatten a wallpaper bubble, inject seam adhesive into the bubble. Then press it down with a seam roller.

Papering over Paneling

Q. *Many of the walls in our home are covered with dark wood paneling. Can we wallpaper over it?*

Yes. But first fill the joints and grooves in the paneling with joint compound to smooth out the walls. Then apply a lining paper, often called blank stock, to give an even smoother base for the final wallpaper. This job gets tricky, so you might want to hire a professional paperhanger to ensure top-quality results.

Sizing Walls for Paper

Q. *Should I size or prime my walls before I hang wallpaper?*

Sizing is a wallpaper undercoat. It acts as a sealer that keeps wallpaper paste from soaking into the drywall or plaster. It makes the walls a little sticky, adding to the holding power of the paste. It also makes it easier to remove the paper later on if you need to strip it off.

If a wall is new and has never been painted, or if it has a lot of patches, apply a primer before sizing. If the wall is painted and in good condition, you can size it without priming. Roll on a single coat of sizing. Use a brush to get close to moldings and ceilings; these areas need the sizing most because they are where the wallpaper edges will be.

If you are papering over existing wallpaper (which you should do only in special circumstances), roll on two coats of oil-base primer, then a coat of sizing. You usually have to wait overnight for the sizing to dry before hanging the paper. There are also primer-sizings available. Ask a knowledgeable salesperson what you need for your project.

how is it done?

REMOVING OLD WALLPAPER

Some wallcoverings are tougher to remove than others. If the wall was not properly sized and primed when the wallpaper was hung, it can be nearly impossible to remove without tearing up the wall.

Newer, strippable wallcoverings have a top layer that peels right off. To remove the backing layer that remains, coat it with water from a sponge or sprayer and let it soak in for a few minutes. Then just scrape the backing off the wall. (If your walls are plaster, use a fine mist of hot water.)

Older wallpapers usually come off easily if you perforate them to help the water get to the glue. You can buy a perforating tool for this purpose. Give the water time to work. If the paper is stubborn, try soaking it with a special wallpaper-remover solution.

If you still can't get the paper off without tearing the drywall or crumbling the plaster, leave the paper in place. Seal loose seams with seam sealer, and prime and size before putting up the new paper.

To see if the paper is strippable, try loosening an upper corner and pulling the surface layer straight down.

If the paper adheres tightly, perforate it with a special perforating tool. Or draw a handsaw across the surface.

Soak the perforated paper with water or wallpaper-removing solution. Then scrape the paper off with a broad knife.

Scrub the walls with an abrasive pad and a cleanser to remove any remaining material.

Wallcoverings

HANGING WALLCOVERINGS

Choosing a Wallcovering

Q. *There are so many wallpapers on the market now. How do I choose one type over another?*

Wallpaper is now commonly referred to as wallcovering because it can be made of vinyl, grass cloth, fabric, or foil as well as paper. New types, patterns, and textures are always being introduced, and you'll find a range in wallcovering quality, too.

Although more expensive than paint, most wallcoverings are moderate in cost; however, exotic papers can be pricey. Though the prices may be tempting, avoid buying cheap wallcoverings—they're more likely to stretch, shrink, tear, or have adhesion problems.

Today most wallcovering comes prepasted—you just wet it and put it up. A single roll will usually cover 25 square feet of wall. Browse through wallcovering books and talk with the salespeople at your local wallcovering outlet. Borrow swatches of the patterns you like. At home, tape the swatches to the wall to see if they are compatible with your carpeting, lighting, and furnishings.

Generally, small prints and light colors make a room seem larger. Big, bold patterns and dark colors will make the feel smaller.

Use a lightly dampened sponge on a seam that needs to be pushed together.

Tight Seams

Q. *How do I get super-tight seams when I hang wallpaper?*

People tend to hang the entire drop, then use their hands to push the seams together. This can stretch the paper causing the seams to come apart later. It's best to unfold only the top half of the drop as you start. Install it about a foot from the ceiling, laying it seam to seam. (Match the

Rolling Seams

Q. *I've heard you should roll seams only once after you hang wallpaper. Is this true?*

Resist the temptation to roll the seams too hard, too many times, or too quickly after the paper has been hung. Wait until the paste has had a chance to set up and get tacky (about 30 minutes); then roll the seam lightly—once.

Rolling too soon, while the paste is too watery, can force the paste out and away from the back of the paper. Rolling with too much pressure can leave visible roller marks. If a seam needs to be pushed together slightly, use a lightly dampened sponge instead of your fingers to adjust it before rolling it. The sponge eliminates fingerprints and distributes the pressure over a wider area.

pattern exactly at eye level where it's most likely to be noticed.) Work it down the wall as far as you can reach, then use a smoother to flatten the paper across the rest of the upper part of the wall. Step off your ladder, unfold the bottom half, and repeat.

If you get off track or create a large crease, pull the entire strip away from the wall and start over. If the back side seems to dry out, rewet it with paste activator and try again.

Paste Activator

Q. *My friend uses something called paste activator when she hangs wallpaper. Would it help me?*

Paste activator can be used instead of plain water on the back of prepasted wallpaper. It increases the stickiness of the paste already on the paper to help it stick even better to your walls and to prevent seam

separations. If you're a beginning wallpaper hanger, you may tend to overhandle the paper, in which case an activator can help keep the glue on the edges. Pros love the stuff, too.

Activator can get a little messy, though. When you roll it on, keep one edge of your paper even with the edge of your table and the other edge on top of your next drop (strip of wallpaper). Be sure to wipe

the seams of the hung paper with a sponge and clean water. Activator can leave a clear, glossy coating on the surface of the paper, so never use it in a water tray (the rectangular pan that is used to completely submerge wallpaper).

Paste activator is cheap insurance against adhesion problems and separating seams. A gallon or two is all it takes to cover an average room.

PAPERING A ROOM

Before you start, turn off the power at the main electrical panel to prevent the risk of shock when working around wall switches and outlets. Remove all faceplates.

The techniques are basically the same for non-prepasted as for prepasted materials. Begin by marking a plumb line for the edge of the first section of wallcovering, called a drop. Plan ahead so that all drops extend 4 inches or more past corners. The best place to start is along a door or in an inconspicuous corner, where any pattern mismatch that occurs where the last drop meets the first won't be noticeable.

Now, thoroughly wet the back of the first drop with lukewarm water until a milky paste forms. Be sure to wet all edges and ends to avoid peeling later on.

Fold the drop in half, with pasted face to pasted face; then fold it again. When you fold, or "book," the wallcovering as recommended by the manufacturer's instructions, the paste can absorb evenly. When the wallcovering is ready, position the edge along the plumb line, starting at the top. The wallcovering should overlap floor and ceiling moldings at this stage.

Using a smoothing brush, flatten the drop against the wall, working large bubbles out toward the edges. Tiny bubbles will disappear as the wallcovering dries. When you're ready to hang the second drop, make certain the pattern matches. Continue to hang the drops in place, taking care not to stretch them.

When the adhesive is tacky, about 30 minutes after hanging the wallcovering, give the seams a single light rolling with a seam roller. Then wipe the seams clean. Trim the excess wallcovering from the top and bottom by pressing a broad knife firmly against the molding, then cutting with a sharp razor knife.

1 Mark a plumb line to indicate the edge of the first section.

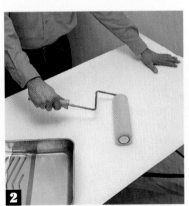

2 Wet the back of the first drop with lukewarm water.

3 Fold drop in half, pasted face to pasted face; then fold it again.

4 Position the edge of the first drop along the plumb line, starting at the top.

5 Roll seams using light pressure—and only roll them once.

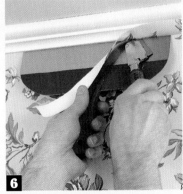

6 Trim excess from the top and bottom with a broad knife and razor knife.

Wallcoverings

Covering Outlet Covers

Q. *I want professional-looking wallpaper results. How do I cover switch and outlet cover plates?*

Anytime you are working around electrical outlets, the first thing you need to do is turn off the electricity at the circuit panel or fuse box. Water, metal tools, and electricity are a dangerous combination.

Remove the covers, wash them in warm soapy water to remove dirt and

Fold the edges back around the cover and secure them with seam sealer. Cut corners diagonally first for crisper folds.

oils, and scuff them with extra-fine sandpaper. Brush on a coat of wallpaper sizing and let them dry overnight. When they're dry, put them back in place.

Put a large scrap of wallpaper over the switch plate (or outlet cover) and position it to match the pattern of the surrounding wall. Remove the scrap and trim it so that it's approximately 1 inch larger than the plate on each side.

Wet the paper, let it set, then place the piece over the plate on the wall, taking care to match the pattern exactly along the edges. Hold the paper in that position and carefully remove the cover, with the paper, from the wall.

Clip the corners of the paper at a 45° angle; then crease and fold the edges over the back of the plate. Secure the edges flat with a thin bead of seam sealer. Make the cutouts for the switch or outlet after the wallpaper has dried. Working from the front, use the openings in the plate to guide your knife. Now reinstall your wallpapered plates and covers.

Hanging Around Windows

Q. *I'm ready to wallpaper my living room, which has four windows. How do I paper around them?*

To paper around a window, drape the wallcovering so that it overlaps the window frame by 5 or 6 inches; take care not to crease it. Make diagonal cuts from the outside corner of the window moldings to the edge of the wallcovering. Now trim the excess wallcovering by carefully pressing it against the molding and trimming it off with your razor knife. Cutting around odd profiles will require many small cuts.

Make diagonal cuts from the outside corner of the window moldings.

Crease the wallcovering and cut along your broad knife with a sharp razor knife.

Making Straight Cuts

Q. *What is the best method for achieving straight edges when trimming wallcovering?*

To make crisp, straight cuts when trimming wallcovering, you need to start with crisp, straight surfaces to cut against. Remove any paint blobs along door and window moldings and any caulk along baseboards beforehand. Use a scraper or sandpaper to even out rough areas along woodwork. If your ceiling is spray textured, use a broad knife turned at an angle to scrape and remove a ⅛-inch line of ceiling spray texture where the ceiling meets the wall.

Trim your paper with a razor knife that holds small snap-off blades. Use a 5- or 6-inch broad knife to keep the wallcovering from lifting and tearing, and to provide a straight guide to cut along. (Slightly round the corners of the broad knife with sandpaper or a file, so they don't dig into and tear the wallpaper.)

For best results, cut along the length of the broad knife; then, without moving the razor blade, leapfrog the broad knife ahead and continue your cut. Don't press so hard that you cut through the underlying drywall tape. Change your razor blade often for sharp, precise cuts.

Pattern Matching on a Wide WIndow

Q. *I have wide windows in the living room. How can I make sure my wallpaper patterns and seams line up by the time I reach the far side of the window?*

The wider the window, the more difficult this can be. The trick is to lightly position the last two or three pieces so you can make adjustments on them while lining up the patterns and widths.

After hanging the piece at one side, install the pieces above the window, and trim them along the ceiling and window frame. Using an easily recognizable part of the wallpaper design as a starting point, draw a horizontal line under the window with a 4-foot level.

Hang the first bottom piece, lining up the pattern along this horizontal line. Lightly lay the other bottom pieces and the full-length piece along the other side, using the horizontal line as a guide. Adjust the pieces until the patterns match and the seams fit tightly, without gaps or overlap. When the patterns are aligned and the seams are tight, finish smoothing out and trimming the pieces.

Make sure you book the individual pieces for equal amounts of time so they will expand to equal widths.

Adjust the bottom and second side pieces before installing and trimming them. The horizontal line acts as a guide.

Hanging a Corner

Q. *What is the best way to hang wallpaper around the inside corner of a wall?*

To hang a corner, measure from the edge of the last full drop to the corner, at the top, middle and bottom of the wall. Then cut the paper ⅛ to ¼ inch wider than the largest measurement. Use a 4-foot level as a guide for your razor knife to cut the booked paper. Install this first piece, wrapping the excess around the inside corner.

Draw a plumb line on the adjacent wall the same distance from the corner as the width of the remaining piece. Install this second piece, matching the pattern in the corner and laying the other edge exactly on the plumb line. Run a small bead of seam adhesive at the corner to secure the overlap if necessary (always do this with solid vinyl wallcoverings).

Measure from the edge of the last full drop to the corner in three places.

Install two pieces. Overlap the seams at the corner and line up the edge of the second piece with the plumb line.

Ceramic Tile

PLANNING A TILING JOB

Choosing Tile

Q. *My tile supplier sells so many types of ceramic tiles. How do I choose the right kind for my new bathroom?*

It's easy to be overwhelmed by the vast array of tile sizes, types, and colors available. If you're a novice tile layer, start by narrowing your choices to tile that has straight edges and even surfaces. Leave wavy edges and uneven surfaces to the pros. Here are some other pointers:

■ Floor tiles are harder and have less glaze than wall tiles. You can use floor tiles on walls, but wall tiles are too slippery and fragile for the floor.
■ Large tiles look impressive and are quicker to install than small ones. You'll also have fewer grout lines to deal with.
■ Don't use floor tiles that are the same size as the wall tiles—it's hard to line up the grout lines where the wall meets the floor.
■ Check on the availability of trim. These are the decorative-edged tiles that you use to finish off a tiled wall surface. Bullnose tile (one rounded edge) is usually available, but double-bullnose (two rounded edges) may not be, or may have to be specially ordered. Check this out before you order tile.
■ When you go shopping, take along a measured drawing of each surface you want to tile. This helps the salesperson better identify what you need.
■ Don't worry about ordering more than you need. Most tile shops will let you return unused tile. It's also a good idea to keep a few tiles and some grout for future repairs.

Tile Layout

Q. *What is the best way to go about laying out a tile pattern?*

Any tile job requires a lot of planning. Once you have a sample of the tile you want to use, make a detailed sketch for each surface that shows:
■ How many tiles go across horizontally and vertically, including space for grout lines.
■ Where the cut tiles will be and approximately how large they'll be.
■ Where the bullnose tiles fit.
■ Where accessories like soap dishes will go.

Lay a row of tiles on the floor, with their spacers if necessary, and measure them to get the dimensions you need. Put cut tiles in less visible areas and whole tiles in the most visible areas. Avoid slivers of tiles by removing one whole tile and placing a cut tile at each end of the row.

Your rows of tile must be straight even though the floor, tub, and walls may not be. Use a framing square and level to measure this. If the surfaces are more than ⅜ inch out of square over 8 feet, you'll get noticeably angled cuts, which look awful. Try to hide them under the

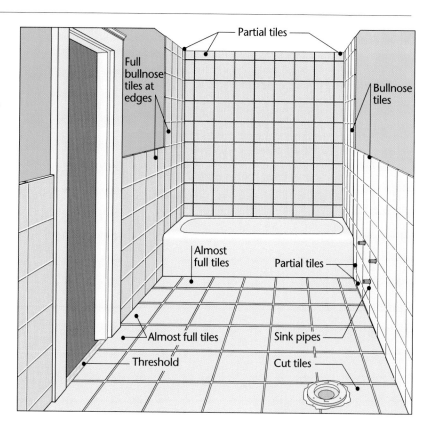

Partial tiles

Full bullnose tiles at edges

Bullnose tiles

Almost full tiles

Partial tiles

Almost full tiles

Sink pipes

Threshold

Cut tiles

sink or toilet. You might want to talk to tile retailers; they will know a trick or two that may help you.

Use full or nearly full tiles along the upper edge of the tub. Be sure to leave a ⅛-inch gap between the tub and the tiles; you'll fill it with caulk later. When you tile a floor, do the area near the door last so you don't walk on the freshly laid tile. Plan for a row of cut tiles (⅔ to ¾ of a full tile) along the wall by the door just in case your grout lines are a bit narrow, or if the room is out of square.

what do you need?

ADHESIVES, GROUT, TOOLS

There are two types of tile adhesive. Latex cement-mortar is mortar mixed with a latex additive for greater strength and flexibility. Also known as thinset, it's the best general-purpose adhesive: waterproof, gap-filling, strong under heavy traffic, and low in odor.

Organic mastic is the other type of adhesive, often used for setting wall tile. It is pre-mixed and is relatively easy to use. However, it is not waterproof, and it isn't recommended for bathroom floors or shower walls. It has a strong odor, and it should not be used to fill gaps larger than ¼ inch.

Grout comes in a sanded form and an unsanded form. Unsanded grout is good for fine grout lines, but for grout lines wider than ⅛ inch, use sanded grout. Like thinset, grout comes as a powder and is mixed with water or a latex additive. When you've finished grouting, use a penetrating sealer to protect the grout lines from stains and water.

Tiling equipment can be rented from a rental outfit or borrowed from the tile shop. The tools you'll need include a notched trowel or two for applying adhesive (ask your tile supplier which one to use with your tile) and a ¼-inch square-notched trowel if you'll be installing cement board on the floor. You'll also need a float to spread the grout, a round-cornered sponge to wipe off grout, a tile cutter to cut straight lines in tile, and tile nippers break off bits of tile. To cut smooth curves, use a rod saw (see Cutting Ceramic Tile, p.50). These general-purpose tools will come in handy, too: a level, chalk line, framing square, masking tape, buckets, and rags.

Tiling over Tile

Q. *My bathroom tile is an ugly pink from the '50s. It's set in a thick mortar bed, so tearing it out seems like a nightmare. Can I tile over it?*

Assuming they're sound and well-bonded, old tiles can be a suitable base for new tiles. To prepare the surface, scratch the tile with a belt sander or a sanding block with 60-grit paper. Next, wash the old tile with a phosphoric acid solution (available at tile stores).

To install the new tile, use a latex-fortified thinset adhesive.

Tiling over Concrete Block

Q. *The backsplash in my kitchen is painted concrete block. Can I tile directly over it, or should I attach cement board as underlayment?*

If the faces of the adjoining concrete blocks are no more than ⅛ inch out of alignment, you can tile directly onto the backsplash. To ensure a strong bond between the tile and the block, however, you must remove the paint with a commercial paint stripper (make sure you have plenty of ventilation). Once you've stripped and cleaned the blocks, apply a ¹⁄₁₆-inch-thick skim coat of thinset cement adhesive to create an even surface; then set your tiles.

If you prefer not to remove the paint or if the blocks are out of alignment, cover the wall with ⅜-inch cement board. Use nails and mastic to attach the cement board to the block. Then tape the seams and you're ready to tile.

Tiling over Laminate Kitchen Counter

Q. *I want to install ceramic tile on our kitchen counter, which is covered with plastic laminate. Can I tile over the laminate?*

Assuming that the laminate is still firmly bonded to the underlayment, you should be able to tile right over it. To prepare the surface, sand the laminate with 100-grit paper to give the adhesive something to grip.

Ceramic Tile

Using Cement Board

Q. *I'm replacing the tile around my bathtub. What's the best backer for the job?*

Cement board is the perfect product to use under tile; it is superior to plaster or drywall, even green water-resistant drywall. In fact, cement board is required by many local building codes for use behind tile in tub and shower areas. Some codes require that you install it above the tub to a minimum height of 18 inches. We suggest you go to 5 feet.

Use wooden shims at the bottom of the cement board to allow 1/4 inch for caulk.

Cement board is made of an aggregated cement slurry with a layer of fiberglass mesh embedded into each side. It is very stable, water-resistant, and hard, yet not too difficult to cut. It is sold at home centers and lumberyards in 3 x 5-foot or 3 x 6-foot sizes, which work extremely well for surrounding standard tubs.

Cement board has a smooth side and a rough side. Keep the smooth side out if you're using organic mastic. Keep the rough side out if you're planning to use thinset adhesive.

Working with cement board is not difficult. To cut it, score it with a utility knife along a straightedge, then snap it along the edge of a workbench or 2 x 4, as you would with drywall. To cut holes for the faucets, drill a series of small holes around the outline of the outlet, then tap the cutout with a hammer. Use a rasp to clean up cuts or to enlarge holes.

To fasten the cement board to the studs, hold it up about 1/4 inch above the tub surface and use galvanized roofing nails or 1 1/4-inch galvanized screws. Be sure to tape the seams with self-adhesive fiberglass mesh. Cover the tape with thinset mortar or organic mastic adhesive.

Thinset or Mortar Bed

Q. *My brother and I are having an ongoing feud. Can you lay tile over a double-layer (3/4-inch and 1/2-inch) subfloor using thinset adhesive, or should you use a concrete bed over the subfloor?*

You can install ceramic tile directly to a plywood subfloor using thinset adhesive, but not all manufacturers recommend that their products be used this way. Check the label

carefully or contact the manufacturer directly before you buy the mortar.

The preferred method of installing ceramic tile is in a reinforced concrete bed at least 1 1/2 inches thick over a 5/8-inch subfloor. However, installing ceramic tile in a concrete bed is a pro job. A do-it-yourself alternative would be to use cement board over plywood screwed to joists with galvanized screws.

Filling Floor Dips

Q. *There are some rolling valleys and peaks across my kitchen floor. Do I have to even it out first, even if I use an underlayment?*

If you don't even out the dips in your floor, the tiles will feel uneven underfoot and your base and wall tile will be out of whack.

To begin, use a 4-foot level to find the high point in the room and then look for the dips. As a rule of thumb, dips greater than 1/8 inch over a 10-foot span are unacceptable.

Large dips (1/4 to 3/4 inch) should be corrected with a self-leveling compound (available at ceramic tile supply stores). To use the compound, simply mix up a batch, pour it onto the floor, and let it dry.

To fill small dips, here's a trick from the pros. Bond layers of 15-pound roofing felt to the subfloor with latex-cement mortar adhesive. Spread the adhesive mortar evenly with a 1/4-inch notched trowel, then press a wide sheet of felt into it. Set the felt firmly into the mortar with the smooth edge of the trowel. Add a second, smaller sheet on top to fill the deeper area. Let the layers harden overnight; then proceed to cover them with underlayment.

To fill small dips (less than 1/4 inch), make a mortar and roofing felt sandwich.

The Thinnest Tile Base

Q. *We want to tile our entryway, but the front door clears the floor by only ½ inch. What kind of underlayment is thin enough so that the tile won't interfere with the door?*

You're wise to plan ahead. A too-high tile floor could not only force you to trim your door and rebuild your threshold, it could also create a toe-stubber where it abuts carpet and a awkwardly short first step where it meets a stairway.

As long as the subfloor is at least ¾ inch thick and you stiffen the joists with blocking every 16 inches, thin (¼-inch-thick) cement board is a good underlayment choice. To attach the cement board to the subfloor, spread latex-modified thinset adhesive on the floor with a ¼-inch square-notched trowel. The rough side of the cement board should face out. Fasten down the cement board with 1½-inch galvanized roofing nails or special flathead screws (available from tile dealers) every 6 inches in all directions. The seams should be offset from those of the subfloor, covered with fiberglass tape, and filled with thinset adhesive when you lay the tile.

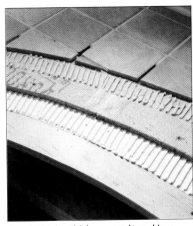

Special ¼-in.-thick cement board is a perfect low-clearance underlayment.

TYPE		USES

Mortar bed
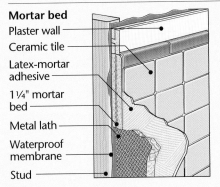
- Plaster wall
- Ceramic tile
- Latex-mortar adhesive
- 1¼" mortar bed
- Metal lath
- Waterproof membrane
- Stud

Mortar beds are strong, durable, and unaffected by moisture. However, they'll need a waterproof membrane, such as asphalt-impregnated felt or plastic, behind them. This method has fallen out of favor because it's labor-intensive and takes a lot of skill to lay a smooth bed of mortar.

Drywall
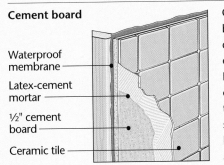
- Organic adhesive or latex-cement mortar
- ½" water-resistant drywall
- Ceramic tile

No membrane under water-resistant drywall

Gypsum-core drywall is a fast and easy backing material for tiling dry locations. However, it will crumble if it gets wet. Special water-resistant drywall (greenboard) is fine for damp locations but can't withstand frequent soakings.

Cement board
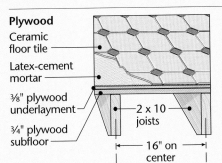
- Waterproof membrane
- Latex-cement mortar
- ½" cement board
- Ceramic tile

Cement backer board combines the convenience of drywall and the durability of a real cement mortar bed. It is made from a thin layer of concrete bonded between two fiberglass mats. The sheets (30 x 60-in.) are heavy, but easy to cut by scoring and snapping.

Plywood
- Ceramic floor tile
- Latex-cement mortar
- ⅜" plywood underlayment
- ¾" plywood subfloor
- 2 x 10 joists
- 16" on center

Plywood is an acceptable underlayment; however, if it gets wet, plywood may buckle or even delaminate. Wood tends to flex more than other materials, resulting in cracked grout lines.

Ceramic Tile

Tile Wall Layout

Q. *What are the correct steps for laying out the wall tiles in my bathroom?*

Begin on the back wall behind the tub. The object is to draw a pair of perpendicular reference lines, one level and the other plumb, that will show where you where to position the edges of the tiles.

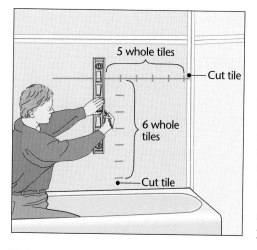

5 whole tiles
Cut tile
6 whole tiles
Cut tile

Use a level to find the lowest point of the tub, and measure up an easy-to-remember number (about 2 feet worth) of whole tiles, including spaces for grout and a ⅛-inch space above the edge of the tub. Mark a level line through that point all the way around the tub enclosure.

Next use your level to mark another line, this time plumb, going from tub to ceiling. Measure out from the corner a convenient number of whole tiles, including grout lines, plus the width of the cut tile in the corner. Your layout drawing should show how large the cut tiles in the corner must be. Mark similar reference lines on each wall. After you've drawn the reference lines, double-check your layout and lines.

When you apply the thin-set, be careful not to cover your layout lines.

Dry-Fitting Your Layout

Q. *What is the best way to plan the pattern for my new bathroom floor tiles?*

Dry-fitting your tiles, or laying out the tiles on the floor without adhesive, is the best way to see exactly how the pattern will look.

First use a chalkline to snap some reference lines; then lay out enough tile to see how the pattern will look and to determine where you will have to cut tiles. Remember to include the space for grout lines. For the best appearance, try to minimize the number of cut tiles and make the pattern symmetrical near the room's most prominent fixtures, like the bathtub or vanity.

Shift the pattern as necessary and snap new chalk lines to help guide your work. On larger floors with more complex patterns, snap guidelines every 2 feet to keep the rows straight.

Dry-fitting is the key to a first-class job. Shift the pattern to minimize cuts and to make the pattern symmetrical at the room's most prominent feature. Snap new chalklines when you're done.

Leaky Sill Problem

Q. *I'm planning to tile the tub surround in my bathroom and to add a little shelf around the lip of the tub. What can I do to make sure that water doesn't seep through the grout and into the wall?*

Use a "trowelable membrane" under the adhesive and tile to prevent water leaks.

The best defense is to apply an additional waterproof membrane on top of the cement board in the wall for extra protection. Without this added layer of protection, the moisture barrier behind the cement board won't keep water from getting to the walls. The easiest membrane to apply is called a "trowelable membrane" (available at tile supply stores). Simply mix up this two-part paste, then spread on a thin layer. Many brands include a fabric for reinforcing corners. After it dries, you can spread the adhesive and set your tile.

For lasting results, remember to slope the shelf slightly so water has a chance to run off into the tub rather than sit and gather around the grout.

Screw a temporary support board to the wall at a horizontal guideline to prevent tiles from sliding out of place.

Stop Sliding Tiles

Q. *Sometimes my tiles slip down while I'm trying to lay them onto the wall. How can I prevent this from happening?*

There are a few things you can do to stop sliders from sliding. To start a row of tiles, try screwing a temporary board to the wall as a horizontal guideline and setting the tiles on top. Leave the board in place for 30 minutes, or until the adhesive stiffens. When working down a wall, prevent sliding tiles by taping loose tiles to an anchored row of tiles above.

You can also use plastic spacers, but watch for misshapen tiles—even a small bump along the edge can throw your rows off. Use a straight-edge to check your progress.

Door Trim in the Way

Q. *How do I fit underlayment and tiles around the door trim?*

For professional-looking results, buy or borrow an undercut saw (at a tile store). Cut the door trim so that the tile can slide underneath.

Rest the blade on top of your flooring materials to make the cut.

Undercut trim for cement board and tile.

Laying Wall Tiles

Q. *I have my reference lines drawn and am ready to begin laying my wall tiles. Where do I begin?*

Start by mixing up a batch of adhesive to the consistency of mayonnaise. Then, without covering up your reference lines, spread a few square feet of adhesive on the lower corner of the back wall of the tub. Spread the adhesive thickly at first, pushing it hard against the wall; then comb it with the notched edge of the trowel. This will give you smooth ridges of adhesive. If the adhesive begins to form a skin or feels stiff, it's starting to set up. Scrape it off, apply new adhesive, and work on a smaller area next time.

Lay whole uncut tiles first, and press them firmly into the adhesive. Avoid sliding the tiles into place because this will displace the adhesive. If you're using plastic spacers, use one at each corner. Use a screwdriver or utility knife to clean up any adhesive that squeezes out between the tiles. It can discolor the grout you apply later.

You'll need to cut the tiles in the row near the corner, and probably in the row above the tub as well. Keep the bottom row of tiles at least ⅛ inch away from the tub.

Move on to another square of adhesive once you're finished, and continue up the wall. When you get to the top and to the sides, finish with single- and double-bullnose tiles on the edges and outside corners.

When you run into plumbing pipes, set all the whole uncut tiles that fit around them. Then cut tiles to fit closely around them. If a pipe ends up in the middle of a tile, cut the tile into two rectangles, nip out a semicircular hole in the edge of each, then reassemble the two parts. Don't be fanatical about getting the tile tight against the pipe; within ¼ inch is fine.

If you have to tile around an outlet or switch, first turn off the power at the main panel. Remove the screws and pull the outlet or switch from the electrical box. Set the tile within ⅛ inch of the box; then replace the switch or outlet so the metal tabs rest on top of the tile. You may have to use longer screws.

After you have finished a few rows, level and bed the tiles. To do this, tap them with a hammer and a wood block wrapped in an old towel.

Apply adhesive between your reference lines. Use the lines to guide your layout.

Laying Floor Tile

Q. *I've just tiled my bathroom walls, and I'm ready to move on to the floor. Is tiling a floor any different than tiling walls?*

Floor tiles are no more difficult, and frequently less time-consuming, to install than wall tiles. To begin, mark your reference lines and dry-fit your pattern. Plan for a row of almost full tiles along the wall nearest the door. Using cut tiles here will ensure that you don't have to use a sliver to correct an out-of-square room or other miscalculation. When you trowel out the adhesive, remember to work from the far wall toward the door.

The threshold should rest directly on the subfloor, and its outer edge should be halfway under the door. Roughen the back of the threshold with 50-grit sandpaper; then glue it to the subfloor with thinset mortar.

Don't walk on the tiles for at least 8 hours or until the adhesive sets. Allow 24 hours before grouting.

Use a square to ensure that your layout lines are perpendicular to each other. Dry-fit the tiles to double-check your layout.

CUTTING CERAMIC TILE

Cutting ceramic tile is a snap—literally. Tile is so brittle that the fastest way to cut it is to break it.

For straight cuts, use a tile cutter. Its hardened wheel scores the glazed surface of the tile. Then, when you push down on the handle, the tile is clamped on either side of the scored line and snapped in two. Most tile suppliers will lend you this tool if you are buying tile from them. If the snapped edge is a little rough, smooth it with a coarse sharpening stone.

For curved cuts, use a nipper. A nipper has hardened teeth that bite away the tile. It's fast and effective but leaves a crude-looking edge. The trick is not to take off too much at one time and to use a corner of the jaws for greater control.

For smoother cuts, use a rod saw—a round carbide blade that fits into a hacksaw frame. It's slow but makes nice smooth curves.

If you have a lot of cutting to do, rent a wet saw. It is great for perfect miters, notches, and L-shaped cuts.

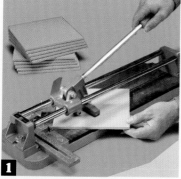

1

A rail-style tile cutter is the fastest and easiest way to make straight cuts. If the snapped edge is rough, smooth it with a coarse sharpening stone.

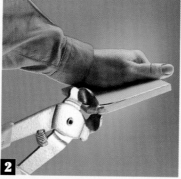

2

Tile nippers allow you to nip out curved cuts. For more control, use the corner of the jaws and work up to the line. Mark your cut line with a grease pencil.

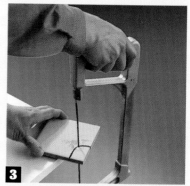

3

A rod saw is a carbide-impregnated rod that fits into a hacksaw frame. It works slowly but leaves a smooth cut.

Installing a Grab Bar

Q. *I need to install a grab bar in our tub. How can I find the studs behind the tiles?*

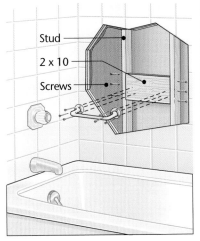

Installing a grab bar involves more than finding a stud. Most bars require three screws at each mounting plate. These screws are spaced so that not all of them will fit on the face of a stud. Also, grab bars don't usually match the typical 16-inch-on-center stud spacing. To do the job right, you'll need to open up the wall and attach a 2 x 10 block between the studs with 3½-inch screws. Then patch the hole with cement board and replacement tiles. Once the patch is completed, mark the location of the grab bar screw holes on the tiles and drill through the tiles with a carbide-tipped drill bit. Most grab bars are made of stainless steel, so be sure to use stainless steel screws to attach it to the wall to prevent rust or other corrosion.

For specific information regarding the placement of handrails and grab bars, call your local or state building department.

If your tub is located on an inside wall, it might be easier to get to the studs from the adjoining room. To install the 2 x 10, you'll only need to cut and then patch the drywall.

Tiles That Stay Stuck

Q. *How do I apply mortar to get the best adhesion?*

To make your tiles stick permanently, spread mortar on the floor or wall in one direction, set the tile in place, and then slide each tile back and forth about ¼ inch, moving at a right angle to the mortar lines as you press it in. Every once in a while, pry a tile back up to check its adhesion. The mortar should cover 80 percent of the back of the tile. If it doesn't, either your mortar is too dry or you need to use a wider-notched towel.

The mortar tends to hide your chalk guidelines, so lay straight-edges along them after spreading the adhesive to keep the pattern perfectly straight.

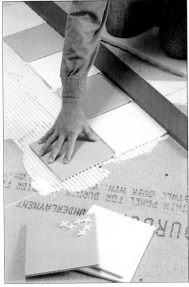

Wiggle in the tiles to bed them into the mortar. To test adhesion, pry up a tile and check that the mortar covers 80 percent of the back.

Adding a Shelf When Tiling a Shower

Q. *I'd like to add a corner shelf when I retile my shower stall. How do I do it?*

A corner shelf made of solid surfacing material or porcelain ceramic is a great convenience for keeping your soap and shampoo within easy reach while you shower.

If you are retiling your bath, simply

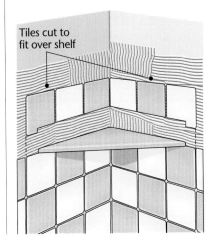

tile the corner up to the height where you want the shelf, then glue the shelf in place against the cement backer board, using thinset mortar. If the corner is out of square, sand the edges of the shelf so that it fits snugly. The shelf should rest on the top edge of the row of tiles beneath it.

When you install the next row, notch or cut the bottoms of the tiles so that they fit over the shelf and keep the rows even.

To install a shelf on an already tiled wall, you could glue it to the surface of the tile with a silicone-base tile adhesive (sold at tile stores). But keep in mind that this isn't the most secure way to install a shelf and should be for light-duty use only. Be sure to install the shelf high enough to deter a child from trying to hang from it or sit on it.

Ceramic Tile

Replacing Caulk

Q. *The grout joint between my bathtub and the ceramic tile is cracked. What's the best way to get a leak-free joint?*

You don't need to regrout between the tub and the tile—a solid bead of caulk will keep the water out. Pry out any cracked grout with a screwdriver; then clean the area with a phosphoric acid solution. Let the surface dry completely before applying a bead of high-quality caulk. Use your finger to smooth the bead, and keep a wet rag handy to wipe away any excess. While you're at it, caulk around the handles and spout to prevent water from getting behind the wall tiles.

Use clear caulk if you can't find a caulk to match the grout color.

Remove cracked or stained grout; replace it with a high-quality caulk.

Caring for Grout

Q. *Our tile still looks good, but the grout is discolored and is missing in a few spots. What can we do?*

Discolored or missing grout requires immediate attention. Cleaning it and making minor repairs can prevent more serious problems later on.

Where the grout is intact, all it needs is a thorough cleaning. Most grout can be cleaned with a phosphoric acid and water solution. If the grout's really dirty, use the acid undiluted. Wear rubber gloves.

The best way to scrub grout is with a nylon-bristle grout brush. The long, stiff bristles let you scrub hard enough to remove the dirt and mildew but won't scratch the surrounding tile.

To repair a small patch of missing grout, try to get grout samples from a tile store to match the color as closely as possible (two or more colors can be blended if necessary). Mix a sample batch and let it dry for 3 days to see how the color compares to the existing grout. Remember to wear gloves; grout is a cement product and contains caustic lime.

Mix the grout with a latex additive instead of water to make it more flexible. To protect the grout lines, use a penetrating sealer (see right).

Sealing Grout

Q. *Can sealing ceramic tile make it easier to clean?*

Yes, it certainly can. A sealer keeps water and dirt from penetrating and staining the grout.

For new tile, allow a week or two for the grout to dry before applying the sealer. Reapply sealer annually to extend the life of the grout. Apply sealer only to the grout lines; it may dull the tile.

When applying penetrating sealer, use a small brush to stay within the grout lines.

Repairing Chipped Ceramic Tile

Q. *We have Italian tiles in our kitchen and some of them have chipped over the years. Can they be repaired?*

The best repair would be a replacement. Unfortunately, unless you have a few leftovers, finding an exact match is almost impossible. The color of all types of tiles varies slightly from batch to batch.

If you don't have any left, try filling the chipped spots with the polyester resin that's used to repair bathtubs. It will be difficult to match the color of the tile, and the repair will definitely be visible. For smaller chips, try using appliance touch-up paint.

Tile Cleaners

■ Specialty cleaning products can work wonders, but their very strength can make them dangerous—unless you follow the directions carefully.

■ Many tile cleaners contain sodium hypochlorite (chlorine bleach), which is an irritant to mucous membranes. For those with respiratory ailments, inhaling this chemical can make breathing more difficult. The fumes can also affect your heart rate and blood pressure and should be avoided by those with heart problems.

REGROUTING TILE

Broken or badly worn grout not only looks bad, it can allow moisture to penetrate behind the tile, which can weaken the adhesive or even damage the substrate. Replacing bad grout now will prevent bigger problems later.

Use a grout saw or an old can opener to scrape out the grout between tiles. For big jobs, you may want to use a rotary-type tool with a carbide tip.

Vacuum the dust and debris out of the joints between tiles. Next, use a tile cleaner to wash off any mineral buildup, soap scum, or grout residue.

Mix a batch of new grout to the consistency of toothpaste. Apply the grout with a float, covering about 2 square yards at a time. Allow the grout to set for 30 minutes; then wipe off any excess with a damp sponge. Next, smooth and pack the grout lines with the handle of a toothbrush. Let the grout set overnight; then wipe off any remaining film with a clean dry cloth.

Wait 2 or 3 weeks before sealing the grout with a grout sealer.

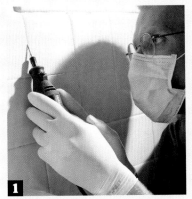

1 Hold the tip of the rotary tool against the grout line and pull down.

2 Sweep a rubber float diagonally across the grout lines to fill the large areas.

3 Run the end of a toothbrush along the lines to pack the grout.

Replacing a Damaged Tile

Q. *What is the best way to replace a damaged tile?*

Starting at the grout line, carefully chisel out the damaged tile. Wear goggles and gloves—ceramic tile tends to chip. Scrape off the old adhesive with a cold chisel. Don't use a heat gun or solvent; they will just create a mess. Chip out most of the old grout with a chisel (or use a grout saw) to make room for the new tile.

After removing the old tile and adhesive, apply adhesive to the back of the replacement tile with a notched trowel, then put the tile in place. Make sure the grout lines align with the adjacent tiles. For floor tiles, use thinset mortar (as the adhesive) and sanded grout. For wall tiles, use premixed mastic adhesive and non-sanded grout.

Using a scrap of wood and a hammer, gently tap the new tile flush with the other tiles. If the tile is lower than the surrounding tiles, remove it and apply more adhesive. Clean off any ooze from the grout lines with the tip of a screwdriver. Allow the adhesive to set for 24 hours before applying grout.

If you use nonmatching repair tile, consider replacing a few others to make a decorative pattern.

Chip away the damaged tile and old adhesive with a hammer and cold chisel.

Don't skimp on the thinset. Any excess can be cleaned up after leveling the tile.

Choosing
Wood
Flooring

IT'S HARD TO BEAT the beauty of a hardwood floor. Wood floors are easy to clean, hypoallergenic, and will last for years. Unfortunately, having a wood floor installed costs much more than most carpeting. You can save a bundle by laying the floor yourself. Here is an overview of the different kinds of wood flooring available, as well a brief description of how to install each product.

Solid Wood

Solid wood flooring is still considered to be the best. Made from hardwood, such as oak or maple, or softwood, such as pine, most floors come in either 2¼- or 1½-inch wide strips. (Pieces wider than 3 inches are called planks.) Each strip is milled with tongue-and-groove joints. The interlocking joint creates a single strong sheet, which adds rigidity to the floor.

PROS & CONS

- Strong, tight floor.
- Can be sanded and refinished.
- Most labor-intensive installation.
- Sanding and finishing can cost as much as flooring material.

FLOOR PREPARATION

The best subfloor is ¾-inch plywood or 1 x 6 boards. Install a layer of rosin paper or 15-pound roofing felt over the subfloor to prevent squeaks. Run the strips at a right angle to the joists for a stiffer installation.

HOW TO INSTALL

Rent a mallet-driven nailer (see picture, right) that drives special 2-inch nails through the flooring tongue and simultaneously drives the strip tight against the previous piece. To finish, rent a floor sander to flatten the joints and smooth the floor. Take care not to gouge the floor. Use a buffer to finish smoothing the floor. Carefully vacuum up any dust, apply stain, and then spread on at least three coats of finish. Sand lightly between each coat.

Prefinished Solid Wood

A prefinished strip floor means the factory has already applied a hard, durable finish to the traditional ¾-inch-thick strips. With sanding and finishing eliminated, the time and effort required to install a floor are significantly reduced.

- Clean installation. Sanding and finishing done at the factory.
- Reduced installation time.
- V-grooves between planks collect dirt and are hard to clean.

Prepare the subfloor as you would for any solid wood floor.

Installation of prefinished solid wood strip and plank is exactly like that for traditional wood flooring. With some prefinished floors, screws are added at the ends of the strips for added reinforcement.

Parquet

Parquet is an eye-catching alternative to strip flooring. There are many intricate patterns you can use to turn your floor into a dazzling wood mosaic, although most homeowners choose the economical finger-block style. Typically, the parquet you'll find is about 5/16 inch thick, prefinished, and milled with tongues and grooves.

Glue-Down Laminate

Laminates feature a prefinished top layer of either a hardwood veneer or plastic. Layers of plywood below stabilize and support the top, making this type of flooring resistant to warps and cracks. Laminate strips are typically 1/2 inch thick, anywhere from 3 to 8 inches wide, and up to 8 feet long. The pieces interlock with tongues and grooves.

Floating Laminate

A "floating" laminate floor is neither glued down nor nailed down, but instead "floats" on a 1/8-inch-thick foam pad that you lay over your subfloor or concrete. The tongue-and-groove edges are glued together, transforming single pieces into a solid mass. Some laminate floors have plastic, instead of real wood veneers.

- Many intricate, eye-catching patterns.
- Easy installation.
- Can be refinished only once or twice.

- Quick and easy installation.
- More stable than solid wood.
- Glues directly to a level subfloor.
- V-grooves between planks collect dirt and are hard to clean.
- Cannot always be refinished.

- Quick and easy installation.
- More stable than solid wood.
- Can be used on basement concrete floors with a plastic vapor barrier under the pad.
- Cannot be refinished.

To lay a top-notch parquet floor, provide a rock-solid subfloor by nailing a layer of 1/2-inch plywood over the existing subfloor. Stagger the joints so they don't match up with those of the plywood below. You can glue parquet to a dry concrete floor that is above ground level.

You can glue laminate strips directly to a firm, level 3/4-inch subfloor. If your subfloor has dips and rises, you need to sand down the high spots, lay a new subfloor, or level the dips with a commercial filler.

You can lay the floating floor over wood subfloors and concrete. However, as with glue-down laminates, be sure the floors are flat and level, with no more than a 1/8-inch rise or fall in every 10 feet; otherwise, the floor will bounce and feel soft.

To lay a parquet floor, snap a pair of perpendicular chalklines to divide the room into four parts. Working out from the center, spread the adhesive and lay the tiles. To press the parquet into the glue, cover a section with a 2 x 2-foot piece of 3/4-inch plywood and tap the plywood with a hammer.

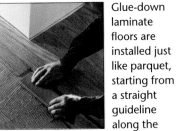

Glue-down laminate floors are installed just like parquet, starting from a straight guideline along the wall. Be sure to use the the mastic and trowel size that is recommended by the manufacturer.

To assemble the floor, run a bead of glue in grooves and tap in the mating piece. Wipe away any squeeze-out before the glue dries. Leave a 1/2-inch gap at the walls for wood movement. (See p.57 for a detailed description of installing a floating laminate floor.)

Wood Flooring

INSTALLING WOOD FLOORING

Uneven Concrete Base

Q. *The slab I want to cover with wood flooring is not perfectly flat. How do I fix it?*

Check a concrete floor for flatness by laying a straight 10-foot-long board on edge in various places on the floor. If there are any gaps of more than ⅛ inch between the floor and the board, you'll need to fill them in with floor patching material. Shave down high ridges with a rented angle grinder.

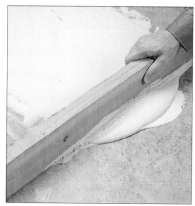

Level the floor, using a straight 2 x 4 to spread patching material over low spots.

Preserving a Wood Floor

Q. *I'm installing new hardwood floors. Is it true that the climate in my home can affect this flooring?*

Yes, it is true. To maintain wood floors, keep the relative humidity inside your home reasonably constant, ideally in the 40 to 60 percent range. Depending on where you live, you may have to run a humidifier in the winter to keep this level up and a dehumidifier in the summer to keep the level down. A properly finished floor should hold up well in these conditions.

Be aware that damp basements, concrete slabs, and crawl spaces can cause high humidity and wood expansion. When things dry out, wood may shrink and crack. Spilled water on the floor can cause problems, too, as can having a furnace directly below a wood floor.

Wood over Concrete

Q. *I want to lay a wood floor over concrete, but I'm concerned about moisture. Is there a way to protect the wood?*

You can glue a wood floor over concrete as long as the concrete remains dry; if moisture is a factor, you'll need to install a floating floor. To determine your need for a floating wood floor, do a "wetness test" by attaching some 2 x 2-foot sheets of polyethylene plastic to the concrete. Use duct tape to seal the sheets down. If after 24 hours the covered areas are dark or damp, you need to install a floating floor.

A floating floor is not nailed or glued, but instead "floats" on a ⅛-inch foam pad that you lay over the concrete. When the floor expands or contracts with changes in humidity, it can move freely, so gaps don't develop between individual planks. A plastic vapor barrier installed under the foam pad prevents moisture in the concrete from reaching the wood.

To allow for expansion, you need to leave a ½-inch gap (larger in extremely humid climates) around the floor's perimeter. Local flooring dealers should be able to tell you how big the gap should be if you give them the dimensions of the room.

Wood Floor in the Kitchen

Q. *I want to install a wood floor when we remodel our kitchen. My husband says a wood floor won't hold up in the kitchen. Is he correct?*

Wood kitchen floors are becoming more common nowadays because the finishes available are tougher than ever and hold up to heavy foot traffic and spills. Of course, you still need to take reasonable care of the floor. When you're out shopping for flooring, tell the salespeople you speak with that you want wood flooring to install in a kitchen. This will help them narrow down the selection of products.

When choosing wood flooring for the kitchen, avoid floorboards that have beveled edges. They collect dirt and are hard to keep clean. Also avoid dark stain colors because they show wear more readily.

To keep the floor looking good, wipe up spills immediately. Place throw rugs in front of the sink, dishwasher, and refrigerator to reduce the potential for water stains.

The biggest enemy of wood floors—in the kitchen or any other room—is sand and dirt from outdoors. You'll want to vacuum frequently. Put dirt-trapping mats at door entrances, place soft protectors on the bottoms of furniture, and wear outdoor shoes as little as possible inside the house.

Although today's finishes are tougher and more durable than finishes from the past, your wood kitchen floor will need to be refinished every 3 to 10 years. As long as the finish doesn't wear down to the bare wood, you can sand it lightly and apply new polyurethane on top of the old. Never use wax on a varnished wood floor because it will prevent any new finish from adhering.

INSTALLING A FLOATING WOOD LAMINATE FLOOR

To prepare a concrete floor, vacuum it thoroughly and make sure it's level (see Uneven Concrete Base p.56). Then cover it with 6-mil polyethylene sheets, overlapping the seams by 8 inches and sealing them with duct tape. The sheets should run at least 3 inches up the walls. The sheets of foam underlayment, which are laid over the poly, should not be overlapped or run up the walls.

Keep the cartons of flooring closed until you are ready to use them; they have a low moisture content and leaving them open could make the planks swell. Begin laying the flooring in a corner, placing the grooved sides against ½-inch plywood spacers. Apply a bead of the adhesive recommended by the manufacturer along the sides and at the ends of each plank. Wipe away excess glue immediately with a damp cloth.

Drive the planks together by gently tapping on a piece of scrap flooring fitted over the tongue of the plank; never strike the tongue directly. Use a jigsaw to cut the planks around outside corners or along walls, and be sure you're cutting the correct end. Force the last planks into place along walls with a pry bar or a hammer and a "tugger." Make a tugger by screwing a block and a metal plate to a 2 x 4 (Step 4, below). If you use a pry bar, be careful not to damage walls. When you lay the planks, try to scatter those with unusual grain or color patterns so they're not all together. Stagger the joints where the wood meets end-to-end. If you lay a plank and then notice that it is damaged, remove it; once the glue sets, it can be impossible to separate. If your room is not perfectly square, you will have to rip a plank (cut it lengthwise) wider on one end than on the other.

The tongue of transition pieces should lap over the flooring but must not be fastened to the flooring.

1 The sheets of foam underlayment, which are laid over the polyethylene sheets, should not be overlapped or run up the walls.

2 Glue the planks together along the sides and at the ends.

3 Drive planks together by tapping on scrap flooring fitted over the tongue.

4 Force planks into place along walls using a "tugger."

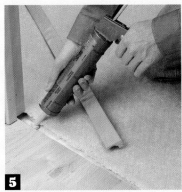

5 Fasten the transition piece to a concrete subfloor with construction adhesive.

Wood Flooring

Patching Wood Floors

Q. *I took down a wall and now there's a gap in the flooring, going across the boards. How do I fill it without it looking patched?*

This job is definitely a challenge, and we recommend it only to seasoned do-it-yourselfers. It takes time and patience, along with some finishing savvy. The toughest job is removing existing pieces to make room for the new ones. Use your judgment about the number of pieces you need to remove to match the random-length boards of the existing floor.

You'll also have to select the right wood flooring at the lumberyard. After you get the new flooring, let it sit in the room for at least a week to stabilize before doing the job.

Begin by cutting out short sections of old strips so you can "weave" in the new strips. Use a ¾-inch spade bit to drill holes at the ends of sections. Split each section with circular saw cuts; then pry the old wood out. Use a sharp combination or carbide-tipped blade. Wear safety glasses, because you'll run into a nail or two.

Square up any rough ends with a wood chisel. Now lay down some rosin paper or No. 15 roofing felt as an underlayment for the new pieces.

Cut the new pieces to exact lengths and lay them in, nailing through tongues. You'll have to face-nail some of the pieces (nail them through the top surface). You'll also have to remove the bottoms of the grooves to fit some of the pieces in place.

When you've finished laying the new flooring, set any exposed nails. Next, use a belt sander to sand the new area to conform with the old. After sanding, you'll need to finish the floor to blend with the existing floor finish.

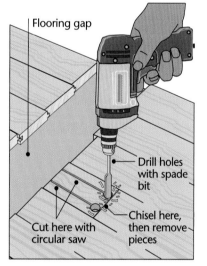

Flooring gap

Drill holes with spade bit

Cut here with circular saw

Chisel here, then remove pieces

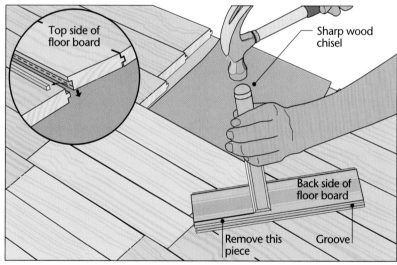

Top side of floor board

Sharp wood chisel

Back side of floor board

Remove this piece

Groove

Popped Planks

Q. *My tongue-and-groove wood laminate floor was installed with adhesive over a concrete slab. Several planks have popped up. How can I fix them and keep them from popping again?*

First check to see that the installer left room for expansion. To find out, remove the baseboards. There should be at least a ⅜-inch gap between the floor and the wall.

If there isn't, chisel out some of the flooring along the walls. When the baseboard is reinstalled, it should cover what's been chiseled out.

The next step? Wait. If the boards pop up in the summer but lie flat in the winter, making room for expansion should take care of the problem.

However, if the boards remain buckled all year long, then it's possible the adhesive has pulled loose, causing a hardened, uneven residue to form under the boards.

To correct this, carefully remove the popped-up boards. It's likely the boards will break in doing so, in which case you'll need to replace them with new boards. To install the new boards, cut off the bottom side of the groove. Trowel new adhesive on the floor, following manufacturer's instructions, and place a bead of glue on top of the tongue. Lay the boards in. Put some weight on them for a few days to make sure they adhere.

Holes in Finished Wood

Q. *There's a 2-inch-long hole in the wood floor in my dining room. What can I fill it in with?*

Fill the hole with wood putty, overfilling it slightly. At the same time, make a test board by smearing a thin layer of putty over a piece of scrap wood. Because putty shrinks slightly as it dries, holes deeper than ⅛ inch or so may require multiple layers of putty.

When the putty dries, use medium-grit, then fine, sandpaper to smooth both the patch and the layer of putty on the test board. Then try polyurethane—you can use gloss, semigloss, or satin—on the test board to find the right sheen.

Stain the patch and apply two coats of polyurethane. An artist's brush is the best tool for finishing small spots.

Shallow nicks and scratches can usually be fixed without wood putty. In most cases they require nothing more than a little stain and polyurethane to do the job.

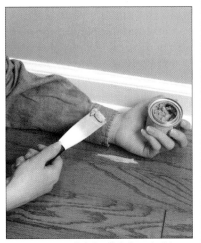

Because putty shrinks slightly as it dries, holes deeper than ⅛ in. or so may require multiple layers of putty.

Squeaky Parquet

Q. *Our 70-year-old parquet floors squeak terribly. We've tried putting in long screws from underneath to stiffen the floors, but it hasn't helped. What next?*

In the 1920's, parquet flooring was laid strip by strip, not packaged in the 12 x 12-inch configuration that is common now. Your floor consists of hundreds of separate strips of oak wood that have become loose and are rubbing against each other. It may help to keep the humidity around 40 percent, which will keep the floors from drying, then shrinking and squeaking. Some people sweep talcum powder into the cracks between floorboards to lubricate the edges to stop squeaks. The only sure solution is to reinstall the existing flooring or to lay new parquet tiles.

Fix Squeaky Floors

Q. *Our second-story floors have become very squeaky. How can we stop the squeaks?*

The first step is to pinpoint the squeak's origin. A floor generally has three layers: the joists, the subfloor, and the floor. Squeaks occur where the layers separate and rub together.

A sprinkling of powdered graphite or talcum powder between the floorboards may silence a squeak temporarily. For a permanent cure, you will need to tighten the parts that are rubbing. If the squeak is from loose hardwood, drive additional nails or screws from the top side. Use nails with a ribbed, spiral, or threaded shank so they'll bite firmly into the joists. You could also use trim-head drywall screws—screws with a tiny head—that easily sink below the surface of the hardwood flooring. Fill the holes with wood putty. Sink

existing loose nails farther into the joist with a nail set, or they'll quickly become loose again. If the joists are accessible from below, have a helper stand on the squeak while you drive new screws into the subfloor.

For carpeted floors where the joists below are concealed by a ceiling, locate the joists with a stud finder.

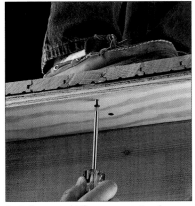

Install screws while someone stands on the floor above. Make sure they penetrate at least ½ in. into the flooring.

Push the carpet nap out of the way over the joist. Next, predrill holes through the flooring that are slightly larger than the shank of the screw; the holes should be drilled at an angle toward the joist, but not into the joist. Stand directly over the squeak and drive pairs of wood screws into the joist.

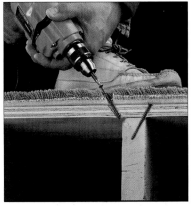

Drive screws into the joists at an angle from both directions. Sink screwheads well below the carpet and pad.

Wood Flooring

REPAIRING A WOOD FINISH

Removing a Stain

Q. *There are stains on my hardwood floor where water dripped from a houseplant. How can I remove them?*

The best way to get rid of water stains is to sand them with a vibrating sander, like a palm sander, then restain the affected area. Don't use a belt sander; it could ruin the floor. Start with 100-grit sandpaper and finish with 150-grit. Vacuum the dust and clean the area with a cloth dampened with mineral spirits

if you'll be using oil-base stain, or water if you'll be using a latex stain.

Matching stain to your floor generally requires mixing different colors. Buy two or three cans of stain that are close to the color of the floor and experiment. Mix oil-base stains with other oil-base stains, and latex with latex. Test the colors on a piece of sanded unstained wood that's the same species as your floor. Check for a match while the stain is wet. Apply the matching stain to your floor, and finish with a matching sealer (gloss, semigloss, or satin).

Use a vibrating sander to remove water stains. Do not use a belt sander.

Test-match two or three stain colors on a piece of sanded unstained wood.

Removing Carpet Glue

Q. *What is the easiest way to remove glue and old carpet backing from a hardwood floor?*

There's no easy way to do this. You'll need to sand off the glue, then sand and refinish the floor. Avoid using solvents and wire brushes.

Remove as much of the backing as you can with an industrial-size floor buffer (you can rent one) fitted with a screening pad. It takes a while to learn how to control a buffer, so start in the center of the room and go easy until you get a feel for the machine. It goes faster if someone else vacuums

up the loose backing as you go. Once the backing is removed, you can remove the glue with a floor sander.

Use 36-grit sandpaper to remove glue, stains, and gouges. Follow with 60-grit paper, and finish with 100-grit. If this is laminated flooring, be careful. If it was sanded once before, it may not withstand another sanding. In that case, consider replacing the floor or covering it with carpet again. Some parquet floors are laminated and should also be treated with caution. To determine if a parquet floor is laminated, look for exposed sections, such as around ducts that are cut into the floor.

Renewing a Finish

Q. *Is there a way to make my hardwood floors look new again without sanding off the old finish?*

If your floor was finished with polyurethane, you should be able to recoat the floor as long as it was never waxed. If it was waxed, a new topcoat will adhere only if you sand off all of the old finish and the wax.

Test for adhesion by cleaning and taping off two 6-inch square sections, one near a wall, the other in a high-traffic area. Sand each section with 100-grit screen or sandpaper. Wipe each clean and coat with oil-base polyurethane or water-base urethane. After 24 hours, scratch the topcoat with a coin. If it doesn't flake off, you can safely recoat.

Quick Touch-Ups

Q. *What's the quickest way to repair little scratches and gouges in my hardwood floor?*

For small scratches, use a furniture touch-up marker in a color that matches your floor; dab it on. Stain from a can will work, too. Cover the repair with polyurethane, applying two or more layers to build it up flush with the existing finish.

Touch-up small scratches with a furniture marker or stain from a can.

REFINISHING A HARDWOOD FLOOR

Putting a new finish coat on a hard-wood floor is a two-step process. First you lightly sand the floor surface. Then you apply a topcoat of finish. But it works only if the floor was never waxed (see Renewing a Finish, facing page). To prepare for recoating, remove all the furniture and clean the floor with a cleaner specially formulated for wood floors. The next step is sanding, which is called screening and requires renting a buffing machine.

Screening roughens the old finish so that the new finish adheres better. If your floor is stained, keep an eye out for uneven or warped boards. Screening may cut through the stain at high points, exposing the natural wood and ruining the floor's appearance. The solution is to screen these boards lightly by hand.

The rental store can supply the special attachments that you need for a buffer: a drive brush, a special pad, and a 100-grit disc screen. If you've never used a buffer, practice on smooth, clean concrete, making sure to clean the pad before putting it on a wood floor. To use a buffer, center it on a 100-grit screen and move it back and forth in the direction of the wood strips. Check the screen every few minutes for grit. Remove any you find to avoid deeply scratching the finish.

For the finish, choose an oil-base polyurethane or a water-base urethane. Make sure it is formulated for floors. Oil-base polyurethane contains solvents; wear a painting respirator with a charcoal filter. Water-base urethane contains little solvent but dries quickly. You have to work fast and use special spreading pads.

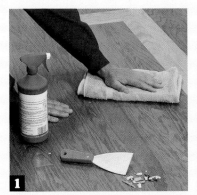

1

Scrape up any dried paint or grime with a putty knife. Then wipe the floor with specially formulated floor cleaner. Spray cleaner on the cloth, not the floor.

2

Remove stubborn stains with a 100-grit screen and mineral spirits. Then sand around the edges of the floor by hand, using a 100-grit screen.

3

Screen the floor with a 100-grit screen on a buffer. Keep the buffer moving, going back and forth with the wood strips until the floor has an even, chalky appearance. Vacuum thoroughly and wipe with a cloth dampened in mineral spirits (for oil-base finish) or water (for water-base finish). After it dries fully, apply a finish as directed.

Carpeting

INSTALLING CARPETING

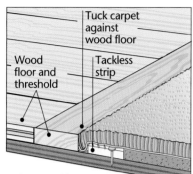

Using a tackless strip

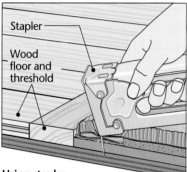

Using staples

Carpet at the Threshold

Q. *I'm recarpeting my living room. The next room has a wood floor, and there's a wood threshold in between. How do I fasten carpet to the floor at the threshold?*

If the difference in height between the wood floor and the uncarpeted living room floor is more than ½ inch, you can safely use a tackless strip to hold the carpet down near the threshold. If the difference in height between the two floors is less than ½ inch, you'll need to staple the carpet to the floor. First cut back the carpet pad about 1 inch from the edge of the threshold. Then tuck the edge of the carpeting under about 1 inch to cover the area that has no padding. Spread the carpet pile apart with one hand while you staple both layers of carpet into the subfloor.

Carpeting over Concrete

Q. *We want to carpet the concrete floor on our raised ranch's lower level. But when our neighbors carpeted theirs, the pad underneath rotted within 3 years. Do we need to lay a subfloor first?*

Putting down a plywood floor over the concrete slab would be a lot of work for the small benefits derived. And it won't solve any moisture problem you might have; this has to be handled with proper drainage and grading on the outside of the house.

Urethane foam padding, which is readily available from carpeting suppliers, will not rot and provides fairly good insulation. Or you can buy carpeting with ¼- or ⅜-inch-thick urethane foam backing already attached.

Choosing Carpet Pads

Q. *Which is better to use as carpet padding, waffle-shaped all-rubber padding or urethane foam? What do the weight ratings mean?*

Most experts recommend a smooth-surfaced urethane foam pad, called bonded or rebound urethane. Waffle-shaped pads, usually made of latex and clay, deteriorate faster than urethane foam. Over time, waffle padding flattens out, making your carpet feel loose on the floor.

Weight rating is a measure of the density of a pad. The more it weighs, the denser it is and the better it will hold up to foot traffic. When choosing carpet pad, squeeze it between your fingers. A good-quality pad won't flatten completely and will return to its original shape as soon as you let go.

Worth Doing Yourself?

Q. *Will I save a lot if I carpet some rooms in the house myself?*

Laying carpet yourself isn't a big money saver. The cost of renting the tools alone can run more than half the amount that a carpet layer might charge for a typical bedroom. But if you do it yourself, you'll have control over when the carpet is laid, the satisfaction of doing it yourself, and the know-how for future repairs.

Beginners should tackle a room less than 12 feet in width, to eliminate having to seam the carpet. Berber carpets are a bit more difficult to work with, so you might want to choose a different type of carpet.

Seaming Carpet

Q. *I plan to carpet a large room. How do I handle seams?*

Seams are best left to a pro. But here's how it's done: Straight-cut the edges of both pieces so that they butt tightly together. Center seaming tape under the joint. Set a warm seaming iron (a rental) on top of the tape. Wait 15 to 20 seconds, then slide the iron forward almost one iron length. While the glue is hot, press the carpet down, making sure the edges meet exactly. Repeat for the length of the seam. Be careful; the iron is hot.

Let the seaming iron rest 15 to 20 sec.; then slide it forward one length.

INSTALLING WALL-TO-WALL CARPETING

Here's how to lay jute-backed carpet, which is secured with tackless strips rather than adhesive. Before you begin, sketch the room on graph paper. Add 3 inches to each carpet dimension to allow 1½ inches along each wall for fitting. Also buy carpet padding, enough tackless strips to go around the room perimeter, and drywall nails to attach the strips. You'll need a hammer, shears to cut the strips, a carpet knife with extra blades, a straightedge, a staple gun to attach the pad, and a screwdriver to tuck in the carpet edges. Rent a power stretcher and a knee kicker. To prepare the room, remove doors from their hinges and grilles from the floor.

Install the pad with the scrim (smooth) side up. Rough-cut a too-wide carpet in a larger space. Cut cut-pile carpet from the back. Spread loop piles apart and cut from the front. Make relief cuts in corners and at doorways so that the carpet lies flat. Lay the carpet over heat ducts; cut the openings later. When stretching carpet, reposition the stretcher often, and never leave more than a 4-inch gap between stretcher-head positions. Your final stretch should be diagonally opposite your starting corner.

At doorways, use metal transition strips for vinyl or tile. For wood, use metal or wood, or trim and tuck the carpet. The transition should occur under the door.

1 Nail tackless strips around the perimeter, ⅜ in. from the wall, with pins angled to the wall. Use drywall nails; put at least two in each strip.

2 Lay the pad and cut it to fit along the edges of the tackless strips. Staple it every 4 in. along walls and seams.

3 Lay the carpet and cut it to fit with 1½-in. extra along each edge.

4 In one corner, press the carpet backing onto the tackless pins by rubbing it hard with a hammerhead. Work out about 5 ft. in each direction.

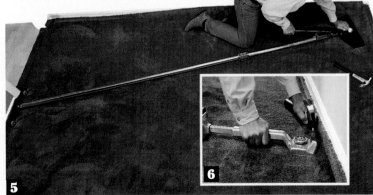

5 Stretch the carpet into each adjacent corner with a power stretcher. Set the heel against a first corner baseboard and the head 4 in. from the opposite wall. Press handle until carpet is taut.

6 Use a knee kicker to bump the carpet onto the strips and a hammer to press it onto the pins. Trim the carpet from the back side, leaving a ¼-in. edge. Tuck the edge behind the strips.

Carpeting

Premature Carpet Wear

Q. *My 2-year-old, expensive, brand-name, stain-resistant carpet needs to be replaced. Why hasn't it lasted?*

Stain-resistant carpeting is just as durable as ordinary carpeting, and just as delicate.

Each fiber of a nylon carpet has little pores (dye sites) where dye is injected to color the fibers. On ordinary carpet fibers, stains can also be absorbed through these pores. On stain-resistant carpet, the pores are sealed so stains are kept on the surface. The sealant has no effect on the wear resistance of the carpet.

If you are maintaining your carpet well (most wear is the result of inadequate cleaning), the premature wear is probably caused by poor installation. Poor carpet padding, for instance, can shorten the life of your carpet and void the warranty. Defective carpeting is rare.

Pet Odor Removal

Q. *Apparently the previous owners of our house had animals that were not housebroken. We scrubbed the area and laid new carpet, but the smell persists. What can we do?*

Use the three-step approach the pros use: Find it, kill it, seal it.

First remove the new carpet and pad. Use a black light to find the spots; it makes the salts in urine visible. Mark all damaged areas with

Rent or buy a black light and use it to locate stains left by a pet.

chalk. Check everywhere—most pets have a favorite spot they repeatedly visit. In addition to the wood underlayment or concrete floor, urine can be absorbed by baseboard, quarter-round moldings, drywall, plaster, even drapes. In severe cases urine may have soaked into insulation and ductwork. Since the bacteria in pet urine can become airborne, spores can wind up on walls, windowsills, and even ceilings.

Let the area air out. Many pros use a fogging machine loaded with an odor counteractant to neutralize the smell. You may be able to rent one from a large rental yard or fire restoration company. If not, saturate the damaged areas with a liquid enzyme product, but don't mix it with other soaps or disinfectants, which can interfere with the reaction that takes place. Let the area dry completely; it may take 2 weeks.

Once the surface is dry, seal the subfloor with a thinned coat of polyurethane. Finally, reinstall the carpet and a new pad, even if the one you're throwing out is only a few months old; pads really trap odors.

CARPET STAIN REMOVAL

CAUSE	SOLUTION
Chewing gum	Freeze gum with ice cubes in a plastic bag; scrape up with a butter knife; blot with trichloroethylene (dry-cleaning fluid, available at drug and hardware stores).
Grease, oil, lipstick, butter	Blot up excess with paper towels; sponge with dry-cleaning fluid; work from edges to center.
Animal urine	Immediately blot up excess with paper towels; soak with carbonated water; blot again; scrub with diluted carpet shampoo.
Fruit juices, soft drinks	Blot up excess; sponge with a solution of 1 tsp. powdered laundry detergent and 1 tsp. white vinegar dissolved in 1 qt. warm water.
Shoe polish, ink, dry paint	Dab with paint remover; if that fails, use dry-cleaning fluid.
Coffee, beer, milk	Blot up excess with paper towels, scrub with diluted carpet shampoo; cover with paper towels and weight down for 2 to 3 hr.
Wax	Scrape off as much wax as possible; then place a brown paper bag over the area and run a warm iron over it. The bag will act as a blotter and absorb the wax.

Removing Surface Burns

Q. *How can I make burn spots on my rug less noticeable?*

Remove surface burns by snipping off the charred tips of the carpet with sharp scissors. If the carpet is plush, it helps to feather out the area by lightly tapering the nap in a circle a little wider than the damaged area.

Snip and feather out burned carpet threads with sharp scissors.

Furniture Footprints

Q. *What can I do to remove indentations in my carpet left by the feet of my furniture?*

To remove furniture footprints, set your clothes iron on *Steam*. Hold it ¼ inch above the dent, then press the steam button. The moisture will make the carpet fibers pop up again and regain their original shape. Use a screwdriver to help fluff the carpet.

Hold the iron ¼ in. above the carpet; don't rest it directly on the floor.

Carpet Snags

Q. *There are several places where yarn has come loose in my level-loop carpet leaving a noticeable run. Can this be fixed?*

If you still have the loose yarn, all you need to repair the snag are scissors, a nail set, and carpet seam adhesive.

First, count the number of loops in the carpet it will take to fill the run. Then count the curls in the loose yarn and cut it to provide the right amount of yarn to fill the entire run. To replace the cut yarn, protect the surrounding carpet with masking tape and squeeze a heavy bead of adhesive into the run. Use a nail set to press each "scab" (where the original adhesive clings to the yarn) down into the carpet backing until each new loop is at the right height.

You can re-affix a loose yarn with seam adhesive and a nail set.

When Carpet Is Too Thick

Q. *I want to install thick carpeting in my family room, but if I do, the door to the garage won't open. I can't cut the door because it's steel.*

Residential steel doors usually have a wood strip at the bottom, which you can trim to fit with a circular saw and carbide-tip blade. You'll probably have to remove and replace the weatherstripping at the door bottom.

Carpet Tears

Q. *How can I fix the tear along the seam in my family-room carpet?*

Most carpet tears happen along seams where two pieces were originally glued or sewn together. To fix them, pull the carpet edges together and hold them in place with nails driven about 6 inches from the tear. Then use a curved upholstery needle and heavy fishing line to sew the pieces together. Make the stitch holes about ½ inch out from each edge and every ¾ inch along the seam. The top of the stitch should be square to the tear, the underside diagonal, for the least visibility.

If you're rejoining a seam that was once glued together, you'll find the old glue tape tough to work a needle through; use needle-nose pliers to help push the needle.

Use needle-nose pliers to help push the upholstery needle through old glue tape.

(See Steel Door Bottom Sweep, p.133.) With some doors, the metal wraps around the bottom and into grooves in the wood. You can trim this type of door, but you must be sure the metal is still bonded in place afterward. Another approach is to remove the door and frame and install a spacer under the threshold.

The simplest solution is to install a small section of vinyl or ceramic tile in front of the door.

Vinyl and Other Flooring

INSTALLING VINYL FLOORING

No-Show Vinyl Seams

Q. *How can I make the seams invisible when I install sheet vinyl flooring in my kitchen?*

Most flooring comes in 12-foot widths, so you may get by without seams. If you're not that lucky, lay out the flooring so the seams will fall in low-traffic areas. Guide your seam cuts by laying a straightedge along a repeating pattern in the flooring. Many vinyl floors, for example, have a grid pattern imitating ceramic tile with grout lines; cut your seam down the center of one of these fake grout lines.

Using the straightedge, cut one sheet of flooring along the fake grout line; then do the same with the other sheet. Lay the two edges together and check the fit. Spread adhesive under the seam and run the roller over it. Use masking tape to hold the seam together. Once the glue has set, the seam can then be cleaned with mineral spirits and sealed with seam sealer.

Cut one sheet of flooring along the center of a grout line using a straightedge. Then do the same to the other sheet.

Lay the two edges together and check the fit. Spread adhesive under the seam and run the roller over it.

Choosing Sheet Vinyl

Q. *What should I know about sheet vinyl flooring before I buy it?*

The cost and quality of sheet vinyl flooring vary widely, so buy the highest quality you can afford. Use the underlayment and adhesive recommended by the manufacturer or you may void the warranty.

Do-it-yourselfers should stick to "rotogravure" vinyl. Designed with the pattern printed on the surface, rotovinyl is available in 6- to 15-foot widths, which minimizes the number of seams required. Inlaid vinyl sheet flooring should be installed by a professional.

Rotovinyl comes with either felt or flexible backing. Flexible costs more but is easier to install. Most felt-backed floors are glued down all over. Flexible-backed vinyl is glued or stapled around the edges and at seams only. Home centers sell helpful installation kits.

If you hire someone to lay the flooring, you can still save money by installing the underlayment yourself.

Good Base for Sheet Vinyl

Q. *I want to put in new sheet vinyl flooring. Can I just nail underlayment over the old vinyl that's there?*

Vinyl can go over any clean, flat sound base. To lay a new floor over old vinyl, remove all baseboards and undercut the door casings (see Door Trim in the Way, p.49), cut out any loose or curling edges of old vinyl flooring with a utility knife, and fill any holes with floor patch. To get a perfectly smooth surface, you may have to sand the floor patch after it dries. Then sweep and vacuum.

If the floor is damaged or uneven, install an underlayment of ¼-inch lauan plywood. Use ⅞-inch chisel-point staples and stagger the seams so that four corners never meet in one place. Flatten any protruding staples with a hammer. Fill underlayment seams with floor patch.

Use a trowel or broad putty knife to fill any area you've cut out and other holes and depressions with floor patch.

Staple ¼-in. underlayment in a 4-in. square pattern and every 2 in. around the edges.

INSTALLING VINYL FLOORING

Laying out sheet vinyl flooring isn't difficult. If you have some experience with tools, you can probably do a first-rate job in one weekend. But you have to be as careful as a surgeon: one false move can leave a permanent scar on your floor.

Most felt-backed floors, such as the one we show here, must be glued down all over. Flexible-backed vinyl should be glued around the edges and at seams only. Different brands—and even different designs—can require different adhesives. Small mistakes can lead to big headaches, so always follow the manufacturer's instructions, right down to the size of the notches in the trowel you use to spread the adhesive.

If the room has a complex shape or if your cutting skills are shaky, make a full-size paper template of your floor and use the template to cut the flooring to fit before you install it. Otherwise, the professional techniques of cutting in place, shown here, are usually faster.

1 Lay the flooring along cabinets or along a wall; then unroll and position it. Use duct tape to keep corners from tearing.

2 Press the knuckle of your pointing finger into the inside corners and mark the point of the corner with your thumb.

3 Pull up the flooring, draw a "horseshoe" on the corner, and cut it out with a utility knife.

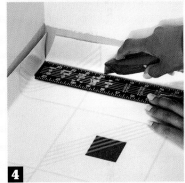

4 Push the vinyl against the wall with your straightedge, and trim off the excess. Change blades often.

5 Roll back the sheet of vinyl about halfway across the room, vacuum the area free of debris, then spread the adhesive. Roll back the other half and repeat.

6 Starting in the middle, roll outward in an overlapping pattern. Use a hand roller wherever the floor roller won't fit.

Vinyl and Other Flooring

VINYL CARE AND REPAIR

Damaged Sheet Flooring

Q. *There are a few small cuts and some larger rips in my vinyl flooring. How can I repair them?*

Cut the damaged piece along the pattern of the vinyl.

Apply the floor tile adhesive with a notched trowel.

For small cuts, apply vinyl floor tile adhesive to the backs of loose edges, then weight the tiles until they're dry.

To repair rips, burns, and cuts, a transplant is the solution.

Remove the damaged section of flooring by cutting along the pattern with a sharp utility knife. Pry up the damaged piece with a putty knife, using a hair dryer to soften the old adhesive if you need to.

Use the damaged piece as a template to cut a replacement patch from a matching remnant you have packed away.

If you don't have a spare, steal one off the floor from inside a closet or from under the refrigerator. Tape the template in place and use a framing square and knife to follow the edges to create your patch. Remove the patch as described above; then glue the damaged one back in its place.

Scrape the old adhesive from the underlayment and test-fit the patch. Apply the floor tile adhesive, wait the recommended time, then position and press the patch in place with a rolling pin. Clean up excess adhesive with a rag, water, and detergent. Weight down the patch for 24 hours while the adhesive dries.

Replacing a Vinyl Tile

Q. *What's the best way to replace a damaged vinyl tile?*

Loosen the tile and the adhesive by heating it with a hair dryer. To avoid damaging surrounding tiles, chip away and pry in the middle of the damaged tile, then work toward the edges. Remove old adhesive with a paint scraper. Trim the new tile as necessary with a sharp utility knife guided by a straightedge. Spread the adhesive and set the tile in place.

Set the new tile, then leave weights in place for 24 hr. while the adhesive dries.

Removing Old Tiles

Q. *I'm having a tough time removing vinyl tiles from my basement floor. Is there an easy way to get rid of them that I don't know about?*

Go to the nearest rental center that caters to contractors and rent a tile stripper. It works like a giant electric chisel to dig tiles out. Using this little powerhouse, you can finish the job in a matter of hours. In really stubborn areas, lift the back wheels off the floor so the machine's entire weight bears down on the blade.

A tile stripper's 75-lb. weight applies pressure to a sharp blade to strip tile.

Moisture on Vinyl Flooring

Q. *When it rains, the sheet vinyl floor on our slab porch turns white from condensation. We want to put down new vinyl but need to solve the moisture problem first.*

It sounds as though your problem comes more from surface water than from condensation. If rain is getting on the floor, the vinyl can blush, or turn white, returning to its normal color only after an extended drying period. If you want a vinyl floor, find a way to prevent water from coming in through the windows. Then seal the concrete with a masonry sealant before putting down new vinyl.

Yellowing No-Wax Vinyl

Q. *I installed no-wax vinyl flooring in my kitchen. Within a year, yellow splotches appeared all over it. What is this and how do I to correct it?*

Unfortunately, these yellow splotches won't come out—you have to replace the floor. Either you have too much moisture in the subfloor below the vinyl or the wrong adhesive was used. Remove the yellowing vinyl and test the floor for moisture.

Replace the flooring with one that the manufacturer specifically states can withstand the moisture, or staple down 4-mil polyethylene sheeting covered with ¼-inch plywood underlayment before installing new vinyl. When applying the vinyl, be sure to use an adhesive recommended by the flooring manufacturer.

MARBLE, SLATE, AND CORK

Restoring Marble

Q. *The marble floor in my home has dulled over time. Is there any way I can restore its shine?*

The best way to restore and preserve the shine of a marble floor is to clean it frequently. Wet and wash it with an all-purpose cleaner. Rinse it well and wipe it dry with a soft, clean cloth. The best finish for marble is actually not a high polish finish, but a flatter, somewhat dull finish. Applying wax to a marble floor is not recommended. Over time and after many cleanings, the floor will take on a shinier appearance as it absorbs oils from the cleaning fluids.

Restoring Cork Floors

Q. *Our home has cork tile floors that are dark and discolored with minor surface wear. What can we do to make them look better?*

You can sand the cork tile with medium-grit sandpaper to remove the remainder of the old finish and the top layer of dust and dirt. For best results, use an orbital finish sander.

After you've thoroughly vacuumed up the cork dust, apply two light coats of polyurethane, thinned slightly with lacquer thinner or another thinner recommended on the label. Be sure the area in which you're working is adequately ventilated. Let the finish cure for about a week. There is no need to wax.

Once the finish is restored, maintain it by vacuuming it regularly. The floor can also be cleaned with floor cleaner mixed with water. Dip a mop in the solution and wring it out well. Too much water may soak between the tiles and cause them to lift.

Dingy-looking Slate

Q. *There's a dingy-looking wax or sealer on the slate floor in our foyer. How can we remove it—and some paint specks? Is it necessary to seal a slate floor?*

Slate is a porous material (it can absorb water), so it does need to be sealed. To clean the slate, you'll have to experiment a bit in a not-so-visible spot. Try to remove the paint drips with a putty knife. If they haven't penetrated the surface of the slate, they should scrape right off. If this doesn't work, you could try a mild dried-paint remover (available at paint stores).

Removing the dingy finish or paint that has penetrated the surface will be tougher. Sometimes slate is sealed with floor wax or penetrating sealer that is absorbed into the slate. If the slate is sealed with floor wax, your best bet is a commercial floor wax remover. For removing stubborn sealers and paint splatters, try washing the floor with trisodium phosphate (TSP) or laundry detergent until the water is clear. Let the floor dry overnight. If that doesn't work, try a water-base paint stripper. Strippers can discolor the slate, so test a small area first. For safety, have plenty of ventilation.

When the floor is as clean as you can get it, apply a paste wax that contains carnauba, or a penetrating tile and brick sealer. Get these at any home center or hardware store. Penetrating sealers can be reapplied from time to time to make the slate look new. Just clean it and put on another coat of sealer. Waxes are less convenient because they leave a buildup that has to be removed periodically, but some people prefer the soft sheen of wax.

BEAUTIFUL WOODWORK is one factor that distinguishes many older homes from modern houses. The rich detail gives these homes a certain character and structure. Besides adding decoration, wood trim also hides gaps and protects walls. Not surprisingly, these traditional treatments are reappearing in many new homes.

Casing

Casing is the trim that wraps around doors and windows. Older homes have substantial-looking moldings that range from simple to ornate. Traditional casings often include rosettes, or corner pieces, and plinths, thicker pieces at the base that the baseboard and casing butt into. Modern casing is simpler and narrower.

Modern casing — Rosette

Traditional casing

Plinth

Baseboard

Chair Rail

Today, chair rail is often all that remains of old-style wainscoting, wood paneling that protected the lower part of a wall. Used alone, chair rail visually divides the wall to accent wallpaper or different wall color schemes. The height is often adjusted in dining rooms to protect the wall from chair backs. Chair rail in other rooms is often set at whatever height looks best.

Crown Molding

The ornamental treatment is used to "top off" a room and to ease the transition between the wall and the ceiling. Crown molding is available in different profiles, such as ogee and cove. Cornice moldings are similar to crown moldings but are more elaborate. They are typically made up of several pieces and are reserved for use in high-style rooms.

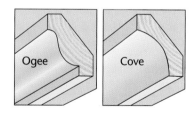

Ogee   Cove

Baseboard

Once called "mop board" because it protected the walls from wet mops, baseboard defines the transition between the floor and the wall. The quarter round is used instead of scribing to hide minor gaps. Because the shorter baseboards can be hidden by thick carpeting, many carpenters install them as much as ¾ inch off the floor.

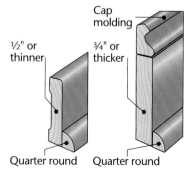

Cap molding

½" or thinner   ¾" or thicker

Quarter round   Quarter round

Types of **Trim**

Reinstalling Trim

Q. *When reinstalling some baseboard molding I tried driving the old nails through from the back side, but they splintered the front. How can I avoid this?*

When you drive an old nail back through the front face, the nailhead pushes out the filler and finish, catches on the wood fibers, and splinters the wood. To avoid the problem, clamp locking pliers on the nail and pull it through the back of the trim. The trim will be unmarred and ready to reinstall.

Loose Woodwork

Q. *The finishing nails I use to secure interior trim sometimes come loose. Is there a simple solution?*

Trim screws are often used for trouble spots because they draw pieces together better than finishing nails.

Trim screws have a thin shank and a tiny (³⁄₁₆-inch-diameter) head that you can easily hide with putty. Drill a ¹⁄₁₆-inch pilot hole and a ³⁄₁₆-inch countersink for the screwhead; then drive in the screw.

Trim screws have greater pulling power for closing gaps or tightening trim.

Picture Molding

Q. *To make repairs, I removed some molding that ran along the walls about ½ inch down from the ceiling. When I reinstall it, should I put it back in its original place or should it be tight to the ceiling?*

The molding you describe is called picture molding and was popular until the early 1900's. It was typically placed a couple of inches to a foot below the ceiling so that hooks with fine wires attached could be used to hang paintings and photographs. This system eliminated the need to drive nails or screws into the wall in order to hang pictures. It also made it easy to change the height or position of a picture on the wall.

If you want to use this molding for its intended purpose, reinstall it in its original position. If you cannot find hooks at the hardware store, make your own from a ½-inch-wide strip

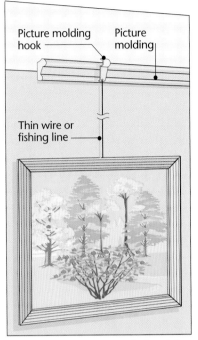

of ¹⁄₁₆-inch-thick steel stock. Bend the metal to the shape of the molding; then attach wire or fishing line down to your pictures.

If you choose not to hang pictures from your molding, you can install it tight to the ceiling.

Pinning Corners

Q. *The miter joints around our doors have developed gaps. What's the best way to tighten them up?*

Joints open as wood dries and shrinks, as your house settles, and doors get slammed repeatedly. The best way to tighten them up for good is to pin them.

Squeeze a bead of carpenter's glue into the opened joint; then use a corner clamp to pull the two miters together. Drill ¹⁄₁₆-inch holes from the side and top, and hammer in a pair of 4d finish nails so that they cross, pinning the miters together. Slide a thin piece of cardboard or sheet metal behind the trim to protect the wall from being damaged by the drill and hammer. Finish the job by filling any remaining gaps or nail holes with colored putty.

Pin the corners of loosened miter joints. Sheet metal protects the wall from dings.

INSTALLING TRIM

Miter Saw Tricks

Q. *I want to rent a power miter saw to speed up trim installation. Are there any special tips I should know about using it?*

The power miter saw lets you make clean, precise cuts as perfect as those made by a finish carpenter. With it, you can change angles in seconds and nibble off the tiniest amount for perfect-fitting joints. To make the slight angle changes necessary for tight joints, it's often easiest to insert a shim between the wood trim and the fence. (See photo, below.)

For more consistency and accuracy when cutting large crown molding, assemble a mitering jig like the one in the photo. First screw or clamp a ¾ x 3½-inch plywood board to the miter box fence. Then screw a stop block on either side of the saw blade to align the crown quickly.

Despite the blade guard on the power miter saw, it is still an extremely dangerous tool if used improperly or carelessly. The blade spins at 5,000 revolutions per minute, so keep your fingers away from it. Be especially careful when cutting small pieces because the blade tends to draw the pieces inward, often catching and kicking them back out at high speed, ruining them in the process. Always wear safety goggles, ear protection, and a dust mask. If you don't feel confident using a power saw, you can get similar results by using a handsaw and a miter box, although it takes longer.

While it's easy to set angles on a miter saw, a shim can be useful for making minor adjustments quickly for tighter-fitting joints.

A stop block helps position crown molding correctly. Place the crown upside down to make the cut.

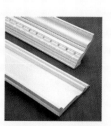

what do you need?

BUYING MOLDING

Molding treatments have changed dramatically in the last 50 years. Traditionally, moldings were very elaborate and often made up of a combination of two or more elements. Today these same profiles can be hard to find and are quite expensive. Contemporary styles are simpler, cost less and are readily available. To save money, you might consider using traditional "high-style" moldings for a formal dining room, and smaller, simpler moldings for the rest of your house.

Whichever style you choose, try to work with the profiles your store has in stock. Custom-milled moldings cost twice as much as stock moldings.

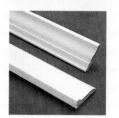

Wood Substitute

Q. *My lumberyard sells a wood product called MDF. What is it, and is it OK to use for interior trim?*

Medium-density fiberboard (MDF), a product made of wood fibers and resins, is an excellent choice for interior trim and panels. MDF cuts easily without the splinters and tear-out associated with particleboard or plywood. MDF also offers a smooth finish for paint or laminate and doesn't swell/shrink like wood.

Cabinetmakers often use MDF because it's cheaper than plywood and because carbide blades and router bits leave well-defined cuts.

INSTALLING BASEBOARD

With some skill and a little practice with a coping saw, you can install base trim that looks good even on walls that are not so perfect (and most aren't). The traditional-style trim we use here has three parts: a baseboard, base cap, and base shoe. Although most modern trim doesn't use a cap, it is installed in basically the same manner.

Outside corners are more difficult to fit and are the most visible, so start with these. Because corners are seldom square, trim usually needs to be test-fitted to fit tightly. However, since the cap will cover the top of the baseboard, you can speed things up by undercutting the baseboard joint (see Tighter Miters, p.74). There will be a slight gap in the back, but the front edge will remain tight when you nail it in. (This trick works only with flat trim, not with curved profiles like the base cap, or where you can see the top edge.)

Working from the outside corners, add sections of baseboard one after another, nailing them to the wall at each stud. For inside corners, butt one length of baseboard against the wall, then butt the second piece against the first. Aim for a "sprung fit"; by cutting the baseboard a hair long, it will hold itself in place and the ends will create a seamless butt joint.

Install the base cap next. Start with the outside corners and work in. To make a clean joint on the inside corners, butt the first piece against the wall, then cope the second piece to fit around the first. (See Coping a Joint, p.74). Continue working around the room.

Install the base shoe just like the cap. Fasten the shoe to the baseboard, so that the floor can move independently of the molding.

1 Fit the outside corners first when you install the baseboard pieces. Tack them to the wall studs using 8d finish nails.

2 The ends of your baseboard should butt tightly together. For carpeted rooms, install the base ½ in. off the floor.

3 Cope the inside corners of the cap molding. The coped end matches the profile to make a tight-looking joint.

Chair Rail

Q. *I would like to know how to install chair rail. How high should it be? How do I end it at an arch that doesn't have a casing?*

First decide how high you want your chair rail to be. You can put it where your chair backs rub against the wall or at the height that looks good with the style of the room. If you plan to install wainscoting (paneling below the chair rail), a good height is 32 inches because it allows you to cut a 4 x 8-foot sheet of paneling or 8-foot boards into three equal pieces.

There are two ways to end the rail at a doorway without molding. The simplest way is to bevel the end at 30°. A better-looking solution is to make a mitered return. A return is simply a small corner piece that makes the molding look as if it turns a corner and heads into the wall. Returns can be tricky to cut with a power miter saw. To avoid having the piece sucked up by the blade, stop the saw before it completes the cut.

To hand-cut a return, miter an extra-long piece, tack it in place, then trim it off after the glue dries. Stop the rail an inch or two short of the opening.

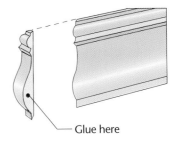

Glue here

Tighter Miters

Q. *Without spending the weekend fitting and refitting each joint, is there an easy way to get tight-looking baseboard miters?*

Walls aren't always straight nor do they always meet at perfect 90° angles. Undercutting removes material from the back edge so that the front surfaces will fit together tightly. The easiest way to do this is by simply shaving material off the back with a block plane or a utility knife. This trick works only on flat trim, and where the top edge isn't exposed.

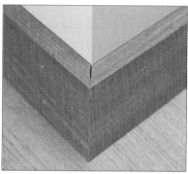

Undercutting the miter joints ensures a tight fit. The base cap will cover the gap.

Mid-Wall Joint

Q. *How do I join two lengths of trim in the middle of the wall?*

Ideally, you should buy all your trim in lengths so that you only need a single piece for each side of your room. For those times when you need to "stretch" a piece of molding, you can splice two pieces together. Make sure to position the joint over a stud so that you can secure the splice with a finish nail. For best results, attach the top piece first, then cut the bottom piece a tad long. Ideally, the bottom piece will spring into place and hide the joint.

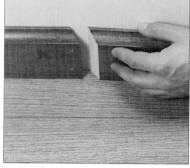

Make splices over a stud so that you can secure the joint with a finishing nail.

Coping a Joint

Q. *With a power miter saw, I can cut perfect outside and inside miters. What's the advantage (if any) of coping inside corners by hand? What's the best way to do it?*

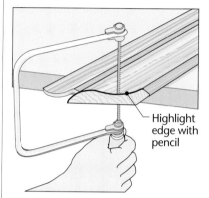

Highlight edge with pencil

Cope joints are used by finish carpenters to join baseboard, crown, and other moldings where they meet at inside corners. Coping has several advantages over mitering. Since wood moves, miters tend to open and close with the seasons. Movement in a coped joint is much less noticeable. Because the molding is back-cut and needs to meet only at the front face to look good, copes are also easier to fit than miters. The downside is that the cope takes longer to cut.

To cut a cope, cut a miter that slopes toward the corner of the joint, as if you were cutting a standard inside miter. Highlight the profile of the molding by rubbing the side of a pencil along the miter's edge.

Using a coping saw, cut along the penciled profile. The idea is to produce a continuous backcut so that only the tip of the original miter remains, creating a crisp profile that fits around the mating piece.

When you finish sawing, try the joint—it might need some fine-tuning. Use a utility knife or file to adjust the fit to the mating piece.

Less-than-Perfect Corners

Q. *We installed a floor-to-ceiling bay window. The drywall tape and compound created rounded, less-than-perfect 45° corners. How do we get the baseboard to fit right?*

Lots of carpenters solve this problem with the "score-and-whap" method. Holding the baseboard in the corner and using the top edge as a guide, score the built-up drywall compound with a sharp utility knife. Then whap the baseboard against the wall with a hammer. This punches the trim through the compound and tape back to where the corner should have been.

Whapping the baseboard with a hammer and beater block will help "straighten out" rounded drywall corners.

INSTALLING CROWN MOLDING

Installing crown molding may look like a simple, straightforward job, but it takes hard work to make it look good. Some of the challenges you may face include making corners fit tightly, keeping the molding straight, and finding solid nailing spots. If you plan to paint the molding, you can get by with a miter box and a handsaw; but for speed and accuracy, use a power miter saw.

Buy your molding first. Buy lengths that will span each side of the room. Add several inches to allow enough material for miters. Sand and paint (or stain) the molding before installation.

Next, plan the order of installation. It's best to cut the outside corners first, because they're the most visible and are the hardest to fit. Once you've installed the outside miters you can proceed around the room.

Mark the locations of the studs and ceiling joists before installation. If the joists run parallel to the wall,

screw a cant block to the wall to provide a solid nailing surface (see Photo 5, below).

Make a template to mark the location of the crown: Measure the bearing point by positioning a scrap of molding on a framing square; then nail together a guide to match.

To cut crown molding, you need to think upside down: Place it upside down in your miter box as if the fence were the wall (see Miter Saw Tricks, p.72).

Most outside corners are not precisely square. Test each corner with a piece of scrap before cutting your molding. To help the front edge fit tightly, undercut the molding slightly. Don't worry if you trim the molding a little short—the gap will be hidden by the next coped section.

Remember to cope the inside corners. The coped piece should clamp the other molding in place and force both pieces into proper alignment.

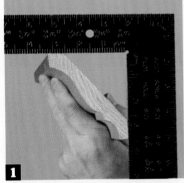

1 Place the molding on a framing square and measure its bearing points.

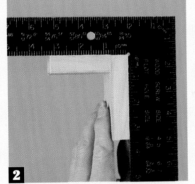

2 Nail together a template that duplicates the molding's bearing points.

3 Use the template to mark the crown's location at each joist and wall stud.

4 Miter the molding upside down. A stop block holds the crown in position.

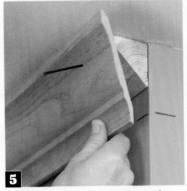

5 A cant block provides a nailing surface where joists run parallel to the wall.

6 Use the coped end to force the other piece into alignment; then nail in place.

Paneling

WOOD PANELING

Salvage the Panels

Q. *I want to take out the knotty pine paneling in my bedroom and paper the walls. Is there a way to remove the boards so I can reuse them to panel the family room?*

Yes, but you'll need to be careful. If you cannot drive the nails in the paneling through the boards, try drilling them out. Use a drill bit the same size as the nails and drill over the nailheads. If this does not work, try using a pry bar to pull the boards away from the framing. Wood dries and becomes brittle with age, so use extra care if you do this. It's a good idea to buy or borrow pry bars in a variety of shapes and sizes. Pry only at the nail location and work slowly. Once you tear out the first board, you should be able to salvage the rest of the wood.

Warped Panel Boards

Q. *The panel boards I want to put up in my living room are a little warped. Can I still use them?*

It's typical to find some waves, or warping, in ¼-inch hardwood plywood paneling. The paneling manufacturing process makes warping nearly inevitable.

Don't let a few waves deter you from paneling your walls. When fastened correctly to the wall, the panels will straighten out by themselves. Use both an adhesive (recommended by the manufacturer) and paneling nails to attach it to furring strips or studs. Follow the manufacturer's instructions for specific nailing patterns.

If your warped paneling is particularly thick, say 7/16 inch, it can't be used and should be returned.

Sweet Smell of Cedar

Q. *My old walk-in cedar closet has lost its wonderful smell. Is there any way I can make the scent return?*

To renew your cedar closet and keep your clothes smelling sweet, lightly sand the surface of the cedar boards with fine-grade sandpaper. (Remove the clothing from the closet before you begin and wear a dust mask.) Sanding will expose new wood that will release the natural scent.

Lighter Paneling

Q. *Our new home has solid pine paneling in the kitchen and den. We love the look, but the boards have really darkened with age. Can I lighten them up somehow?*

Try scrubbing a small hidden area with mineral spirits and fine steel wool, working with the grain of the wood. If that doesn't work to your satisfaction, you'll need to strip the old finish off.

Follow the specific directions on the can; use a paste-type paint stripper. Work in sections of about 2 feet wide and the full height of the paneling to avoid lap marks. Protect the floors with polyethylene sheeting taped at the edges with duct tape and covered with layers of newspaper. Protect yourself by wearing a respirator, goggles, and rubber gloves. Make sure that there is plenty of ventilation.

If you want the wood even lighter, try applying household bleach. (Let it dry between applications.) You can also try using a pickling stain (available at paint stores) to get a whitewashed effect.

Paneling High Walls

Q. *How can I panel a room with 8-foot 8-inch-high walls when paneling comes in 8-foot lengths?*

First, check with your supplier. You may be able to order paneling in 10-foot lengths. If not, consider using an extra-high baseboard and wide crown molding to make up the difference. You might also try splitting and spreading the panels, using chair rail molding to fill the space between them (see figure, below). The simplest, yet still elegant, solution is to cap the 8-foot-tall panels with a simple cap molding. Paint the remaining wall the same color as the ceiling.

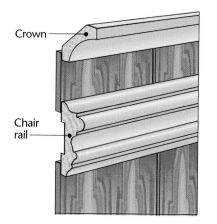

Crown

Chair rail

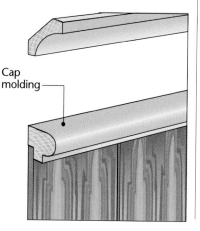

Cap molding

Shrinking Wood

Q. *Last summer I installed tongue-and-groove pine boards in our family room. This winter some boards shrank and now there are gaps between them. Can the wood shrink that much? Will it be OK this summer when the humidity changes again?*

Wood will always expand and contract with changes in humidity. In fact, it's not uncommon for a 1 x 8 pine board to change ⅛ inch or more in width. The tongue-and-groove pine was probably not dry enough when you installed it. If the wood was stored in a moist area before installation, it could have absorbed moisture and swelled.

Whenever you plan to install wood paneling or wood trim, stack it horizontally in the room where it will be installed and allow it to acclimate for at least a week. This will ensure less dramatic changes in dimension after installation.

Your tongue-and-groove boards will probably not swell enough to close the gaps, nor can you solve this problem without removing all of the affected boards. If the shrinkage was extreme, you may have to add a ripped section of tongue-and-groove board in the corner of the wall.

If you live in an area where the winters are cold, the constant running of your furnace can cause excessive dryness. Long periods of low humidity can cause wood to dry and shrink. To counteract the dryness, install a humidifier and run it during the winter months.

Replacing Tongue-and-Groove Paneling

Q. *Some of the tongue-and-groove knotty pine paneling in our summer cabin was damaged by water last season. I chiseled out the damaged boards; now how do I get new boards in?*

The solution will be a bit like making a puzzle, but an easy one. First, make sure you select the new boards carefully. Don't get boards with any warps or bows, and buy boards of the same thickness and width as the old ones, with tongues and grooves that match. Position the new boards in a slight V-shape, then press on the

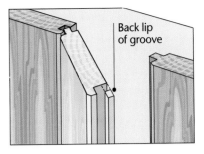

middle until they snap in place. Nail the boards in place, as shown below.

If you need to replace only a single board, use a chisel or a utility knife to remove the back lip of the groove on the replacement board. Push the tongue into the groove of the adjacent board, then face-nail the board to the wall. Putty over any nail holes.

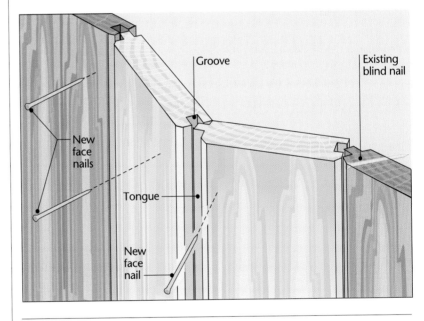

Paneling Changed Colors

Q. *When I was rehanging pictures, I found that the paneling under them was much lighter in color than the rest. How can I correct this?*

You have a problem that only time can erase. Natural light has caused the paneling to darken. This process will continue gradually and there is no way to reverse it, short of

stripping and sanding the wood. Don't worry—after a few months the light patches will catch up with the surrounding wall and the ghost images will become less noticeable.

The best way to avoid this problem is to periodically move the pictures and furniture. But you won't have to do this forever; most of the color change takes place in the first few years after installation.

Stairs

REPAIRING STAIRS

Remount a Handrail

Q. *The handrail on my staircase is starting to feel loose. What can I do to secure it to the wall?*

To remount a loose handrail or install a new one, use a stud finder to find the studs along the entire length of the stairway. Next, choose a stud that is located at the front edge of one of the stair treads. Measure up from that tread and mark the wall somewhere between 31 and 35 inches. Attach one of the brackets to this wall stud. (To meet code, the top of the handrail must be between 34 and 38 inches above the front of the tread.) Install additional brackets about every 3 feet; the top and bottom ones should be secured 12 to 16 inches from the ends of the handrail.

To position a bracket to a stud that is not located at the front edge of a tread, pick the stud you want to mount the bracket to. Then go to the step just above and measure up from the front of the tread to the desired bracket height. Repeat this for the step just below the stud. Now draw a straight line between these marks. Mount the bracket where the line intersects the stud. To ensure that the bracket screws bite into the stud, angle them slightly inward as you drive them. Once the brackets are attached, secure the handrail to the wall by attaching the bracket straps to the underside of the rail.

According to code, a replacement handrail can be the same length as the old one, but to be safe, it should extend 12 inches beyond the top step and all the way to the bottom step. Also, new handrails are required to have a return at both ends. Returns prevent you from catching a sleeve on the open end of the railing, which could cause a fall.

Child-Safe Balusters

Q. *Our second-floor landing has a 36½-inch balustrade. How can I tell if it's safe for small children?*

According to the Uniform Building Code, the height of the handrail must be at least 34 inches. Guardrail balusters (decorative railings with spindles) need to be spaced so that a 4-inch sphere cannot pass through them. The space between the floor and the bottom rail must also be a maximum of 4 inches.

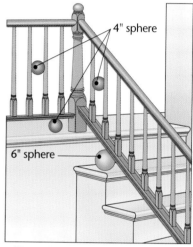

If your balusters are too far apart to meet this safety code, add an additional baluster between each pair or attach an acrylic plastic sheet shield across the balustrade. Horizontal slats are never safe, no matter how they're spaced, because children can climb them like a ladder.

The handrail code for open railings and stairways is a little different. The spacing of the balusters is the same (4 inches or less), but the height of the top rail may be between 30 and 38 inches. The space between the lower rail, the riser, and the tread cannot allow a 6-inch sphere to pass through. Also, for a safe, comfortable grip, the handrail must not be more than 2⅝ inches wide.

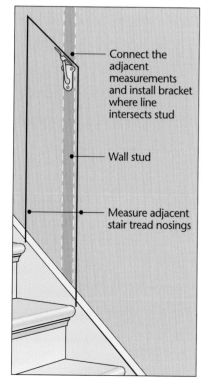

Connect the adjacent measurements and install bracket where line intersects stud

Wall stud

Measure adjacent stair tread nosings

To attach the bracket strips, drill pilot holes in the rail before installing screws.

Nail and glue short returns to ends of rail.

Silencing Squeaky Stairs

Q. *How do I stop the squeaks in my stairs before they drive me crazy?*

Before you can silence squeaks, you'll need to find them. Get underneath the stairs and have someone walk on the stairs so that you can mark the noisy spots.

Once you've identified the squeaks, eliminate any gaps between treads, risers, and stringers so that the loose boards can't rub against nails or other boards. Fill small gaps with shims covered with construction adhesive. To secure loose treads, risers, or stringers, use wood blocks or metal brackets

To secure blocks or brackets, drive screws into the loose tread or riser first. Leave the screws untightened by about ⅛ inch. Next, drive screws tightly into the solid part, and then tighten the first set of screws. The boards should draw together as you tighten the screws.

If you can't get underneath the stairs, just screw from above. The centers of the two outside stringers should be about 1½ inches from the ends of the treads. There may be a third stringer in the center of the stairs. Use trim screws; their small heads are easy to hide with putty and can be driven through carpet.

Glue wooden shims in gaps from beneath stairway so that treads can't move.

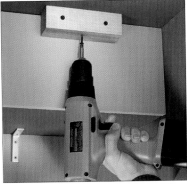

Lock treads, risers, and stringers together with wood or metal brackets.

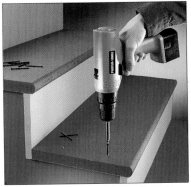

Drive trim screws through treads and into stringer. Conceal screwheads with putty.

Wobbly Newel Post

Q. *How can I fix the wobbly newel post at the bottom of my staircase?*

There's no single solution for wobbly old newel posts, because posts were installed in a variety of ways.

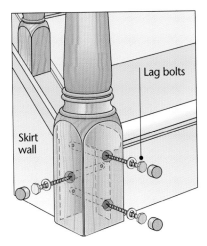

Lag bolts

Skirt wall

In newer homes, most posts are bolted to the framework or to the short skirt wall that follows the angle of the stairs. In this case, the original screws were concealed behind wood plugs and are almost impossible to get to for tightening. You'll have to install additional lag screws from each side to firm up the post.

If the post was secured to the floor with a metal plate, the only way to steady it is to install larger screws in the stripped-out holes. First, cut back the carpet or remove the tile and remove the newel post. Next, install bigger screws and then reattach the post to the floor.

If the post is attached to a joist, you can add blocking, shims, or additional screws. This procedure may require you to remove a section of the basement ceiling.

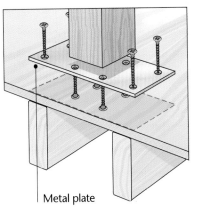

Metal plate

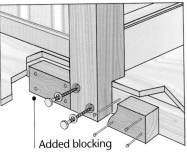

Added blocking

Interior Doors

INSTALLING INTERIOR DOORS

Cutting a Hinge Recess

Q. *What's the best way to cut a door hinge recess?*

With so many kinds of power tools at our disposal, we forget that some jobs are best done using the simplest of tools. Chisels are the best tools for three tasks—making sharp plunge cuts, removing stock, and smoothing. All three techniques are used to cut the recess for a door hinge.

Plunge cuts are made with the blade's beveled edge facing the waste side of the cut. These cuts are used first to outline the hinge shape, then to score the area to a consistent depth so the wood can be removed in small manageable chips rather than one large chunk. Remove the chips with the bevel side down, so you can control the depth of cut by slightly lowering and raising the handle as you work. Smooth the area with the chisel bevel facing up. Use angled or circular motions to prevent tearing the grain.

Make a series of vertical plunge cuts that are as deep as the hinge is thick.

Remove the small wood chips, cutting at a low angle.

Replace Door Locks

Q. *I'd like to replace the doorknobs in my house, but the new locksets won't fit in the old holes. How do I cut bigger holes in the doors?*

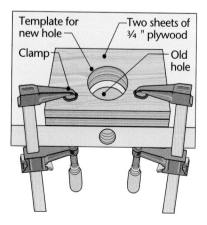

Cutting a bigger hole shouldn't be a problem. First, determine the backset: the distance from the edge of the door to the center of the hole that holds the doorknob.

Make a drilling template by gluing together two 12-inch squares of ¾-inch plywood. Measure and mark the backset distance from one edge of the template. Using the correct-size hole saw, drill a hole in the template, centering it on the mark.

Clamp the template to the door, making sure the edge of the template is flush with the edge of the door. The template will hold your hole saw steady while you cut the new hole. If your door is metal, you'll need a carbide hole saw.

Left- or Right-Handed Doors

Q. *The plans for our remodeling project call for left- and right-handed doors. What does this mean?*

Right-handed door

Left- or right-handedness refers to the direction the door swings when it is opened, or simply the side of the door the hinges are on. Stand in front of a door on the side where you can push it open. Are the hinges on the left? If they are, you have a left-handed door. On the right? You have a right-handed door (above).

For exterior entry doors, determine handedness by standing outside facing the building. These doors are either left- or right-handed as just described. However, if exterior doors swing out from the building toward you and the hinges are on the left, they are called "left-handed reverse." And if the hinges are on the right? Then they're "right-handed reverse."

Left-handed reverse door

Shorter Hollow-Core Door

Q. *We want to put a door below the main support beam in our basement. But there's only enough room for a 6-foot-6-inch door. Our home center carries only 6-foot-8-inch doors. What are our options?*

You can special-order a shorter door, but you'll pay premium price and may have to wait weeks to get it. Your swiftest, cheapest solution is to cut the bottom off a standard hollow-core door.

Mark your cut-off line with a sharp utility knife; then cut with a circular saw just to the scrap side of the line to avoid splintering. Remove the plywood from the sides of the door bottom crosspiece with a chisel. Use the chisel to push the cardboard core farther up into the door so there's room to glue and clamp the crosspiece back in place. If it's a prehung door, you'll need to cut 2 inches off the doorjamb too.

Don't forget to thoroughly seal the bottom of the door with paint or polyurethane before installing it in the jamb. An unsealed door—especially in a damp basement—will absorb moisture and warp.

Clamps help the crosspiece stay in place while the glue dries.

 HANGING A NEW INTERIOR DOOR

Because your existing door will act as a pattern for the new door, you want it to fit perfectly before you remove it. Tighten all hinge screws, and if necessary, use a plane or a belt sander to shave down tight spots. Remove the lockset, and then the door.

Align the new and old doors along their hinges on a worktable or sawhorses. Trace the old door onto the new. Along edges where the new door should be wider or longer, measure and mark with a straightedge instead of tracing. Put the old door aside. Prior to cutting it with a circular saw, score the new door deeply on the face-up side with a straightedge and utility knife.

This prevents splintering. Cut the door along the waste side of the line. If the new door is only slightly longer than the old one, shave it with a plane instead of cutting it. If it's beveled (cut at an angle) on the strike side, make sure you angle the bevel in the correct direction, toward the doorstop. Use a guide (a straight 1 x 4 works well) when you cut the door. Measure from the end of the saw's shoe to the edge of its blade. Set the guide so the blade will cut about 1/16 inch from the cut line. Then smooth the door's edge with a plane or belt sander. When you finish cutting, lay the old door over the new one again to mark the hinge mortises and the holes you'll need to drill for the lockset.

1

On your worktable or sawhorses, trace the old door onto the new.

2

Score the door deeply, using a straightedge and utility knife, before you cut it.

3

Use a guide to help you make a perfectly straight cut.

REPAIRING INTERIOR DOORS

Doors Won't Stay Open

Q. *The wooden doors in our 90-year-old house close by themselves; one of them even opens on its own. How can I make them stay put?*

Your old house has settled with age. Some of the door frames are out of plumb; that is, the hinges are no longer in line with each other. The quick approach is to remove the hinge pins (the rod that holds the two hinge leaves together) one at a time and hit them with a hammer. You want to bend the pin slightly so that the hinges are tight enough to prevent the door from swinging by itself.

A more permanent fix is to rehang the doors so they are plumb. First, take the door off its hinges. Then use a level to see in which direction the door frame is crooked. Is it parallel with the wall? Perpendicular to it? Both? Hold a 6-foot level if you can get one, or a shorter level, against a very straight board. Place the board and level against the barrels, or round part, of the hinges to check for perpendicular to the wall; hold it against the leaves, or flat part, of the hinges to check parallel to the wall.

If the hinges seem out of plumb parallel to the wall, slip a shim (a piece of cardboard, metal flashing, or a thin piece of wood) under the hinge that needs it. To fix hinges that are out of plumb perpendicular to the wall, move one of them sideways. You may need to chisel out the hinge recess (see Cutting a Hinge Recess, p.80) to make it bigger. You may also need to remove the doorstop and reposition it after you install the door.

If you'll be moving the hinge only a small amount, the screws may insist on going back into their old holes. If this happens, break a toothpick in

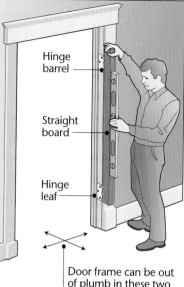

Door frame can be out of plumb in these two directions

half and dip the sharp ends in carpenter's glue before tapping them tightly into the old hole with a hammer. Cut them off flush when the glue is dry. Now you should be able to get the screws in where you want them.

Free a Binding Door

Q. *No matter what the season, the door to my son's bedroom sticks and catches. What can be done to solve this problem?*

Sounds like the door needs to be planed. Begin the repair by tightening all the hinge screws. Replace any

Mark the edge of the door wherever it rubs against the frame.

stripped screw holes with a 3-inch-long screw that will sink into the framework behind the door frame.

A light sanding may be enough to free a sticking door. A whack with a hammer on a block of wood held along the nonhinged side of the door frame may widen the opening enough to stop the binding, too. In severe cases, use a small block plane or belt sander. Belt sanders can make a mess and they remove wood quickly, so cover your floor and/or rug and go slowly.

Don't be surprised if you need to trim, rehang, and check your door more than once to get the right fit. Finally, be sure to paint or stain and seal the newly exposed wood or the door may absorb moisture and need to be trimmed all over again in a few months.

Self-Closing Door

Q. *My bedroom door closes on its own every time I open it. The house isn't even old! Why does it do this and how can I fix it?*

Most likely, the person who built your house did not use a level often enough. To avoid the hassle of rehanging the door and door frame, try tightening all the hinge screws. If a screw just spins, install one that's an inch longer so it will sink into solid wood; pull the hinge tightly against the door or door jamb.

If the door still closes on its own, bend one or more of the hinge pins (see Doors Won't Stay Open, above). Or, screw a magnetic cabinet door catch to the door. Affix the metal plate to the wall or door bumper to hold the door open.

Door Won't Latch

Q. *On several doors in our house, the latches are lower than the holes in the strike plate. How can I re-align them?*

Check the wear marks on the latch plate (or strike plate) and observe how the latch hits the plate as the door closes. To make small adjustments, it's easiest to slightly enlarge the latch opening in the plate with a file. Shift the latch plate only as a last resort, because it can turn into a big job. You'll have to rechisel its mortise (the pocket cut into the jamb in which the plate sits), then fill the old mortise and redrill screw holes.

If the old plate and jamb are worn or damaged, buy a slightly larger latch plate from a well-stocked hardware store and install it in place of the old one. It looks best if it completely covers the damaged area.

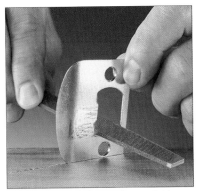
File the latch hole larger. Saw a slot in scrap wood to hold the plate steady.

Door Frame Repair

Q. *I removed a door and don't intend to replace it. How do I patch the stained oak door frame where the hinges and strike plate were?*

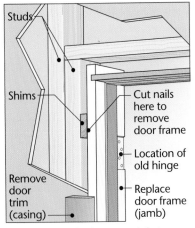

Studs

Shims

Remove door trim (casing)

Cut nails here to remove door frame

Location of old hinge

Replace door frame (jamb)

Like it or not, the best repair is to replace the door frame. Any patches would be obvious. Fortunately, it's not hard to replace a door frame. Carefully remove the trim (casing), cutting the nails holding the frame in place with a hacksaw blade (wrap one end with tape to make a handle). Then make a duplicate frame. Your lumberyard can probably rip new boards for you if you don't have the tools. You don't need to match any fancy joints at the top of the old frame; just butt the pieces together and nail them (after you predrill for the nails). Reinstall the new frame so it's in the same place, using new shims. Be sure the sides are plumb. Then replace the trim.

Your biggest problems will be getting the door trim off without damaging it and finding a stain that matches the old trim. To remove the trim, use a wide putty knife and a flat pry bar. Drive the nails all the way through the wood, rather than trying to pull them out. You'll do the least amount of damage this way.

Some paint stores have a stain-matching service, but the results are usually not precise. You must mix colors to fine-tune the match, comparing test samples with the old trim in both daylight and artificial light. Varnish your samples, too, because that usually makes them darker.

Easy Door Removal

Q. *I need to take a heavy door off its hinges. What is the safest and easiest way to do it?*

Stick a shim under the outer edge to support the weight of the door and keep it stable while you remove the hinge pins.

Hinge pins vary, but most hinges today have a small hole on the underside, so you can tap the pin up and out with an 8d nail. If there are no holes, tap a flat-bladed screwdriver under the head of the pin to drive it upward. To keep the door balanced, start with the bottom hinge pin and remove the top one last.

If you plan to rehang the door later, just reverse this process: Place a shim under the outer edge and put the top pin in first. If the leaves on the bottom hinge don't match up, lift the door from below and tap one leaf gently to nudge the two together. If that doesn't work, loosen the screws in one of the leaves, position the hinges together, then retighten the screws.

Tap the pin up and out of the hinge barrel with an 8d nail.

Interior Doors

Replacing a Doorknob

Q. *The doorknob in my bathroom is damaged and needs replacement. Is replacing a lockset difficult?*

The workings of a lockset are a little complex, but replacing one is not. Before you buy a new lockset, determine the backset, or the distance between the edge of the door and the center of the doorknob. Standard backsets are 2⅜ inches or 2¾ inches, and a new lockset will probably fit one of these.

The trickiest part of the job will be getting at the retaining screws behind the inside knob. You can remove some knobs by pushing on a tiny latch. Most of them, however, require that you work around them with a long screwdriver or an offset screwdriver. Next, pull the inside and outside knobs apart. The spindle is attached to the outside knob and will slide out of the inside knob when you separate them.

Use pliers to pull the latch unit out of the door and be careful not to splinter the wood around the faceplate. Unless the new strike plate doesn't fit perfectly into the original mortise and you choose to keep the old one in place, detach the old strike plate.

To install a new lockset, simply repeat the previous steps in reverse, beginning with the new latch unit.

Have an assistant hold the outside knob so that the spindle goes through the latch unit while you are positioning the inside knob and inserting the retaining screws.

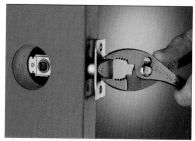

Pull the inside and outside knobs apart. The spindle is attached to the outside knob and will slide out of the inside knob and latch unit as you pull.

Try not to splinter the wood around the faceplate as you remove the latch unit.

Loose Screws

Q. *The hinge screws on some of my doors won't tighten no matter how hard I try. How can I fix them?*

Old screw holes, especially for the top hinge, often become stripped, preventing you from tightening the screws. If this is the case, plug the old screw holes with toothpicks or wooden matchsticks dipped in carpenter's glue. When the glue dries, shave off the ends with a sharp chisel or utility knife and drill new pilot holes for the screws. A 9/64-inch hole should handle most situations. Then screw the hinge into place again.

Two other tricks you can use to retighten a loose hinge leaf: (1) Drive a long screw (the same diameter but at least 2½ inches long) completely through the frame and into the wall stud behind. Angle it slightly to make sure it penetrates the stud. Avoid overtightening this screw, because it can pull the frame out of square. This trick works only with the hinge's inner screws. The outer ones won't hit the stud. (2) Simply drill a new screw hole in the hinge. To make the screwhead flush, you have to countersink the hole. If you don't have a countersink bit, start the hole with a ¼-inch drill bit. Then dimple the hinge with a ⅜-inch bit.

Stuff toothpicks or matchsticks dipped in glue into the old screw holes. Trim the ends flush when the glue dries.

Drill new pilot holes and drive the screws. A special Vix bit automatically centers the pilot hole when you drill it.

Door Rattles

Q. *How can I stop my bedroom door from rattling every time I walk past it?*

Try slightly bending the flange…

To stop a rattling door, try slightly bending the flange on the latch plate with pliers. Another solution is to move the doorstop tighter against the door at the bottom. Use a utility knife to cut through the paint or varnish on both sides of the stop so it can break free. Then use a block and hammer to move the stop over about ⅛ inch. When you test it, the door should hit the stop and latch at the same time. Finally, drive a couple of 1¼-inch finish nails through the stop to anchor it in its new position.

Or move the stop a bit to stop rattles.

FIXING A SAGGING DOOR

Doors that sag or bind in their jambs and drag unevenly across the carpet are a common problem in new and remodeled homes. The new framing takes years to dry, shrink, and settle, and as it does it can pull away from the jamb. If the jamb on any of your doors is more than ⅜ inch out of level, a sagging floor may be your problem, and you should contact an experienced contractor or structural engineer before you attempt to fix the door. However, if a doorjamb is level within ¼ inch, you can do the job. You'll need a pry bar; a stiff putty knife; a drill; a nail spinner or drill bit; a handful of precut shims; a 2½-inch No. 8 screw in a finish that matches your hinges; 4d, 6d, and 8d finish nails; and safety glasses.

Tighten the upper hinge by drilling a 2½-inch screw through the center hole. Angle it so it hits the stud and pulls the hinge tight. If you miss the stud, plug the hole with a glued-in dowel; redrill at a sharper angle.

Next, repair the lower hinge. With the casing partially removed, pry the door and jamb away from the stud until the gap around the door is uniform. Do not attempt to remove the casing above the upper hinge because it may break. Insert a pair of shims above and below the lower hinge. Shims prevent the lower hinge from bowing in under the weight of the door. If you need to make the shims thicker, trim their tips. Nail each pair in place with two 6d finish nails, and cut the shims flush with the wall by scoring them with a utility knife and then snapping them. Refasten the casing to the jamb with 4d finish nails, and to the wall with 8d finish nails. Predrill the trim first to avoid splitting. If the door doesn't strike the stop evenly after you've adjusted it, remove the stop and renail it, using the door as a guide.

1 *Drive a 2½-in. No. 8 screw through the center hole.*

2 *Use two 6d nails to secure each pair of shims in place.*

3 *Use 4d finish nails to refasten the casing to the jamb.*

Interior Doors

Hole in Hollow-Core Door

Q. *We have several hollow-core doors with holes in them. Can they be repaired or would it be cheaper to replace them?*

Hollow-core doors are cheap, but since replacing a door involves mortising the hinges, drilling a hole for the lockset, and finishing the new door, it's easier to make a patch.

If your door is painted, the easiest way to fix it is to inject some foam sealant into the hole. Let the foam ooze out and harden. Once the foam has cured, use a utility knife or sharp putty knife to trim away the excess so that the surface of the foam is just below the surface of the door.

Level the depression with wood filler, sand it smooth, then apply a coat of paint.

Use foam sealant to fix holes in hollow-core coors.

POCKET AND FOLDING DOORS

Repair Pocket Doors

Q. *Our pocket doors keep coming off track. Can we repair them without ripping out the walls?*

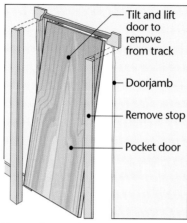

Tilt and lift door to remove from track

Doorjamb

Remove stop

Pocket door

Depending on the repairs needed, you may not have to rip out the wall. If the rollers are worn, they can be replaced. If the track has become loose, you might be able to tighten it. But to do either of these repairs, you'll need to remove the door.

First, remove the stop molding on the doorjamb. You'll probably need to remove all four pieces, two on each doorjamb. Be careful not to crack or break the stop molding: If the door is old you may have trouble finding a replacement piece.

To remove the door, slide it to the closed position. Grasp the door by the sides, tilt it slightly, and lift it off the track.

Check the rollers first. If the roller wheel is worn or broken, replace the entire roller mechanism.

Check the track next. If the track is loose, you may be able to reach into the opening and tighten the screws. The opening to the track is only a few inches wide, so the reach may be a little tricky. If the track is bent, you can replace it. To install a new track, you'll have to tear out the wall that forms the pocket. Replacing the track is usually more work than most folks care to get into, so you may want to make the best of the existing track.

French Pocket Doors

Q. *I love the look of French doors but have no room for them to swing open. Is there a way to get around this problem?*

French-style pocket doors don't require room to swing, but they do require a wall free of internal obstructions like plumbing, electrical wires, and heating ducts. The wall also has to be twice the thickness of the doors to provide an adequate pocket.

If your wall is a bearing wall, you can't remove part of it without installing a suitable replacement beam. Contact an architect to size the correct beam for the load. If you need wires rerouted, hire an electrician. Work that affects the structure of your home should be checked by your building inspector.

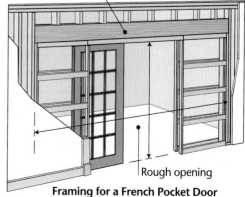

New header beam

Rough opening

Framing for a French Pocket Door

BIFOLD DOOR TUNE-UP

It's not unusual for bifold doors to become misaligned and then bind on the frame or sit unevenly in the opening. Here's how to get your bifold doors into good working order. The hardware on your doors may differ somewhat, but the basic tune-up is the same.

If misalignment is the problem, adjust the top of the door by loosening the small screw on the sliding bracket, moving the bracket left or right, then retightening the screw. If the surfaces of double sets of doors don't meet evenly when closed, adjust the clips on the backs. These clips are intended to overlap and lock into one another. If they're bent, straighten them with pliers. If the screw holes in the door are stripped, remount the brackets an inch higher up the door.

Replace broken roller guides by compressing the internal spring, swinging the door into the closet, then removing the old guide with a pry bar.

Another common problem occurs when the holes for the mounting pins become distorted from years of heavy-handed opening and closing. The trouble spots are located in the upper and lower corners and the top center where the doors meet. The best way to fix this problem is to drill out the enlarged hole, plug it with a wood dowel, and redrill for the pin. You'll have to remove the door from the track to fix this.

Remove the door by opening the two-door sections, grabbing them, and lifting up and out at the bottom. Remove the pins from their holes. The pins are usually in good condition and can be reused once the holes are plugged and redrilled. If the track or pins are damaged, buy replacement parts or a complete hardware kit at a home center or full-service hardware store. Note the holes drilled into the top and bottom corners of each pair of doors. Three of the holes are used—two for pins and one for the roller. The fourth hole isn't used. However, you'll need that fourth hole as a reference.

Measure the fourth hole's distance from the edges of the door. These measurements are where you'll need to redrill the plugged area to reinsert the mounting pin. Drill out the enlarged hole with a hole saw the same diameter as the dowel plug. Use a wood template as a guide to keep the drill straight; a scrap of wood cut to the same thickness as the door will work. Once the drilling is complete, apply wood glue to the dowel plug and insert it into the hole. Measure where the fourth hole is drilled and transfer those measurements to the newly plugged area. Redrill for the pin, using a drill bit the same diameter as the pin.

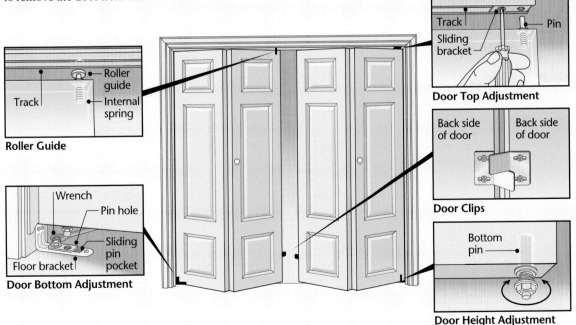

Roller Guide

Door Top Adjustment

Door Clips

Door Bottom Adjustment

Door Height Adjustment

Cabinets

INSTALLING CABINETS

Cut Costs: Install Cabinets Yourself

Q. *I'd like new cabinets for my kitchen, but having someone install them costs a lot of money. Is this a job my husband and I could tackle ourselves?*

Remodeling a kitchen is a big investment, but you can cut costs by installing the cabinets yourself. The key to a successful installation is careful planning. Some useful tips:
■ Buy your appliances before you order your cabinets so you'll know their exact measurements.
■ Buy quality, national-brand-name stock cabinets—cabinets built to standard measurements—at a large home center.
■ Create a computerized plan of your kitchen layout. The home center where you buy your cabinets most likely offers this service.
■ When placing cabinets, be sure the doors do not obstruct or swing into each other.
■ Before you begin, shut off water lines and turn off electrical power to the kitchen at the main electrical panel.
■ Remove the old cabinets with care; you might be able to use them in the basement or garage.

Hang Cabinets Straight

Q. *We're going to install new kitchen cabinets. What's the best way to ensure they hang right?*

Start by marking the height of the base cabinets on the wall. Measure 34½ inches up from the floor and snap a chalk line. Check first that the floor is level, and measure up from the highest point on the floor. If the floor is more than ¾ inch out of level across its entire run, you'll have to use a jigsaw to trim off about half or more of this amount from the base of the cabinet at the high spots. Be sure to allow for this cut-off amount when placing the chalk line. The remainder of the difference can be eliminated by using shims under the cabinet.

Mark a horizontal line 19½ inches above the lower line to mark the bottom of the wall cabinets (18 inches from the counter to the wall cabinet; 1½ inches for the counter thickness).

To ensure level cabinets, mark the walls with a level chalk line at the height of the base cabinets. Mark vertical lines along both edges of the studs so you'll have no trouble finding them when it's time to attach the cabinets to the walls.

Buying Stock Cabinets

Q. *I want to order kitchen cabinets from my home center. How do I go about choosing and ordering the right sizes for my house?*

Regardless of style, stock cabinets are built to standard dimensions. Most base, or lower, cabinets are 34½ inches high by 24 inches deep and are available in widths ranging from 9 to 48 inches, usually in increments of 3 inches. Wall, or upper, cabinets are normally 12 inches deep, 12 to 42 inches high, and are available in the same widths as base cabinets. If you find that you have odd size requirements, you can have a few cabinets custom-made or you can modify the stock cabinets themselves.

Bring the exact dimensions of your kitchen, including the locations of windows and doors, and the dimensions of your large appliances, when you shop. Most stores provide free computerized layout and design assistance to help get sizes right.

Framed vs. Frameless

Q. *What's the basic difference between framed and frameless cabinets?*

Framed cabinets have a "face frame" applied to their fronts. The frame is wider than the cabinet sides, and cabinet door hinges are mounted on the frame. Face-frame cabinets are more traditional looking and a bit sturdier, but they can be more difficult to install.

A frameless, or "European-style," cabinet makes more of the interior space inside the cabinet accessible. Frameless cabinets have door hinges that are mounted on the inside of the cabinets.

INSTALLING KITCHEN CABINETS

To demonstrate how to install kitchen cabinets, we've chosen a project that includes a corner unit. Your project may vary from ours, but the basic process is the same.

BASE CABINETS

Remove all the cabinet doors. Clamp the corner base cabinet to the cabinets next to it. Line up the cabinet frames at the top and bottom, and along the face. Push the assembled cabinets into position. Level the cabinets with shims. Later, after all the units are in place, pry up the cabinets slightly and slide the shims out. Place a dab of wood glue on the bottom of the shims and slide them back in place. When the glue dries, cut off the excess shim with a small handsaw.

Screw the leveled cabinets together near the top, bottom, and middle, through their face frames. Use screws that are long enough to extend at least ¾ inch into the receiving frame. We find that it saves effort to use a three-stage bit to predrill the holes (Photo 3).

When you are ready to install the base cabinet that will hold the sink, measure and mark the openings for the drain and supply lines; then cut them with a jigsaw (Photo 4). Slide the cabinet into position, level it, and secure it as shown in Photo 3.

Allow the space required for your dishwasher next to the sink base cabinet (Photo 6). Be sure the cabinet tops are level across the span and from front to back. Position and level base cabinets on both sides of the stove and refrigerator in the same way.

Secure the entire assembly of base cabinets to the wall using 2½-inch-long Phillips-head screws.

COUNTERTOP

We began the countertop installation by screwing 1 x 2 cleats to the wall in the open area behind the corner base cabinet. The cleats support the back of the counter. We used 2½-inch screws and kept the top of the cleats on the 34½-inch level chalk line.

If you're using a two-piece mitered plastic laminate countertop, join the premade sections. Place both sections upside down on a level surface. Test-join the sections with the connector bolts; then loosen. Spread wood glue on the joining edges. Lightly tighten the connector bolts with an open-end wrench. Align the front edges by rapping with a hammer on

(continued on next page)

Remove the cabinet doors. Clamp together the corner base cabinet and the cabinets that adjoin it. Place the clamps close to the spots where you'll be screwing them together.

Use shims to level the cabinets. Make sure they are level in all directions, and that the top edges of the cabinet backs are smack on the chalk line.

An easy way to hide screws in cabinetry is to use a three-stage bit like the one shown. It drills a pilot hole into the receiving frame and a clearance hole and countersink in the nearer frame, all in a single drilling operation.

Cut out the back of the sink base cabinet. Or if your water lines come up through the floor, drill holes for them in the cabinet floor.

INSTALLING KITCHEN CABINETS (CONTINUED)

a wooden block; then tighten the bolts. Let the glue dry.

Clamp the countertop to the base cabinets. Fasten it down with screws driven up through the cabinet frames. *Carefully* predrill clearance holes in the frames. If your screw is too long it will ruin the laminate. Be sure the countertop is down tight on the cabinets over its entire length, including the back edge. If is isn't tight enough, carefully drive screws wherever necessary.

WALL CABINETS

We joined the three corner wall cabinets in much the same way as the base cabinets shown in Photo 1. Place the cabinets upside down on the floor and clamp the frames together. Because you can't drive screws into the angled frames of the corner cabinet, screw the cabinets together through the sides. We had to cut four filler blocks to fill the extra space between the angled cabinet sides. Drive screws through the cabinet sides into the filler blocks from both directions to secure the sides.

Install temporary support cleats on the wall where the bottom of the wall cabinets will be. Predrill holes in the cabinet backs, located to hit the studs. Place the screws in the holes, then lift the wall cabinet assembly into place, resting it on the cleats. Drive in the screws.

5 When securing cabinets to the wall, predrill clearance holes near the top edge of the cabinet back, and drive a screw into each stud.

6 Allow the required space (almost always 24 in.) for your dishwasher next to the sink base cabinet.

7 Screw 1 x 2 cleats to the wall in the open area behind the corner base cabinet to support the corner of the counter.

8 Join the preformed counter sections if you're using a two-piece mitered plastic laminate countertop.

9 Check to see that the countertop is down tight on the cabinets over its entire length, including the back edge. If not, drive screws, carefully, wherever necessary. You can also secure the countertop to the cabinets with dabs of construction adhesive.

FINISHING TOUCHES

Clamp the wall cabinet end panels in place, squaring them with the cabinet top and bottom. Secure them with screws driven from inside the cabinet. Nail the crown molding to beveled backing strips screwed to the cabinet tops. Use ¼-inch-thick matching baseboard to finish the cabinet bases. Lay out the sink opening in the countertop by tracing the upside-down sink positioned so that it will be centered over the sink base cabinet. The sink directions will tell you how far inside the traced line your cutting line should be. Drill a starter hole; then cut with a jigsaw. Reattach the doors and adjust the hinges until the doors align and work properly.

Once the countertop is clamped to the base cabinets, fasten it down with screws driven up through the cabinet frames.

Place wall cabinets upside down on the floor and clamp the frames together. Cut four filler blocks to slide in place. Drive screws through the filler blocks and into the cabinet sides.

Lift the joined wall cabinet assembly into place, resting it on temporary support cleats.

Clamp decorative wall cabinet end panels in place, squaring them carefully with the cabinet top and bottom.

Reattach the cabinet doors. Good-quality hinges will allow for door adjustment in at least two directions: up and down, and left to right.

Cut the sink opening in the countertop with a jigsaw, drilling a starter hole for the saw blade.

Cabinets

RENEWING CABINETS

New Cabinet Pulls

Q. *The hardware on my kitchen cabinets is older than I am. Can I replace it without damaging the doors or drawers?*

Replacing old hardware is a quick, inexpensive way to update the look of your cabinets. If the distance between screws (referred to as the "bore") is the same, simply remove

A hole-drilling jig/template.

the old pulls and install new ones. If you're switching to a different bore, fill the holes with wood putty or hide them behind a backplate.

To get perfectly positioned pulls without repeated measuring and marking, build a hole-drilling jig (see photo, below left). Center the new pull and backplate on the cabinet door until you find a position that looks good. Mark where the pull's screw holes will go, then transfer these marks to a board to make the drilling template. Remember to flip the jig around to drill holes in doors with hinges on the opposite side.

The backplate covers old screw holes and wear marks while adding a touch of class.

Fading Lacquer Finish

Q. *Four years ago we had our cabinets refinished with lacquer. It isn't lasting well; can we apply polyurethane over the lacquer?*

Lacquer is not the best or most durable finish to use on kitchen cabinets, and it's surprising it lasted as long as it did. The good news is that you can apply polyurethane over the lacquer if you follow a few simple steps to ensure a good bond.

First, remove any hardware. Then scrub the cabinets to remove any dirt and grease (a mixture of ammonia and water works well). Follow the cleaning with a clear water rinse. Next, roughen up the old surface with 220-grit sandpaper to give the new finish something to adhere to. Remove the dust from the cabinets with a vacuum or tack cloth.

When refinishing, lay the doors and drawer faces on a flat surface; then brush on the polyurethane in several thin coats.

Cabinet Finish

Q. *We want to refinish our oak cabinets in a finish that won't show wear around the handles. What should we use?*

Any finish will wear eventually, so the trick is to catch it before it becomes obvious. Stain the oak to your liking; then apply three coats of satin-finish polyurethane, rubbing each coat down with fine steel wool when it is completely dry. Finish the back side of the doors the same way. When the door starts to look worn around the handles, simply apply another coat of polyurethane. It's also a good idea to choose door pulls with backplates to protect your doors from wear.

Aging New Hinges

Q. *The new brass hinges I bought for my cabinets look too shiny. Is there a way to make them look old?*

You can age brass pieces by suspending them above nonsudsy ammonia in a covered bucket. They will turn black in a day or two. Scrub off the black until they look the way you want them to. Do just one hinge for starters to be sure it's the look you want.

REFACING KITCHEN CABINETS

Refacing cabinets is a great way to give your kitchen a face-lift without the hassle of tearing out old cabinets or the expense of installing new ones. If the cases are solid, the drawers are in good working condition, and you're satisfied with your kitchen layout, it makes sense to reface.

Refacing involves putting a new veneer of real wood on cabinets and replacing the doors and drawer fronts.

Before starting, make a list of the exact measurements of the existing doors and drawer fronts; then order *unfinished* doors of the same dimensions. (If you buy prefinished doors, it will be difficult to stain the veneer to match.) To order veneer, add up the surface area of all the cabinet face frames, then add 20 percent. Peel-and-stick veneer is easiest to work with. Use ¼-inch plywood that matches the veneer to cover the visible sides and toe-kick areas.

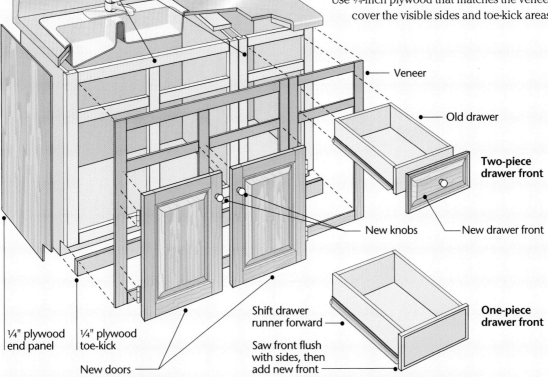

Cabinet frames

Veneer

Old drawer

Two-piece drawer front

New knobs

New drawer front

One-piece drawer front

Shift drawer runner forward

Saw front flush with sides, then add new front

¼" plywood end panel

¼" plywood toe-kick

New doors

To avoid wasting veneer, test-fit each strip first; then peel the backing and lightly fit it in place, then roll it to anchor it.

Finish the job by putting the newly stained and finished cabinet doors in place.

Cabinets

REPAIRING CABINETS

Straighten Cabinet Doors

Q. *My kitchen cabinets are starting to sag. How can I straighten them?*

Chances are it's not the cabinets that are sagging—just the doors. Examine the hinges; if they're bent, replace them. If the screw holes in a door or cabinet frame are stripped, remove the door and fill the screw holes with toothpicks or dowels dipped in wood glue. When they are dry, trim the excess with a utility knife. To remount the door, snap a chalk line along the entire row of cabinets to establish a level line, then clamp the door in place and redrill the holes.

Snap a chalk line; then clamp the door in place and redrill the hinge holes.

Replace a Cutting Board

Q. *My pull-out cutting board looks terrible and is difficult to clean. Can I fix it or must I replace it?*

A badly scored cutting board is a breeding ground for bacteria, and it's best to replace it with a new one.

Strips of "butcher block" hardwoods such as maple or birch glued together are the ideal replacement material for your cutting board, since they make a hard cutting surface that is easy to maintain. To install a new board, cut a board to size, then attach the face piece from your old board with wood glue and clamps.

A board that is not too severely scored can be sanded clean and oiled. First, remove the board from its slot and carefully knock off the wood face piece if it has one. Use a nontoxic finish (vegetable oil works well). Rub the oil into the wood and rub off any excess with a dry cloth. Reattach the face piece. You can re-oil the board as often as necessary to keep it looking good.

Knock the face piece off the cutting board, using a wood block and hammer.

Attach the face piece to the new board, using wood glue and clamps.

Smoother Sliding Drawers

Q. *My kitchen drawers constantly get stuck. Is there a permanent fix you can suggest to make them slide more easily?*

If the gap between the side of the drawer and the side of the cabinet face frame is at least ½ inch wide, consider stepping up to full-extension, ball-bearing drawer slides. They will eliminate stuck drawers and make the back of your drawer fully accessible.

First, remove the old slides from the drawers. Install furring strips inside the cabinet to mount the new slides to the case. The surface

of the furring strips should be flush with the inside edge of the cabinet face frame. Mount the new slides to the center of the drawer sides and to the furring strips in the center of the drawer opening.

Secure furring strips in the cabinet frame. Center them in the drawer opening.

To install the drawer, line up the two halves of the slides and then push the drawer into the opening. To remove the drawer, use the release lever.

Mount the slides on the center of the drawer sides and drawer opening.

Countertops

REPAIRING COUNTERTOPS

Scratched Laminate

Q. *How can I remove the scratches in our relatively new plastic laminate countertop?*

Unfortunately, there is no way to remove scratches from plastic laminate. This is true even if you have color-through laminate, where the color is impregnated through the thickness of the countertop. (The color-through type is less likely to show scratches, however.)

To hide small scratches, try using a seam filler, available from plastic laminate distributors. The filler comes in a variety of colors that you can custom-mix yourself. Spread the filler in 1/16-inch layers until the scratches are no longer visible. For deeper gouges, try a porcelain repair kit containing a colored epoxy (look for them at home centers). Again, you may need to blend the colors to get a good match.

MENDING A BROKEN COUNTERTOP EDGE

Mend a chipped or broken laminate countertop edge before water seeps into the particleboard base and loosens even more laminate. To replace a missing piece, first cut through the laminate, using a utility knife and straightedge, to create a clean edge. Scrape and remove the old adhesive from the particleboard base.

Next cut the laminate patch about 1/8 inch larger than needed in all directions. Apply contact cement to the patch and the base; then let the glue dry for about 15 minutes. Position the patch carefully (contact cement grips instantly) and press it in place. Allow the adhesive time to set; then file the patch to shape. Hide the joint (or small chips) with laminate seam filler.

1 Cut chipped laminate away with a utility knife to create a clean edge. This may take as many as 10 to 15 passes.

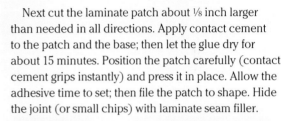

2 Apply the contact cement to the base and the patch, let it dry, and then apply the patch.

3 File the patch to fit, filing only towards the laminate edge.

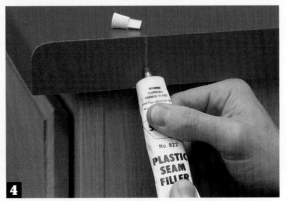

4 Use a special laminate seam filler to hide the joint.

Countertop Materials

Plastic Laminate

Most countertops and some cabinets are covered with a high-pressure plastic laminate. Plastic laminate countertops are easy to keep clean and fit with most decors. Durability is pretty consistent from one brand to the next, so choose this material by style, not by the manufacturer's name. Laminate countertops are relatively inexpensive and the color and style choices are endless, especially if you custom-order the top from a home center, lumberyard, kitchen showroom, or fabricator. You can find ready-made countertops at home centers and lumberyards, too, but the styles will be limited.

The downside to plastic laminate is that it can be scorched, scratched, and chipped. Unless you choose more expensive "color-through" laminate (which is more expensive), any exposed backing will create a dark line along the edges.

Most moderately skilled do-it-yourselfers can install a finished countertop of this kind, but leave the fabricating (building a particleboard substrate and attaching the laminate to it) to the pros.

Ceramic Tile

Ceramic tiles intended for countertop use are impossible to scorch and very difficult to keep clean. Tile is available in a variety of colors and shapes. Glazed tiles are easier to keep clean than unglazed ones, and tiles with a matte finish hide small scratches better than those with a high-gloss finish. Tile is easy for most do-it-yourselfers to lay themselves.

Grout is a high-maintenance substance. It can be difficult to clean, and needs to be resealed every few months and replaced every few years.

For the best results, lay tiles on cement board or on a mortar bed. Use latex or acrylic additives to strengthen the grout, or consider investing in epoxy grout.

Solid Surface

Essentially a dense slab of solid plastic, solid-surface counters are heat-resistant, extremely durable, and easy to repair with a little sanding or buffing. Solid surface comes in solid colors, granite-like speckled patterns, and marble look-alikes.

Solid surfacing is expensive and almost always requires a professional installation. Installing-solid surface material yourself may void the manufacturer's warranty.

Countertop Face-Lift

Q. *I am remodeling my kitchen and want to redo the countertop. Can I put new plastic laminate right over the old stuff?*

Assuming the old surface is in good condition, you can put new laminate over old as long as your countertop is flat and has a squared-off backsplash. If the countertop has a rounded backsplash, it is a postformed countertop, and you'll need to hire a professional or buy a new countertop.

To do the job yourself, make sure the old laminate is secure and that the edges are in good condition. Roughen the surface with 80-grit sandpaper. Don't use quick-drying solvent-base adhesive, because it will require a special respirator and an extremely well-ventilated work area, free of pilot lights, stoves, or furnaces. Instead, use a water-base adhesive; it takes longer to dry, but it is a safer product to use.

Flat backsplash

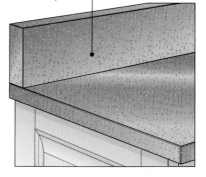

Rounded (postformed) backsplash

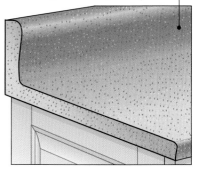

Burns on Laminate

Q. *There's a dark brown burn mark on our laminate countertop where someone placed a hot pan. Is there any way to repair the damage?*

If a burn or stain on your laminate countertop is light brown, you may be able to remove it by covering it with a thick paste of baking soda and water. Let the mixture sit for 20 minutes, then scrub it all off.

Unfortunately, in your case it sounds as though the burn has eaten through the laminate. Your best bet may be to cut out the burned area and replace it with a heat-resistant drop-in insert. The replacement board will provide a safe space for placing other hot pans and can be used for cutting food.

First, trace the insert's outline onto the counter. Check the underside of the counter to make sure there are no obstructions. Then drill some starter holes and cut out that section with a jigsaw. Some premade inserts come with a special retaining rim, but you can also make wooden support blocks and screw them to the underside of the counter.

Use a jigsaw to cut out the damaged area of laminate.

Secure a drop-in board in place with inserts or custom-made wooden blocks.

Choosing a Substrate

Q. *Can I use plywood as a substrate for my laminate countertop?*

We don't recommend it. Because plastic laminate is so thin, the surface underneath it (the substrate) must be sturdy and smooth.

If you do use plywood, use sheets that have one face with an "A" grade. Lower grades usually have surface imperfections as well as twists and warps that inevitably spell distaster.

The most popular choice for a substrate is ¾-inch high-density particleboard, because it's relatively cheap. High-quality plywood and MDF (medium-density fiberboard) work well but will cost more. All these substrates are sold at home centers in 4 x 8-foot sheets.

If you want to make a countertop that's more than 8 feet long, you'll need to connect two substrate pieces together with dowels. Then, using 1¼-inch screws, attach a 2-foot-long piece (trimmed to the width of your top) to the bottom.

You'll need to let the substrate and laminate adjust to the climate of your assembly area for at least 2 days before starting your project.

Plastic Laminate to Go

Q. *How do I transport sheets of laminate?*

Plastic laminate is brittle; it cracks easily if stressed. Treat it with kid gloves. You can't force it into submission, and it's not as forgiving as wood. Also, plastic laminate is thin and unwieldy, making it tricky to transport. Roll the sheet into a cylinder about 20 inches in diameter, then bind it with twine until you get it into your workshop.

Stone Countertops

Q. *The glaze on our ceramic tile countertop is almost gone. I'd like to replace the tile with slate, but I'm concerned about the porous surface. Will germs be a problem if I use slate?*

You're right to be suspicious about slate countertops for the kitchen. Unpolished stone surfaces provide a ripe environment for bacterial growth; they also stain easily.

If you're set on using slate, we suggest treating the surface with

three coats of waterborne satin urethane varnish. The varnish, which is available at your local home center, will seal the stone and the grout.

If your countertop takes a lot of punishment, after a few years you may have to rub the surface with steel wool and reapply the varnish.

BUILT-INS

Sagging Shelves

Q. *For a built-in bookcase, I'd like to use ¾-inch plywood shelves supported by brackets at each end. If I leave the shelves unsupported in the middle for 36 inches, will they sag when loaded with books?*

All wooden shelves sag a little; the question is how much sag you find acceptable to look at. Usually a sag of more than ⅛ inch over a 30-inch span is obvious. You might consider adding a ¾ x 1⅛-inch apron (a solid wood edge) to the front, rear, or both edges of your shelf.

A wood apron glued and nailed onto the front edge can increase the span length by 50 percent. By adding an apron to both sides, you can almost double the span.

Glue and nail every 8"

¾" x 1⅛" apron   ¾" x 8" shelf

HOW APRONS AFFECT SPAN LENGTHS

Use this table as a guide for maximum spans using ¾ x 8-inch shelving (35 pounds per foot).

MATERIAL USED	SHELF ONLY	WITH FRONT APRON	BOTH APRONS
Particleboard	20 in.	30 in.	40 in.
Plywood	28 in	42 in.	52 in.
Softwood	28 in.	42 in.	52 in.
Hardwood	34 in.	51 in.	60 in.

Sagging Closet Shelves

Q. *Why do the wooden shelves in the tops of closets always seem to sag? I'd like to know how to fix mine.*

Closet shelves sag for two reasons: we overload them, and most were not installed properly in the first place. Here's what to do to: Pry the old shelf off the side cleats (you may have to remove some nails first). If you're careful not to split or crack the shelf when you remove it, you can reuse it.

Install a 1 x 4 wooden cleat that is approximately the same length as the back wall. Make sure the cleat is

level; then secure it to the wall studs with drywall screws.

Flip the old shelf over so the sagging portion is convex and screw it to the side and back cleats. The sag will disappear once you reload the shelf.

Install an extra cleat along the back wall for additional shelf support.

Floor-to-Ceiling Bookshelf

Q. *Should I strengthen the floor before I build a floor-to-ceiling bookshelf in my home office? If so, how would I do it?*

A typical residential floor is designed to carry a load of about 50 pounds per square foot (psf). A bookshelf like the one you described could weigh more than 100 psf when full, so you will definitely need to reinforce the floor.

The most common floor joist system is 2 x 10's or 2 x 12's spaced every 16 inches. To bring this up to a 100-psf rating, you'll need to add an additional 2 x 10 to each joist. If the joists span more than 14 feet, you'll have to add even more joists or support the floor some other way.

Contact a local building inspector before you proceed with this job. Bear in mind that a floor is strongest where it is supported by a wall underneath; for example, exterior walls are supported by the foundation wall. Also, try to plan the shelf so that its length runs perpendicular to the floor joists.

Cabinets over Carpeting

Q. *I'm making a built-in entertainment center for our newly carpeted family room. Can I build the system right over the carpet?*

Carpeting isn't stable enough to support a built-in cabinet. You should pull back the carpet and padding, then cut it to fit around your built-in.

After you finish building your unit, install tackless strips (available at any home center) around the perimeter of the cabinet to secure the carpeting. Be sure to stretch and trim the carpeting and pad to fit around the cabinet just as you would trim and stretch it along a wall.

MARKING A PERFECT FIT

In a world where houses settle, walls wave, and ceilings sag, it's up to you to make a successful marriage between the material being installed and the space it's installed into. Objects that fit right look better and perform better. For example, a tight door will keep out the cold better, and a snug-fitting countertop will prevent water from seeping into places it shouldn't go. To get materials to fit seamlessly, professionals rely on a technique called "scribing."

Scribing involves copying an irregular shape or angle from one material to another. The two most common ways of doing this are by "direct" and "indirect" scribing. Direct scribing uses the edge as a guide, such as when installing countertops or cabinets against wavy walls in a kitchen. Indirect scribing uses a tool, such as a bevel gauge, to "remember" a curve or angle, which is then transferred to the material being installed.

Back-Cutting Basics

Q. *What does it mean to "back-cut" a joint, and how exactly do I do it?*

"Back-cutting" is an installation technique used to make tighter-looking joints. When you back-cut a joint, you remove more material from the back edge than you do from the front. The pointed front edge makes it easier to fine-tune the joint (with a plane or files) and allows the workpiece to be squeezed into place.

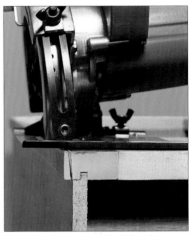

Use a circular saw to cut cabinet face frames at a slight bevel, or back-cut, so that the visible edge can be easily fine-tuned for a tight fit.

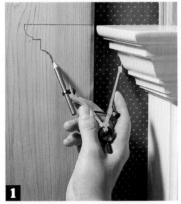

1 Use a compass to transfer tight curves. Set the legs equal to the widest gap, and hold the tool perpendicular to the piece being copied.

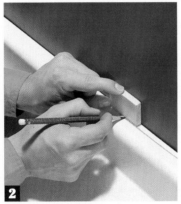

2 Use a spacer block to transfer the curve of an irregular wall onto a countertop. Make the block the same thickness as the widest gap.

3 To use a sliding bevel, adjust the two legs to match the desired angle, then turn the wingnut to lock the legs. Transfer this angle to the next board.

4 A contour gauge conforms to and records complex curves. Push the gauge toward the curve until all the feelers make contact.

A belt sander is best for back-cutting laminates without chipping and for working up to wavy scribe lines.

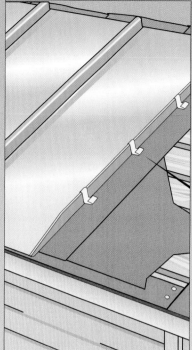

Siding

102	Wood Siding
103	Stucco Siding
104	Vinyl and Other Siding
106	Brick Siding

Exterior Trim

108	Trim

Roofs

110	Installing a New Roof
112	Repairing Asphalt Shingles
114	Cedar Shingles and Shakes
115	Metal and Tile Roofs

Gutters

116	Installing and Repairing Gutters

Windows

118	Window Repair
122	Storm Windows
124	Replacement Windows
126	Energy

Your
House
Outside

Exterior Doors
128 Installing Doors

132 Door Repairs

135 Security

138 Garage Doors

Housepainting
140 Selecting Paint and Gear

142 Surface Preparation

145 Painting Siding

146 Painting Brick and Stucco

148 Painting Doors and Details

149 Cleaning Up

WOOD SIDING

Nailing Siding

Q. *I plan to install traditional 6-inch cedar lap siding on my 60-year-old house. The wood sheathing underneath seems in good shape. How should the siding be nailed?*

Real wood siding is expensive, so you want it to last. To prevent the siding from cracking as it expands and contracts with the seasons, it's important to install it correctly.

Never nail wood siding through the course just below it: this impedes its ability to expand and contract. If you did, the resulting cracks would leave gaps for moisture to infiltrate on the back side, against the sheathing. Get the nail as close to the top edge of

the piece below as possible (⅛ to ¼ inch) without actually nailing into it. If you nail too far above the lower course, you'll be more likely to split the piece of siding you're nailing. When nailing close to the cut end of a piece of siding, drill a pilot hole for the nail. Otherwise you're almost guaranteed a split.

Use nails specifically made for wood siding. Ring shank nails, either galvanized steel or aluminum splitless,

work best because they hold well and don't pop or rust. Drive the nails into the studs behind the sheathing, then drive the heads flush with the surface of the siding.

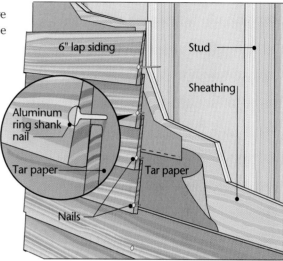

Labels: 6" lap siding · Stud · Sheathing · Aluminum ring shank nail · Tar paper · Tar paper · Nails

---

REPLACING DAMAGED WOOD LAP SIDING

Repairing wood clapboard siding is a fairly simple job. Whether it's made of redwood, pine, or cedar, in 3-inch- or 12-inch-wide strips, the method is the same. To remove the damaged section, gently pry up the siding and cut the nails with a mini-hacksaw. When you are removing more than one damaged clapboard, start with the top

board and work down. Cut the siding over the studs where possible, and stagger the joints to make the repair more weathertight and less obvious. Install the new clapboards from the bottom up. To finish, caulk the seams where clapboards run into a window, a door, or corner trim. Prime and paint. You can find new siding at a lumberyard or a large home center.

1 Pry up the damaged siding, and cut the nails with a mini-hacksaw.

2 Stagger cuts, starting at the top and working down. Reverse the blade in a keyhole saw to make close-in cuts.

3 Install new boards from the bottom up. Use rustproof siding nails. Caulk at windows, doors, and corners.

Darkened Cedar Shingles

Q. *My house has cedar shingles that have never been stained or sealed. The front is beautiful, but the sides are weathered and dark with mildew. How can I get the sides to look new again?*

Wood left to the elements naturally discolors. Sometimes the results are favorable as the siding weathers to a silvery gray. But black mildew is not attractive. Products are available at home centers for stopping mildew and cleaning and renewing wood. If you buy one, follow the manufacturer's directions.

To make your own solution, mix 1 gallon of household bleach with 2½ gallons of water and 1 cup of *nonammonia* detergent. Cover your plants with a plastic tarp. (In summer, work in the morning so that the plants don't overheat.)

Wearing safety goggles and rubber gloves, spray the solution generously onto the siding with a garden sprayer. Wait about 15 minutes; then rinse the siding thoroughly with a garden hose. Let it dry. If the siding is still darker than you want it to be, mix 4 ounces of oxalic acid (available at hardware stores) in 1 gallon of water. Spray it as before, but this time, scrub it with a stiff nonmetallic brush; then rinse and let dry. To help prevent mildew from returning, apply a transparent sealer or semitransparent stain that contains a mildewcide once the siding is completely dry.

If the problem persists, hire a reputable contractor to determine the cause. The contractor may suggest that you add vents to eliminate moisture. You might also remove other conditions that could be causing mildew. For example, cut back trees that create too much shade, preventing the sun from drying the siding.

Fixing a Hole in Stucco

Q. *I changed the location of a handrail on our stucco house. How can I patch the hole this made?*

To fix the hole where your handrail was located, chisel the edges of the stucco back to expose at least 1 inch of the old metal lath to allow a tight bond. Use a staple gun to staple a piece of roofing felt over the wood sheathing. Cut a piece of metal lath the shape of the hole, and secure it to the wood sheathing with 1-inch roofing nails.

Moisten the old stucco around the hole; then mix 1 part Type M masonry cement with 3½ parts washed sand to create a mixture that will hold its shape and not fall.

Fill the hole to within a ¼ inch of the finished surface. After 30 minutes, scratch the surface with a large nail so the next coat will bond. Spray the patch lightly with water every few hours to help it cure.

The next day, mix another batch and build the patch up even with the surrounding surface. Smooth it with a trowel or wood float. Moisten the patch a few times a day with a spray bottle for the next 2 days.

Mix the final batch for texturing. This layer is usually a thin veneer about ⅛ inch thick and contains 2½ parts white Portland cement to 3½ parts washed sand. Experiment using a large paint brush on a piece of scrap plywood. Strike the handle of the brush against a broom handle to get a stippled texture. For a troweled finish, use a flat steel trowel.

Cracks in Stucco

Q. *How can I repair a crack in the stucco on our house?*

Seal a crack in stucco as soon as you notice it to prevent moisture from seeping in and ruining the sheathing behind it. If the cracks are ⅛ inch wide or less, buy premixed stucco patch in a cartridge that fits into a caulk gun. Remove any loose dirt with a stiff brush; then apply the patch material as you would caulking. Smooth the surface, let it dry, and if you need to, mix some paint to cover the patch.

If you have large cracks, consult a stucco contractor immediately—they could be a sign of a structural problem, settling, or water damage.

Siding

VINYL AND OTHER SIDING

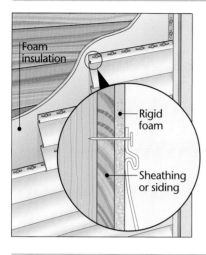

Foam insulation
Rigid foam
Sheathing or siding

New Vinyl Siding

Q. *Can I install vinyl siding over existing wood siding?*

Vinyl siding can be installed over old siding that is solid, but if the new siding sticks out in front of the old window and door trim, it won't look good. Before residing, you will need to replace any rotted wood and correct the causes of the rot. Renail loose boards, and nail a ⅜-inch layer of foam insulation over the old siding to provide a flat base for the vinyl.

Melted Vinyl Siding

Q. *I placed a grill too close to the house. When I lifted the lid, it hit the house and melted the vinyl siding. Is there any way to fix this?*

If you can find new siding to match the panel that melted, you can fix it. Vinyl siding is installed from the bottom up, so each piece interlocks with the section below it. To remove a section in the middle of the wall, first unhook it from the section above. Don't work in cold weather or the siding may crack. Vinyl siding will flex a bit, so first try freeing the damaged section by pushing up on the bottom edge while pushing down on the section above it.

If this fails, you'll need to use a zip tool, which is a little piece of metal shaped like a toboggan. You can buy a zip tool from a siding contractor or at a home center. Hook the curved end of the tool under the bottom edge of the section above the damaged one, and pull down and out. Once the sections are unlocked, use a flat pry bar to remove the nails that hold the damaged piece in place.

Cut your new piece of siding to size. Slip the bottom of it over the lip on the section below it, and nail it in place. The top section can be locked to the new section by pressing against it or by using the zip tool to pull down while you push in.

Before you remove the damaged siding, make sure you can match the style and color. Vinyl siding fades over time, so you may not get a perfect color match. Ask the contractor who installed the siding if he can supply you with a piece that matches.

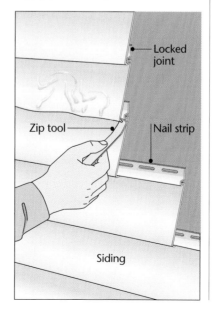

Locked joint
Zip tool
Nail strip
Siding

Chalky Siding

Q. *The original vinyl siding on our 15-year-old house is getting a whitish, chalky look to it. Is there a way I can make it look new again?*

"New" might be asking a lot, but you can certainly get rid of that chalky appearance. Look for a product specially formulated for cleaning siding at a home center or hardware store. It will clean aluminum and vinyl siding and remove any chalk, mildew, and dirt film.

The solution will come in a gallon container. Mix 2 cups of it with 5 gallons of water and apply it to your siding with a mop, a garden sprayer, or a pressure sprayer. If you use a pressure sprayer, be careful: the high pressure can break glass and damage the siding. You may have to clean the siding a second time if there is any stubborn dirt and grime.

Cleaning Vinyl Siding

Q. *The winter left my vinyl siding very dirty, especially under the eaves. How can I clean it?*

Rinse the siding, using a garden hose with a long-handled car-washing brush. To prevent streaking, start at the bottom and work up. For stubborn dirt, wipe the siding with a solution of ⅓ cup biodegradable household cleaner in 1 gallon water. Rinse with clear water. Wear protective clothing, rubber gloves, and goggles. Protect plants and shrubs with plastic drop cloths. You can also rent a power washer to clean the siding.

Asbestos Shingle Removal

Q. *I want to remove what appear to be asbestos shingles covering the cedar clapboards on our house. How can I do this safely?*

It is unlikely that your shingles contain asbestos, but to be sure, call your local environmental protection agency for a list of laboratories that can test the shingles. They will tell you the best way to take a sample.

If the shingles contain asbestos, hire a specialized contractor to remove them. Your local EPA may have a list of qualified contractors you can call. The price for this service will vary depending on local disposal and insurance costs.

Asbestos is dangerous if not handled properly, so keep the following in mind as you speak with contractors about doing the job: The shingles must not be broken or sawn—this generates dust. Hosing down the shingles can cut down on dust. The workmen should always wear full-body protective clothes, including a mask designed to protect against inhaling asbestos fibers.

REPAIRING ALUMINUM SIDING

Metal siding is largely maintenance-free, but it's not immune to dings, dents, and accidents.

When metal siding is installed, the bottom edge of each piece is hooked onto the top lip of the piece below. This interlocking system allows metal siding to be installed with no exposed nails, but it also makes repairs more difficult. The trick is to use a siding replacement tool, available from home centers and siding suppliers. Called a zip tool, it helps you unlock the siding so you can cut around the damaged piece and pull the nails to remove it.

Force the tool up and under the lap of the damaged piece and hook the bottom edge; start at a corner or a splice if possible. Pull down and toward you as you move the tool toward the damaged section. Unlock the bottom edge of the siding above the damaged piece too. Use aviation snips to cut along each side of the damage; then pull the nails out with a pry bar. Remove the damaged section.

Cut a replacement piece long enough to overlap the adjacent siding by ¾ inch. Cut a ¾-inch notch from each corner to accommodate this overlap. Relock the bottoms of the adjacent pieces and of the replacement piece onto the lip of the piece below. Nail the top of the new piece in place. Use the zip tool to hook and relock the upper piece onto the repaired section.

Hook and unlock the damaged piece of siding from the pieces below and above. Pull down and toward you as you move the tool sideways.

1

Pull the nails that secure the damaged section to the house. Prop the upper piece of siding up and out of the way with blocks or scrap wood for easier access.

3

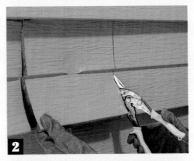

Cut out the damaged section of siding, using aviation snips. Wear gloves to protect your hands from sharp edges.

2

Install the replacement piece. Cut the new piece so it overlaps the existing siding ¾ inch on each side. Notches cut from each top corner accommodate the overlap.

4

Siding

BRICK SIDING

Sprinkler Stains

Q. *My brick home has water stains from the garden sprinklers. Is there a way to clean off these deposits?*

Hard-water stains left by your sprinklers can be difficult to remove. Generally the stains are composed of calcium carbonate, and you'll need an acid-base cleaner to get rid of them. However, don't use muriatic acid (which is often suggested), because it can stain or bleach many types of brick and can corrode aluminum window frames. Look for a brick cleaner that contains special buffers that prevent these problems. Your local brick dealer probably carries these products.

When cleaning, remember that you are using an acid-base product. Follow precautions and directions.

After cleaning the brick, you can avoid some future headaches by sealing the surface with a siloxane- or silane-base sealer.

Scrub water stains off brick with an acid-base cleaner and a stiff-bristle nylon brush. Protect nearby plants, shrubs, and grass with plastic sheeting.

Chalky Bricks

Q. *The bricks on my house look like they've been whitewashed. What caused this and how can I make them look better?*

Bricks naturally contain salt. When it rains, they absorb moisture. The salt dissolves in the water and when the bricks dry, salt crystals are left on the surface. The process, called efflorescence, typically occurs in the first few years after the brick is installed.

Assuming the brick was properly installed, rain will eventually wash the salt away. If you don't want to wait, scrub the bricks with water or a mild masonry detergent. If you suspect that the bricks may be soaking up water in places other than the face, ask a masonry contractor for advice on how to solve the problem.

Thin Bricks

Q. *We live in a 1960's ranch with hardboard siding. We'd like to jazz up the front with brick. Is this possible? And can I do it myself?*

When a brick face is planned during initial construction, the contractors provide a ledge to support the brick. The brick ledge extends down below the frost line, so that freezing and thawing don't disturb the brick. Retrofitting a frost footing can cost several thousand dollars.

A simpler and less expensive alternative is to use a thin brick veneer. Thin bricks are real brick, but because they're glued onto the exterior wall, there's no need for a brick ledge. You can install them yourself—the job is about as difficult as laying tile. To prepare the wall, you need to to apply wire mesh and a stucco-like scratch coat for the setting compound and brick to adhere it to. Once the bricks are in place, use a grout bag to squeeze mortar into the joints. Each manufacturer's brick veneer system comes with instructions and an array of corner pieces and top caps for a realistic look.

Thin bricks are applied to a substrate of wire mesh and a stucco-like scratch coat.

Attaching Window Boxes

Q. *How do I attach window boxes to my brick-exterior house?*

Attach the boxes just below the upper course of bricks under your windows. Make a bracket from ⅛ x 1-inch steel, which is available at hardware stores. The strap will support the bottom and back of the box and keep the back side away from the brick so air can circulate.

Using a vise and a hammer, bend the steel to conform to the shape of the box. Next, paint the brackets with rustproof paint and predrill them with ¼-inch holes.

Mark your anchor locations on the wall. Use a masonry bit to drill into the mortar for a lag shield.

Transfer the hole locations from the wall to the back of the planter and bracket. Attach the bracket to the box with ¾-inch wood screws, as shown. Drive the lag screws through the back of the box, into the wall anchors. For window boxes longer than 4 feet, use three brackets.

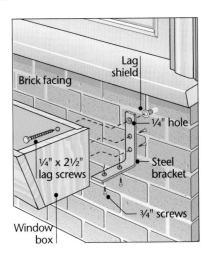

Brick facing · Lag shield · ¼" hole · ¼" x 2½" lag screws · Steel bracket · ¾" screws · Window box

REPOINTING BRICK MORTAR JOINTS

Brick seems maintenance-free, but over time the years take their toll. Cracks and gaps appear in the mortar joints first. If you don't repair them, moisture can get behind the brick and cause extensive structural damage. To avoid a major repair bill, you need to repoint failing joints. Also called tuck pointing, the process involves removing and replacing cracked or missing mortar. If large pieces of mortar are missing, or if bricks are falling apart or missing, call a pro.

The tools you'll need include a cold chisel that's no wider than the mortar joint, a 2-pound sledgehammer, a stiff brush, a trowel for mixing and holding the mortar, a plastic tub or wheelbarrow to mix the mortar in, a pointing tool for getting the mortar into the joints, a rake or jointing tool to match the existing mortar joint shape, and a stiff-bristle scrub brush to sweep away excess mortar.

You can use premixed mortar, but to get a seamless repair, you should mix the mortar yourself. Combine 3 parts sand to 1 part Type N masonry cement, then add water until you get a stiff paste that retains its shape when it's formed into a ball. Let the mortar stand for 1 to 1½ hours so it will be stiff enough to stay in place. Once the mortar is ready, you'll have 30 minutes to use it. If it gets a bit stiff, you can add a little water, but if it gets very stiff, mix another batch.

If a gap is deep—¾ inch or more—pack the mortar in ¼-inch layers. Each layer should be "thumbprint hard" before adding more mortar.

1 Remove loose mortar with a cold chisel to a depth of 1 in., or until you reach sound mortar. Brush out the debris, then rinse the surface.

2 Push the mortar into the joint with a pointing tool. Hold the trowel upside down, with the mortar on the bottom of the trowel.

3 Once the final layer of mortar is thumbprint hard, pack it in with a wheel rake or jointer. Use a scrub brush to clean away any dried excess.

Exterior Trim

Hanging Shutters

Q. *I'd like to install shutters around my windows. Is it easy?*

If your shutters are the right size and you use appropriate hardware, hanging them is not difficult. Shutters look best if each one is half the width of the window.

There are two ways to hang shutters: functional and non-functional. Functional shutters are fastened to the window trim with hinges, just like the old-fashioned variety. Decorative holdbacks hold the shutters in the open position and are fastened to the wall with lag screws.

Nonfunctional shutters can be fastened to the wall with a galvanized screw at the top and bottom. The edge of the shutter should abut the side of the window trim. If the window trim sticks out a little beyond the siding, use a short piece of plastic pipe as a spacer between the siding and the back of the shutter.

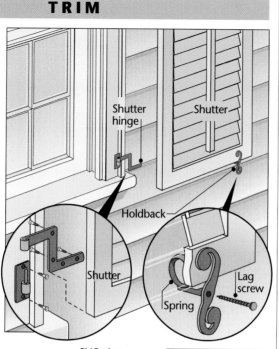
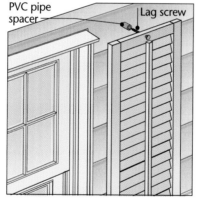

Replacing a Sill

Q. *I've found extensive rot in an exterior windowsill. Will I need to remove the window to replace just the sill?*

While it is possible to replace a rotten windowsill without removing the window, this is a job that's best left to a professional. With older windows, you may have to mill a replacement sill yourself. A rotten sill may also indicate other damage to the rough sill or to the wall that should be looked at and corrected while you're making the repair.

Depending on the extent of the damage, you may be able to stop the rot and rebuild any damaged wood with an epoxy filler (see Using Epoxy to Repair Wood Trim, next page).

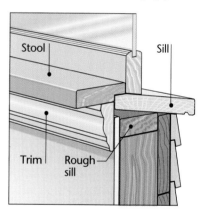

Gingerbread Trim

Q. *We'd love to add a Victorian touch to our home. Where can I go to get gingerbread trim, spindles, and other doodads?*

Adding decorative trim is back in fashion, which means that finding what you're looking for isn't that hard. You should be able to find a wide variety of ornamental spindles, brackets, and rails at your local home center. For more options, ask a salesman to see the product catalog.

Decorating your home with gingerbread trim can bring back turn-of-the-century style.

USING EPOXY TO REPAIR WOOD TRIM

Two-part epoxy is an excellent wood filler for repairing rotting windows. The epoxy bonds well to wood, holds up under all weather conditions, and won't shrink.

Before you make the patch, it's important to use a wood consolidant, or hardener, to stop rot from continuing to eat away at the wood. Probe the rotted areas with a screwdriver to see how deep the damage is; then remove the rotted areas and loose paint. Make sure the wood is bone-dry before applying the consolidant. Drill small holes to help the consolidant sink in; then soak the repair area with consolidant.

Next, mix the epoxy. For small repairs, shape the putty with your gloved hands to roughly rebuild the missing areas of the trim. Smooth it before it hardens. To keep the epoxy from sticking to your putty knife, dip the blade in lacquer thinner. If you're making flat or square repairs, you might consider packing the filler into a wooden form: Make a temporary form and screw it in place on the window sash. Wrap the form in polyethylene to prevent the epoxy from sticking.

It will take the epoxy about an hour to harden. Once it has fully cured, you can shape it with a rasp and sand it smooth just like real wood trim.

Prime and paint the epoxy as soon as possible so that ultraviolet light doesn't have time to damage it. Although it's difficult to stain the filler to match the surrounding wood, you can cut fake grain lines in it to make the patch less noticeable.

It's always a good idea to figure out the cause for the moisture problem that rotted the wood in the first place. Check your gutters for leaks and drips from the roof. Trimming back branches gives the sun a chance to dry out damp areas and stop rot before it can start.

1 Gouge and scrape away loose, spongy wood with a chisel.

2 Give the spot time to dry out, then soak the area with consolidant.

3 For large repairs, use screws to anchor and reinforce the built-up epoxy.

4 Smooth the filler with a putty knife before it hardens.

5 Build a wooden form for repairing large sections or square corners.

6 Once cured, epoxy can be shaped and sanded like wood for a seamless repair.

INSTALLING A NEW ROOF

Tear Off and Reroof?

Q. *How do I know it's time to reroof my house? Also, how do I know if I can shingle over the old or need to tear everything down to the sheathing?*

Look to your roof for answers. First, study the top layer of shingles; if they are slightly curled, brittle, or if you notice any patches where the granules have worn away, then it's probably time for a new roof.

Next, check the flashing. It may need to be replaced. If it has been patched or tarred over, it is probably well beyond its useful life. Typically, flashing lasts 30 to 40 years—twice as long as a shingle layer of shingles.

Finally, count the layers of shingles on the roof edge. The roof shown below has three layers of shingles. While building codes differ slightly on whether you can shingle over existing roofing, shingle manufacturers recommend not reroofing over more than two layers of old roofing.

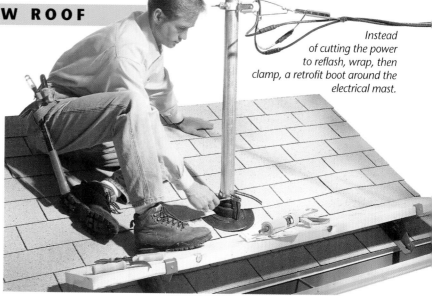

Instead of cutting the power to reflash, wrap, then clamp, a retrofit boot around the electrical mast.

Count the layers and check the condition of the top course to decide if it's time for a tear-off.

Flashing for Electrical Mast

Q. *In reroofing my house, should I replace the flashing around the electrical mast? Do I need to disconnect the electrical supply?*

In most cases, it's best to remove old flashing since it won't last as long as the new shingles. You can use retrofit flashing to flash the mast without having to cut the power.

Basically, retrofit flashing wraps around the pipe instead of slipping over the top. To install it, apply a bead of asphalt roof cement, install the flange, and tighten the two band clamps. Cut the shingles so that the top half of the flange is covered.

Retrofit flashing is a specialty item; you might find it at a roofing supply store or you may need to have it specially ordered.

Why Use Roofing Felt?

Q. *My local building code requires that roofing felt be used under shingles. What purpose does the felt serve?*

Roofing felt actually performs several important functions.

For starters, it protects the roof deck (the wood part of the roof) and the interior of the building from the elements while the roof is being applied. It also offers extra protection if the wind rips off shingles. In addition, it keeps wind-driven water, snow, or backed-up ice from getting under the shingles and damaging the wood roof deck underneath.

Need a New Roof?

Q. *Last year I bought a 35-year-old house with its original asphalt roof. The home inspector and a few contractors told me to get a new roof, but it doesn't leak and I say I can wait a few years. Am I right?*

You're both right. You can wait until it leaks, but it doesn't always pay off. Unnoticed leaks can cause roof rot, lift paint off the exterior and stain and damage interior walls. If you're short of cash and you are willing to climb up into your attic periodically to check for leaks, you can probably get a few more years out of the roof. Otherwise, replace it.

Membrane for Ice Dams

Q. *For the past few years we've had problems with ice dams. We're reroofing this spring. Is there anything we can do to prevent them from forming in winters to come?*

You can take steps to stop the dammed water from entering your house, but the best way to prevent snow from melting and damming in the first place is to create a cold roof. Do this by improving the insulation and ventilation in your attic.

As long as you're reshingling, consider applying a weatherproofing membrane directly to the sheathing along the eaves. The membrane bonds to the boards and seals itself around nail holes to form an impenetrable layer. The membrane should extend at least 2 feet beyond the plane where the inside of the exterior wall intersects the roof. You may need to install two rows of membrane if your house has wide eaves. For added insurance, use this membrane in valleys and around dormers. This material is sticky, so install it in the cool part of the morning. Once it's in place, shingle over it.

ROOF SAFETY

Working on a roof is inherently dangerous. To start, you need a good ladder and a sound base under it. Make sure your ladder is rated for your weight and the weight of any material you're hauling up with you. Make sure the ladder is at the correct angle, as shown, and that it protrudes at least 3 feet above the roof edge. If the ground is soft, tip down the safety shoes so that they dig into the soil. If the ground isn't level, put wood blocks under one side (keep the safety shoe up). If you must set the ladder on concrete or asphalt, have someone hold it for you.

As you climb, always maintain three points of contact with the ladder. When you get to the top, keep your feet on the rungs below the roof's edge; otherwise, the ladder can kick out below. On a steep roof, use a hook ladder to get from the edge to the peak.

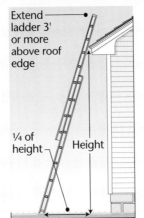

Extend ladder 3' or more above roof edge

¼ of height — Height

Roofing contractors are required to wear safety harnesses. A homeowner doesn't have to wear one, but it makes sense to rent one. A harness relies on an anchor that is fastened to a truss or rafter. Use a stud finder to locate the structural lumber; then attach the anchor with six 3-inch deck screws. Make sure the harness fits comfortably. Always adjust the cinch so there's no more than 6 feet of slack in the rope.

Roof brackets that support a 2 x 10 work platform are also helpful on a steep roof. Nail the brackets into a truss or rafter, then screw a plank to the brackets. Don't span more than 6 feet; for a longer platform, buy more brackets and a longer plank.

A snow and ice membrane sticks to the roof sheathing, keeping ice-dammed water from seeping into your home.

Wheel a hook ladder to the top of the roof and then flip it over to secure it.

A safety harness can be attached to an anchor (inset) at the peak of the roof. A plank set on top of roof brackets makes a good foothold.

Installing a New Roof **111**

REPAIRING ASPHALT SHINGLES

Shingle Repair

Q. *A few roofing nails have worked loose and worn through the top course of shingles. How can I patch these holes without having my roof look like a patchwork quilt?*

Small holes from nails, screws, or staples can let in enough water to cause a noticeable stain. Luckily, the holes are easy to repair.

To patch small holes, simply drive the nail below the shingle and seal the head with a dab of roofing cement. For larger (dime-size) holes, gently pry up the dam-

Patch a nail hole by driving the nail through the shingle, then slip in a piece of flashing for a lasting repair.

aged shingle with a putty knife. Next, spread a bead of roofing cement on both sides of a piece of flashing tin and slip it under the damaged tab.

Detecting Ice Dams

Q. *My neighbor told me that my house has ice dams, but I don't know what to look for. How can I find out if I have a problem?*

Ice dams form when snow melts from the top of your roof, and trickles

Matted insulation, areas darkened by water stains, and rot are interior signs of ice dams.

down toward the eaves, where it refreezes. A dam starts as a sheet of ice, then grows as snow continues to melt and freeze. Ice dams are known to hide under blankets of snow, so they're not always easy to find. Try to recall what your roof looked like over the past few winters: was it sometimes bare toward the peak but snow-covered toward the eaves, with icicles hanging off? If so, you probably had ice dams. Other signs include damaged shingles near the eaves; stains running down exterior walls; or rot, rusty nailheads, or blistered paint on soffits or fascia.

The only way to know for sure if water is leaking in is to check your attic the next time it snows. In the meantime, look for matted insulation and areas darkened by water stains or rot.

Holes in Metal Flashing

Q. *Is there a fast and easy way to plug a small hole in metal flashing?*

Fixing a puncture in roof flashing is easy. First scrub the damaged spot with a wire brush to clean and roughen the metal surface. Then fill the hole with gutter sealant (available at hardware stores) and smooth the patch with a putty knife. Wetting the knife with paint thinner will help you put a smooth finish on the patch.

Fill small holes in flashing with gutter sealant. Dip the putty knife in paint thinner to smooth the patch.

Buckled Shingles

Q. *My roof, which has five different levels, was redone about 5 years ago with asphalt shingles. Now some of the shingles on certain levels are badly buckled and leaking while the shingles on other levels are perfectly flat. What happened?*

Sounds as if your roof deck is not properly ventilated. Moisture and heat can build up to cause shingles, or even the deck, to buckle and shingles to fail prematurely. Improper ventilation can also create ice dams during the winter. A roofing contractor should be able to suggest ways to improve ventilation, such as by adding ridge vents.

Preventing Ice Dams

Q. *I'm building a new house in northern New England and have been warned about ice dams. How can I protect my roof against them?*

The main problem with ice dams is the water that pools up behind the dam. This standing water can seep up between the shingles, enter your attic, and leak into the space below. This can stain walls and rot rafters.

The best way to prevent ice dams is to prevent warm air buildup in your attic. You can do this by improving insulation so less heat enters the attic, and improving ventilation so warm air has an escape route.

Ice Dam First Aid

Q. *Can I use the salt I sprinkle on my driveway to melt ice dams off my roof?*

No, never use salt to melt ice on your roof. It can damage shingles, gutters, and wood. In an emergency, you can use a hammer, hatchet, or ice pick to chip grooves in the dam every 3 feet or so to drain the water. Be careful not to break the cold, brittle shingles. Better yet, hire a roofing contractor to steam away ice dams. The job will cost you some money, but it will be the best thing for your roof.

how is it done?

REPLACING A SHINGLE

Replacing a damaged shingle is a relatively simple job. You'll need a putty knife, a pry bar, galvanized roofing nails, a hammer, a caulk gun, and a tube of roofing adhesive. If you don't have a matching replacement shingle, bring the broken one to a home center or roofing supply store to select the best match.

Schedule your repair for a warm day; the shingles will be more pliable and less likely to crack. If the temperature gets above 80° F, wait for it to cool down: walking on hot shingles could cause additional damage.

Because the shingles overlap, you'll need to remove the nails from the damaged shingle and the one just above it. Use your putty knife to lift the two rows of shingles above the damaged one. Make sure the entire length of the shingle is loose before bending back any tabs. Once you remove all the nails, the shingle should slide out. Slip the new shingle into position and nail it in place. Replace all nails; then apply a thin bead of adhesive to the nailheads and under the tabs of any shingles you bent back. Press down on the tabs so that they stick to the adhesive.

1 To remove roofing nails, tap the flat end of the pry bar under the nailhead.

2 Slip the new shingle into place. The bottom edge should align with the rest of the course.

3 Drive nails into the new shingle in approximately the same locations as the old nails.

4 In addition to the new shingle, secure any bent tabs with a thin bead of roofing adhesive.

Roofs

CEDAR SHINGLES AND SHAKES

New Cedar Shake Roof

Q. *I love the look of cedar shakes and would like to have them on my own house. What's the best way to install a cedar shake roof?*

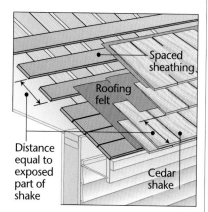

First, let's be sure we're talking about cedar shakes and not cedar shingles. Cedar shingles are sawn on both sides and have a smooth appearance. Shakes are hand-split, have a rougher texture, and are thicker.

There are two methods for installing cedar shakes: They can be installed over solid plywood sheathing or over a spaced sheathing (sometimes called "skip sheathing"). Solid sheathing is more weather-resistant and is recommended for areas that receive heavy snow and/or experience earthquakes. Spaced sheathing is preferred in hot and humid areas because it helps the roof dry quickly, preventing rot. This method uses 1 x 6's installed with a gap between them. The size of the gap is equal to the distance from the bottom of one shake to the bottom of the next.

Because of the rough texture of shakes, wind-driven rain and snow can work their way in through gaps. To prevent this, lay an 18-inch-wide strip of roofing felt under the courses to act as a baffle.

Care of Cedar Shingles

Q. *My cedar shingle roof is 6 years old and is in good condition. Do I need a wood preservative?*

While an untreated cedar roof will last about 25 years, using a wood preservative can extend the life of the roof by an additional 10 years.

Prior to treatment, make sure the roof is free of loose debris and mildew. Use a commercial mildew cleaner, or mix 1 cup of laundry detergent and 1 cup of bleach with a gallon of water. Apply this solution with a garden sprayer, let it sit for a few hours, then hose it off. Let the roof dry for several days; then apply a roof preservative. Caution: Wet cedar is very slippery.

Expect to treat the roof about every 5 years, or when the shingles start to look dry and brittle or dirty.

Roof Moss Remedy

Q. *There are dark streaks and moss all over our cedar shingle roof. I tried power-washing, but the problem has come back. What can I do?*

The dark streaks are most likely algae growth. Moss and algae are fairly common in humid regions. To prevent new growth, install zinc strips (available in roofing supply stores) near the ridge of your roof. These strips release zinc ions, which are carried down the roof by rainwater, and inhibit algae growth. You'll have to clean old streaks with a bleach solution to get rid of them. (Be sure to protect your plants below the roof with a plastic tarp.) Starting from the top and working your way down, pour the solution and then carefully sweep off the algae. When you're done, rinse the roof with a hose.

Replacing Cedar Shakes

Q. *How can I repair my cedar shake roof without damaging shakes in the process?*

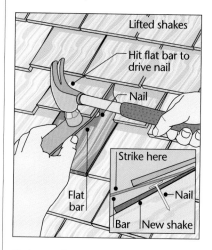

Cedar roof repair requires careful work and patience. To do the job yourself, mark an X on the shakes that need to be replaced. Then, starting four or five courses above the topmost damaged shake, slide a flat pry bar under the shakes and work the nails loose so you can raise the shingles ¼ inch at the point where they are nailed. (Put a piece of sheet metal under the pry bar to protect the shingles.) Move to the next course down and repeat. You can lift this course ½ to ¾ inch. By the time you reach the shakes that need to be replaced, you should be able to remove them easily.

Select a new shake that is the same width as the old one. Start two nails in the new shake so that when it is in position, the next course will overlap the nails by 1½ inches. Slide the new shake into position; then slide the flat pry bar over the head of one nail. Drive the nail by holding the end of the bar and hammering on it close to the shake. Repeat with the other nail.

METAL AND TILE ROOFS

Cleaning Copper Roofs

Q. *I've tried everything to clean the copper roof over my bay window: paint stripper, TSP, ammonia, drain cleaner, and several polishes. Nothing works. How can I restore its original luster?*

Copper cannot be restored to that shiny metal you saw when it was new. Copper goes through a natural weathering process, called oxidation, that takes a number of years. It is this corrosion process that makes copper roofs appealing and maintenance-free for the life of your roof.

A copper roof will look brown when it is in the first of three stages of oxidation. The second stage is characterized by green streaks, and the third stage occurs when the whole roof turns a soft green color. If you don't want to wait, you can hire a professional to artificially induce the final green stage by applying a specially formulated solution.

Rolled-Edge Metal Roofing

Q. *I love the way rolled-edge metal roofs look and would like to install one on my house. They're pretty expensive and I'm wondering: Is there anything a do-it-yourselfer can do to reduce the cost of one?*

Rolled-edge metal roofing (more correctly called standing seam metal roofing) costs about twice as much as wood or premium asphalt shingles. However, metal roofing will last twice as long. (It's not unusual for metal roofs to outlast the structures they're installed on.) Also, since metal roofs shed snow quickly, they rarely get ice dams. If you plan to own your home for a long time, the investment in this low-maintenance roof can be worth it.

Unless you have experience working with sheet metal and the proper tools, you'd better leave this one for a pro. You might be able to save a few hundred dollars by stripping off the old roofing material yourself, instead of having the roofer do it.

Sealing a Metal Roof

Q. *My old farmhouse has a leaky metal roof. Is there a product that will seal it against leaks?*

There are many water-base roof sealants that you can apply with a brush or roller. They come in various grades that differ in longevity and price. Keep in mind that they are meant for temporary fixes. Eventually you'll need to replace your old roof with a new one. Get a replacement-cost estimate from a local roofer to make sure that the seal will be the most cost-effective solution.

Tile Roofs

Q. *We bought a home with a tile roof and have no idea what maintenance it requires. Any suggestions?*

Tile roofs are virtually maintenance-free. Unlike other roofing materials, tiles need no patching, sealing, or recoating. A tile roof should last the lifetime of your house.

Because they are made of clay or concrete, tiles may break every now and then, especially in cold climates. Tiles are fragile and difficult to handle, so repairs are best left to a pro.

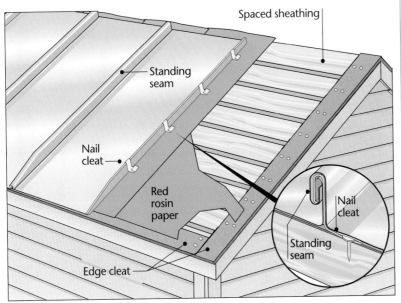

Spaced sheathing | Standing seam | Nail cleat | Red rosin paper | Edge cleat | Nail cleat | Standing seam

SAFETY CHECK

When working on the roof:

■ Be sure your ladder is in good condition before you use it.
■ Wear work boots or shoes with soft rubber soles.
■ When climbing onto the roof, keep three points of contact with the ladder. Keep your feet on the rungs below the roof edge and step up to the roof.
■ If there's moss or algae on the shingles, they will be slippery.

Gutters

INSTALLING & REPAIRING GUTTERS

Choosing Gutters

Q. *We're ready to replace the gutters on our house. What's the best system to install?*

Most gutters are made of vinyl, aluminum, galvanized steel, or copper. Each type of material has advantages, but each also has vulnerabilities.

At the high end of the price scale are soldered copper and galvanized steel. These systems are custom-fitted on site and are usually the strongest and most attractive. Left unpainted, the copper weathers to a dull brown. Soldered galvanized steel gutters must be painted.

"Seamless" aluminum and steel gutters are formed on site on a special machine that molds factory-coated sheet metal. Single sections can run almost any length, so the system has fewer joints (it's not actually seamless). Joints are usually riveted or caulked or sometimes strapped. Caulked joints can leak, and though you wouldn't expect the steel coating to rust, it will if water is left to sit in it for a long time. Seamless gutters are moderately priced.

Multipiece aluminum, vinyl, and steel gutters are the least expensive and can be installed by a homeowner. They are assembled from 10-foot lengths of gutter and joined with special fittings and caulk. Most metal types have a baked-on finish that resists corrosion. However, some cheaper lines suffer from leaky joints and look flimsy. If you opt for this type, look for heavier-gauge systems.

Regardless of the type of gutters you choose, you'll need to buy enough material to run the length of your roof's fascia, as well as enough for one downspout for every 700 square feet of roof area and one at every corner of the house.

Sagging Gutters

Q. *We've insulated and ventilated our attic to eliminate ice dams. Now the problem is the sagging gutters the dams left behind. How can we resecure the gutters?*

The quickest and easiest way to reattach aluminum and steel gutters is with spikes and ferrules. The ferrule acts as a spacer and support while the long spike tightens up the gutter and secures it to the eaves. Try to drive the spike into something solid, like the ends of the rafters. To find the rafters, look for nailheads in the fascia (the horizontal board directly behind the gutter).

Some people will argue that punching holes in a gutter designed to carry water is not so smart. The alternative method is to use brackets that wrap around the gutter, and then securing them to the roof with nails driven under the shingles. The problem with this method is that shingles tend to get brittle with age and may break as you lift them to drive the nails. Then you have both gutter and shingle repairs to tackle.

The spike and ferrule method of fixing sagging gutters is quick and easy. Wrap-around brackets may cause more harm than good.

Patch a Leaky Gutter

Q. *Every time it rains I am reminded that my front gutter leaks water into my basement. What's the best way to fix it?*

Here's a solution that will work on leaky metal and vinyl gutters. Begin with a thorough cleaning. Rinse out any debris with a garden hose, then scrape away loose rust or paint with a wire brush.

Once the area surrounding the leak is clean and dry, use an old putty knife to spread plastic roofing cement at least 6 inches beyond the leak in both directions. Embed a piece of repair mesh or metal flashing into the cement; then recoat it with a second layer of cement.

Embed repair mesh into plastic roofing cement, then coat with a second layer.

Sealing Gutter Seams

Q. *I have seamless aluminum gutters on my house. Despite the name, there's a seam where two sections meet, and it leaks. How can I seal it? Caulk doesn't seem to work.*

Drill out the pop rivets holding the gutter sections together. Clean them off, and apply a ⅜-inch-wide bead of caulk (specifically labeled for aluminum gutters) to the gutter overlap. Press the joint together and install new pop rivets.

INSTALLING VINYL GUTTERS

Vinyl gutters are easy to work with and can be installed by a homeowner with moderate skill. Here we provide some helpful tips, but you should consult the manufacturer's instructions for specifics.

The first step is to establish a line on the fascia board for hanging the gutter; the screws will be attached along this line. For effective water runoff, start at the point farthest away from the downspout and slope the line downward toward the downspout. This slope also ensures that overflowing water in a clogged gutter won't flow back under the shingles or into the wooden roof overhang. Beginning ¾ inch below the shingles, snap a chalk line that slopes down about 1 inch for every 20 feet toward the spout. Also:

■ The front gutter edge should be about ½ inch lower than the back so water will overflow in front rather than soaking the fascia board in back.

■ If your house doesn't have a conventional soffit and fascia—for example, if the ends of the roof rafters are exposed—you'll have to attach the gutters with roof brackets.

■ To be sure the downspout doesn't deposit water near or on sidewalks, use an adequate length of downspout.

Once you've marked a line for the position of the gutter, install the drop outlet for the downspout between 12 and 24 in. from the corner of the house; this lets you secure the downspout bracket to the siding.

Slide the gutter brackets onto the gutter. Use three or four per section. Don't worry about their position since they slide easily.

Attach adhesive-backed seals to each end of the gutter sections. Don't overstretch the seal or it will leak.

Snap the slip joint onto the end of the gutter section that will be connected to another section of gutter.

Snap the end of the gutter into place in the drop outlet. Space the remaining gutter brackets evenly, and attach them to the fascia with galvanized screws along the chalk line.

Measure the distance between the ends of the elbows; add 3 in. to this and cut a section of downspout to this length. Install it between the elbows. The lower elbow is secured to the house with a bracket.

Windows

WINDOW REPAIR

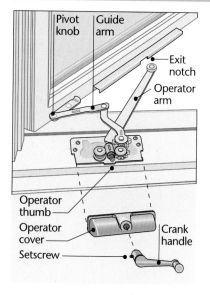

- Pivot knob
- Guide arm
- Exit notch
- Operator arm
- Operator thumb
- Operator cover
- Setscrew
- Crank handle

Window Lever Fixes

Q. *The windows in our summer cottage are the casement type. A few years ago a couple of the levers stopped working properly. Do they need to be replaced, or is it possible to fix them?*

Casement windows, awning windows, and hopper windows all rely on levers called "operators" for opening and closing. Several things can go wrong with these levers, but you can usually fix the problems easily.

First, inspect the levers by making sure the latches (not shown) are fully released. If paint has glued the window to its frame, cut the paint bond with a sharp utility knife; then tighten the setscrew with a small screwdriver. If tightening doesn't help, loosen the setscrew and check the teeth inside the crank handle. If the teeth are rounded over, replace the handle. If the teeth on the operator thumb are also worn, you'll have to replace the entire operator.

Next, remove the operator cover (if it's removable). If the gears inside are corroded, bent, or broken, replace the operator. If they look OK, try cleaning them with a toothbrush and spraying them with a silicone lubricant. To install a new operator, simply reverse the steps you took to remove the old one.

Replacing Broken Glass

Q. *Is replacing a single pane of broken window glass something I can do myself?*

Replacing a broken single-pane window is both easy and inexpensive. The materials you'll need are available at home centers and hardware stores. You have the choice of either leaving the sash in place or removing it to do the job on your workbench.

First, remove the broken glass and glazing compound. If the compound is old and crumbly, you'll be able to chip it away with a chisel. If not, try softening it with a hair dryer before chipping and scraping. Under the compound you'll find tiny metal tabs, or glazing points; remove them with pliers.

Take the window measurements and ask the hardware store for a piece of glass 1/8 inch smaller than the opening. When you have the new piece of glass, line the opening of the window with a thin bead of glazing compound and firmly press the new glass into place. Secure the glass by placing glazing points every 4 inches around the perimeter. Be sure to use points that have "ears" that allow you to press the points into place with a putty knife.

Apply compound around the edges of the glass with your fingers, and then smooth it with a putty knife. Dip the putty knife in linseed oil so it skims smoothly over the sticky compound. Let the putty cure for at least a week before painting the window.

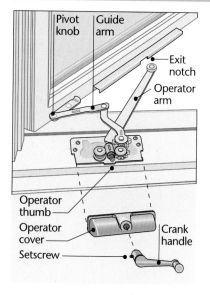

Apply a thin new bead of glazing compound and press the new glass into it.

Use glazing points that have "ears" that can be pushed into the compound with a putty knife.

A flexible putty knife dipped in linseed oil works well at smoothing the compound around the window.

how is it done?

REPLACING A WINDOW SASH

Today, replacing a window is easy. Replacement window sash kits available from quality window manufacturers let you replace just the sashes without removing the interior trim or tearing out the frame. They are airtight, come with insulated glass, and allow you to do the job from the inside of your house.

You'll need the following tools for this job: a hammer, a pry bar or wide, stiff-bladed putty knife, a utility knife or heavy-duty scissors, both straight-tip and Phillips-head screwdrivers, pliers, and 6d finish nails. Paint or stain the sashes before you install them, and follow the manufacturer's instructions carefully, because each brand is a little different.

Begin by removing the existing part-ing stop with your pry bar or putty knife. Then angle out the lower sash, cut the window weight cords, and remove the sash. Be careful not to damage the window casing trim. Now do the same for the upper sash. Remove the access hole cover in the jamb, and remove the weight and cord. Unscrew the pulleys for both sashes and fill the entire area behind the jamb with insulation. When it's filled, replace the access hole covers.

The next step is to install the jamb liner bracket clips. The vinyl jamb liner then snaps in place over the brackets to provide an airtight track for the new sashes. To install the new sashes, start with the top one and follow the manufacturer's instructions for locking the lift mechanisms. That's all there is to it.

Pry off the stop and pull the nails carefully. You'll reuse the stop later.

You'll need heavy-duty scissors to cut the window cords.

Remove the access hole cover in the jamb, and remove the weight and cord.

Follow the manufacturer's instructions for the number of bracket clips for each liner and the spacing between clips.

Snap the airtight vinyl jamb liner onto the brackets.

Install the top sash first. Replace the window stop.

New Screen Material

Q. *After a few summers of kids and the dog pushing on our aluminum screen door, it looks pretty shabby. What tools and materials do I need to fix the screen?*

Fixing a screen door is an easy project, and the materials you need are readily available. There are several types of screen to choose from. Fiberglass is flexible and the easiest to use; if you make a mistake, you can take it out of the frame and try again. Aluminum screen is sturdier, but you get only one chance to install it because the grooves you make with the roller are permanent. Sun-shading fabric is becoming popular as a screen material because it helps cool your home and keeps carpets from fading. It is also stronger than fiberglass or aluminum, so it's great for pet owners.

All three materials come in gray or black to match your other window screens. You can also get shiny aluminum and sun-shading fabrics in bronze and brown tones.

To repair your screen you'll need new screen material, a new rubber spline, and a screen rolling tool. If your screen is longer than 36 inches, you will need a center support to keep the frame from bowing.

With these few tools and materials, you can easily fix your own window screens.

REPLACING A TORN SCREEN

To replace a screen, first remove and discard the spline (the rubber strip that holds the screen). Pry it out with a narrow-tipped screwdriver and remove the damaged screen.

Prepare the frame for the new screen next. Screw wooden stop blocks to your work surface along the inside edge of the two longest sides of the frame. The blocks will keep the frame from bowing in when you install the new screen material.

Lay the new screen over the frame so that it overlaps by about 1 inch, and cut the corners of the screen. Starting in a corner of the frame, use the screen rolling tool to push the spline and screen into the groove. Finally, trim the excess screen material with a sharp utility knife. Cut with the blade on top of the spline, pointed toward the outside of the frame.

1 *Screw wooden blocks to the work surface to help keep the frame straight and square as you install the screen.*

2 *Cutting the corners of the screen at a 45° angle keeps the screen from bunching in the corners.*

3 *If large wrinkles and bulges appear when you are rolling the screen and spline into the groove, remove the spline and reinstall it.*

4 *Be sure to use a new blade on your utility knife when you trim the excess screen; a dull blade will just pull the material, not cut it.*

Leaky Skylight

Q. *The 10-year-old skylight in our kitchen has begun to leak badly. The ceiling plaster is falling and we've tried every type of caulk imaginable to fix the problem. Do you think we'll need to replace the entire skylight?*

Have you tried removing the old caulk down to the shingles and/or flashing before recaulking? Do this first; then use a silicone caulk that will stay flexible through various weather conditions and over a long period of time. If the skylight itself is still in good condition, you might want to consider removing the window unit and reinstalling it with new flashing and caulking.

Drafty Skylight

Q. *There's a cold draft that comes down directly under the bottom edge of the large skylight in my living room. The skylight is double-glazed and I don't think there is any air leaking in around the edges, since they are completely watertight. I feel the draft more at night than during the day. Any ideas what the problem might be?*

You probably have an uninsulated shade on your skylight. Warm air is passing through this shade, striking the glass, and cooling down. The cooler air then sinks back into the room by way of the shade's back surface. To solve the problem, install an insulated shade cover that seals all around the edges of the skylight well. A simpler solution, though far less energy-efficient, is to leave your existing shade open so that the falling cool air won't be concentrated into the steady stream that you feel at night.

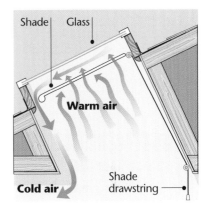

Skylight Condensation

Q. *We get condensation on our bathroom skylight that runs down the glass onto the wall, then onto the woodwork. How can we solve this problem before the water causes more damage?*

Condensation on skylights forms when warm, humid air (like the air in your bathroom) meets the cold surface of the glass. It can be lessened, but keep in mind that it's almost impossible to stop condensation completely, especially in regions that have freezing temperatures.

Condensation can be either persistent or periodic. Persistent condensation is moisture that forms on a skylight and stays for days or weeks. This is the worst kind because walls and surrounding areas can become soaked, mildewed, and stained. The problem is that the humidity level in the house is too high. To reduce it, remove sources of moisture: seal damp basement floors and walls, cover crawl spaces with plastic, make sure your gas- and oil-burning appliances are properly vented, and consider reducing the number of houseplants in your house. Improving the airflow in your house with proper ventilation will also help considerably (see Ventilation, p.290-293).

Periodic condensation happens when there is a sudden drop in temperature outside or a short-term increase in the humidity level inside. This type lasts just a few hours or so at a time. Most manufacturers put small gutters or weep holes along the lower edge of their skylights to control any runoff. These little holes are essential for skylights in kitchens and bathrooms, where humidity levels can jump quickly. You can keep periodic condensation under control by improving airflow to flush out the high humidity: use exhaust fans in kitchens, bathrooms, and laundry rooms and ceiling fans in other living areas. Open the skylight slightly, or open a vent in the skylight if there is one; also, open any inside shading device that covers the skylight.

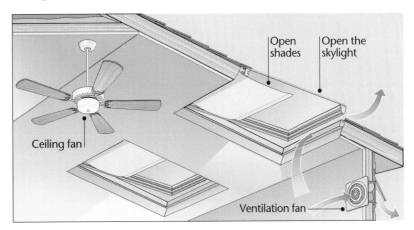

Windows

STORM WINDOWS

Interior Storm Windows

Q. *Is it difficult to make and install interior storm windows? I'd like to learn how.*

Interior storm windows block noise and eliminate drafts on the interior side of windows. They are not difficult to make or install, and they add extra insulation by creating dead air space between the existing window and themselves. They are also the only type of add-on window that will work with casement, awning, or other tilting or swinging windows. In addition, these acrylic windows offer a shatter-resistant buffer between occupants and the glass of the primary window. Their only drawback is that all or part of the storm window must be removed in order to work the primary window.

There are several types of interior storm windows. The photos below illustrate how to install a window with magnetic edging.

Nail wood stops to the top and sides of the window. Space the stops so the new window doesn't touch the old hardware.

Cut acrylic to size according to the manufacturer's instructions. Leave room for the acrylic to expand and contract.

Slip the magnetic edging over the top and side edges of the acrylic, seating it firmly with a rubber mallet.

Position the interior window so that the foam cushion rests on the window sill.

Wood Storm Windows

Q. *Our 1910 home has storm windows with separate screen and glass sashes that need to be changed every spring and fall. We think aluminum combination windows will ruin the look of the house. Do we have any choice?*

There's no denying that aluminum and vinyl windows don't look right on an old house. You may choose to stick with traditional wood storms, or you can step up to wood-frame combination windows.

Wood-frame combination windows (the storm and screen are combined) will match the look of your old house. While the aluminum models are available in many stock sizes, you will probably need to have the wood combination windows special-ordered.

Traditional wood storm windows require annual installation and periodic maintenance, but they are a lot less expensive. Since they are full-size and custom-fit, they eliminate winter drafts. In addition, if you have basic carpentry experience, you can build the frames yourself.

Whether you choose storm or combination windows, you need to measure the openings carefully. Before you measure the opening, place a framing square in each corner of the window frame to check it for square. If the opening is out of square, measure the width at the top, middle, and bottom. Measure the height along both sides. Use the widest dimensions to order your window, and then plane it to fit.

Whatever type of window you choose, remember to prime and paint the wood frames with a good exterior primer and paint to protect them from moisture.

Sealing Storm Windows

Q. *Will sealing storm windows yield better protection against the elements?*

No, storm windows—whether they're made of wood, metal, or vinyl—should never be caulked or sealed with a gasket. The main purpose of storm windows is to protect the interior sash and frames from wind and foul weather. Sealing the storm window can trap moisture between the interior window and the storm window. This moisture will cause condensation problems on the window sash and can eventually rot both the frame and the sash. The sill is especially prone to rot, so be sure rainwater can run off it through weep holes or a small gap at the bottom of the storm sash.

If you have aluminum or vinyl combination screen/storm windows, they probably have weep gaps built in on the bottom sash to let water out. Assuming this is so, it's a good idea to make sure the weep gaps are not clogged or caulked. It doesn't take a lot of air movement to solve condensation problems, so the small gaps around the outside of the storm sash will be enough.

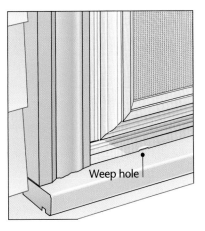

Weep hole

Choosing
Combination
Storms

COMBINATION STORM WINDOWS eliminate the seasonal climbing, switching, and storing required with traditional storm and screen units. The screen and glass panels ride in tracks so that they can be raised, lowered, or removed from inside your house. A do-it-yourselfer can install this kind of unit in about 30 minutes.

Here are a few features to look for when buying combination storms:

■ **Solid construction.** Solid reinforced corners and a sturdy frame insure weathertightness and longevity. Triple-track construction allows the storm and screen inserts to be positioned anywhere within the frame.

■ **Low-E glass.** This glass blocks out sun in the summer, and in winter redirects heat back into your home. Low-E glass also filters out ultraviolet rays that can fade fabrics.

■ **Weatherstripping.** Thick, resilient pile on the window inserts and frame provides the tightest seal against the elements and cuts down on rattling.

■ **Tilting windows.** Some models feature panes that tilt inward so both sides of the glass can be cleaned from inside.

Windows

REPLACEMENT WINDOWS

Look of Wood

Q. *I like the look of wood windows, but I want a maintenance-free exterior finish. What are my options?*

You can have both in the same window: the beauty of wood on the inside and attractive, maintenance-free options like vinyl or aluminum on the outside. A vinyl or aluminum cladding protects the exterior window sashes, frame, and moldings and has a durable factory finish. Some manufacturers offer a variety of colors. You can expect this painted finish to last up to 15 years or more, depending on the severity of your climate.

Newer replacement windows can have maintenance-free aluminum- or vinyl-clad exteriors, attractive wood interiors, and special features such as tilt-down sashes for easy cleaning.

New Panes

Q. *My old windows are the kind with all the small panes. Can I get new windows in the same style?*

Yes, you can. "True divided light" windows feature individual glass panels held in a real wood framework. A newer option is the "simulated divided light" window, which has a solid piece of glass with either a glued-on wood divider or a grill that snaps out for easier glass cleaning. One-sided (just the interior) or two-sided (interior and exterior) grills are available. A simulated divided light window has better thermal performance because it has fewer seams and joints for cold air infiltration.

Need Deeper Windows

Q. *My home was built in 1923 when window jambs were deeper than they are today. I want to replace the windows but can't find any that will fit. What can I do?*

You can use new standard-size windows if you make a jamb extension. This is done by adding strips of wood to all four sides of the window frame so that they extend completely through the wall. If you order your window from a dealer, specify the window jamb width you need. A jamb extension will be attached in the shop to make a stock window the right depth for your window.

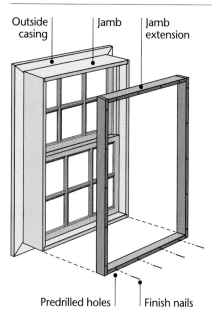

Outside casing | Jamb | Jamb extension

Predrilled holes | Finish nails

Buying New Windows

Q. *It's time to replace my drafty old windows with new ones. How do I go about choosing them? I don't know where to begin.*

The first thing you want to look for in a replacement window is a style that matches your old windows. The two most common styles are double-hung and casement (the kind that swings outward when you turn a crank).

You have a choice of buying all-wood, aluminum- or vinyl-clad wood, or all-vinyl windows. Wood windows are traditional and look good painted or stained but need periodic repainting to protect against decay. Aluminum- and vinyl-clad windows have attractive wood visible on the inside but have maintenance-free aluminum or vinyl covering on the outside. All-vinyl and all-aluminum windows are maintenance-free but many people find them less attractive than wood. Both the clad and all-vinyl windows are usually easier to install than all-wood windows. Look at each type and compare prices; the higher-quality (and more expensive) windows will operate better.

As for the window glass, most windows come with double panes for energy efficiency, erasing the need for storm windows. Other options include argon gas sealed between the panes, a third pane of glass for greater thermal efficiency, and partially reflective coatings and tints. The value of these options depends on the climate you live in.

Always consider how long it will take for the energy savings to pay for the extra cost of the feature. A 7- to 10-year "payback" period is usually worthwhile. Finally, make sure the glass has a 10-year warranty, at minimum, against seal failure, which causes a fog to build up between the panes, obstructing your view.

REPLACING OLD WINDOWS

Before you buy replacement windows, take detailed measurements of the old ones. Carefully pry the trim from around the inside of the frames (you may want to reuse it). Measure the height and width of the jamb (the window frame), the "rough opening," (the width between the trimmer studs and the height between the rough sill and the header). Finally, measure the depth of the window frame (the wall thickness, excluding the siding).

After removing the window trim, stop, and sashes from the inside, pull the old frame from the opening, cutting the nails in the frame (Photo 2). Slide building felt under the edges of the siding to keep moisture out. Begin at the bottom and finish at the top, overlapping the felt as you go. Staple the pieces in place.

Now slip a metal drip cap up under the siding at the top of the window opening; the window trim will hold it in place. Your new window might take a couple of test-fits; center and level it until it's right, then measure the exterior trim sizes. Leave a ⅛-inch gap between the trim and the siding for caulk. Squeeze the caulk behind the trim around the opening.

You can now slide the window into place. Tack it through the trim to anchor it temporarily. Level the sill and plumb the sides. Make sure the window operates freely; then anchor it with 10d galvanized casing nails, spaced 16 inches apart, through the exterior trim. Nail the interior trim to the window frame with 6d finish nails and to the wall with 8d finish nails. If you use expanding foam to insulate around the frame, use it sparingly. It can bow the frame as it expands and interfere with the operation of the window.

1 Remove the window trim, stop, and sashes from the inside.

2 Use a mini hacksaw to cut nails driven through the sides and top of the frame.

3 Apply No. 15 asphalt-impregnated felt 2 in. under the edges of the siding.

4 Slip a preformed metal drip cap up under the siding, but don't fasten it. The window trim will hold it in place.

5 Test-fit your window; then measure the exterior trim sizes. Leave a ⅛-in. gap for caulk.

6 Caulk around the opening (behind the trim); then slide the window into place.

Replacement Windows **125**

Windows

ENERGY

Old, Cold Windows

Q. *Why are my old windows so cold?*

Almost all old windows are single-pane glass, which loses heat through conduction. Conduction occurs when you pour ice water into a glass, and the glass gets cold as well. Window glass, single-pane in particular, is no different. It will allow cold or heat to come in from the outdoors or escape to the outdoors.

Because the sashes of old windows are often worn or damaged, heat is also lost through infiltration. If the weatherstripping on a window is poor or the glazing no longer fits tightly, air is able to move through that opening, causing a draft.

Argon-Filled Windows

Q. *I know the space between the glass of my new thermal-pane windows is filled with argon gas. What is the advantage of having argon-filled windows?*

Argon is an inert gas, which means it is very stable and has a low reaction rate to changes in temperature. It is used in the space between the panes of glass to slow down the rate of heat transfer from one pane of glass to another. The air we breathe (a combination of oxygen, hydrogen, and nitrogen) allows heat to move from one pane to another much faster than argon does. The argon is sealed in place with high-quality sealants placed along the edges of hollow aluminum spacers; the spacers are filled with a moisture-absorbing material to capture any water vapor that might seep through the seal. Check the warranty to see how long the seal should last.

Low-E Glass

Q. *What is low-E glass and how is it helpful?*

"Low-E" stands for low-emissivity. The glass has a special coating of metallic oxide that improves its energy efficiency in both winter and summer. Windows with this coating can reduce solar heat gain in the summer by reflecting radiant heat back outdoors. During the winter the heat from your furnace is reflected back into the room as it hits the window glass. Low-E glass windows should be used in hot or cold climates. Nearly all new windows sold today offer low-E glass as an option.

Some windows also feature a type of low-E coating that provides extra dead air space, essentially creating a triple-glazed window.

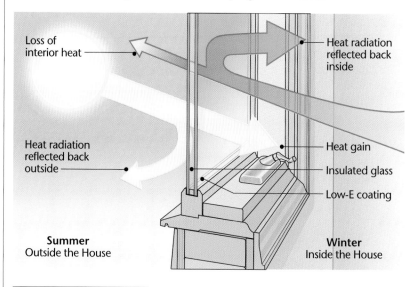

Loss of interior heat

Heat radiation reflected back inside

Heat radiation reflected back outside

Heat gain

Insulated glass

Low-E coating

Summer
Outside the House

Winter
Inside the House

Comparing Efficiency

Q. *How do I compare windows for energy efficiency?*

Look for the NFRC (National Fenestration Rating Council) sticker. It certifies that the window has been evaluated for energy efficiency according to standards set by the NFRC, a window industry organization. Manufacturers voluntarily submit their windows for evaluation by independent agencies, then display the results using the standard NFRC sticker (right).

The U-value measures how much heat escapes through the window. The lower the number, the better the thermal performance. Figures on solar heat gain, the ability to reflect solar heat, and visible light transmittance, may not be displayed.

NFRC
National Fenestration Rating Council
CERTIFIED

World's Best Window Co.
Millennium 2000⁺ Casement
CPD#0098-xyz-001

ENERGY Performance

Winter Heating Rating	Summer Cooling Rating
3.3	**3.0**

- A Higher Seasonal Rating = Lower Energy Consumption
- Energy savings will depend on your specific climate, house and lifestyle
- For more information, call 1-800-WBW-1234 or visit NFRC's web site at www.nfrc.org

Technical Information - Residential Products

U-Factor	Solar Heat Gain Coefficient	Visible Light Transmittance
.32	**.45**	**.58**

Manufacturer stipulates that these ratings conform to applicable NFRC procedures for determining whole product energy performance. NFRC ratings are determined for a fixed set of environmental conditions and specific product sizes.

REPLACING INSULATED GLASS

The best way to replace insulated glass is to remove the sash and take it to a window repair specialist who can tell you the size and thickness of the glass and determine if it is still under warranty. If it's not, you can buy a new unit from a window manufacturer and install it yourself using one of the following two methods.

If your window is sealed with a one-piece rubber gasket, remove the broken unit from the frame. Next, remove the gasket and wrap it around the new insulated glass unit. Push the frame back together, tapping it lightly with a hammer. Seal any openings in the corners with a small bead of silicone sealant.

If your windows are sealed with a two-sided "setting" tape, pull out the stops on one side of the tape, using a thin pry bar or thin-bladed putty knife. Next, flip the window over and slice the tape bond. Only continue if the glass can be removed without being broken. Scrape the old tape from the frame and remove any old adhesive with paint thinner. Lay new tape along the frame; if it won't adhere, coat the edge with contact cement. Position the new glass against the setting blocks, center it, and drop it into place. Replace the stops, and caulk the gaps at the corners with silicone.

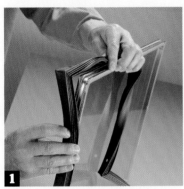

Some insulated glass windows have gaskets that can be removed from the broken window and wrapped around the new glass unit.

Once the glass touches the two-sided tape, it adheres and can't be adjusted.

If your insulated glass is caulked in place, the glass should be knocked out by and replaced by a window repair specialist.

Warmer Picture Window

Q. *What type of window can I use to replace my 3 x 5-foot single-pane plate glass picture window to make it more energy-efficient?*

For improved energy efficiency, replace your single-pane window with a double-pane insulated window. A glass company will make the window to your specifications. Order it slightly undersize so there will be a 3/16-inch gap on each side between the glass and the frame.

The single-pane window you have now is held in place with stops on the inside and outside. Remove all of these; then remove the single pane of glass. It will be heavy, so get someone to help.

Place rubber spacer blocks in each lower corner and every 12 inches along the bottom. Be sure that both panes are supported on the spacer blocks; if the window rests on the bottom, where water collects, the seal will break and the window will fog between panes. Next, stick neoprene glazing tape to the back of the exterior stops (get this tape from the glass dealer). Lift the new window into place, and push it firmly into the glazing tape. Finally, reinstall the interior stops.

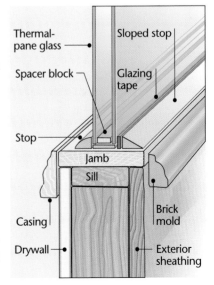

Exterior Doors

French Patio Doors

Q. *I want to replace my old aluminum patio door with wood French doors. Can you offer any tips on what to look for when ordering and replacing the door?*

You have made a good decision. Replacing an old aluminum sliding patio door with new swinging French doors will improve the appearance, energy efficiency, and security of your home.

Because of the high demand for French patio doors, many door companies offer replacement door units in special sizes for fitting the existing patio door rough opening. To determine the size doors you need, remove the interior trim and measure the exact width and height of your old door opening. Next, check the sides of this rough opening to make sure they're plumb. Then check the top and floor of the opening to make sure they're level. You'll have to reduce the available opening (the first measurements you took) by the amount the sides, top, and floor are not plumb and level. You'll also need to allow a minimum of ¼ inch on the sides and top of the new door to allow for shimming and expansion. If you cannot find the exact door size, get one that is slightly smaller; you can use spacers and wider trim to fill in the gaps. Don't forget to measure your existing doorjamb depth from the exterior sheathing to the interior wall surface.

Also before you order the new doors, decide whether you want one or both doors to open, and if you want them to swing inward or outward. If you want screen doors, you are limited to doors that swing inward. An experienced do-it-yourselfer can complete the job of replacing the old patio door with a new French door in a day. It probably won't take too much longer for a novice if the new doors are a fully assembled unit and are the right size.

Old aluminum patio doors (below) are easily damaged and look outdated. Swinging French doors can improve the look, energy efficiency, and security of your home. You can buy fully assembled doors to fit right into the old rough opening.

SELECTING AN EXTERIOR DOOR

TYPE	PROS	CONS	MAINTENANCE	WARRANTY
Wood	Warmth, solidity, and traditional elegance.	Expensive. Can split, warp, or crack. Less energy-efficient than fiberglass.	Must be painted or revarnished periodically.	1 year
Steel	Inexpensive. Won't crack or split. Foam-core filler is energy-efficient.	Must be painted rather than varnished. Can dent.	Dents can be filled with auto-body filler.	10 years
Fiberglass	Energy-efficient and durable. Can resemble the grain of wood doors.	Limited choice of styles and sizes.	Can be stained.	Lifetime

Products for Accessibility

Q. *My son is in a wheelchair and I'm looking for special offset hinges for my doors, the kind that let the doors swing clear of their frames. Any suggestions where I might begin looking?*

You can buy offset hinges from any major hardware supplier. They cost a lot more than ordinary hinges, but they allow someone in a wheelchair to pass through most doorways without any problems.

If the holes in your new offset hinges don't line up with the existing screw holes in the doorjamb, fill the old holes with epoxy and short lengths of wooden dowel. When that's dry, you can drill new holes.

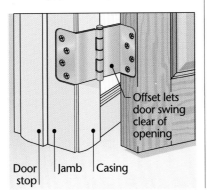

Offset lets door swing clear of opening

Door stop | Jamb | Casing

Tips on Buying Doors

Q. *What should I look for when I buy a new door?*

■ If steel, buy one with 24-gauge or thicker skin (the lower the number, the thicker the steel).
■ Buy one with quality weatherstripping to help stop drafts.
■ A wood door and its finish will last longer if it's not exposed to direct sunlight and is protected by a deep overhang.
■ Glass reduces the insulation and security value of your door. Keep glass components to a minimum.

---

how is it done?   ADDING AN AUTOMATIC DOOR-CLOSING HINGE

In many areas of the country, automatic door closing mechanisms are required by code on the door between your house and garage. The mechanism keeps fire, carbon monoxide, and unwanted animals out of your home. Spring hinges can be used as a door closer on doors between the entryway and main house, on garage service doors, on basement doors (especially if there are small children and crawling infants around), or on any door you want to keep closed. They are discreet and you can install them in less than an hour. Most doors require two special spring hinges; heavier ones take three.

To install spring hinges, you'll need a drill, screwdriver, hammer, and chisel. The hinge usually comes with an adjustment wrench. The hinges come in two sizes—be sure you get the right size. For a successful installation, the centers of the hinge pins must align vertically or the door will bind. No mechanism will close a door that binds or drags.

Remove the old hinges, and install the new spring hinges one at a time so that the door can remain on the jamb. Begin by marking the outline of the new hinge and new screw holes with a sharp utility knife. Chisel away the wood so the new hinges fit; then predrill the holes for the new screws. Install the new spring hinge, with extra-long screws that will secure the hinges to the house framework. This will add security against break-ins. Finally, adjust the closing tension by tightening the internal spring. Readjust the tension as needed on the hinges after a week.

1 Hold the new hinge in place, and mark around the outside edge with a utility knife.

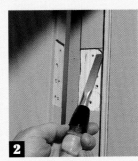

2 Carefully chisel up to your cut lines so that the new spring hinges fit perfectly.

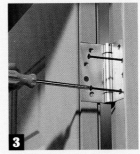

3 Extra-long screws secure the hinges to the frame of the house, adding durability and extra security.

4 Most hinges adjust with a hex wrench; some require inserting a small pin to set the tension.

REPLACING AN ENTRY DOOR

Thanks to prehung door kits, a do-it-yourselfer with basic carpentry experience can get professional results. Since a prehung door comes already hinged into its jamb, getting a smooth-fitting, weathertight fit involves simply removing the old entry door and putting in a new one. The whole job usually takes less than a day. (To be on the safe side, it's best to start in the morning and have all the materials on hand. Once the door is installed, plan to spend another day taking care of touch-up work—reattaching interior trim, caulking, priming, painting, and installing the lockset and deadbolt.)

To replace an exterior door, you'll need a few basic tools: a utility knife, putty knife, large and small pry bars, hammer, handsaw, level, framing square, caulk gun, nail set, and drill.

Buy a new door the same size as the old so that you can install the new one in the same rough opening. If you remove the old door carefully, you can eliminate a lot of repair work later. Use a sharp utility knife to slice through the paint and caulk where the moldings meet the interior wall and exterior siding. Carefully remove the interior casing by prying it off with a stiff putty knife. Rip out the old jamb and dispose of it (see Photo 1).

Use a level and framing square to inspect the rough opening (Photo 2). This will give you a preview of what it will take to install the jamb plumb and level. A rough opening is sized for a particular door size, so your new door has to be the same nominal size as your existing door. You may need to replace rotten wood around the rim joist (see below). If you want a larger door, or one with added sidelights, you will also need to rebuild the rough opening.

Once the rough opening is ready, test-fit the new door. Set the jamb into the opening for a trial fit. To do this, set the threshold on the sill, then tilt

1 Cut through the jamb with a handsaw; then rip out both the side and head jambs to reveal the rough opening.

2 Check the condition of the rough opening with a level and a framing square. A straight board compensates for bows in the trimmers.

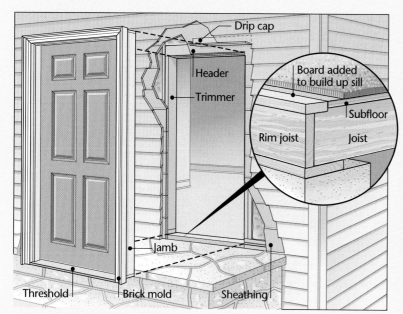

Drip cap

Header

Trimmer

Board added to build up sill

Subfloor

Rim joist

Joist

Jamb

Threshold

Brick mold

Sheathing

the jamb upright into position (Photo 3). Hold the brick mold tightly against the sheathing as you check that the side jambs are plumb. Enlist a helper to adjust the door's position from inside as you keep an eye on the weatherstrip at the top and bottom. Continue to shift the door's position in the opening until the jamb is flush with the wall and the gap between the door and jambs is consistent. When the fit looks good, tip the jamb out of the rough opening, and lay three heavy beads of caulk on the sill and one bead around the rough opening. Be sure to remove any screws or nails from the latch side, otherwise your door won't open. Then reinstall the door.

Tack the door in place by driving 10d galvanized finish nails through the brick mold every 16 inches (Photo 4). Don't drive any nails home until you've opened and closed the door and double-checked the fit.

Working first on the hinge side of the jamb, wedge pairs of shims in between the trimmer studs and jamb; then drive one 3½-inch screw alongside each hinge. Remove two screws at each hinge nearest the weatherstrip and replace both of them with 3½-inch screws. Drive the screws through the shims (otherwise they may distort the jamb). Attach the latch side next. As you screw the jamb in place, test the door to make sure it works smoothly.

The last step is to adjust the height of the threshold. Many thresholds have adjustment screws (Photo 7). Cut off any protruding shims. Fill the gap between the door and the jamb with fiberglass insulation only. Finally, seal any remaining cracks with caulk and replace the interior trim.

Use a shim to hold the finish nails and protect the molding from bad hammer blows. Don't drive the nails home until you're certain the door works smoothly.

Secure the jamb with 3½-in. screws instead of nails in case you need to reposition the jamb. Replace a pair of short screws with 3½-in. screws at each hinge.

Place the door in the rough opening so the brick mold is tight against the sheathing.

To conceal the screws on the latch side, drive them behind the weatherstrip. Install two screws near the middle, and one each near the top and bottom.

To adjust the height of the threshold, remove the caps and turn the setscrews until it's level and forms a tight seal with the door.

DOOR REPAIRS

Replacing Patio Door Rollers

Q. *The rollers on my sliding glass patio door are worn, making it difficult to open and close. Do I have to remove the entire door to replace the old rollers with new ones?*

Yes, you probably will have to remove the door, but most patio doors can be removed easily. Adjust the roller height adjustment screw with a screwdriver to bring the door down as close to the track as possible. You can then lift the door up and out from the bottom track.

Some patio doors have a stop (retaining strip) along the top inside edge of the door frame that acts as a sliding guide. You may have to remove it to get the door out. Look for screws holding the stop at the top of the door frame. As you remove the stop, have a helper hold the door to prevent it from falling into the room.

Look for replacement rollers at a well-stocked hardware store or home center; otherwise, you can always order them directly from the manufacturer.

Patio door

Height adjustment screw

Bottom track

Repairing a Fixed Door

Q. *On a sliding glass door, is the fixed door always the exterior door while the sliding one always goes on the interior? Whoever installed mine reversed the process.*

The company that makes the doors decides whether the fixed panel goes on the interior or exterior. The door probably wouldn't work at all if the panels were reversed. Most patio doors have the fixed panel on the exterior, but some (including Pella and Peachtree patio doors) don't.

To make sure your doors are installed properly, do this simple check. With the door closed, note the location of the weatherstripping where the two panels come together. If your exterior panel opens, the weather stripping should be on the interior side of that panel. The weather stripping on the fixed panel should be on the exterior side. This forms a seal when the door is closed.

Worn Threshold Gasket

Q. *Is it possible to replace a worn threshold gasket in my front door?*

Because vinyl gaskets wear out, manufacturers no longer use them as seals on the wood thresholds of exterior doors. You can still find replacements for existing doors.

To get the right replacement, remove the old gasket and take it to a home center or hardware store. You'll probably have to cut your new gasket to the right length with a sharp utility knife.

Typically, the gasket has two splines that fit into grooves cut into the wood threshold. When you pull away the old gasket, the splines sometimes rip off and stay in the grooves. You can pry them out with a narrow screwdriver or chisel.

Some gaskets snap into place with a little thumb pressure and others require more force. If your new gasket is stubborn, press the spline into the groove as far as you can with your finger; then use a block of wood to apply the even pressure needed to finish the job. You may need to rap the block with a hammer a couple of times to secure the gaskets.

Try to remove the old gasket in one piece. Pry out the old splines from the grooves.

Use a block of wood to help push your new gasket into place.

Steel Door Bottom Sweep

Q. *The vinyl weatherstrip at the bottom of my steel door is wearing out. I love having a steel door, but will I always have to replace this bottom piece?*

Steel doors are great because they're easy to maintain and insulate well. Eventually the vinyl weatherstrip will tear and wear out, ruining the tight air seal that steel doors are known for. The good news is that the strips are very easy to replace.

The hard part might be taking the door off its frame. First take out the hinge pins or unscrew the hinges from the door, whichever is easier. Once the door is off, lay it on a pair of sawhorses. Get a new sweep that matches the old one in design, with the same flange configuration and the same door attachment. Some sweeps snap into place, while others slide in. If you can't find one that matches, you can buy one that slips over the door bottom and is secured with screws. Replacement sweeps are sold at home centers.

Install a new sweep by snapping it into place. You may need to trim the length.

Stubborn Deadbolts and Latches

Q. *I have to give my door a big shove for the deadbolt to catch. How can I fix this?*

Try filing the inside edge of the strike plate. File a little away, then see how the deadbolt works. If you file back

If you find that your deadbolt won't catch, try filing the inside edge of the strike plate.

Sagging Storm Door

Q. *My aluminum storm door is sagging in the upper corner opposite the hinge side. The top of the door is glass and I'm wondering: Is there a way to fix it that would look better than adding a brace?*

Check to see if the storm-door frame has been installed properly and is square. To do this, remove the glass panel from the door, then put it back in place. If the glass doesn't fit in easily, the frame of the door is probably out of square.

Also check the corner key to see if it's bent or broken. If you see any damage, simply replace that corner key. If neither of those checks helps, try to determine if the frame of the exterior door is square. You'll probably need to remove the storm-door frame completely to do this.

too far, the door won't seal tightly against the weatherstripping, so be careful and go slowly.

If your deadbolt and strike plate are only slightly misaligned, you can make the bolt slip more easily into the plate by lightly rounding both the inside edges of the strike plate and edge of the deadbolt.

If there's just a slight misalignment, try rounding the edges on both the strike plate and the edge of the deadbolt.

If the exterior door frame isn't square, you'll need to shim the hinged side of the storm-door frame.

The type of hinge that is on your door (whether it be full-length or piano hinge) is harder to shim than a door with three or four butt hinges. If you try to shim, be careful not to cause the door to bind or start to rub on the other frame pieces.

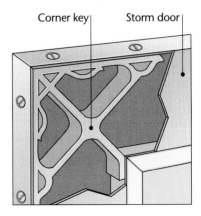

Corner key | Storm door

Storm Door Closer

Q. *The storm door closer on our back door is all bent and out of whack. How do I replace it?*

When the plunger shaft on a storm door closer gets bent and/or the screws that hold the bracket to the doorjamb get ripped out, it's time for a replacement.

The secret to a replacement job that will last is in the type of screws you use. Don't use the 1-inch screws that come with most closers; they aren't long enough. Instead, get 3-inch-long screws to fasten the closer bracket to the doorjamb. You want the screws to go through the doorjamb and into the 2 x 4 framing in the wall.

To begin the repair, open the door and lock the plunger into the open position. Pull out the pin that holds the plunger in the mounting bracket. Then remove the pin on the other end of the closer. Remove the old bracket and screws from the doorjamb. If the screw holes are only slightly damaged, don't worry about them; they'll get covered by the new mounting bracket. However, if the damage is more extensive, you'll want to fill in the holes with wood putty.

Secure the new closer bracket to the doorjamb with the 3-inch-long pan-head screws. This is done most easily using a drill/driver. If you don't have a tool like this, use a screwdriver with a long handle.

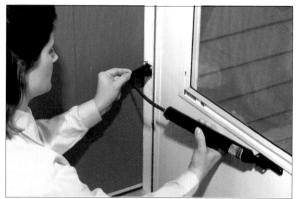

Pull out the pin that holds the plunger inside the mounting bracket; then remove the pin that holds the closer to the storm door bracket before removing the bracket.

Remove the old screws and bracket and fill badly damaged holes with wood putty.

Drill the screws through the doorjamb and into the 2 x 4 framing in the wall.

Use a fast-drying auto-body filler to patch a dent or hole in a metal door.

Dented Metal Door

Q. *There's a big ugly dent in my metal door. What is the best way to fix it?*

With some filler and paint, you can fix that ugly dent, or even a hole, in your metal door.

First you'll need to sand the damaged area down to bare metal with medium-grit sandpaper. Then, mix up and spread on some auto-body filler (check your home center or auto supply store) with your fingers (wear gloves). This stuff hardens fast, so mix up only as much as you can use in 5 minutes or so.

Sand the patch of filler with medium, then fine, sandpaper. If you have a raised panel door, shape the patch to match its contours. Lastly, prime the patch and paint the door.

Foggy Patio Door

Q. *The 30-year-old sliding glass door in our kitchen has accumulated moisture between its two sheets of glass. Can a do-it-yourselfer fix this problem, or must we get a new one?*

A failing seal is usually caused by water splashing on a deck or patio and ruining the wood rail at the bottom of the door. Repeated exposure to moisture will eventually break the seal and moisture will appear between the panes. Unfortunately, once a seal fails, the only option is to replace the glass, a job for a pro.

If the door is in good shape otherwise, a glass replacement company can replace the glass. If the door shows signs of warping, cracking, or rot, replace both door and frame.

Safer Than Hiding a Key

Q. *Somebody in our family manages to get locked out of the house every couple of months. We tried hiding a key, but everyone in the neighborhood soon knew where it was. What can we do?*

Install a key box, the ones real estate agents use, on the outside of the house. The key box is a small safe for keys with a combination dial on the front. Mount it in a visible location to discourage tampering, and secure it to solid framing with the long screws provided. Change the combination periodically if you give it to cleaners or workers outside the family. The boxes are available from locksmiths for about $30.

With a box installed, members of the family who forget their key can still get in the house at any time.

INSTALLING A NEW DEADBOLT LOCK

Every exterior door should have a good-quality deadbolt lock. If your door has a window or is so close to a window that someone could break the glass and reach the deadbolt from the outside, get a deadbolt that is key-operated inside and out. (Be sure local fire codes permit use of this type of deadbolt.)

When you buy the deadbolt, read the packaging. It will tell you what size hole saw and spade bit you need to install it. Along with the deadbolt, you'll also get a template that fits over your door and shows you exactly where to bore the holes.

To bore the lock hole, first drill a 1/8-inch pilot hole. Then drill halfway through with a hole saw; finish the hole from the opposite side. Use a spade bit to drill the bolt hole in the door edge; it should meet the center of the lock hole. Slide the bolt into the hole; position the plate, outline it, and remove it. Chisel a mortise about 1/8-inch deep into the door for the plate. Insert the bolt and plate, and screw in place. Install the cylinder assembly with the bolt in the locked position; be sure to follow the manufacturer's directions. Using a key, test the bolt for smooth operation.

Smear lipstick on the end of the deadbolt; then place masking tape on the doorjamb where the deadbolt will strike. Close the door and twist the thumb turn so that the deadbolt presses against the masking tape. Center the strike plate over the lipstick impression and trace around the plate. Drill a recess for the deadbolt, and chisel out a 1/16-inch-deep mortise for the plate.

1 Chisel a 1/8-in. mortise for the plate; then insert the bolt and plate and screw them into place.

2 Be sure to install the cylinder with the screw holes on the interior if your deadbolt is key-operated from both sides (and has two cylinders).

3 Smear lipstick on the deadbolt and put masking tape where the bolt will strike. The lipstick will mark the exact position of the bolt recess.

4 Center the strike plate over the bolt recess, and trace its outline before mortising.

Always reprogram a garage door opener security code after you've installed it.

Randomly reset the transmitter switches; then reset the receiver switches to match.

Extra Security

Q. *There have been a couple of robberies in my neighborhood in the past few months. How can I add extra security to my exterior door?*

For added security, replace the existing lockset and deadbolt strike plates with "strike boxes" that have a metal pocket and oversized plates that are secured to a stud in the wall.

Use a 1-inch spade bit to enlarge and deepen the hole in the jamb to accommodate the new strike box. While you hold the strike box in position with one hand, trace the outline onto the doorjamb with the other hand. Use a chisel to create a ⅛-inch-deep recess for the strike and cover plate. Finally, reposition the new strike box and cover plate and predrill small pilot holes. Then install 3-inch-long screws.

You can easily strengthen your door hinges by replacing short

Changing Frequency

Q. *How do I change the frequency on my garage door opener?*

To individualize your garage door opener's frequency, remove the covers from the transmitters and receiver. Randomly reset the tiny switches in the transmitter; then set the switches on the receiver to match. If your transmitter doesn't have a set of switches in it, your opener has a unique factory-set code that doesn't require changing.

Some burglars (mostly on the East and West coasts) have been using electronic "code grabbers" that record garage door opener codes. Major manufacturers have developed systems that deter this, but you'd have to install a new receiver and buy new transmitters to take advantage of this technology.

screws with 3-inch-long screws that will bite into the stud behind the doorjamb, not just the fragile doorjamb itself. Predrill slightly wider and deeper holes to accommodate the heftier 3-inch screws; but don't overdo it. You want the screw threads to be able to bite into plenty of wood.

Take care not to drill or install any screws into adjacent sidelights or double doors.

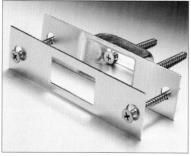

Enlarge the hole for the new strike box to fit into, and create a larger recess for the cover plate to nestle into.

A Good Lock

Q. *I'd like to know what makes a good cylinder lock. What are the features I should look for?*

Though all cylinder locks have the same basic components, they vary in the quality of the metal, the accuracy of the milling or machining, and the fit of their parts.

The critical components of a lock are the bolt, the cylinder, the cylinder housing, and the tailpiece. The bolt should be made of hardened steel with at least a 1-inch throw (the distance it will extend beyond the edge of the door into the strike plate). The longer and tougher this part is, the better. To check if a bolt is made of steel, put a magnet up to it. If the magnet sticks, it's steel.

Solid brass cylinders operate smoothly because brass, by nature, is easily shaped and causes little friction when in contact with other brass components. Cylinders with six pins and keys with six cuts are less easily tampered with than those with five. The best cylinder housings are made of crush-proof solid steel or brass with chambered or honeycombed reinforcement. The bigger the screws holding the two sides of the locks together, the more difficult it will be for a burglar to get past the door. Burglars use a variety of tools ranging from huge monkey wrenches that can snap a cylinder housing to pry bars that can snap the screws.

The tailpiece is the connecting link between the inside and outside mechanisms, and it needs to be strong enough to withstand all the twisting and turning it takes. The stronger and thicker it is, the longer it will last through everyday use and attempted sabotage.

Home Security Improvements

■ Keep your windows and doors locked. In almost 50 percent of burglaries, thieves get inside the house through an unlocked window or door. This might seem obvious, but in many cases people forget about them. Insurance companies won't cover your losses unless there's evidence of forced entry.

■ Reinforce deadbolt strike plates. Too often strike plates are secured with short screws that will pull out with a couple of swift kicks to the door. Strike plate screws should be 3 inches long so that they extend all the way through the jamb and deep into the framing behind it.

■ Install a peephole. Drilling a hole is all you need to do to install a peephole. If you hear a knock and don't see anyone through the peephole, don't open the door. Some crooks knock and duck away, waiting for you to open up.

■ Replace exterior lights with motion detector lights. Burglars who work at night hate motion-activated lighting. If you already have exterior light fixtures, replacing them with motion detecting lights is a simple task. Keep these security lights out of the reach of burglars who can tamper with them.

■ Make sure windows are visible. Hidden windows and doors are a burglar's dream because no one will see them break in! Keep this in mind as you plan a fence or landscaping project. Trim existing trees or bushes that could provide cover for a crook.

■ Secure your windows. Casement windows, the kind that crank open, are usually difficult to break into. Double-hung windows offer less security, but you can cut a dowel to fit in the track to pin the sashes. Jalousie windows (made from several slatted panes that open like a louver) are the least secure and should be replaced or covered with metal bars.

■ Change the frequency on your garage door opener. Many garage door openers come with an individualized frequency code. Some, however, have standard factory-set codes that homeowners never bother to change once they install the door. Thieves can drive around the neighborhood with a few common brands of transmitters, clicking them until they find a garage door that responds (see Changing Frequency, p.136).

■ Secure sliding glass doors. Burglars love sliding glass doors because many of them have flimsy locks or can be lifted out of their tracks. To prevent lift-out, drive a couple of screws into the top track, leaving the heads protruding so the door can't be removed unless the screws are removed first. You can supplement your existing lock by simply laying a cut-to-fit dowel in the lower track. This will prevent the door from being slid open.

■ Install strong doors. Hollow-core doors are not intended for exterior use. Exterior doors should be made of steel, fiberglass, or solid wood.

Exterior Doors

Replace an Extension Spring

Q. *The extension spring on our garage door broke. How can we prevent this from happening again?*

If you've ever heard an extension spring on an overhead garage door break, you know the kind of force that's generated. The springs never break when the door's open because they are slack then. Instead, they break when the door is closed, when the springs are fully extended. When a spring breaks, the flying piece(s) can do serious damage to anyone or anything inside the garage. To prevent this kind of damage, install a new set of springs with safety cables. The cables will keep the spring pieces from flying around the garage if the spring breaks.

Hold your garage door open by clamping locking pliers on the track. The spring and the lift cable will hang freely. Remove the pulley and spring from the lift cable, and install the new spring. Run the safety cable through the spring, securing it to the hanger bracket. The front connection of the safety cable (usually an eye bolt or a lag bolt) is attached to the door header or to the front of the door track.

Always replace springs in pairs.

SAFETY CHECK

Torsion Spring Safety

Unlike extension springs, you should never handle torsion springs yourself. If your garage door operates roughly or slowly, or if it hasn't been inspected within the past year, call a professional garage door installer to have a look.

Clamp locking pliers on the door track to hold the garage door in place.

Remove the pulley and old spring from the lift cable.

Install the safety cable through the new spring, securing it to the hanger bracket.

Choosing a Garage Door

Q. *I need a new garage door. Can you give me some general information so I can make the best choice?*

It's a good idea to know some things about garage doors before you go out and buy one and/or attempt to install one. First, realize that a garage door can weigh 400 pounds or more; they only seem light because the springs balance the weight as you lift the door. Steel doors are actually lighter and more stable than wood doors, and you can get ones that are insulated and finished on both sides. Steel doors come already painted, so there's nothing to do once you install one. Aluminum doors are still manufactured, but steel doors are stronger and more durable.

Wood and hardboard doors require painting after installation, but dents and scratches are easy to fix and they have a nice traditional appearance that most people like best. Today fiberglass doors look better than ever. Their translucent panels let in natural light—a plus for folks who have a work area in their garage.

Your new garage door kit should include all the hardware, the springs, and the tracks. Make sure the kit has extension springs, not torsion springs. Extension springs are easy to replace and most come with a safety cable to hold back the spring if it breaks. Torsion springs are under extreme tension and can cause serious injury.

If you're replacing an overhead door, just measure the old door. If your old door is the one-piece tip-in type, measure the width and height of the opening so you can order the right size overhead door. If there is less than 10½ inches between the top of the opening and the ceiling, you'll probably need to special-order a low-headroom kit from a supplier.

GARAGE DOOR TUNE-UP

Your garage door probably doesn't work as well as it used to. After hundreds of trips up and down, roller shafts get bent, hinge screws loosen, and the rubber seal gets ripped. Here's how to fix these three common problems yourself.

First, open the door, unplug the automatic door opener, and put a C-clamp or locking pliers on the track above and below one of the rollers to lock it in place. For manually operated doors, you'll need to remove the bottom bracket and roller by disconnecting the extension spring, which runs parallel to the door track. (Never attempt to disconnect the spring when the door is closed.)

Replacing a damaged roller is easy; just remove the hinge and twist the track. Give the new roller shaft and roller bearings a few drops of oil about every 6 months to keep them in good condition and working smoothly.

Wobbly hinges are caused by stripped screw holes. Remove the old hinge and screws; then drill completely through the door to install the new bolts. Replace the old screws with ¼ x 2½-inch carriage bolts, lock washers, and nuts.

On wood doors, the rubber seal is usually secured with roofing nails. To replace it, pry out the nails and remove the old seal. In cold regions, install the new seal with the long flange facing into the garage; this will keep the flange from freezing to the driveway.

On metal and fiberglass doors, the bottom seal slides into grooves. The bottom bracket and roller assembly cover the ends of the grooves to keep the seal in place. Disconnect the extension spring, lift cable, bottom roller, and bottom bracket. Slide out the old seal and install a replacement.

HINGES AND ROLLERS

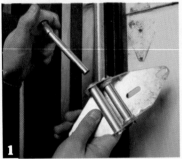

To remove a roller, unscrew the hinge and twist the track. Tighten loose hinges by replacing screws with carriage bolts. Use a combination nut/washer or a lock washer to prevent the hinge from loosening again.

WOODEN DOOR BOTTOM

Pry out the roofing nails and remove the old bottom seal. If you live in a region with hard winters, install the new rubber seal with the angled flange toward the inside of the garage.

METAL DOOR BOTTOM

You'll need to disconnect the extension spring and remove the bottom bracket and roller assembly to replace the bottom seal. Bend the ends of the grooves to remove the old seal.

Housepainting

Tools for Painting

Q. *When I buy tools for painting my house, I want to get ones that will give me the best results. Which ones should I buy?*

Start your housepainting arsenal with this terrific trio of tools.

Despite the variety of painting tools and timesaving devices available at your paint store, your best bet is to start with a trio of top-quality tools.

As for brushes, you can probably get by with two sizes: a 2½-inch angled brush for window sash and small trim, and a 4-inch brush for wide trim and siding. Use nylon or other synthetic-bristle brushes for latex paint and natural Chinese bristle brushes for oil paints. As with anything, you get what you pay for. Better-quality brushes hold more paint and can last for years.

Many professional painters use rollers to spread paint onto the exterior of a house, then follow up with a brush. Applying paint with a roller can save you from having to constantly dip your brush into the paint can; it also spreads the paint more consistently than a brush.

Primer vs. Paint

Q. *My neighbor says two coats of paint are as good as a coat of primer and a coat of paint. I say primer is essential to a good paint job. Who's right?*

You are. A coat of primer adheres and seals better because it contains more binders and less pigment than paint. On bare wood or metal, a base coat of primer is absolutely necessary. On surfaces that have been previously painted, primer gives the new paint something to stick to.

Instead of two top coats, ask your paint dealer to tint the primer to match the top coat of paint and you may be able to save yourself a step. Also, make sure the primer you use is compatible with the top coat you use. An oil-base primer can always be used under latex or oil paint, but a latex primer should be used only under latex paint.

Repainting: Latex or Oil?

Q. *How can we determine if the existing paint on our wood siding is oil or latex? We want to repaint it and don't know what to buy.*

The type of paint that is on your house doesn't have to determine what type of paint you decide to put over it. Today latex paints are the best choice in most situations. They dry faster, stay more flexible, breathe better, and are easier to clean up than oil-base paints. And, as long as the surface is well prepared, you should be able to use latex, even over old oil-base paints.

Oil-base paints still have their place; they're good for binding existing and chalky paint to old surfaces. Some people prefer oil-base paint on porch floors, doors, and trim because it levels out without brush marks.

Choosing the Right Paint

Q. *What kind of paint should I use for my wood siding?*

Exterior paint has to be tough to protect wood siding from the weather, but flexible enough to stretch as the wood expands and contracts with changes in temperature and humidity. It must also resist dirt, mildew, air pollution, and occasional scrapes from branches. High-quality exterior paints contain premium resins and pigments; the better the quality, the better a paint will do its job and the less often you'll have to repaint.

Acrylic latex paints are more flexible and let damp wood dry out better than oil-base alkyd paints. They also don't break down as easily under intense sunlight. For these reasons most painters choose latex over oil. However, oil-base alkyd primers soak into bare wood well, which helps paint adhere better. Many painters still like to apply an oil-base primer to bare wood, then cover it with a water-base acrylic top coat. You can put water-base paints over oil-base, but not oil-base over water-base for outdoor use.

Don't necessarily equate a high-price paint with high quality, though price can often indicate as much. There are a few things you can do to ensure you get the best paint for the job. First, read the label. Look for an exterior house paint that contains at least 20 to 25 percent resin for durability (you may have to ask a knowledgeable salesperson). Better-quality paints often carry a 15- or 20-year wear guarantee. You can usually trust advice from a paint specialty store; they should know what paints are best for your area and climate.

Paint for Trim

Q. *Should I use the same type of paint for window, door, and corner trim as I use for my siding?*

You can use the same paint for trim as you do for siding, but many people prefer to paint trim with a gloss finish rather than with the same flat paint that is typically used for siding. Glossier paints make the color seem brighter, and they last longer, too.

Adding Mildewcide

Q. *When I bought my exterior paint, the store clerk suggested I have a mildewcide added, but the can indicates that the paint already contains mildewcide. Was the clerk trying to pull a fast one?*

Probably not. The mildewcide that's already in the paint is often there to preserve it in the can—not on your house. If you have a mildew problem where you want to paint, or if it's a common problem in your area, it would be good to add a mildewcide.

Paint for Rough Shingles

Q. *What type of paint should I use on my rough-surfaced wood shingles? They have never been painted.*

Rough wood shingles have more exposed surface area than standard shingles and consequently give rain more places to penetrate. Wet wood will eventually cause even the best-quality paint to blister and peel. Latex paint works best because it lets any trapped water vapor pass through. It's also flexible enough to withstand changes in humidity.

Exterior stain is an excellent alternative. Unlike paint, stains won't peel and will allow the rough texture of your siding to show through.

what do you need?

BUYING A LADDER

It can be difficult to decide what type of ladder is best for your needs. Your first consideration is strength. All ladders work basically the same way, but the higher-priced ladders generally feel sturdier and last longer. Fiberglass ladders are the most expensive, but they are stiff, tough, and weatherproof. They're used by electricians and professional painters because they don't conduct electricity. Aluminum is the lightest ladder material and is only slightly more expensive than wood. Ladders made of aluminum are weatherproof, but you should avoid using them around electrical wires because the metal conducts electricity. Wood ladders are stiffer than aluminum ladders, non-conductive, and the least expensive; however, they also tend to be the heaviest. If you store a wood ladder outside, it might rot.

The higher the weight rating of the ladder, the stiffer and less wobbly it will be. Type IA ladders are heavy-duty industrial units, rated to 300 pounds. Type II, rated to 225 pounds, are medium-duty commercial ladders. Type III, light-duty household ladders, are rated to only 200 pounds. Most do-it-yourselfers should have either Type II or Type IA.

There are also specialty ladders available for people who want to do more than simply climb up and down. Platform ladders are more secure and comfortable when you need to do an overhead job. Many painters like flip-up ladders that convert from a 6-foot stepladder into a 10½-foot straight ladder. An articulated ladder has three sets of hinges that let you use it as a 6-foot stepladder, a 12-foot straight ladder, and a 3-foot scaffold. Specialty ladders are compact but are often heavier than an equivalent stepladder.

Stepladders made of wood, aluminum, and fiberglass come in a variety of sizes. A platform ladder (center) provides good support for overhead work, while flip-up and articulated ladders can double as straight ladders.

Housepainting

SURFACE PREPARATION

A power washer with a sandblast attachment can blast off tough whitewash.

The special nozzle, sand inlet tube, and suction hose hook to the washer's wand.

Sandblasting with Water

Q. *I just bought a house with a brick chimney that has been painted white and I don't like the way it looks. I tried to strip the paint off, but it didn't work. What can I do?*

If paint strippers don't work, your brick is probably whitewashed. Whitewash is a mixture of white portland cement, lime, and water. To test if it is, buy a quart of muriatic acid at the hardware store, mix it 50:50 with water (slowly add the acid to the water), and brush it on the brick. If it fizzes, you have whitewash. The only way to remove it is to sandblast it off.

Sandblasting a large area requires heavy equipment and is best left to professionals. For smaller areas, a power washer with the capacity of at least 4 gallons per minute at 3,000 pounds per square inch (psi) with a sandblast attachment will work fine.

Test a small area first to make sure the brick is hard enough to withstand sandblasting. Wear protective clothing because water sprayed at this speed can shoot right through the skin. Rent a sandblast hood and rain suit, and wear rubber gloves. Cover the ground with tarps, and protect windows and trim.

Peeling Stain

Q. *I used an oil-base stain on my rough cedar siding about 3 years ago. Now it's peeling and almost impossible to scrape off. What happened?*

If the pigmented stain was applied too thickly to the cedar siding it will peel, much like paint. Stain should be applied so that it's absorbed by the wood immediately, with no excess stain remaining on the surface of the wood. Don't expect a thin-bodied stain to cover the grain completely like paint would.

A power washer will help you remove a lot of the peeling stain; you can rent one from your local home center or paint supply store. Let the siding dry for at least a week before you apply a new finish.

Using a Heat Gun

Q. *Can I use a heat gun to strip paint from the surface of my house? I hate scraping.*

You can use a heat gun to soften the old paint, but you'll still need to scrape it off. Remember that you don't have to strip the surface completely; just try to remove the loose, peeling, or flaking paint.

Heat guns are powered by standard household electric current. If you need to work on a ladder, the extension cord might make the job awkward and dangerous. It's probably a good idea to reserve your heat stripping to low areas of the house and to scrape or sand the rest, to avoid any accidents.

Never try to heat strip paint with an open flame, such as a propane torch. A hot ember can smolder for hours within the walls of your house before starting a dangerous fire. Never heat strip lead paint.

GETTING A HOUSE READY FOR A PAINT JOB

The best way for your house to look its best and to prolong the life of your home's exterior is to paint it every 5 years or so. Careful prep work takes time, but it is the key to a lasting paint job. (Don't be surprised if the prep work takes longer than the painting itself!)

The first step in preparing your house for a new coat of paint is to wash off dirt and flaking paint. For best results, rent a power washer and use a good cleaning agent like trisodium phosphate. If your siding is wood, be careful not to spray any closer than 12 inches or you could gouge the surface. Power-wash stucco carefully; the pressure can destroy the surface. Rinse with clean water.

Scrape off any remaining loose paint with a wire brush or a long-handled scraper. Scrape with the grain to prevent gouges. Finish with a sanding block and 100-grit sandpaper.

Fill any nicks or uneven spots with exterior-grade spackling compound, using a 6-inch putty knife. After the filler dries, smooth it with 100-grit sandpaper.

To prevent water penetration and indoor drafts, and to get a good-looking paint job, caulk all the joints where the siding meets the windows, door trim, and other openings. Don't forget to caulk around outdoor electrical boxes, water faucets, and exterior lights. Apply fresh glazing to any windowpanes that appear loose. (See Replacing Broken Glass, p.118.)

Don't ever paint without priming. Prime all new wood, scraped wood, and all the spots filled with surfacing compound. Now you're ready to paint.

1 *Keep the power-wash nozzle at least 12 in. from wood siding to prevent gouging. Don't spray up under siding laps, and never use a power washer to clean windows. Wear eye protection and work on calm, non-windy days.*

2 *If the paint you're scraping won't come off, leave it. Paint that's bonded to the wood surface is OK to paint over.*

3 *Use an exterior-grade surfacing compound to fill holes and low spots; then sand the area smooth with medium-grit sandpaper.*

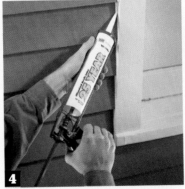

4 *Small gaps let heat out and water in. Remove all of the old caulk and recaulk the joint with a good-quality paintable acrylic latex or silicone acrylic caulk.*

5 *Prime all bare wood and scraped and sanded areas before you paint. For better coverage, have your paint dealer tint the primer to match the top coat.*

Housepainting

THE RIGHT WAY TO USE A LADDER

Tens of thousands of people are injured every year working on ladders. In most cases it's because they failed to use them correctly. By simply following a few basic safety practices, you can perform your home improvement tasks effectively and avoid injury at the same time. Remember, there's more to ladder safety than making sure the ladder's feet are secure.

EXTENSION LADDERS

Inspect an extension ladder every time you use it. Make sure all rivets, nuts, and bolts are tight. Each rung should be clean and secure; if any part looks bad or feels wiggly, don't use the ladder. Take extra care around electrical lines, especially if the ladder is made of aluminum.

All ladders sold in the United States are rated and labeled according to the weight they can safely carry (see Buying a Ladder, p.141). When judging a ladder's capacity, remember to take into account the weight of the tools and materials you'll be carrying in addition to your own weight. If you plan to do a lot of second-story work, it makes sense to buy a better-rated ladder that will feel sturdy even at full extension.

The problem with lightweight aluminum ladders is that they can easily blow over on a windy day; but heavier wood and fiberglass ladders can tip, too. To prevent your ladder from falling, secure it to the top of the house. Drive 2-inch-long construction staples into the fascia board; then wrap a wire around an upper ladder rung and thread it through the staple.

If you are painting or doing something else that requires you to move around a lot, don't get lazy and overreach—get down and move the ladder. There are also stabilizers (or stand-offs) that help keep a ladder securely in place by giving it a wider stance; they also keep you 8 to 10 inches away from the wall so you can work comfortably.

2

The ladder should rest about 1 ft. away from the wall for every 4 ft. it rises. To make sure a ladder is at the correct angle, place your feet against the feet of the ladder. When you extend your arms at shoulder height, you should be able to grasp the rungs without stretching or leaning.

3

A stabilizer, or stand-off bar, keeps the ladder away from the wall and helps keep the ladder from twisting.

1

To walk an extension ladder into the upright position, place the ladder feet against a solid surface, then use a hand-over-hand motion to raise it.

4 For extra safety, push the spiked end of the ladder's feet into the ground; step onto the bottom rung to drive the spikes fully into the dirt.

5 Use the flat, rubber-faced side of the feet when working on hard surfaces. Make sure the feet are free of dirt and debris. If you're working on a wood surface, like a deck, screw or nail a wood cleat to the decking to prevent the ladder feet from slipping.

STEPLADDERS

Make sure the ladder is open wide and the spreader (the metal hinge part between the ladder legs) is locked. To help stabilize the ladder, keep the pail shelf open.

Stepladders are meant to be used only in the open position. Don't try to climb a closed ladder that's leaning against a wall. It can easily kick out at the bottom.

Painting Aluminum Siding

Q. *My aluminum siding is 30 years old and looks pretty faded. Can I paint it?*

The most important step in painting siding is the prep work. In order for the paint to adhere properly, the siding has to be free of any chalk, dirt, grease, and oil. The best way to clean the surface is to power-wash it.

Rent a power washer with a rating of at least 1,200 psi (pounds per square inch), and use a trisodium phosphate (TSP) solution. If you cannot find TSP, use an exterior-use all-purpose cleaner. Start washing from the top of the siding and work your way down, rinsing the surface with clean water after you wash it. Let the siding dry for 2 days before you paint it. (Always wear eye protection when

you use a power washer, and don't ever spray any glass with it.)

The factory coating on most metal siding usually stays firmly intact, so you shouldn't need to prime before you paint. Use a 100-percent acrylic, high-quality latex paint (read the label to be sure that it will adhere to metal). Don't use an oil-base paint; it will fade quicker and might not adhere very well. Start on whatever side of the house is in the shade so that the paint doesn't dry too quickly. Use a brush to apply the paint along the edges, then follow up with a roller for good coverage.

Your paint job should last 6 to 8 years if it's applied correctly to a clean surface. Be sure to follow the directions on the can; the biggest cause of paint failure is not following the directions.

Once your siding is clean and dry, paint along the edges with a brush.

After the edges are painted, use a roller to cover the remaining area.

Painting Asbestos Shingles

Q. *Our house has asbestos shingle siding. Instead of removing it, we want to repaint it. What type of paint should we use?*

If the siding is in good condition, simply clean it with a garden hose and a soft-bristle brush. Allow the shingles a few days to dry; then prime

and paint with either a top-quality latex or an oil-base paint.

Asbestos is hazardous to your health if its fibers are inhaled, so if any of the shingles are cracked, you must take the necessary precautions. Wear a respirator as you work, and wash the clothing you wear during the job separately from the rest of your laundry.

Housepainting

PAINTING BRICK AND STUCCO

A masonry brush works best for applying whitewash to a stucco surface.

Whitewashing Stucco

Q. *The stucco around the downspouts of our house is stained. I've tried washing it without luck. How can I freshen up its appearance?*

What you need is a whitewash, a mixture of white portland cement and water. To make a batch, simply mix cement and water in a pail to the consistency of pancake batter. Wet your stucco with a garden hose and apply the whitewash with a masonry brush or a whisk broom. You can color whitewash with masonry dye, but in that case you should plan to do the entire wall. Getting an exact color match is almost impossible.

what do you need?

ELASTOMERIC PAINT

Your house is always moving with the changing weather. The paint over stucco can stretch enough to handle small movements, but more extreme changes can stretch paint beyond its limit. The resulting cracks are both an eyesore and an invitation for moisture to enter your walls and cause structural damage.

Elastomeric paint handles movement better than regular latex because it's more elastic. It lasts longer, too. This extra resiliency is due in part to the paint's thickness: one coat may be more than 10 times as thick as a coat of regular paint.

Because they're thicker, elastomerics are harder to work with than regular paint. They'll also cost more to use because you'll need more to coat your house.

If your stucco has only a few hairline cracks, you probably don't need to use elastomeric paint. But if the cracks are sizable and there are a lot of them, it would be cheaper than having to replace the stucco. Since elastomeric paint is fairly new, you may need to stop into a few stores and ask where you might find it.

Thick, tough, and elastic, elastomeric paint outperforms regular latex for covering cracked stucco walls.

Painting Brick

Q. *Do people ever paint brick? I want a new look for the exterior of my house but can't afford to replace all the bricks.*

You can paint your brick, but you should consider your decision carefully. Removing paint from brick is expensive and the results will not be perfect. Plus, you'd be turning a virtually maintenance-free exterior into one that will require fresh paint every 5 to 7 years.

If you decide you want to paint your brick, the key is to choose the right kind of primer and paint. Use an alkali-resistant primer and paint made for masonry (ask the paint dealer for help finding it).

Power-wash the brick first (it may be that that is all the brick needed to look great). To save time, use an airless paint sprayer to apply the primer and paint first, then roll out the paint with a thick-napped roller.

Should I Seal Stucco?

Q. *Is there a way to seal the stucco on our house so it won't absorb so much water when it rains?*

The moisture should evaporate without damaging your home. Sealing the stucco will keep it from breathing and might actually seal the moisture into the stucco, which you don't want. Sealing would also make it harder to renew the stucco finish, which generally lasts 20 to 30 years. If you apply a sealer, it will have to be sandblasted off when it's time to re-stucco (a messy procedure).

Most moisture damage occurs when water seeps in through cracks, especially around windows and doors, and rots the wood behind the stucco. You can seal up these cracks yourself with a silicone acrylic caulk.

PAINTING STUCCO

Stucco is relatively maintenance-free. However, in time it can crack and fade. The only fix short of applying new stucco is to paint it. Think twice before painting unpainted stucco; left unpainted, it will last decades before needing attention. Painted stucco will need a new coat every few years. Also, never paint new stucco until it has cured for at least a month; otherwise the paint might discolor and peel right off.

PREPARATION APPROACHES

Depending on the condition of your stucco, preparation can mean days of hard work or a couple of hours of light scrubbing.

If your stucco has never been painted, or if it's just dirty with a few areas of mildew or peeling, you can loosen grit and grime with a nylon brush and then rinse it clean with a hose. Use a wire brush to scrub those spots where the old paint is peeling.

If you don't have the patience for scrubbing, or if there are large areas of peeling paint, rent a pressure washer rated between 1,500 and 2,500 psi. Begin by holding the nozzle of the washer 3 feet away from the house to avoid blasting off the stucco. Gradually move closer until you reach a distance where the water jet removes the paint but doesn't eat into the stucco.

COMMON PREP PROBLEMS

Gray or black stains on your stucco are probably mildew. Scrub these stains away with a solution of 1 part chlorine bleach and 3 parts water. A white crust is more serious. Called "efflorescence," this crust forms when moisture passes through the stucco from the inside out. If you wash and paint it, it will come back. If ignored, the moisture could eventually cause structural damage. In this situation, the smartest thing to do is to call in a professional.

CAULK THE CRACKS

Fill any cracks wide enough to get a fingernail into with acrylic latex caulk. Bear in mind that big, wide cracks may be a sign that the stucco is falling off the wall, in which case you need new stucco, not paint.

BUYING AND USING PAINT

Use a top-quality acrylic latex or elastomeric paint. Since a thick film of latex paint is more resilient than a thin film, plan to apply two coats. Use a thick-napped roller for rough-textured stucco and a masonry brush to get paint into all the crevices. For painting along trim, use a smaller paintbrush with synthetic bristles. Work the first coat into the stucco's rough surface by brushing or rolling in several directions.

Use a paintable caulk to fill any gaps between the stucco and door or window trim, and any cracks wide enough to get a fingernail into.

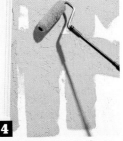

1 *Scrub dirty stucco with a coarse nylon brush; use a wire brush on peeling paint and efflorescence. A long-handled brush makes this tedious job easier.*

2

3 *A power roller pumps paint directly into the roller and will speed up the job.*

4 *Work the paint into the surface by brushing or rolling in several directions.*

Housepainting

Steel Railing

Q. *The steel railing on our front steps looks like it's gone through a war. What's the best way to repaint it so that it lasts a few years?*

A wire brush accessory for a power drill will help remove flaking paint and rust. Be sure to wear eye protection.

First use a wire brush to remove any loose paint and flaking rust. You may also need to use a liquid rust remover to reach deep recesses. Rinse the railing thoroughly and wipe every inch clean with lacquer thinner. Use a direct-to-rust primer before you paint to absorb any lingering rust and prevent it from spreading. Let the primer dry completely before you apply the top coat of paint.

High-gloss oil-base enamel paints are best for railings because they last the longest and wash clean easily. Aerosol spray cans provide the best coverage as long as you keep the can at the right distance and apply several light coats. Use newspapers or plastic to protect your house and landscape from the overspray.

Coat the railing with a primer before you paint it; look for a primer that solidifies rust and prevents it from spreading.

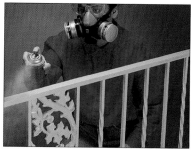

Finishing the railing with spray paint may take three or four coats, but it's easier and quicker than using a brush.

Paint Both Door Sides

Q. *My 14-year-old garage door is made of plywood. I want to paint both the inside and outside faces, but I've been advised to leave the inside unpainted so it can breathe. What should I do?*

All garage door manufacturers recommend that you paint both the interior and exterior faces of a garage door. In fact, you can do more damage by not painting the interior.

The coat of primer that is applied when the door is made is not enough protection for the door. Heat from your car and the sun draws moisture from outside. As it passes through the door the moisture can cause the door panels to warp, crack, or split.

To be safe, use both exterior primer and exterior paint to seal both sides and all the edges of the door.

how is it done? WOOD GRAIN OVER STEEL

Painted steel doors don't always look right in a house with lots of woodwork. Wood-graining kits can duplicate the look of wood on steel and previously painted doors. Graining isn't difficult, but you may want to practice on a scrap of plywood.

First, paint the door with a wood-tone latex and let it dry. Then wipe on a thin, uniform coat of the stain. While the stain is wet, move the graining tool slowly across the door while gently rocking the tool back and forth. Just a little movement of this tool can produce an impressive natural-looking appearance.

If you don't like the way it looks, wipe off the stain and start over. To protect the stain, wait about 24 hours and then apply polyurethane.

Use the figure as a guide for the correct grain direction and painting sequence.

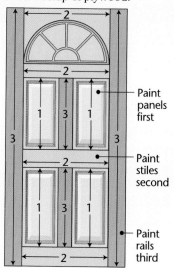

Paint panels first

Paint stiles second

Paint rails third

Shiny Garage Door Finish

Q. *The stain and varnish on both sides of our six-panel redwood garage door looked great for about a year. How can we restore that nice luster it used to have?*

Sounds like you're fighting the age-old battle between varnish and the elements. Keeping a glossy varnish finish on natural wood is a continuous job. To restore the shiny finish on your garage door, you'll need to sand, scrape, and revarnish it every year or two. For best results, use a marine-grade spar varnish containing an ultraviolet screening agent.

If you don't mind giving up the gloss, you'll get a much longer lasting finish (one that can be renewed without stripping) from a tinted or clear wood preservative, solid or semi-transparent exterior stain, or exterior oil finish. Ask for these products at your local paint store.

Peeling Steel Doors

Q. *The paint on my steel doors peels in winter. Last year I stripped and repainted them, but they still peeled, especially around the decorative plastic design. What am I doing wrong?*

Your problem is that metal and plastic expand and contract at different rates as the temperature changes, and this breaks the paint seal where the two materials join. If possible, remove the decorative plastic trim and paint it separately.

If you cannot remove the trim easily, place masking tape on the trim when you paint the door, then place tape on the door when you paint the trim. This creates a break in the paint between the materials and permits them to expand and contract independently of one another.

Stain on Vinyl Windows

Q. *I got stain on my white vinyl window frames when I was staining the cedar siding. How do I remove it without damaging the frame?*

Try a hand cleaner with lanolin; it works slowly, but it's the least harmful to vinyl. If that fails, step up to naphtha, mineral spirits, or turpentine. Test the products in a small area first. Never use sandpaper, razor blades, or steel wool to remove stain or paint—they'll damage the vinyl.

Removing Graffiti

Q. *Graffiti on the garages lining the alley behind our home is a big problem. What's the best way to get rid of it and keep it away?*

The best thing to do is to get rid of it quickly; fresh paint is easier to remove than cured paint. Also, the quicker you remove these statements, the quicker the culprits might find a better area to display their words more permanently.

For painted siding, the quickest cover-up is paint. Coat the surface with a primer that prevents bleed-through, then repaint the area. Gloss paint will withstand future scrubbings better than flat paint.

Brick and stucco are absorbent and present a more difficult problem. Try scrubbing or pressure-washing the surface with a solution of hot water and TSP or a TSP substitute.

If none of these solutions work, you'll need to step up to a commercial stripper. Check your local hardware center for a commercial graffiti remover. You might also want to ask about paints and wall textures that discourage future "artists."

Paint Spatters on Stucco

Q. *How do I remove paint spatters on my stucco siding? I don't want to damage the surface.*

Any commercial paint remover can be used to remove paint from stucco. Paint removers that have a jelly-like consistency are the easiest to work with since they won't run down the wall as easily as thinner-bodied ones. Dab the paint remover on the spatters with a paintbrush or rag. Clean the surface with water after you've removed the paint.

Cover the area below the paint spots with plastic, and wear rubber gloves. Follow the label directions carefully, and always try any cleaning procedure in a small inconspicuous area first. Do not use acid to remove paint from stucco.

Paint Spots on Brick

Q. *The previous owners of my home let paint drip from the trim onto the brick and never bothered to remove it. What's the best way to remove these blemishes?*

The first method you could try is to use a soft-bristle brush and a solution of TSP (trisodium phosphate). Several applications may be needed before the paint can be completely removed. If some stubborn spots remain, try a commercial paint remover. Experiment first in an out-of-the-way spot.

Another method of removing paint spots is to use a water-base paint stripper—but again, experiment first in a hidden spot. Be sure to follow the recommended safety precautions for any of these chemicals. Never rinse TSP or a paint stripper down the drain or let it run into the soil.

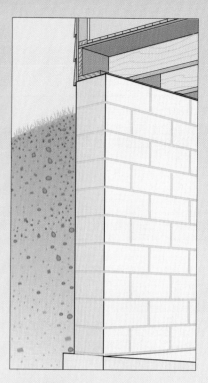

Building
and
Remodeling

Foundations

152 Foundation Repair

House Structure

156 Structure Basics
158 Bearing Walls
159 Structural Problems

House Framing

160 Buying Lumber
164 Nails and Fasteners
166 Framing Walls
168 Framing Floors
169 Framing Ceilings

Carpentry

170 Tape Measures
172 Measuring and Marking
174 Nailing Techniques

Workshop Tools

176 Tooling Up for DIY Projects

Remodeling

178 Heavy Lifting
180 Regulations
182 Basement
186 Storage Solutions
188 Design Considerations
190 Converting Decks and Porches

Foundations

FOUNDATION REPAIR

Replacing a Damaged Sill

Q. *Termites have eaten through a 3-foot-long section of a sill plate. What's the best way to replace the damaged section?*

If your house has siding and the damage is on a side of the house where the joists run at right angles to the sill, you can replace the damaged portion yourself. You'll need to jack up the wall slightly, cut away the damaged sill, and replace it with pressure-treated lumber. If the damage is on the side where the joists run parallel to the sill, jacking up the wall can get tricky and your best bet is to get a professional opinion.

To jack up the wall, you'll need to install pole jacks (plan to use two jacks for every 4 feet of sill) and a 6-foot 4 x 4 beam under the floor joists. You can rent pole jacks from a construction equipment store. You'll also need 2 x 12 x 12 jack pads to distribute the weight on the jacks and prevent damage to your basement floor.

Tie the beam to the joists so it can't fall on you. Center the jacks under the beam between the joists. Next, slowly lift the joists by turning the handles on the jacks. (They will be hard to turn. You may need to tap the handles with a hammer.) Raise the joists just enough (no more than ¾ inch) to take the pressure off the sill. Cut out the damaged wood and any anchor bolts or straps with a reciprocating saw. Depending on your situation, you may also need to remove some of the exterior siding, sheathing and rim joist to remove the sill.

Cut a section of 2 x 6 pressure-treated lumber to size and slide it into place. Seal the joints with latex or butyl caulk to prevent further pest and moisture problems. Lower the jacks, slowly easing the joists back into place. Finish by replacing any siding and sheathing you removed.

Minor cracks may appear in the interior walls due to this slight uplift, but it's unlikely. Work carefully to prevent injury.

Cracked Foundation

Q. *The concrete foundations under my house and garage were poured separately. A crack has developed where the two foundations meet. Should I be worried?*

When a foundation is poured in two parts, it's very common for a crack to occur at the construction joint between them. What you need to do is to determine if the two foundations are actively moving apart. To test for movement, paint a horizontal line over the crack and note its width and the date. Watch the crack for 6 months. If you find that the walls on either side are moving, contact a structural engineer.

If the crack has stopped widening, you should fill it with a urethane caulk or neutral-cure silicone caulk. Since concrete expands and contracts, brittle patching compounds, such as mortar or concrete, are likely to fall out.

Stopping Stone Leaks

Q. *How can I seal my stone foundation to stop it from leaking into the dirt crawl space?*

First, you'll need to seal the joints between the stones to stop the leaks. Start at the outside of the house. Rake out any crumbling mortar and brush out the joints until you hit solid mortar. Use prepackaged mortar mix to repoint the joints, following the manufacturer's instructions. Repeat this process on the inside joints.

Once the stones are repointed, seal the interior surface with a masonry waterproof coating. You can also seal the exterior for extra protection, but know that you will lose the natural look of the stone.

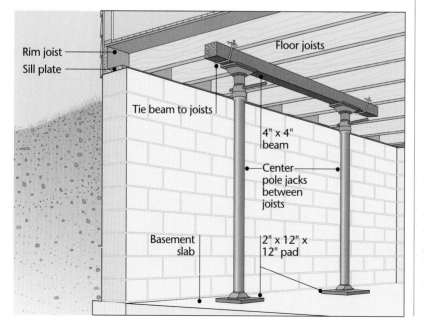

Rim joist
Sill plate
Floor joists
Tie beam to joists
4" x 4" beam
Center pole jacks between joists
Basement slab
2" x 12" x 12" pad

THE SOURCE OF MOISTURE

If the walls of your basement feel damp but you don't know where the moisture is coming from, try this simple foil test to help determine the source.

Secure all four sides of a rectangular piece of aluminum foil or plastic wrap to the wall with duct tape and leave it for 2 days; then remove it. If moisture has collected on the exposed face of the foil but the concrete behind feels dry, the moisture is due to interior basement humidity. If water has accumulated on the side facing the wall, the moisture is seeping through the wall.

If the wall behind the patch is dry, the moisture is inside the basement.

If the wall is wet, moisture is seeping in from the outside.

White Powder on Concrete

Q. *There is a white powdery substance growing on the concrete floor in our basement. What is it and how can we prevent it?*

What you see is a salt deposit, called efflorescence. When water travels through the concrete, it picks up soluble salts. When the water evaporates on the surface, the salts are left behind. Efflorescence can be cleaned up with a wire brush, wet rag, or mop.

These white deposits are an indication that water is seeping into your basement. Check to make sure your yard is sloped away from the foundation, and that the downspouts and gutters are clean and attached properly. If you have a sump pump,

make sure it's working. If the staining occurs infrequently and in small amounts, it's not a problem. Severe efflorescence suggests a more serious problem. Have a professional water-proofer take a look.

Efflorescence (salt deposits) can be scrubbed off with a wire brush.

Damp Basement

Q. *My basement is always damp. I'm not sure if the moisture is coming from the soil outside or the laundry room inside. What can I do to keep the humidity level down?*

If the walls feel damp, use the aluminum foil test (see The Source of Moisture, left) to help determine if the dampness is coming from inside or outside. If the moisture is coming from inside the house, check to make sure the bathroom fans and clothes dryer are vented to the outside. If that doesn't solve the problem, buy a dehumidifier to help remove excess moisture. During damp weather you could also run a bathroom-type exhaust fan. Leave a window open in the laundry room for ventilation during dry weather.

If moisture is coming in through the walls, check to make certain your gutters and downspouts are directing water away from the foundation. You may need to redo the landscape so the ground slopes away from the house; a minimum slope of 6 inches over 10 feet is advised. Excessive foliage around the foundation can create a lot of shade and keep air movement from drying the soil. If your walls or floors visibly leak or seep water, plug these areas with hydraulic cement.

Finally, clean the walls and coat them with a waterproof masonry paint. Newer latex-base products are just as effective as the older types and have far less odor. Let your basement sit through an entire season, or at least a rainy spell, to see if you've conquered the moisture problem before trying a more drastic remedy.

If you have major water problems, you may have to dig a trench around the interior or exterior of the foundation and install a drain tile system.

Foundations

Building a Dry Well

Q. *Every time it rains, we get water in our basement. We have long gutters and downspouts, but the water still pools next to the foundation. What can we do?*

The best solution is to regrade the soil around the house so that it slopes away from the foundation. If this isn't an option, consider installing a dry well at each downspout.

A dry well is like a holding pit where you send the runoff until the soil can absorb it. The water is diverted underground, so you don't have a puddle waiting to evaporate. It's not perfect, especially if you have clay soil, because heavy rain can make it flow back against the house.

To make a dry well, first dig a 3- to 4-foot-diameter hole that is 6 to 8 feet deep (see drawing, right). Next, dig a 2-foot-wide, 2-foot-deep trench to connect the downspout to the well. Line the trench and the well with landscape fabric (not plastic). Fill the bottom of the trench with 6 inches of small gravel. Run a

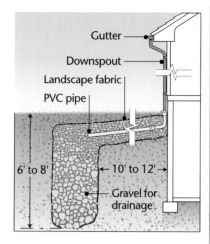

3-inch-diameter PVC pipe from the downspout to the middle of the hole. Fill the hole and trench with gravel until it's a foot below the surface. Fold the landscape fabric over the trench and hole. Bury the entire trench and dry well with soil, replace the sod, or reseed the soil. The land-scape fabric will keep the gravel from filling with dirt and silt while the water drains out into the soil.

Another option is to run an underground pipe to a low area where you can safely dump the water.

Sump-Pump Backup

Q. *The last time we lost power, we had to carry the water in our basement out in buckets. Is there a sump pump backup system I can buy?*

One option is to buy a portable gas-powered pump. This tool will pump out not only your sump basket but also any other flooded area. Maintain good ventilation to prevent carbon monoxide buildup from the engine.

A more convenient solution might be to get a battery-powered backup pump. Powered by a 12-volt marine battery, the unit will beep to warn you of a power failure, then will kick in when needed. A backup pump will also take over if your sump pump

breaks down. Installation will require you to have minor plumbing skills; you will have to install a T in the water discharge pipe a few inches above the electric unit.

A battery-powered backup unit for your sump pump warns of a power failure and takes over if the sump pump fails.

Holes in Basement Walls

Q. *My basement wall sprang a leak this week during a huge rainstorm. Is there a magic potion that I can use to plug it up before it starts gushing?*

Hydraulic cement may not contain magic, but it performs as if it does. It hardens fast (even under water), expands as it cures, and will plug even a gushing leak in minutes. Of course, you're better off using it to plug cracks and holes before the water starts pouring in.

Chip away any loose material from around the hole with a cold chisel. Mix a heaping handful of hydraulic cement with water. When it becomes stiff enough to form into a ball—after a minute or two—it's ready to use. Wearing rubber gloves, push the cement into the hole and hold it there for a few minutes until it hardens. This should do the trick.

Once you've inserted the cement plug, hold it in place until it hardens.

Crawl Space Moisture

Q. *How can we keep our ventilated dirt-floor crawl space drier?*

Install a 6-mil plastic vapor barrier over the ground and on the crawl space walls (don't cover the vents). Kill any mold that grows by spraying a bleach solution onto the plastic and wiping it off. Wear safety goggles.

WATERPROOFING A BASEMENT FROM THE INSIDE

Crystalline waterproofing material, or CWM, is a product that has been used for the past 20 years on large commercial projects, like dams and subway systems. Luckily for us, it's now available to homeowners. Look for CWM under brand names such as Xypex or Hi-dry.

CWM is a powdered blend of cement, sand, and a chemical catalyst. You mix it with water and brush it onto the interior of your poured concrete or concrete block basement walls. (There's no need to treat the areas above ground level, so keep this in mind when you calculate how much you need.)

If your moisture problem is concentrated in one area, first try treating the area plus a couple of feet on either side of it. The concrete must be solid and nearly bare before CWM is applied. Chisel away any loose chips of concrete. If the paint was applied before 1979, test it for lead before you scrape any of it.

CWM penetrates several inches and makes the concrete itself waterproof. This is unlike other "barrier" coatings that form a paintlike film on the surface but eventually loosen and peel. Unlike other coatings, CWM can be applied any time, not just when the concrete is dry. There are no fumes or toxins in CWM; however, CWM is more expensive than other barrier coatings and comes only in a cement-gray color.

Before you decide to do any waterproofing inside your basement, inspect the outside of your house. Solving a water problem may be as simple as repairing leaky gutters or extending downspouts. Correcting the cause of the moisture on the exterior is better than trying to rememdy the problem inside your home.

1 Chisel or scrape away any loose concrete or existing coatings (wear eye protection). You should remove at least 85 percent of all the existing coatings and leave no patches larger than a silver dollar.

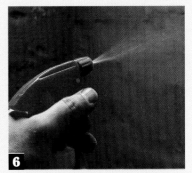

2 To seal cracks, lay a bead of silicone caulk in the crack and later fill it with some hydraulic cement.

3 Fill large holes with hydraulic cement. The cement sets quickly; mix as much as you can use in 3 min.

4 For CWM to work, the concrete must be thoroughly soaked but not dripping wet. If the concrete begins to dry while you're applying CWM, wet it again.

5 Spread a 1/16-in.-thick coat of CWM over concrete, using a stiff masonry brush. Mix only as much material as you can use in about 10 min.

6 Moisten the coating as needed after it begins to harden. The coating should remain damp for 48 hr. after application to fully cure.

House Structure

STRUCTURE BASICS

Live and Dead Loads

Q. *What's the difference between live load and dead load?*

Engineers divide the stress carried by the structure of a house into two categories: dead load and live load. Dead load refers to the weight of the building materials themselves (typically several tons of wood shingles, drywall, nails, etc.). Live load refers to temporary weight, such as people, furniture, and snow on the roof.

Dead loads vary based on the materials used and the design of the house. Live loads vary considerably from region to region due to snowfall and wind variations. Your local building inspector will tell you the standards for your region.

Settling House

Q. *How do you stop an old house from settling?*

New houses settle, then stop; old houses shouldn't be settling unless something is wrong. You probably see the effects of settling (cracks in the ceiling and foundation walls, for example) that occured when the house was new. For a new house, there's not much you can do other than try to maintain the status quo. Make sure drainage patterns stay the same or improve. For example, if you do any paving projects, direct the surface water away from the house. Water can also work its way in through the walls. Repoint brick and stone, and repaint the exterior early, before the paint fails and lets water in.

Good home maintenance practices will also help. Maintain your roof and gutters so they won't spill water around the foundation. Water can also work its way in through the walls. Repoint brick and stone, and repaint the exterior early, before the paint fails and lets water in.

Pick the Best Beam

Q. *What's the difference between the way wood joists and manufactured beams carry structural loads? Which type is best?*

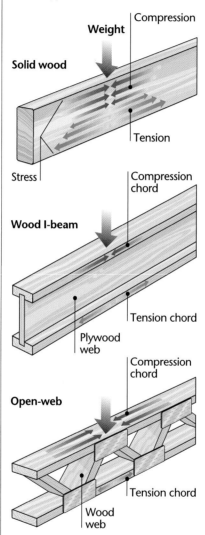

Regardless of what they're made of, all beams and joists (beams that support floors) perform the same job—they support horizontal loads. Weight (or load) from the room above places stress on the top of the beam. This stress compresses the top layer of wood fibers and stretches the bottom layers, putting them in

tension. A joist transfers the weight out to the walls. Understanding the compression/tension principle of a joist can help you understand the odd shape of manufactured beams. The bulk of the wood is concentrated at the top and bottom. These "chords" carry most of the stress.

In most cases, solid wood 2 x 10 joists are more than adequate for a stiff floor. But the desire for bigger rooms and bigger houses, and the increasing scarcity of good dimensional lumber are all factors that have led to the development of a variety of manufactured beams.

Wood I-beams have several advantages over solid wood. These manufactured beams require half as much wood as a solid beam to carry the same load. And, unlike solid wood, each joist is absolutely straight and uniform—producing a flat, squeakproof floor. Larger I-beams can also carry longer spans. Wood I-beams cost more than solid wood, and your supplier may need to review your plans to provide the right beams.

Open-web joists have several advantages over solid wood and wood I-beams: They're easy to handle; they have plenty of room for ductwork, plumbing, and electrical wires (they even eliminate the need for notches and cut-outs); and the wide nailing flanges are more forgiving of layout errors. One drawback of open-web joists is the need to order exact lengths, but some are available with trimmable ends so that they can be cut to length on the job site.

Be careful how you handle any kind of beam. Notches or drilled holes in either the top or bottom third of a beam eliminates wood in the zones where the stress is greatest and thus will weaken the beam. Open-web and wood I-beams are flexible and can be damaged if they are improperly stored or lifted.

The Stressful Life of a Beam

Q. *What does it mean to "size a beam"?*

Through a process of testing and trial and error, engineers have learned how much weight a beam can support and why it might fail. Beams typically fail in one of three ways: They shear near a vertical support, bend and break near the middle, or simply sag. Shearing almost never occurs with wood beams in residential construction, so engineers focus on a beam's resistance to sagging (stiffness) and its bending strength.

The stiffness of a beam determines the amount of bounce you feel when you jump on a floor or deck. Stiffer beams feel more solid and are less likely to lead to sagging floors or cracked walls.

The bending strength of a beam determines how much weight a beam can hold before the wood

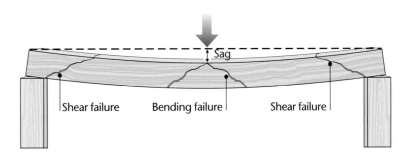

Shear failure Bending failure Shear failure

fibers hit their maximum stress points and break. Wood fibers that run lengthwise along the beam are quite strong. Under moderate loads, a beam bends slightly as the fibers at the top compress and those at the bottom stretch. When you overload a beam, the fibers at the top crush, the ones at the bottom stretch and snap, and the beam cracks roughly at its midpoint. That's why you should never drill holes or cut notches near the top or bottom of a beam.

Selecting the right size beam is straightforward because all structural materials have been tested for stiffness and bending. To size a beam,

engineers look up the strength of the wood species and grade they want to use and select a size to withstand the the estimated load.

Cost and space requirements usually determine which species of wood or which engineered beam is used. Most often carpenters nail together two-by lumber to achieve the required strength, but this is often the bulkiest option. One-piece wood beams can cost more than twice as much and don't offer much additional strength. When you're trying to save headroom, manufactured beams offer compactness at a reasonable price.

Build a Better Beam

Q. *I'm thinking of building a small addition with a cathedral ceiling. I've read about a variety of different types of beams that can serve as the ridge beam. What's the best type?*

All the beams will do the same thing. Your choice really comes down to appearance and cost.

A solid wood beam would be a traditional and attractive option. However, large solid wood beams

can be expensive and can be difficult to transport and raise in place. It's for that reason that carpenters prefer to build up beams on site, using nailed-together pieces of two-by lumber.

Another option would be a glue-laminated (or glu-lam) beam. A glu-lam is a stack of lumber glued together under pressure. It's stronger than the sum of the strengths of the individual boards, so it can be small. Glu-lams are fairly attractive (and expensive) and can be left visible.

A less costly alternative is a laminated veneer lumber beam, or LVL. LVL's are more compact than glu-lams, but they look like a long strip of plywood.

Steel is an excellent beam material. For appearance, you can box the steel beam in solid wood. Unfortunately most carpenters shy away from steel because they can't work with it as quickly or easily as with wood (most cutting and drilling must be done before delivery).

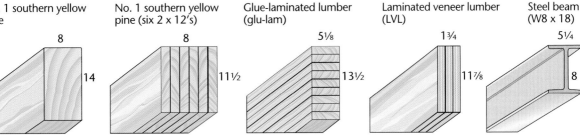

No. 1 southern yellow pine
8
14

No. 1 southern yellow pine (six 2 x 12's)
8
11½

Glue-laminated lumber (glu-lam)
5⅛
13½

Laminated veneer lumber (LVL)
1¾
11⅞

Steel beam (W8 x 18)
5¼
8

House Structure

BEARING WALLS

Bearing and Nonbearing Walls

Q. *What's the difference between a load-bearing and a non-load-bearing wall? What clues can I look for to tell them apart?*

Load-bearing walls shoulder the bulk of your home's weight: the wood and other construction materials that make up your house; the weight of weather, such as high winds and piles of snow; and you and your furniture. If you tear out bearing walls without compensating for the lost support, your house is in for big trouble. While it may not collapse in a cloud of debris, you can expect sagging floors and roof, cracked walls, sticking doors and windows, and other structural damage. In comparison, non-load-bearing walls contribute little to your home's strength. These walls divide your house into rooms, closets, and storage areas. You can usually tear them out without worrying about the roof or floors caving in.

Identifying bearing walls can be tricky; consult a carpenter or structural engineer if you are not absolutely sure that a wall you plan to remove is non-load-bearing. To help identify a bearing wall, ask yourself these two questions:
■ Do the floor or ceiling joists run perpendicular to the wall?

Look to the top of your wall to see if it's supporting anything. A bearing wall will have joists crossing it or ending on it. To find out, you can check the attic to see which way the ceiling joists run. In most cases, rafters will run at right angles to a bearing wall.

If you find that the joists or rafters run parallel to the wall, the wall is probably not load-bearing. Realize that some walls that have joists or rafters crossing them, such as closet walls, are not bearing walls. To know for sure, ask yourself the next question:
■ Is the wall supported from below, all the way down to the foundation or concrete slab?

Assuming that the original builders and remodelers did a good job, a bearing wall will have another supporting wall directly under it on the level below, and so on down until it reaches the foundation. Most exterior walls are load-bearing walls, and in most homes the middle wall is load-bearing too. Usually the support for this central wall isn't a continuous wall, but a beam and a series of posts in the basement.

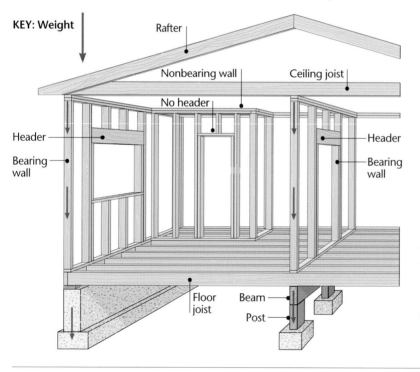

KEY: Weight

Rafter

Nonbearing wall

No header

Ceiling joist

Header

Header

Bearing wall

Bearing wall

Floor joist

Beam

Post

Bearing Walls on a Slab Foundation

Q. *My home was built on a concrete slab. How can I check if a wall is load-bearing?*

In your case, the entire slab is a foundation, so every wall resting on it is directly supported by the slab. For slab-built homes, you need to ask yourself the same two questions listed above, plus one more:
■ Do the ceiling joists end after crossing over the wall?

Climb into the attic to find the joint between the two joists. You'll always find a bearing wall where one joist ends and another begins.

The exception to this rule is a truss roof, where the ceiling joists and rafters are connected by a wooden web. A truss bears on the exterior walls, but depending on how it's constructed, it may not depend on the interior walls. In this case, your best bet to is to ask a structural engineer.

STRUCTURAL PROBLEMS

How Big a Load

Q. *I'd like to move a post in my basement so that one section of the beam spans 10 feet instead of 8 feet. Does it make much difference?*

It's easy to understand that a beam supports weight, but it's difficult to appreciate just how much until you add up everything that's stacked on top of it.

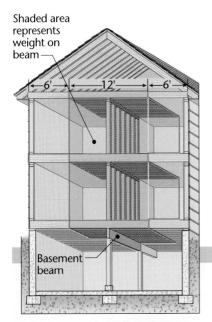

Shaded area represents weight on beam

6'   12'   6'

Basement beam

The pink shaded area on the drawing below represents the load shouldered by the basement beam. To calculate the load on a beam, you need to start from the top and work downward. In this case the roof doesn't count, since this type of roof transfers its load to the side walls. It does, however, support half the attic (the outer walls support the other half). Continuing down through the house, add up the live and dead loads for each floor. Walls typically weigh in at 48 pounds per foot. Beams that span doorways and archways can complicate the calculation; they shift the weight to a different section of the beam. (One more reason to call an expert.)

The weight on this 10-foot section of beam is almost 2 tons more than the load carried by the 8-foot beam. Your best bet would be to leave the post where it is; otherwise you would need to install a larger beam.

WEIGHT

The beam supports the shaded area. Moving the beam 2 feet increases the load by 25%.

	LIVE LOAD/ DEAD LOAD (LB. PER SQ. FT.)	WEIGHT ON 8-FT. BEAM (LB.)	WEIGHT ON 10-FT. BEAM (LB.)
Roof	15 / 35	None*	None*
Attic	10 / 20	2,880	3,600
Wall	48 (lb./ft.)	384	480
Second floor	15 / 40	5,280	6,600
Wall	48 (lb./ft.)	384	480
First floor	20 / 40	5,760	7,200
Total weight on beam		14,688	18,360

*Weight supported by outside walls

How Much Stuff on a Truss?

Q. *How much stuff can I store on my garage's roof trusses?*

According to the truss manufacturers we contacted, you shouldn't store anything on, or hang anything from, the bottom chord of a truss. However, off the record, if you're going to put stuff up there, here's what they advise:

■ Never cut through or remove any wood member of a truss, metal fastening plate, catwalk, or brace. Trusses are designed as a system, and removing any part of it can lead to truss or roof failure.

■ Never suspend heavy objects—like a car engine—off a single point of a truss. The metal fastening plates can pull away from the wood.

■ Store only light objects on top of the bottom chord. Attach ⅜-inch plywood to the bottom chord with drywall screws, then distribute light items along it. Keep it to about 5 pounds per square foot, or 80 pounds per 2 x 8-foot sheet of plywood.

■ Contact the manufacturer. Often the name will be stamped somewhere on one of the trusses. They may be able to give you some suggestions for reinforcing the truss.

Use trusses solely for light-duty storage. Plywood can help distribute the weight.

House Framing

BUYING LUMBER

Dealing with Defects

Q. *Most of the studs sold at my local lumberyard have all sorts of twists, turns, and bends. Should I believe the yard guy when he says that they're "good enough"?*

The truth is, lumber doesn't need to look perfect to do the job. But you will need to decide if the defects you see will affect your project. For example, if you're making deck furniture, your standards will be higher than if you're building a compost bin. You should avoid bowed, crooked, and twisted lumber when framing corners or door openings. Badly misshapen lumber should be cut into short lengths and used for blocking.

The best way to search for straight lumber is by eye. Pick up each piece by its end and sight down its length. You should have no trouble spotting crooked, bowed, or twisted stock like the examples shown below.

■ Bow. Studs and joists can bow a half inch or more and still be acceptable for framing. You can usually straighten bowed lumber as you apply the drywall or sheathing.

■ Crook. When you frame with crooked studs, try to orient the crooks so that they all face upward on joists or toward the exterior on walls. Usually ½ inch of crook on an 8-foot stud won't matter in a wall. But mismatching will give floors and walls a really uneven surface.

■ Twist. As long as the twisting isn't too serious, these boards can be used in framing and straightened out as you nail them in place.

■ Whenever you buy dimensional lumber, try to use it as soon as possible. If left standing around in a heated environment, it may start to move on you. If you plan to store lumber for more than a few weeks, keep it stacked out of the weather in an unheated garage or shed.

Lumber Numbers

Q. *Why isn't lumber sold by its actual size (for example, why is a 2 x 4 actually 1½ by 3½ inches)? How much can a 2 x 4 be cut down and still be a 2 x 4?*

Even though a 2 x 4 piece of lumber isn't really 2 inches by 4 inches, both the lumber industry and consumers are so comfortable with the terms, they're not likely to change them.

The first mills sold lumber by its nominal, or green undried, size. Once it's surfaced (planed) and dried (which results in shrinkage), the lumber's actual size ends up smaller than its nominal size. In addition, thickness and width can vary as much as ⅛ inch from the standard sizes because of differences in moisture content and variances in sawing. The American Lumber Standards Committee sets and enforces minimum limits that planed and dried lumber must meet. Refer to the table below for nominal lumber sizes.

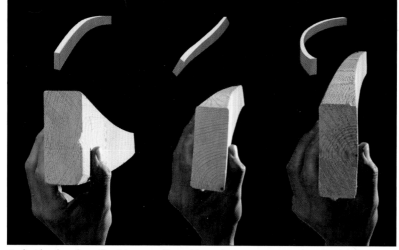

Perfect lumber doesn't exist, so you'll need to make some compromises. By sighting down the edge of each piece, you can watch out for unusable studs like these, which are good only for kindling. Shown, from left to right, are crooked, twisted, and bowed stock.

LUMBER SIZES

NOMINAL	ACTUAL
2 x 2	1½ x 1½ in.
2 x 4	1½ x 3½
2 x 6	1½ x 5½
2 x 8	1½ x 7¼
2 x 10	1½ x 9¼
2 x 12	1½ x 11¼
4 x 4	3½ x 3½
1 x 2	¾ x 1½
1 x 3	¾ x 2½
1 x 4	¾ x 3½
1 x 6	¾ x 5½
1 x 8	¾ x 7¼
1 x 10	¾ x 9¼
1 x 12	¾ x 11¼

Quick Material Estimates

Q. *I'm trying to get a rough idea of how much material to buy and how much it will cost to finish our basement. Are there any rules of thumb to estimate how much stuff I'll need?*

The amount of materials varies according to your project's design and your carpentry expertise. If your basement plan contains lots of corners, doors, and closets, you'll use more studs per foot of wall than if the walls were straight. Here are a few rules to help you come up with a rough estimate:
■ Wall plates (the horizontal top and bottom members of the wall): figure out the total length of all walls in feet, then multiply by 2.
■ Studs: Figure one stud per linear foot of wall.
■ Drywall: Multiply the square footage of the floor by 4.5; then divide this number by 32 to get the number of 4 x 8 sheets you'll need.

Boards vs. Dimensional Lumber

Q. *Is there a difference between board and dimensional lumber?*

While it may seem as if we're splitting hairs, technically, yes. And understanding the difference will make it easier for you to ask for and find the wood you need. *Boards* are any piece of lumber 1½-inches thick or less. *Dimensional lumber* is cut 1½-inches thick and greater. As a general rule, most board lumber is kept under a roof to protect it from the weather. The better grades of dimensional lumber, especially redwood and cedar, are often stored inside as well, because they're expensive. Lesser grades of dimensional lumber are usually stacked outside.

Wood Defects

ONCE YOU'VE FOUND a relatively straight piece, here are some other blemishes to watch out for:

■ **Cup, or warp,** occurs when the flat side of the lumber curves up due to shrinkage along the face. Since cupping can hold water as well as create a tripping hazard, avoid cupped wood for decking.
■ **Knots** are common in softwoods. Usually knots don't affect the strength, but large loose knots, especially near the edge, can weaken the lumber. Avoid using such pieces for joists or rafters.
■ **Splits** can be dangerous flaws if they continue along the length of a board. Short cracks near the ends are common as the wood continues to dry, and these usually can be cut away as you build your project. Avoid using if the split travels a foot or more past the cut-off point.
■ **Shakes** look like cracks but are actually a separation between growth rings in the wood that may run the whole length of the board. When choosing rafters and joists, avoid pieces with full-length shakes.
■ **Wanes** are bark edges on a piece of lumber. Pieces with this defect are OK for framing because you can usually work around them. If it's an otherwise straight piece, it's a keeper.

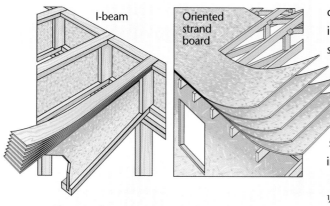

I-beam

Oriented strand board

R e i n v e n t i n g
Wood

chips that have been oriented by grain and pressed into thin mats. The mats are stacked to create 4 x 8 sheets. OSB is engineered to be as strong as plywood of the same thickness, but it costs 10 percent less than plywood. Though OSB looks similar to other compressed board products, such as wafer-board, chipboard, or particleboard, OSB is stronger. Look for the OSB label or a "Rated Sheathing" grade stamp if you plan to use it for structure.

When nailing OSB to framing members, leave ⅛ inch between the sheets to allow for expansion. OSB is more sensitive to moisture than plywood: The edges will swell if water soaks into them. If it gets really soaked, the panel may start to sag or weaken.

ENGINEERED WOOD PRODUCTS are made from rejected waste wood, sawdust, scraps, and wood from trees that can't be cut into decent lumber. Yet they're strong, stable, and consistent in size. Oriented strand board (OSB) and wood I-beams are two engineered products that are strong enough to be used as structural components.

Oriented Strand Board

Oriented strand board is the coarse-grained sheathing you often see on the sides and roofs of homes under construction. The panels are made of wood

Wood I-Beams

Wood I-beams consist of two laminated wood flanges connected by an OSB web. By varying the size of the flanges or the width of the web, manufacturers can engineer the beam's strength precisely while using less, and often lower-quality, wood than needed for standard 2 x 10's. Although wood I-beams cost slightly more than a 2 x 10, they can span longer distances and are lighter. However, you can't cut, drill, or nail into a wood I-beam as you can a 2 x 10; wiring and plumbing must be planned to pass through preperforated knock-outs. They also require special joinery techniques.

Getting Hitched

Q. *What's the best knot to use when you want to tie down a load?*

The trucker's hitch is the ideal knot for tying down a load. This knot, shown below, allows you to cinch

down the rope with a ratchetlike action. It's a complex knot, but it's worth adding to your tying arsenal.

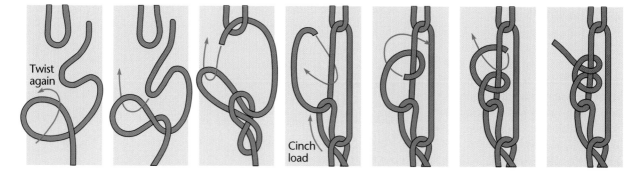

Twist again

Cinch load

Hauling Lumber Home

Q. *I have a roof rack. How do I use it to safely transport lumber?*

There are three basic kinds of tie-downs you can use with a roof rack: rubber tie-downs with hooks at each end, flat nylon straps with buckles or ratchets, and rope. Here are some tips about each type:

■ Elastic tie-downs: The best kind for lumber are the heavy-duty black rubber straps, rather than the lighter and thinner multicolored tie-downs. The rubber grips the wood, preventing lumber at the center of the pile from sliding out. Four 2-foot straps and two 3-footers should take care of most of your needs.

■ Don't rely exclusively on elastic straps, because they will allow your load to move. Use additional rope or nylon straps to stabilize the load.

■ Nylon straps: Look for flat nylon straps that have either a self-cinching buckle or a ratcheting tie-down. These straps cost more, but they'll allow you to bind down a load really tight and will last a long time.

Tie down boards with rubber straps first.

Next use nylon straps with self-cinching buckles to hold the load securely in place.

Tie sheets down with ¼-in.-dia. hemp rope running front to back.

■ Rope: Sometimes the original tie-down tool is still the best. Use a good-quality ¼-inch-diameter hemp rope. Nylon or plastic rope is slippery and stiff; knots in the coarse-textured hemp hold better and are easier to tie. Invest the time it takes to learn at least one good knot. With practice, the "trucker's hitch" (see Getting Hitched, p.162) can be done quickly.

Rating Roof Racks

Q. *A set of roof racks for my car is a lot more affordable than a pickup. Considering the fact that I'll be hauling plywood and lumber, what should I look for?*

Roof racks fall into two main groups: the really good expensive ones and the inexpensive. As with anything, you get what you pay for.

Most of the inexpensive racks are held in place with straps that you have to fiddle with every time you mount the racks. The expensive racks snap on and off your car in about 10 seconds; what's more, they won't mar the paint. Better-quality racks also have accessories available

for carrying bikes, skis, canoes, and luggage containers.

All types of roof racks have weight limitations, ranging from 150 to 200 pounds. That's about eighteen 8-foot

2 x 4's or three sheets of ¾-inch plywood. Too much weight will dent the roof. If you plan to carry heavy loads, buy a roof rack that has cushioned bases or broad feet.

Inexpensive racks have straps that you mount on your car's rain gutters.

Higher-end racks snap on and off your car in seconds. Custom accessories are available for different carrying chores.

NAILS AND FASTENERS

Nail Knowledge

Q. *Whenever I go to the hardware store to get nails, I'm confused about what length nail to use for the best holding power.*

It's impossible to come up with a rule that applies to all situations, but there

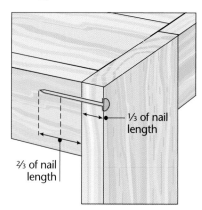

⅓ of nail length

⅔ of nail length

are a few general guidelines that will work most of the time:

- Always nail the thinner piece to the thicker one. Try to use a nail that's three times as long as the thinner piece. If both pieces are equal thickness, use 2 or more nails, ¼ inch shorter than the combined thickness. (Use the figure below to select the right "d"-size nail for the job.)
- To increase the holding power of a nail, drive it in at a slight angle. Driving nails at opposite angles will create an even stronger joint.
- Splitting the wood greatly affects a nail's holding power. To avoid splitting, drive nails in a staggered pattern, rather than along a grain line. Blunting a nail's point also helps prevent splitting.

Nail Weigh-In

Q. *My hardware store still sells nails out of wooden barrels. Just how many nails are there in a pound, anyway?*

There's no easy formula, but many hardware stores can provide you with that information if they have a computerized scale. Below is a close approximation for steel nails.

NAILS PER POUND

SIZE	COMMON	BOX	FINISH
4d	315	450	600
6d	190	225	300
8d	105	140	200
10d	70	90	120
16d	50	70	90

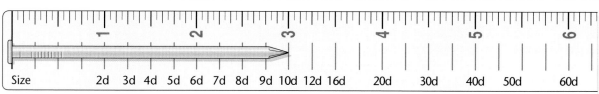

| Size | 2d | 3d | 4d | 5d | 6d | 7d | 8d | 9d | 10d | 12d | 16d | 20d | 30d | 40d | 50d | 60d |

A common nail's length is designated by penny size (d), a term that once indicated the price per hundred.

Trim Screws

Q. *My house was framed with metal studs. I'd like to install new moldings, but finish nails don't seem to work. What should I use?*

Put your hammer down. To fasten trim to metal studs, you'll need to use a drill with a screwdriver bit and special trim screws. Trim screws have a very small head (slightly larger than a finish nail) with either a square or

a Phillips head. Be sure to bury the screw just below the surface so you can fill the hole with putty.

Use trim screws for metal studs or to pull loose molding to a wood-stud wall.

Box Nails vs. Common Nails

Q. *What's the difference between box and common nails?*

The primary difference is diameter. Box nails have a thinner shank and are less likely to split the wood. They're good for applying sheathing to roofs or subfloors, building soffits, and other light assembly work.

Common nails have a thicker shank and a greater shear strength, which means they can hold larger weights without sagging or breaking. They're best for general framing.

Better-Gripping Nails

Q. *Why do some nails have ridges? And where would I use these types of nails in my home?*

When a nail needs more holding power, as in flooring or roofing, manufacturers "deform" the shank to give the wood fibers a rougher surface to grip. Deformed nails usually have ring-stamped or spiral shanks. You can use these nails anywhere, but they're used primarily for floors and drywall. Galvanized ring-shank nails are especially good for split-prone siding, like redwood and cedar. The thin shanks avoid splitting, yet the rings hold as well as thicker nails. Roofing nails are also deformed to increase their holding power in thin plywood sheathing.

Once they're driven in, these nails are difficult to pull out; you may pull off the head. Also, because thin nails tend to bend easily, manufacturers heat-treat them to stiffen the shanks. This heat treatment makes the shanks brittle; if you bend a nail, it may break if you try to straighten it.

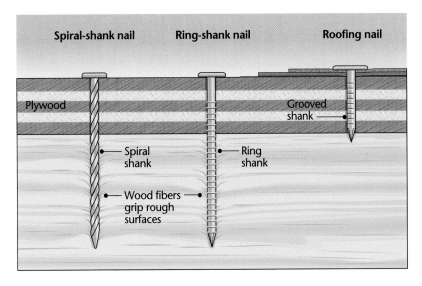

what do you need? THE NOT-SO-COMMON COMMON NAIL

On the job, 16d nails are not as common as they used to be. The common 16d nail is so thick that it's hard to drive, and when driven near the end of a board it tends to split the wood. Instead, for most applications carpenters use easier-to-drive 16d box nails, 16d cement-coated (glue-coated) sinkers, or 16d power-driven cement-coated nails. These three substitutes retain the same size label as common nails, but none has the same holding power.

The longer and thicker a nail is, the better it holds—unless you split the wood when you drive it. Splitting sharply reduces a nail's holding power. Box nails and air-driven nails are as long as common nails, but they're slimmer. Because of this difference in diameter, the holding power of a 16d box nail is only slightly higher than that of an 8d common nail. However, these fasteners make up for this by splitting the wood less often.

Cement-coated sinkers are slimmer than commons and shorter than box nails. However, because of the grip of the cement coating, their initial strength is about the same as common nails. Air-driven nails are even thinner, but their extra length and cement coating provide extra holding power.

While these lighter-duty nails may not be as strong as common nails, they're more than strong enough to meet the design specifications of your house. And because they speed up the building process, using box nails, sinkers, and power-driven nails can cut your overall construction costs.

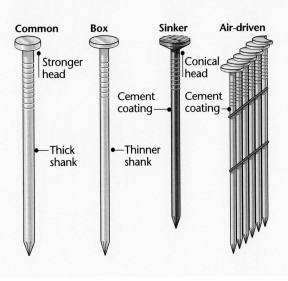

FRAMING WALLS

Laying Out Stud Walls

Q. *I tried laying out a stud wall, but the first sheet of drywall completely covered the stud that the next sheet was supposed to start on. How do I frame a wall using 16-inch centers so that the drywall ends in the middle of the stud?*

To get the first drywall panel to end on the middle of a stud, you need to subtract ¾ inch from the second stud in the wall section. Space the other studs 16-inches on center from the second stud.

There are two ways to do this. Some carpenters prefer to lay out the second stud at 15¼ inches, then mark the rest of the stud locations at 16-inch intervals. Another option is to mark all the studs at once, but ¾-inch less than the 16-inch on-center marks.

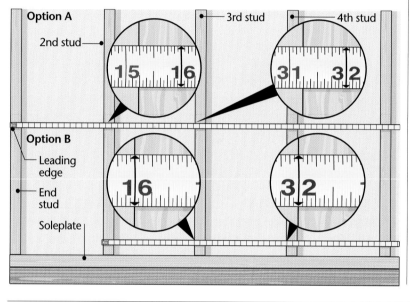

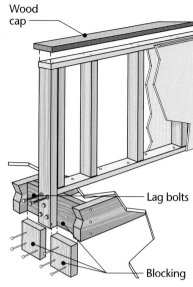

Rock-Solid Half Wall

Q. *We'd like to build a half wall between our dining room and living room. What do we need to do to keep it from wiggling?*

Stabilize the wall by going down through the floor. Extend the end stud of the new half wall so it protrudes down through the floor. Nail blocking to the existing joists; then nail or bolt the protruding part of the end stud to the blocking.

Soundproof Walls

Q. *I am going to finish a room in my basement and would like to soundproof the walls. What acoustic materials should I use?*

The acoustic value of a wall or ceiling is measured in its Sound Transmission Class (STC). Ordinary wall/ceiling cavities have an STC of 32–34. Installing insulation in a wall/ceiling increases the STC to 36–38. Using resilient metal channels and screws to mount the drywall raises the STC about 12 points, to 44–46. The most effective sound-deadening solution is to build a

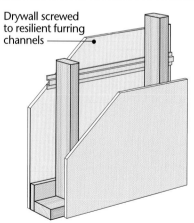

double wall with staggered studs, as shown. The combination of the separated wall surfaces, the added mass of the double-thick drywall,

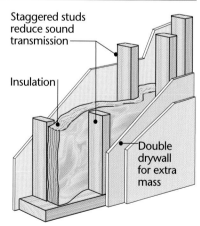

and the core-filled with insulation adds up to a wall with an STC of 53–55.

FRAMING A CURVED WALL

Framing a curved wall is a lot easier than you may think. It takes more time, but it's not much different than framing a straight wall. Following are the steps involved in framing a section that forms a one-quarter turn. To build an oval wall, you'd use the same basic methods, but you'd need to lay out the wall a little differently.

First, lay out the curve. To do this, snap chalk lines marking the locations of the straight walls. Next snap two more parallel lines as far in from the original lines as your desired radius. The point where these second lines meet is your pivot point. Using a wire tied to the pivot nail, draw the outline of the wall on kraft paper. You'll use this pattern to make the curved plates. The first arc will connect the outer wall lines. Draw the second 3½ inches in from the first to establish the inside edge. Don't forget to mark the ends of the arc.

Make each plate from two layers of ¾-inch plywood. Cut out the plates with a jigsaw, and smooth the curves with a belt sander. For a radius of more than 5 feet, use four pieces of plywood. Alternate the seams when you glue the pieces together to form the plate.

Build the straight walls, install the curve plates, then nail in the studs. Around the curve, place the studs closer together than you would on a straight wall in order to help the drywall bend smoothly. Install inset blocks between the studs to support the ends of the drywall. Cut the blocks ½ inch narrower than the studs so they'll create a depression at the butt joints.

Once you have installed the studs, drywall the ceiling, then the wall. (The curve template can also be used to cut the drywall for the ceiling.)

1

Snap two lines parallel to the wall lines to establish the curve's radius. Drive a nail at the pivot point.

2

Using a wire tied to the pivot nail (string stretches), draw two arcs on paper to make the plate template.

3

Cut the arcs out of ¾-in. plywood. Glue the pieces together to form one plate.

4

Install studs closer than you would on a straight wall to make a smooth curve.

5

Fasten drywall to inset blocks. Recess blocks by ¼ in. for smoother joints.

House Framing

FRAMING FLOORS

Bouncy Floor

Q. *We have an extremely bouncy floor. Normal foot traffic causes the grandfather clock to shake and rattle as if it's in an earthquake. How can we fix it?*

To eliminate the bouncing, you'll need to stiffen the floor joists. One way to do this is to nail sister joists alongside the old ones. Unfortunately, this would involve removing any plumbing, wiring, or heating vents that run through the old joists, drilling holes, and then reinstalling the plumbing, wiring, and vents.

The simplest option is to install a permanent support beam and jack posts under the center of the room.

However, the size and location of the beam and locations of the posts must follow building codes and may not fit into your decorating plans.

A good alternative is to glue a 2 x 3 flange to the bottom of the existing joists. To do this, remove the furniture from the floor upstairs to reduce any bowing. Next, spread construction adhesive along the flange and

the entire edge of the joist. Use screws to hold the flange in position until the glue dries. Insert wedges under temporary posts to support the joist and take the load off while the glue is drying. Support the joist in the center and about 4 feet to each side of center. You may not need to stiffen every joist. Reinforce every second or third joist; if the floor still bounces, stiffen additional joists. Then remove the temporary posts.

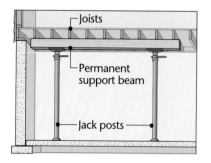

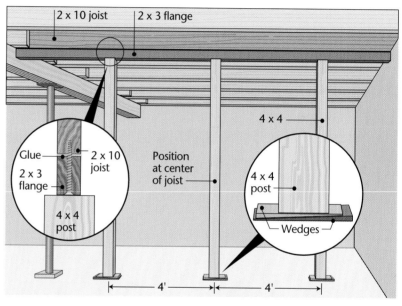

Floor Joist Support

Q. *We're planning to add on to both the main floor and the basement of our house. How do we support the ends of the floor joists after we knock out the foundation wall? (Supporting the joists with a beam underneath wouldn't leave enough headroom in the basement.)*

Since you can't put a beam under the joists, you'll need to beef up the rim joist so it'll take the load once the foundation wall is removed. The best way to strengthen the rim joist is to attach a laminated wood beam.

The most important step is to deter-

mine the correct beam size and the best way to fasten it to the rim joist. Start by making a detailed drawing of what you want to do. The drawing should include the length of the beam, what will rest on top of it, and what the foundation is made of. Also include a sketch of what your house looks like now and what it will look like after the remodeling.

Working from your sketches, a structural engineer can size the beam and show you how to fasten it in place (the number and type of fasteners will vary by locale). When you apply for your building permit, the building inspector may not allow you

to start unless your plans have been approved by a professional. Remember that while your building department approves your plans, they aren't liable for any errors you make.

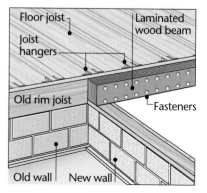

FRAMING CEILINGS

Seasonal Ceiling Gap

Q. *Each winter, the ceiling in our upstairs hallway comes away from the wall and leaves a ¼-inch-wide gap. Everything returns to normal in the spring. What's going on?*

Assuming you have a truss roof, it sounds like the top chord of the truss is absorbing a lot of of moisture, causing it to expand. As the chord lengthens, it bows outward. Because it's fastened at each end, the interior walls keep it from bowing in. As it bows, the bottom chord pulls the ceiling up, causing the gap to appear in the colder months.

Short of removing the drywall on the ceiling, the best solution is to hide the gap with crown molding. Nail the crown molding only to the wall, not to the ceiling. The gap will still come and go, but at least it'll be less noticeable.

If you decide to replace the ceiling with new drywall, use metal clips to fasten the edges of the ceiling to the walls instead of to the trusses. That way, the drywall will be able to flex and prevent the seasonal gap from forming. These clips can be found at drywall supply houses.

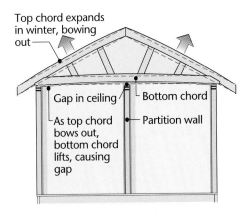

Top chord expands in winter, bowing out

Gap in ceiling

Bottom chord

As top chord bows out, bottom chord lifts, causing gap

Partition wall

Framing a Cathedral Ceiling

Q. *We'd like to build a great room with a cathedral ceiling. How do we frame the ceiling?*

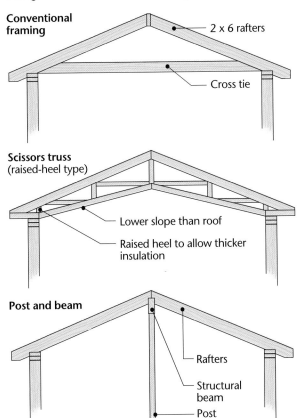

Conventional framing

2 x 6 rafters

Cross tie

Scissors truss (raised-heel type)

Lower slope than roof

Raised heel to allow thicker insulation

Post and beam

Rafters

Structural beam

Post

A cathedral ceiling is a great eye-catching feature. Not only does it make a room feel more spacious, it allows you to add tall windows in the gable end of a house. However, a cathedral ceiling does make the roof framing more complicated. Here are three good ways to do it:

Conventional stick framing is the simplest and least expensive option, but you will have exposed cross ties at least every 4 feet across the entire ceiling. The biggest problem with this kind of framing is that it may not provide enough space for adequate insulation. For example, if your room has 2 x 6 rafters, you'll have to use some type of rigid insulation in addition to insulation batts in the rafter spaces in order to meet the energy requirements of most building codes.

Scissors trusses don't require cross ties and leave enough space for insulation. The downside of using scissors trusses is that they reduce the slope of the ceiling to about half the slope of the roof. A lower ceiling slope may not look as dramatic in some situations. Scissors trusses work best on roofs with steep slopes. You can order scissors trusses for about the same cost as regular trusses.

Post-and-beam construction is the ideal way to frame a cathedral ceiling, but it is the most difficult and expensive. The end result is a wide-open space, without cross ties, and a ceiling that has the same slope as the roof. Post-and-beam construction directs the weight of the roof to the ridge beam and the side walls. You'll need to hire a structural engineer to calculate the proper beam size and other structural details. Structural beams are expensive, and installing adequate insulation and good roof venting can be tricky and time consuming.

Carpentry

TAPE MEASURES

Accurate Measurements

Q. *Even though I "measure twice and cut once," my scrap bin is still too full for my taste. What am I doing wrong?*

First, check to make sure that your tape isn't out of adjustment (see Tape Measure Tune-Up, right). Next, review these steps for reading and marking a measurement.

First, hook the tape measure's tip over one end of the board and pull the blade taut. Make sure that you haven't hooked one of the rivets that secures the tip to the blade. Next,

pull the tape measure's case 6 inches past the dimension you wish to mark off, tilt the blade so one edge lies flat on the board, and draw a V with your pencil so that the tip marks the exact measurement. Mark an X on the scrap side of the piece so that you know which side of the mark to place the blade on when you make the cut.

When you've finished marking the workpiece, lift the tape from the board and apply light pressure along the bottom of the blade as it retracts, so that the tape doesn't snap back too quickly and damage the tip.

Tilt the edge of the blade against the workpiece. Mark the measurement with the tip of a V and the waste with an X.

Eating an Inch

Q. *What exactly do they mean when they say, "Eat an inch"? Is this really necessary?*

Carpenters will frequently "burn" or "eat" an inch, especially when they need a really accurate measurement. What they're doing is starting their measurement from the 1-inch mark, then subtracting an inch from the final reading.

Why is it necessary to burn an inch? You'll notice that your tape

measure's tip is loosely riveted to the blade so that it moves slightly. Ideally, this movement is equal to the thickness of the tip. This is so the tip can adjust to zero to give a correct measurement whether you're making an inside measurement (with the tip pressed against the board) or an outside measurement (with the tip hooked over a board). But few tapes are perfect. And in some situations, such as when measuring mitered stock, it's impossible to hook the blade over the workpiece.

Tape Measure Diamonds

Q. *My tape measure has diamond-shaped markings at about 19³⁄₁₆ inches, 38⁷⁄₁₆ inches, and so on. What are these marks for?*

The special markings you're referring to are used by carpenters when they want to save material without sacrificing strength. If you were to frame an 8-foot-long section of wall using these measurements, you'd use one less stud than the traditional 16-inch on-center spacing, but one more stud than with 24-inch on-center spacing. Because the numbers aren't whole numbers, the spacing system is more difficult to use.

The hook is slightly loose to adjust for its own thickness when making inside or outside measurements.

Start at the 1-in. mark when you can't hook your board. Remember to "eat," or subtract, an inch from the measurement.

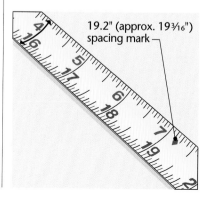

19.2" (approx. 19³⁄₁₆") spacing mark

Tape Measure Tune-Up

Q. *Why do I get different results measuring the same distance with two different tapes?*

Most problems with irregular measurements are caused by a damaged slip hook. The hook can bend when the tape is dropped and you may not notice it until you've measured something, cut it, and found it doesn't fit. A bent or otherwise stuck hook can also lead to frustrating differences between inside and outside measurements or cause you and your helper to get different readings from different tapes.

To check your tape, try both inside and outside measurements, then double-check your results by "eating an inch" (see p.170). If your tape's hook is out of adjustment, you should be able to bend it back with a pair of pliers.

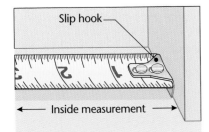

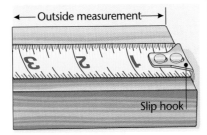

Carpenter's Pencils

Q. *Why are carpenter's pencils flat? Is there any significance to their size and shape?*

Few tools are as well designed or work as hard as the lowly carpenter's pencil. Their thick, flat bodies make them easy to grip, especially in the cold, and keep them from rolling off surfaces like roof decks and planks. They are also easy to sharpen with a utility knife.

Carpenter's pencils can be used instead of a compass to scribe small gaps. When used with the smaller flat side against a wall, the carpenter's pencil will mark a line about ⅛ inch from the wall. If you scribe with the wide side, you'll get a line about ¼ inch in from the wall.

how is it done?

GETTING EVERY INCH FROM YOUR TAPE MEASURE

Your tape can serve as a giant compass, a straightedge, or even a simple hand-held calculator. Here's how:

■ To create a circle or arc, first drive a nail at the center of your circle as a pivot point. Next, hook the tip of your tape over the head of the nail. Holding a pencil against the tape at the desired radius, draw your arc. (You may find that it's easier to draw a series of small arcs rather than an entire circle.)

■ To mark a line parallel to the edge of a board, hook the tip of your tape over the edge of the board. With the pencil held firmly on the desired measurement, pull the tape along the edge. Keep the blade perpendicular to the edge.

■ To quickly divide a board into halves, thirds, or any fraction, angle the blade across it with one end on zero and the other on a number that's easily divided by the number of pieces; then mark it into equal sections.

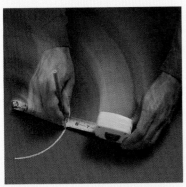

Use your tape measure to help draw circles of any size. Keep tension on the blade to prevent it from kinking.

Mark lines parallel to the edge of the board by hooking the tip over the edge and guiding the pencil toward you.

Divide boards into equal parts by angling the blade to an easily divided number, then marking off the parts.

Carpentry

On-the-Level Level

Q. *I've been using the same level for years, and I am beginning to think that it might be slightly out of whack. How can I check to be sure?*

An inaccurate level is a disaster waiting to happen. Levels can be damaged by being dropped, bent, or stored in extreme hot or cold.

To test your level, set it on a table, then shim one end until the tool reads perfectly level. Next flip the level end for end. The bubbles should still be centered between the lines on the vial. Repeat this test in the plumb (vertical) position on a vertical surface.

A cheap level that's not reading true should be discarded. With better-quality levels, you can adjust the vials yourself. Some manufacturers will replace the vials and, if necessary, straighten the level.

Just because a level is new doesn't mean that it's accurate. Test a new level in the store before you buy.

To test a level, shim one end until the bubble is centered, then flip end-for-end.

Splitting an Angle

Q. *I'm trying to install trim in a room with several oddly angled corners. What's the best way to measure the angles to set my saw?*

While you could use a drafting protractor to measure the exact angle, an easier and more precise method for making the cut does away with numbers altogether. Here's how to do it:

■ First draw two lines parallel to the walls. The simplest way to do this is to lay your trim against the floor and draw a pencil line along the outside edge of the wood.

■ Next draw a line from the corner of the wall through the intersection of the two lines. The line you just drew is the bisected angle. Use a bevel gauge to transfer this angle to your saw, and make your cut.

■ To ensure that the front edges fit tightly together, ease the back edge of the molding with a block plane.

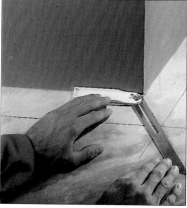

Use a bevel gauge to transfer the angle to your power miter saw.

Use the lines to position the wood. Shave the back face to make the front fit tightly.

Chalk Colors

Q. *My hardware store carries several different colors of powdered chalk. Does it matter what color I use, or are certain colors used for special applications?*

While there is no formal code dictating which colors should be used where, most carpenters will use certain colors of chalk for different jobs because they're easier to brush off, especially tenacious, or more visible. Before you fill up your chalk box, here are some of the attributes of each color:

■ White chalk is the most easily removed of all the colors. It's often used to snap lines for wallpapering or to mark dark surfaces.

■ Blue chalk is highly visible, yet it is easy to brush off most surfaces (except very porous ones), making it ideal for marking lines you will want wash off. Most carpenters use blue as their all-purpose chalk.

■ Red chalk is permanent. It's used by roofers, tile layers, and carpenters for marking lines they want saved for several days.

■ Fluorescent orange and yellow are also permanent. Both are easily seen in low light, such as in basements.

Chalk Line Defined

Q. *I'm a fairly new DIY'er, so could you tell me what a chalk line is, and what it's used for?*

A chalk line is nothing more than a reel of string with a crank (like a fishing reel) that's enclosed in a plastic or metal case, which is filled with powdered chalk. The chalk clings to the string as it's pulled from the case, and releases when the string is pulled taut and snapped against a surface. This leaves a long straight line that you can use as a guide for cutting, nailing, straightening, or positioning.

To snap a line, simply hook the end over a board or bent-back nail, flip the reel out of the lock socket, then keep the string taut as you let it unwind from the case. Raise the string 3 or 4 inches squarely from the surface, then let go. If you're working with a partner, you can usually get two or three "snaps" without rewinding (and rechalking) the line.

If you need a very precise line, give the line a midair snap before lowering it on the surface to make the mark. This preliminary snap will get rid of the extra chalk that can make a blurry line. For lines over 20 feet long, press the line down at the mid-point, then snap both sides.

To mark long lines, use a double snap. Press the line down at the midpoint, then snap each side.

Measure Once, Cut Twice

Q. *I'm planning to finish my basement. The wall studs need to be 92½ inches long. What's the easiest way to cut a roomful of studs down to size?*

Building a cut-off jig will save time and eliminate the errors that can creep into making the same measurement over and over again.

To build a jig, measure and cut your first piece very carefully; then use it as a template to mark the rest of your cuts. Attaching a stop block at one end will make it easier to line up your stock. It's best to attach the block with screws; nails can wiggle loose and cause you to make progressively longer cuts.

Speed Square Secrets

Q. *What exactly is a Speed Square, and what's the advantage to having one?*

Speed Square is a brand name for a fairly recent invention that has replaced the try square in just about every carpenter's tool pouch. Not only can this square give you measurements and reliable 90- or 45-degree angles, but the tongued lip also allows you to hold the square securely in place against the edge of a board so you can use it as a guide for your circular saw.

The Speed Square is also a quick and nifty angle finder. Using the end of the tongued lip as a pivot point, tilt the triangle to read the angle stamped on the diagonal arm. Some squares have a pivoting guide that locks in place to make repeated angle cuts (for stairs or rafters), replacing a standard framing square.

Because a Speed Square is a single triangular piece of metal, it won't lose accuracy if dropped.

Use a Speed Square to make accurate 45° and 90° cuts. Hold the lip of the square against the board; then use the edge to guide your circular saw.

To find an angle, hold the pivot point against the board, rotate the triangle, then read the angle on the diagonal arm.

Carpentry

NAILING TECHNIQUES

How to Toenail

Q. *What is "toenailing" and how do I do it?*

Toenailing is joining two boards together by nailing at an angle through the end, or toe, of one board into the face of the other. You need to toenail when you attach a stud to the bottom plate of a wall.

Driving toenails will frequently split your stock, but sometimes they are the only way to join two boards.

To toenail a stud, position the stud on end about ¼ inch to one side of your layout line. Hold the opposite side of the stud with your foot, a block nailed to the plate, or a partially driven nail. Hold the nail pointing slightly down about an inch above the bottom of the stud and tap the point in about ⅛ inch; then push the head up to a 60° angle and drive it in. Don't worry if the last few blows move the stud a bit beyond the mark; it should slide back into position when you drive nails in from the other side. To drive the nails in farther without moving the stud, use a nail set. Toenail both sides for maximum strength. Stagger the nails so that they don't hit each other.

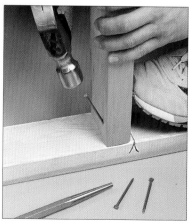

When toenailing, start each nail at a 30° angle, 1 inch above the end of the stud.

A Perfect Finish

Q. *How do I set finish nails without denting the surrounding wood with my hammer?*

A nail set is a punch-shaped tool designed to sink, or set, nails beneath the surface of the wood. To use a nail set, position its point over the head of the nail and strike the top with a hammer. Fill the hole with wood putty.

Pulling Nails

Q. *Are there any tricks to pulling out nails?*

There's nothing complex about removing nails—you just grab and pull. However, you do need to be careful when pulling nails with a wood-handled hammer—it's easy to break the handle. If the nail is stuck, use a crowbar for extra leverage.

If the nailhead is slightly recessed into the wood and you can't get the hammer's claw under it, give the wood next to the nail one good whack. This sudden jarring often loosens the nail enough to get the claws under it. If the nailhead is still buried in the wood, use a cat's paw. Hit the cat's paw with a hammer to dig its claw around the nailhead and lever it out.

To remove trim, drive the nails all the way through with a nail set. You can also use nippers or locking pliers to pull nails through the back side of the trim without marring the surface.

Be sure to pull out or bend over nails that are in the boards you take apart. The extra time spent pulling or bending will prevent someone from stepping on a nail and puncturing their foot.

Set finish nails about ⅛ inch below the surface of the wood, and fill with putty.

Hit the cat's paw with a hammer and the claws will dig around the nailhead so you can lever it out.

Grip finish nails with carpenter's nippers and pull them through the back side of the wood to keep the good side intact.

Nailing Without Splitting

Q. *I'm embarrassed to say how many times I've tried to drive a nail and wound up splitting the wood. What can I do to prevent this from happening?*

To avoid splitting the wood, try blunting the point of the nail with a light hammer blow. Sharp nails spread the wood fibers apart as they're driven in; blunt nails crush the wood fibers. Another option is to try nailing into the lighter part of the wood, not on the grain lines. The darker grain lines are harder and are more likely to be the start of a split.

The best solution is to drill a pilot hole for the nail. To do this, select a drill bit that's slightly smaller in diameter than the nail. (An old-time trick is to clip the head off a finish nail and use it as a drill bit. Finish nails are readily available but tend to get dull rather quickly. For bigger jobs, use a drill bit.)

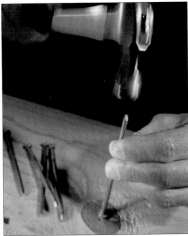

Blunt the nail tip to keep it from splitting the wood. Place the nail's head on a hard surface; then hit the tip with a hammer.

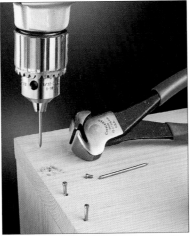

Make a makeshift drill bit by cutting off the head of a finish nail and tightening the nail in your drill chuck.

Clinching a Nail

Q. *The pickets on my picket fence keep working themselves loose. What can I do to keep things tight?*

Ever hear the expression, "dead as a doornail"? Doornails were clinched, or "deadened," to make them impossible to remove. Clinching is also a safe way to deal with protruding nails. To clinch a nail, bend the tip with the hammer claw, then pound it down until it bites into the wood.

Clinching nails will keep them tight. Bend the nail's tip with your hammer; then pound it until it bites into the wood.

Need a Hand?

Q. *I'm building a deck by myself. Do you have any tricks for positioning joists single-handedly?*

There's a lot more that you can do with nails than just pound them in. To install joists single-handedly, try driving a common nail about ¾ inch into the top edge of the wood, then bending the nail over so that it sticks out over the end. Use the bent nail as a hanger to position the joist.

Bent-over nails can act as an extra set of hands for positioning lumber.

Holding Little Nails

Q. *What can I do to avoid hitting my fingers or denting the wood when I drive finish nails?*

A small strip of cardboard will hold the nail in place and will also protect the woodwork if you should happen to miss the nailhead with your hammer. (Cedar shingles also make excellent nail holders.)

Begin by pushing the nail halfway through the cardboard. Position the nail and drive it in. Once the nail is driven, pull the cardboard free and set the nail with a nail set.

Workshop Tools

what do you need?

TOOLING UP FOR DIY PROJECTS

You don't need a garage full of tools for most home improvement tasks. Many jobs don't require a lot of tools, but they do require the right tools. To help decide which tools you need to buy, we have created a three-tiered approach. First buy a set of "survival" tools to handle home emergencies and minor do-it-yourself chores. As your skills improve and your projects become more complex, buy more tools as you need them. Our "home improvement" list shows what you typically would need. You may never need the tools in our "wish list," but they can make many jobs easier.

SURVIVAL TOOLS

■ Stepladder. A must for painting rooms or cleaning gutters. Wood ladders are twice as heavy as fiberglass or aluminum. Do not use an aluminum stepladder if you do electrical work.

■ Miter box and miter saw. These tools work for square cuts and molding jobs.

■ Drill. A ⅜-inch corded, variable-speed drill is the tool for putting up curtain rods, mounting deadbolts, and screwing down deck boards. A heavy-duty model should last a lifetime.

■ Handsaw. 15-inch saws that fit in a toolbox are great for cutting shelves.

■ Putty knife. For filling nail holes and scraping paint.

■ Utility knife. Takes care of all sorts of cutting jobs.

■ Measuring tape. A 25-foot-long metal tape might be bulky, but the 1-inch-wide blade is stiff enough to measure long spans like ceiling heights and wall widths without bending.

■ Hammer. A 16-ounce steel-handle hammer drives nails and serves as as a pry bar, nail puller, and wrecking bar.

■ Plunger. The cure for stopped-up plumbing. The extra bell-type collar on the newer models creates a better seal for better plunging.

■ Groove-joint pliers. Plumbing repairs are inevitable. Large (10-inch) pliers can tighten those 1½-inch slip nuts that hold the P-trap under the sink.

■ Four-in-one screwdriver. This tool has two sizes of both slotted and Phillips tips in the handle. This avoids the hassle of hunting down the right screwdriver for the job.

■ Slip-joint pliers. This tool's jaws have flat and curved areas to grip or crimp a variety of objects. The jaws slip on the pivot post to adjust the size of the jaw opening.

HOME IMPROVEMENT TOOLS

■ Level. Any level at least 24-inches long will do the job. Higher priced models offer ruggedness and long-term accuracy. Consider buying a case to protect your level from job-site mishaps.

■ Caulk gun. To seal a tub, fix a drafty window, or glue insulation panels, simply load the gun with the right tube of caulk or adhesive.

■ Framing square. In addition to framing and stair-building, a square makes a great straightedge and is also good for checking 90° angles.

■ Safety equipment. Glasses and hearing protection are essential companions.

Leather gloves protect your hands during heavy work. A half-face respirator offers the best protection against insulation particles and sawdust.

■ Pry bar and cat's paw. These are two essential tools for pulling boards and pulling nails.

■ Clamps. Buy a few to get started, then add more to your collection as needed.

■ Angle square. This triangular-shaped tool can do almost everything that a framing square can, plus it fits in your tool pouch.

■ Chisels. Pick up a set for installing locksets and trimming wood. Be sure to learn how to sharpen them.

■ Tool belt. This companion keeps essential tools close by. Look for one that has extra pockets for screws and nails.

■ Block plane. The tool that shaves wood for great-fitting doors, floors, and trim.

■ Extension cord. Buy a heavy-duty 12- or 14-gauge 50-foot cord to deliver the power where you need it.

■ Chalk line. Makes marking drywall cuts and rows of shingles a snap.

■ Circular saw. The power tool for any carpentry project.

■ Shop vacuum. The perfect clean-up companion for wet or dry jobs.

WISH LIST

■ Jigsaw. This portable tool can make straight or curved cuts in wood and other materials. A 3.5-amp motor will provide enough power for all cutting chores.

■ Power miter saw. A "chopsaw" is great for trimming studs or cutting miters. Shop for a saw that has the capacity to cut the widest stock you may want to cut.

■ Router. From decorative edge treatments to joinery, this is the ultimate portable woodworking tool. With a variety of bits, jigs, and accessories, a router can do the work of a shop full of large stationary machines.

■ Cordless drill. Cordless drills can do almost anything corded models can and offer unlimited freedom of movement around the job site. A 12-volt or larger drill will have plenty of power. Buy an extra battery to eliminate down time.

■ Bench-top table saw. Table saws are ideal for ripping and crosscutting lumber and plywood. A bench-top saw is less powerful than the larger contractor's saw, but you can carry it wherever it's needed.

Remodeling

HEAVY LIFTING

Adjustable post

Bottle jack

Brains over Brawn

Q. *How can I temporarily lift up a corner of my deck to replace a damaged post?*

A hydraulic, or "bottle," jack is cheap, fast, and very powerful; a jack that is rated for 10 tons costs about $40 at home centers.

The tool is simple to operate, but you need to know a few things to lift safely and effectively. For starters, don't leave weight on the jack for more than a day; otherwise the fluid will leak and the jack will begin to lower. If you need to keep something lifted for a long duration, instead of a jack use a block for a low load or an adjustable post for a higher one.

When extending the jack's reach with a post, make sure it's plumb; otherwise it may kick out. Nail diagonal braces to the post for additional support. Use the jack on firm ground or on a solid footing; otherwise it may pump itself into the ground.

Perfect Post Puller

Q. *My fence was installed before the days of pressure-treated wood, and the posts have rotted out. What's the best way to lift out a damaged post?*

You can use the handyman jack, or "hi-lift." This type of jack resembles a king-size bumper jack; most are rated to lift 3 tons up to a height of 3 feet. The toe of the jack will fit into an opening of just 4 inches, and you can attach a rope or chain onto the top of the jack to use it as a winch. There is nothing better for lifting logs, pulling stubborn fence posts, or lifting a trailer tongue.

Preventing Injuries

■ The best ways to prevent injuries are to exercise, stay fit, and use proper body mechanics when lifting, carrying, climbing, or working with tools.
■ Many aches and pains are the result of many, many "micro-injuries" or Cumulative Trauma Disorders (CTD's). These injuries are caused by the sum total of thousands of hammer blows or hundreds of improper lifts. If you perform these kinds of tasks, look for special wrist, elbow or back supports. These kind of personal protection devices can reduce the risk of injury from repeated stress and vibration.

Tilt-In 2 x 4's

Q. *I want to replace the small window in our dining room with one that's 3 feet wider. What's the best way to support the wall? And how can I lift the new header in place?*

First, you'll need to build a temporary shoring wall within 2 feet of the exterior wall to prevent the wall from shifting or sagging.

To protect the floor and ceiling, tack plywood strips to them. Then nail horizontal 2 x 4's to these plywood strips. Cut temporary studs ¼ inch longer than the space between the 2 x 4's and wedge and hammer the studs into place between the horizontal plates. Position the strips directly beneath the existing overhead floor joists. (You may want to nail a horizontal 2 x 4 midway up one side of the temporary wall to prevent the studs from bowing under the weight.)

Use the same tilt-in technique to install the new header tightly in place over the window opening (see photo, right). In this case, you will need to clip both upper corners of the header so that it can clear the surrounding wood.

Cut the 2 x 4's to the exact height of the opening minus the height of the header. Place one end of the header on top of one of the studs; then use a 3-pound sledgehammer to tap the opposite stud in place. As you straighten the 2 x 4, it will lever the header into place.

A 2 x 4 cut ¼ inch longer than the ceiling height can be used to lift and support the wall. Place plywood under the stud wall to protect the floor.

Use a 3-lb. sledge to straighten the stud and lift the header. Cut the top corners off the header so that it can be tilted into the opening.

Better Back Support

Q. *I've noticed that all of the employees at my lumberyard now wear back belts. Do back belts really work? When and how do I use one?*

Back support belts will not make you any stronger, but they can help prevent injuries. Back belts are designed to stabilize and support the muscles in the lower back (where 95 percent of all back injuries occur). The belts also work psychologically to remind you to use the correct body mechanics while lifting.

Most belts are secured in two stages. First secure the waistband snugly, with the upper edge about 1 inch below the navel. Then, just before lifting a heavy object, pull the outer elastic bands forward and tightly fasten them for additional support. Loosen the outer bands when not lifting.

When selecting a back support, choose one made of breathable material to prevent overheating. Look also for models with a slight dip in the back to provide extra support. The suspenders don't add support, but they do help you to quickly and correctly position the belt before tightening the outer bands and lifting.

Back supports promote proper body posture and lifting position while also helping support the muscles of the back.

Remodeling

REGULATIONS

Home Inspectors

Q. *I've heard about the American Society of Home Inspectors and would like to know more about the services they provide. What will one of their inspections reveal?*

According to the American Society of Home Inspectors (ASHI), a home inspection is a visual examination of the physical structure and systems of the house. It includes a visual exam of the heating system, the central air-conditioning system, the interior plumbing and electrical systems, the roof and visible insulation, walls, ceilings, floors, windows and doors, the foundation, basement, and the visible structure.

The report doesn't give a home a failing or passing grade. It provides an examination of the current conditions of the property and indicates which item(s) will be in need of immediate or near future repair or maintenance. A routine inspection usually costs about $350.

To locate a home inspector, check the Yellow Pages under "Building Inspection Services." To find the ASHI member nearest you, or to obtain a free pamphlet, "The Home Inspection and You," write to American Society of Home Inspectors, 932 Lee Street, Suite 101, Des Plains, Illinois 60016, or call (800) 743-2744.

how is it done?

FIGURING SQUARE FOOTAGE

There are two basic methods for figuring the square footage of a house. If you're comparing two houses, you need to ask how the square footage of the house was determined.

Builders, appraisers, and tax assessors mostly use "overall square footage." They measure the outside foundation of the house and multiply the length by the width. Then they multiply this number by the number of floors; basements are included if they're finished living space. This figure tells you the physical size of the house, but it doesn't tell you how much actual living space there is.

Most people are interested in knowing the living space. If you measure the floor area of each room that you'd actually live in (bedrooms, bathrooms, kitchen, and living room, but not closets, halls, storage areas, or garage) and add them all together, you get the "usable" or "livable square footage."

Add up the square footage of the closets, pantries, and other storage areas to get the square footage of storage space. Unfinished basements either are considered storage space or aren't considered at all.

Insurance Coverage During Remodeling

Q. *I've been told that homeowner's insurance won't cover our house during remodeling. Is this true?*

We aren't aware of any insurance company that will suspend your home's insurance just because you're remodeling. But let your agent know if you are making changes that could affect your coverage.

If you're doing the work yourself, your insurance should cover the remodeling, including any materials stored in your home. Keep receipts in case you have a claim. If contractors do the work, it's their responsibility to provide insurance—ask to see a certificate before you sign a contract. They should be covered for any injuries or damage to your home connected with the remodeling.

No Building Code

Q. *I'm restoring an older house in a township that doesn't have a building inspector, just a zoning inspector. Am I even subject to building codes in my area?*

It's entirely possible that you aren't covered by any building code.

There is no national building code, and individual states can either choose to adopt one of the "model" codes, have no code, write their own, or have one that affects only public buildings. Local city governments are usually responsible for enforcing building codes, although in unincorporated or rural areas, they sometimes choose not to do so.

Check with your city and county government first. If there are no requirements, check at the state level. While you're asking, check on the electrical code, which is separate from the building code.

Home Seller's Disclosure Obligation

Q. *My brother did most of his own remodeling work (including a new kitchen and master bath) in his home, which he's now trying to sell. No major plumbing or electrical changes were made, but none of the work was inspected. Is my brother required to tell a prospective buyer that he did the remodeling?*

The requirement for on-site inspection of home improvement or remodeling work, whether it was performed by the homeowner or a professional, is controlled by local building or zoning codes. These codes are different from city to city, so check with your local building inspector for accurate information.

Generally speaking, it's the seller's obligation to disclose to the buyers only those material defects of which he or she is actually aware. Where the sellers have performed work that they believed followed local codes, they can't reveal a defect if they believe that no defect exists. On the other hand, if the seller knows that the work was not up to code, then he or she is obligated to disclose those facts to potential buyers.

The safest course for home sellers is to advise all potential buyers that they performed certain repairs or improvements to their home. This way, the buyers can satisfy themselves that those improvements are acceptable.

Frequently, buyers will have a house professionally inspected. The cost of the inspection is minimal when you consider that it may detect a major defect in the house. Sellers can also hire a inspector to check their home for any potential trouble spots that may slow down a sale.

Identifying House Problems

IF YOU'RE THINKING OF BUYING A HOME, chances are you will hire a home inspector to identify and report on any problems before you buy. Since you can't know everything about plumbing, electricity, carpentry, and roofing, hiring an inspector makes sense.

Here's a list of the fifteen most common house problems:

- Damaged exterior paths and steps
- Inadequate attic ventilation and insulation
- Inadequate crawl space insulation
- Wet-basement problems
- Electrical problems
- Heating system problems
- Deteriorating roof shingles
- Missing or damaged gutters
- Fire hazards
- Deteriorated or improperly vented plumbing
- Termites
- Hazardous steps/stairs
- Water heater improperly installed
- Windows with damaged sash cords
- Problems with the garage

Not all of these are major concerns. The inspection report will identify the repairs that are essential and those that will involve significant costs, and if necessary, will suggest further investigations.

Remodeling

FINISHING A BASEMENT WITH STEEL STUDS

When it comes to making warm, clean finished walls in your basement, steel studs beat wood every time. Steel framing is easy to work with in confined basement spaces, costs less than wood, and screws together like a giant erector set. Because steel doesn't soak up water, it won't shrink or swell the way wood framing does. Walls are straighter and the drywall won't be as likely to develop cracks or pop-outs.

To finish the typical basement wall, you can use 25-gauge, 1⅝ x 1¼-inch studs. Compared to the more common 3⅝ x 1¼-inch steel studs, these skinny studs are easier to work with and are less expensive. They're a good choice for finishing a basement, but they can't be used for load-bearing walls. For doorway or partition walls, you should use wider studs.

To work with steel studs, you'll need a screw gun, hammer, drill, level, tin snips, clamps, tape measure, chalk box, plumb bob, pliers, leather gloves, dust mask, and hearing and eye protection.

The first step is to fasten the bottom plate, or track, to the floor. To do this, you can use self-tapping masonry screws or drive concrete nails with a power-activated nail gun. Position the studs about ¾ inch away from the foundation walls at the closest point. Snap a line on the floor 2½ inches away from the walls, and fasten the track along the line.

Framing a room with steel studs is as easy as twisting and popping the steel studs into the track, and then fastening them with a screw gun and pan-head screws.

Next use a plumb bob to align the upper track with the lower track (Photo 2). Screw the track to the floor joists with drywall screws. If the floor joists run parallel to the track, install short 2 x 4 bridges between the rim joist and the first joist into the room. Fasten the track to the bridges every 32 inches.

Install the corner framing first, using three studs with the two inside studs fastened together (as shown top right). Measuring out from the corner, mark the location

1

Overlap longer runs of track by a couple of inches and screw through the overlap. Use masonry screws or concrete nails.

2

Punch a hole in the track to start a screw. Use a clamp to hold the plumb bob along the outside of the track. If floor joists run parallel to the track, install short 2 x 4 bridges between the joists and attach the track 32 in. on center.

wall studs every 16 inches. Make sure that the end of an 8-foot sheet of drywall installed horizontally can be fastened to the center of a stud. (Remember to add ½ inch to the layout of the second wall, since it butts the drywall on the first wall.) Generally, you should position the studs so that they all face in the same direction. However, to frame the windows, you'll need to place studs at each side of the opening so that their webs face in. Position the studs so that the webs line up with the edges of the concrete window cuts.

To attach the wall studs to the floor track, clamp the front stud flange into the track and fasten them together with a pan-head screw. Fasten the rear stud flange to the track after flattening the back edge of the stud and placing a temporary backer block behind the track (Photo 3).

Build the windowsill from a length of track 2½ inches longer than the distance between the window studs. Make two cuts 1¼ inches deep on the end of the track and bend the web 90°. Install the windowsill flush with the bottom of the opening and level from side to side (Photo 4). Install wall stiffeners at the midpoint of the wall by fastening 3-inch-long angles to the foundation and to the webs of the wall studs (Photo 5). Create these angles by removing one flange from a 3-inch piece of stud.

Install ½-inch plywood to the window surrounds. Fasten the plywood to the steel framing with drywall screws and to masonry with construction adhesive or masonry screws. Hang the drywall; then install metal corner bead. Finish the plywood with conventional drywall taping techniques.

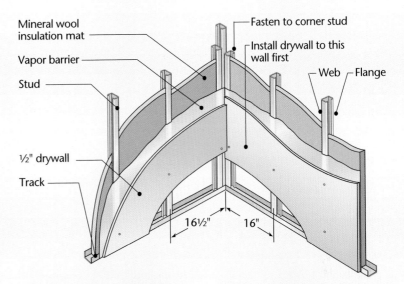

- Mineral wool insulation mat
- Vapor barrier
- Stud
- ½" drywall
- Track
- Fasten to corner stud
- Install drywall to this wall first
- Web
- Flange

16½" 16"

3

Use a temporary backer block to prevent the bottom flange from bending as you install the pan-head screw.

4

Make the sill from a length of track 2½ in. longer than the opening. Install a pan-head screw through the bent web.

5

Install the sill flush with the frame. Note the wall stiffener (bottom of photo) made from a 3-in. piece of stud.

6

Use ½-in.-thick plywood to finish the window surrounds. Butt the plywood against the window frame.

Remodeling

BASEMENT

Finished Basement Window Guidelines

Q. *We're finishing off the basement to include a bedroom for our son. How big does the window have to be to be used as a fire escape?*

A bedroom egress window must conform to a number of safety regulations. First, it must have a minimum clear area of 5.7 square feet. The minimum height of the opening is 24 inches and the width is 20 inches; the maximum height from the floor to the bottom of the opening is 44 inches. The window well also has to be at least 3 feet wide and 3 feet deep.

If the well exceeds 44 inches in depth, you must include steps or a ladder. If the window well is over 30 inches deep, you may also need to install a guardrail.

These codes are confusing, and inspectors interpret them differently.

Your best bet is to talk with a building inspector early in the planning stages. Keep in mind that furnaces, water heaters, and other carbon monoxide-producing equipment might be sharing the basement with your son. Be sure to install both carbon monoxide and smoke detectors.

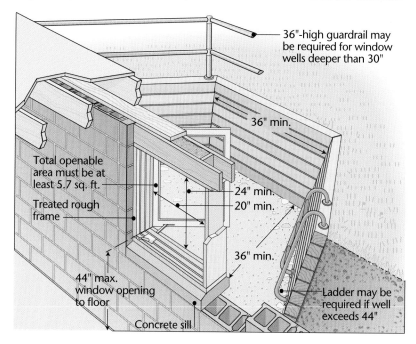

36"-high guardrail may be required for window wells deeper than 30"

36" min.

Total openable area must be at least 5.7 sq. ft.

Treated rough frame

24" min.
20" min.

36" min.

44" max. window opening to floor

Ladder may be required if well exceeds 44"

Concrete sill

Installing Window Wells

Q. *To improve drainage during heavy rains, I'd like to raise the grade along the foundation of our house. What do I do about the area in front of the two windows?*

First, you need to make sure that the new grade level will be 6 inches below any untreated wood such as the siding and framing members of your house.

What you now need are window wells. Start by marking the new grade line on the foundations with chalk. A slope of 2 inches per 10 feet is adequate for most areas. Dig out the area around the windows. Apply an exterior brush-on sealer up to the new grade mark and let it dry.

You can find galvanized steel window wells at your local lumberyard

or home center. Select wells that are at least 6 inches wider than the window openings and 6 inches deeper than the bottom of the windows.

Test-fit the wells in place against the foundation. Remove the wells temporarily and drill pilot holes for the anchors. Coat the back sides of

the wells' flanges with asphalt mastic; then fasten the wells to the foundation. If you need to install larger steel window wells, brace the insides of them while backfilling to prevent the wells from bending. Finally, add 3 inches of crushed rock at the bottom of each well.

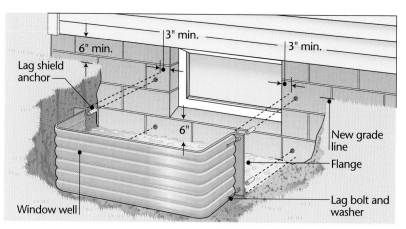

3" min.

6" min.

3" min.

Lag shield anchor

6"

New grade line

Flange

Window well

Lag bolt and washer

Framing Around Basement Windows

Q. *We'd like to hang drywall in our basement. What's the best way to frame around basement windows?*

When it comes to framing and hanging drywall, the space around basement windows can be tight. Install the framing flush with the masonry around the window. Glue ½-inch water-resistant drywall directly to the masonry, and then screw the edges of the drywall to the framing. You may need to temporarily brace the drywall in place while the adhesive sets.

If the space around the window frame is very tight, you can use ⅜-inch plywood instead, so that the window can open and close freely.

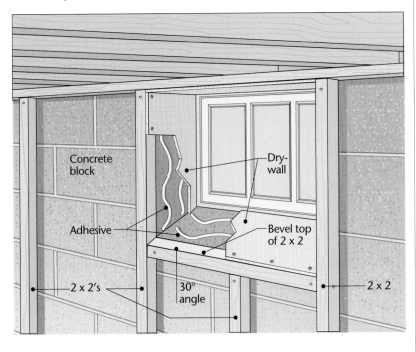

Leveling a Concrete Floor

Q. *My wife and I would like to convert our basement into a family room. How do I level the floor?*

If you have to deal with only a handful of low spots, leveling the floor is a job that you can easily do yourself. Place a long, straight 2 x 4 on the floor of the basement. Shine a flashlight on one side and mark the areas where the light shines through beneath the 2 x 4. Do this for the entire floor.

Once all the low spots are marked, fill them in with a self-leveling topping compound. Be sure to follow the directions carefully. Some mortar mixes require special floor preparation or a separate bonding agent. Pour the mix into the center of each low spot. The mortar will level itself, but you might want to use a trowel to feather out the edges.

If the floor is sloped or badly cracked, call a professional. Leveling a large area requires experience and special tools. A damaged floor may indicate other structural problems. If you have to add more than 2 inches of concrete to the floor, not only will you lose headroom, but it will cost about as much as tearing out the old floor and starting from scratch.

Fill cracks and level sloped sections of floor with a topping or leveling compound.

Sawing Concrete Walls

If your basement walls are poured concrete, you'll need to hire a pro to cut any door or window openings. The saw that the pros use for cutting masonry has a diamond blade and weighs about 150 pounds. Even if you can rent one, you may end up ruining the wall or injuring yourself.

Remodeling

Finding More Closet Space

Q. *We've run out of closet space. Is it better to build an extra closet in the basement or in the garage?*

Of those two choices, we'd pick the garage, but we don't advise storing your best clothing there. Try to re-examine your indoor storage possibilities. For example, are items being stored in clothes closets that could instead be kept elsewhere? The area under each bed offers a wealth of storage space. The backs of closet doors can be equipped with holders for shoes and other items. Almost any closet can hold more if properly organized. Consider making additional shelving or purchasing a closet organizer system. If the closet is deep enough, adding a second hanger bar can double existing storage space.

Closet Space Cures

Q. *My closets are just too small. Is there any way to design more closet space in the layout shown here without losing much floor space?*

If you are willing and able to sacrifice a bit of floor space, we may have an answer. Replacing your old closet doors with sliding or bifold doors will give you better access to the existing closets. You might also consider making better use of the dead space behind the door of bedroom B. By filling in one doorway to one closet and removing the opposite wall, you can create a double-wide closet for bedroom A. There are several storage solutions for bedroom B. Our illustration shows a new built-in wardrobe and a built-in dresser.

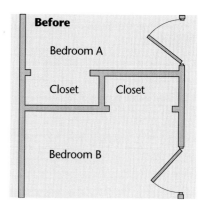

Before

Bedroom A

Closet   Closet

Bedroom B

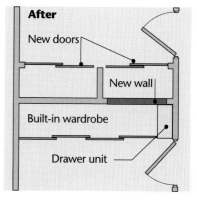

After

New doors

New wall

Built-in wardrobe

Drawer unit

The key to efficient storage is making the best use of every square inch. Consider making a custom cabinet, or buying a shelving system, that will give you the flexibility to size the height of the shelves to fit what they're holding. Below are some height guidelines for the things that fill up our shelves:

Compact discs	6 inches
Paperbacks	9 inches
Average books	11 inches
Magazines	11 inches
Display books	11 to 14 inches
Record albums	13 inches
Stereo equipment	17 inches
Television	24 inches or more

Attic Storage

Q. *There's a lot of room in my attic, but it's filled with blown-in insulation. What's the easiest way to make storage space up there?*

Strange as it may seem, most attics are not designed for storage. Heavy objects such as boxes of books and furniture can cause ceiling joists to sag and can damage plaster or drywall. However, lightweight objects, such as clothing or decorations, shouldn't cause any problems if they're stored properly.

If you decide to use the space for lightweight storage, you can build a simple plywood platform as shown. It will give you a solid reinforced area for setting boxes. The raised platform will also allow plenty of room underneath for the insulation.

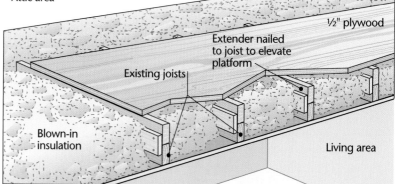

Attic area

½" plywood

Extender nailed to joist to elevate platform

Existing joists

Blown-in insulation

Living area

Safe Keeping

Q. *Exactly how safe are home safes? What's the strongest kind and how can I install one?*

If fire is your main concern, purchase a fire-rated safe. They're designed to withstand temperatures of 1,700° F for 1 hour without papers within being charred. Some can be bolted to the floor from inside to slow would-be thieves. Many home centers offer them for around $100.

If you want a safe that really stymies burglars, buy an in-floor safe. They're not only difficult to remove (though persistent burglars have been know to do so) but also easy to disguise (a rug can lay flat over them). Since they're encased in concrete, they also offer excellent fire resistance. A 1-cubic-foot in-floor safe costs about $400.

To install an in-floor safe in your existing home, you'll need to jack-hammer out a section of concrete at least 6 inches larger than the safe itself, position the safe, then pour concrete. In new homes, an area can be blocked off before the concrete is poured. Most in-floor safes are made of polyethylene or have a nylon inner lining to guard against moisture.

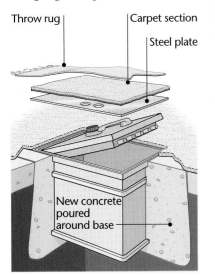

Throw rug | Carpet section | Steel plate | New concrete poured around base

BUILT-IN IRONING BOARD

One of the best ways to make more space is by taking advantage of unused space. This stowaway ironing board folds up into the wall and hides behind a cabinet door. With some units, installation is as simple as cutting away the drywall and screwing the premade cabinet in place. Other models, like the one shown here, have electrical outlets and indicator lights to let you know when the iron is on. (Installing a powered unit can take a few extra hours to a day, depending on the availability of power.) You can usually tap power from a nearby outlet, but keep in mind that irons draw up to 10 amps, so make sure you don't overload the circuit.

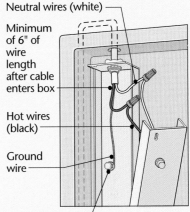

Neutral wires (white)

Minimum of 6" of wire length after cable enters box

Hot wires (black)

Ground wire

Ground screw

First, use a drywall saw to cut out a section of drywall between two studs. Position the opening so that the board will be at a comfortable ironing height. While the wall is opened up, run the electrical cable (if required) to the opening.

Mount the unit to the studs. The frame on most cabinets will cover the rough edge left by cutting. As you slip the unit into place, feed the electrical cable into the raceway or electrical box inside the cabinet.

Cut out a section of drywall between two studs just large enough for the ironing board cabinet.

Fasten the ironing board's case to the sides of the studs with 2-in.-long drywall screws.

Remodeling

DESIGN CONSIDERATIONS

Classic Columns

Q. *I own a small home that has a number of very small rooms. Apart from building an addition, is there a way to make the house feel bigger?*

A great way to transform smaller rooms, such as a cramped living room and dining room, into a great room is to knock out a wall and install decorative columns. The columns visually divide a large room into separate areas while simultaneously opening up the space.

Installing decorative columns isn't difficult. To keep the project simple, consider using paint instead of stain and varnish—your workmanship won't have to be perfect since you can putty over any imperfections.

The complexity of the project depends on the wall you're removing. Tearing out a non-load-bearing wall is a relatively easy task. Having to deal with a load-bearing wall and/or rerouting cable, pipes, and ducts will at least double the complexity of this job (see Bearing and Nonbearing Walls, p.158).

You can custom-order decorative columns from many home centers, but expect to wait at least one week for delivery. Consider using synthetic columns made of polyurethane or fiberglass instead of wood. They may cost a little more, but they are knot-free and are ready to paint. And, unlike wood, they will never develop hairline cracks. Be sure to note the column's "trimmable" measurement; overcutting a column could make it look out of proportion.

Removing a non-load-bearing wall and installing decorative columns can have a dramatic effect on your living space. Columns can be painted to complement other trim.

Work Triangle

Q. *I'm planning to remodel my kitchen and install new cabinets. I keep hearing about the "work triangle." Can you explain what this is and how it might improve my kitchen?*

Professional kitchen planners use the concept of a work triangle to help them design an efficient kitchen. Here's how it works:

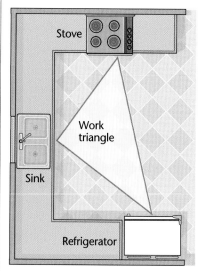

■ The kitchen has three primary work stations: the sink, the range/cook top, and the refrigerator. There should be countertop workspace next to each station.
■ These work stations should form a triangle with the sink in the middle to avoid long hikes to the stove or refrigerator.
■ The ideal distance around the whole triangle should be more than 12 feet (so you'll have enough counter space) but less than 23 feet. The same rule applies for L-shape or galley kitchens
■ If you use a microwave oven, be sure to locate it somewhere within the triangle.

Placing a Bay Window

Q. *I'd like to install a bay window in the kitchen, but my wife insists that it would look better in the living room. How can we decide who's right?*

You can put a bay window just about anywhere, but some locations work better than others. Here are a few guidelines to help you decide:

■ Structural limitations. Your local building inspector might make the decision for you. Structural limitations can limit the size of the window in a particular wall or determine if it's feasible to install one in the first place.

■ Interior limitations. Bay windows are cooler than regular windows during cold weather, and they tend to fog up faster, too. To compensate for this, you might have to adjust your heating system to avoid having a "cold spot."

■ Realize also that add-on bay windows aren't designed to serve as window seats. If you want a window seat, you'll need to frame out a walk-out bay, which is more work.

■ Exterior design. You'll want your new bay to look as though it were designed to be part of the original house, rather than a glued-on afterthought. Avoid projecting the bay out beyond the overhang of the roof, or it'll look like a mistake. Instead, use a shallow bay or extend the main roof over the bay.

■ Light. Considering the amount of light that a bay window lets in, you'll need to think about the effect of the extra sunlight. For example, a south-facing bay lets in the most sunlight. The east collects the morning sun and the west the evening sun. The north side gets the least sun. Unshaded south-facing windows can make a room hot.

■ View. Take advantage of the best view. A bay window is like a wide-angle camera lens—you'll see more through the sidelights and window than you would through the window alone. You will be maximizing your view by selecting a 30° bay or bow window.

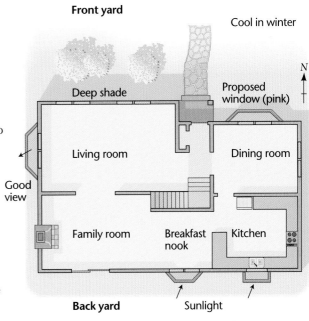

Front yard
Cool in winter
N
Deep shade
Proposed window (pink)
Living room
Dining room
Good view
Family room
Breakfast nook
Kitchen
Back yard
Sunlight

Choosing a Dormer

Q. *I want to add a couple of dormers to my house. How do I decide on an appropriate size and style?*

Consult with an architect, structural engineer, or builder to help you determine the type of dormer (a structure that projects from a sloping roof) that best fits the style and structure of your home. You may learn that your attic floors will need reinforcement if you intend to use the attic as a room.

Roof structure also plays a role in your decision. A hand-framed roof is the easiest to work with. A truss roof is much more complicated and requires detailed structural analysis.

The style of dormer you choose depends on structural concerns, your home's design, and your budget. The three basic styles are shed, gable, and hipped. The slope-roofed shed dormer often is the easiest to build, but you may have limited headroom at the exterior wall. The peaked gable dormer offers more design opportunities for the interior but is more complicated to build than the shed. The pyramid-shaped hipped dormer is attractive but the most complex and expensive to build.

Shed dormer

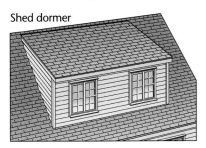

Gable dormer

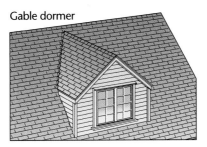

Hipped dormer

CONVERTING DECKS AND PORCHES

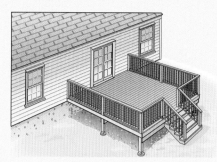

Converting a deck to a screened porch, or a screened porch into a three-season porch, is a tempting upgrade. With the basic structure in place, it seems as if it should be easy to do and relatively inexpensive. But this is not always the case.

The key to a simple conversion is to keep an eye to the future. In this example we'll start with a simple deck, then show what it takes to convert it to a screened porch. Then we'll make the screened porch into a three-season porch. As we go along, we'll alert you to common pitfalls and expenses.

CONVERTING A DECK TO A SCREENED PORCH

The first conversion is the toughest because you have to cover the deck with a new roof and attach the roof to the house. Compared with the cost of building a screened porch from scratch, this conversion can save you about 50 percent.

There are three questions you need to ask yourself before starting this project:

■ Is the deck sound? Inspect the deck carefully. If it shows signs of rot or is structurally inadequate to begin with, you're probably better off starting from scratch.

■ Is the deck really in the best spot for a screened porch? If not, then you probably will not be happy with your investment.

■ Can you attach the porch roof to the house? Stand back and imagine how the porch roof will meet the house. Windows, intersecting roof lines, and other details affect the shape of the roof. Again, consider whether a screened porch would fit better somewhere else.

Once you've decided to go ahead with the conversion, you'll need to focus your attention on the construction details:

■ Footings. The added weight of the new roof usually requires an increase in footing size. Unfortunately, the only way to inspect the footings is to dig them up (most building inspectors will require this). Rather than enlarging existing footings, many contractors prefer to install additional footings and posts to support the roof.

■ Structure. Unless you have building experience or can copy a preapproved design, you'll have to hire an architect or structural engineer to help design the roof and frame. A screened porch has to meet the same structural requirements as a full addition. You'll have to submit your plan for approval when you apply for a building permit.

■ Screening. The easiest way to install screening is to staple the screen to the post or framing members, then screw trim over the edges. It's easy to unscrew the trim and replace the screen if it gets damaged. You'll also have to staple screening to the bottom of the deck

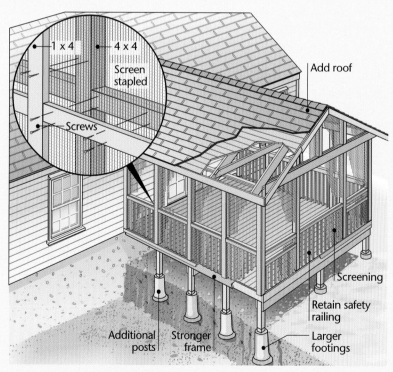

1 x 4

4 x 4

Screen stapled

Screws

Add roof

Screening

Retain safety railing

Additional posts

Stronger frame

Larger footings

to keep mosquitoes from sneaking in between the deck boards. If you choose to lay a solid floor covering, be sure that it has drain holes to allow for the rain that will blow in from time to time.

■ Railing. Screening itself isn't an adequate barrier. If your deck is more than 30 inches above the ground, you'll need a safety railing that satisfies the building code.

■ Electrical. Plan for overhead lighting. If you add wall receptacles, they must have waterproof covers.

CONVERTING A PORCH TO A THREE-SEASON PORCH

Technically, a three-season porch is not much more than a screened porch with windows. Still, finishing the interior will make it feel more like an interior room. Since the structure is already in place, converting a screened porch into a three-season porch can save at least half the cost of starting from scratch. The biggest cost is doors and windows, which will run you about $300 apiece.

Again, you should ask yourself a few questions before committing to this project:

■ Are you willing to lose your screened porch? From a building standpoint the job is a small one, but the effect is large. It'll be more comfortable during cool periods in the spring and fall, and it'll remain cleaner and drier, but you'll probably feel more closed in and cut off from the outdoors.

■ Size and shape. Each conversion that you decide on increases your commitment to a particular size, shape, and location. Are you sure this is the configuration you want?

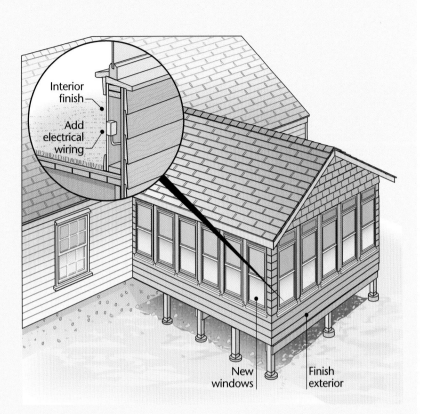

Construction Details:

■ Windows. Standard insulated windows are your best choice for all-around comfort. If you plan to finish off the interior, they also look the best. However, you can get by with combination storm windows at about one third of the price. Combinations have an upper and a lower pane of glass and a lower screen, so you can slide up the lower pane and catch the summer breezes. If you think that you might eventually convert the porch to a four-season room, the investment in regular double-pane windows will pay off.

■ Framing and exterior walls. Ideally, you can leave the structural members in place and frame the walls for standard-size windows. In this example, however, we had to reframe the walls so that the double-

hung windows would match the rest of the house. When the framing is complete, you'll also want to finish the exterior to match the house.

■ Insulation. Adding insulation while the walls are still open is an easy and inexpensive way to extend the comfort zone of a three-season porch by 2 months or more, even without heating or air conditioning.

■ Interior finish. Without a heating or cooling system, materials such as hardwood floors and carpeting will take a beating from humidity and temperature extremes. Select materials than can withstand fluctuating temperatures and moisture levels without significant damage.

■ Electrical. Wire the porch as if it were a regular room in your house. Be aware that you will be required to obtain an electrical permit.

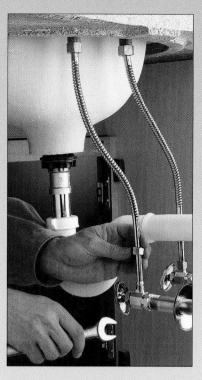

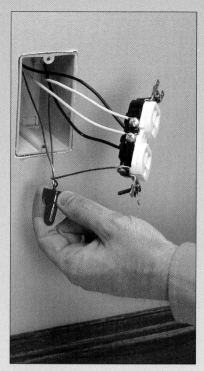

Plumbing

194 Small Bath Plumbing
196 Metal Pipe
200 Plastic Pipe
202 Toilet Repair
206 Installing Toilets
208 Clogged Pipes
210 Drains
214 Faucets
218 Shower Repairs
220 Kitchen Sinks
222 Fixtures
224 Bathtubs
226 Water Heaters
228 Water Heater Repairs

Electrical

230 Circuit Breakers and Fuses
232 Electrical Grounding
234 Electrical Safety
236 Electrical Wiring
238 Outlets
240 Ground Fault Circuit
       Interrupters
242 Switches
244 Lighting Fixtures
246 Recessed Lighting
248 Light Bulbs
250 Ceiling Fans
252 Motion Sensors and Doorbells

House
Systems

Appliances

254 Ovens and Stoves
256 Refrigerators and Freezers
258 Dishwashers
260 Washing Machines
262 Dryers

WHEN IT COMES TO understanding plumbing, the principles are elementary—but there's a lot more going on than meets the eye. It has taken generations of plumbers to perfect the system we now take for granted. Here's an overview explaining how the various pipes and fittings work together to bring water into, and take water out of, your home.

Drains, Traps, and Vents

The main waste line is a 4-inch-diameter cast-iron or PVC pipe. This pipe is called a "soil stack" when it runs vertically inside the house, and a "building drain" when it runs horizontally underground. Cast iron was once the standard material for all waste lines, but today most plumbers use white PVC plastic pipe. In some regions

you can also use black ABS plastic.

Ells (90° and 45° elbows), tees, and wyes are types of fittings used to direct the water flow from the plumbing fixtures through the waste lines and to the soil stack. All the fittings and lines should drop to the stack at a slope of ¼ inch per foot. A sanitary tee is a fitting designed so that when the vent and drainage pipes are plumb, the waste arm is at the proper slope.

Draining the waste water was never that difficult. For many years, the problem was keeping the sewer smells out of the house. Traps and vents work together as one-way valves, allowing water and waste to go down the drain while preventing sewer gas and and other unwanted house guests from coming in. Traps (such as the P-trap under your sink) hold a plug of water that

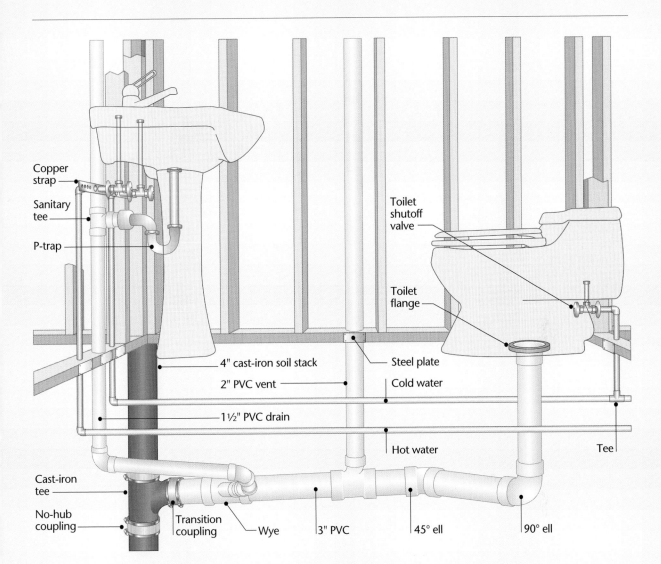

Copper strap

Sanitary tee

P-trap

Cast-iron tee

No-hub coupling

Transition coupling

Wye

3" PVC

45° ell

90° ell

4" cast-iron soil stack

2" PVC vent

1½" PVC drain

Steel plate

Cold water

Hot water

Tee

Toilet shutoff valve

Toilet flange

seals off the pipe. Vents equalize air pressure in your plumbing system so the traps remain filled with water. Without a vent, the water plug can be siphoned out by the vacuum created when water runs down a common drainpipe. Every fixture has a trap to keep sewer gas from entering the house, and every trap is vented.

Some fixtures, like second-story bath fixtures, can use the main stack for venting. Others, like a first-floor bath or kitchen sink, must use additional vent pipes. The vent may connect to the soil stack above the uppermost bath, or it may require a separate vent stack through the roof, depending on your house's requirements and the local codes. Always have an inspector review your venting plan before adding or moving plumbing fixtures.

Water Supply Lines

Because of their flexibility, water supply lines are installed after the drains and vents. Water lines can be snaked to fit almost anywhere, however the trick is to maintain water pressure. As a rule, ½-inch pipe should serve only two cold-water fixtures; for additional fixtures you'll need a ¾-inch-diameter water pipe. (Hot-water lines can serve more than two fixtures since hot water is used less frequently.) To save soldering time and help maintain good water pressure, the ells and tees in supply lines should be kept to a minimum. Supply lines to fixtures should each have a shutoff valve to make future repairs and replacements easier.

Remember that the building inspector must approve all plumbing work before pipes are enclosed in walls.

Plumbing

No-Leak Pipe Joints

Q. *When you're joining iron pipe, which gives you a tighter seal—pipe compound or Teflon tape?*

Pipe compound and Teflon tape serve several functions: They seal the threads to prevent leaks; they lubricate the pipe and fittings so they screw together and come apart more easily; and on galvanized pipe where threads have been cut outside of the factory, tape or compound also helps rustproof the threads.

The trick to using Teflon tape is to wrap it around the male threads clockwise so it doesn't bunch up when the fitting is screwed on (also clockwise).

The only trick to using pipe compound is to use plenty of it on the male threads—but not so much that globs of it wind up inside the pipe.

Which works better? Compound and tape both work well. Some pros apply tape and then compound for the tightest possible seal.

Wind Teflon tape around the male threads in the clockwise direction.

Copper and Galvanized Pipe Incompatibility

Q. *Several years ago I used copper tubing to extend some existing galvanized pipes. Now the copper pipe has greenish "pit holes" in it and is starting to leak. A friend told me I shouldn't have connected copper to galvanized. What do I do?*

Your friend is right. Copper and galvanized pipe should never be connected directly together. Since your copper pipes are beginning to leak, you should replace all of the piping that is showing signs of deterioration and where there is a direct copper-to-galvanized connection.

When you replace the pipes, connect the copper to the galvanized with a dielectric fitting. These can be couplings, unions, or nipples. Dielectric fittings separate the two metals, preventing the interaction that corrodes the pipe. Nipples that are at least 4 inches long do the best job of stopping this chemical process.

Not all hardware stores or home centers carry dielectric fittings; you might have to go to a plumbing contractor or plumbing supply house to find them.

Old Lead Joints

Q. *I'm rerouting some water pipes. Since the original copper piping is pretty old, I'm sure it contains lead. Is it safe to reuse the fittings if I resolder them with no-lead solder?*

We don't recommend that you reuse the old copper fittings. Small amounts of lead solder will probably remain on them and possibly leach into your drinking water—presenting a health hazard. It's also difficult to get the new joint to seal when you

use lead-free solder over old solder, because the two have different melting points.

It's aggravating when a plumbing joint leaks, so don't increase the odds of it happening to you by using an old fitting. Cut the old ones out and replace them. It's fine to use the old copper pipe.

⚠️ When you have finished working on an older plumbing system, remove the faucet aerators and let the water run for a full 5 minutes. This will flush out any particles that may have been dislodged.

The Lead Dilemma

■ Ingesting or inhaling lead can lead to high blood pressure, kidney damage, muscle weakness, and damage to reproductive organs. Children are at the greatest risk of lead poisoning.

■ Your home's plumbing system may contain lead in several forms: pipes installed before 1930; the solder used to join copper pipes and fittings until about 1987; and faucets with brass fittings and spouts. The distribution system delivering water to your home may also contain lead. Other sources of lead in the home include flaking or peeling paint and lead-contaminated dust.

■ If you suspect your plumbing contains lead, don't drink, cook, or make baby formula with water from the hot-water faucet. (Hot water dissolves lead more readily than cold water.) Also, if water has been sitting in the pipes for 6 hours or more, flush the pipes by running water through them for a minute.

■ Call your local health department for more information.

Freezing Pipes

Q. *Each winter, when we get a string of really cold days the water supply line to my kitchen sink freezes. The pipes haven't broken yet, but I feel I'm on borrowed time. How can I correct this?*

Most kitchen sinks are located against an outside wall, where the supply pipes are prone to freezing in cold climates. The problem is usually found in older homes with poor insulation. Here are a few suggestions:

■ Reinsulate the area behind the sink base cabinet.

■ If the pipes are in the exterior wall, move them inside the cabinet.

■ If the pipes aren't in the wall, add vents or louvers to the doors of the sink cabinet to help air circulate around them.

■ Wrap heat tape around the pipes to keep them warm during cold days.

Removing Mineral Deposits

Q. *My 40-year-old home has its original steel plumbing. Is there any way to remove the mineral deposits that have collected in the pipes? I'd like to avoid replacing all the pipes.*

You can try lightly tapping on the pipes with a hammer, or running electrician's fish tape into them, to knock the deposits loose. This process can be time-consuming and difficult, and the success rate is unpredictable. The particles are difficult to remove, and when loosened may then plug faucets and drains.

The most reliable solution is to replace the horizontal pipes in your basement, and the verticals you can easily get at, with new copper piping. To learn more about this kind of job, talk to a plumber.

The four major types of water supply tubes are (from top) flexible plastic, braided stainless steel, ribbed chrome, and chrome-plated copper.

Water Supply Tubes

WATER SUPPLY TUBES connect sinks, toilets, and shutoff valves to the water supply lines that protrude from the wall. There are four types:

■ **Braided Tube**

Braided tube is easy to install because you don't cut it. You buy the size closest to the length you need, then flex it to fit. Unlike other supply tubes, the connector nuts at both ends are preattached; they take the place of the connector nuts that come with the faucet, toilet tank, or shutoff valve. The label tells you whether the tube is for a toilet or a sink. These are available in stainless steel, white braided vinyl, or nylon.

■ **Chrome-Plated Copper Tube**

Chrome-plated copper is a rigid but bendable type of tube, usually used where appearance is important. It's also available in bright brass or antique brass plating. The flat-head type is for a toilet tank hookup and the tapered-head type is for sinks.

■ **Flexible Plastic Tube**

Flexible plastic tubes are inexpensive, and you can cut them to length with a utility knife. They require a plastic compression sleeve, which comes with the tube. They're not very attractive and are almost never used for an exposed connection.

■ **Ribbed Chrome Tube**

Ribbed chrome tube is easy to bend without kinking. It's more attractive than braided tube, but not as clean-looking as smooth chrome.

Some types of water supply tubes look better than others. Know the advantages of each before you buy.

Plumbing

how is it done?

SOLDERING COPPER PIPE

If you want perfect leak-free plumbing joints, you need to know how to solder copper. Everything you need for soldering copper pipe is available at home centers, hardware stores, and plumbing supply stores. Soldering is not difficult if you follow some basic steps. If you use common sense, it also shouldn't be a dangerous job.

CLEANING AND FITTING

You need to clean the outside of the pipe and the inside of the fittings both physically and chemically. If you don't, you'll have leaky joints. Physical cleaning means rubbing the outside of the pipe with emery cloth, an abrasive cloth that's designed for cleaning metal. Rub a piece of it back and forth until the pipe is shiny; it's not clean until it shines. Clean the inside of fittings with a wire fitting brush. Brushes come in different sizes to match the inside diameters of the fittings.

To chemically clean the pipe, you need a paste cleaner called flux. The flux must be lead-free if the water lines supply potable water (water for human consumption). Using a flux brush, apply the flux on the end of the pipe, covering slightly more than the distance the pipe will extend into the fitting.

SOLDERING

For proper soldering, the fitting must be hot enough to melt the solder and draw it into the joint through capillary action. The best way to heat a fitting is with a propane torch. A propane torch kit includes a propane tank, a control head, and a round-flame tip. You'll also need a striker tool to ignite the propane.

All plumbing codes require lead-free solder for drinkable-water supply lines. Check the package label carefully, because solder that contains as much as 50 percent lead might still be available in some areas.

When you solder, remember to heat the fitting, not the pipe. Position the flame tip so it touches the fitting but doesn't wrap around it. The tip is the hottest part of the flame. The fitting is hot enough when the solder touches the joint, melts immediately, and is sucked in. Wipe away any excess solder with a wet rag. Don't try to melt the solder by heating it with the flame. If you do, the solder won't be drawn into the joint, and you'll end up with a leaky joint.

A joint with too much solder not only looks ugly but also restricts water flow. Solder is drawn into a fitting as long as heat is applied. When the joint is full, the excess drips into the pipe and forms a glob. To avoid using too much solder, here's the rule of thumb: If you're using ½-inch-diameter pipe, use ½ inch of solder per joint; for ¾-inch-diameter pipe, use ¾ inch of solder. There should be a solid shoulder of solder all the way around the joint, with no gaps.

If you're soldering a threaded dielectric fitting (used to connect copper pipe to galvanized pipe), keep the threaded end of the fitting raised slightly. This will prevent the solder from melting on the threads and ruining the fitting.

1 Clean the inside of fittings with a wire fitting brush. They come in various sizes, and they clean the inside of fittings faster than emery cloth.

2 Apply flux to the outside of the cleaned pipe ends and the inside of the cleaned fittings to chemically clean these areas.

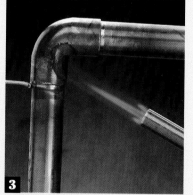

3 You'll know it's hot enough when the solder melts and is sucked into the joint. If the solder isn't drawn in quickly, keep heating the fitting until it is.

Soldering Safely

Q. *What safety precautions should I take when soldering copper pipe?*

If you are careful, you shouldn't have any accidents, but you should always have safety equipment within easy reach. Keep a fire extinguisher close by, and use a fireproof cloth when you're heating fittings that are close to flammable building materials, like plywood and wood studs. Place the cloth between the fitting and the building material. Fireproof cloth is available at any hardware store. Use a spray bottle filled with water to douse any sparks and a wet rag to wipe away any excess solder or flux.

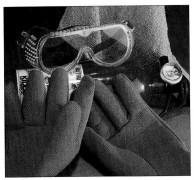

Working overhead increases the risk that solder will drip on your skin or in your eye. Wear goggles, gloves and a long-sleeved flannel shirt to protect skin and eyes.

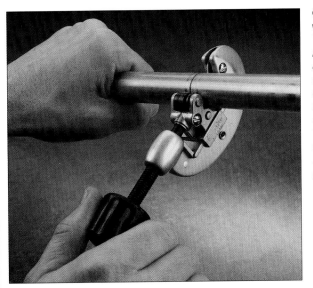

Cut copper pipe with a tube cutter. The cutting wheel makes a smooth, even slice through the wall of the copper as you rotate the tool around the pipe. This cutter's jaw can open to fit 2-in.-dia. copper pipe.

Cutting Copper Pipe

Q. *How do I cut copper pipe?*

The easiest way to cut copper pipe is with a tube (pipe) cutter. This tool has a movable jaw that grips the pipe between two guide wheels, and against a cutting wheel. Place the pipe in the jaw against the guide wheels and turn the knob clockwise until the jaw lightly clamps the pipe against the cutting wheel. Rotate the tool clockwise around the pipe, tightening the cutting wheel a quarter turn with each rotation.

Whatever you do, don't try to race through a cut by cranking the cutting wheel into the copper. You'll either crush the pipe or end up with a distorted cut. Then, if you try to use the pipe, the joint will leak.

Once the pipe is cut, remove any burrs on the cut edge. Use the triangular reaming tool on the back of the pipe cutter to remove burrs. Place the reaming tool inside the pipe and twist the tool back and forth a few times, applying just enough pressure to remove the burrs.

Fixing Holes in Plumbing

Q. *I have a small leak that would require major work to repair. Is there some kind of sealer I could use that can withstand water pressure?*

The best way to deal with a leak is to replace the section of pipe. Here's a temporary fix for a small leak: If the hole is in a supply line, turn off the water pressure at the main or at a shutoff valve. Cut a section out of a rubber coupler (available at hardware stores) or an inner tube and place it over the hole. Secure the rubber patch with hose clamps. Small holes require only one clamp; larger holes will require two or more clamps. Don't draw the clamps too tight or you may damage the pipe.

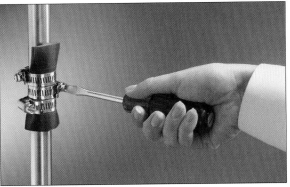

A piece of a rubber coupler and a few hose clamps provide a temporary fix for a hole in a water supply pipe.

⚠ Quick fixes like this one are for water pipes only. Gas lines should be repaired by a pro immediately.

PLASTIC PIPE

Buying Plastic Pipe

Q. *How many different types of plastic pipe are there?*

There are four types of plastic pipe:
■ ABS (acrylonitrile butadiene styrene) is a rigid black pipe used for drains and vents. It is available in 1½ inch and larger diameters; the joints are solvent-welded.
■ PVC (polyvinyl chloride) is a rigid white pipe used for drains and vents. PVC is available in ½-inch and larger diameters, and is typically used for waste and vent lines. The joints are solvent-welded.
■ CPVC (chlorinated polyvinyl chloride) is a rigid cream-colored pipe used for hot- and cold-water lines. It's normally used in 1-inch and smaller sizes. The joints are solvent-welded.
■ PB (polybutylene) is a flexible, gray pipe used for hot- and cold-water lines. It's usually used in 1 inch and smaller diameters and is joined with compression fittings.

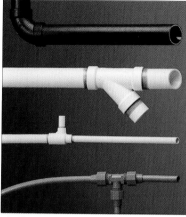

The four types of plastic pipe include (from top): ABS, PVC, CPVC, PB.

Cutting and Fitting

Q. *How do you cut and fit plastic pipe?*

Cutting and fitting plastic pipe is easy for the do-it-yourselfer. The fittings all have molded "hubs"—enlarged ends—into which you slide the pipe. Simply remember to include the hub depth when you measure the length of each section of pipe.

Use a fine-tooth (about 14 teeth per inch) handsaw to cut plastic pipe. Don't use a narrow-bladed hacksaw. Make cuts at exact right angles so that when two pipes are joined, there are no interior gaps that can slow water flow or collect debris. Use a miter box to make the cut square.

Cut completely through the pipe to avoid chipping off the last ¹⁄₁₆ inch. Use a half-round file or sandpaper to bevel the edges slightly, allowing the pipe to nest into the hub more precisely. To ensure the components have been cut accurately, dry-fit (put together without glue) each connection. Realize that the pipe may not seat completely in the hub and may slip in an additional ⅛ inch or more when you apply solvent. This could throw your measurements off for the run. To avoid this problem, dry fit only two or three fittings at a time, then glue them together. Mark the pipes and fittings to make sure they line up again when you glue them.

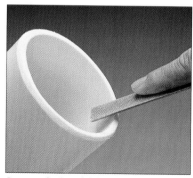

Cut the pipe off perfectly square, using a miter box and a fine-tooth handsaw (about 14 teeth per inch works well).

Remove the burr left by the saw with a file or sandpaper. Bevel the edges slightly for a smoother fit.

Metal vs. Plastic Pipe

Q. *Which is better: plastic pipe, or copper and cast-iron pipe?*

Plastic pipe is light, inexpensive, and easy to connect; it requires no soldering. You can cut and assemble it without special tools. It won't rust, lasts almost indefinitely, and has a smooth interior surface that allows water and waste to flow better than in metal pipes. However, plastic pipes are noisier than metal. Consult your local code to find any restrictions on the use of plastic pipe.

Coated Plastic Pipe

Q. *A plumber told me I can use only coated PVC pipe for drinking water. What is coated PVC?*

There's no such thing as coated PVC. The plumber is probably talking about CPVC, or *chlorinated* polyvinyl chloride, pipe. CPVC pipe is used for potable (consumable) water instead of PVC because it can handle hot water without softening. CPVC pipe is usually cream or light brown in color, but when you're buying it, make sure the sides of the pipe are stamped "CPVC."

Plastic Pipe Tips

Q. *We plan to use plastic pipe in the bathroom of our new addition. Do you have any tips before we start?*

■ Support. All pipe must be supported, and plastic requires more support than metal. Support ABS, PVC, and PB every 32 inches when it runs horizontally and every 4 feet when it runs vertically. Support CPVC every 3 feet. Confirm these distances with your local plumbing inspector, because codes vary. Studs and other framing count as support when the pipe runs through them.

■ Protection. Whenever a pipe passes through wood and comes within 1¼ inches of its edge, cover that area with a ¹⁄₁₆-inch-thick steel plate. This protects the pipe from misguided nails and screws.

■ Pipe movement. Cut slightly oversize holes through wood members so plastic pipe can expand and contract easily when hot and cold water run through them. This prevents squeaking noises when the pipe moves.

■ Transitions. To make a transition from galvanized pipe or copper water lines to plastic, use special plastic transition fittings that have one threaded side. Be sure to buy the right size. For transitions to larger galvanized drains or vents, you should use rubber transition couplings with a steel sleeve. For hubless cast iron, use rubber and steel transition couplings as well.

■ Noise. Plastic doesn't muffle the sound of draining water nearly as well as cast-iron or steel pipe. Lessen the noise by tucking insulation around plastic drainpipes before you close up the wall or ceiling.

GLUING PLASTIC PIPE

In the gluing process, properly called solvent welding, the solvent melts the plastic. When you push the pipe and hub together, the two fuse as the solvent evaporates. Each type of plastic has its own solvent. Be sure to use the type that's meant specifically for the plastic you're working with.

Dry-fit the pipe and fittings first. Make a mark at each pipe and hub connection to help reassemble it after you apply the glue. Apply the primer next. PVC and CPVC pipe require a special purple cleaner/primer. ABS does not require a primer.

Next, liberally coat the surfaces to be joined with solvent. Ventilate your work area well and/or wear an organic fume respirator. Quickly push the pipe into the fitting, giving the pipe a quarter turn to make sure it seats fully in the hub. The joint will harden in seconds, so try to align your marks as you twist the joint together. Hold the joint together for about 15 seconds to make sure it stays tight.

You can buy solvents, cleaners, and primers at home centers, but for the best selection and good advice, shop at a plumbing supply store.

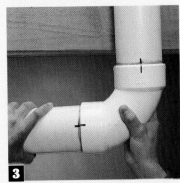

1 Dry-fit the fittings and mark their proper positioning. If the joints stick together, tap them with a hammer.

2 Spread purple primer liberally on the inside of the hub and the outside of the pipe.

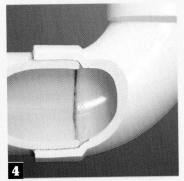

3 Push the hub and pipe together and twist the pipe a quarter turn so that it seats in the hub. Align the positioning marks and hold tightly for 15 sec.

4 The finished joint should be completely seated so water flows smoothly, without obstruction.

Plumbing

TOILET REPAIR

Stopping Tank Sweating

Q. *My toilet tank sweats so badly in the summertime that it makes puddles on the floor. What can I do to stop it?*

Just like a glass of cold water, a toilet tank filled with cold water condenses moisture out of the air. Warm air holds more humidity than cold air, so when the warm humid air hits the cold surface of the tank and cools down, it gives up its moisture, which drips to the floor. On very humid days, water can condense on surfaces as warm as 70° F to 80° F.

Correcting the problem ranges from the expensive total fix to the temporary fix. Air conditioning is the most permanent but most costly solution; it removes enough humidity from the air to prevent condensation from occurring on the toilet tank. Running a dehumidifier can also help, but it's difficult to dehumidify the bathroom on a hot day when other windows are open elsewhere in the house. You can also try:

Sweating toilets are no fun; they can cause puddles that ruin nearby wood.

Solution 1: Line the Tank

Most toilet manufacturers carry foam liners to fit their toilets, or you can make your own pretty easily from foam insulation. A liner works best when combined with a tank heater or tempering valve. On its own, it does nothing to stop condensation on the lower part of the toilet or on the supply line.

A foam tank liner is a cheap way to fix the problem quickly, but not completely.

Solution 2: Install an Aquarium Heater

Place a 20-watt aquarium heater in the tank. This is a quick but more obtrusive solution. The heater takes about an hour to raise the tank temperature above the condensation point, so you may get some dripping in the meantime. Also, condensation will continue to form on the supply line since it's filled with cold water. Avoid using an aquarium heater if there is a chance that the cord would be damaged by the tank lid.

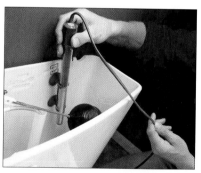

An aquarium heater is another quick fix, but it won't stop the supply line from dripping.

Solution 3: Install a Tempering Valve

This is the best solution, but it requires some additional plumbing. A tempering valve, added to your toilet supply line, mixes hot water into the cold toilet water supply so the water in the tank is warm enough to prevent condensation. It takes only a few hours to install. Only a little bit of hot water is used in each flush, so the it adds only a few cents a day to your energy bill. The valve is a bit more expensive than the aquarium heater and is available at plumbing supply stores.

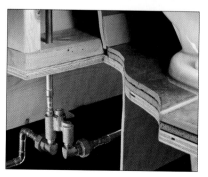

The best fix is a tempering valve, which mixes hot water into the cold.

Gurgling Sink

Q. *My bathroom sink gurgles every time the toilet is flushed. It's driving me crazy and I'd like to know how to fix it.*

Gurgling is a sign of a serious problem with your plumbing, namely lack of venting. Chances are your sink and toilet were not properly vented when they were installed.

What's happening is that when someone flushes the toilet, water goes down the soil stack. As it travels, it sucks air in behind it—air that is normally supplied by a vent stack. If there is no venting, the water produces a suction so strong that it pulls water out of the sink trap, making a gurgling sound. Your pipes are gasping for air. Not only is it annoying, but without water in the trap, smelly and poisonous sewer gases can enter your house.

For a permanent solution, you should add vent stacks, a complicated job that must be done in consultation with a licensed plumber. As an interim solution, however, you could run water in the sink after you flush the toilet, to refill the sink trap.

On rare occasions, a bathroom that is properly vented will have a gurgling problem. That means the vent stacks are clogged. The best thing to do is call a plumber for help.

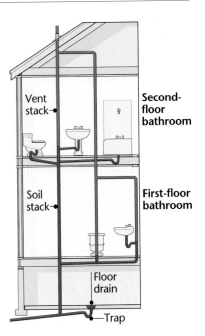

Vent stack

Second-floor bathroom

Soil stack

First-floor bathroom

Floor drain

Trap

UNCLOGGING TOILET PIPES

It has happened to many of us. The toilet gets clogged and we experience a twang of panic because we don't know what to do. Unclogging pipes is easy, and it's something everyone should learn how to do.

Don't ever flush a toilet you suspect is clogged; it might flood your floor. First check to see if the water level is up to the mark on the inside of the tank. If it's not, adjust it by bending the metal rod that holds the float. Also, if you have put anything inside the tank (like a brick) to limit the amount of water in the tank, take it out. You can also lift the flapper valve to let just enough water out to see if it's going down. Check that the flapper valve stays open until only an inch or two of water remains inside the tank. If it's closing too quickly, replace the flapper valve.

Plunge a clogged toilet with the flange on the plunger pulled out, and enough water in the toilet to cover the plunger. Plunge hard and often, and be prepared for splashing by putting old towels on the floor.

Use a closet auger to snake out the clog in a toilet. This specialized snake has a bent shaft to get around the first bend, and a crank so you can get some strength going behind it.

If all your efforts fail, the toilet probably has to be removed—something a plumber should do.

1 *Lift the flapper valve to see if water is going down.*

2 *Plunge with the flange on the plunger pulled out.*

3 *A "closet auger" will help you snake out whatever is clogging your toilet.*

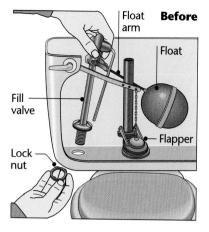

Float arm **Before**

Float

Fill valve

Lock nut

Flapper

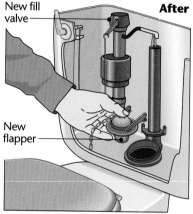

New fill valve **After**

New flapper

Trickling Toilet

Q. *We have an old 5-gallon toilet that trickles constantly. What could the problem be?*

A constantly trickling toilet is not only an annoyance, it can waste more water than a leak in any other fixture in your house. Most toilet leaks are caused by a stuck fill valve that can't close or by a hardened flapper that won't seal. Both can be replaced easily and inexpensively. Complete replacement kits are available at most hardware stores.

Before making the repair, shut off the water supply to the toilet, flush the toilet to empty the tank, and then sponge out any remaining water. Keep a bucket and rags handy. Remove the old fill valve (the float is also part of the fill valve) by unscrewing the locknut on the underside of the tank on the handle side and replace it with the new one. You can regulate the amount of water used in each flush by adjusting the fill valve.

Mysterious Toilet

Q. *My basement toilet has two problems: (1) When the toilet hasn't been used for a day or so, the water in the bowl is siphoned out; and (2) when the water is low in the bowl and the toilet is flushed, the bowl overflows. Is it not properly vented?*

Venting equalizes the air pressure in your plumbing system, which helps to maintain the water plugs in your sinks' traps and to keep drains running smoothly. Improper venting can cause the problems you describe.

The vent for your basement toilet should be located on the drain line somewhere before it joins the main line. The vent can tie into other plumbing vents in your home or can terminate through the roof independently. It must not terminate within 10 feet horizontally of a window.

Check to see if the existing vent is clogged first. If you think that you need to install an additional vent line, consult a licensed plumber.

Replacing a Toilet Seat

Q. *The toilet seat in my kids' bathroom is worn out and starting to crack. How can I replace it?*

The trick to removing an old toilet seat is to avoid damaging the porcelain bowl in the process. To remove a newer seat—one held in place with plastic bolts and nuts—pry up the bolt covers and unscrew the bolts.

Older seats that have the metal bolts molded directly into the hinge assembly are tougher to remove because the bolts can rust in place. If you can't loosen the nuts on the underside of the bowl with a wrench, spray penetrating oil on the rusted parts, then heat them with a hair dryer and try again. Still no luck? Cut the bolts with a hacksaw.

Remove the old seat and clean the hinge area. Flip up the bolt covers on the new seat hinge assembly. Slip the two bolts through the hinge holes and position the new seat. Hold the nut with one hand while tightening

the bolt from the top with a large screwdriver. Snug it just over finger-tight. Don't overdo it; you could crack the bowl. Snap the bolt covers back in place. Retighten the bolts after 2 or 3 days.

Remove the nuts that hold the old toilet seat in place. The rag keeps the wrench from cracking the toilet bowl if it slips.

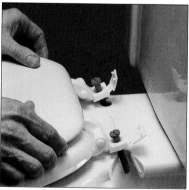

Slip the plastic bolts through the holes in the hinge and the toilet bowl. Tighten the nuts; then snap the bolt covers in place.

Slow-Flushing Toilet

Q. *Our downstairs toilet has begun to flush very slowly. We hired a plumber to clean the main drain line, but that didn't help. Our neighbor had a similar problem and says it might be the toilet itself. What do you think?*

The first thing you want to do is to check the water level in the toilet tank. It must be high enough to enable flushing action. Someone may have bent the lift arm in order to stop the toilet from running. This allows less water into the tank. Sometimes people will put objects in the tank so there's less water used per flush. That can also limit the flushing power.

If your water is hard, mineral deposits can clog the rinse and siphon jet holes, slowing the water flow. To clean both rinse and siphon holes, first shut off the water and flush the toilet to get rid of most of the water. Use a metal coat hanger to ream out the rinse and siphon holes. In some toilets, the siphon jet hole is toward the back of the bowl; in others it is up in the rim. Next, use wet paper towels to block the rinse and siphon jet holes and plumber's putty to keep the towels in place. Pour lime remover down the overflow pipe or valve seat and let it sit in the rinse and siphon jet hole chambers for 8 to 24 hours to dissolve the deposits. Remove the putty and towels; then flush several times before using.

A clogged vent can also cause a slow-flushing toilet. The pipe that runs up and through the roof can become clogged with almost anything, including sticks, nests, frost, leaves, and pipe scale. The debris can often be removed with a plumber's snake or blasted down the drain with a garden hose. To keep the problem from recurring, you can secure screening over the top with a hose clamp.

Finally, there is a chance that you may have a bum toilet. Several years ago, toilet manufacturers switched from 3.5-gallon- to 1.6-gallon-flush models. Some of the new designs didn't work very well—so there are a number of chronic-problem toilets out there. If after these treatments your toilet still doesn't flush properly, you should consider replacing the toilet or calling a plumber.

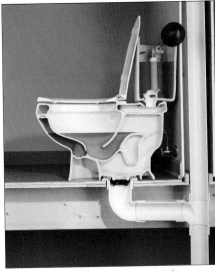

If the water level is too low, there might not be enough water released to get the siphoning action (the flush) in motion.

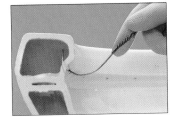

Ream out the rinse holes with a metal coat hanger.

Block the rinse and siphon holes with wet paper towels and plumber's putty.

Pour lime remover down the overflow pipe to remove any built-up mineral deposits in the rinse holes.

Toilet Tidal Wave

Q. *The water level in my toilets rises and falls on windy days. What could be causing this?*

You're seeing one of the laws of physics in action. The wind blowing across the plumbing vent on the roof creates low air pressure inside the vent pipe, which causes the water level in the toilets to fall. If the wind were constant, the water level wouldn't change. Gusting wind causes the water level fluctuation.

You can re-create this effect with a glass of water and a plastic straw. Put a straw in the water and blow across the top of the straw. The water in the straw should rise, lowering the water in the glass. If you blow short puffs across the top of the straw, the water level will fluctuate.

Plumbing

Up-Flush Toilets

Q. *We're converting our basement into an in-law apartment. We want to install an up-flush toilet to avoid making a hole in the floor to connect to the waste line. Is there anything in particular we need to know about up-flush toilets?*

If it's feasible, you're better off getting a standard flush toilet. Up-flush toilets cost more than standard units, must be professionally installed, and can be problematic in certain instances.

Up-flush toilets are designed for situations where a direct connection to a lower waste line is impossible—for instance, where a toilet is installed below the level of the sewer line. Up-flush toilets liquefy waste and then use your home's water pressure to lift the waste to the drain. If you have poor water pressure, don't even think of installing an up-flush toilet.

If you still think you must have an up-flush toilet, another possible solution is a sump ejector system. This system uses an electric pump instead of water pressure to lift waste up to the sewer line. These systems work well—until you have a power outage.

Although it will mean tearing through your concrete floor, you're better off installing a standard toilet. Standard toilets are less expensive, and you can do the plumbing yourself. Gravity also has a dependability that is hard to match.

Before installing any toilet below the sewer level, check to make sure that it's allowed by your local building code. For more on basement conversions, see Remodeling, p.182-185.

Finding Space

Q. *I'd like to install a small powder room under my stair landing. What is the smallest space that I can squeeze a toilet into?*

Most building codes now include space requirements for half baths. At a minimum, a toilet needs to sit in a 30-inch-wide space and have 24 inches of open floor space in front. You can use this figure as a guide, but you'll need to get the measurements of the fixtures you intend to use in order to plan the exact dimensions of the room. For example, toilets vary in length from 24 to 28 inches. Sink basins measure from 13 to 24 inches deep. To find smaller sinks and toilets, check the supplier catalogs at a full-service plumbing supplier or consult a professional bath designer. You might also save space by positioning the sink on either side of the toilet or in a nook off to one side.

Other building codes you'll need to follow specify ceiling height and ventilation. The ceiling must be at least 7 feet high, and the bathroom must have either a window that can open or a ventilating fan.

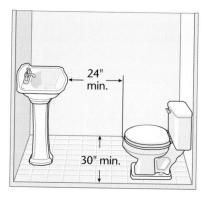

Unruly Toilet Flappers

Q. *The new flapper I installed on my toilet won't stay up long enough to allow the toilet to flush. What's wrong and how can I fix it?*

Toilet flappers seem to add a lot of frustration to people's lives. To fix the flapper, first make certain that the chain has only one link of slack. Next check to see if you have a water-saving flapper. These models must be "dialed in" in order to work properly. Last, check with the manufacturer of the toilet to see if you have the right type of flapper on your toilet.

A water-saving flapper may need to be adjusted in order to work properly.

Tightening Toilets

Q. *I've read that I'm not supposed to overtighten the bolts when I fasten a toilet to the floor or the tank to the base. How do I know if I've tightened them too much?*

To get a watertight seal, the toilet must be solidly seated. Tighten the tank and flange bolts to a "firm" tightness, about one-quarter-turn beyond hand tight. In a 2-piece toilet, there are bolts (tank bolts) connecting the tank to the bowl as well as bolts (flange bolts) connecting the unit to the floor. Above all else, your objective is to avoid cracking the bowl.

There are a great variety of toilet mounting systems; tanks may be fastened with two, three, or four bolts. Some models have rubber gaskets that can make you wonder whether the wing nuts are tight enough. When in doubt, have a helper sit on the bowl as you hand-tighten the nuts.

Toilet Flanges

Q. *What type of closet flange should I use under my new toilet?*

The two basic types of closet flanges are all-plastic (either black ABS or

An all-plastic flange (left) costs less than a comparable metal-ring flange.

white PVC) and plastic with a metal rotating ring. The flange is the part of the toilet that gets screwed to the floor. The toilet is bolted to the flange and the wax ring makes the tight connection between the two.

The metal-ring flange may cost a few dollars more, but it's worth it. If the toilet bolts are overtightened, the all-plastic flange can break. You can't easily replace the flange, so your only recourse is to install repair rings—a messy and often less than perfect fix.

The sliding metal ring also prevents a common installation mistake: gluing the flange with the holes for

the closet bolts not parallel to the wall behind it. The rotating metal ring can be adjusted during installation.

Metal repair rings can fix a cracked plastic flange, but you'll need to lift the toilet.

REPLACING A WAX RING

When water leaks out from under your toilet, it usually means that the wax ring between the bottom of the bowl and the floor flange has failed. You should replace it right away to avoid major repairs later on.

The only tricky part of this job is not dropping and cracking the toilet. You'll need a wrench to remove the flange nuts that hold the bowl to the floor and a putty knife to scrape off the old ring from the bottom of the toilet and the flange. You may also need pliers to disconnect the toilet from the water line. Keep a sponge handy to sop up any remaining water in the tank. As with most plumbing projects, it's always a good idea to keep a bucket and some rags handy.

Shut off the water supply, disconnect the supply tube to the tank, and empty the tank. Use a sponge to get as much of the water out of the tank as possible. Remove the flange bolt nuts (sometimes hidden by vinyl covers), located on both sides of the bowl. Grab the toilet bowl and gently rock it back and forth to loosen it from the floor flange. When the bowl is free, lay it on its side. Stuff a rag in the drain opening to block waste odors.

Scrape the old wax ring from the flange and the bottom of the toilet with your putty knife. Place the new wax ring on the flange. The wax ring should be room temperature or warmer so that it makes a firm seal. Lift the toilet bowl over the bolts and lower it onto the wax ring. Press down firmly on the toilet to compress the wax ring. Align the bowl with the wall behind it and tighten the flange bolt nuts.

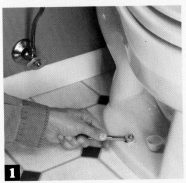

1 *Remove the flange bolt nuts, located on both sides of the toilet bowl.*

2 *Scrape the old wax off the flange and the bottom of the bowl.*

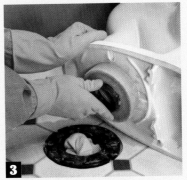

3 *New wax rings have a plastic collar to direct water and waste into the drain.*

Plumbing

CLOGGED PIPES

Proper Plunging Technique

Q. *Is there a "right way" to use a plunger?*

Actually, there is. First of all, do yourself a favor and use a plunger that has a flange. The flange folds in for normal use on sinks and folds out for use on toilets. Next, cover any place where water can escape. The best tool to use for this is a rag or sponge inside a plastic bag. For a bathroom sink, cover the overflow hole, and on a double-bowl kitchen sink, cover the drain on one side of the sink and plunge the other side.

Whenever you plunge, make sure there are at least a couple of inches of water around the plunger. Because water can't be compressed, it will transmit the pressure of plunging straight to the clog, and you're much more likely to break it up. Keep some rags or towels handy because you might make a mess. Steady back-and-forth plunging—twenty or more times—can break up a clog that a few huge plunges won't be able to.

Plunge a sink while there are a few inches of water in it, for a good seal. Cover the overflow hole with a rag or sponge in a plastic bag.

Disposer Smells

Q. *How do I get rid of the mildew smell coming from my garbage disposer? Does the smell mean it's not working properly?*

What you smell is a buildup of bacteria and probably not a sign of anything wrong. Run some ice cubes and baking soda through your disposer every week. This will clean the unit and remove the offensive smell.

Do Dishwashers Destroy Disposals?

Q. *Is it true that dishwasher detergent is hard on the metal parts of garbage disposal units?*

Some lower-priced disposer models manufactured before 1987 were prone to damage from dishwasher detergent. The bleach in the detergent caused the aluminum alloy housings and drain inlet to corrode. Manufacturers have since solved the problem, but some corrosion-prone disposers remain in service.

If your disposer is more than 10 years old, check the drain inlet for signs of discoloration and leaking. If it's in bad shape, the $60 for a new disposer is a lot cheaper than the potential cost of repairs if the drain inlet breaks and causes a flood.

Homemade Drain Cleaner

Q. *What's the safest way to deal with a sluggish kitchen drain?*

Commercial drain cleaners work, but we don't recommend using caustic chemicals on a regular basis. Here's a safer, homemade remedy that fights buildup and deodorizes your drain:
- Combine 1 cup baking soda, 1 cup salt, and ¼ cup cream of tartar in a jar. Pour about ¼ cup of this dry mixture down the drain, followed by 2 cups of boiling water. After 1 minute, flush the drain with cool tap water. Repeat this procedure weekly.

Detergent from your dishwasher can corrode the drain inlet and may even cause it to break off.

UNCLOGGING PIPES

If the plunger didn't unclog your drain, don't call in the plumber yet.

REMOVING THE TRAP

First, with a bucket in place under it, remove the trap underneath your sink. Use a wrench to loosen the slip nuts that hold the trap in place. If the nuts are shiny and new, wrap a rag around them while you use the wrench so they don't get scratched. You may find that the clog is right in the trap; just push it out with a coat hanger. Look through the mass to see if there's jewelry or anything else stuck in it.

When it's time to replace the trap, remember to use new washers; the old ones are probably dried out or distorted. Also, don't overtighten the nuts. Hand-tight plus a quarter turn with a wrench is enough. If the joint leaks, don't tighten more; disassemble the trap and try a new washer.

SNAKE

A plumber's snake can save you the expense of calling a plumber. However, this tool also gets filthy and can spring at you with no warning, so be careful with it. The snake is a long wire coil with a corkscrew-like tip that you feed into a pipe until it encounters the clog. When you hit the clog, turning the snake clockwise will screw the tip into the clog and let you pull or push it free. For dense clogs, you can grind away until it breaks up. Snaking is messy, so wear old clothes and work gloves. You might want to pull the snake through an old towel as you extract it from the pipe.

HYDRAULIC RAM

A hydraulic ram won't replace a plumber's snake, but it's easier and faster to use, makes less mess, and does the trick for most clogs. The contraption is a rubber bladder that fits on the end of your garden hose. If you decide to buy one, also get a threaded brass adapter that will let you attach the garden hose to your kitchen or bathroom sink.

Insert the bladder 6 inches or so into the clogged pipe and turn on the water. The bladder will inflate to form a tight seal inside the pipe. A valve then opens at the clog end of the bladder, filling the pipe between the bladder and the clog with water. The pressure of this water builds up until it reaches a certain point. With luck, the water pressure fires the clog down the pipe, into oblivion.

The advantage of a hydraulic ram is that when it works, it works completely. It's also easier to use than a snake, and a lot less messy since the clog goes down the pipe, not back up at you. If you are having trouble getting the bladder around a bend in a pipe, try coating it with petroleum jelly. Remember to turn the water off when you want to remove the bladder; it won't deflate until you do.

Run the snake into the drain until it hits the clog; then twist it clockwise and pull.

Hydraulic rams seal into the pipe and blast clogs with a forceful shot of water.

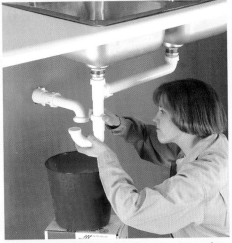

Keep a bucket underneath the trap as you work. Try to poke out the clog with a coat hanger.

Plumbing

DRAINS

Slow-Draining Tub

Q. *The bathtub in our house drains so slowly that I usually end up standing in a couple of inches of water at the end of a shower. What will it take to make it drain better?*

Before you take apart the trap under your bathtub, take a look at the stopper. If it's the pop-up type, operated by a lever mounted on the overflow drain, jiggle the lever and pull the stopper out. There's a good chance that the linkage is covered with a messy wad of hair. Remove the hair, rinse the stopper, and your problems may be over. See Adjusting a Bathtub Drain, p.211.

If your tub is slow to drain, check to see if the stopper needs cleaning.

Sink Oozes

Q. *My son installed a new kitchen sink and drain for us. Sometimes a greasy bead of gunk oozes out from around the ring in the bottom of the sink. What could it be?*

Have no fear. It's plumber's putty.

The gray-colored putty gets its name because it is often used by plumbers to create leak-free seals when installing sinks and drains.

Your son did a good job of applying enough of it to seal the strainer flange to your new kitchen sink. Because the seal is tight, occasionally excess putty is squeezed out.

To get rid of it, simply scrape it away whenever you see it appear. It will soon go away for good.

Leaky Shower Drain

Q. *My fiberglass shower leaks because the floor of the shower moves up and down whenever someone stands on it. How do I fix this problem?*

You need to support the shower floor to keep it from flexing. The best approach is to remove it. This usually requires tearing out the walls, which is a big job. With the shower floor out, check to make sure the drain was installed correctly. If not, replace the drain. Unfortunately, not all drains come with instructions, so be sure to note the correct order of its parts.

With the drain taken care of, mix up a bag of mortar mix and spread it over the subfloor. Slip the shower floor over the drainpipe and into the bed of mortar, working it down until the edges rest on the subfloor. If necessary, add more mortar so the shower floor makes good contact; then set the shower floor back in place while the cement is still wet. Wait a day or two before you use the shower.

There are other solutions, though they may not work as well. Sometimes you can get access to the area under the shower floor by removing the molding and a little drywall from the bottom of an adjacent wall. Then pile some mortar on a narrow piece of plywood, slide the plywood into the space between the shower floor and the subfloor, and pack in the mortar with a 2 x 4.

Another alternative is to fill the space with aerosol foam. Again, gain access to the area by removing the molding and drilling a hole in the wall. Be careful not to overfill the space; the foam expands.

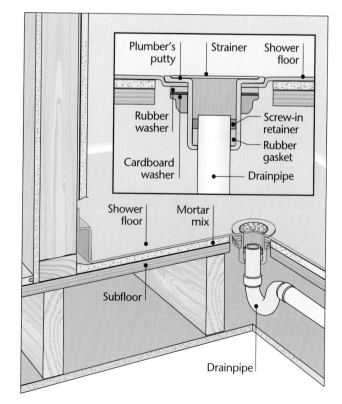

Removing a Drain Stopper

Q. *Our antique bathtub has a drain stopper with a lever mechanism built into the wall. The drain needs to be cleaned, but I don't know how to remove the stopper or replace it. Can you help?*

You don't need to remove the stopper. If the handle that opens the drain is on the wall, your drain stopper is probably attached to the bottom of a vertical rod that lifts it up and down. In this case, when you open the drain the stopper moves up and out of the way for cleaning the drain.

Many houses with the arrangement you've described have a drum trap, and you must be careful with it when you clean the drain. If the trap is made of lead, a motorized snake can run right through the wall of the trap, leaving you with disastrous results.

Most drum traps are fitted with a removable cover, and if you can reach it, unscrewing the cover will make

it easier for you to clean the drain. Don't use a lot of force, however; if the cover is stuck, try carefully heating it with a heat gun or hair dryer, or lightly tapping it with a mallet.

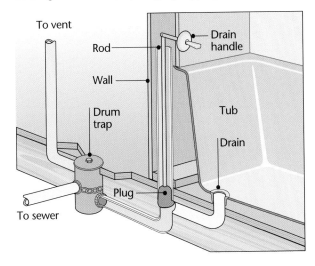

ADJUSTING A BATHTUB DRAIN

Drain moving too slowly? Pop-up drains are adjustable. They consist of two separate parts: the overflow assembly and the stopper assembly. To adjust the overflow assembly, remove the two screws on the overflow plate and completely or partially withdraw the assembly. If the tub is draining slowly, turn the lift rod assembly to lengthen it so it pushes the stopper higher. If your stopper leaks water, you should shorten the striker rod.

Adjust the stopper assembly by withdrawing it from the drain and moving the small nut and stopper up or down; lengthen the short rod to speed draining, or shorten it to stop leaking. There are many different bathtub drain mechanisms, but most of them work the same way. While you are down there in the tub, you might want to clean out the pipe and the P-trap with a plumber's snake; the overflow assembly hole provides the most direct route.

1 Remove the two screws that secure the overflow plate in place. Note how the overflow and stopper assemblies are not directly connected.

2 Now adjust the length of the lift rod: longer to speed up sluggish draining, shorter to stop leaks when the bathtub is full of water.

3 Withdraw the stopper assembly and adjust the height of the stopper: higher to speed a sluggish drain, lower to stop leaks.

4 Clean the pipe and P-trap through the overflow assembly hole. Feed a snake in 6 in. at a time and rotate it.

SINK DRAINS

Sink Overflows

Q. *Bathtubs and bathroom sinks have built-in overflow drains to prevent spills. Why don't kitchen sinks and laundry tubs have them?*

Overflow drains are designed to handle water displacement as you get into the tub or put your hands into the sink bowl. Overflows also help prevent disaster by draining away excess bath water if you accidentally leave a filling tub unattended.

Traditionally, kitchen sinks do not have overflows because the small drain can trap food waste, which would eventually rot and cause a foul odor. Also, unlike tubs, kitchen sinks are usually attended while they're filling. Laundry tubs don't need overflows because they're usually placed in the basement near a flood drain.

Manufacturing standards for bathroom sinks and tubs no longer require overflows, and many fixtures are available without them. However, plumbing codes in some areas may still require overflows on bathroom sinks and bathtubs.

Leaky Sink Drain

Q. *I need to replace the drain to my kitchen sink. Where do I begin?*

Before you begin, take a photo or make a simple sketch of the existing drain setup so you can put it back together properly. Next, disassemble the drain and take all of the old parts with you to the hardware store so you get the right replacements.

Using the photo as a guide, dry-fit the new parts together first, and mark the ones that need to be cut. Note that the slip nuts fit onto the unthreaded ends of the pipe. When you slide a slip washer onto a pipe, be sure that the taper points away from the nut. If the washer is installed backwards, it won't seal.

Assemble the pieces of the new drain system with the slip nuts loosely fastened. The trap should be the last piece assembled, because it's the one piece you can adjust back and forth and up and down. Hand-tighten the slip nuts and then check for leaks. If you find a leak, tighten that nut an additional quarter turn.

Wrap masking tape around the pipe where you need to cut. The tape's edge acts as a guide to ensure a straight cut.

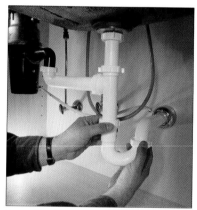

Leave the slip nuts on the P-trap loose so that you can adjust the trap to connect the sink's tail piece to the drain line.

Leaking Basket Strainer

Q. *How can I fix the basket strainer so that my kitchen sink stays filled with water?*

The basket strainer that lifts in and out of the drain has two jobs—to strain the water as it goes down and to plug the sink compartment when you want it to stay filled with water. The stopper at the bottom of these basket strainers can wear out. Take yours to a home center or plumbing supply store and replace the whole thing with a new one that will fit.

There are three types of basket strainers. One has a drop-down rubber stopper. Another has a fixed stopper and a rigid flat spindle on the bottom; you turn the whole basket to seal the drain. The third and most expensive type has a threaded center piece that spins and locks the basket in place. This type works the best.

Fixed stopper

Drop-down stopper

Spin-and-lock stopper

FIXING A POP-UP SINK STOPPER

Sometimes all you need to do to fix a broken stopper is to adjust the lift rod, but knowing how to remove and replace the entire assembly will enable you to accomplish whatever repairs are needed. The parts you need are available as a package at hardware stores. Even if you find that just one part needs replacing, it's easier to replace the entire assembly. You'll have a hard time finding the parts to fit the old assembly.

Begin by removing the old drain assembly. Loosen the nuts that secure the stopper seat and pivot rod to the drain body. Remove the setscrew, lift rod, and lift-rod strap. Use a hacksaw to remove stubborn nuts and penetrating oil to loosen the setscrew, if necessary. Depending on the design of your sink, you may also have to remove the P-trap.

Install the new stopper and drain body. Place a ring of plumber's putty about the thickness of a pencil around the bottom of the stopper seat and Teflon tape on all threaded parts. Tighten the mounting nut until it's hand-tight, then about another quarter turn, making sure the pivot rod opening faces the rear.

Position the lift rod through the hole in the faucet body, and secure it to the lift rod strap with the setscrew. Lightly tighten the setscrew; you may need to lengthen or shorten the lift rod for final adjustments.

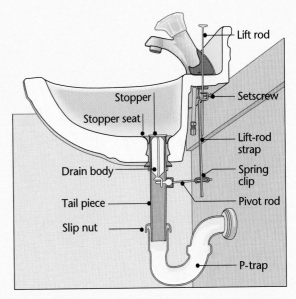

Labels: Lift rod · Stopper · Setscrew · Stopper seat · Lift-rod strap · Drain body · Spring clip · Tail piece · Pivot rod · Slip nut · P-trap

Drop the stopper in place and insert the pivot rod tip through the stopper hole. Loosely tighten the retaining nut; then raise and lower the pivot rod end in the adjustment holes until the stopper works correctly. Finally, install the spring clip.

(Even if you don't break the P-trap, this is a good opportunity to replace all of the old plumbing. See Leaky Sink Drain, p.212.)

1

To prevent leaks, place a ring of putty around the the stopper seat and Teflon tape on all the threaded parts before you install them.

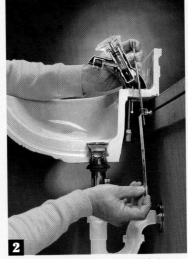

2

Slide the lift rod through the hole in the faucet body, and secure it to the lift strap with the setscrew.

3

Adjust the pivot rod end in the adjustment holes until the stopper sits high enough for water to easily drain and drops low enough to seal the drain.

Plumbing

FAUCETS

Drippy Tub Spout

Q. *The faucet in my bathtub dribbles when the shower is turned on, which means I don't get as strong a stream of water as I should. Replacing the spout didn't help. How can I get all the water to go up to the shower head?*

Replacing the spout was the first thing that had to be done, so that wasn't a wasted effort. A combination tub/shower faucet has a diverter that is triggered when the button on the spout is pulled up. Diverters can wear out, causing the problem you describe.

Since you're still experiencing the problem even after installing a new spout, it's likely you have low water delivery—a situation common in older homes. Over time, mineral deposits collect inside water pipes, reducing the amount of water that can flow through. If there's not enough water flow, the pressure is reduced as well. The result is weak showers, because the diverter is unable to send all the water up to the shower head.

To solve the problem of low water delivery, you may have to replace your home's main water pipes. This is a fairly expensive undertaking, so before you start, get professional advice from at least two plumbers who can take a closer look at the whole plumbing picture.

Slow-Flowing Faucet

Q. *I replaced the old faucet on my kitchen sink. Why does the water seem to run only half as fast?*

Your old faucet probably had a flow rate of 3 gallons per minute (gpm). A few years ago standards were enacted to decrease the allowable gpm; your new faucet has a maximum flow rate of 2.5 gpm.

Another possibility is that debris shook loose from inside old pipes and clogged your shutoff valves, reducing water flow. Try opening and shutting the valves several times while gently rapping them with a wrench. Debris can also clog the aerator at the tip of the faucet. If your aerator unscrews, remove it and use a toothbrush to clean it.

Bad Sink Sprayer

Q. *The sink sprayer in our kitchen doesn't work anymore. I don't know if it's clogged or just broken, but I'd like to know how to make it operable again.*

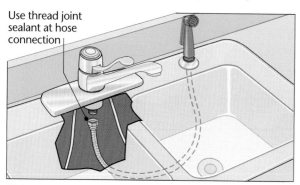

Use thread joint sealant at hose connection

Sink sprayers can get clogged in the same way a faucet aerator can. The sprayer head unscrews at its base. Pay attention to the washers; there's a thick hard one and a soft thin one. When it's time to reattach the sprayer head to the base, make sure these washers are in the proper sequence. Use a needle to clean out debris from around the nozzle and inside the connecting joint of the base; then reattach the head.

If you cannot get the sprayer head cleaned out, or if it's worn or broken, replace it. You'll find that most brands of sprayer heads are interchangeable. Bring the old one along to a home center or plumbing supply store, and pick out one you like.

If your sprayer head is good but the hose needs replacing, use a small screwdriver to pry off the small C-shaped metal ring that secures the bottom part of the sprayer head to the hose. The other end of the hose connects to the underside of the faucet. Sometimes this hose connection is threaded on the outside, and sometimes on the inside. Most hose replacement kits have adapters to accommodate either type of thread. Before you connect the hose end to the underside of the faucet, use your finger to dab thread joint sealant onto the threads.

Clear out everything stored under the sink to give yourself enough room to work when it comes time to connect the hose to the faucet bottom. Give yourself plenty of light, too, and a piece of carpet to cushion your back. Since you will be working in a small space above your head, pliers or an adjustable wrench about 6 inches long is the best tool to make this connection.

When you reassemble the sprayer head, make sure the two washers go back in the right order.

Clogged Aerator

Q. *We have hard water, and I think the minerals are building up and clogging our faucet. How do I clean it out?*

Whether it comes from your city's system or your own well, hard water contains minerals and sediment that will eventually build up and restrict the water flow from the faucet. A sediment-encrusted aerator needs to be removed and cleaned, perhaps even replaced.

Remove the aerator by unscrewing it from the faucet spout. Try cleaning it with hot water and an old toothbrush. Then reinstall it and turn on the water. If that doesn't help, you'll need to replace the aerator. Take the old one with you to the hardware store or home center. The new aerator or the replacement cartridge must be the same size to fit inside the aerator body.

Use your fingers to remove the aerator; it unscrews from the spout clockwise.

The new aerator or replacement cartridge must be the same size as the old one to fit correctly inside the aerator body.

Sand in the Faucet

Q. *Twice a week for a long time, I've had to clean sand out of the aerators on my faucets, and now all the faucets in my house are in need of replacement. How can I get rid of this sand? We're on a private well.*

The sand is getting into your water system through the well, and unfortunately, most of the fixes are expensive ones. Consult a licensed well driller in your area. There may be a hole in the well casing. In this case, a new well is the best solution. Another possibility is that you need a new well screen (the main screen at the bottom of the well).

If you have a "rock bottom" well, where the well is open to the rock at the bottom, there is no screen. Sand may have accumulated at the bottom of the well and the pump is pumping it into your system. In this case you can have the sand air-lifted out, and it's likely to stay out.

Homeowners who are annoyed by sand in their faucets, but aren't faced with the quantity you're dealing with, can install in-line sediment filters on the faucets, or a sediment filter big enough to serve the entire house.

Trickling Faucet

Q. *I have an older home with two outside faucets. One works just fine; the other barely trickles. Could you help me out with this problem?*

If you're getting good water flow and pressure at the rest of the faucets in the house, it's likely that something is plugging the line to the faulty faucet.

Start by turning off the water to the problem faucet. Disassemble the faucet without removing it from the pipe. Look for broken washers or mineral deposits that could block the flow of water.

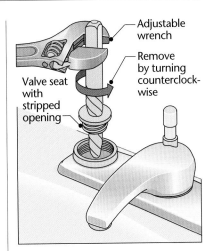

Stubborn Valve Seat

Q. *When I tried to remove the worn valve seat from my bathroom faucet to repair a leak, I rounded the square opening for the valve wrench. How do I get it out?*

The easiest way to get the valve seat out is with a screw extractor, commonly referred to by the brand name Easy Out. A screw extractor looks like a tapered drill bit, except it has wide spirals that run in the opposite direction of a drill bit. The top of the extractor has flat sides so you can grip it with an adjustable wrench (shown above), locking pliers, or the T-handle that is used with taps.

Insert the extractor into the valve seat opening and gently tap it tight. As you turn the extractor counterclockwise, it is forced tighter into the valve seat opening. Tap on the extractor as you turn it to make sure it gets a good grip. You can help loosen the valve seat by heating it with a hair dryer.

A screw extractor is also good for removing a bolt whose head has snapped off. Simply drill a hole down the middle of the bolt and insert the extractor into that hole.

how is it done?

FIX A LEAKING FAUCET

Regardless of the internal design—cartridge, ball, or washer—a faucet can (and usually will at some point!) drip or leak. All types can be repaired. Repair kits containing O-rings, washers, and rubber seals are available at home centers, hardware stores, and plumbing supply stores.

To begin, first shut off the water supply to the faucet. Remove the decorative cap or button on all styles of faucets (a straight-tip screwdriver is typically all you need to pop it off); then unscrew the small screw that is inside the handle. Follow the instructions below for your type of faucet.

CARTRIDGE FAUCET

When a push-on, pull-off cartridge-style faucet leaks from the handle, the upper O-ring is the problem. If the faucet drips from the spout, the other O-ring needs to be replaced. If the faucet drips or doesn't mix hot and cold water as it should, you need to replace the cartridge.

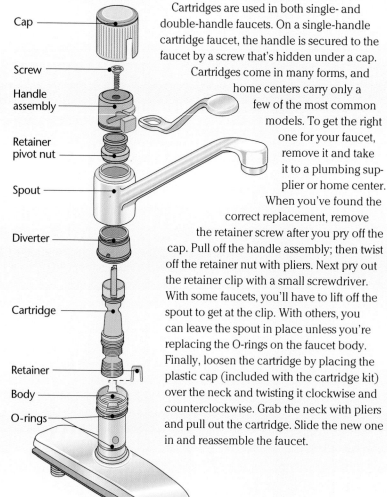

Cartridges are used in both single- and double-handle faucets. On a single-handle cartridge faucet, the handle is secured to the faucet by a screw that's hidden under a cap. Cartridges come in many forms, and home centers carry only a few of the most common models. To get the right one for your faucet, remove it and take it to a plumbing supplier or home center. When you've found the correct replacement, remove the retainer screw after you pry off the cap. Pull off the handle assembly; then twist off the retainer nut with pliers. Next pry out the retainer clip with a small screwdriver. With some faucets, you'll have to lift off the spout to get at the clip. With others, you can leave the spout in place unless you're replacing the O-rings on the faucet body. Finally, loosen the cartridge by placing the plastic cap (included with the cartridge kit) over the neck and twisting it clockwise and counterclockwise. Grab the neck with pliers and pull out the cartridge. Slide the new one in and reassemble the faucet.

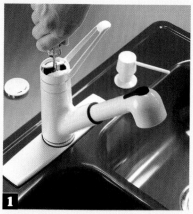

1 Remove the retainer screw after you pull the cap off.

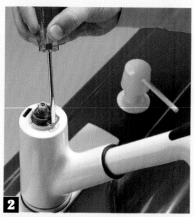

2 Pry out the retainer clip with a small screwdriver.

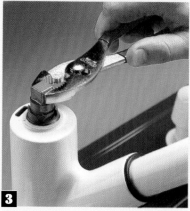

3 Place the plastic cap over the neck of the cartridge, and twist it back and forth.

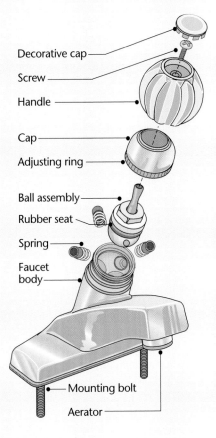

Decorative cap

Screw

Handle

Cap

Adjusting ring

Ball assembly

Rubber seat

Spring

Faucet body

Mounting bolt

Aerator

BALL-STYLE FAUCET

If a ball-style faucet leaks at the handle, tighten the adjusting ring, which is part of the faucet cap and is located under the handle. If you can't find the wrench that came with the faucet, use two narrow-blade straight-tip screwdrivers. Cross the screwdriver blades to form an X and place the tips in the slots in the adjusting ring. Then tighten the ring clockwise.

If the faucet drips from the spout, replace the rubber seats and springs. Remove the faucet cap with a pair of adjustable pliers. (Wrap a rag around the cap to avoid marring the finish.) Lift out the ball assembly. Replace the rubber seats and springs (located inside the ball assembly opening) for both the hot- and cold-water supply even if only one looks bad.

Tighten the plastic adjusting ring if your faucet leaks at the handle.

Replace the rubber seats and springs if the faucet drips from the spout.

WASHER-STYLE FAUCET

If your leaky faucet has rubber washers and O-rings, you need to replace the O-ring on the valve stem. Replace the rubber washer on the bottom of the valve stem only if water is dripping from the faucet spout.

To do this quick repair, remove the faucet handle. Next remove the bonnet from the faucet body with adjustable pliers. The valve stem is inside the bonnet and must be removed to replace the O-ring and washer. The valve stem unscrews through the bottom of the bonnet and is reverse-threaded, so turn the screwdriver clockwise to back it out.

The valve stem is inside the bonnet and must be removed.

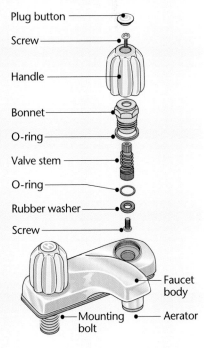

Plug button

Screw

Handle

Bonnet

O-ring

Valve stem

O-ring

Rubber washer

Screw

Faucet body

Mounting bolt

Aerator

Plumbing

SHOWER REPAIRS

Detachable Shower Head

Q. *I want to install a detachable shower head in my newly remodeled bathroom. Is it hard to do?*

Not at all. A detachable hand-held shower head is great for the elderly or disabled who must sit in the shower, for washing children and dogs, and for cleaning the tub and shower walls. The new head simply screws on in place of the old.

Remove your old shower head with pliers. Use a small pipe wrench or pliers to keep the shower arm from turning while you work on it. Pad the wrench teeth with a piece of cloth so they don't mar the shower arm.

Next, after cleaning off the old threads and wrapping them (clockwise) with Teflon plumber's tape, mount the shower attachment clip to the shower arm. Use your pliers to tighten it and use a folded cloth to protect the finish.

Finally, screw the shower hose to the attachment clip and tighten it. In most cases, you won't need Teflon tape on these threads, but check the instructions that come with your new shower head.

Mount the shower attachment clip to the shower arm.

Screw the shower hose to the attachment clip and tighten it.

Tub/Shower Diverter Valve

Q. *How does that knob on the bathtub spout route water up to the shower head? And how do you fix one that leaks?*

The knob you're referring to is a diverter valve or gate. When the rod is raised, this gate prevents the water from flowing through the spout. The backed-up water climbs the shower pipe and overflows through the shower head. Unfortunately, the diverter gate can't be repaired; the entire spout must be replaced.

If your plumbing is copper pipe, the spout is most likely secured to the pipe with a small Allen-type setscrew on the underside of the spout. Unscrew this, twist the old spout off, and install a new one.

If your plumbing is threaded pipe, the spout is screwed on. Insert a wrench into the spout and unscrew it. Wrap Teflon tape around the threads of the pipe sticking out of the wall; then screw the new spout on.

Diverter valves that are not built directly into the spout can be repaired. They're built like faucets with washers and O-rings.

When the plunger rod on the spout is pulled up, the water is blocked and rerouted up to the shower head.

Cold Shower

Q. *If I'm in the shower and someone turns on the dishwasher or washing machine, I get blasted with cold water. How can I solve this problem once and for all?*

The change in water temperature is actually caused by a change in water pressure. When the dishwasher or washing machine is turned on, hot water that was being directed to your shower is now directed elsewhere, causing the cold blast. You can solve this problem by installing a pressure-balancing shower faucet. Pressure-balancing faucets will maintain the temperature no matter what other demands are placed on the system.

Another solution is to install a pressure-balancing valve on the hot and cold lines just before the faucet. Do this if you have an access panel behind the shower or somewhere along the hot and cold supply lines.

You can find pressure-balancing faucets and valves at plumbing showrooms and home centers.

Clogged Shower Head

Q. *I'm tired of showering under the narrow streams of water that trickle from my shower head. What can I do about this problem?*

Most likely, lime scale buildup is blocking the water holes. Soak the shower head in vinegar and clean out the holes using a straight pin. If the shower head needs replacing, you may want to buy a self-cleaning model. These shower heads are designed to push mineral buildup outward where it can be wiped away.

To install a new shower head, first remove the old one by unscrewing it from the shower arm. Hold the shower arm as you unscrew the shower head to keep it from twisting and getting damaged. If you do damage the arm, replace it. Next, unscrew the shower arm from the water supply pipe located inside the wall. Most shower arms have external "male" threads on the shower head end.

If yours has a ball-end design, replace it with one that has external threads on both ends because most shower heads have internal "female" threads in the mounting nut.

Wrap Teflon thread-sealing tape on the threads of both ends of the shower arm. Wrap in a clockwise direction when looking at the end of the pipe threads. The clockwise wrap prevents the tape from being twisted off when you install the arm and shower head. Be careful not to misthread the new arm into the hidden fitting. If the arm doesn't screw on smoothly, take it out and try again. Replace any damaged tape before reinstalling the arm.

Install the new shower head on the shower arm until it's finger-tight; then hold the shower arm and continue to tighten the shower head. Turn on the water and check for leaks. If you find one where the head is attached to the threads, remove the head and add a few wraps of Teflon tape on the shower arm threads. Reinstall it and test it until there are no leaks.

Unscrew the shower arm from the brass fitting on the shower water supply pipe. The pipe is in the wall.

Wrap Teflon tape on the threads in a clockwise direction to prevent it from twisting off when you install the new shower head.

If there is a leak after you install the new shower head, remove it and add more tape around the shower arm threads.

Unsealed Cover Plates

Q. *What is the best way to prevent water from trickling down between the shower handle cover plate and the wall?*

Any water that gets in between the cover plate and the wall, or behind the tub spout and the wall, can cause rot and other deterioration to wood framing and other wall materials. If left unstopped, you'll eventually have to tear out the shower wall and rebuild it. This is definitely something you want to prevent from happening.

The best thing to do is to seal the entire edge around the shower handle cover plate, and the edge where the tub spout meets the wall. Use a good-quality tub-and-tile caulk. Allow the caulk to dry for 24 hours before using the shower. If your shower has separate hot and cold handles, caulk behind each handle ring, then secure the rings tight against the wall.

Caulking around the cover plate and tub spout will prevent water from seeping into the wall behind.

Plumbing

Choosing a Water Filter

Q. *Our tap water is cloudy and smells bad. We'd like to install a water filter. Which kind is best?*

Water filters can't solve all water problems, but they can improve the taste and appearance of water. Even better, they can be easily installed in less than half an hour. They are also cheaper, per gallon of water, than bottled water, faucet-mounted filters, or countertop filters. Three types of filters help three sorts of problems: bad taste, lead, or sediment.

■ Bad taste or odor. Use an activated carbon filter to help get rid of bad-tasting and bad-smelling tap water. The carbon filter removes odors and unpleasant tastes, including chlorine, from your cold water. It also reduces pesticide residues. However, if you have well water with a rotten-egg smell, see a water treatment dealer for better options. Carbon filters are plastic cylinders that hold a replaceable carbon filter and are mounted under your sink. This is the easiest type of filter to install.

■ Lead. If you're concerned about lead, call your health department. They can recommend labs that will test your water. The federal Safe Drinking Water Act recommends that you take action to reduce lead if your first-draw water has more than 15 parts per billion (ppb) of lead.

A multistage filter will remove 85 percent or more of the lead from your water. This filter is similar to a carbon filter except that it has two or three cartridge holders. The other difference is that a multistage filter typically uses a separate faucet (supplied with the filter) that mounts on your sink or countertop. This makes the filters last longer, and allows for better filtration because the flow is slower.

If you suspect high levels of lead in your water, there are precautions you can take: Use only cold water. (Hot water dissolves more lead from pipes.) Cook with cold water, and heat up cold tap water to make infant formula. Also, don't consume water that has been standing in the pipes for more than 6 hours. Let it run until it's cold, then 15 seconds more.

■ Sediment. If the problem with your water is cloudiness, or if there are flakes of rust or sand, a whole-house filter will help. Inside the screw-in filter housing is a spun polyethylene filter that traps particles. You can also get two-stage units that include an activated carbon filter for taste/odor improvement. However, if there is dissolved iron in your water, which often results in rust stains in the toilet, a filter won't help. You need a special iron-removal filter (consult a water treatment professional). Units with a built-in shutoff valve are recommended. Install the filter vertically in the main water line, downstream from the main shutoff. Leave enough room below the unit to change filters.

An activated carbon filter mounts under your sink and removes tastes and odors from your water. It filters cold water and attaches easily with compression fittings.

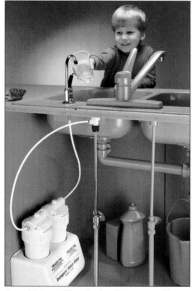

A multistage filter for lead connects like the one-stage unit, but the filtered water comes out of a separate faucet on your sink or counter.

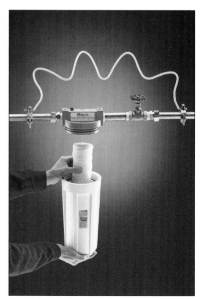

A whole-house sediment filter is installed on the main water line, after the shutoff valve. It removes scale, cloudiness, and rust flakes. A jumper wire should be installed across it.

CHOOSING A KITCHEN SINK

Your kitchen sink will be with you for a long time; know the options available so you can choose the one that's best for you.

SINK MATERIAL

You can buy a kitchen sink made of stainless-steel, enamel, porcelain, or solid-surface material.

Stainless-steel sinks are rated by thickness and composition. Thickness is measured by gauge; the smaller the number, the thicker the steel. Eighteen-gauge is good quality; thinner will dent more easily. Check noise-reducing coatings on the undersides of stainless-steel sinks—some coatings thickly blanket the whole underside; others are thin and patchy.

Enamel is a tough but brittle material. The quality of an enamel sink is determined mostly by what's under the enamel. Stiff cast iron is better than steel, which can flex, causing the enamel to shatter. Enamel comes in several colors; the darker ones highlight soap scum and mineral deposits.

Metal-based porcelain-finished sinks are half the weight of cast-iron yet more resistant to impact damage. Sold under the brand name Americast, the sound-deadening qualities of these sinks significantly reduce kitchen sink garbage disposal noise.

Solid-surface sinks are made from the same material used for solid-surface countertops. They have all the characteristics of the material used for counters, plus very low dishwashing-noise levels.

MOUNTING METHODS

Self-rimming sinks are supported by the sink rim, which overlaps the surrounding countertop. Sinks can

An undermount allows a clear path for sweeping food crumbs into the sink, unlike the self-rimming mount.

also be undermounted—attached to the underside of the counter with clips or adhesive. Just about any sink can be undermounted, but this method is not recommended if you have a laminate or tile countertop.

Solid-surface sinks can be self-rimming, undermounted or integral. Made from the same piece of solid-surface material as the countertop, an integral sink is part of the counter, rather than attached to it.

FAUCETS

To ensure that the faucet you buy is a quality product, stick with established brand names. Don't be concerned about the type of valve you choose—all of today's faucet technologies are durable and reliable. Decide which you prefer—a one- or two-handle faucet. Metal finishes, such as chrome and the new brass finishes, are the most durable. Colorful powder-coated finishes—color granules baked onto the faucet's surface—are tough but can chip.

A self-rimming sink sits atop the counter.

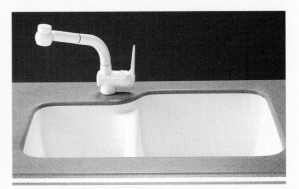

This is an integral sink arrangement. The contrast between the blue and white gives it the appearance of an undermount.

FIXTURES

Drilling Through Porcelain

Q. *I plan to install a point-of-use water purifier and need to know how to drill through my porcelain sink. What tools do I use?*

Plumbing experts agree that you cannot drill through porcelain without damaging it. If you try, you'll chip and crack it. Instead, try to install your point-of-use purifier at the edge of the sink, on the counter. Often the spout of the purifier will be long enough to reach the sink, even if it's installed on the counter.

If your sink has a sprayer hose, you may be able to install the purifier's spout in its place.

Finding Old Fixtures

Q. *The beige toilet in our 25-year-old home is damaged and can't be repaired; we've looked everywhere for a replacement and cannot find one. We don't want to replace our tub and sink because they're in great shape. Is there a solution we're just not thinking of?*

Contact local plumbing contractors who specialize in remodeling. They may know of salvage yards that deal in used fixtures, or they can keep an eye out for one from a remodeling job. Old toilets can be rebuilt to work as well as new. In the meantime, you can install an inexpensive toilet until you find a "new" old one.

Refinishing a Tub

Q. *Is it possible to refinish a bathtub with a porcelain finish? If so, is it a job for a do-it-yourselfer?*

Tubs cannot be refinished with true porcelain. They can be refinished with an epoxy-base coating, but it's generally not a DIY job. If you buy a kit, the coating will last a maximum of 5 years, and usually less. A professional recoating will be much more durable, lasting 10 to 12 years with normal use. The difference is the result of the way the tub surface is roughened up to accept the coating—pros use a very powerful etching agent (hydrofluoric acid), but homeowners need to use sandpaper. Don't try muriatic acid, either, because it releases toxic fumes.

REPAIRING CHIPS

Chips in sinks, bathtubs, appliances, and even glazed tiles don't have to be permanent. The repair is quick, inexpensive, and easy. There are several types of repair materials available, ranging from simple paints to tough epoxies. Epoxies are usually available in a variety of colors, so you should be able to find one that matches the damaged area.

First, scrub the chipped area with soapy water. Next, rough it up with a small piece of medium-grit sandpaper to remove rust and give the damaged area some tooth for the repair material to cling to. Mix together equal parts of hardener and color; then wait about 10 minutes for the mixture to thicken. Brush the epoxy onto the damaged area. If the chip is deep, wait 8 hours, then apply a second coat. Repeat the procedure if necessary. Wait 24 hours before getting the area wet and 7 days before scrubbing it.

1 Sand the damaged area to remove rust or debris and to provide a rough surface for the repair material to cling to.

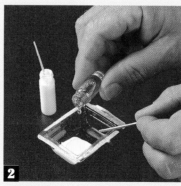

2 Mix together equal amounts of color and hardener, using the plastic bubble package as a mixing tray.

3 Confine your repair to the damaged spot rather than trying to feather it out or blend the old with the new.

The Right Caulk

Q. *I want to recaulk my tub, shower, and sinks, but I'm having a hard time choosing a product. Can you tell me what to look for?*

Look for a caulk that is designed for use in wet areas, that adheres well to nonporous surfaces, and that contains a mildewcide or fungicide. Beyond those traits, what you use depends on how you prioritize these three characteristics: durability, workability and appearance.

If durability and adhesion are most important to you, nothing beats solvent-base silicone. It will stick well, and last a long time, doesn't shrink, and is waterproof. However, silicone is tricky to work with because it skins over quickly, and it can be a nightmare to clean up because nothing dissolves it. Also, once you use silicone, you will need to always use silicone; nothing else will stick to it.

If workability is most important, choose sealants that clean up with water. Two drawbacks with these types of sealants are shrinkage and the lack of color choices.

If you need a particular color, ask the sales staff at your hardware store or home center about kitchen and bath sealants made of high-quality acrylic latex. They are available in a wide range of colors.

To choose caulk, determine which qualities are most important to you: durability, workability, or appearance.

Removing Adhesives

Q. *I've used everything short of a crowbar to remove the shower-door track which is affixed to our tub—and still it won't come loose. Any good ideas?*

Try to determine what type of adhesive is holding this track in place. If it feels very hard, it is possibly an epoxy resin, which is just about impossible to remove from surfaces such as bathtubs. You'll damage the tub if you try to remove it. If you can push a fingernail into the adhesive, it is probably not an epoxy resin.

If the adhesive feels soft, try to pry up the track, but be careful not to damage the tub. You might try heating the track (not the tub) with a heat gun. If your tub is fiberglass, do not use heat; you could damage the surface beyond repair.

Start at one end of the track and try to loosen it for 6 to 8 inches. If you can do this, you can most likely pry off the rest of it. Also, check to see if there are any bolts or other metal fasteners holding the track in place.

Rust Marks

Q. *We have hard water in our house, and together with a dripping faucet, it has caused rust marks in my bathtub. How can I get rid of them?*

You can buy rust and iron remover products for removing stains from porcelain and enamel fixtures, or you can be adventurous and try a home concoction.

First try mixing lemon juice and salt, then scrubbing the stains with this mixture and a sponge. For hard-core stains on vertical surfaces, dip a rag in the mixture and lay it over the stain for several hours before scrubbing.

If that fails, put on some protective goggles and rubber gloves, then mix 1 part oxalic acid with 10 parts water, and stir in cornmeal to make a paste. Sometimes called wood bleach, oxalic acid is sold in paint and hardware stores. Pack this paste over stains on the bottom and sides of the tub and let it sit for 3 or 4 hours; then rinse it away with water.

Stains on Cultured Marble

Q. *The cultured marble base in my shower has stains that I can't seem to get rid of. Some are black and some are white. Can you help?*

The two stains need different remedies, but you should be able to remove both types. For the dark stain, try soaking a clean white cotton cloth with hydrogen peroxide and leaving it on the stain overnight. Rinse with cold water in the morning.

For the light-colored stains, which are generally caused by hard water, use a mixture of ½ cup ammonia, ¼ cup vinegar, and ¼ cup baking soda in ½ gallon of hot water. Mix this in a 2-gallon bucket, because the vinegar and baking soda will foam up. Apply it with a clean sponge. Let the solution stand for 5 minutes; then rinse it off well. Test it in a small area first, before doing the whole shower floor, and wear rubber gloves.

If these solutions don't help, you'll probably have to have the shower floor refinished.

Plumbing

Removing a Bathtub

Q. *I'm remodeling my bathroom and I want to replace my old cast-iron bathtub. How do I get it out so I can get the new tub in?*

If you don't want to use it elsewhere, you can break the bathtub up with a sledgehammer and take it out in pieces. This works only with a heavy cast-iron tub. Wear eye protection and hearing protection, and remove mirrors and other breakables from the walls before you begin.

You'll want to shut off the water supply and remove the drain and overflow before doing anything with your 22- or 28-pound sledgehammer. Drape a heavy blanket or dropcloth over the tub to prevent flying shards, and then use the sledgehammer.

If the tub is steel rather than cast iron (the tub bottom flexes when you stand on it) or if it's fiberglass, you'll have to cut it into pieces with a reciprocating saw using a metal blade.

Save your sight and hearing by wearing full goggles and hearing protection when you break up an old tub to remove it.

You'll also need to cut out the old tub faucet valve, spout, and shower head. On copper pipe, use a minitubing cutter that allows you to make a complete turn. Old-fashioned galvanized pipe can simply be unscrewed with a couple of pipe wrenches.

The old faucet valve, spout, and shower head will need to be cut out with a minitubing cutter.

Cracked Fiberglass Tub

Q. *After wallpapering our bathroom, my wife and I discovered several dings and cracks in the bottom of our fiberglass tub from when we dropped some tools. Is there something we can patch them with?*

Some home centers sell repair kits to patch this type of damage. If you can't find one, ask your local hardware or bath showroom if you can order one.

To repair surface cracks, use a

Dremel or similar rotary tool to widen the crack so the repair material has something to grab onto. Mix the color into the gel, then add the hardener. Use a toothpick to apply the mixture and a scraper to smooth it out. Apply two layers to fill deep gouges. Once the gel hardens, sand with 600-grit sandpaper and buff.

Structural cracks that go all the way through must be repaired by a professional. Look in the Yellow Pages under "Fiberglass Repair."

Widen a surface crack in fiberglass with a rotary tool.

Apply the gel and hardener; then sand and buff.

Installing a Tub Surround

Q. *Can a tile or drywall bathroom wall be replaced with a fiberglass tub surround?*

A tub surround can be installed in any conventional tub/shower area that has a 5-foot bathtub. Using a surround will very likely be much less expensive and much quicker than installing new ceramic tile. You'll find a wide variety of tub surrounds with features such as built-in shelves and towel bars.

Three-piece tub surrounds can be applied directly over the old wall surface, but we don't recommend doing this unless you know the wall is sound and will last a long time. Otherwise, you need to remove the old wall materials—all of the old plaster or drywall—and replace them with new cement board. The tub surround is then installed over the cement board with adhesive.

REPLACING A BATHTUB

Replacing a bathtub is a project an ambitious do-it-youselfer can do with careful planning. If you haven't already, remove the old tub and any floor tile within 4 inches of the tub. This will allow you to get the new tub in place, resting directly on the subfloor. To make enough room to move the new tub into place, you might have to temporarily remove the sink and toilet.

If your tub is on the first floor with an open, unfinished basement or crawl space below, you're in luck. You can get at the drain and trap from below. For a second-floor tub, or a first-floor tub over a finished basement or on a cement slab floor, you might have an access opening in the wall behind the plumbing end of the tub. If you don't, just cut a hole to provide a small door or hatch for future access. Make the hole large enough to get at the tub faucet valve and the water supply lines running to it.

Hook the new faucet valve so it is centered over the new tub. The front-to-back positioning of the valve is critical to allow the cover plate to fit flush with the finished wall, so be sure to follow the instructions that come with the valve.

Solder fittings that are close to the valve body before screwing the threaded adapters into the body, because heat from the torch can melt plastic parts in the valve body. Use Teflon tape on the threaded adapters. Now you can secure the assembly to the wood crosspiece with ½-inch copper pipe straps.

Reposition and level the 2 x 4 ledger board that supports the far side of the tub. Calculate the height so the tub will sit exactly level. Slide the tub into position. Later, you will finish the walls with cement board to a height of 72 inches above the tub bottom. The cement board's bottom edge should be about ⅛ inch above the tub's vertical flange; tile will overlap the flange.

Finally, connect the new drain and overflow. Hook up a 1½-inch-diameter two-piece PVC trap. In most cases, you can connect it directly to the existing drain line with a threaded PVC coupling and a small length of 1½-inch PVC pipe. Cut the drain's extension arm to length to accommodate the trap.

Slide the tub into position on two 2 x 4 skids. Gently remove the skids when the tub is in position, and make sure it doesn't rock.

Mount the faucet body high enough so you won't have to bend to adjust the water when showering; position the shower head high enough so tall users won't have to duck.

Connect the new drain and overflow to the tub; then a two-piece PVC trap.

Plumbing

Anatomy of an Older Electric Water Heater

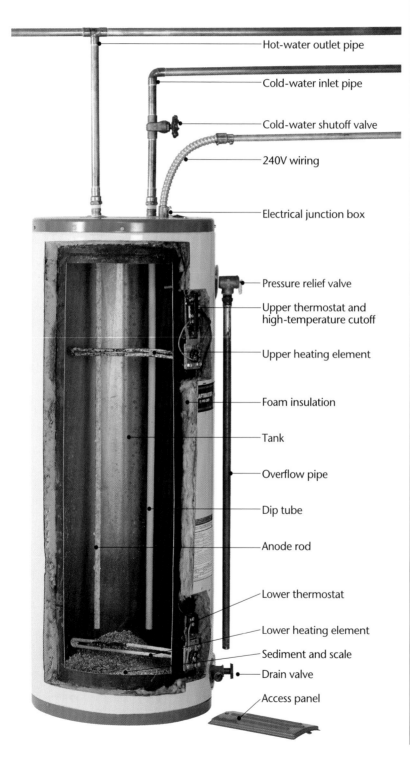

- Hot-water outlet pipe
- Cold-water inlet pipe
- Cold-water shutoff valve
- 240V wiring
- Electrical junction box
- Pressure relief valve
- Upper thermostat and high-temperature cutoff
- Upper heating element
- Foam insulation
- Tank
- Overflow pipe
- Dip tube
- Anode rod
- Lower thermostat
- Lower heating element
- Sediment and scale
- Drain valve
- Access panel

Buying a Water Heater

Q. *We need to replace our water heater but don't know the first thing about them. Is bigger better? Can you give us some tips?*

Bigger isn't always better in new water heaters, unless you run out of hot water frequently. Water heaters with larger tanks use more energy, so if your old water heater has consistently delivered enough hot water, you don't need a larger one.

The prominent yellow energy guide label on each water heater gives you some idea of its efficiency and average annual operating cost. This average helps you compare different models. Electric water heaters generally cost 2 or 3 times as much to operate as natural gas water heaters. But they don't need the vent (a class B chimney) that is required for gas models, making them easier to install in homes without chimneys.

In recent years, manufacturers have developed venting systems for gas water heaters that eliminate the need for a chimney. The power vent draws combustion gases from the heater with a blower and exhausts them through a 3-inch PVC pipe (white plastic drainpipe) that runs out through an exterior wall. The blower mixes the hot exhaust with room-temperature air, and prevents the plastic pipe from overheating.

The direct-vent system draws its combustion air in through the outer chamber of a double pipe and expels the exhaust through the center chamber. It too can exhaust through an exterior house wall. One drawback with these systems is that the vent pipe cannot be very long, so you have to put the water heater within a few feet of an outside wall. Both power-vent and direct-vent water heaters cost at least twice as much as regular gas models.

Tankless Water Heater

Q. *We want to replace our 40-gallon water heater. Can we replace it with a tankless heater? Is this kind of water heater fast enough for a family of four?*

Tankless, also called "instant" or "on demand" water heaters, heat water as needed with a blast of gas or electric resistance heat.

The pros? Tankless heaters fit into small spaces, last a long time, and will provide limitless hot water as long as they're not overtaxed. The cons? They're expensive; they may require larger gas or electric lines and vents; and they're foreign to most repair people. Your monthly utility bill would most likely be lower with a tankless unit—but it takes a long time to offset the substantially higher purchase price. The biggest drawback may be their inability to keep up with demand when more than one fixture or appliance calls for hot water. Only the largest units can keep pace with a family of four.

Their perfect use? In weekend cabins where keeping a conventional heater working full time is a waste of energy, and in 1- or 2-person dwellings where hot-water use is minimal and predictable.

Fiberglass Blanket

Q. *I've heard you can save energy by covering an electric water heater with a blanket. Is this true?*

Yes, it is true. Special fiberglass blankets that wrap around your water heater can save energy when used properly. To wrap your water heater safely, follow the directions that come with the blanket. In particular:
■ Do not insulate the top of the water heater.
■ Do not cover the air intakes for gas burners.
■ Leave the controls and all valves exposed.
■ Don't cover any warning labels.
■ Don't wrap a gas water heater.

⚠ To reduce the risk of scalding, set the water temperature on your water heater no higher than 120° F. This will also reduce energy usage.

When wrapping your water heater, be careful not to cover any warning labels.

Foul-Smelling Water

Q. *Our water comes from a well. Since installing a new water heater, we have been plagued with a sulfur odor, particularly in the shower. What's causing this odor, and is there any way to get rid of it?*

The odor is the result of sulfur in your water reacting with the magnesium contained in the anode rods of your water heater.

Pulling out the anode rods is certainly one way to eliminate the problem, but it could mean a shorter life for your water heater and a voided manufacturer's warranty. The reason? The anode rods (sometimes called sacrificial rods) minimize deterioration of the heater by attracting corrosive elements, thus keeping these elements away from the inside walls of the heater.

Another way to get rid of the odor is to chlorinate your well water. This can be done periodically or through a continuous feed. You may be able to do this yourself, depending on the type of pump system you have. But because chlorine is toxic and can harm your pump if improperly added, we recommend that you contact your local well contractor for advice.

One other option is to replace the magnesium rod with an aluminum anode rod. Be sure to use an aluminum rod that is produced, or at least recommended, by the water heater manufacturer (the aluminum must have 2 percent tin in it to work properly). Under no circumstances should a zinc rod be used. At temperatures above 150° F, zinc and steel reverse roles, and the steel tank corrodes instead of the anode rod.

Plumbing

WATER HEATER REPAIRS

Faulty Heating Element

Q. *We no longer get very much—or very warm—water from our electric water heater. Can I track down and fix this problem myself, or do I need to call a plumber?*

Most likely one of your water heater's two heating elements has gone bad. Since the lower element does up to 90 percent of the heating, that one usually wears out first. If you're comfortable with plumbing and electrical tools, you can do the repair yourself.

First, shut off the power to the water heater at the fuse or breaker box. In almost every case, you'll remove two fuses or click two breaker handles. At the water heater, remove the two access panels and use a voltage meter or other voltage-sensing device to make sure there's no electricity running through any of the wires. Don't skip this step! Water and high-voltage wires create a potentially dangerous combination.

Disconnect the two wires attached to the element. Use a water heater continuity tester to test each element. To do this, attach the alligator clip to one screw and touch the probe to the other screw; no light indicates a burned-out element. Perform a second test: Keep the alligator clip in place and touch the probe to the metal plate surrounding the element. If the element is shorted out, the tester bulb will light up.

To replace the element, first shut off the cold-water inlet valve. Next open the nearest hot water faucet—then drain the unit through a hose connected to the drain valve. The element may be held in place with four bolts, or it may screw directly into the tank. In the second case you'll need to use an element wrench. Take the faulty element to an appliance parts store to match the wattage, voltage, length, and mounting style of the old element.

Install the new element and gasket, reconnect the wires, close the drain valve, refill the tank, and check for leaks. If all systems are go, you can turn the power back on.

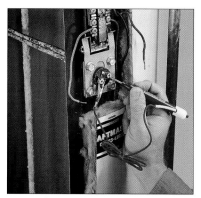

Use a voltage meter, neon voltage indicator, or other voltage-sensing device to ensure no voltage is running through the wires before you begin any repairs.

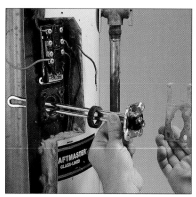

You may need a special element wrench to remove the element. The new heating element should slide in easily.

Pressure Relief Valve

Q. *The pressure relief valve on my water heater drips about a gallon of water every week. I've replaced it several times with no improvement. What else can I do to try to stop the leaking?*

It sounds as if the real problem may be with the pressure regulator on your main water line. Pressure regulators are designed to allow for thermal expansion of the water, but it appears that yours isn't working.

When water in the tank is heated, it expands and needs somewhere to go. Usually the water can expand back into the main water line. If the pressure regulator is blocking that line, the expanded water just increases the pressure inside the water heater and the household plumbing. When the pressure reaches about 150 psi, the pressure valve does what it's supposed to do—it begins to leak.

To test the pressure regulator, have a plumber hook up a pressure gauge to a hose-thread adapter; then screw it onto the water heater drain or onto an outside hose bib (faucet) that's on the house side of the regulator. If the pressure builds while the water heater is operating, you've found the problem.

There are three ways to solve it. However, they all require a professional plumber. Your are options are:
■ Install an expansion tank near the water heater.
■ Install an adjustable relief valve and set it about 20 pounds higher than the pressure regulator setting. Be sure to direct the water to a drain.
■ Replace a toilet's existing flush valve with a Watts Governor 80 Fill Valve. This valve relieves the line pressure above 80 pounds and the excess water simply overflows into the toilet bowl. This device not only handles water expansion, it's also a safeguard in case the house's pressure regulator fails.

Water Heater Noise

Q. *In the past few weeks I've noticed a rumbling and popping sound coming from my gas water heater. Should I be concerned?*

The noises you hear are probably caused by a buildup of sediments from minerals in the water. These sediments pile up on the bottom of the tank and trap heat from the gas burner, raising the temperature on the bottom higher than normal and stressing the steel tank and its protective inner glass coating. Electric heaters won't rumble, but sediment buildup can still decrease burner efficiency.

Some new water heaters have self-cleaning systems to help reduce sediment. These heaters have a curved dip tube that causes the incoming cold water to stir up the sediment so it flows out with the hot water. If your present water heater doesn't have this feature, drain the tank through the drain valve and flush it according to the instructions in your owner's manual. Do this once or twice a year to prevent buildup.

how is it done? LIGHTING A GAS WATER HEATER

Lighting a natural gas or propane water heater can be intimidating if you've never done it before. Even though every water heater has step-by-step instructions pasted on its side to safely lead you through the lighting procedure, they don't tell you what you're actually doing when you turn a knob or what to do if the pilot does not light. Here's a detailed step-by-step sequence.

To begin, turn the thermostat to its lowest setting and the gas control knob to *Off*. (You may have to depress the gas control knob slightly to turn it to the *Off* position.) Before moving to the next step, wait about 5 minutes to allow any escaped gas to dissipate. If you continue to smell gas, leave your house immediately and call the gas company from a neighbor's house.

Turn the gas control knob to *Pilot* and depress it completely (or push down the adjacent red button on some models). This allows gas to flow through the pilot tube only; gas cannot yet flow to the main burners. With the knob depressed, immediately hold a lighter to the tip of the pilot tube to ignite the gas. Usually the gas lights within 10 seconds, but if the gas line also contains air (common in new installations), it might take up to 5 minutes for the air to bleed out and the pilot to ignite. For this reason, a log starter or long fireplace matches work better than paper matches. If the pilot doesn't light and you begin to smell gas, release the button and turn the gas control knob to *Off*. Wait a minute or two, then start over.

Continue to hold the button down for 60 seconds after lighting the pilot. In that time, the pilot should heat the thermocouple enough to automatically open the valve. By holding the button down, you're manually keeping the gas valve open to the pilot and heating the thermocouple. Release the button and check to make sure the pilot remains on. Once the pilot remains lit, you can turn the gas control knob to *On* and replace the panel door.

Finally, reset the temperature control knob. (Check your owner's manual to find out what temperatures the high, medium, and low settings actually represent.) Usually you'll hear the burners ignite within seconds. However, if the water in the tank is still hot, the burners might not start immediately. Turn the temperature control knob to a higher temperature until the burners come on. Turn the control knob back to the desired temperature level immediately to make sure you don't scald anyone with unusually hot water. If the burners still refuse to start, call a repair specialist.

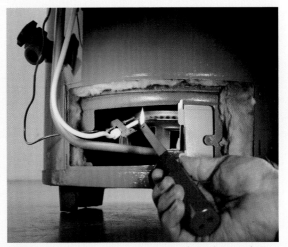

Lighting a water heater is easy once you know how to do it correctly. If the pilot doesn't stay lit, you may have a faulty thermocouple or some other problem. Turn the control knob to Off *and call a professional.*

Electrical

Fuses and Circuit Breakers

Q. *Is there a difference between a fuse and a circuit breaker? Are circuit breakers safer?*

Fuses and circuit breakers are "over-current protection devices." Their job is to protect your home from electrical overloads, which happen when too many appliances are drawing power from the same circuit. When too much power is drawn on a circuit, fuses and circuit breakers cut off the power before an overloaded circuit can cause a fire.

The National Electrical Code allows each electrical circuit to carry a certain number of amperes (a measure of electrical current). This wiring might serve switches, lights, and wall outlets or just a single appliance, like the refrigerator. To guard against overloads, each circuit is protected by a circuit breaker or fuse in the main panel. When the current exceeds the circuit's limit, the breaker or fuse shuts off or breaks.

Fuses are still common in homes built before the 1960's, before the invention of inexpensive circuit breakers. All of the current in a circuit flows through a flattened wire in the fuse. If the current exceeds a certain limit, the flattened wire overheats, burns, and breaks. When this happens, the power goes off. To restore power, you must unscrew the old fuse and install a new one. Fuses do their job as well as any circuit breaker, but they are less convenient because you have to replace them.

Most circuit breakers have a current-sensitive device that triggers the switch. In addition, many circuit breakers have a heat-sensitive plate that deforms as current passes through it. When it gets too hot, the metal expands and triggers a switch to shut off the electricity. Circuit breakers are an improvement over fuses because you can easily reset them by flipping the switch—there is no component to replace when you reset a breaker switch.

⚠ Sometimes when you're faced with repeated overloads, you might be tempted to replace a fuse or circuit breaker with one that is higher-rated and can endure more electrical current running through it before it shuts the power off. This is a bad idea and you should never do it; the wiring will no longer be protected from overloads and could overheat and cause a fire.

Flickering Lights

Q. *Every time we start our dishwasher, the lights upstairs flicker momentarily. What causes this and how can it be fixed?*

When the lights flicker briefly as you describe, the electrical system is experiencing a voltage drop. This could be caused by insufficient power being brought into the house. In the old days houses had only 30- or 60-ampere electrical service. In most homes these have been upgraded to 100 or 200 amps. Voltage drops can occur if the service was upgraded with a new circuit breaker panel but without an increase in the amperage coming into the house.

Another possibilty is that the dishwasher is on the same circuit with the lights and the circuit is not large enough for all of them. When the dishwasher kicks on, a momentary power drain dims the lights. The dishwasher should be on its own circuit without any other lights or outlets.

Power Off!

Before you even think of starting to do any electrical work yourself, shut off the power to the area you will be working on. Here's a trick that comes in handy when you're trying to find which circuit to shut off before you begin work: Plug a radio into the outlet you want to work on and turn it up loud so you can hear it when you're standing at the main electrical panel. Switch off circuit breakers or unscrew fuses until the radio shuts off. If the main panel is in a damp location, stand on a dry board. Wear rubber-soled shoes in all cases.

When a fuse burns and breaks you must replace it.

When a circuit breaker trips, you can reset it with the flip of a switch.

What
Causes an
Overload?

YOU PLUG IN A POWER TOOL to do some work in the garage and the lights go out, the refrigerator goes off, and the clock stops. You've done it again: caused an overload. If it hasn't happened to you yet, it will.

An overload occurs when you try to draw too much power through part of your home's electrical system; too much electricity is trying to get through too small a wire. Toasters, refrigerators, air conditioners, table saws, and many other electrical appliances demand a lot of power. If enough of them draw electricity at the same time through the same wire, the wire heats up. If the overload lasts too long, the wire can melt through its plastic insulation and start a fire.

A properly designed electrical system will not allow fires to occur. The wiring has special "overcurrent protection" devices—circuit breakers or fuses—that are located behind the metal door in the main electrical panel. A properly installed system will sense an overload, opening a circuit breaker or burning a fuse to shut off the circuit. The shutdown is a signal for you to stop what you're doing and find out why the overload occurred. Go to the main panel and reset a circuit breaker by flipping its switch or replace a blown fuse with a new fuse. Then make sure no one is making toast or ironing clothes on the circuit your paint-stripping heat gun is plugged into.

Preventing Overload

When an overload has occurred, you know you have to transfer the appliance to another outlet, but you may not know which outlets belong to each circuit. You can map out your electrical system by first turning off a circuit or loosening a fuse at the main panel. Then walk through your home with a utility light or radio, plugging it into each outlet and turning on light switches as you go. If the light or radio doesn't come on, you'll know that the outlet or switch is on the dead circuit. Repeat the process with the other circuits, recording the results on a sketch of your home's floor plan. Shift appliances around to more evenly distribute the load.

If you are plagued by overloads, the best solution is to run a new circuit from the main panel directly to the appliance with the heaviest power draw. This is the preferred option for air conditioners and refrigerators. You can do the job yourself, but if you are not experienced, hire a licensed electrician. Make sure a local electrical inspector checks the work.

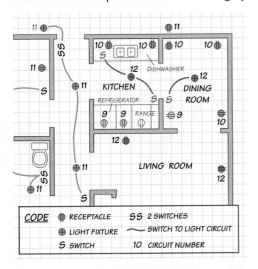

CODE
- ⏚ RECEPTACLE
- ⏀ LIGHT FIXTURE
- S SWITCH
- SS 2 SWITCHES
- ⌐ SWITCH TO LIGHT CIRCUIT
- 10 CIRCUIT NUMBER

CURRENT NEEDED

Two or more of these common household appliances plugged into the same 15-amp circuit can easily cause an overload and blow a fuse or open a circuit breaker.

APPLIANCE	AMPS
Window air conditioner	8–16
Table saw	13–15
Refrigerator	6–15
Microwave (countertop)	6–12
Hair dryer	10
Clothes washer	10
Portable heater	10
Toaster	7–10
Garbage disposer	5–10
Clothes iron	9
Freezer (new model)	5

Electrical

ELECTRICAL GROUNDING

If armored cable has slipped, pull it back up into the clamp. To lift the cable, slide a screwdriver between the box and the wall. In some cases you may need to break into the wall.

Grounding Wires with Metal Cable or Conduit

Q. *The wires in my home are enclosed in metal conduit. Can the conduit serve as part of the grounding system?*

Steel armored cable or steel conduit provide grounding as long as the metal cable or conduit is properly connected to the outlet box. Loose connections can be hard to trace, but the breaks usually occur where vibrations have loosened a screw or clamp. Check the connections if an outlet tests as an open ground (see Finding Ungrounded Outlets, p.233). If the bad connection isn't at the box, check any visible conduit for breaks.

Protecting Home from Lightning

Q. *Our old farmhouse has been struck by lightning twice, even though there are two lightning rods on the roof. How can I protect my electronics in case it happens again?*

Lightning is attracted to tall structures; if your house is one of the tallest in the area, that may explain why lightning has struck twice.

You can do a few things to reduce the chances of damage to your electrical equipment in the event of a power surge caused by lightning. For starters, have an electrician check the lightning rods to make sure they are functioning correctly. The rods are supposed to attract lightning to themselves, keeping it away from the rest of your house, and then redirect it into the ground via a thick wire connected to a metal rod.

Ask your local electrical supplier if they sell a surge suppressor that mounts on the main electrical panel or meter to protect your house from lightning-induced power surges. Power surges can also enter your home through antennas, phone lines, and cable TV cables; it's a good idea to install a second surge protector that has connections for coaxial cable (used for cable TV and antennas) and 110-volt plugs. This type plugs into a standard wall outlet. If you use a computer, get a separate surge protector designed specifically for computers.

Last, you might consider buying a homeowner's insurance policy to cover lightning damage. If you work at home and use equipment such as copiers and computers, make sure that your policy also covers business-related equipment.

Supply Pipe Grounding

Q. *My house's electrical system used to be grounded to the water supply pipe coming into my house, but the utility company has replaced the iron pipe with plastic pipe. Do I need new grounding?*

Yes, you must provide new grounding! An earth ground provides a place for a house's stray electrical voltage to dissipate. Without an earth ground in the house, there is nowhere for excess voltage to leave your electrical system if a fixture or appliance shorts out or if you have an electrical surge.

How you add an earth ground depends on soil conditions, and often involves driving an 8-foot-long by 5/8-inch-diameter copper or copper-plated rod into the ground or burying a ring of heavy wire around your house. Never use a natural gas line for grounding. Ask a local inspector about the method used in your area.

Buying an Outlet Tester

Q. *What should I look for when I go to buy a new circuit tester?*

Circuit testers are handy because they let you safely check your outlets without turning off the circuits or opening up electrical boxes. A tester has three lights in arrangements that vary among brands. Use the guide on the tester to interpret the patterns.

There are two types of testers available at hardware stores. One type has a GFCI (ground fault circuit interrupter) test button and costs under $25. The other has no GFCI button and costs about $12. Spend a little more and buy the type with the GFCI test button. GFCI's are important safety devices for every household and should be tested regularly.

A circuit tester will catch the common wiring errors and circuit problems. If you find more than one or two simple errors in the outlets in your home, call in a pro.

FINDING UNGROUNDED OUTLETS

Certain wiring errors, such as a bare hot wire, are immediately dangerous, but others can exist for years, never causing a problem until something else goes wrong. One common invisible error is the case of an outlet with an open ground. An open ground occurs where there is a break or "opening" in the ground wire circuit and electrical current cannot flow through it to the main panel. This wiring error becomes a problem only when something else fails—current needs to flow through ground wire only if there is a problem— but if the ground is not there when you need it you could end up getting a dangerous electrical shock.

The bare copper or green wire you see in most outlets today is the ground wire. (It corresponds to the rounded slot in an outlet and the round prong on a three-prong plug.) The ground wire circuit is supposed to form a continuous path back to the main electrical panel. The ground wire is designed to siphon off electrical leaks from hot and neutral wires that have broken loose, worn out, or been incorrectly connected and bring them back to the main panel, eventually causing a circuit breaker to trip or a fuse to burn out. The shutdown alerts you to an electrical problem.

The best way to detect an open ground is with a circuit tester. To do this, plug the tester into the outlet; the combination of lights will indicate whether or not the ground is working. If the tester indicates an open ground, turn off power to the circuit at the main panel and remove the outlet. Check for loose or discon- nected ground wires. Sometimes the bad connection is somewhere other than at the outlet. You may need to call in an electrician to help you find the problem.

The tester cannot detect an open ground when the ground terminal on the outlet is directly wired to the neutral terminal, a common wiring error. To find out if there are errors like this, you'll need to shut off the power to the outlets and pull them out one at a time.

Open grounds are most common in older homes where owners have upgraded outlets to the three-slot type, but never upgraded the electrical system to include an equipment ground. In this case the tester will indicate an open ground, and you'll find the equipment ground wire missing when you pull out the outlet. Your options are to install a GFCI to offer shock protection (see Ground Fault Circuit Inter- rupters, p.240), install an ungrounded two-slot outlet, or run new cable that has ground wire (the best solu- tion, especially if you plan to plug large or sensitive equipment, like a refrigerator or a computer).

Plug a circuit tester into the outlet; the three-light display will let you know if the ground is working. You can test all the outlets in your home in a matter of minutes.

1

The ground wire (technically called the equipment ground) is the bare copper or green wire that's in most outlets.

2

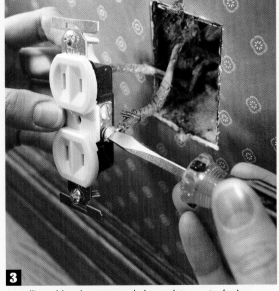

3

Installing old-style, ungrounded two-slot receptacles in a house with older wiring is an acceptable solution if you need to plug in only lamps, radios, and other two-pronged devices.

Electrical

ELECTRICAL SAFETY

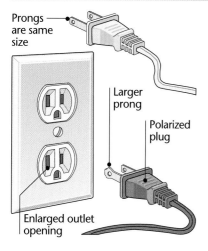

Prongs are same size

Larger prong

Polarized plug

Enlarged outlet opening

Polarized Plugs

Q. *My neighbor files down the wide prong of polarized electrical plugs to fit into the older outlets in his home. He says he's never had a problem doing it. Is this safe?*

Although his electrical equipment will still operate if he files down the wide prong to fit into the outlet, he is putting himself and others at risk for a severe, even fatal, electrical shock.

Only very old wall outlets and some extension cords do not accept polarized plugs. If your extension cords don't have polarized ends and your electrical plug requires one, buy a new cord at a home center or hardware store. If your electrical outlets won't take polarized plugs, have an electrician update them for you.

The National Electrical Code is very specific about polarized electrical connections. Polarized plugs are required on electrical equipment that would be hazardous without them. You'll find that some plugs on electrical equipment aren't polarized, but only when the equipment has extra built-in protection.

AVOIDING COMMON ELECTRICAL HAZARDS

Everyone uses them: screw-in outlets, taps, and adapter plugs. In most cases these little helpers are more a hazard than a help. They are easy to avoid, however, and here's how.

Before you do anything involving electrical outlets, be sure to turn off the power at the main panel. Always test the wires with a voltage tester to make sure the power is off. When you are finished with the work, have it checked by an electrical inspector to make sure you did everything correctly.

SCREW-IN OUTLETS

You can easily overpower an outlet that screws into a light socket. Light sockets typically have a maximum power rating of about 60 watts or less than 1 amp, well below the 15 amps available through most regular outlets. If you plug a 10-amp appliance into the light socket receptacle, it will overheat, the wire will melt, and there could be a fire.

The circuit breaker will not shut off to protect the light socket because the electrical current still falls within the circuit's safety limits. It's safer to provide regular receptacles for all plug-in devices and to use extension cords for temporary needs.

TAPS

Sometimes called octopus plugs, taps allow you to plug more than one cord into a single outlet. Taps can make it easier for you to overload the circuit and cause a circuit breaker to shut off or a fuse to burn out at the main panel. If an overload occurs, move some of the plugged-in appliances to other circuits.

Taps also wear out; the result is a poor connection, which causes the outlet to heat up, eventually ruining the electrical contacts and causing the electrical wires to harden and become brittle. This is a definite fire hazard!

The best solution is to provide enough wall-mounted outlets for your plug-in appliances. For instance, you can install a larger electrical box in the wall and convert a duplex receptacle to a double duplex outlet.

DO

Double duplex outlet

1 *Install a larger electrical box that can handle more outlets rather than using temporary multiple plug devices.*

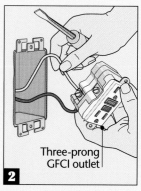

Three-prong GFCI outlet

2 *Install a GFCI when you need a three-prong outlet but don't have a ground wire at the electrical box.*

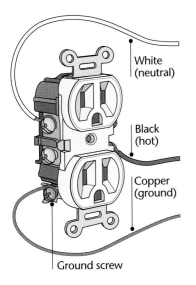

White (neutral)

Black (hot)

Copper (ground)

Ground screw

Electrical No-No

Q. *I've replaced many of my old two-slot electrical outlets with new ones that have a third hole for a ground. I don't have a ground wire, however. Can I ground the outlet by running a wire from the ground screw on the outlet to the white (neutral) screw on the outlet?*

Absolutely not. You cannot run a wire from the ground screw to the neutral (white) screw on the outlet. This would be a very dangerous situation. If you have already done this, *do not* use these outlets.

Disconnect all the outlets that have been wired this way. The National Electrical Code requires that you must provide a separate and continuous ground that runs from the outlet's ground screw to the house's main electrical control panel.

Most appliances will work with this improper wiring configuration, so this common mistake often goes unnoticed. When all of the outlet grounds have been connected to the neutral wire at the outlet, they are energized. Whenever someone plugs anything into these outlets, they'll send electricity through the ground wires, a potentially dangerous situation. Also, sometime in the future when someone needs to replace one of the outlets, the black and white wires may be accidentally reversed when they're connected to the new outlet.

If the wiring error goes undetected and the neutral wire is accidentally disconnected somewhere between the outlet and the circuit breaker box (because of a loose or missing wire connector, a broken wire, or a poor connection), you will lose all grounding. You'll be able to plug in a tool or appliance, but when you turn it on, electricity could flow through the tool or appliance's ground, causing a severe shock. The worst part about this situation is that you'll never know anything is wrong until you're electrocuted.

Instead of providing an independent ground, you could install a GFCI (see Outlet Grounding, p.240). If you don't provide a new ground, replace the old fashioned two-pronged outlets so no one mistakenly thinks the outlet is grounded.

ADAPTER PLUGS

Adapter plugs, also called "cheater" plugs, allow you to plug a three-prong plug into an old-fashioned two-prong outlet; in doing this, you bypass a safety feature. That third prong represents the ground wire in the cord, which helps to protect you from lethal shocks. The screw on the cover plate is rarely a substitute ground.

It's usually difficult to add a ground wire to an existing outlet, but there's a simple, safe alternative: Replace the two-prong outlet with a ground fault circuit interrupter (GFCI) outlet. The GFCI outlet provides shock protection even without the ground wire. Whenever you upgrade an electrical box, remember to make sure the box size meets the current National Electrical Code requirements.

DON'T

Screw-in socket and outlets

1

Screw-in outlets can be easily overpowered, causing overheating, melting wires, and a possible fire.

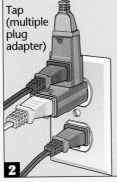

Tap (multiple plug adapter)

2

Taps (multiplug adapters) can overload a circuit and can be a fire hazard when they wear out.

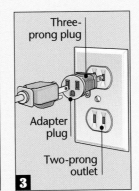

Three-prong plug

Adapter plug

Two-prong outlet

3

Avoid using adapter plugs; they allow you to bypass an important safety feature.

Electrical

ELECTRICAL WIRING

Connecting Aluminum to Copper Wiring

Q. *Our 30-year-old home has aluminum wiring, but our new light fixtures are prewired with copper wire. Some of our wall switches have to be replaced, too. How can we install the new light fixtures and new switches safely?*

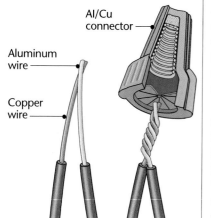

Al/Cu connector

Aluminum wire

Copper wire

You will need a special connector to join aluminum and copper wiring. The connectors are available at hardware stores, home centers, and electrical supply stores. The package should indicate that the connector is for "Al/Cu" connections.

This device has a dielectric paste inside to stop corrosion and the possible loosening of the connection over time. The connectors are designed for the specific wire sizes stated on the package. You may have to run an additional copper wire from the copper wire on your fixture to accommodate the wire size required by the connector.

Remember that this special connector is designed for copper to aluminum only and must not be used for aluminum-to-aluminum connections. And as with any home wiring project, have it inspected by a local electrical inspector.

Aluminum Wiring Bad?

Q. *Why is aluminum wiring in houses considered bad?*

Aluminum wiring is not bad, it's just incompatible with common copper devices. If you have aluminum wiring, it's safe as long as any rewiring or additional wiring is done correctly. Aluminum wire expands and contracts at a different rate than copper. If aluminum-to-copper connections are not done properly, they can fail over time by corroding. Corrosion can lead to hot connections, and ultimately fire.

There is a special connector that must be used whenever aluminum is connected to copper (see Connecting Aluminum to Copper Wiring, left). Switches and outlets marked "Co/Alr" are the only devices for direct connections with aluminum wiring. Co/Alr devices are available at electrical wholesale distributors.

I-Beams Can't Be Notched

Q. *I've chiseled notches in the bottoms of solid wood joists in order to run wire through. Can I put notches in wood I-beam joists, or is there a better solution?*

The rules for I-beam joists are different than for standard solid wood joists. Notching the top or bottom

New Wiring in Foam-Insulated Walls

Q. *The exterior walls of my house are filled with a foam insulation. I want to rewire my house and wonder if I should rewire when the house is being resided next year or try to rewire now, from the inside?*

There is no easy way to run wire through foam insulation except for short runs from below—and that is only feasible if you have an accessible basement crawl space.

One possibility is to remove your baseboards (if they're wide) and open the wall behind them. Run the wires through the studs behind the baseboard. Another solution is to use surface-mounted wiring strips on interior walls, but some people find these devices to be unsightly.

The best solution may be the one you already suggested: removing the siding and sheathing behind it and running the wires through the studs from the outside. As always have your work checked by an inspector.

flange severely weakens the joist, even if you make just one notch. Instead, knock out the perforated holes for running wires. If you need to drill a bigger hole, drill it toward the center of the span rather than near the ends or bearing point, just as you would with standard joists. Contact a joist manufacturer or lumberyard for specific information.

You will weaken your I-beam joists if you put notches in them. Instead, punch out the perforated knock-out holes to run wire through.

RUNNING NEW WIRES THROUGH WALLS

If you want to add a new switch, outlet, or wall light fixture where none exists, you will need to fish new electrical cable through the wall cavities. You'll need to be able to access the wall from either the basement, the crawl space, or the attic.

Identify where you want the new switch, outlet, or fixture to be, and follow the steps shown at right. To determine the cable size you will need, find the circuit breaker or fuse that controls the circuit you will be adding to. If it's labeled "15" (15 amps), buy cable labeled "14-3 with ground." If it's labeled "20" (20 amps), buy "12-3 with ground." The electrical box will have to be large enough to safely contain all the wires and devices.

■ Use a handsaw to cut the holes in the walls; it will let you feel if you've hit a wire and give you enough time to stop cutting.

■ Fasten the cable to the floor joist every 2 feet with special wire staples.

■ Cut a pocket in the insulation for the new electrical box. Avoid compressing the insulation, and caulk around the box so air leaks won't reduce the insulation's effectiveness.

■ Be sure to fasten the ground wires to metal boxes as well as to the switches.

■ If your home has aluminum wiring, have a licensed electrician do the job.

■ Always have an electrical inspector check any work you have done yourself.

1 *Position the new switch or outlet box, mark the hole size needed, and cut away the drywall.*

2 *Drive an 8d finish nail through the floor so you can see the spot from below. Drill a ⅝-in. hole through the floor, into the stud cavity under the new box.*

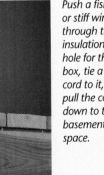
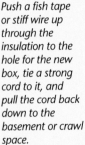

Push a fish tape or stiff wire up through the insulation to the hole for the new box, tie a strong cord to it, and pull the cord back down to the basement or crawl space.

3

4 *Tie the cord to the cable. Wrap it with tape so it won't snag the insulation, and pull the cable up through the hole.*

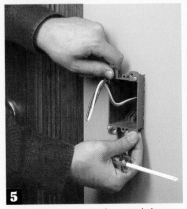

5 *Install the correct-size box, and clamp the cable to it.*

OUTLETS

Installing an Outdoor Electrical Outlet

Q. *How difficult is it to install an outdoor electrical outlet? I'm tired of running extension cords out the windows every time I want to use my weed trimmer.*

You can usually add a new outdoor outlet in just a few hours. You must install a GFCI outlet (see p.240), which will provide protection from shock in outdoor and damp locations. The process is actually the same as if you were going to install a new outlet between two studs inside your home (see An Easy Way to Add an Outlet, p.239); you'll be drawing power from an outlet on the interior side of the wall. You can also supply power to a new outdoor outlet by tapping into a basement junction; this requires more extensive fishing of wires but allows you to put the outlet almost anywhere you want. If you need an outlet for heavy-duty use (big power tools, lots of

Christmas lights, or anything over 300 watts), have a licensed electrician run a new circuit from the main electrical panel to the new outlet.

When you decide to install a new outdoor outlet, be sure to obtain a permit and check with your inspector on any special restrictions or requirements. Before doing any work, turn off the power to the outlet at the main panel and make certain you aren't overloading the circuit you intend to branch out from. Also, make sure the interior outlet box you will be running an additional wire from has a volume of at least 20 cubic inches. If the existing box is too small, replace it with a larger one. Be careful not to nick other wires and pipes when you cut the holes and fish for wires, and make sure you're between the same pair of studs as the inside outlet box. On brick, masonry, and stucco walls, you can surface-mount a special exterior electrical box. With narrow lap siding, use GFCI outlets and covers that can be installed horizontally.

Outlet Guidelines

Q. *What are the specific guidelines for installing electrical wall outlets in a house?*

The requirements for outlets, technically called receptacles, are stated in article 210-52 of the National Electrical Code. Basically it says that you shouldn't have any electrical or extension cords traveling more than 6 feet in any room, more than 2 feet along countertops, or stretched across doorways where someone might trip on them. Keep in mind:

■ From the edge of a doorjamb, opening, or fireplace, there must be an outlet within 6 feet.

■ On a continuous expanse of wall, there must be one outlet every 12 linear feet. This 12 feet can include one corner but can't be broken by a door, opening, or fireplace. The railing along a stairwell is counted as a wall for these purposes.

■ There must be an outlet on all walls over 2 feet long.

■ There must be at least two small-appliance outlets along a kitchen countertop, and no point on the kitchen counter should be more than 24 inches from an outlet.

■ You can place wall outlets at any height within 5½ feet of the floor.

The code is vague when it comes to the number of "openings" (outlets and light fixtures) on one circuit. Most electricians and inspectors agree that there should be no more than eight openings on a 15-amp circuit and no more than ten on a 20-amp circuit. Your local codes may require kitchen and bathroom outlets to be on separate 20-amp circuits. Outlets for large appliances also require their own dedicated circuits.

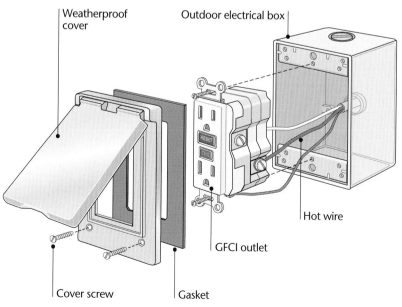

Weatherproof cover

Outdoor electrical box

GFCI outlet

Hot wire

Cover screw

Gasket

AN EASY WAY TO ADD AN OUTLET

When you want to add an electrical outlet to a room in your house, sometimes there's an alternative to fishing wires from the basement or attic. By working within one bay (the hollow cavity between two studs), you can add a new outlet on either side of the wall. The drawback to this method is that you can't place the outlet just anywhere; you can add one only inside a bay that already has an outlet in it (and sometimes not even then).

To determine if you can add an outlet, first you need to determine whether an additional outlet will overload the existing outlet. Keep in mind that if an outlet is on a circuit that often blows its fuse or breaker, you don't want to connect another outlet to it. Also, electrical codes restrict the number of outlets that can be connected to one circuit (See Outlet Guidelines, p.238). Codes also limit the number of wires that can enter an electrical box, depending on the inside volume of the box and the gauge of the wires. If the circuit is 20-amp (usually with thicker, 12-gauge wire), or if the existing box is smaller than 18 cubic inches, you need to replace the box with a larger one.

Note that if the box that holds an outlet has only three wires entering it, there is no way to draw power from that particular box. If there are more than six wires (two black, two white, and two bare copper) entering the box, you cannot connect your new outlet

as shown in these photos unless the outlet box is larger than 18 cubic inches.

Before you take any steps to tackle this project, turn off the power to the circuit at the main panel. Use a voltage tester to make sure the power is off before you touch any bare wires or terminals on an outlet. If the existing wires are aluminum, they require special connectors (see Connecting Aluminum to Copper Wiring, p.236). If you have old fabric-insulated wiring, call in a licensed electrician.

Once you've chosen a power source, use a stud finder to locate the studs on both sides of the old outlet. You can put the new outlet anywhere between the studs on either side of the wall. Hold the open end of the new electrical box against the wall, trace around it with a pencil, and cut out the hole for the new outlet with a drywall saw. Be sure to buy a box that can be fastened to the drywall, not mounted on a stud.

Next, unscrew the existing outlet from its box and feed the new cable through the box into the wall cavity (you'll have to either pry out a round knock-out with a screwdriver or force open a rectangular plastic tab). When you've fed in the cable—enough to reach the new outlet plus about 1 foot—pull it out through the new outlet hole, feed it into the new box, and mount the box inside the wall. The photos below show how to make the electrical connections for the new outlet.

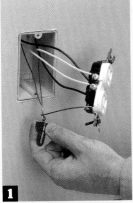

1

First disconnect the ground (bare copper) wires. Also disconnect one neutral (white) and one hot (black) wire from the existing outlet. Run the new cable through this box and into the wall.

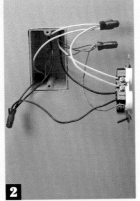

2

Connect the new hot and neutral wires to the ones you disconnected from the outlet. Your final results should look like this. Wires connected to terminals must always hook around the screws clockwise.

3

Use a stiff wire hook to fish for the new cable. Then strip about 9 in. of plastic sheathing off the end of the cable, insert the cable into the box, and mount the new box in the wall.

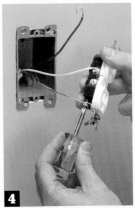

4

Connect the new wires to the new outlet. With the outlet facing you, the neutral (white) wires connect on the left; the hot (black) on the right. The cable sheathing must end inside the box.

Electrical

What Is a GFCI?

Q. *What exactly is a GFCI, and how does one work?*

You usually see GFCI's (ground fault circuit interrupters) in a kitchen or bathroom; they're the outlets with the tiny *Test* and *Reset* buttons. A GFCI is basically a super-sensitive switch that can detect leaks of electrical current that could cause deadly shocks or fires. When the GFCI detects a problem, it instantly shuts off power to everything plugged into it.

The National Electrical Code began requiring GFCI's in 1971. The Code now requires them in bathrooms, garages, outdoor locations, unfinished basements, and crawl spaces, as well as within 6 feet of the kitchen sink and within a certain distance of pools and spas. Check with an electrician if you are unsure where to install them. Know, too, that medical equipment and devices containing microprocessors might not work if plugged into a GFCI.

GFCI Doesn't Reset

Q. *Last week the GFCI in my bathroom triggered. Now I can't get it to reset or to trigger. What do you think the problem is?*

Either your GFCI is bad, or it's good and responding to a leak in electrical current and keeping the power shut off. There's no easy way to tell the difference, but the problem often lies in a plugged-in device like a radio or hair dryer; before you take anything apart, unplug everything from the GFCI outlet and from any other standard outlets on the same circuit. GFCI outlets should have a "GFCI Protected" label attached to them.

Retest the GFCI with the *Test* and *Reset* buttons. If it still doesn't work, turn off the power at the main and replace that GFCI with a new one. Retest the new one; if it doesn't reset, you have a problem in the electrical system. Call in an electrician to track it down. If the new GFCI works, get rid of the old, worn-out one.

Shock from a GFCI?

Q. *We didn't have a grounded outlet in our kitchen, so I installed a GFCI outlet for my refrigerator. Whenever someone touches the refrigerator and the stove at the same time, they get a shock. I thought GFCI's were supposed to prevent this.*

GFCI's will prevent you from receiving a *lethal* electrical shock, not from receiving any shock. It sounds as though you might have a short in your refrigerator; it should be repaired immediately. While the National Electrical Code allows you to use a GFCI in place of a grounded outlet, these outlets are not intended for major appliances.

An electrical ground needs to be installed to this outlet by having a ground wire run to the closest grounded electrical outlet or to the circuit breaker box. Contact a licensed electrician to do the work.

Outlet Grounding

Q. *The old house I live in has no grounded electrical outlets. Is there a way I can ground them without having to go back to the electrical panel with new wires?*

Adding a ground wire to your existing outlets can be difficult and should be done by a licensed electrician. However, there is an easier way to minimize the risk of shock: Install a GFCI outlet. The outlet still won't be grounded, but it will protect you from dangerous electrical shocks. It also has a slot for three-prong plugs. You must affix labels to these outlets that say "No Equipment Ground."

Another advantage to installing a GFCI is that if it's wired at the first location where the line comes in from the electrical breaker, any outlets "downstream" from that one can be replaced with standard three-prong outlets. Remember to label the downstream outlets with stickers marked "GFCI Protected" and "No Equipment Ground." The stickers are available at electrical supply retailers.

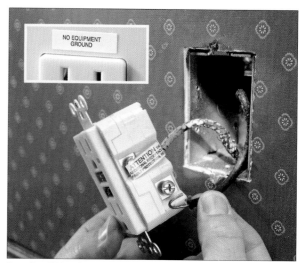

Install a GFCI when a ground wire isn't present. Be sure to connect the power supply wires to the "line" terminals. (The "load" terminals are covered by a warning label.) You might have to install a new, larger electrical box if the old one isn't big enough.

INSTALLING A GFCI

Many of the thousands of electrical accidents that occur every year can easily be prevented with the installation of a GFCI, the switch that detects hazardous leaks of electrical current. Installing a GFCI is not difficult, but if you don't feel comfortable doing electrical work, hire a licensed electrician to do the job. If you do the work yourself, obtain a permit from your local building department so that an electrical inspector will check your work when you're finished. You will need a screwdriver, a wire cutter/stripper, a tape measure, and a circuit tester.

Once you have turned the power off at the main panel and have tested the circuit you're about to work on to make sure it is dead, remove the cover plate and the two screws that hold the existing outlet in its box. Carefully pull out the outlet. Use the circuit tester to check both the hot and the neutral wire to see if either is live. Hold one tester lead against the bare ground wire and touch the other lead to the hot (black) wire, then to the neutral (white). If the tester lights up in either case, one wire is still live and you have a problem somewhere in your system; put everything back together and call in a licensed electrician to find the problem before you do any more work.

If there are no live wires in the box, you can begin work. Two terminals will be labeled *Line* and two *Load*. You will be connecting to the "line" terminals. Connect the black (or other color except green, white, or gray) hot wire to the brass screw and the white neutral wire to the silver screw (or a screw marked "white") on the

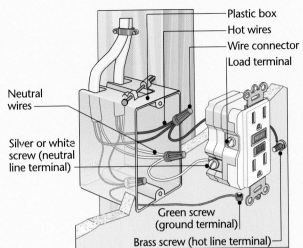

Plastic box
Hot wires
Wire connector
Load terminal
Neutral wires
Silver or white screw (neutral line terminal)
Green screw (ground terminal)
Brass screw (hot line terminal)

GFCI. Connect the ground wire to the ground screw. Fold the wires back into the box, screw in the GFCI, install the cover plate, and turn on the circuit.

The wiring in many older homes has hot and neutral wires, but not a ground wire. The GFCI will still work if you connect it to the hot and neutral wires. However, two complications can occur. First, the old metal boxes were sometimes grounded by metal tubing (conduit) or other metal pathways leading to the main or other ground. If so, you are required by code to attach a ground wire to the metal box and to the GFCI ground terminal. Let a licensed electrician tell you if the metal box is grounded. Second, most old electrical boxes are too small by current standards to hold a GFCI, so you may have to install a larger box. Test the GFCI as shown in Photo 3.

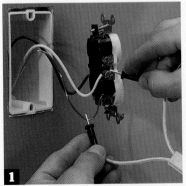

1 When the power is off, check for live wires with a circuit tester. With one lead touching the ground wire, touch the neutral (white) wire, then the hot (black) wire with the other lead.

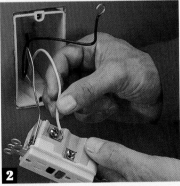

2 Connect the ground wire to the green ground screw, the white wire to the neutral (silver) screw, and the black wire to the hot (gold) screw on the side of the GFCI labeled Line.

3 Turn the circuit back on at the main panel, and test the GFCI by plugging in a radio and pushing the Test button. The radio should go off. Push the Reset button to restore the power.

Electrical

Buzzing Light

Q. *Why do lights sometimes buzz when a dimmer switch is set on anything but the highest setting?*

Dimmer switches work by interrupting the flow of power to the light. These interruptions cause little surges of power that can vibrate some filaments, like a pick striking a guitar string, causing the bulb to make a buzzing sound. The buzzing stops at the highest setting because there are no more interruptions, just a steady flow of power.

Try using 130-volt bulbs or Rough Service (RS) bulbs to get rid of the buzzing. These types have a sturdier filament that not only lasts longer, but is less likely to shake. If heavier-duty bulbs don't work, replace your dimmer switch with a new one.

Hot White Wire?

Q. *Can a white wire be the "hot" wire when it is used in a three-way switch?*

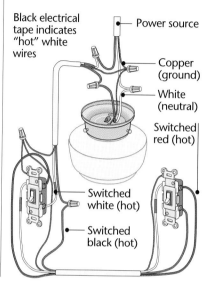

Black electrical tape indicates "hot" white wires — Power source

Copper (ground)

White (neutral)

Switched red (hot)

Switched white (hot)

Switched black (hot)

Although the white wire is usually the neutral wire in an electrical box, it is not always the neutral wire. If the white wire is the hot wire, it should be identified with a piece of electrical tape, but often it is not marked—so be careful!

The National Electrical Code makes an exception from the normal "black-hot, white-neutral" rule for wires in a "switching situation." This means that in a properly wired three-way switch (see drawing, left) the white wire will be a hot wire. In fact, any wire connected to a switch is a hot wire, unless it's a ground wire.

This code exception has been in force for a long time, and only requires that the wires be "manufactured" cable. This includes the non-metallic sheathed cable you use for house wiring—the one that has the black, white and ground wires together in a plastic cover.

Good-Bye Pull String

Q. *I'm always fumbling in the dark basement to find the pull string on the ceiling light fixture. Is it possible to put a switch on this type of light?*

To wire a new fixture to a wall switch, first turn off the power at the main electrical panel and use a temporary work light from another source. Remove the fixture from

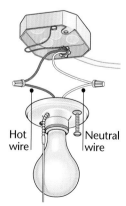

Hot wire | Neutral wire

the junction box and disconnect the hot and neutral wires from the fixture. If you plan to reuse the old porcelain pull-chain fixture, make sure the chain is left in the On position.

Push out the knock-out in the box in a convenient location to run two-wire-with-a-ground nonmetallic (NM) cable. Since you are replacing a basement fixture, it is fine to run the cable on the surface of the wall to the new switch box that you should locate about 48 inches from the floor. Attach the cable to the wall with cable staples no further than 12 inches from

each box and at least every 4½ feet along the run. Install a new light fixture as shown in the diagram below.

If you don't want to run wire, you could also install a transmitter/receiver system. With this system, a transmitter, which runs on a 9-volt battery, is surface-mounted. It works like an ordinary wall switch as long as it is located anywhere within 50 feet of the fixture. The receiver screws into the socket with the light bulb.

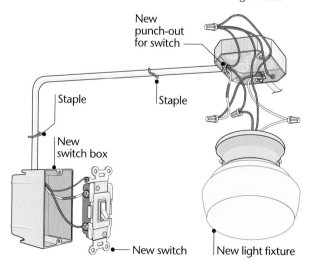

New punch-out for switch

Staple | Staple

New switch box

New switch | New light fixture

Do Dimmer Switches Save Electricity?

Q. *I've read that installing dimmer switches can lower the electric bill. How can a dimmer switch actually save electricity?*

Modern electronic dimmers do save electricity. The old-fashioned "rheostat" dimmers controlled the flow of electricity by adding resistance; power that wasn't going to the bulb was lost as heat and no electricity was saved.

Today, electronic dimmers work differently. Those used on incandescent bulbs switch the flow of electricity on and off very quickly, at a rate that keeps the filament glowing at the intensity you want. Fluorescent lights and low-voltage lights require "full-wave" dimmers, which don't turn the electricity on and off, but instead change the voltage. Both types save electricity, but not a lot of it. To really save electricity on your lights, try using compact fluorescent bulbs instead of incandescent bulbs.

how is it done? REPLACING A BAD LIGHT SWITCH

Replacing a bad light switch is a quick, simple job. You can replace standard switches with dimmers, decorative switches and most timer switches. The photos below show you how to do it.

Don't worry if the wiring inside your switch box doesn't look exactly like what we show here. Your switch may be connected to one white wire and one black, for example. There may be more wires in the box than we show, but you only need to deal with the two connected to the switch.

Before you unscrew the switch's cover plate, shut off the power to the switch by flipping the circuit breaker or removing the fuse at the main electrical panel. Don't touch any bare wires or terminals until you've tested to make sure they are not powered. To make sure the power is off, hold one probe of a test light against a ground wire. With the other probe, touch one terminal screw, then the other. If the test light glows, the circuit is live; that means you switched off the wrong circuit. If the light doesn't glow, you can loosen the terminal screws and disconnect the wires.

⚠️ If you have old, fabric-insulated wiring, have a licensed electrician inspect the wiring before you do any electrical work yourself. Also, check to see if you have aluminum wiring. With the power off, scrape a bare wire with a utility knife; if you see silvery metal instead of copper, it's aluminum and you must call in a licensed electrician to handle the job.

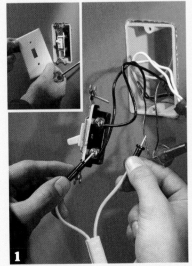

1 Remove the switchplate. Use a voltage tester to determine if you've switched off the correct circuit.

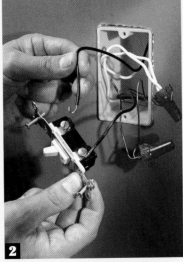

2 Connect the new switch by hooking the bare leads clockwise around the terminal screw. If the bare leads of the wires are badly nicked or cracked, cut them off and strip new leads.

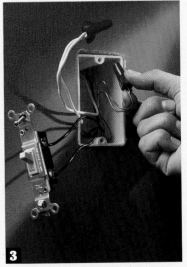

3 Fold the wires back into the box, ground wires first; they shouldn't touch the terminals or they'll cause a short circuit. Screw the switch into the box and reinstall the cover plate.

LIGHTING FIXTURES

Undercabinet Lighting

Q. *I want to install undercabinet lighting in my kitchen. Should I install fluorescent or halogen lights?*

Both fluorescent and halogen under-cabinet fixtures add light to the work surfaces in a kitchen. Fluorescent fixtures are less expensive and easier to install, while halogen fixtures provide a brilliant white light that shows colors vividly. However, halogens also create intense heat. Halogens can actually warm the bottom of the cabinets, so you cannot keep perishable food in the cabinets or on the counter. Fluorescents give off little heat and consume less than one-third the electricity of halogens. They are available in a range of lengths between 12 and 42 inches. Fluorescents are wired like any other fixture, and they are available in sizes that fit easily under a cabinet.

Despite the seeming impracticality of halogen lights, the high-quality light that they provide makes them a popular choice for kitchen upgrades. Halogen undercabinet systems use tiny low-voltage bulbs that operate on 12 volts, so you will need to install a special low-voltage transformer. These low-voltage systems are packaged either in the form of an easy-to-install modular system, which includes the transformer and bulbs in one fixture, or as a more complicated multiple-piece system, which would include a separate transformer, low-voltage wires, and a variety of fixtures to choose from. More expensive halogen fixtures have more openings for convenient hardwiring, dissipate heat better, have frosted or textured glass to cut glare, and have longer-lasting, quieter transformers.

Some undercabinet fixtures can be plugged into outlets, while others are designed to be wired directly. Keep in mind that the cords on plug-in systems get dirty, hang down, and can clutter the countertop: According to the National Electrical Code, these cords cannot be hidden away inside or fastened to the cabinet. Finally, always buy fixtures stamped with the UL (Underwriters Laboratories) label to be sure that they meet certain safety standards.

Halogen fixtures installed underneath your cabinets create dramatic kitchen light that illuminates workspaces and shows colors better than fluorescents.

Humming Fluorescent

Q. *I'm getting a very loud humming noise from the fluorescent fixtures recently installed in my home. Is there any way to eliminate this problem?*

The annoying hum you are hearing is a mechanical vibration from the magnetic forces in the ballast (or transformer) located inside the fixture. It's typical in all fluorescent lights, although it does vary in volume from one fixture to another.

Check the label on the ballast in your fixture. It should give a sound rating (determined by laboratory and manu-facturing standards) from "A" to "F," with "A" being the quietest. If yours is rated "B" or lower, replace the ballast with one rated "A." Ballasts with labeled sound ratings are sold at hardware stores, home centers, and electrical supply stores. To replace the ballast, shut off power at the fuse box, disconnect the two wires on the old ballast, and connect the new ballast.

You might also check to see if the hum is coming from the fixture's mounting. Occasionally the surface which the fixture is attached to can act as a sounding board, causing excessive noise. Remounting it with some vibration-dampening fasteners will help to minimize the problem.

Track Lighting

Q. *I want to install track lighting in my family room. What do I need to know before I buy and install it?*

Track lighting can be powered by either standard 120-volt or 12-volt (low-voltage) power. You can use standard incandescent bulbs in a 120-volt system, but halogen bulbs of equal wattage will give you whiter and more focused light. Low-voltage lighting provides a very narrow beam, allowing for dramatic accent lighting of objects and artwork. And while low-voltage systems cost more (they require transformers to reduce the standard voltage from 120 to 12 volts), they use slightly less energy.

Before you buy and install:

■ Think about how you want to use the room and what objects, such as plants or artwork, you want to emphasize. This will help you decide how many lights you'll need.

■ Don't try to mix brands or modify the fixtures of one brand to fit the track of another.

■ Track is sold in 2-foot increments, usually up to 12 feet long. Keep this in mind when you are planning the layout for track lighting.

■ Make sure you have a light and an electrical box in the the ceiling (controlled by a wall switch) to which you can hook up the track system.

■ Make sure the ceiling is high enough. The lights may hang down as much as 6 inches, so if your ceiling is less than 8 feet high, as it might be in a basement, it will be a problem.

■ Decide whether you want a dimmer switch. Some low-voltage transformers require a special dimmer that's available from lighting retailers.

■ Consult an electrician if you have aluminum wiring or knob-and-tube wiring with fabric insulation on the wires. Working with these types of wires requires the skill and knowledge of a qualified professional.

---

how is it done ? REPLACING A LIGHTING FIXTURE

Replace a light to update the look of a room. Start by turning off the power to the light at the main service panel; then remove the old light fixture. Unscrew the mounting plate and gently pull the wires out of the electrical box—you don't want to pull the box loose. Separate the wires that are connected together into bundles. Attach the new fixture's wire leads to the correct wires in the ceiling box—usually white to white and black to black. Use the correct-size wire connector.

Many of today's light fixtures use lamp-style cord for leads, rather than one white and one black wire.

If your fixture has a lamp-cord lead, examine the two wires closely. The neutral wire of the cord will be identified with writing, squared corners, indentations, or ribs on the sheathing. Connect this wire to the white wires from the electrical box. The other lead should be connected to the black wire.

To ground the fixture, secure a 6-inch piece of bare copper wire (called a "pigtail") to the ground screw. Connect the other end of the pigtail to the ground wires from the box and the ground wire of the fixture. Tuck the wires back up into the ceiling box; then install the new mounting bar to the box.

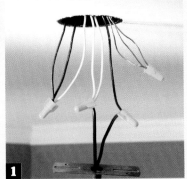

1 *The only bundles you need to work with are the ones that are connected to the wires from the old fixture and the ground wires (bare copper or green).*

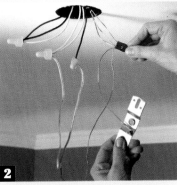

2 *Connect the fixture's ground wire to the ground wires that are in the box. The mounting bar on the new fixture has a green ground screw.*

3 *Ask a helper to hold the light while you tuck the wires back up into the ceiling box and install the new mounting bar to the box.*

RECESSED LIGHTING

Intermittent Recessed Lights

Q. *Two of the four recessed lights in our living room occasionally shut off, then go back on after a while. What's going on?*

This on-off-on action is called "nuisance tripping"; the "nuisance" may be preventing your house from catching on fire. Recessed lights, which are enclosed and prone to overheating, contain a thermal protector that turns off the light if temperatures exceed a certain level, usually around 190° F.

One situation that causes overheating is too-tight packing of insulation around the outside of the housing. Some regions of the country require this insulation, but it can keep the heat from dissipating. The label on the housing should indicate whether the fixture is "rated" or "not rated" for direct contact with insulation. If your fixture is "not rated" and is in an insulated ceiling, this can cause the problem you are experiencing. A way to resolve this problem is to hold the insulation away from the fixture with a cage of wire mesh.

Another situation that may be causing the problem is a bulb that's recessed too far into the fixture. Look for a pair of wing nuts or screws in the housing that will allow you to adjust how far the bulb is positioned inside the fixture housing.

A third reason this may be happening is that the wattage of your bulb is too high for the fixture, or you're using the wrong type of bulb. Recessed light housings have a label that tells you the maximum-wattage bulb you can safely use in the unit and if you should use a reflector-type bulb which directs heat downward and away from the fixture.

Regardless of the cause, this may be a potential fire hazard. Resolve the problem as soon as possible!

Recessed lights may overheat if insulation is trapping heat in the fixture.

Use wire mesh to hold back the insulation. This will allow air to circulate around the fixture and prevent overheating.

Many fixtures use a reflector-type bulb, which has a silver back to direct heat downward and away from the fixture.

Recessed Lights in an Old House

Q. *Can I install recessed lights in an old house? There's an old light fixture in the kitchen that I want to replace.*

There are a few questions you need to ask yourself before you install recessed lighting. First of all, what is on the other side of the ceiling? If the answer is "the attic," you can most likely use the standard recessed light housings. If there's living space above, you'll have to fish cable inside your ceiling and you'll need remodeling cans designed for installation without access from above. Most cans require at least 7 to 8 inches of space between floors. If your house has fabric-insulated wiring or aluminum wiring,

you'll have to call in a licensed electrician to do the work.

How many lights do you plan to install? If you want to install a lighting system that uses more watts than the existing fixture, first make sure the circuit can handle the added demand.

What do you hope to do with the old fixture? One option is to remove it, tap into the junction box above it, and place a cover plate over the box. The junction box must remain accessible, however; you can't patch over it with joint compound. You could also remove the fixture and the box above, then install a recessed light in its place. For this, you'll have to disconnect all the wires in the existing box and reconnect them inside the new junction box attached to the can.

how is it done?

INSTALLING RECESSED LIGHTS

If you have some DIY experience, you can install recessed lights yourself. The amount of time and money involved depends on the existing electrical wiring, the lights you choose, and the number of lights you put in. If your room already has a light fixture, you should be able to install four good-quality recessed fixtures in a weekend.

Aside from the cans and trim pieces for the recessed fixtures, you'll need a drywall saw to cut holes for the cans, an electronic stud finder to find the ceiling joists and decide where to locate the lights, and an electrical test light to make sure the power is off before you ever touch a bare wire. Cans must be at least ½ inch from joists, braces, or anything else that can burn.

The electrical cable you use for this job must be the same gauge as the cable you'll be connecting it to. In order to secure the wire connections, you'll want to get some wire nuts. Cable clamps also come in handy whenever you want to secure cables as they enter junction boxes. If you plan to fish cables through joists, buy some protector plates and drywall clips. In spots where the cable must cross joists, cut 5 x 5-inch access holes in the drywall and chisel notches in the joists just deep enough for the cable. You'll also need a drywall patch, drywall screws, and joint compound to repair the holes you'll be making in the ceiling.

Chances are, the ceiling will have to be painted after you've patched the holes.

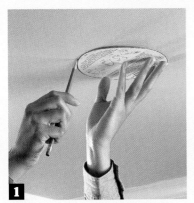

1 Mark openings for the cans using the template; then drill a hole in the ceiling to probe for obstructions.

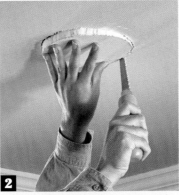

2 Cover the floor with a drop cloth, and put on eye protection and a dust mask; then use a drywall saw to cut out the light openings.

3 Run cable from the power source to the nearest light opening, then along to the next light openings, leaving at least 16 in. of cable hanging from each opening.

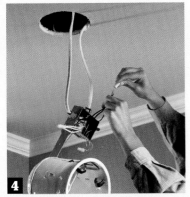

4 Make connections at the power source and at each can, securing all connections with wire nuts.

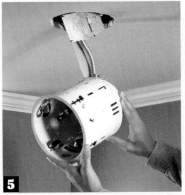

5 Lift the cans into the openings. Different cans use different methods of mounting; this one has built-in clips that lock onto the drywall.

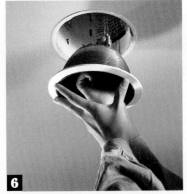

6 Install the trim pieces and screw in the light bulbs. Do any painting and touch-up before you install the trim.

LIGHT BULBS

Lumens Versus Watts

Q. *When I buy light bulbs, I notice that the package has the number of "lumens" printed on the box. What are lumens?*

A lumen is a unit of measurement that defines the amount of light a bulb produces. When bulbs were first manufactured, they were rated in comparison to candles. One lumen is equal to the amount of light a standard taper candle sheds onto a 1-square-foot surface held 1 foot away from the candle.

Don't confuse lumens with watts, a unit of measurement that defines the amount of power used. For example, a 60-watt incandescent light bulb produces about 850 lumens. A 16-watt fluorescent can produce 700 lumens—nearly an equal light output for about a quarter of the energy.

Stubborn Bulbs

Q. *Our home has several exterior light fixtures. By the time the bulbs burn out, their bases have fused to the socket and we wind up breaking the glass. How can we safely remove broken bulbs and avoid this problem in the future?*

To safely remove a stuck bulb first turn off power to the fixture. Remove the glass from the bulb (break it if it's not already broken). Then insert needle-nose pliers into the center of the bulb base. Spread the pliers apart and slowly unscrew the bulb. The outward pressure from the pliers should loosen the base.

To prevent this from happening in the future, buy better-quality bulbs with brass bases. Brass will not rust inside the receptacle.

Bulbs Burn Out Too Fast

Q. *One of my two porch light bulbs burns out every 4 to 5 weeks. Both are wired to the same switch and are sheltered from rain and snow. I replaced the socket in the problem light and checked all the wires, but the problem persists.*

If the light bulbs are enclosed in globes, it's possible that excessive heat is building up within the one globe, resulting in fast-burning bulbs.

You might consider stepping up to a 130-volt bulb instead of the standard 120-volt. A 130-volt bulb has a stronger filament that can better resist voltage surges, heat, and vibration. The bulb life is nearly triple that of standard 120-volt bulbs, and they consume 10 percent less energy. The downside is that they produce about 11 percent less light. To compensate for this use a bulb of the next higher wattage if the fixture allows it.

Another possibility is the quality of the bulb. Poor-quality light bulbs burn out rapidly and unpredictably. Generally, the established name-brand light bulbs have a reliably long life. Compare brands by the hours listed on the package.

Leave the Light On

Q. *A salesman told me that turning a compact fluorescent on and off too much can shorten the life of the bulb. Is this true?*

Yes, frequent on-off switching will shorten a compact fluorescent's life span. If you leave a room where a compact fluorescent bulb is on and you'll be back shortly, leave the light on. The energy costs aren't that much and you'll lessen wear and tear on the bulb.

COMPARISON OF BULBS FOR INDOOR USE

TYPE		WATTS	LUMENS	HOURS
Soft white Incandescent		40 100	445 1,710	750–1,500
Halogen spot- or floodlight		50 90	600 1,300	2,500–3,000
Halogen bulb		60 100	960 1,850	2,250–3,000
Compact fluorescent		11 15 23	600 925 1,580	8,000–10,000
Compact fluorescent reflector		15 20	725 1,000	10,000

New Ideas in Light Bulbs

THE ENERGY POLICY ACT (EPACT) of 1992 was enacted to reduce the use of electricity nationwide. As a result of this legislation, manufacturers redesigned various products, including light bulbs, to be more energy-efficient.

Among the many products developed since the act was passed are long-life compact fluorescent light bulbs. Unlike fluorescent bulbs of the past, which worked off a ballast that often hummed and buzzed, the new compact fluorescents light up a room silently, providing a warmer light, more like that of an incandescent bulb. They're more expensive than incandescents, but they last 10 times longer. And, unlike their predecessors, compact fluorescents can be screwed directly into an incandescent light or lamp socket, making the conversion to these bulbs convenient.

To help consumers who are replacing an incandescent bulb with a compact fluorescent, most packages list the fluorescent's wattage rating and its incandescent equivalent. There's also information on recommended areas of use for the particular bulb. When you read the package, keep in mind that the wattage-equivalency numbers don't tell the whole story. Lumens, not watts, measure a bulb's brightness.

Other ratings you'll find on light bulb packages are the color-rendering index (CRI) and lumen-per-watts (LPW) rating. The CRI states the accuracy with which a bulb renders colors. The LPW measures how efficiently the bulb converts watts into lumens (see chart, left, for a comparison of some typical bulbs).

Although not as new to the consumer market as the other bulbs discussed here, halogen bulbs can offer energy savings. The bulbs contain halogen gas, which allows the tungsten filament to burn hotter and cleaner, producing a whiter, brighter light. Compared to conventional incandescent bulbs, halogen bulbs produce more light. Finally, you can also find "smart" bulbs, which dim themselves to a preset level or turn themselves off after a specified amount of time. No special switches or fixtures are required. These bulbs have microchips embedded in their socket bases to outsmart and outlive ordinary bulbs.

A trip to the store for a few light bulbs may take a bit longer than it used to because there are so many more to choose from.

CEILING FANS

Ceiling Fan Out of Balance

Q. *One of our ceiling fans has developed a bad vibration at medium and high speeds. How can we correct this?*

To troubleshoot this problem:

■ One or more of the blades could be warped. Remove the blades from the fan and lay them on a flat surface. They should lie flat. If any blades are warped, replace the entire set. Blades are matched as a set at the factory.

■ Check the blade irons for defects. These irons are matched and set at the factory at an angle of about 12°. Stack the irons atop one another; you should be able to tell if one doesn't have the same angle as the others. If you find one that doesn't match the others, replace the defective iron. Irons can be replaced individually.

■ Check the fan motor. With the blades and irons removed, turn the fan on to the fastest setting. There should be no wobbling. If there is,

send the motor in for repair. Check your owner's manual for the closest authorized service center.

■ If everything else checks out OK, balance the fan blades by attaching small weights to the top of the out-of-balance blade or blades. This is strictly a trial-and-error process. First, reassemble the fan. Use any small weights like washers, coins, or fishing sinkers. Attach the weight with tape temporarily and experiment until you find the right spot and weight; then glue the weight in place to keep it from flying off.

INSTALLING A CEILING FAN

A ceiling fan offers both a practical and a decorative solution for keeping a hard-to-cool room comfortable without air conditioning. There's a wide selection of styles, colors, and finishes available to fit just about everyone's taste and room decor. And if the room has a center ceiling light fixture, you can easily install a ceiling fan without any major rewiring (though you can't use the existing electrical box as the fan support). That's the kind of installation we discuss here.

There are two space requirements to be aware of before you begin: There must be at least 24 inches

between the fan blade tips and the wall. And the bottom of the fan (and its attached light, if there is one) must be at least 7 feet from the floor, so people can walk under it safely. If your home has aluminum wiring, have an electrician do the entire installation.

Start by turning off the power to the circuit. Remove the old light fixture. Put a piece of tape on the black wire (power supply hot) and the white wire (switch loop hot) that were connected with a wire connector inside the box. These wires deliver power to the wall switch and must be reconnected later in order for the switch to work. The other black wire and white wire are the switch

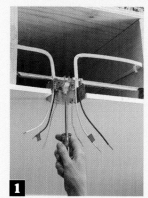

1 Place a piece of tape on the black wire (power supply hot) and the white wire (switch loop hot) that were connected inside the box.

2 Pull the hanger brace bar through the ceiling opening. It's best to feed the brace into the cavity along the length of the joists, then turn it 90°.

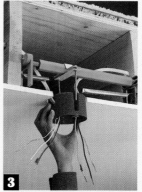

3 Push the power cable wires through the knockouts in the box; then secure the cable to the box with the clamps. Attach the new junction box.

4 Mount the fan's hanger bracket on the supported junction box. Check the manufacturer's instructions.

If you have a four-bladed fan, you can cut the trial-and-error time considerably. Remove two blades

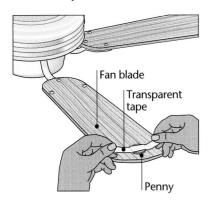

Fan blade

Transparent tape

Penny

that are opposite each other. If there is a wobble with the remaining set of blades, balance them using the weight trick mentioned above. When they're balanced, attach the other two blades, making sure you mark which blades you just attached. If there still is a wobble, balance those two blades as well. There's no time-saving trick for five-bladed fans!

Some manufacturers offer balancing kits, with instructions on how to balance your fan. If the dealer who sold you the fan doesn't stock the kit, check with the manufacturer.

Ceiling Fan Maintenance

Q. *I have had many ceiling fans in the various homes I've owned and have always wondered: Do they require any preventive maintenance?*

All that's necessary is a periodic dusting. About every 3 months (or more if you feel it's necessary), clean the blades and the housing around the motor, using a paper towel sprayed with an all-purpose window cleaner. While it doesn't seem like much, this regular cleaning will extend the life of any ceiling fan.

---

leg and neutral of the power supply and will be connected to the corresponding black and white wires of the fan. Green or bare copper ground wires will be secured together with a pigtail to the fan's grounding points (wire or screws).

Remove the old metal ceiling box by unscrewing the center fastener. Once it's removed, loosen the cable clamp screws to release the cable. Now remove the box. Cut off the old support bar at both sides of the ceiling opening with a mini hacksaw.

Work the hanger brace bar through the ceiling opening (Photo 2). Place the feet of the bar on the ceiling and turn the bar so it expands until the legs are secure against the joists. Make sure the brace remains centered over the opening.

Feed the power cable wires through the knockouts in the box; then secure the cable to the box with the cable clamps. Attach the new junction box to the hanger bracket assembly. Check the kit instructions for details.

Connect the power supply neutral (white) and the switch leg (black) wires to the appropriate fan and light wires. Attach the light kit to the fan to complete the wire hookups; consult your fan's instructions. The general rules regarding wire colors and connections are: green to green (ground); white to white (neutral); and black to black (and red or light blue if there's a light) for the hot wires. Remember, however, to reconnect the marked black and white wires to feed the switch loop.

Mount the fan's hanger bracket on the newly

supported junction box; again, check the instructions. Create a ground pigtail using the junction box ground wires. Then use a wire connector to secure the hanger bracket ground wire, the fan motor ground wire, and the ground pigtail. If you don't, the fan won't be grounded and you could receive a severe shock.

5

Connect the power supply neutral (white) and the switch leg (black) wires to the appropriate fan and light wires. To finish, attach the light kit to the fan. Consult the fan's instructions.

Electrical

Placing a Motion Detector

Q. *I just bought a motion detector. Where should I install it to get the most security?*

For safety, position motion detectors to cover the walks leading to your front and back doors and your driveway, so the light will come on when you come home at night. These lights are also good for decks and any potentially dangerous areas, such as stairways and swimming pools.

If your goal is to improve security, aim sensors to cover every approach to your home, including fence gates and patio doors. Also, be sure to direct light into the darker areas of your yard. Good lighting is an inexpensive yet effective way to discourage unwanted intruders.

Ideally, it's best to mount motion sensors 6 to 10 feet above the ground, and to position them so that most movement will occur across the sensitivity zone rather than directly toward the detector. If you are using existing light locations, you can easily mount the sensor separate from the lights. The low-wattage wire connecting the sensor to the light doesn't require conduit sheathing.

Front walk and front door

Dark or deeply shaded areas

Deck

Back walk and back door

Driveway and garage

Oversensitive Motion Detectors

Q. *How can I adjust my motion detector so that it doesn't go on at the slightest movement outside?*

You can prevent most unwanted activations simply by adjusting the detector's sensitivity and by aiming it correctly onto your property.

Sometimes heat from a light bulb can also confuse the sensor. Try to keep the bulb and detector as far apart as possible.

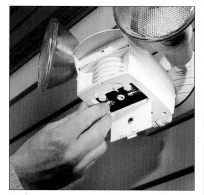

To fine-tune a motion detector, adjust the sensitivity and timer controls as described in the manufacturer's instructions.

Too Short Wires

Q. *When I tried to replace my old doorbell, the ends of the wires broke. Now there isn't enough wire to attach to the new doorbell terminals. What should I do?*

Fortunately, you have a few options to try before you buy a door knocker.

First, try splicing extension wires onto the old ones. Buy some 18-gauge insulated wire and a package of heat-shrinkable tubing sized for that wire. Cut two pieces of wire about 6 inches long; then twist the new wires around the ends of the old wires. (You won't need to turn off the power to the doorbell because it's low voltage.) Solder the joints with a soldering gun; then slip the shrink tubing over the joints. Heat the tubing with a match so it shrinks tight around each joint.

If you don't have enough wire to splice onto, you might be able to run new wires from the transformer to the doorbell. This could be fairly easy if you have a basement with exposed floor joists. You might also need access to the bell button, which may involve removing some of the trim surrounding the door.

If neither option works, consider calling a licensed electrician. There may be other ways to get your doorbell working again that require the knowledge of a skilled professional who can study the problem up close.

Finally, a less expensive option may be to simply forget the old wiring and buy a wireless doorbell at your home center.

Adding a Door Chime

Q. *Our home's door chimes are located toward the rear of the house, and we can't hear them when we're in the front. How can I add a second chime?*

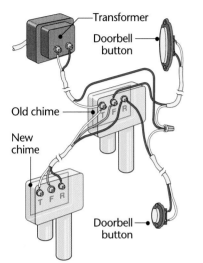

Transformer

Doorbell button

Old chime

New chime

Doorbell button

Decide where you want the new chime. Then run a new low-voltage wire, the same size as the present wire, from your old chime to the new one. Connect the wires according to the wiring diagram.

After installing the new chime, you may discover that your present transformer isn't big enough to handle a second chime. If this is the case, you'll need to replace the existing transformer with a larger one.

Finding a transformer can be difficult. They're often installed in an unfinished basement or utility room. There may be more than one transformer in this area, so make sure you have the right one by tracing the wire to the doorbell, or by disconnecting one wire and testing the door chime. Be careful, transformers are powered by standard household current.

Make sure the new chime's operating voltage matches the output voltage of the transformer. The operating voltage should be printed on both the chime and the transformer.

REPLACING A DOORBELL

Three components make up a doorbell system: the doorbell button, a chime unit, and a transformer. Unless you suspect a break or a short in one of the wires, replacing a doorbell is a simple job that you can do yourself.

Working on the doorbell button or chime with the power on is safe because the transformer reduces the 120-volt electrical supply to a lower voltage, usually 24 volts or less; so unless you have a heart condition or wear a pacemaker, you need not shut off the power at the main service panel. However, if you need to replace the transformer, you must turn off the power at the main panel; it's connected directly to a 120-volt circuit and you could get a severe or fatal shock if the power is not turned off.

First, remove the bell button and touch the two wires together. If the bell chimes, replace the button. If the bell doesn't ring, take the chime off the wall and clean its parts with denatured alcohol to make sure the unit's plungers aren't sticking. If this doesn't solve the problem, it's time for a new chime.

Before you buy a new door chime, check the old chime's voltage rating (it's usually stamped near the screw terminals). The new and old chimes' voltage ratings must be the same.

To remove the doorbell button, disconnect the two wires from the terminal screws. It doesn't matter which wire goes to which terminal.

Attach the new doorbell button to the house. Fill in any gap between the decorative plate and the siding with a bit of exterior-grade caulk.

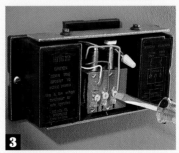

Disconnect the wires from the chime's screw terminals. Note which wires go to which terminals. The wires must be attached to the corresponding terminals on the new chime.

Mount the new chime on the wall and attach the low-voltage wires to the correct terminals. Check the operation of the chime and the doorbell buttons before you attach the decorative cover.

how is it done?

HOOKING UP A GAS RANGE

Afraid to hook up a gas appliance? You should be! A gas leak in your home can be fatal.

However, it's a relatively simple job requiring just basic tools and readily available supplies. And if you use the right materials and follow instructions carefully, you can safely do the job yourself. A professional may charge as much as $200 to hook up a gas appliance.

BUYING A PIPE AND CONNECTORS

The most important step for a safe installation is to buy the appropriate connector. Don't reuse old flexible connectors.

Flexible corrugated gas connectors and gas pipe and fittings are available at most home centers and well-stocked hardware stores. Stainless steel or coated brass connectors are the only type of flexible connectors sold these days, and the only type you can safely and legally use. Older types of corrugated connectors—sold until about 15 years ago—made of uncoated brass or other metal have been found to be unsafe. If you have one in your house, replace it now!

When you buy a connector, the package should be clearly marked "stainless steel" or "coated brass" and have the AGA (American Gas Association) stamp of approval. Be sure it is clearly marked for use with a range. Typically the corrugated tube of a range connector is ½ inch i.d. (inside diameter). Buy a connector that comes packaged with the end connector fittings you need, and make sure it is long enough for you to work between the stove and the wall.

Usually the gas line coming into your kitchen will be ½-inch threaded black pipe, and the connection to the stove will be either a male (external threads) or female (internal threads) ½-inch fitting. If you cannot find a connector package with end fittings that match what you need for the gas line, use a black gas pipe fitting on the line to accommodate the end connector fitting.

Faithfully follow the instructions on the package for installing the connector. Be careful not to kink or force the corrugated connector into sharp bends, which could eventually cause a break.

 Always check for gas leaks. *Never* screw the connector nuts on the ends of the corrugated tube directly to a black gas fitting or pipe. This will surely leak.

1 ◆ Pull out the old range, and shut off the gas cock. The gas is off when the lever is at a right angle to the pipe (see Photo 2). This shutoff may be located behind the range or in the basement just below. A shutoff is required in the line to the range, and should be added if you don't have one.

2 Wrap Teflon pipe-joint tape twice clockwise around the threads. Yellow Teflon tape, heavier than white, is meant to be used for gas fittings.

3 Remove the end connector, wrap the unbeveled end with Teflon tape, and screw it to the gas line. This end fitting can be either male or female.

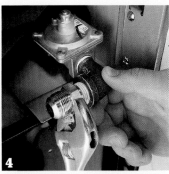

Screw a ½ x ½-in. street elbow (male threads at one end, female at the other) into the range gas port. Screw the connector's other end fitting into the street elbow. Use Teflon tape.

Tighten the connector nuts to the two end connector fittings. While tightening the nuts, hold the tube straight against the fitting. Do not use Teflon tape on these threads.

Turn on the gas cock (vertical position), and light the range burners for about a minute to get the air out of the gas line. Spray all the joints you've made with gas leak detector. Or use soapy water: Bubbles indicate a leak.

Replacing an Electric Range Element

Q. *How can I fix an electric range burner that has stopped working?*

This repair is a simple one; all you need is a replacement element. There are two types of elements: flip-up elements that are wired, using screws housed in a ceramic insulator block, and plug-in elements that plug into a prewired ceramic receptacle.

To begin the job, turn off the power at the main electrical panel. If you have flip-up elements, flip the element up, remove the mounting screw, and gently pull the unit out of the opening. Remove the clips that hold the halves of the insulator block together; then use a nut driver to remove the screws that connect the wire leads to the element. Reconnect the wire leads to the new element and put it all back together again.

If you have plug-in burners, conduct a test before turning off the power: Unplug the nonworking burner and insert it into the receptacle of a working burner. If it works, you have a good element and a bad receptacle. If it doesn't work, buy a new burner and plug it in.

To replace a bad receptacle, first unplug the range or turn off the power at the main electrical panel. Lift the top of the stove, and disconnect the wire connectors that join the receptacle wires to the control panel wires; then install a new receptacle. Be sure to use the ceramic wire connectors that are supplied. In some cases, both the receptacle and the burner will need to be replaced.

Flip-up elements are wired with screws housed in a ceramic insulator block.

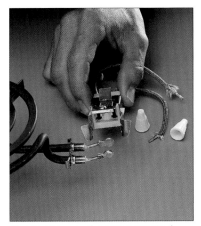

Plug-in elements plug into a prewired ceramic receptacle.

Repaint a Range?

Q. *The home we purchased has an electric stove. It works well, but we don't like the color. Is there a safe and effective way to paint a stove?*

Repainting a stove is just not worth the time and effort. Its surfaces are subject to such a combination of hard use and high temperatures that a repaint won't hold up long enough to make it pay off; and taking it to a supplier for a baked-on enamel finish probably isn't worth it either.

Appliances

Getting Rid of Water in the Refrigerator

Q. *Water accumulates under the crisper drawers at the bottom of my refrigerator even when the tube that carries defrost water from the freezer to the drip pan underneath isn't clogged. How do I stop this?*

This is usually caused by a "frozen lake" inside the drain trough in your freezer. You need to melt the lake.

Freezers defrost themselves from time to time; the defrost water is supposed to drip down into the trough and drain pan. If the drain trough opening is obstructed, the drain hole will freeze over and the defrost cycles will add water to the frozen lake.

To fix the problem you will need to unplug the refrigerator and put the contents of the freezer in a cooler. Remove the screws that hold the evaporator cover in place, and remove the cover. Remove the two air-duct extensions, too. To speed the

Remove the screws that hold the evaporator cover in place; then remove the cover.

defrosting of the freezer, remove the freezer floor (six screws secure it). You should be able to see the piece of ice that is causing the problem.

Use a hair dryer to help defrost the ice in the drain trough. Aim the heat along the length of the trough until the ice is gone and the water has drained. The water in the trough will travel down the drain tube into the drip pan underneath the refrigerator.

Next, check the drain trough for an obstruction such as a piece of insulation or a food package label. Then pour a cup or two of very hot water into the trough to check the drain system. Reassemble the freezer compartments, empty the drain pan that's under the refrigerator, and plug the appliance back in. It may take a few days for the dripping to stop.

Test a Refrigerator Switch

Q. *The interior light of our refrigerator has gone out, and simply replacing the bulb hasn't done the trick. Any suggestions, short of buying a new refrigerator?*

This sounds obvious, but make sure the bulb is screwed all the way into the socket. If the bulb is properly seated and there's still no light, check the door switch. There are two types—a rocker style (which we show) and a plunger type. Both are tested the same way. Here's what to do:
- Unplug the refrigerator.
- Release the tabs on the sides of the body of the switch with a putty knife or a small screwdriver. Wrap the putty knife blade with tape to avoid scratching the refrigerator.
- Pull the switch and the wires connected to it out of the cabinet.
- Make sure each wire is firmly connected to its terminal. If they're not, connect them and try the switch.

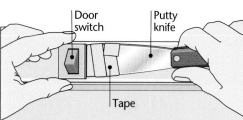

If this doesn't fix the problem, you can replace the switch or test it with a multitester. To test the door switch:
- Disconnect the wires from the switch terminals. Mark each wire so that you can reconnect it to the correct terminal. To keep the wires from falling back into the cabinet once they're detached, tape them to the cabinet.
- Set the multitester dial to the highest RX setting. The multitester's needle should be resting on the "∞" (left) side of the tester's display face.
- Attach one of the multitester probes to one of the switch terminals; attach the other probe to the other switch terminal. The multitester needle should swing to the right (zero) when both

probes are attached.
- Press the rocker arm into the switch body to test the switch. If the needle deflects or moves to the left at all, the switch is bad and needs to be replaced.

Replacement door switches are sold at appliance parts stores. Take the old switch along with you when you go to buy a new one.

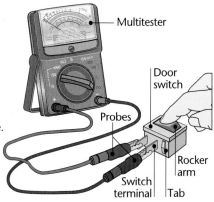

Moving Old Refrigerators

Q. *We have an old refrigerator and we need to transport it to our new home. Can we lay it on its side for the move?*

If at all possible, you shouldn't lay a refrigerator that is more than 10 years old on its side. Transport the fridge in a standing position to avoid damaging the compressor and refrigerant lines. If it was manufactured in the last 10 years, it will not be harmed if you transport it on its side or back.

If you transport a new refrigerator on its side, let it sit upright for several hours at room temperature before plugging it in and turning it on. This will allow any oil that may have traveled from the compressor area to drain back into the proper position for normal operating lubrication.

Refrigerators that have their condenser coils on the outside of the back of the units should never be placed on their sides or backs! If you do this, you'll damage the coils and the refrigerator won't work anymore. If you suspect that your refrigerator is more than 10 years old, play it safe and transport it upright.

Switching a Door

Q. *I just moved my old refrigerator into a new house and it would makes sense for the door to open on the opposite side. It appears the manufacturer has drilled holes for switching the hinges and handles. Is this something I can do myself?*

It's quite a simple job. You'll need a Phillips screwdriver, a nut driver, and about a half hour. Start at the top and work your way down.

Unscrew the top hinge and lift the top door off its lower hinge. Do the same for the bottom door.

To remove the refrigerator door, begin at the top by unscrewing the top hinges and taking the doors off; then remove the caps on the new hinge side.

Remove the small plastic caps on the new hinge side of the fridge. Then, starting at the bottom, install the lowest hinge, the bottom door, the middle hinge, then the top door and hinge.

Switching the hinges and handles should have no effect on the door gaskets. And if you hate the idea of letting out all that cold air while you're making the switch, stretch plastic wrap across the opening while you're working. You can install the screws right through the wrap, and you'll keep most of the cold air in.

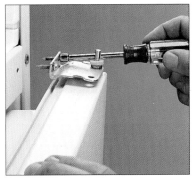

Reinstall the hinges, doors, and screws on the side you want the door to open from.

Freezer Runs Continually

Q. *My freezer seems to be running almost all the time. I am constantly having to scrape frost away just to close the door. What's the problem?*

Your freezer probably needs periodic manual defrosting; you should unplug it and get rid of the frost whenever it reaches a thickness of ¼ inch on the freezer walls and interior shelves. Never use salt or sharp instruments to remove the frost—no spatulas, forks, putty knives, or screwdrivers! If you use a hair dryer or heat gun, use caution and never leave it unattended.

Pans of hot water placed inside the freezer will speed defrosting. Blowing a fan into the freezer also works. Place food from the freezer in a cooler; it will stay frozen for the couple of hours it takes to completely defrost the freezer.

High-Priced Repair

Q. *The estimate I just received to install a new compressor in my old refrigerator is twice what it cost a few years ago for the same work on another refrigerator. Why is it so expensive now?*

Nowadays when a repair technician services a Freon system in a refrigerator or freezer, the refrigerant must be recovered and reprocessed. Recovered refrigerant is sent to a certified reprocessor to renew the substance to new or virgin purity specifications. As of 1996, the production and use of Freon refrigerant in refrigerators has been discontinued. All of the following factors contribute to a higher repair bill: additional training required for the technician; new tools and the expensive recovery equipment; and the significant additional time required to complete this type of EPA-approved repair.

Appliances

Dishwasher Wiring

Q. *I'm adding a dishwasher and need to get power to it. I want to connect it to one of the existing kitchen outlets. Is this OK?*

No, it's not OK. Most local codes require that any fixed kitchen appliance be on a separate circuit (usually 15 amps). You could hard-wire the dishwasher by connecting sheathed cable directly to its connection box. However, many electricians prefer to wire dishwashers so they can be unplugged. Installing an outlet avoids any inconvenience if you should have to move the unit.

To do this installation, place a metal electrical box, with an outlet, within easy reach of any person who might do repair work on the appliance. One good place is on the floor just behind the dishwasher's toeplate (see photo below); another is inside the sink cabinet. Make sure the electrical box won't be in the way of the dishwasher motor when you need to slide the dishwasher in and out.

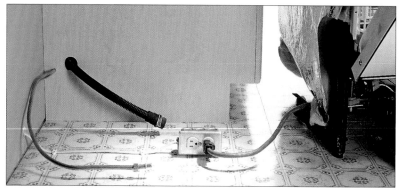

A dishwasher should have its own electrical outlet. A floor-mounted metal electrical box located just behind the toeplate is convenient when you need to move the dishwasher.

Bugs in the Dishwasher

Q. *Living in Miami means living with palmetto bugs, and occasionally I discover one scurrying about inside my dishwasher. I assumed that a dishwasher is a sealed unit. So how do they get in? And how do I keep them out?*

Those nasty critters have learned what most dishwasher owners don't know: A dishwasher isn't the airtight container that people envision. In fact, there are several possible routes palmetto bugs can take. The solution is to call an exterminator to eliminate the bugs, because you should not modify your dishwasher in any way. The three most likely entry areas are:

■ The tub flange area where the bottom of the door meets the front of the tub. By design, the bottom of the door is not sealed tightly.

■ The fill spout area, located on the side of the unit.

■ The venting area where hot water vapor escapes, generally located in the upper portion of the door.

Sudsy Dishwasher

Q. *After my dishwasher completes all the cycles, there are still soap-suds inside the tub; they don't go away no matter how many times I run clear water through the cycles. How do I get rid of them?*

Though not a convenient solution, you could add buckets of cold water to the dishwasher instead of allowing the machine to fill automatically with hot water; this will speed the removal of the suds. Of course each time the cold water is added, you must interrupt a pump-out portion of the cycle to get rid of that cold water and a portion of the suds.

Another tactic you might try is adding ½ teaspoon of liquid fabric softener at the start of the cycle which will reduce sudsing action. Also, be sure you are using dishwasher detergent and not dishwashing detergent; dishwashing detergent is designed solely for hand-washing and will add loads of unwanted suds if used in a machine. If you are using dishwasher detergent, make sure you're not using more than the box calls for; a general rule is to use 1 tablespoon per full load of dishes for each grain of water hardness. A local water-conditioning company or your water utility can tell you the water hardness in your area.

Water temperature is also important. Some dishwasher manufacturers require that the temperature be 140° F to activate the detergent and dissolve greasy food soil. Fill a glass with hot tap water and check the temperature with a candy or meat thermometer; if it reads less than 140° F, consider raising your water heater setting. Be careful—tap water at 140° F can scald.

One final tip about ridding your dishwasher of soapsuds: Run the hot water at the kitchen sink before starting the dishwasher. This clears the line of any cold water, which reduces the detergent's cleaning ability.

Dishwasher Stops Prematurely

Q. *Our dishwasher stops at the beginning of every wash cycle. We've had the motor replaced because it had what the repair person called "start winding problems," but that repair didn't last. What could the problem be?*

It's not uncommon for a service technician to diagnose this problem as a bad start winding and to repair it by replacing the motor. However, this situation may also require a new relay switch along with the new motor, even if the switch is OK. This should prevent failure of the new motor. The technician should be able to get a new motor under warranty from the parts supplier. A start relay switch is not normally shipped with a new motor; ask the technician to replace the relay at the same time the new motor is installed.

Adding A Dishwasher

Q. *I'd like to add a dishwasher in my kitchen. Do I need to change my cabinets to make room for it, or can I modify the existing cabinets? What sort of plumbing do I need?*

Installing a dishwasher involves cabinetry, plumbing, and electrical work; unless you're an experienced do-it-yourselfer, leave this job to a pro. You'll need a minimum distance of 34 inches from the floor to the bottom of the countertop for starters. The space under the countertop must have a depth of at least 24 inches. The width of the opening must be 18 inches for a small dishwasher, 24 inches for a standard model.

The existing cabinet to the right or left of your sink base cabinet will have to be removed or modified to make room for the dishwasher. It's a good idea to keep the dishwasher adjacent to the sink cabinet because you'll need to run a hot-water line and a waste line between the dishwasher and the plumbing for the sink. Having the dishwasher near the sink is also more convenient when it comes time to load the dishes.

If you cannot place the dishwasher next to the sink, be prepared to use up valuable cabinet space as you run the plumbing through it. If you have a basement, you can run the plumbing under the floor.

As for electricity, a separate electrical line will have to be run directly to the dishwasher. Check with a local electrical inspector, and make the hookups according to the manufacturer's instructions.

If you have a 24- or 18-inch-wide cabinet next to the sink, you're in luck; if not, you'll have to modify the existing cabinets. After these modifications, you'll need to connect a separate hot-water line and to replace the sink drain tailpiece with one that has a drain nipple for the dishwasher drain hose. If you have a garbage disposer, you might be able to connect the dishwasher waste line to it. You will need to drill holes in the side of the cabinet to run the water and waste lines. The electrical line should come from the back wall near the floor and should have about 2 feet of extra length for hookup.

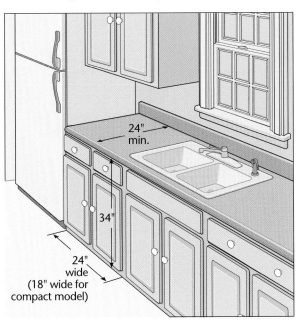

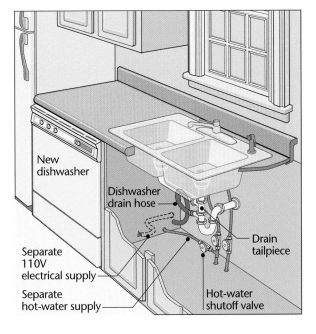

Appliances

Slow-Filling Washing Machine

Q. *It takes 20 minutes for my washing machine to fill with water for each cycle. What's going on?*

You probably have clogged inlet valve screens. Fortunately, they're easy to clean. First, turn off the hot and cold water to the washing machine; then unscrew the inlet hoses from the back of the machine. Use a sharp awl to pry the thimble-shaped screens from the inlets.

Use an old toothbrush (and a lime-deposit-removing product if they're really encrusted) to scrub the screens, or just replace them. To reinsert, use a small piece of pipe, the same diameter as the screen, to seat the screens firmly in place. Be careful when tightening the hoses back onto the water inlets; the plastic threads are easy to strip or misalign.

Don't ever consider removing the screens and not replacing them. Dirt and grime will quickly ruin the inlet valve. If cleaning or replacing the screens doesn't cure the problem, you'll most likely have to replace the entire inlet valve (see Replacing a Water Inlet Valve, below).

Clogged inlet valve screens can slow the rate at which a washer fills. To correct this problem, remove and clean the screens; then reinsert them.

REPLACING A WATER INLET VALVE

To check this valve, always unplug the machine first and shut off the water. Check the machine's manual to find out how to remove the back panel. Unbolt the inlet valve from the cabinet, and disconnect the wire terminals, using masking tape to identify them for reinstallation. Use a multitester to check the condition of the valve (Photo 1). Set it to its lowest ohm rating, and probe each pair of terminals on the solenoids. Look for a resistance of between 100 and 1,000 ohms.

If the test fails, replace the water inlet valve. First, using pliers, unclamp and disconnect the hose connected to the valve; then connect the wires to the replacement unit. Attach the replacement to the mounting plate and cabinet (Photo 2).

If the solenoids pass the resistance test, unscrew them from the valve. Dissassemble the valve and clean it thoroughly with a toothbrush under running water. Reinstall the valve, then reattach the hoses and replace the back panel. Test-run the machine.

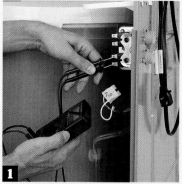

1 *Set the multitester to the RX100 scale and hold the probes to the terminals. If the multitester gives an infinity (∞) reading or doesn't move at all, the valve is bad and must be replaced.*

2 *Using pliers, unclamp and disconnect the hose connected to the water inlet valve. Connect the wires to the replacement unit. Attach the unit to the mounting plate and cabinet.*

3 *If the solenoids pass the resistance test, unscrew them from the valve. Dissassemble the valve and clean it thoroughly with a toothbrush. Then reassemble and install it.*

No Warm Water in Washer

Q. *Our washing machine won't mix the hot and cold water. When the warm-wash cycle is selected, we get hot water, and when we choose the cold-water cycle, we get only a small stream of cold water. What area of the machine controls the temperatures and needs adjusting?*

You may need a new water inlet valve (see Replacing a Water Inlet Valve, p.260). Before you do this, however, check a few more possibilities. First, be sure that the cold-water faucet is opened completely. If this doesn't help, shut off the hot and cold faucets and disconnect both fill hoses from the washer's inlet valve. Keep a bucket handy to catch the water still in the hoses.

Next, place the disconnected ends of the hoses in the laundry tub or washer, turn on both faucets and see if the water flow out of both hoses is similar. If the cold-water flow seems slow, check the filter screens in the faucet end of the hose and in the water inlet valve. (See Slow-Filling Washing Machine, p.260). Then hook everything up again and try the warm-water cycle. If there's still no warm water, you'll need to replace the water inlet valve.

Oil-Staining Washing Machine

Q. *There are oily stains on our clothes when we take them out of our washing machine. I've cleaned the tub, but that didn't help. Where could this be coming from?*

If the grease or oil isn't already on the clothes being washed, the stains are probably being caused by a buildup of detergent and fabric softener that has accumulated inside the washer over the years. This buildup can give clothes an oily look and feel.

To get rid of this stuff, empty the washer, set the water level selector switch to the highest setting, and let the tub fill with hot water. As the agitation begins, lift the lid and pour in 2 cups of bleach. Close the lid and let the machine run for 2 or 3 minutes; then turn the washer off and let everything sit for 30 minutes.

After that time, turn the machine back on and let it go through the rest of the washing cycle. Finally, wash a load of old rags or old clothes (ones without grease on them). The staining should be gone, or at least mostly diminished. If the stains persist, repeat this procedure.

Leaky Washing Machine

Q. *After every wash cycle there is a small puddle of water on the floor under our 10-year-old washing machine. How can I determine what is causing this?*

When a small amount of water leaks directly under a washing machine, it's usually coming from one of four places: the water inlet hose, the drain hose, the water-level air hose, or the pump. To check each one, begin by turning off the power to the machine and unplugging it. The water inlet hose extends along the top rear edge of the washer. To inspect the hose for cracks, lift the top of the washing machine. For some models, you may need to remove the entire cabinet.

The hoses that carry dirty water from the basket to the drain pump and from the pump to the standpipe drain or laundry tub (depending on the machine's draining setup) can often be seen from the back of the washer. If not, take the front panel off the washer or remove the cabinet.

After the panel is off, plug the washer in and run it through the drain phase of a wash cycle to check the hoses. At this point you'll want to check the pump for leaks as well; if you find any leaks in the hoses, simply replace them. If the pump is leaky, you might be able to repair it with a pump seal kit, or you could replace the pump with a new one.

The water level (pressure) air hose may be faulty. Usually, this hose is located in the top console panel and can be reached by removing the back of the panel. If it's not behind the console, you'll have to remove the cabinet.

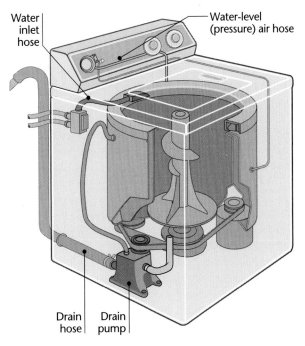

Water inlet hose

Water-level (pressure) air hose

Drain hose

Drain pump

Appliances

D R Y E R S

Ink-Stained Dryer Drum

Q. *There is a ballpoint pen ink stain on the inside of my clothes dryer drum. How do I remove it so it won't stain my clothes?*

For almost any stain inside the drum, first remove as much of it as you can with a clean dry cloth. Clean the area thoroughly with a spray cleaner, a laundry presoak product, or a mild abrasive cleaner. Then wipe the area with a cloth and clean water to remove any residue.

Next, take a bunch of damp old rags or towels and dry them for 20 to 30 minutes on normal heat. You may still see a little bit of the ink stain on the inside of the drum, but don't worry; by now the stain has set into the drum's finish and should not transfer to your clothes.

If you want your dryer drum to look like new, you can spot-paint the inside with special high-temperature paint made for dryer interiors. Ask someone in an appliance store to recommend one for you.

Inside Dryer Vent

Q. *In the cold of winter I'd like to save some heat by venting the gas clothes dryer directly into the basement. Is this a good idea?*

No, it's definitely a bad idea to vent a gas dryer anywhere but outside. The exhaust from the dryer contains sulfur dioxide, nitrous oxide, and other unhealthy by-products of combustion. You can safely vent an electric clothes dryer into the basement, but keep in mind that all the moisture and a fair amount of lint from the clothing will end up in the house.

Non-Spinning Clothes Dryer

Q. *My daughter's clothes dryer runs, but the drum refuses to spin. The belt is not broken, and the drum will spin if you push it. What could be broken?*

Since the belt is intact, the problem is most likely the idler pulley—the pulley that keeps tension on the drive belt and keeps the belt in line as the drum rotates. If the idler pulley is weak, it will cause the belt to come right off the motor pulley, or it may not be able to keep enough tension on the belt to spin the drum.

To check out the pulley, begin by unplugging the dryer. Remove the lower access panel. If there's no lower access panel, remove the front panel: Remove the two screws under the lint filter cover, then release the top hinge clips. Lift the top next, and remove the two side screws that hold the front panel to the cabinet sides. You can now remove the front panel and get to the idler pulley.

If the idler pulley rolls freely and the tension spring is not broken, it's likely that the belt has just jumped off the motor pulley. If the idler pulley appears defective, you'll need to install a new one.

To replace the idler pulley, first release any tension on it by moving it to the right; then remove the belt from the motor pulley. Lift the idler pulley up to release the tabs which are in slots in the dryer cabinet. Reverse these steps to install the new idler pulley.

To install the belt, make a loop in it and feed the loop below the idler pulley toward the motor pulley. Push the idler pulley toward the motor and place the loop around the motor pulley. Now let go of the idler pulley and everything will be aligned.

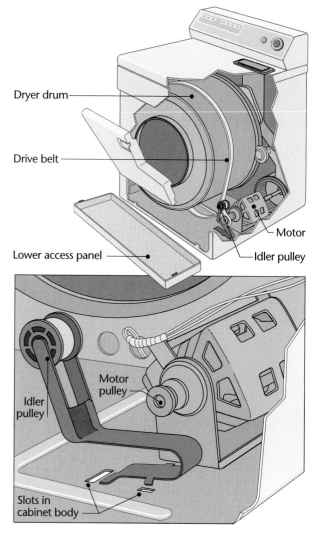

Dryer drum

Drive belt

Lower access panel

Motor

Idler pulley

Idler pulley

Motor pulley

Slots in cabinet body

INSPECTING A DRYER

A clothes dryer works by circulating heated air through wet clothing, causing the moisture to evaporate. If your clothes aren't drying, there are many possible reasons why the dryer isn't working. Here's a guide to identifying common dryer problems and their solutions:

■ Poor drying is often caused by lint buildup in the screen or in the exhaust system. Check the lint screen and remove any buildup with your fingers. You should do this after each load of laundry. Next, vacuum any lint that may have accumulated in the heater area, lint screen, blower housing, and exhaust duct connection. You should also check for lint on the flapper of the outside duct outlet.

■ If lint is not the culprit, check for a leaky door seal. Hold a piece of tissue near the door when the dryer is running. If the tissue is drawn in, or if you see signs of wear or damage on the seal, replace it.

■ Another common clothes dryer problem is a broken drum belt or idler pulley, which would prevent the drum from turning even when the motor is running. A thumping sound usually indicates a worn belt, and steady rumbling or rolling often means worn rollers or a bad idler pulley bearing. These parts are available where large appliances are sold. Check your appliance manual for specific repairs to the belt or idler pulley.

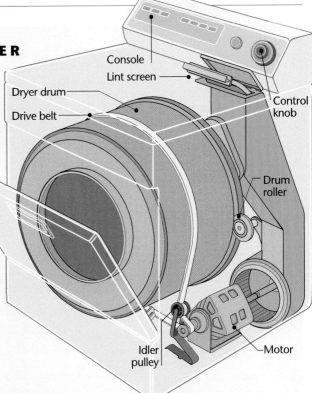

Console
Lint screen
Dryer drum
Drive belt
Control knob
Drum roller
Idler pulley
Motor

■ If you suspect that your electric dryer is not heating properly, look for a circuit breaker that has tripped or a fuse that has blown. Problems having to do with a dryer's electrical system (including switches and timers), motor, and blower are best left to a professional. Internal dryer wiring is heat-resistant and should never be replaced with ordinary wiring.

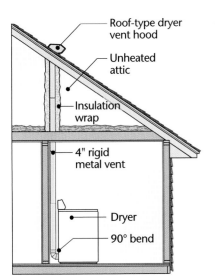

Roof-type dryer vent hood
Unheated attic
Insulation wrap
4" rigid metal vent
Dryer
90° bend

Venting a Dryer Through the Roof

Q. *What is the best and safest way to vent a clothes dryer through an unfinished attic to the roof? Do I need a special vent hood on top of the roof?*

There is a special dryer vent hood made for roof mounting. It has a screen and a flap that is designed to open when the dryer is exhausting. You can buy one at a hardware store or home center.

To vent your dryer safely, limit the total length of the duct to 22 feet for a straight run. For each 90° bend, subtract 5 feet from the 22-foot total. To keep air resistance to a minimum, use smooth sections of galvanized steel or aluminum vent pipe that are sized for your dryer. Don't use flexible plastic vent pipe because it can melt from the heat of the dryer.

Whenever the vent runs through an unheated attic space, the duct should be wrapped with fiberglass insulation to prevent condensation on the interior. (Condensation will moisten the lint flowing through the vent, causing the wet lint to stick to the sides and block the airflow.)

Home Comfort

Weatherproofing

266 Types of Insulation
268 Upgrading Insulation
270 Insulation Strategies
274 Air Leaks

Heating

276 Ducts and Heat Pumps
278 Furnaces and Thermostats
282 Fireplaces
286 Chimneys

Cooling

288 Air Conditioners

Ventilation

290 Fans
292 Vents

Air Quality

294 Indoor Pollution
297 Fire Prevention

Humidity

298 Condensation, Mildew, and Moisture

Weatherproofing

Blowing In Wall Insulation

Q. *When we bought our 1930's-vintage home, it had no insulation. We installed fiberglass insulation in the attic and are considering filling the walls with blow-in insulation. Is this a DIY project? If it is, would I approach it from the inside or the outside?*

Serious DIYers can buy loose insulation and rent a blowing machine, but you need special tools and know-how to do the job right. It's probably not a job you'll ever have to do again, so hiring a pro isn't a bad idea in this case. If you decide to do it yourself, work from the outside because loose insulation creates a huge mess.

Begin by drilling 2½-inch holes in each stud cavity, fill the holes with insulation, then close them with tapered plugs. If the house has original lap siding or has been resided, a pro would remove rows of siding, do the work, plug the holes, then reinstall the siding. Some contractors remove a single strip of siding in the middle of each wall, blow the top half of the cavity first, then blow the bottom half. Others bore holes at the top or both midway and at the top, then blow insulation down through the holes. Odd-size cavities and spaces below windows should also be insulated, though it's not always cost-effective to fill every little space.

Houses with brick exteriors must be insulated from the inside. Stucco homes can be insulated from the outside, but the dozens of plug holes can be an eyesore if the patches don't match perfectly. This is a challenge even for stucco experts. Working from the inside makes sense if the house is vacant or if remodeling is under way and the insulation holes will be painted, wallpapered, drywalled, or paneled over.

Cellulose insulation is a popular choice because it's inexpensive, easy to blow, minimally irritating, and good for packing around ducts, electrical boxes, and wires. Fiberglass, mineral wool, and foam insulation are also available to blow in.

Foil-Faced Insulation

Q. *Is the foil on foil-faced insulation supposed to reflect heat away from the side the foil faces? Can you tell me exactly where and how it should be used?*

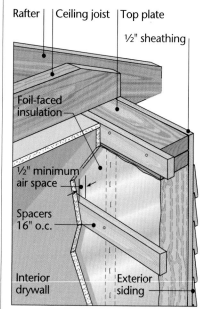

There are several types of foil-faced insulation available. One type is made of rigid sheets of urethane or isocyanurate and usually has foil on both sides. These sheets have the highest R-value of any insulation and are also the most expensive. They typically come in 4 x 8-foot panels, in ½-, ¾-, or 1-inch thicknesses. Fiberglass batt insulation is also available with foil glued to one side.

In all cases, the foil works as a moisture barrier; however, if there are cracks or gaps between pieces of insulation, air currents carrying moisture can work their way through. While the foil's primary purpose is as a moisture barrier, it can also be used to reflect heat—as a radiant barrier—provided you leave at least ½ inch of air space between the reflective surface and any other surface.

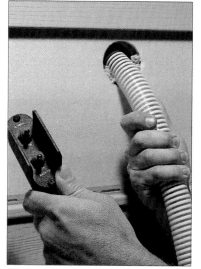

Fill the wall cavity with an insulation blower. A remote control regulates the flow.

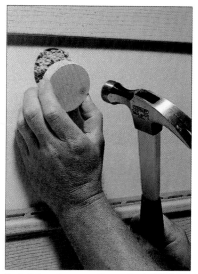

Install the plug once the cavity is filled; then patch or reinstall the siding.

Urea Formaldehyde Foam Insulation

Q. *My house was insulated with urea formaldehyde foam. Is this type of insulation dangerous? Will it lower the value of my home?*

Urea formaldehyde foam insulation (UFFI) is dangerous when first installed, but the risk is low once the insulation has aged. UFFI is a foam-like product that was commonly sprayed into wall cavities to insulate older homes during the 1970's, until researchers discovered that the formaldehyde gas given off by the foam as it cures is a suspected carcinogen. The curing stage happens mainly during the first year after the insulation is installed, so the risk of cancer drops substantially after that.

Some people, however, are extremely sensitive to the formaldehyde gas given off by this type of insulation as well as by carpeting, furniture, and many kinds of building materials. If you experience eye, nose, and throat irritation, persistent cough, skin irritation, nausea, headaches, or dizziness, and especially if these symptoms disappear when you are away from home, see a doctor and have your house tested for formaldehyde gas.

If you need to check your walls to see if they're insulated with UFFI, remove some switch and outlet cover plates (on outside walls) and use a flashlight to look for the foam of insulation in the cavity behind the electrical box. If you're not sure what you see, consult an insulation contractor or house inspector to help you out.

Itchless
Insulation

TRADITIONAL FIBERGLASS insulation is no fun to install: The fibers break off, become airborne, and make your skin itch and your eyes water. Fortunately, manufacturers have responded to this problem by producing "encapsulated" insulation, which has a porous plastic bag around the exposed sides of the batt or roll. The perforated bag lets moisture through but keeps the glass fibers together and off of you. Fibers are released, however, when you cut the insulation and handle the end, so you still need to wear a dust mask, goggles, gloves, and skin covering when you install it.

Encapsulated products are available from several manufacturers. In addition, at least one company also makes insulation that not only is encapsulated but is made of a completely new type of glass fiber that's springy, flexible, and soft. The fibers don't break off and become airborne as easily, so the rolls don't carry a cancer warning.

The downside to these new products is their cost (about 20 percent more than traditional insulation). Also, you may not be able to find the insulation you want in encapsulated form. Availability in your area depends on your local retailers, who might carry just one brand. It's likely that eventually all fiberglass insulation for do-it-yourselfers will be encapsulated. For now, if you can pay the few extra dollars and can find what you need, you, your skin, and your lungs will appreciate the difference.

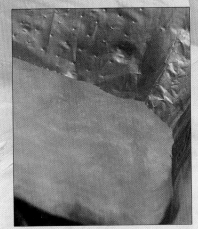

Encapsulated insulation has a porous plastic bag around it to let water vapor flow through but keep the loose fibers in.

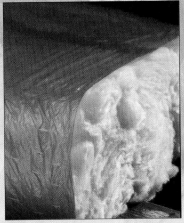

One of the newest types of glass fiber insulation is flexible and less likely to break off and irritate your skin or lungs.

Weatherproofing

Double-Ceiling Insulation

Q. *The ceilings in our older home are 10 feet high. The previous owner installed a second ceiling of plasterboard at 8 feet but did not remove the original ceilings. Since there is no insulation in either ceiling, we want to install some ourselves. Where should it go: above the original ceiling or above the newer, lower one?*

If you have a one-story house, put the insulation between the joists of the original ceiling (assuming you can reach them from the attic). If you have a two-story house and the dropped ceiling is on the first floor, there is no need to insulate; insulation should only go between heated interior spaces and areas with outdoor temperatures. If the dropped ceiling is on the second floor, place the insulation between the joists of the original second-story ceiling.

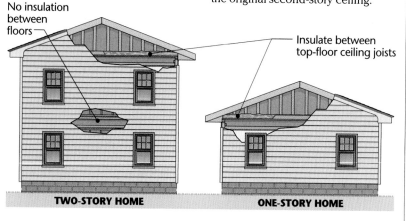

No insulation between floors

Insulate between top-floor ceiling joists

TWO-STORY HOME

ONE-STORY HOME

Between-Floor Insulation

Q. *The upper level of our 1½-story home is unfinished and has loose-fill insulation in the floor. Do I need to remove this insulation when I finish the space? How much air space should I leave between the roof sheathing and the insulation?*

You don't have to remove the existing insulation. It will continue to keep the first level warmer in the winter and cooler in the summer. However, you'll need to heat the second floor independently of the first.

Leave a 2-inch air space between the roof sheathing and the insulation. To ensure a cooling airflow, vent each joist space from the soffit at bottom and to the roof peak at top.

Vapor Barrier

Q. *I have a 1950's-era house that has loose cellulose attic insulation. I want to add more. Should I install a new vapor retarder between the old insulation and the new?*

If you want to add more insulation to your attic, you can put it right on top of the old insulation, but don't put a vapor retarder between the layers. It would only trap moisture inside the insulation, decreasing its effectiveness and possibly causing rot in nearby wood. For the additional insulation, we suggest laying down unfaced fiberglass batts (that is, without a paper or foil covering). Be careful not to block the ventilation, especially in the eaves.

Insulating an Attic

Q. *We have an unfinished attic with insulation just above the ceiling. Would it be a good idea to insulate right under the roof to keep the heat from entering the attic in the first place?*

No; although this seems like a logical idea, insulating right under the roof in the attic wastes energy. In the winter you need to keep the heat from escaping, and in the summer, the heat from entering. If you insulate just under the roof at the top of the attic, you will be heating the attic in the winter in addition to the rest of your house. If you have central air conditioning, the same would be true in the summer, when you'd be forced to cool the attic.

Another reason not to insulate the attic roof is ventilation. The attic area above the insulation needs to be kept cold in the winter in order to prevent ice dams from forming on the roof and to keep moisture from condensing on the insulation and on the roof framing. This is achieved by ventilating the attic. In the summer months, a well-ventilated attic and the roof will stay cooler by allowing excess heat to escape, thereby keeping the living space below cooler.

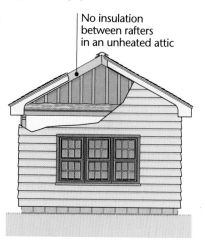

No insulation between rafters in an unheated attic

MAKING YOUR HOME ENERGY-EFFICIENT

Every home has its own unique way of losing energy. Insulation, windows, and foundations vary from house to house, and even the skill of the builder can make a difference in your home's energy efficiency. Therefore, the best way to evaluate your home is to hire an energy auditor. Many utility companies have conservation programs that include energy audits. You could also call your local building inspector and ask about local or state programs.

How Efficient Is Your House?

From looking at your annual utility bills and the size of your house, an auditor can tell you how well your house performs compared to similar houses in your area.

You'll find your home wastes energy in three ways: bad family habits, inefficient appliances, and heating or cooling losses through exterior surfaces.

Bad family habits that waste energy include forgetting to turn off the lights, setting the thermostat unnecessarily high in winter or low in summer, and setting the water heater temperature too high. The auditor can suggest simple changes that will cost nothing, won't sacrifice comfort, and yet can cut energy costs.

An auditor can inspect your appliances, like the water heater and furnace, determine which are eating up the most energy, and suggest improvements. By inspecting the basement, the attic, the thickness of the walls, the number and condition of the windows and walls, and the overall condition and the insulation in your house, an auditor will estimate where the greatest heat losses occur in winter and where the heat gains occur in summer. Infiltration— the air that continually leaks into a home from outside—generally ranks as the biggest problem. The auditor will point out where to caulk cracks, fill holes, and weatherstrip doors and windows to reduce the leakage. You can use this energy report to plan future home improvements.

Seeing Results

An energy auditor can help you decide which improvements will make a good investment. The key is to base the value of an energy improvement on how much money it saves on your utility bills. Here's a rule of thumb: An energy-saving improvement is worthwhile if it pays the improvement cost back within 7 to 10 years. There's no better measure of energy performance than your utility bills. When comparing your utility bill with one from the previous year, remember that the price of gas, oil, and electricity may have changed; average temperatures may also rise or fall from year to year.

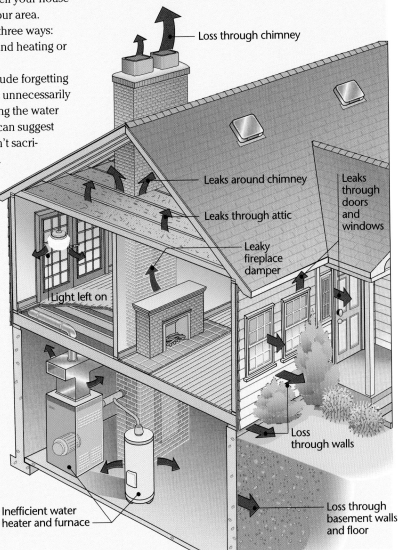

Loss through chimney

Leaks around chimney

Leaks through attic

Leaks through doors and windows

Leaky fireplace damper

Light left on

Loss through walls

Inefficient water heater and furnace

Loss through basement walls and floor

Weatherproofing

Crawl Space Insulation

Q. *What is the best way to insulate the crawl space under my house? What should I do about air vents in the block walls?*

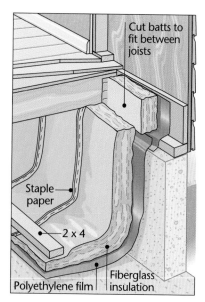

Cut batts to fit between joists

Staple paper

2 x 4

Polyethylene film | Fiberglass insulation

The crawl space under a house can be a source of cold floors, drafts, and unwanted moisture if it is not properly weatherproofed and insulated. You can cut your heating costs by plugging the potential heat leaks.

First, to prevent moisture from damaging the floor joists or insulation, lay a vapor barrier of 6-mil polyethylene film over the bare earth. If you need to use more than one piece of film, make sure to overlap the edges at least 6 inches. Use staples to secure the polyethylene to the rim joist and sill.

Fit short fiberglass insulation batts between the floor joists and against the band joist. This will give you full insulation protection. Next, place longer fiberglass insulation against the foundation. Make sure that the length of the batt will allow it to cover the wall and at least 2 feet of the ground.

Don't leave any gaps between the insulation batts. Staple the paper flanges together. Lay a 2 x 4 across the batts to help hold them in place.

Remember to wear the right gear whenever you work with insulation. A long-sleeved shirt, gloves, a dust mask, and protective eyewear will keep you sufficiently protected from stray fiberglass particles.

Air vents can be left open in the summer to help ventilate the crawl space. You should close the vents in the colder months to conserve energy. If the vents can't be closed, you can seal them yourself with a piece of plywood or rigid foam insulation. Remember to remove the covers in the warmer months.

Protecting Exterior Foam Insulation

Q. *Our foundation is insulated with 2-inch-thick rigid foam insulation. From the ground to the bottom of the siding, the foam is exposed. Can we somehow cover it?*

Not only is the protruding foam unattractive, but it will deteriorate if it's exposed to sunlight for any length of time. There are a number of ways to cover and protect exterior foundation insulation. Because extruded polystyrene isn't affected by soil acids or water, it isn't necessary to extend this protective coating below the grade line.

First, clean the insulation board of any mud or dirt. Roughen the surface of the insulation with a wire brush. To prevent the protective coating

from cracking at the insulation joints, apply a latex caulk between the joints, or tape the joints with fiberglass mesh tape.

One way to cover the insulation is with panels of cement board, aluminum or rigid vinyl, or pressure-treated plywood. These panels are glued, nailed, or screwed through the foam to the foundation wall. Another way to cover the insulation is to use a foundation coating. There are several brush-on coatings that come premixed in 2- and 5-gallon pails. A 5-gallon pail will cover about 225 square feet. Follow the directions on the label.

A third, and most expensive, solution is to cover the foam with stucco. Either ¼-inch-thick latex-modified stucco with fiberglass mesh reinforcement, or ⅝-inch-thick

stucco with metal lath, can be applied over the foam. If you decide to stucco the foundation, your best bet is to hire a professional to do the job.

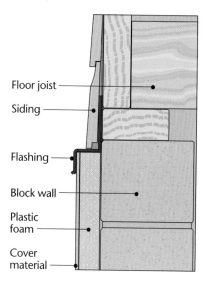

Floor joist

Siding

Flashing

Block wall

Plastic foam

Cover material

Soffit Vents Blocked

Q. *Our bedroom walls and ceiling become wet in freezing, windy weather, and the wallboard is deteriorating. There is no roof leak, and the ceilings are insulated. There are both roof vents and soffit vents.*

It's possible that moisture is condensing on the underside of your roof, then running down toward the eaves and coming through the ceiling. This problem occurs when insulation is shoved into the soffit area over one or more of the soffit vents and blocks the venting of moisture-laden air. Without proper ventilation, the insulation covering the soffit vents will get wet and transfer the water back to the walls and ceiling.

Ceiling insulation should cover the top plate of the wall but should not block the air space between the roof sheathing and the ceiling. Air should be able to enter the attic freely via the soffit vents, then pass out through roof or gable vents.

To prevent this from happening again, install baffles between the attic rafters. Cardboard baffles may be waxed or plastic-coated to resist moisture. Plastic baffles also work well. Thin foam baffles must be handled gently since they're quite brittle.

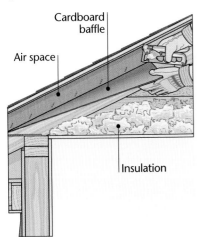

Cardboard baffle

Air space

Insulation

Even the best insulation job will still allow cold air to leak into your house (and heated air to leak out). Before you insulate, stop leaks and drafts by following the steps shown here.

ELECTRICAL BOXES

Seal holes on the outside of electrical boxes with caulk or expanding foam to make them airtight. Do not put foam or caulk on the inside. Do not seal recessed light fixtures.

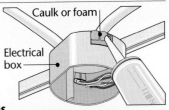

Caulk or foam

Electrical box

PARTITION WALLS AND OUTER CORNERS

Tuck fiberglass insulation into gaps at partition wall–exterior wall junctions before the sheathing goes on. This helps prevent condensation and mildew growth on walls.

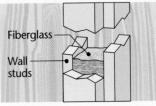

Fiberglass

Wall studs

AROUND WINDOWS

Apply expanding foam (a bead only) to the outer edge of windows to seal the gap between the studs and the window jamb on all four sides. Fill the gap with fiberglass.

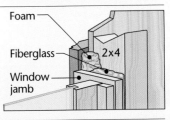

Foam

Fiberglass

2x4

Window jamb

HOLES TO ATTIC

Seal holes to the attic and between floors around wiring, pipes, and heating ducts with expanding foam. Maintain proper clearances from flues and chimneys.

Wiring

Vent pipe

RIM JOISTS

Caulk the joints around the rim joist at each floor level. See The Right Caulk, p.223, for more information about caulk selection.

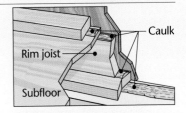

Caulk

Rim joist

Subfloor

BEHIND DUCTS

Place rigid insulation behind forced-air ducts in exterior walls before the ducts go in. Ask a heating specialist where the ducts will run and what insulation thickness will fit.

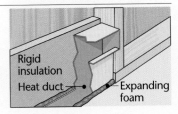

Rigid insulation

Heat duct

Expanding foam

Weatherproofing

Is Housewrap Worth It?

Q. *I'm planning to build an addition to my house and am wondering if I should put on a housewrap product. What does a housewrap do? Is it worth the money?*

Housewrap is an air barrier that's installed between the sheathing and the siding. Properly installed, it does two things: (1) It reduces air leakage, so heated or cooled air stays inside your house and outdoor air stays outside. Researchers have discovered that air leakage is a major source of energy loss in most houses, even ones with well-insulated walls and ceilings. (2) Unlike tar paper, housewrap allows moisture to pass through, so it doesn't get trapped inside your walls, leading to rot. But housewrap is not porous enough to let rainwater through if a leak develops in the siding.

Is it worthwhile? Yes, it is. Housewrap is certainly one way to control air leakage and make your home more airtight and energy-efficient. Also, it's not very expensive.

Can you make your house airtight and energy-efficient without housewrap? Yes, you definitely can. Using a combination of tight vapor barriers, thorough caulking, taped sheathing or foam insulation, sealed electrical boxes, and other techniques, you can tightly seal a house against energy leaks and air infiltration.

Housewraps are great, but don't be fooled into thinking they are a magic solution for energy efficiency. Caulking, insulation, weatherstripping, and an effective vapor barrier are essential elements of a weathertight home.

If you choose to wrap your addition, be sure that you tape all the edges of the wrap with contractor's sheathing tape, especially around windows and at seams. Sheathing tape is a long-lasting tape designed specifically for this use.

Paint as a Vapor Barrier

Q. *I live in an old two-story house that has balloon-frame construction, where the wall studs go all the way from foundation to roof. I'd like to blow insulation into the stud cavities from the exterior. I'm concerned that the insulation will absorb moisture and cause structural problems, because there's no moisture barrier behind the plaster. Someone told me that paint can be an effective moisture barrier. I'm not convinced. What should I do?*

Paint can be an effective vapor barrier to keep interior moisture from penetrating into the wall cavity. But just as important, you'll need to stop any air filtration from gaps around window and door trim, baseboards, and electrical boxes. Air infiltration can cause warm, moist air to condense onto the insulation as the air works its way into cool wall cavities.

If you live in an area with cold winters, you'll need a vapor barrier on the warm side of the insulation. Name-brand paint manufacturers have latex-base products that are effective moisture barriers when any finish paint is used over them. Shellac-base primers, such as BIN, are also effective vapor barriers. Other paint manufacturers recommend an alkyd enamel undercoat as a primer with an oil or latex finish coat, or a latex primer with a semigloss latex finish coat. Flat latex paint, by itself, is not an effective vapor barrier.

Housewrap can be good insurance against moisture damage.

Where to Place a Vapor Barrier

Q. *I'm confused. Where should I install the vapor barrier in a wall?*

A vapor barrier can be in either of the two places, depending on the climate you live in. In some areas of the country, you may not even need one.

Warm air holds more moisture than cold air, and if that warm, moist air moves through your wall and cools off, condensation will form, leading to rot. Vapor barriers are designed to keep moist air out of your wall.

In cold and moderate climates, moisture moves from the inside of the house outward, so the vapor barrier should be installed on the inside of the wall. It is typically installed between the insulation and the drywall. In Gulf and southeastern coastal areas, which are warm most of the year, the vapor barrier should be installed on the outside of the wall.

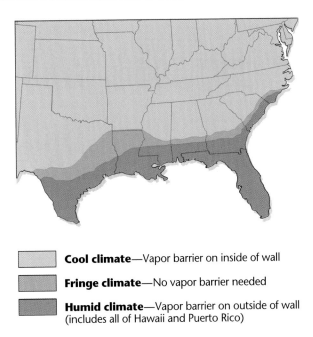

Cool climate—Vapor barrier on inside of wall

Fringe climate—No vapor barrier needed

Humid climate—Vapor barrier on outside of wall (includes all of Hawaii and Puerto Rico)

Warming a Slab Floor

Q. *My kitchen and dining room have a concrete slab floor covered with carpet. This floor is always cold in the winter, and I'm wondering if there is anything we can put under the carpet to make it warmer.*

Put down the densest and thickest 100-percent-urethane foam pad you can find—one that's rated at 8 pounds per yard—under your carpet. Though you may sacrifice some cushioning (a dense pad won't give as much), you'll block some of that cold migration that is coming through the slab.

Ideally, a layer of rigid board insulation should have been placed underneath the concrete slab when it was originally poured, but it's too late for that now. Putting down some sort of rigid insulation, such as sound-deadening board or plywood, on top of the concrete slab at this time is not practical: It's difficult to securely fasten the insulation to the slab, and the insulation might crush under the weight of heavy traffic or furniture.

Settled Insulation

Q. *How can I tell if the loose cellulose insulation that was installed in my walls years ago is doing its job? Can I add more insulation?*

The first step in determining if you need to add more insulation is to have a thermogram done—an infrared picture of your house that will show you where the heat losses are. Call your local heating utility for this service. Once you know where the weak insulation spots are in your walls, you can treat just those areas.

To add more insulation, whether it's cellulose or loose-fill fiberglass, drill a 2-inch-diameter hole at the top of the inside wall where the thermogram shows a heat loss. Blow more insulation into these wall spaces with an insulation blower. (See Blowing In Wall Insulation, p.266). Make sure you get a wall reducer for the hose so that it will fit into the hole you cut in the wall.

Force the end of the hose into the wall cavity and down the wall as far as you can. As the cavity fills, the insulation will stop flowing through the hose. To help pack the insulation, move the hose around and slowly pull it out of the wall as the wall fills. Go slowly, pulling on the hose only when the insulation stops flowing. Have a helper keep the blower filled with insulation.

Once the wall cavity is filled with insulation, cover the holes with drywall patches; then apply drywall compound, sand, and finish.

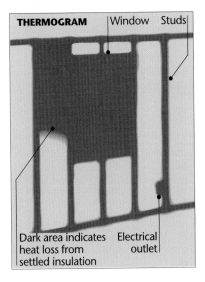

THERMOGRAM | Window | Studs

Dark area indicates heat loss from settled insulation | Electrical outlet

Weatherproofing

Attic Bypasses

Q. *I've caulked and weatherstripped my house and added 12 inches of insulation in the attic, but I still feel cold drafts. Is there anything else I can do?*

Air is probably still leaking through attic bypasses—areas in the ceiling where gaps in the vapor retarder exist. While you do lose heat through attic bypasses, that isn't your biggest concern, moisture is. Moisture from the lower floors will enter the attic and condense on the inside surfaces, causing wood to rot and insulation to get wet. In an extreme situation, the ceiling drywall below will be damaged and water will leak into the house from the attic. To prevent moisture and cold air from getting into the attic, seal all bypasses with caulk or insulation.

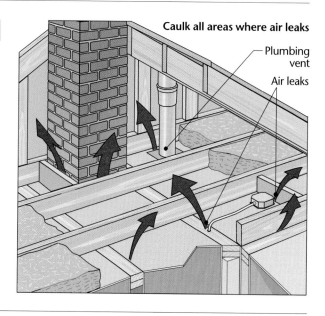

Caulk all areas where air leaks
- Plumbing vent
- Air leaks

Caulking Technique

Q. *What's the best way to lay a perfect bead of caulk?*

Caulk is the perfect solution for drafty basements and attics, and for gaps around windows and siding. But choosing the best caulk for a job is only part of the weatherproofing battle. How you apply the caulk is equally important. A too-thick bead of caulk doesn't flex much, so the bead might crack along one side, breaking the bond between the caulk and the wood.

The illustration below shows the ideal caulk joint: The hourglass shape allows for movement without a significant chance of breaking the seal. Make the bead about half as thick as the gap it bridges. It should stick to the sides of the joint (wood in this illustration) but not to the back, so that when the wood dries out, causing the gap to widen, the caulk can stretch like a rubber band. You can always stuff loose fiberglass or foam backer rods (available in various sizes) into deep cracks to keep the caulk from getting too thick or sticking to the back of the gap.

To mold the bead of caulk into that ideal hourglass shape, use one of these two techniques: For silicone, shape the bead with a concave-shaped tool such as a spoon. Silicone doesn't shrink, so the shape you see after you apply it is the shape it will dry. For latex- and solvent-base caulks (urethane or butyl, for example), simply flatten the bead. As the caulk dries, it will shrink into the concave shape.

Contrary to what you might expect, narrow joints (less than ⅛ inch) tend to crack open more readily than wider ones. Think of it this way. If an ⅛-inch gap widens just an additional 1/16 inch, its width has just increased by 50 percent. Not even the best brand of caulk can flex that much without breaking in the middle or along one side of the joint. However, if there is a ¼-inch gap that widens by that same 1/16 inch, its width has increased by only 25 percent. This is about the maximum flexibility of the best caulks, so in this case the joint should not break.

In reality, few of us make perfect caulk joints, and we'll caulk any size crack that we find. These are the best reasons for buying high-quality caulk. Its superior adherence and flexibility help compensate for a less-than-ideal application. If you make sure the surfaces are dry and free of grease and old hardened caulk, and then apply a good-quality caulk, you can make a long-lasting caulk joint despite any minor shortcomings in your technique.

Foam backer rod
Paper flashing
Depth
Width
Hourglass shape
1¼" x 4" window casing
½" x 6" bevel siding
Continue caulk

how is it done?

WINTERIZING LEAKY DOORS

Thanks to a wide variety of do-it-yourself weatherstripping products, you can stop chilly winter drafts from blowing in around a door. Most weatherstripping is inexpensive and easy to install. Before you install it, though, check for leaks. Most air leaks occur because the door has sagged, has loose hinges, rubs unevenly against the frame, or has a loose latch plate.

Most doors today have weatherstrips built into both the frame and the door bottom. If these are worn out, buy exact replacements. If you can't find a replacement, use a spring-metal or surface-mounted type.

SPRING-METAL WEATHERSTRIPPING

Spring-metal weatherstripping is a thin V-shaped strip of bronze, aluminum, or stainless steel that compresses against the edge of the door when you close it. It's long-lasting, adjustable, and inconspicuous, a good choice for a handsome front door. You can't use spring metal if the door fits too tightly; it needs at least a ⅛-inch gap around all edges. Also, if the door sags and rubs against the jamb, the metal could be damaged. And finally, if the hinge screws should loosen, you'll have to remove the section of the strip that covers the hinge, tighten the screws, and then replace the strip.

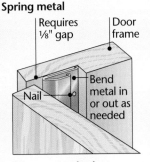

Spring metal

Requires ⅛" gap — Door frame — Nail — Bend metal in or out as needed

Spring metal is a bit trickier to install than other types of weatherstripping. Handle each strip carefully so it doesn't bend and crease; you won't be able to smooth it out. The nailing process takes patience, and you have to install a narrower strip around the latch and lock plates so that it won't interfere with the latch.

SURFACE-MOUNTED WEATHERSTRIPPING

This type of weatherstripping consists of a tube, wedge, or flange of flexible material backed by a metal, wood, or plastic stiffener that you tack or screw to the face of the jamb. To install it, cut it to length, leaving the tube ¼ inch longer than the stiffener, press it gently against the closed door, and screw it to the jamb.

Surface-mounted weatherstripping doesn't always look nice and may not be acceptable for a front door. If it's too bulky, it can also narrow the space between the jamb and the doorknob and make the door difficult to open from the outside.

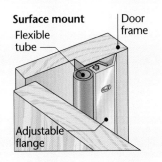

Surface mount

Flexible tube — Door frame — Adjustable flange

FOAM FLAPPER SEAL

Foam flapper seal comprises a foam strip encased in a plastic skin. This type of weatherstripping is easy enough to replace but tough to install. You'll probably have to rent special tools to trim the frame and cut the grooves. Once you cut the groove from the top to the bottom of the jamb, simply press the foam flapper seal in place with your fingers.

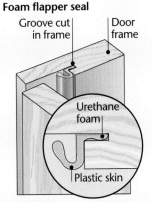

Foam flapper seal

Groove cut in frame — Door frame — Urethane foam — Plastic skin

DOOR SWEEPS

The best door sweeps are the ones that mount under the door and have several flexible flaps that seal against the threshold. Unfortunately, you may need to remove and trim the door. A multi-flap surface-mounted sweep is a good second choice. Mount it with the screws on the inside of your door. Swing the door open to make sure the sweep doesn't catch on carpeting or a floor mat. If clearance is a problem, buy a sweep that drops into place when the door closes.

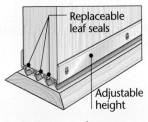

Under-door sweep

Replaceable leaf seals — Adjustable height

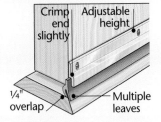

Surface-mounted sweep

Crimp end slightly — Adjustable height — ¼" overlap — Multiple leaves

Heating

Fitting Metal Ducts

Q. *How do I cut and join sections of round ductwork?*

You could use aviation snips to cut round ductwork, but it is much easier and faster to use a hacksaw with a metal-cutting blade. If you need to make a new male-end duct connection, crimp the end of the duct with needle-nose pliers or a special crimping tool. The sections should be installed so that the male end points downstream from the airflow. Finish the seam with sheet-metal screws and aluminum-faced duct tape.

The easiest way to cut circular ducts is with a hacksaw.

You can make a new male-end connection by placing plier jaws on the duct and twisting them every ½ in. or so.

Wasted Heat

Q. *The exhaust stack on my furnace gets very hot and I think I might be losing a lot of heat up the chimney. Is there some device that could save some of the heat and reduce my fuel bills?*

You have an older furnace that relies on high stack temperatures to vent the products of combustion such as harmful carbon monoxide. Since it depends on the fact that heat rises, exhaust temperatures may be as high as 550° F. This venting method was designed so that the stack will exhaust even on mild days. This old type of system is wasteful. Modern furnaces have improvements such as inducted drafts and recuperative cells that extract more usable heat while venting combustion gases more efficiently. Check with a local heating contractor for retrofit products, such as stack heat reclaimers and automatic vent dampers. If you cannot get either of these, consider replacing your furnace with a new high-efficiency model.

Turn Off the Pilot Light?

Q. *We have a gas-fired cast iron boiler in our home. Should I leave the pilot light lit in the summer?*

Go ahead and turn off the pilot light; by doing this you can cut your gas consumption (and utility bill) by 2 to 5 percent. Be aware that if your boiler is located in a cool, moist area like a basement, condensation can form around the heat exchanger when the pilot light is left off. If the heat exchanger is not corrosion-resistant, it could be damaged. Call the manufacturer to get information on your specific boiler model.

Duct Tape for Ducts

Q. *I use duct tape to fix everything in my house. Can I use it on ducts?*

Don't use cloth-faced duct tape on heating duct joints—this type of tape deteriorates quickly. Instead, secure each section of a heating duct run with sheet-metal screws and aluminum-faced duct tape. Building codes in some areas actually require that this kind of tape be used. The protruding ends of screws can catch lint, so use just the tape on dryer ducts to avoid a potential fire hazard.

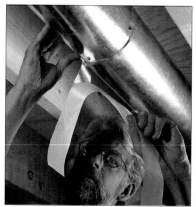

Aluminum-faced duct tape is much more durable than cloth-faced duct tape for sealing heating duct joints.

Heat Exchanger Hole

Q. *A heating contractor says there is a hole in the heat exchanger of my 20-year-old gas forced-air furnace. He wants to replace it, but how do I know he isn't just trying to sell me a new furnace?*

Call your local gas utility and tell them you suspect there is a leak in the heat exchanger. They should take the report seriously and, for a fee, inspect it promptly for you. The average life of a furnace is about 20 years, and a major cause of failure is the heat exchanger rusting out.

Ground-Source Heat Pump

Q. *Would I be better off with a ground-source heat pump or an air conditioner? How does it work?*

Whether you should buy a central air conditioner or a ground-source heat pump depends on several factors. The big advantage of a ground-source heat pump is that it will heat and cool your home. This system is also much more energy efficient since it transfers heat to and from the earth rather than burn fuel to heat or cool (it still needs electricity to run the pump). The only disadvantage of a ground-source heat pump is its higher purchase and installation price—as much as twice the cost of central air.

Think of a heat pump as a two-way air conditioner: It can remove heat from the inside of the house and also remove heat from the outside air and bring it inside through your existing heating system. Remember, a heat pump supplements your furnace; it doesn't replace it. If you're heating your home with fuel oil, electricity, or propane, a heat pump will probably lower your heating bills. Because a heat pump requires little maintenance and will decrease the wear and tear on your existing system, you will also save in maintenance costs.

A closed-loop heat pump system circulates an antifreeze solution through pipe buried underground. The pipe can be buried in trenches, circulated beneath ponds, or run in a series of deep vertical well holes. The antifreeze mixture is warmed by the surrounding earth, then the heat is withdrawn by a heat pump.

An open-loop system relies on a supply of water (usually a well) rather than antifreeze. Water is circulated through the heat pump, heat is extracted, then the cooled water is discharged, usually to a pond.

In either system, the heat pump withdraws heat energy from the antifreeze or water. This energy is absorbed by a refrigerant, which is compressed and rises in temperature to about 160° F. Air passing over a heat exchanger is warmed and then distributed throughout the house via ducts. In the summer, heat is gathered from the house and returned to the ground via water or antifreeze.

Concern over possible contamination of groundwater has slowed the acceptance of this system in some areas. Because of the major excavation required, heat pumps are often not feasible on small lots. Many people, however, view ground-source heat pumps as the energy source of the future because the energy is free.

Cutting Ducts

Q. *One of the toughest jobs I have ever done in my house was to add a couple of heating duct runs in the basement. How are you supposed to cut the stuff?*

To do this job right, you need some specialized tools. Since it's easy to cut yourself on a sheet-metal edge, heavy gloves and a long-sleeved shirt are a must. To cut ductwork you'll need three types of aviation snips—they are easy to identify since each is color-coded: straight-cutting snips for straight cuts (yellow handle), left-cutting snips for cutting circles to the left (red handle), and right-cutting snips for cutting circles to the right (green handle). To cut in the middle of a duct, use a hammer to drive the tip of a straight-bladed screwdriver inside the area that needs to be cut. Once the slit is started, use the tip of the screwdriver to twist the slit open enough to use your snips. Make the first cut with either the right- or left-cutting snips and cut half of the circle; then use the other snips to cut out the other half of the circle.

Use a straight-tip screwdriver and a hammer to make a slit. Keep the screwdriver from slipping when you hit it.

Begin your cut with right-or left-cutting aviation snips. Wear gloves and a long-sleeved shirt to protect yourself.

Finish the other half of the circle with the opposite-cutting snips.

Heating

FURNACES AND THERMOSTATS

Sizing a New Furnace

Q. *I'm purchasing a gas forced-air furnace for my home and have received bids from several contractors. However, none of them agree on the size of the furnace required. How do I decide what size furnace is correct for my home?*

The amount of heat a furnace produces is measured in British Thermal Units (Btu's). Heating contractors are supposed to size furnaces according to the calculated heat loss rate of your house. To do this, they need to account for factors such as the insulation level, number of windows, and the regional climate.

When you buy a new furnace, make sure your contractor makes this calculation and doesn't give you a seat-of-the-pants estimate or simply replace the old unit. When in doubt, ask him to explain how he came up with his heating estimate.

For both efficiency and longevity, you want a furnace that is sized just right for your house. The correct-sized furnace will run consistently during cold weather. An oversize furnace will cycle on and off more often, which is inefficient.

When reviewing the bids, make sure the furnaces are comparable. Some are rated according to their efficiency. With a very efficient furnace, you will use less fuel. If one contractor suggests a furnace with a high efficiency rating while another suggests one with a lower efficiency rating, it makes it difficult to compare furnace size recommendations. For easier and more accurate comparison, all the bids should be for furnaces with the same efficiency rating.

Programmable Thermostat Problems

Q. *When I installed a programmable setback thermostat on my furnace, it did not function properly. The dealer said our furnace was not able to work with a programmable thermostat—is this possible?*

Your furnace may be unable to meet the power requirements of a programmable setback thermostat. Some older oil and gas furnaces rely on nonprogrammable thermostats that operate on only 0.75 volts of electricity. Programmable thermostats require more power, 12 or 24 volts, to operate.

Fortunately, you can step up the power by adding a switching relay and transformer. (You may need only a switching relay; contact your furnace's manufacturer to see what your system requires.) The transformer is wired into a 120-volt outlet and steps down the voltage to 12 or 24 volts to run the thermostat.

The actual wiring configuration and necessary controls depend upon your particular heating system, the number of heating zones in your home, and whether or not you also have a cooling system (wiring diagrams are included with the switching relay).

Switching relays and transformers are available at heating supply stores or directly from the manufacturer. Consider hiring a heating contractor to ensure a safe and proper hookup.

Heat Register Placement

Q. *Why are heat registers often placed under windows? Won't energy be wasted?*

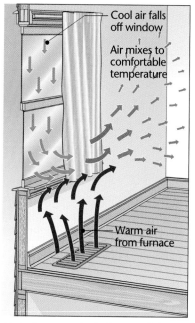

Cool air falls off window

Air mixes to comfortable temperature

Warm air from furnace

Air leaks around windows and doors are usually the cause of most of the chilly drafts inside your home.

Weatherstripping the windows and caulking around the interior trim are the best remedies to prevent drafts. Windows are often the culprit in another way, too. Cold window glass is like an open refrigerator door; cool air literally falls off it, creating a draft down to and across the floor.

Heating contractors try to solve this problem by locating warm-air registers and radiators under windows to counteract those drafts and to mix the cold air with warm air.

In forced-air systems, floor registers work best, especially in front of patio doors, which are always drafty because of the large area of glass.

So it may seem strange to put warm air registers and radiators in drafty places, but it really makes the most sense for your comfort.

Buying a Furnace Filter

Q. *How important is it to change my furnace filter? Are some filters better than others?*

A dirty air filter restricts the airflow, reduces heating and cooling effectiveness, lowers the furnace or air-conditioner efficiency, and can seriously damage furnace or air-conditioner parts, all of which are costly. Check the filter monthly during furnace and air-conditioning operation. Change it whenever it looks dirty, but at least every 3 months. Dust-producing activities like remodeling can clog it in just a few days.

There are four types of filters available. The pleated fabric filter is designed to capture a high percentage of particles such as dust, pollens, molds, animal dander, and bacteria. Pleats expand the total filter area and reduce the filter's air resistance so it won't constrict airflow as much. This filter protects the furnace and air-conditioner coil from dust and reduces household dust, sometimes offering relief for people with allergies. Check this filter monthly and replace it at least every 3 months.

The flat 1-inch-thick fiberglass filter is the cheapest one to buy and is designed to capture larger dust particles to protect the blower motor and other furnace parts. It is not designed to improve air quality and provides minimum protection for furnaces with central air conditioning. This type should be changed every month; dust and grease can bypass a dirty fiberglass filter.

An electrostatic reusable filter is somewhat less effective than a pleated filter because the electro-static charge weakens. You can wash and reuse this kind, but keep an extra one on hand to use while you wash the dirty one. If you wash and dry it monthly, this filter should last 5 years.

The last type of filter is the pleated fabric filter that is electrostatically charged. The charge of static electricity attracts particles and makes the filter more efficient. It is also capable of catching smoke particles and bacteria. This filter offers the same benefits as the pleated fabric filter.

Here, a used pleated fabric filter (bottom, right) is replaced with a new one. Inset (from left): pleated fabric, fiberglass, electrostatic reusable, and electrostatically charged filters.

Unheated Houses

Q. *I own an unoccupied house that is expensive to keep at 60° F for the heating season. Will cold temperatures do any damage if I don't heat it in the winter?*

To leave a house unheated in the winter, you must first turn off all the thermostats. Have the utility company shut off the water main at the street. Drain all water lines, including the drain traps and water heater. Use compressed air to blow water out of drain traps, or fill them with antifreeze. Turn off the electricity at the main panel. If your foundation area is well drained, the basement or foundation walls should not suffer from the frost. Furniture and appliances can remain in unheated storage for years.

Furnace Inspection

Q. *How often should I have my furnace inspected?*

Furnaces should be inspected annually. Half of the fatal poisonings in the United States are from carbon monoxide (CO), one source of which can be a malfunctioning furnace. It is *not* recommended that homeowners do their own furnace inspections. Your local gas or oil supplier will either do the inspection or recommend an inspection service company. Furnace inspections should include a complete inspection of the heat exchanger for cracks and a carbon monoxide check. Have your furnace inspected at the end of the summer, just before the heating season, even if it's brand-new.

Heating

TUNING A NOISY FURNACE

If your furnace squeals whenever it starts up, most likely it has an improperly tensioned, worn, or misaligned drive belt; you can fix it yourself. First, find the service manual or get a new one from the manufacturer.

Turn off the furnace to begin the repair. Both the switch on the side of the furnace and the appropriate fuse or circuit breaker must be turned off.

The service manual describes how to tension the drive belt for your particular model. Remove the access panel and inspect the drive belt for cracks and frayed areas. If in doubt, replace it—belts are inexpensive. Loosen the bolts that hold the motor and slide it toward the blower to loosen the V-belt. Take it to a hardware store for the correct replacement. Don't overtighten the new belt or you'll wear out the bearings. When you press on the belt between the pulleys, there should be ½ inch of deflection. Check the alignment by placing a straightedge against the faces of both pulleys and sighting along the belt. Tighten the motor bolts to finish the job.

Most belt drives have two blower motor bearings and two fan shaft bearings that require yearly oiling. Lift the caps or remove the rubber plugs and apply several drops of 20-weight machine oil to the bearings; don't fill them to overflowing. Some bearings have grease caps that must be filled with axle grease. Newer furnaces often have permanently lubricated bearings that don't need oiling.

Dirt can block the small holes in the burners and cause the furnace to burn inefficiently. Clean the burners annually by removing the main compartment cover and a small access panel to expose the long burner tubes. Vacuum dirt from above and below the burners.

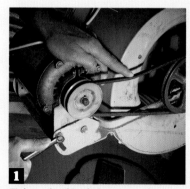

1 Tighten the drive belt once you have determined that it's in good shape or after you've replaced a damaged one.

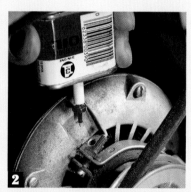

2 Oil the blower motor bearings and shaft bearings every year. Use 20-weight machine oil.

3 Clean dust and dirt from the burners annually, using a refrigerator coil brush and a shop vacuum.

Balance a Forced-Air System

Q. *We have combined central heating and air conditioning. Whenever the seasons turn, the temperature in the house seems to change, getting either too hot or too cold. Why does this happen, and how can we correct this problem?*

A change of season can easily throw the temperature in your home off if you have central heating and cooling combined. The problem occurs because heated air and cooled air mix differently, yet the duct system treats them virtually the same. Warm air mixes best when its natural buoyancy lets it rise, but cooled air mixes best as it falls.

Heating contractors usually balance a forced-air system differently for heating in winter and cooling in summer. They do this by adjusting the dampers (metal plates inserted into the ducts). Dampers must be adjusted seasonally to control the volume of airflow in the heating and cooling ducts.

Chances are, no one told you about these settings when you bought your house. And the maze of ductwork can be intimidating to the untrained eye. So don't hesitate to call in a heating contractor to explain how your system works, help you locate the dampers, and show you how to adjust them. The contractor can balance the ducts for you if you don't feel comfortable doing it yourself.

Feeling Temperature Swings

Q. *I keep the thermostat set at a constant 68° F in the winter, but I still feel wide temperature swings. Is the thermostat working the way it should?*

Even when you set your thermostat at a constant temperature, chills can creep in. In operation, the thermostat allows about a 2- to 4-degree temperature swing, turning the furnace on when the temperature drops to 66° F and off when it hits 70° F. Most people can tolerate a 4-degree swing, as long as the temperature range stays between 67° and 76° F. Sensitivity to chills increases when you're tired or feel ill and as you age.

Sometimes, however, that temperature swing is too wide, especially in rooms that are distant from the thermostat. You can lessen these swings by adjusting the heating anticipator, located under the removable cover of the thermostat. The anticipator tells your furnace to cycle on and off more frequently, keeping the temperature more constant. Keep in mind that the more often the furnace goes on and off, the less efficiently it will burn.

Another possible reason for the temperature fluctuation is the location of your thermostat. Make sure the controller is in a place that represents the average temperature of the whole house. If it's in a cool room or hallway, it will cause the other rooms to overheat. If it's close to a radiator or catches the sun's rays, it will let other rooms get cold. You can move the thermostat by turning off the furnace at its switch or at the electrical panel and then

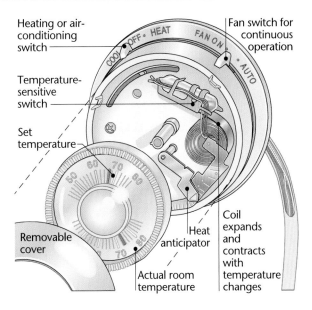

Heating or air-conditioning switch

Temperature-sensitive switch

Set temperature

Removable cover

Fan switch for continuous operation

Heat anticipator

Coil expands and contracts with temperature changes

Actual room temperature

rerouting the low-voltage thermostat wiring to a better location in your house.

Sometimes a chill may be due to the air in your house getting drier. Lower humidity in cool weather can cause your house to dry out unless you use a humidifier. A temperature drop outside can cause the air inside your house to stratify, so the warmer air is close to the ceiling and the chilly air is at your feet. To chase this chill, turn up the thermostat or wear warm socks. Try running the furnace fan continuously or running a ceiling fan on low to mix the air for a more consistent temperature.

Duct Booster

Q. *Our bedroom, located at the end of a long hallway, stays about 10 degrees cooler than the rest of the house. How can we direct more (forced-air) heat to that one room?*

First check to make sure all the dampers are open. You can see the damper in a floor or wall-mounted register by using a flashlight, and you can adjust it by moving a lever or wheel on the register. Often there's a second damper in the branch duct leading to the register. This one is controlled by a wing nut on the side or bottom of the duct; when the wing nut is aligned parallel to the duct, the damper is open. In some cases there

can even be a damper in the main trunk line, usually controlled by an L-shaped lever on the side of the vent.

If all the vents are wide open, consider installing an in-duct air boosting fan. It won't create more heat, but it will pull more warm air to the cool spot. Install this type of fan as near as possible to the cold room in your house. You can wire it to either a manually controlled switch or to the furnace's blower fan. If it's wired to the fan, it will turn on every time the blower fan kicks in.

If you go this route, remove a few duct support brackets and then remove one or two sections of round duct. Install the booster fan; then reinstall the whole works.

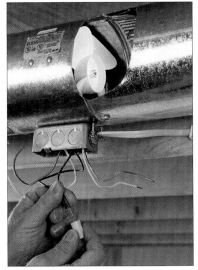

A duct booster fan will pull more warm air from the furnace to a room that is colder than the rest of the house.

Heating

FIREPLACES

Measuring a Cord of Wood

Q. *How do I measure out a cord of wood? I want to make sure I'm getting all that I paid for.*

A cord of wood is 128 cubic feet of cut and split firewood. It could be stacked in any way. For instance, it can be a pile of wood 8 feet long, 4 feet wide, and 4 feet high, or it could be a stack 16 feet long, 2 feet wide, and 4 feet high. The width of the pile depends on the length that the logs are cut to. A 4-foot log can be cut into two 24-inch, three 16-inch, or four 12-inch pieces. These standard sizes make the stacking and measuring easier; one of them should work best in your woodstove or fireplace.

To be certain you are getting a good deal on a cord, make sure the wood is stacked with a minimum of gaps and spaces. The tighter the stack, the more wood you get.

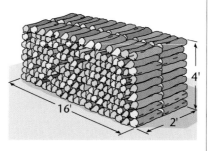

Warming Up to Fireplaces

Q. *I swear my house gets colder every time I use the fireplace. Why are fireplaces so inefficient?*

When you light a fire on a cold night, many things happen. First, as you open the damper, heavy cold outside air pushes its way down the chimney and into your house. When you light the kindling, the fire creates a strong updraft and pulls smoke up the chimney. If you crack a window to get more air into the room, the fire eventually creates a stronger draft and begins pulling air in from the window and around the room. A vacuum is created by the air loss in the room and the fireplace begins to suck in fresh cold air from around doors and windows and even electrical outlets.

When the fire is going strong, it will return only about 20 percent of its heat into the room. If you place a spark screen in front of the fireplace, the heat entering the room drops to only 12 percent. As the fire dies down, the draft up the chimney becomes a freeway for the heated house air to escape. In all, the fire draws more heat out of the house than it generates.

To improve the efficiency of your fireplace, burn hot, blazing fires because the combustion of wood and gases is more complete and the fire will radiate the heat better.

When the fire is burning, adjust the damper to the smallest opening that doesn't allow smoke to spill out into the room. Keep the damper open until the fire is completely out to avoid carbon monoxide poisoning. Keep the damper completely closed when the fireplace is not in use. You could also install tempered glass doors with adjustable air intake slots that will help prevent room air from escaping up the chimney when the fireplace is not in use or when a fire is waning.

If you really want your fireplace to provide heat for your home, you should consider installing a gas or wood-burning fireplace insert (see Efficient Fireplaces, p.283).

Removing Soot

Q. *I just bought a house with a beautiful brick-front fireplace. Unfortunately, the brick is covered with black soot. How should I clean it off?*

First wet the bricks with water. Then, using a stiff-bristle brush, clean the bricks with a scouring powder that contains bleach. Rinse the bricks off with water when you have finished scrubbing them.

It may take a couple of scrubbing sessions until you are satisfied with the results. Remember to put down plastic drop cloths to protect the surrounding area when you tackle this messy job.

Wood for Burning

Q. *Which is the best wood to burn in fireplaces?*

No species of wood is absolutely unsuitable for burning, but some are much better than others. Hardwoods—which come from trees with leaves, like maple or oak—generally burn longer and produce more heat than softwoods, such as pine, which come from trees with needles.

Any wood you burn should be bone-dry. Wood with high moisture content crackles pleasantly but burns poorly, throwing more sparks and less heat. Worst of all, wet wood produces more creosote, a dirty, dangerous deposit that coats the inside of your chimney. Well-dried or "seasoned" wood isn't hard to recognize; it's dry to the touch, has loose bark, and usually has cracks in the end grain. Nine months in a dry place is generally ample time for wood to dry out. But climate makes a big difference; 3 months may be enough in sunny Santa Fe, while it make take more than a year in rainy Seattle.

EFFICIENT FIREPLACES

New metal fireplaces offer significant energy advantages over older open masonry fireplaces. Enclosed-combustion fireboxes allow for efficient burning without robbing fresh air from the house, and a heat chamber behind the firebox unit circulates fire-heated air with a blower, warming the room in the process.

WOOD AND GAS-FIRED INSERTS

If you have a masonry fireplace, you can install a top-venting wood or gas fireplace insert. A fireplace insert is a metal unit that sits inside the original fireplace and can increase the heat output of the fireplace significantly, yielding an efficiency rate of 50 percent or more. An insert uses the old chimney as a chase for a new metal flue liner. It has metal faceplates to cover the space between the insert and the fireplace opening, and glass doors to enclose the fire. Gas fireplaces use artificial logs—you can't burn wood, roast marshmallows, or burn paper in a gas fireplace, but you don't have to haul wood or lose heat.

The most difficult part of either installation is snaking the new metal liner up the chimney. If you plan to install a gas insert, hire a licensed plumber to install the gas line. You could probably do the rest of the installation yourself.

Before you do anything, have a professional chimney sweep clean and inspect your fireplace. Some chimneys are encrusted with creosote, which presents a serious danger. Consult a local building inspector if you want to alter your fireplace in any way.

GAS FIREPLACE INSERT

- Special chimney cap
- Exhaust
- Combustion air intake
- Damper removed or clamped open
- Sealed combustion chamber
- Heat exchange chamber
- Sealed glass front
- Blower
- Hinged faceplate
- Gas shutoff

A new direct-vent gas fireplace can be installed without a chimney.

A special duct on the side of the house provides air intake and exhaust.

NEW DIRECT-VENT FIREPLACES

If you want to install a new fireplace, the most efficient type is an enclosed direct-vent gas fireplace. You can install these units without a chimney and vent them through the wall of the house (see photos, left). These sealed units are airtight, meaning combustion air is brought in, heat is created, and exhaust gas is released all within the firebox. No air from the house is used for combustion or escapes up a chimney. These units are about 75 percent efficient.

Heating

Protect Walls and Floors from a Woodstove

Q. *The space is limited where I want to install a wood-burning stove. How can I protect the walls and floor and have the least amount of required clearance?*

The National Fire Protection Association (NFPA) has standards and clearance guidelines for fireplaces and wood-burning stoves. Check with your local building official or fire marshal for local requirements.

The floor around and directly underneath the stove should be protected since sparks from the stove, as well as the heat radiating from the stove, have the potential to start a fire. There should be a minimum of 18 inches between all edges of the stove and the unprotected floor.

If the stove has legs or pedestals that provide more than 6 inches of ventilated open space beneath it, you can use masonry such as bricks or concrete blocks that are at least 2 inches thick. If the stove has legs that provide 2 to 6 inches of open space, use 4 inches of hollow masonry, with the holes laid to provide airflow. In either case, you should cover the top surface of the floor with 24-gauge sheet metal or better. If the stove has less than 2 inches of open space underneath, only a fully noncombustible floor will provide protection.

You can also buy manufactured wall/floor protector panels made from ceramic fiberboard that are used in place of sheet metal. Use the manufacturer's recommended method for installing any of these, and make sure you buy only UL-listed panels. A UL-listed panel will provide the heat and fire protection for reduced-clearance installation. If you use a ceramic fiberboard panel, you still need the required ventilated open space between the woodstove and the floor.

NFPA guidelines require a minimum of 36 inches between the stove and an unprotected wall. To help reduce the clearance needed between the woodstove and the wall, install a noncombustible wall, like ceramic board, with fire-proof spacers that hold it 1 inch away from the wall and 1 inch above the noncombustible floor, allowing air to circulate and keep the wall cooler. This allows you to reduce the clearance needed by as much as two-thirds, depending on the material you use and your local code. Ceramic electric fence insulators or lengths of electric conduit are good noncombustible spacers.

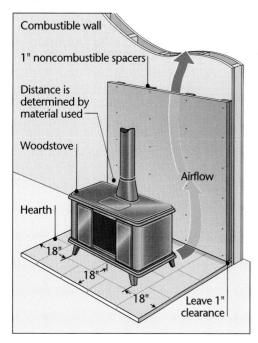

Combustible wall
1" noncombustible spacers
Distance is determined by material used
Woodstove
Airflow
Hearth
18"
18"
18"
Leave 1" clearance

Prepare a Woodstove for Winter

Q. *Before the heating season begins, what should we do to keep our wood-burning stove in good working order all winter?*

At the beginning of each heating season, make sure your stove is safe for use. The stove should rest on a noncombustible, fire-resistant base. Check the legs, hinges, grates, and draft louvers for defects. If it's new, have your local building inspector check the stove for proper clearance and installation. Also, inspect your chimney and connectors for structural problems and creosote buildup. A buildup of $\frac{1}{8}$ to $\frac{1}{4}$ inch could be a fire hazard. To maximize efficiency and cut down on creosote buildup, burn small, hot fires rather than large, smoky ones.

Cleaning Out Ashes

Q. *The wood-burning season is over and I'd like to clean out my fireplace. Can I use my wet-dry vacuum to get the job done quickly?*

No, absolutely not. Using a shop vacuum to clean out a fireplace is dangerous and can make a huge mess. Coals can burn for days after a fire, and then start a fire in your vacuum. Wood ash is very fine, it may go right through the vacuum's filter and create a lot of dust. Chimney sweeps use a vacuum to clean up after they're done, but their machines have a special filter and a metal canister.

You should shovel the ashes into a covered metal container, then use a whisk broom to remove the remaining ash. Let the covered pail sit outside for several days for any coals to burn out. Dispose of the cooled ashes or add them to your compost pile.

No-Vent Fireplaces and Heaters

Q. *I'd like to add a fireplace in my third-floor apartment. I've heard it's possible to install a gas fireplace that needs no chimney or even a vent to the outdoors. Are these safe?*

You've heard right. A vent-free gas heater or fireplace requires no venting to the outdoors and can be installed safely along an interior wall. They are much safer than old-fashioned space heaters because they have better burners that minimize by-products like carbon monoxide. They also have an oxygen depletion sensor, that shuts the gas off if the oxygen falls below a safe level.

It may seem odd to let combustion products from a fire go right into your home to pollute the air. But vent-free devices have a good safety record; over 4 million of them have been installed in American homes since 1982 and the U.S. Consumer Product Safety Commission (CPSC) has not identified a single death from their emissions. A recent study determined that vent-free heaters, when properly sized, installed, and used, will produce pollutants and combustion by-products that are below the levels established by the CPSC, OSHA, and other regulatory agencies.

Vent-free gas appliances add a large amount of water vapor to your home. If you have a winter condensation problem, this added water vapor might make it worse; if you suffer from dry air, it will help.

If you plan to use a vent-free heater or fireplace, check with your local building inspector first; these units are not allowed in some areas. If you have one installed, use it for decoration or supplemental heat only; these units are not designed to be your primary heat source.

Vent-free gas fireplaces and heaters require no venting to the outside and have a good safety record.

New Fireplace Smokes

Q. *We cannot use two of the brick fireplaces in our new home because smoke from the chimneys pours into the house. The chimneys are clear of debris. What do you think the problem might be?*

Modern houses are built very tightly, and fireplaces need large quantities of air to burn properly. Open a window or door to let in outside air for combustion if your unit doesn't have a vent to supply outside air. Open the damper fully, then light a crumpled piece of newspaper in the fire pit to start an upward draft of warm air. Then light the kindling.

Use a steel grate to hold the logs in the fireplace if you don't already have one in place. A grate will raise the logs so air can circulate underneath for better combustion; it also raises the fire to help the smoke go up the chimney rather than curl out the top of the opening. You could even try raising the grate higher than it is by setting it on bricks. If this works, you may want to raise the fireplace floor permanently with an additional layer of bricks.

To help determine the cause of the problem, try getting in touch with the mason who did the work on your fireplaces. This is a complicated problem, and you'll probably need to call in an expert to help you.

Steel grate with bricks

Built-up hearth with steel grate

CHIMNEYS

Avoiding Costly Chimney Repairs

Q. *My neighbors had their chimney rebuilt and it cost them a fortune! My chimney appears sound, but how can I prevent ever having to make costly repairs?*

Concrete caulk is sticky—use an ice cube to smooth it out.

A chimney cover keeps water and animals out of the flue.

The easiest way to avoid expensive chimney repairs is regular maintenance. Taking care of the crown is one way to prevent moisture from working its way in and damaging the masonry below.

The crown is the concrete cap covering the top of the chimney. It acts like a roof to protect the brickwork. If the crown fails, water gets behind the brick. Once moisture gets into the brick, it can freeze and thaw, causing mortar to pop out, layers of the brick face to break off, and ultimately the entire chimney to split apart.

To determine if you have a problem, look for brick and mortar lying on the roof. Check the top of the crown for cracks, and make sure there is flashing between the brickwork and the crown. Finally, check the condition of the caulk between the crown and the flue.

ANNUAL CHIMNEY CHECKUP

Checking your chimney annually can help prevent chimney fires. The springtime, right after the heating season is over, is a good time to make the inspection. Learn to spot common problems and what causes them so you can correct them before disaster strikes.

A chimney draws smoke out of the house by creating an upward draft when a fire in the fireplace heats up the flue and the warm air is naturally drawn upward. A good draft will occur only if all parts of a chimney and fireplace are in tune with one another. For instance, the flue has to be the right size to draw the right amount of air in.

The smell of smoke in your home is a common sign that the chimney isn't drawing the smoke up and out. To figure out the problem, put on some old clothes, a hat, and safety glasses, and grab a flashlight. First make sure all ashes in the fireplace are out and cold; then open the damper. Look up into the chimney for blockage like sticks and leaves (including animal nests) and broken flue tiles or bricks (if you find these, call in a chimney expert immediately). If you are comfortable working on the roof, you could also take a flashlight up onto the roof and look down into the chimney. While you are up there, check the condition of the chimney crown (see Avoiding Costly Chimney Repairs, above).

BACK DRAFTS

If you don't find any blockage, the draft problem could be caused by a back draft, which occurs when air is being pulled down the chimney instead of up. If you have the furnace, clothes dryer, and kitchen or bath fan running at once, they are all pulling air from your house. If you don't have adequate ventilation in your house, air to make up for this loss can be sucked down in from the fireplace flue; smoke from a fire or exhaust from a furnace will spill into the house in this case. Tighter, more energy-efficient homes are most likely to have this problem. If you suspect a back draft, open a window or door to the outside in the same room as the fireplace. If the chimney begins to draw the smoke upward, you at least know there is an air shortage and that you should to bring a fresh-air duct into your house near the fireplace. Most prefabricated metal fireplaces already have their own outside air supply ducts, but most traditional masonry fireplaces do not.

DOWNDRAFTS

If opening a window doesn't solve the problem, you might be experiencing a temporary downdraft. A downdraft happens when wind blows down the chimney flue instead of across the top. This problem is sometimes caused by nearby obstructions like roof peaks, trees, or other chimneys on your roof and is usually just a sporadic problem. Sometimes a good draft in one chimney flue in a multiple-flue chimney will cause a downdraft in another, and sometimes air leaks in the flue tile will seriously weaken the draw. The best solution is to call in an expert if you think there might be a downdraft problem.

Don't try to repair a badly cracked or crumbling crown, especially if it doesn't have flashing—have it replaced by a professional mason. Insist that the mason install flashing and use concrete mix rather than mortar mix.

Routine checks and maintenance will make your chimney last longer. Caulk the crown with caulk specified for concrete—apply it to the gap between the flue and the crown. Install a cover to keep water and animals out of the flue and prevent rust from forming on the fireplace dampers and the metal flue liner. Finally, seal the crown and the brickwork with a penetrating water repellent called siloxane, which repels water but allows moisture from furnace gases to escape through the brickwork. Note that siloxane is combustible. Turn off gas appliances and extinguish fires before treating your chimney.

New Furnace Needs a New Flue Liner

Q. *I want to install a new high-efficiency furnace in my house. Will I have to install a new flue liner too?*

When you install a new furnace, you usually need a new flue liner. A high-efficiency furnace produces cooler exhaust gas, so the old flue may be too large, allowing destructive moisture and chemicals to condense on the flue walls.

The good news, however, is that if you buy a furnace that's even more efficient, you don't need a flue at all. A furnace that's 90 percent efficient can be vented directly to the outdoors with PVC pipe—no flue liner, not even a chimney. You pay more up front, but besides not needing a new flue liner, you save on fuel.

CREOSOTE BUILDUP

Look up the chimney past the damper and you'll see a black coating on the brick and the flue tile. The coating might be powdery, crusty, soft and sticky, or hard and shiny. This buildup is made of soot, tar, and creosote, but we'll call it all creosote. Creosote forms when unburned waste products from a wood fire stick to the sides of the fireplace and chimney. Over time, it can build up so much that it blocks the flue; it's also so corrosive that it can dissolve mortar joints and allow smoke to leak through the sides of the flue.

The worst danger of creosote is that it can ignite and burn inside your chimney, causing a chimney fire. If it spreads through cracks in the flue and chimney and heats the wood frame of your home, it can burn your house down. Even if the chimney is able to contain the fire, damage will have been done to the tile or metal liner and it may cost thousands of dollars to replace it.

Check for creosote buildup annually. If the buildup is more than ⅛-inch thick, have it cleaned. To help prevent a buildup of creosote, burn dry wood and maintain a hot fire. A buildup of more than ¼ inch is dangerous; don't use the fireplace again until you have had it cleaned by a professional chimney sweep who is certified by the Chimney Safety Institute of America. Hire a sweep in the spring, when it is easier to schedule an appointment; most people wait until the fall and have a hard time getting prompt service.

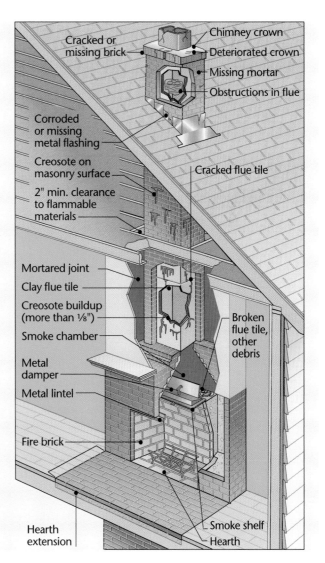

Chimney crown
Deteriorated crown
Missing mortar
Obstructions in flue
Cracked or missing brick
Corroded or missing metal flashing
Creosote on masonry surface
Cracked flue tile
2" min. clearance to flammable materials
Mortared joint
Clay flue tile
Creosote buildup (more than ⅛")
Smoke chamber
Broken flue tile, other debris
Metal damper
Metal lintel
Fire brick
Hearth extension
Smoke shelf
Hearth

Cooling

AIR CONDITIONERS

Cleaning a Window Air Conditioner

Q. *How do I clean my window air conditioner?*

A good cleaning of your window-mounted air conditioner will keep it operating efficiently. Room air conditioners have two sets of coils: the condenser coil on the outside and the evaporator coil on the inside. Keeping the coils clean is 90 percent of keeping an air conditioner in good shape. The most important maintenance steps are easy, but if this is your first time cleaning the unit, allow a few hours to take the machine apart and put it back together.

You cannot clean your window air conditioner unless you unplug it and remove it from the window. Hold on to it when you remove the window support. It can weigh 100 pounds or more, so have a helper stand by to help you lift it out. The cleaning process we show here applies to most air conditioners, but refer to your owner's manual for details about your brand and model.

When the conditioner doesn't seem to be cooling well, most people assume that the coolant needs recharging (a job for pros only).

But most often the coils are just dirty. The evaporator coil is protected by a filter. Rinse it out or replace it, and vacuum the fins if they're dusty.

The condenser coil is usually the dirtiest and is harder to get to. Since you usually cannot vacuum the fins from the fan side, spray water back through the fins from the outside. Do this outdoors or inside near a floor drain. Wrap plastic around the fan motor to protect it and to keep the wiring compartment dry. Let the unit dry for 24 hours before setting it in the window and plugging it in again.

Be sure to use the correct oil for fan motor lubrication. Don't use all-purpose or penetrating oils. Buy oil made specifically for electric

how is it done? CLEANING A CENTRAL AIR SYSTEM

When spring-cleaning time comes around, don't forget your central air-conditioning system. You can bet that a year's worth of dirt and debris has clogged the cooling fins and lowered the unit's efficiency. A dirty unit may stop cooling altogether in extreme cases.

A central air conditioner has two basic parts: an outdoor unit and an indoor unit that's located in the duct above your furnace. Allow at least a few hours to clean both units, especially if it's your first time doing it. Refer to the owner's manual for specific instructions. Before you begin, turn off the power at the main electrical panel that controls both the outdoor and indoor units.

THE OUTDOOR UNIT

Clean on a day that is above 60° F; compressors won't cool properly in temperatures below that. Your main job is to clean the condenser fins and coil (Photo 1). Unscrew the top grille and hold it open. The fan usually comes with it, so support it carefully to avoid stretching the electrical wires and stressing the connections. If the fan doesn't lift out, avoid hitting it with a lot of water when spraying it with the garden hose (Photo 2).

Compressors are quite fragile and must be treated with care. If the 240-volt power to your compressor has been off for more than 4 hours, don't start the outdoor unit immediately after cleaning. Instead, move the

Vacuum the condenser fins with a soft-bristle brush. The fins are delicate, so try not to bend them. Clear any debris that blocks the airflow through the coil. You might have to unscrew a metal case and lift it off to get to the condenser fins.

Spray the fins with a garden hose from the inside outward to clear away any dirt. Remove the debris that has collected on the bottom, then screw the top back on.

motors (usually non-detergent SAE 20 motor oil) unless your owner's manual suggests otherwise.

A handy tool to use when you're cleaning the fins is a fin comb; it can easily straighten out the delicate fins that may have become bent as you handled the unit.

Replace the filter, or wash and reuse the old one. Vacuum the fins with a soft brush attachment.

Wash the condenser coil with a spray of water from the outside inward. Cover the fan motor with plastic to keep it dry. Rinse and wipe up as much dirt as you can.

Winterize an Air Conditioner?

Q. *Can I winterize my window air conditioner and leave it in place all year?*

An air conditioner doesn't need winterizing, but a storm window won't fit with the air conditioner in place, and the seal between the air conditioner and the window probably isn't very good. To prevent air from getting in, you can cover the outside of the window and the air conditioner with an outdoor window insulation kit, or you can cover the inside of the window with an indoor kit. But it may be just as easy to haul the air conditioner to the basement every year!

switch to *Off* at the inside thermostat. Then switch the 240-volt power back on and let the outdoor unit sit for 24 hours. Whenever you switch off the system at the thermostat, wait 5 minutes before switching it back on. Once off, the compresser needs time to decompress so it won't stress the motor when it starts up again. To restart, switch the thermostat to its cooling mode and set the temperature so that the outdoor unit comes on; then check the unit. Listen for noises that might indicate damage. After 10 minutes, pull back the insulation on the insulated pipe. It should feel cool—about 60° F. The other pipe should feel warm, about skin temperature. If either doesn't, call in a pro to check the refrigerant level.

THE INDOOR UNIT

You probably won't have access to the evaporator coil that's in the plenum above the furnace, so you can't clean its fins. What you can do is keep the air that flows through it clean. Replace the furnace filter if it's dirty, and vacuum up any dust in the blower cabinet.

The evaporator coil in the plenum dehumidifies the indoor air as it cools it. The water flows out through a condensation tube; check to make sure it isn't clogged by sludge and algae. Flexible drain tubes are easy to pull off and clean, but rigid plastic tubes might have to be sawn off with a hacksaw, then rewelded with the proper pipe solvent and coupling.

Open the blower compartment and vacuum up any dust and dirt that has collected there. With the power turned off, lubricate any accessible ports on the blower motor with electric motor oil.

Check the condensation drain for sludge and algae growth. If it's partially clogged, pour a bleach solution (1 part bleach to 16 parts water) through the tube. Remove and clean the flexible tubes.

INSTALLING A BATHROOM FAN

A bathroom fan gets rid of odors and keeps the mirror from fogging; most importantly it removes humid air from your home. Moisture that fills the air while you bathe condenses on the walls, causing mildew and peeling wallpaper. If it gets inside your walls it can lead to rot. An exhaust fan takes care of this moist air by blowing it outside. Installing one is fairly simple.

If you just want to replace an existing fan, be sure the new fan uses the same size duct and has a housing at least as large as the fan housing now in your ceiling. Otherwise, you'll need to patch the ceiling.

TOOLS AND MATERIALS

The tools you'll need include a screwdriver, drill, jigsaw, metal snips, utility knife, hammer, wire strippers, an electronic stud finder, a drywall saw, and a voltage test light. A home center will carry the materials you need: duct tape, foam sealant, roofing cement, roofing nails, 1-inch self-tapping screws, two hose clamps, a rigid metal duct, a vent cap, electrical cable (Romex), wire connectors, cable clamps, and a switch box.

You may have to visit a heating supplier for insulated flexible duct. It is important to use only insulated duct, because moisture can condense in uninsulated duct, leak out, and damage the ceiling below. Your fan can be controlled by a regular light switch, but a timer switch is a lot more convenient.

Follow the manufacturer's instructions for specifics on installing and wiring your model of fan.

IN THE BATHROOM

Bathroom fans are usually installed over the toilet or near the shower, but you can put one in any spot that's not obstructed by objects in the attic above. A fan placed directly above the shower must be rated for that wet location and installed on a GFCI-protected circuit. (See Installing a GFCI, p.241.)

To begin the installation, locate the joist nearest to the spot where you want to install the fan, using an electric stud finder. Wear a dust mask and eye protection, and put down a drop cloth, too; then drill a ⅛-inch hole in the ceiling about 3 inches from the joist. Next, push a straightened piece of wire clothes hanger up through the hole and into the attic.

IN THE ATTIC

Lay a plank or a piece of plywood near the fan location to use as a work platform. Step only on the platform or the joists or you'll fall into the room below.

Find the wire hanger and pull back any insulation to check for obstacles (wiring, ducts, structural members) that might prevent you from placing the fan there. Remember that the fan duct route through the attic should be as short and straight as possible—sharp bends obstruct the airflow. If there are no obstacles, trace the outline of the fan housing. (For easier handling, remove the motor from the housing first.) Then cut the hole, using a drywall saw.

Install the housing flush with the finished ceiling below. Extend the mounting brackets to the joists on either side and then nail or screw them in place. Attach the duct to the housing.

ON THE ROOF

Watch out for power lines (see Roof Safety, p.111). To make a hole in the roof for the vent cap, use the 6-inch section of rigid duct as a template and mark the hole with chalk. Drill a hole for your jigsaw blade; then cut out the hole. Put roofing cement under the top and side flanges of the vent cap and slide the top edge under the shingles. Nail the bottom corners and fill the nail holes with roofing cement.

From the attic, slip the inner layer of the duct over the vent cap collar and secure with duct tape or a self-locking plastic tie.

ADDING POWER

The most accessible source of electricity for a fan is usually a junction box in the attic. Look for a box mounted on a joist or rafter, or you may have to pull up insulation to find a box connected to a light fixture below. Bathroom fans use very little electricity, so you can tap into almost any junction box without fear of overloading the circuit. Still, avoid circuits you sometimes overwork (such as kitchen circuits). If you don't feel comfortable doing electrical work, hire a licensed electrician to do this part of the installation.

Ultra-Quiet Bathroom Fans

Q. *The buzz of my bathroom fan is so loud that it wakes me up whenever someone turns it on during the night. Do bathroom fans have to make this much noise?*

There are new models of fans that are whisper-quiet and very affordable. Some of these newer fans produce about 1 sone (a measure of sound), similar to the loudness of a running refrigerator. Others are practically inaudible, producing 0.3 sone; this type often comes with a special switch to remind you when the fan is on. Quiet fans will cost more than the louder older models, but these new fans are built better and can last a decade or more.

A few manufacturers produce quiet fans that turn on and off automatically. Some models turn on when a user-set level of humidity is reached. Others turn on only when there is a sharp increase in dampness (and they can't be fooled by high outdoor humidity). Still others have motion detectors to turn the fan on when someone enters the bathroom. These fans can be programmed to turn off a certain time after the humidity or motion sensor is off.

Your bathroom fan doesn't have to keep you up at night. New models are much quieter and often come with automatic on-off switches.

Venting a Bathroom Fan

Q. *Our bathroom fan is vented into our attic. Most homes in my area don't have roof vents. Do I need to add one? What do you think?*

Never exhaust bathroom air into your attic. Your bathroom fan should be vented through the roof or through an outside wall to prevent moisture buildup. The reason you don't see roof vents in your neighborhood is probably because the bathrooms are vented through walls or soffits, eliminating the need for a roof vent. (Venting through a wall reduces the heat loss and the chance of leaking.) If you want to add a new vent, buy a venting kit that comes with an exterior vent, 8 feet of duct, mounting clamps, and hose clamps.

Loss of Heated Air

Q. *We have a large family and the bathroom exhaust fan, which is wired to the light, is always running. Are we losing a lot of heated air in the winter?*

Yes, you are losing a lot of heated air. The average exhaust fan can pull all the bathroom air out in a few minutes; this air has to be replaced by heated air from the rest of the house.

During the winter months, it's best to use ventilation fans sparingly. To do this, you can rewire the fan to a separate switch. You'll notice the savings on your fuel bills. You will keep some of that humid air in your house, but the extra humidity may improve your indoor comfort during the dry winter months.

Ventilation

VENTS

Swift Soffit Venting

Q. *We're turning our unfinished attic into a home office. To provide ventilation along the peak of the roof, we plan to install a continuous ridge vent. What's a simple way to vent the lower soffit?*

Circular soffit vents work well for vaulted ceilings and old or high soffits.

Use circular soffit vents, available at most home centers. They're especially handy for vaulted ceilings because you need to ventilate each rafter space individually. They're also good when you're dealing with old soffits that won't stand up to a lot of banging and cutting, or high soffits where cutting with a circular saw is awkward, messy, and dangerous.

Drill a hole for the vent, using a hole saw; then run a bead of caulk around the lip of the vent and tap the vent into place. When you're drilling, be careful. If the bit bogs down, the drill will start spinning, even if you're holding on to it. Use a drill with a side handle, and brace the handle against the house, if you can, to prevent an accident. And remember, vents won't do any good if you don't leave space between the roof boards and the insulation for airflow.

Attic Vents in Winter

Q. *There are two large attic vents in my house, one on each of the gable ends. Should I close these vents in the winter when the humidity is low? Would this keep the attic and the rest of the house warmer?*

Don't close your vents. The moisture that gets into your attic has no way to escape if the vents are closed. Moisture reaches the attic from your living area through air leaks (like around plumbing pipes) and by seeping through the ceiling. Trapped moisture accumulates as frost, which diminishes the effectiveness of your insulation and can even damage your ceiling as it melts. Instead of closing the vents, the best thing you can do to help warm your house is to install more insulation.

Calculating Roof Vents

Q. *I'm not sure my house has enough ventilation. How many vents should I have?*

According to the Uniform Building Code, you need 1 square foot of free venting area per 150 square feet of attic floor space. The code allows you to halve the venting area if you place half the vents 3 feet lower than the others. This low-high arrangement allows better ventilation.

Net free venting area (NFVA) is the open area of a vent after subtracting the thickness of the louvers or screens that run across it. Most vents have a label that lists the NFVA so you can calculate the number of vents you need to install.

Gable, or triangle, vents *are installed under the triangle formed by the end of the roof's ridge.*

Roof vents *are installed over an opening that's cut between rafters.*

A ridge vent *is installed over a 1½-in. to 2-in. gap in the sheathing and roof felt, along the ridge.*

Soffit, or eave, vents *replace part of the soffit. They can be continuous, rectangular, or circular.*

Square attic vents *are similar to gable vents, but they don't provide as much free ventilation area.*

HOW TO VENT A ROOF

how is it done?

Venting a house is an inexact science; the building's location and design greatly affect how air moves underneath the roof. Most experts agree that both the amount and the pattern of airflow are important. You want air to flow freely from the eaves to the peak of the roof. You need enough ventilation to allow the house's excess heat and moisture to escape and to keep the roof cool in winter to prevent ice dams from forming. For proper airflow, half the roof ventilation must be positioned at the peak and half near the eaves.

The photos below show how to install basic box-type roof vents. Locate them near the peak, but not so high that any part sits higher than the peak. Space the vents evenly across one side of the roof—it doesn't matter which side. In a house with eaves, you would also install soffit vents like those shown on the facing page to provide air inlets. On a house with no eaves, you can install the same basic box vents 3 feet up from the lower edge of the roof to serve as air inlets.

When you install box vents near the peak, make sure that air can get in through the eave vents. In the attic, look closely at the area where the roof meets the outside walls. Open an air path by knocking out or drilling holes through any short blocks of wood or rigid insulation that is blocking the airflow. Be careful not to weaken any structural blocking; consult an engineer if you are unsure. If insulation is in the way, install baffles between the rafters to keep the space between roof and soffit vents open (Photo 6).

1 Drive a nail up from the attic to identify the space between rafters; then saw holes through the roof sheathing equal in size to the opening in the roof vent.

2 Cut and remove shingles so the top of the roof vent can slide under the two uppermost courses of shingles. The hooked shingle blade simplifies cutting.

3 Pull nails that could interfere when you slide the vent under the two upper courses of shingles. Apply roofing tar around the perimeter of the hole.

4 Slide the roof vent under the top two courses of shingles and over the bottom two courses. Carefully lift old, fragile shingles. Nail the vent in place.

5 Apply roofing cement to seal out wind-blown rain. Add dabs of caulk over exposed nailheads. Do not apply caulk along the bottom edge of the vent.

6 Install insulation baffles if needed to provide an unobstructed airway from the eave to the peak of the attic.

Air Quality

INDOOR POLLUTION

Electrostatic Air Filters

Q. *Do electrostatic air filters work? My son has bad allergies and I'm thinking of installing some type of air cleaner. Do I need to be an electrician to install one of these?*

Electronic air cleaners and electrostatic filters depend on the principle of static electricity to trap airborn particles. Electronic air cleaners are installed in your furnace ductwork and do require electricity. Electrostatic filters are a different product. They slip in as a replacement for your regular filter and are charged with static electricity at the factory; there is no electrical work involved. These filters need to be replaced every 3 months.

Manufacturers claim the cleaners and filters will remove up to 97 percent of most dust, pollen, and animal dander. The only real way to find out if they'll help the allergy sufferers in your family is to install one and try it out for a few months.

Another thing you can do is to leave the blower on your furnace and air conditioner running continuously and change your regular filter every few weeks. This will drastically cut down on particles in the air. If your thermostat doesn't have a setting that does this, an electrician can set one up inexpensively.

Cleaning an Electronic Air Filter

Q. *I installed an electronic air cleaner a few months ago and I think it's time to clean it. How do I do it?*

Check your owner's manual. For most electronic air cleaners, you can wash the elements in a dishwasher. Place them in the bottom rack with the airflow arrows pointing up. Run the washer through one cycle and let them air-dry.

Another way is to soak the elements. Dissolve ¾ cup of automatic dishwasher detergent in very hot water. Soak the elements for 15 to 20 minutes; then rinse. Next, re-soak the elements in clean hot water for another 5 to 15 minutes; then let them air-dry.

Air Cleaners

Q. *I suffer from allergies while I'm inside my house. I want to buy an air cleaner, but I'm confused by all the competing products that claim to clean the air. How do I pick the right one?*

Air cleaners like this one trap pollen, dust, and other allergy-causing particles in your home; some can even catch things as small as harmful bacteria and viruses.

Before you buy an air cleaner (sometimes called air purifiers), make sure you are taking other steps toward clean indoor air. This includes frequent vacuuming with a high-quality, high-filtration vacuum and the removal of dust-trapping furnishings like shag carpeting and heavy draperies. If you still suffer from allergies, or if you want to reduce airborne contaminants like smoke and pollen, try an air cleaner.

If your home has forced-air heating and cooling, a central air cleaner that's connected to the furnace is your best bet. Look for an air cleaner that will trap large particles with a pre-filter and smaller ones with electrically charged collector plates. Most models have charcoal post-filters for odor removal. Electronic air cleaners are effective on the bulk of pollutants, including tobacco smoke, bacteria, cooking grease and smoke, dust, mite feces, mold, pollen, and animal dander.

The price of a central electronic air cleaner, installation included, is a few hundred dollars, but operating costs are very low. Manufacturers even claim that you can cut air-conditioning costs by up to 10 percent because an air cleaner keeps the cooling coils clean.

High-efficiency particulate air (HEPA) cleaners are the most effective and most expensive approach. They have hundreds of feet of filter folded into a small space, and they remove even the smallest particles, like viruses. The cost of an installed whole-house HEPA can be more than $1,000, and they cost more to run than standard air cleaners.

If a central air cleaner is not a possibility, the best models of portable air cleaners are nearly as effective, at least for a single room. Buy one with a cfm (cubic feet per minute) rating that will give you four changes of air per hour in the room the unit is in.

There are two types of carbon monoxide detectors: One plugs into the wall and may have an electronic readout, and the other is battery-operated with a replaceable battery/sensor.

Buying a Carbon Monoxide Detector

Q. *Should we buy an electric carbon monoxide detector for our home or one that is battery-powered? What is the best place to install one of these?*

Most battery-powered carbon monoxide detectors require you to change the battery/sensor unit every 2 years. With plug-in or permanently wired units, nothing needs replacing. However, during a power failure, they won't work. And it's during a power failure that your family is most likely to use generators, gas-powered pumps, and kerosene and propane space heaters; all these machines, when not properly vented, can produce high amounts of carbon monoxide.

The Consumer Product Safety Commission recommends that one detector be placed outside each sleeping area at any height on the wall. People with small children might consider placing battery-operated detectors high on the wall, out of their reach. Most manufacturers suggest keeping detectors 10 to 15 feet away from furnaces, water heaters, and other fuel-burning appliances. Garages are also bad locations because they often cause nuisance alarms when a car starts up; false alarms can occur in high humidity and from cleaning supply fumes.

Detectors can fail to sound if you place them too close to a window, where dangerous carbon monoxide can be diluted and quickly whisked away. Also, don't place one behind furniture or curtains that block airflow. Finally, be sure not to plug an electric unit into an outlet that is controlled by a wall switch; these detectors need to be on at all times to do their job correctly.

Checking for Back Drafting

Q. *How do I test to make sure my gas furnace and water heater are properly vented?*

Your furnace, water heater, and woodstove need air in order to exhaust properly. If your home is too air-tight, air from outside will be sucked down the furnace or chimney. This is called back drafting, and it allows all of the dangerous carbon monoxide to stay in your house instead of going up the chimney.

To see if your home is getting enough air, do this: Close all the doors, windows, and fireplace dampers, then turn on all exhaust fans, like the ones in the kitchen and bathroom. Next, turn on all vented gas appliances, such as the furnace and water heater. Wait 10 minutes for drafts to stabilize, then hold a wood match or incense stick below the furnace draft hood air intake. If the smoke is pulled up toward the draft hood, you have sufficient fresh air. If the match flame goes out or the smoke is blown away from the draft hood, back drafting exists and you need to call your local utility for assistance immediately.

If you have a fireplace, start a fire and repeat this back draft test at your furnace and gas water heater draft hoods. If back drafting exists, you may have to install a duct to provide the fireplace with outside air.

Make sure your house is breathing properly. Hold a smoking match or incense stick to the vent hood on the top of your water heater and furnace while they're operating to see if there is proper draft, like the one shown here.

If the smoke is not pulled up the vent hood, there is back draft. Call your local utility immediately. Install carbon monoxide alarms in your home.

PREVENTING CARBON MONOXIDE BUILD UP

Carbon monoxide is an invisible, odorless gas that kills hundreds of people in their homes every year. You cannot be too cautious about guarding your home against dangerous levels of carbon monoxide.

SYMPTOMS

■ Persistent headaches, dizziness, blurred vision
■ Nausea and vomiting
■ Confusion, disorientation, and loss of muscle control
■ Sleepiness
■ Rapid heartbeat, or tightening of the chest
■ Abnormal cherry-red color to the skin

Because many of the symptoms are similar to those of the flu and because poisoning is most likely to occur during the winter months when furnaces are in operation and windows are closed, many cases of carbon monoxide poisoning are misdiagnosed as "bugs." If all the family members experience the same symptoms, or feel sick at home but are OK after leaving the house, then carbon monoxide may be the culprit.

SOURCES OF CARBON MONOXIDE

The colorless and odorless gas is a by-product of incomplete combustion. The diagram below shows the major sources of household carbon monoxide. Other less obvious sources include lawn mowers, some paint strippers, and cigarettes.

Some houses are so energy-efficient and tight that they don't provide adequate airflow for carbon monoxide to escape to the outside. In older homes, added enclosures around furnaces or water heaters may create traps for carbon monoxide gas. If insulation has been added, check to see if extra ventilation is needed.

CLUES

Even though carbon monoxide is colorless and odorless, persistently stuffy, stale, or smelly air may be a clue to accumulated carbon monoxide gas. Another clue might be high humidity, often showing up as moisture on windows. Look for soot around the outside of the fireplace, furnace, or chimney, especially when there is no draft in the chimney.

WHAT TO DO

■ Check your chimney every fall for signs of blockage.
■ Have all heating appliances (including your water heater) checked by a professional every year. Utility companies sometimes provide this service at low cost.
■ Make sure your furnace space has access to outside air. A properly adjusted gas flame should be crisp and blue, not orange.
■ Consider getting a sealed-combustion furnace if you are buying a new furnace.
■ Install a carbon monoxide detector and periodically conduct a back-draft check (p.295).

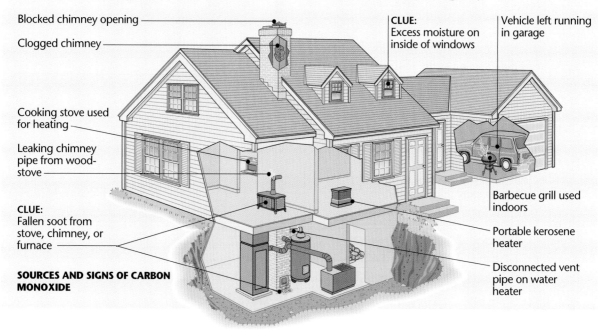

Blocked chimney opening

Clogged chimney

Cooking stove used for heating

Leaking chimney pipe from wood-stove

CLUE:
Fallen soot from stove, chimney, or furnace

SOURCES AND SIGNS OF CARBON MONOXIDE

CLUE:
Excess moisture on inside of windows

Vehicle left running in garage

Barbecue grill used indoors

Portable kerosene heater

Disconnected vent pipe on water heater

Reducing Radon

Q. *I tested our basement for radon recently and the results showed high levels of this gas in our home. What do I do to get rid of it?*

Don't be alarmed yet. Environmental and health organizations say that if you find high levels of radon based on one test, you should do some follow-up long-term testing. Radon is tested in picocuries per liter of air (pCi/L). If you get a short-term result of more than 4 pCi/L, you should do more extensive testing.

There are two strategies to reducing radon levels: Stop it before it enters your home, and remove the radon that does get in. Stopping it from getting in involves sealing up the entry points. Cover your sump pump, caulk cracks in the foundation, and seal crawl spaces. Removing radon involves increasing the ventilation in the house. This will replace radon-contaminated air with fresh outside air.

For detailed information on how to test and deal with radon in your home, contact your state department of health or the local office of the Environmental Protection Agency.

Radon Pump

Q. *It is necessary to run my radon pump constantly?*

Yes, leave the pump (actually it's a blower or fan) on at all times. It's part of a sub-slab depressurization system (SSD). An SSD pulls radon and other soil gases from under the foundation slab and vents them outside before they have a chance to enter your home. If you have a radon pump in your home, it is likely that there was a high radon level in the past. If you don't know the radon level in your home, get it tested as a baseline.

FIRE PREVENTION

Deadly Fire Extinguishers

Q. *I've heard that certain old fire extinguishers are dangerous to have because they can explode. I have a couple of old ones; how can I tell if I should get rid of them?*

Many extinguishers manufactured years ago have since been banned; some of them can be as deadly as the fires they are meant to put out. Some have been known to explode while they hang on the wall; others give off deadly fumes when used on a fire. Many states and national safety organizations have banned the use of the types of extinguishers shown in the chart below.

Fire Extinguishers

Q. *At my local home center I found fire extinguishers with an "A" rating and others with a "BC" rating. What type should I get for my kitchen and garage?*

You're better off getting a third type of extinguisher that can handle class A, B, and C fires. Class A fires involve wood, paper, and cloth. Class B fires involve grease, gasoline, chemical solvents, and other oils, while Class C fires involve electrical equipment. Extinguishers with an ABC rating are more expensive, but they handle all types of fires. Kitchen and garage fires usually involve grease or oil products, so a BC extinguisher is usually recommended for those areas.

All extinguishers eventually lose their charge, so look for one that can be recharged. Those with plastic heads and nozzles tend to lose their charge quicker than those with metal heads and nozzles. Check the charge three times a year and call a recharging service when the level is low.

HAZARDOUS FIRE EXTINGUISHERS

If you own one of these bombs, or have questions about any extinguisher, call a qualified fire equipment company or your fire department. Don't discharge a prohibited extinguisher yourself or put it in the trash.

CANISTER CONSTRUCTION	EXTINGUISHER TYPE
All	Carbon tetrachloride
All	Chlorbromethane (CBM)
Brass	Dry chemical (stored pressure)
Brass	Dry chemical (cartridge-operated)
Brass, copper	Foam
Brass, copper	Soda-acid
Brass, copper	Water, antifreeze (cartridge-operated)
Brass, fiberglass	Water, antifreeze (stored pressure)
Copper	Loaded stream (cartridge-operated)

Humidity

Interior Condensation

Q. *We have a moisture problem in our home that we can't solve. We have electric radiant heat in the ceiling. Every day during the heating season, we have to wipe moisture off our windows. What can we do to reduce the excess moisture?*

Many factors can cause excess moisture in a home. Older homes often have plenty of air leaks that help dry the place out, but newer and remodeled homes are tighter and can trap moisture inside. The radiant heating system you have does not circulate warm air, which would help prevent condensation on the windows. You can, however, install ceiling fans to increase air movement.

One common source of excess humidity is ground moisture migration. Water can be seeping into the foundation, adding to humidity levels inside your house. To prevent this, add drain tile around the outside perimeter of the house, or use gutters to divert the runoff from the roof.

Firewood stored inside the house can also cause excess levels of humidity; store wood outdoors. Do you have a lot of houseplants? Consider giving some of them away.

Cooking, dishwashing, and mopping floors can add a great deal of moisture to your home, especially if you don't have a ventilation hood in your kitchen to expel moisture outdoors. Remember, too, that each shower a family member takes adds a cup of water to the air. Baths add less. If you don't have a bathroom fan, consider installing one. Wet bath towels and drip-dry laundry also add to high humidity levels. Instead of air-drying them, put them in the dryer, and make sure that the dryer is properly vented to the outside.

Also make sure your fuel-burning heating appliances, such as your water heater, are vented correctly. Back drafting (when the appliance actually draws air in from the exhaust flue and spills exhaust into the house; see Checking for Backdrafting, p.295) can cause excess moisture and carbon monoxide poisoning.

If these remedies don't solve your problem, you may have to open a window slightly for about an hour each day to get rid of the extra moisture in the house. You could also consult a heating and ventilation contractor and have a heat-recovery ventilator installed; this would bring in lots of fresh dry air without losing heat. Installing a dehumidifier that drains into a laundry tub or floor drain is a good idea.

Musty Odors

Q. *Our summer cottage is near a river and is used only 6 to 8 weeks a year. How do we get rid of the mold and musty odors that accumulate throughout the year?*

Use paint that contains a mildewcide to help control mold.

Getting rid of mold and musty smells is possible, but not always easy, especially because of the cottage's location and the short time it's occupied. For starters, air out the cottage thoroughly before closing it up for the season. When you aren't there, have someone ventilate it when the weather is dry and cool. Also, repair all external and internal leaks, especially if you have a basement. You should also trim overhanging tree branches and clear away excess plant growth around the cottage.

If you have a crawl space, cover its floor with 6- or 8-millimeter polyethylene plastic and apply a concrete sealer to the interior foundation walls to help prevent moisture from seeping in. Installing a dehumidifier with a continuous drain will also help, but you'll need to keep the temperature around 65° F in the cottage for it to work. You can use electric baseboard units for this, and run the heaters part-time with a timer.

A mixture of trisodium phosphate (TSP), bleach, and water (facing page) is good for washing the mold-infected areas. If TSP is banned in your area, use a solution of $2/3$ cup powdered cleanser, $1/3$ cup nonphosphate detergent, 1 quart bleach, and 3 quarts warm water. Scrub the areas with a soft-bristle brush and rinse with warm water. Paint the affected walls and ceilings with mildew-resistant paint. Consider replacing carpeting, upholstery, ceiling tiles, and other porous furnishings that are likely to contain mold spores that could reinfect your cottage.

One final solution would be to install an air filtering/cleaning system. However, since your cottage is used very little, this is a costly option.

Dealing with Mildew

Q. *There is black mildew growing in some of the corners of our house and in the shower stalls. What's the best way to get rid of it for good?*

The black web-like fungus called mildew is the result of chronic moisture problems. It's easy to get rid of mildew for a short time, but it will return unless the underlying problems are corrected. The best way to remove mildew is to apply a solution consisting of 1 quart bleach, 3 quarts water, and ⅔ cup trisodium phosphate (TSP). Wear rubber gloves to avoid skin irritation. The solution will lighten, if not eliminate, the dark stains.

You can prevent mildew by using a paint or wallpaper paste that contains a mildewcide, but the only way to eliminate it altogether is by depriving it of moisture and darkness. To improve ventilation and lighting, leave lights on and doors open in bathrooms and closets. If you install closet lights, they must be at least 16 inches from shelves to avoid a fire hazard. Also, put louvered doors on closets.

To lower humidity in a bathroom, install an exhaust fan. Chemical dehumidifiers such as calcium chloride can lower humidity, but they can be difficult to find in certain parts of the country. Use an electric dehumidifier or air conditioner to lower humidity throughout your home.

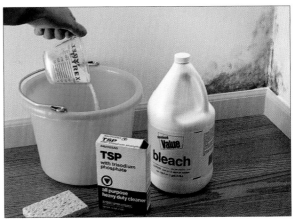

A solution of TSP, bleach, and water can clean away mildew.

Attic Moisture

Q. *The plywood on the underside of my roof is wet with condensation. There are vents at each end of the house with a turbine-type roof ventilator. What causes the condensation? What can I do to stop it?*

You need to evaluate your whole house to answer this one. Warm air can hold more water in vapor form than cold air can. When that warm air reaches the underside of your roof, it cools rapidly and condensation forms. To stop it, check several things. First, make sure that warm, moisture-laden interior air isn't being vented directly into the attic, such as from a bathroom or kitchen fan. To prevent moisture vapor from penetrating to colder areas, a vapor retarder should be installed on the warm-air side of your attic insulation. Insulate the attic door, hatchway, or stair walls, using a vapor retarder, and weatherstrip the door or hatch. Attic ventilation should then remove the water vapor that does penetrate.

Dew-Covered Floor

Q. *I built a screen-enclosed patio with a concrete floor and, after 2 years, applied a water sealant to the floor. Before that, I never had a water problem, but now it's slippery from beads of water any time it rains or is damp outside. I want to put asphalt tile on the floor but wonder if it would stay down. I never had any sweating problem before I put the sealer on.*

The sealant you applied is simply doing its intended job of preventing water from being absorbed into the concrete. Before you applied the sealant, moisture was absorbed into the floor. We can't endorse your plan to install asphalt tile, because resilient flooring is meant for indoor applications only. A much better choice is quarry tile. As long as the sealant you used was not an epoxy-type (check the label), you should be able to install the quarry tile with an appropriate tile-to-concrete mastic without problems.

New-House Condensation

Q. *Not long after we moved into our brand-new house, we began to notice that our windows were fogged over. What's going on?*

New building materials such as wood, drywall, concrete, and paint naturally contain a lot of moisture. A new house will experience a high indoor humidity level for a year or so until it dries out.

Increase ventilation as much as possible, and open your doors and windows for brief periods during the day to flush out the moist air.

Solutions for Curing Condensation

WHEN COOL WEATHER ARRIVES, so does the wet window season. The moisture that shows up on your windows during the cool months is condensation caused by moist air inside your home meeting the cool surface of the window glass. The lower the temperature outside, the more condensation will build up on windows and walls.

If condensation persists, it can rot windowsills, cause mildew to grow on walls and ceilings, and lead to a damp, musty smell throughout the house. Solve these common problems before they do serious damage. The easiest and least expensive solutions to each problem are listed first.

OCCASIONAL CONDENSATION

MORNING CONDENSATION

Windows fog or frost up during the night when the outside temperature drops. Also, when you lower the thermostat at night, you increase the relative humidity inside the house, which causes condensation to occur more easily.

As the day warms up and you turn the heat back up, the windows should warm up and clear within a few hours. As long as water doesn't run down onto your window sash and sills, temporary condensation isn't a problem. Open the curtains so circulating air can warm and dry the windows faster.

AUTUMN CONDENSATION

Homes absorb moisture like a sponge during the summer months and dry out in the winter. High indoor humidity may cause your windows to fog up every time there's a cold spell. After a few weeks of cool weather, your house will be dry enough for the windows to remain clear for the rest of the winter.

Open your doors and windows for 5 minutes several times a day to flush out the moist air. This is an inexpensive way to help your house dry out faster. If you have a forced-air heating system, set the furnace blower to run continuously until the condensation problem stops. Circulating air warms the window glass and causes more rapid air turnover in most homes. A dehumidifier can also help.

CONSTANT CONDENSATION

CONTINUAL CONDENSATION

Chronic condensation is a bad problem that calls for immediate attention. Either the humidity level in your home is consistently high, or your windows or walls are poorly insulated and cause condensation to form on them because they're consistently too cold.

Increase air circulation by running the blower on your forced-air furnace continuously. Upgrade single-pane windows by installing interior or exterior storm windows or double-pane windows. Hire a pro to increase your wall insulation. Have a whole-house ventilation system installed.

DIRT AND MILDEW

Moisture often condenses on cold spots in corners, in closets, or over wood framing in walls and ceilings. This moisture collects dirt and promotes mildew. It often appears as the shadow-like outlines of studs and joists.

Improve air circulation by running the furnace blower continuously or by operating a fan in the room. Open closet doors or install louvered doors. All these can warm the surface of the walls and ceilings above the condensation point. Reduce the indoor humidity as you would for a continual condensation problem, and consider hiring a professional to improve your wall or ceiling insulation.

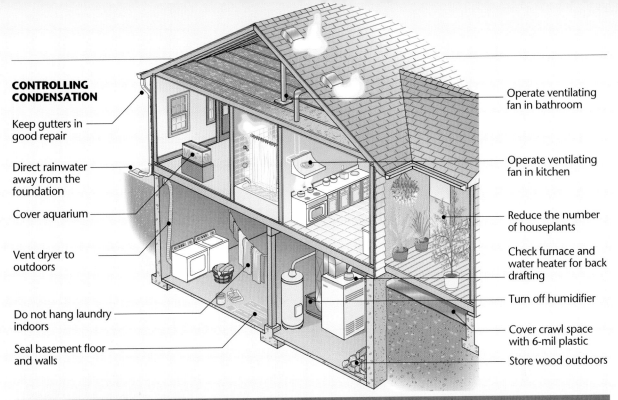

CONTROLLING CONDENSATION

Keep gutters in good repair

Direct rainwater away from the foundation

Cover aquarium

Vent dryer to outdoors

Do not hang laundry indoors

Seal basement floor and walls

Operate ventilating fan in bathroom

Operate ventilating fan in kitchen

Reduce the number of houseplants

Check furnace and water heater for back drafting

Turn off humidifier

Cover crawl space with 6-mil plastic

Store wood outdoors

SITE-SPECIFIC CONDENSATION

CONDENSATION ON METAL DOORS AND WINDOW FRAMES

Metal is a good heat conductor, so it cools rapidly in cold weather and provides a handy surface for moisture to condense on.

There is no inexpensive solution to this problem except to lower the humidity level inside your house. Look for metal doors and windows that have thermal breaks—gaps filled with heat-resistant material so they lose heat more slowly.

LOCALIZED CONDENSATION

Cooking, showering, washing and drying clothes, or the presence of a large group of people can all radically raise the humidity level in certain rooms.

If the windows dry off within an hour or so, don't worry. If water runs down the glass and soaks the sash or sills, turn on a ventilating fan to flush out the moist air. If there is no fan, open a window just a little to air out the room until the condensation disappears.

DAMP BASEMENT

In the warmer months, warm, humid air from outdoors condenses on the cool concrete walls and floor of the basement. Dampness can also seep through concrete floors and foundations from the soil.

Operate a dehumidifier and keep the basement closed up as much as possible in humid weather. If the condensation problem is ongoing in the winter, seal the concrete walls and floor of your basement with a concrete sealer. This will stop dampness, but it won't stop water from entering your basement through cracks, nor will it stop efflorescence, a whitish powder that appears on walls.

CONDENSATION ON CERTAIN WINDOWS

The windows on the north side of your house might fog up because they're colder than the rest. Storm windows on the side away from the prevailing wind can fog up, too, because cold, dry air tends to infiltrate on the windward side, while moist, warm air exits on the opposite side through leaks. This moist air often condenses when it hits a cold storm window.

For foggy window problems on the north side, install storms and double-pane windows. This is the best long-term solution, although expensive. You could also run the blower on a forced-air heating system continuously to clear the windows. Windows that get foggy and are away from the wind should not be airtight, and should have weep holes at the bottom to let water escape.

Workshop Safety

304 Safety Gear

Tools and Materials

306 Small Shop Strategies

308 Wood

310 Tool Repair

311 Clamps

312 Sharpening

314 Cutting Skills

316 Table Saws

318 Routers

320 Sanders

322 Drills

324 Grinders

326 Glues

Workshop

Repair and Finishing

328 Finishing Wood

330 Clear Finishes

332 Finishing Problems

334 Furniture Finish Repairs

336 Furniture Repairs

Workshop Safety

SAFETY GEAR

Blocking Out the Noise

Q. *I spend almost every weekend puttering around in my shop. Can my woodworking machines damage my hearing?*

Noise-induced hearing loss can be caused by cumulative exposure to loud noises over a long period of time. Since there is no immediate indication of injury, this kind of damage sneaks up on people. The Occupational Safety and Health Administration (OSHA) recommends that industry workers wear hearing protection when the noise equals or exceeds 85 decibels (dB) for 8 hours or more. At 95 dB, the allowed exposure without protection drops down to 4 hours, and that time decreases by half for each additional 5 dB.

Most woodworking machines are loud enough to damage your hearing. Some machines, like routers, table saws, and wet/dry vacuums produce more of the high-frequency (high-pitched) noise that's even more likely to cause hearing damage.

Here's a general guide for determining noise levels: If you're within 3 feet of a tool and have to raise your voice to be heard, the noise level is probably above 85 dB. If you have to shout, the noise level is above 90 dB.

There are several different types of hearing protectors to choose from (see chart, below). Whichever type you choose, it's important that they fit correctly. To test earplugs, try cupping your hands over your ears. If the earplugs are fitted correctly, you won't notice much difference in the level of outside noise.

HEARING PROTECTION

TYPE	NOISE REDUCTION RATING (NRR)	DESCRIPTION	PROS AND CONS
Earmuffs	16–20 dB NRR (Cuts noise level by 16–20 dB.)	Fit over the outer ear and seal against the head. Some are designed to increase protection as noise levels rise.	Convenient for intermittent use. Fit a wide range of head sizes. May be bulky and heavy. Most expensive type.
Semi-aural (canal caps)	25 dB NRR	Combine the protection of an in-ear device with the convenience of a hearing muff.	Lightweight and easy to use. Can be worn with safety glasses. Tips may be uncomfortable after long periods of use.
Formable foam	29–31 dB NRR	Made of compressible foam. When inserted in the ear, they expand to provide a snug fit.	Inexpensive and comfortable. Offer most protection when properly fitted. Inconvenient for intermittent use.
Premolded	26–27 dB NRR	Made of a flexible material to fit the ear canal. Some must be individually fitted for size.	Washable, reusable, and comfortable. Require some practice to insert correctly.

SOUND CHECK

HOW LOUD IS LOUD?

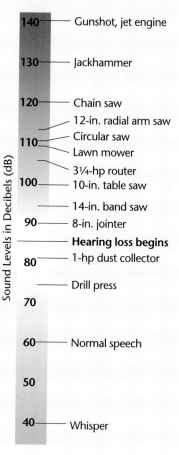

Sound Levels in Decibels (dB)

- 140 — Gunshot, jet engine
- 130 — Jackhammer
- 120 — Chain saw
- — 12-in. radial arm saw
- 110 — Circular saw
- — Lawn mower
- — 3¼-hp router
- 100 — 10-in. table saw
- — 14-in. band saw
- 90 — 8-in. jointer
- — **Hearing loss begins**
- 80 — 1-hp dust collector
- — Drill press
- 70
- 60 — Normal speech
- 50
- 40 — Whisper

Better Dust Mask

Q. *What are the best dust masks available these days?*

To choose the best mask, first determine what substances you're trying to avoid inhaling. Most pollutants fall into one of two categories: dusts and mists, or vapors and gases.

Dusts and mists are small, solid or liquid particles that float in the air and can be trapped easily by a mesh filter. Sawdust, drywall dust, and dust from various types of insulation are in this category. Disposable masks work well if they fit correctly; the mask must seal tightly around your face in order to protect you. Change the filter or discard the mask if breathing becomes difficult.

Vapors and gases, such as those you'd encounter when working with paints or strippers, are too small to get trapped in a mesh. Special charcoal (organic vapor) filters absorb these substances. If you begin to smell a solvent through your mask, replace the cartridge.

Only buy respirators carrying the official test mark "NIOSH Approved." NIOSH stands for the National Institute for Occupational Safety and Health. The mask and filtration device will list the categories of pollutants for which they're approved.

Masks for dusts and mists: disposable fabric (right); plastic frame (left) and silicone (center) with replaceable filters.

what do you need?

SAFETY GLASSES

Most eye injuries can be avoided if you take precautions when working around anything that could accidentally fly at your face and into your eyes. Make a habit of always wearing eye protection in the workshop or when using hand or power tools, even when you're only cleaning up.

GLASSES, GOGGLES, OR FACE SHIELD

Protective lenses will be stamped with the manufacturer's logo to show they have passed safety tests. The frames will also bear a "Z 87.1" stamp to show they have passed certain tests. Polycarbonate is considered stronger than other plastics or glass. (Ordinary prescription eyeglasses do not offer adequate eye protection.)

Safety glasses with side shields will protect you from particles entering at the sides and are more comfortable than goggles. Use them when you use hand tools (including a hammer) or slow-moving electric tools. You can get prescription safety glasses, too.

Goggles provide front, side, top, and bottom protection. The direct-vent type offers good air circulation and minimizes fogging. Indirect-vent goggles offer additional protection from fine particles and chemical splashes. Buy a comfortable pair that can fit over your prescription glasses.

Full-face shields offer complete face protection and are ideal for blocking chips and shavings from lathes or routers. Always wear safety glasses or goggles with full-face shields because the shields do not offer total protection against heavy impact. Wear a shaded shield whenever you are welding or brazing to cut down on brightness and infrared light.

Safety glasses with top and side shields are a must for all types of building and wood-working tasks.

Goggles offer the best all-around protection. Indirect-vent goggles protect from liquid splashes.

Face shields offer eye and full face protection, but you should still wear safety goggles or glasses with them.

SENSIBLE TIPS

■ Choose eye protection that's comfortable enough to use every day.
■ Keep an extra pair of eye protection for visitors or helpers.
■ Get your children in the habit of wearing protective eyewear whenever they help you or work on projects of their own.
■ Store a set of safety glasses in the case along with the power tool you would use them with, such as your circular saw or reciprocating saw.
■ Keep your eyewear clean with an antifog, antistatic solution.

Tools and Materials

SMALL SHOP STRATEGIES

Tools on Wheels

Q. *The good news is that I own several large professional-quality stationary machines. The bad news is that I don't have a professional-size shop. Any suggestions?*

One way to make your shop feel bigger is to put your tools on wheels. Table saws, band saws, drill presses, assembly tables, clamp racks, and scroll saws can all become mobile. Most manufacturers offer mobile bases with locking wheels so that the tools won't "walk" while you are using them.

Lathes and workbenches need a more solid footing. For these, the best choice is retractable casters that allow the legs to rest firmly on the floor during use (see photo). Use two casters if you can lift one end of the tool; otherwise, use two at each end.

Put racks and shelves for smaller tools and supplies on casters, too. To save even more space, hang the tools you seldom use on the wall and put the rolling racks in front of them.

Casters can help you rearrange your shop as needed. To make them retractable, bolt the wheels to a hinge, then screw the caster assembly to a plywood base.

Soundproof Solutions

Q. *My shop is in the basement directly below my son's room. What can I do to noiseproof my shop so I don't disturb him at night?*

Most people think that you can block sound with insulation and cushiony materials. In fact, it's density and mass that best reduce noise. Here are a few things you can do:

■ Use drywall compound to plug any holes in the walls and ceiling, even the little gaps around outlets or ducts.
■ Put up an extra layer of ⅝-inch drywall on the ceiling. To help further isolate the sound, install wood or metal furring strips perpendicular to the ceiling framework first.
■ If the existing door is hollow, replace it with a solid wood door, and install a tight-fitting sweep at the bottom.
■ Place cork pads under the feet of your stationary tools.

Double-Duty Bench Top

Q. *I'd love to have a workshop. Unfortunately, I have to share my "shop" with the family car. Do you have any advice to help me make the most of my space?*

Thanks to bench-top tools, people with limited workshop space no longer have an excuse not to hone their woodworking skills.

Most portable planers, belt sanders, and scroll saws work just as well as larger machines. Bench-top jointers work fine as long as you don't try to straighten very long edges (over 6 feet). Small three-wheeled band saws work quite well unless you need the power of the larger tool. For an accurate cut-off tool, go for a miter saw rather than the larger radial arm saw. The one tool you should always buy full-size, however, is a table saw.

There are many options for storing bench-top tools. One is to use a portable folding workbench like the one shown here. Attach a plywood base under every tool, and use bolts or cleats to fasten them to your work surface. Build some strong shelves to rest your tools on when they're not in use.

Bench-top tools, like this jointer, are great space savers. A plywood base allows you to attach the tool to a portable base or workbench.

A folding workbench can serve double duty as a tool stand and as a drafting board. Bevel the inside edges of the cleats to keep the table from popping off while you work.

Multitasking Table Saw

Q. *My table saw takes up a lot of room. How can I make better use of the space?*

To make better use of the space reserved for your saw, try sharing the space with other tools. For example, attaching a router to the extension table is like having two tools in one. Make your own table (a piece of plastic laminate countertop works great), and buy a couple of angle brackets to attach it to the saw.

A piece of plywood and two cleats can also transform your saw into a finishing table. When you use the table, be sure the saw is unplugged.

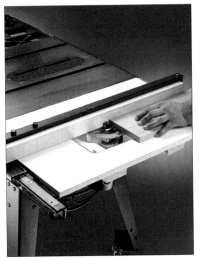

Installing a router under your saw's extension table saves space, and you can use the saw's fence for router cuts.

Turn your table saw into an extra work surface. Screw cleats onto a ¾-in. plywood top for a no-slide fit.

Cutting Plywood Down to Size

Q. *Cutting a full-size sheet of plywood on my small table saw makes me nervous. Is there a better way?*

You're not alone. Even if you own a full-size table saw, cutting a 4 x 8 plywood panel requires a lot of space on all sides of the saw, plus several work supports. A safer and more space-savvy method is to make your initial cuts with a circular saw. You can then trim the smaller pieces to their exact dimensions on the table saw.

You can get straight, splinter-free cuts with your circular saw by using a straightedge and a fine-tooth blade. For a good straightedge, use plywood factory edges or a piece of aluminum bar. For super-smooth cuts, use this straight-edge setup with your router and a straight bit.

Cut plywood down to size with a circular saw rather than than balancing it on a small bench-top saw. Cut the plywood on a set of saw-horses or rest it on a couple of 2 x 4's.

Dealing with Dust

Q. *My whole basement (including the clothes washer and the furnace) is covered with a layer of superfine sawdust. What can I do to avoid this mess in the future?*

Airborne dust is not just an annoyance; it can also ruin bearings and electrical switches. Short of buying a dust collector, there are a few simple and inexpensive options to help you cope with workshop dust.

First, try catching the dust at the source. One easy way to do this is by attaching a furnace filter to an old room fan. Put the makeshift filter on your bench when you're working so it can catch the dust before it becomes an airborne cloud. When the filter is full, vacuum up the dust.

You might want to consider improving your shop's ventilation by installing a window fan. Reverse the fan's direction so that it blows the dust-laden air outside.

Attach small metal L-brackets to a fan to create a slide-in filter holder.

Tools and Materials

Plain-Sawn or Quarter-Sawn Wood

Q. *What's the difference between plain-sawn and quarter-sawn wood?*

Plain-sawn and quarter-sawn stock differ not only in the way they are cut from the log but also in stability, appearance, and cost.

Plain-sawn boards are cut from a log in parallel slices. This method results in very little wasted wood. The grain pattern usually consists of long, drawn-out arches. Because plain sawing uses most of the log, these boards are less expensive than quarter-sawn stock. However, plain-sawn boards are much more prone to cupping and shrinking.

Quarter-sawn boards come from a log that has first been quartered and then been cut in parallel slices. This procedure is more time-consuming and wastes more wood, but quarter-sawn boards are more stable and less prone to shrinking and cupping. Some species, such as oak, display an attractive flecked or ray pattern

Two ways to saw lumber from a log: plain-sawn, top; quarter-sawn, bottom.

when quarter-sawn. This is caused by the wood cells running perpendicular to the surface. Quarter-sawn stock can cost 50 percent more than plain-sawn lumber.

Rough Stock

Q. *Is there any advantage to buying rough-sawn stock?*

In a word, yes. Buying rough-sawn stock is one way of ensuring that you get all the wood you're paying for. For starters, you're paying only for the material, not for the additional labor of planing and storing finished lumber. In addition, if you're planning to store your lumber, the wood may shrink, bow, or cup. Rough-sawn stock allows you to plane out these imperfections and still use the thickest possible board.

Before you buy any quantity of rough-sawn lumber, you'll need to invest in a thickness planer. If you plan to buy a pickup truck-size load of wood, this tool will pay for itself.

A planer will produce lumber of uniform thickness. You'll also need a jointer to make the edges straight and perpendicular to the faces. If you don't own a jointer, some lumberyards will cut one side of your boards straight for an additional fee.

When buying rough stock, try to select wood from a single tree to ensure consistent grain and color.

Wood Moves

Q. *I built a harvest-style kitchen table. For some reason, the boards that make up the top have started to separate. What could have caused this to happen?*

Sounds as though you may have been working with wet wood. Wood tends to dry out until its moisture level is in balance with the relative humidity of the air around it. And as the wood dries, it shrinks. This phenomenon becomes painfully clear when working with wide planks. For example, a 1 x 10 pine board can shrink more than ½ inch in width as it dries to indoor moisture levels. A similar drying/shrinking effect can occur during the winter if you have central heat and do not use an auxiliary humidifier.

Some gaps are caused by a process called compression set, which happens when wood absorbs moisture, swells, and then has no room to move. When wood has no room to move, the cells get crushed—permanently. Then, when the wood returns to its normal moisture level, it stays narrower. This might happen if the top was accidently soaked.

Unfinished furniture has no defense against seasonal swings in humidity and is especially prone to moisture-induced movement.

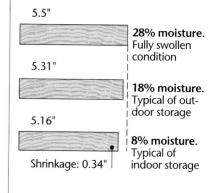

5.5"

28% moisture. Fully swollen condition

5.31"

18% moisture. Typical of outdoor storage

5.16"

8% moisture. Typical of indoor storage

Shrinkage: 0.34"

Buying Boards by the Foot

Q. *My hardwood dealer sells wood "by the board foot." How do I go about ordering the material I need?*

Buying hardwood, from either a specialty lumberyard or a mill, is different than buying a 2 x 4 at your home center. For example, hardwood stock is sawn in a variety of thicknesses up to 4 inches. The thickness is measured as the boards come rough-sawn from the mill in quarters of an inch. For example, "four quarter" is 4/4 or 1 inch thick, while "five quarter" is 5/4 or 1¼ inches thick, and so on.

Hardwood lumberyards use the board foot system to measure lumber. One board foot is equivalent to a piece of wood that measures 1 inch thick, 1 foot wide, and 1 foot long.

Here is the formula to calculate board feet:
- Board foot = width (ft.) x length (ft.) x thickness (in.)

Most lumberyards can plane your wood to any thickness for an additional fee. No matter how thin it's planed, the price is based on the rough thickness.

Here are the maximum-size pieces you can expect from the standard-thickness stock:
- 1¾-inch-thick piece from a rough 8/4
- 1⁵⁄₁₆-inch-thick piece from a rough 6/4
- 1¹⁄₁₆-inch-thick piece from a rough 5/4
- 1³⁄₁₆-inch-thick piece from a rough 4/4

Hardwood Plywood

Q. *My lumberyard sells several different grades of oak plywood. What's the difference? Is it worth buying the best plywood I can afford?*

Hardwood plywood is made of a veneer and a core. While it might make sense to use cheap stock for some jobs, understanding the differences will help you decide when it's a good idea to spend more.

Rotary-cut veneer core plywood is the standard hardwood plywood sold at home centers. The core is made from softwood veneers and is economical, stiff, and lightweight. The face veneer is rotary-cut hardwood; the result is a distorted grain pattern.

Plain-sliced face veneer is sliced from the log as if it were a board, and the pieces are glued side by side. The result is a more natural appearance to the grain. This plywood can be ordered in any species, including cherry and walnut, and is great for making cabinets.

MDF, medium-density fiberboard, is a less expensive alternative to veneer core. It's more warp-resistant but less stiff than veneer core and doesn't hold fasteners as well. It is an excellent choice for cabinet construction.

Lumber core is made of strips of basswood, edge-glued together. This core holds screws well in the side grain, but not in the end grain. When stained dark, the edges look good enough that you might be able to leave the sides exposed.

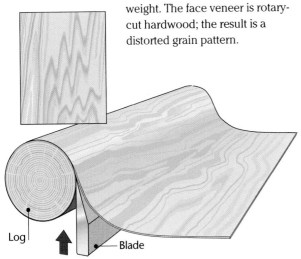

Rotary-cut face veneers are more economical to produce, but they have a wilder and more distorted grain pattern.

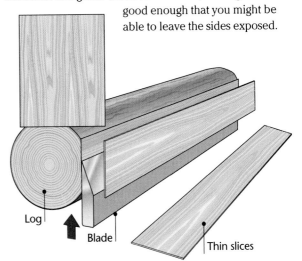

Plain-sliced face veneers have a more natural, boardlike grain pattern and are used for higher-quality work.

Tools and Materials

Wood Hammer Handle Replacement

Q. *Can you tell me the right way to replace a wooden hammer handle?*

First, remove the handle by cutting it even with the bottom of the hammer's head. Drill a series of holes through the remaining part of the handle and then use an old chisel or nail set to punch the pieces out.

Bring the head and the broken handle with you to the hardware store so you can find a nearly identical replacement. Closely match the throat of the replacement handle to the eye of the head. The shims and wedges used for securing handles can close up small gaps, but they can't make up for a undersize handle. The new handle's length should also be close to that of the original, or the tool will feel unbalanced.

Set the head on the new handle and strike the butt end of the handle onto your workbench. Some wood will curl at the bottom of the head near the swell on the handle; remove just the curled wood with a sharp utility knife. You may also need to use a knife or rasp to make it fit. Never use another hammer to drive on the new head—metal-to-metal contact could damage both tools.

Once the head is snug, cut off the protruding wood flush with the top of the head. Drive a wood wedge into the top of the handle with another hammer, and saw off any extra wood. Then drive metal wedges into the wood at a 45° angle as shown. File the top of the wood smooth; then seal the top with polyurethane paint.

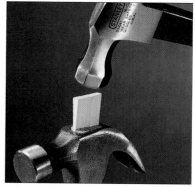

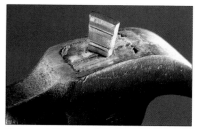

Drive a wood wedge into the top of the handle until it fits tightly.

Drive metal wedges into the wood as shown; then tap off the excess wedge and seal the top of the handle.

Extension Cord Repair

Q. *My 50-foot extension cord was accidentally cut near the end. Can I repair the cord?*

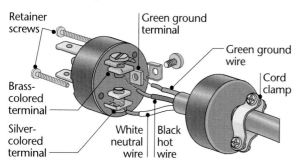

All you need to do is attach a new plug. Match the plug size and type with your cord. Strip the exterior skin of the cord back 1½ inches from the end; then remove about 5⁄16 inch of plastic insulation from each wire. Slide the lower part of the replacement plug over the cord; then screw the wires to the terminals of the plug.

Make sure to match the wires to the correct terminals: green to green, white to silver, and black to brass. Then attach the plug end to the base and tighten the clamp around the cord, as shown.

Rusty Hand Tools

Q. *I inherited a entire shed's worth of rusty tools. How can I restore these tools to usable condition?*

First, scrub the tools with a wire brush or steel wool to get off most of the rust. To speed things up, you can attach a wire wheel to your electric drill or grinder, but be sure to wear eye protection and heavy clothes; wire bristles can be dangerous.

For tools such as planes, and chisels, saturate the tool with WD-40, allow the oil a few hours to penetrate the rust, then start scrubbing with medium-grade steel wool or a nylon scrubbing pad. Wipe off the rusty solution and repeat until all the rust is gone. Once the tools are clean, they'll need to be sharpened.

To clean rusty files, soak them in a solution of 4 parts muriatic acid to 1 part water for 4 to 6 minutes. (Be sure to wear a full face shield, rubber gloves and a protective apron when working with acid, and have a bucket of water ready in case of spills.) After you soak the files, rinse them in clean water and scrub them with a file card; then rinse them again.

To keep tools rust-free, keep them clean and dry, and give them a light coat of oil or paste wax.

Clamping Panels Flat

Q. *I tried to glue some boards together to make a tabletop, but the panel came out cupped. What did I do wrong?*

Pipe clamps can bow when they're overtightened, in turn warping the panel you're gluing up. While you can't prevent the pipes from bowing, you can avoid problems by making sure that the boards fit together without excessive pressure. Make sure that the joints mate well with the clamps in place before you use glue.

Alternate the clamps on the top and bottom of the piece. In addition, use C-clamps to hold wood battens across the assembly. (This trick also forces the edges of the boards into alignment.) Wrap the inside face of each batten with tape so that it can't stick to your work.

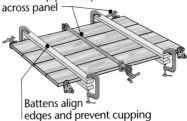

Alternate pipe clamps across panel

Battens align edges and prevent cupping

CLAMPS

Clamps can do a lot—hold projects together while gluing, serve as a vise for tools while sharpening, and even act as an assistant by holding the opposite end of a long board. Through the years, cabinetmakers, carpenters, welders, and hobbyists have developed specialty clamps for different tasks. Here's an overview of some of the most common woodworking clamps, what they're used for, and which ones to buy for a small workshop.

LIGHT DUTY

Spring clamps

Spring clamps are good for holding templates or boards together for marking or drilling. They're not able to apply lots of pressure or withstand heavy vibration. Start off with a pair of large and small clamps. Look for ones with soft tips to protect your work.

Bungee cords

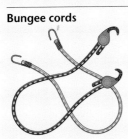

These inexpensive band clamps are perfect for holding together oddly shaped objects, such as a chair, but do not apply a lot of pressure. If you plan to do a lot of furniture repair, invest in a half-dozen.

Bar clamps

Consisting of a bar with a fixed jaw and either a screw- or squeeze-type sliding jaw, bar clamps combine the compactness of C-clamps with the versatility of pipe clamps. Different types are available for delicate or heavy-duty work. Start off with at least one pair of medium-duty clamps.

HEAVY DUTY

C-clamps

These strong, inexpensive, and versatile clamps have a ball-and-socket shoe that tilts to adjust to angled surfaces. Buy four each of 4- and 6-inch clamps.

Hand screws

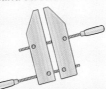

With the ability to evenly spread pressure over a broad surface and with wood jaws that won't mar surfaces, these clamps are good for more than woodworking. Start with a pair of 6-inch clamps.

Pipe and I-beam

These heavy-duty clamps are best for clamping large objects or edge-gluing boards. Use one every 12 to 18 inches when edge-gluing. The length of pipe determines the length of the clamp. Buy three sets.

Band clamp

Tighten the bolt in the head to apply even pressure around regular and irregular shapes. Steel corner pieces allow the band to tighten corner joints. Start off with two clamps.

Tools and Materials

Flattening a Waterstone

Q. *I bought a Japanese waterstone to sharpen my plane blades and chisels. After a few uses, it has become dished in the middle. How can I flatten it?*

Waterstones work quickly because the dulled particles wear off to reveal crisp new grits. However, these stones are relatively soft and can become dished in the center. To flatten a dished waterstone, place a sheet of drywall sanding screen on a dead-flat surface, such as a piece of ¼-inch-thick plate glass, and scrub the stone across the screen.

Slipping Screwdriver

Q. *Can I sharpen my screwdriver to keep it from slipping off screws and gouging the wood?*

Use a single-cut file to restore the tip of a slipping screwdriver.

If your screwdriver tends to slip, it's a good idea to sharpen, or rather restore the shape and size of the screwdriver's tip. For a straight-tip screwdriver, clamp the screwdriver in a vise, then push a file diagonally across the tip until it's flat. Next shape the edges so the tip is the desired width. As a final step, lightly dress the faces of the tool so the tip is the desired thickness.

If you do a lot of woodworking, consider reshaping the sides of a straight tip so they're parallel rather than tapered. This allows you to sink screwheads below the surface of the wood without creating a crater around the edge of the hole with the wide part of the taper.

What *Not* to Sharpen

Q. *I have a collection of old steel circular saw blades. How do I sharpen them?*

You don't. In order to cut properly, a circular saw blade's teeth must be set to the right height and angle, a task best left to a pro. You'll probably discover, as we did, that it costs less to buy a new blade than to sharpen the old one.

The pros know not only what they can sharpen, but also what isn't worth sharpening and what should be left to the professional sharpeners. In general, bargain basement bits and blades aren't worth sharpening. Anything with carbide cutting teeth should be professionally sharpened. Most hardware stores offer sharpening services, or you can mail tools out to a specialist. Price may give you some indication of what's worth sharpening, but here are a few more considerations for frequently sharpened tools:

■ Handsaws. Leave this tool to the pros. Your granddad may have sharpened his saw, but nowadays you can have the teeth professionally ground and set for a low cost.

■ Carbide-tipped blades must be sharpened by a pro. This service is relatively costly, so it may be worth doing only on your best blades. Ask your sharpener about adjusting the cutting angle of the teeth to match the materials you cut most frequently.

■ Router bits. Some woodworkers can restore a lightly worn edge, but when it's time for sharpening, carbide-tipped and high-speed steel bits are best left to a pro. Weigh the cost of a new bit against the cost of sharpening.

Sharpening Chisels

Q. *What's the best way to sharpen a dull chisel?*

Wood chisels should be sharpened to an angle somewhere between 25° and 30°. To do this, place the bevel edge of the chisel on the coarse side of the sharpening stone and rock it up and down until you feel the existing angle. Move the chisel over the stone in a figure-8 pattern. After five or six passes, check the bevel. If it's uniformly shiny, you're doing a good job; if only the heel or toe is shiny, adjust the angle so the bevel makes full contact. Repeat this process on the finer side of the stone.

As a final step, polish the back of the blade on a fine stone. Sharpening creates a slight wire edge that must be polished away. Breaking off this burr will ruin the edge.

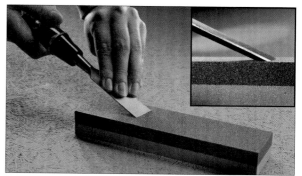

Move the chisel over the stone in a figure-8 pattern. The heel and the toe of the chisel (see inset) must make contact at the same time for good sharpening to occur.

Home-Ground Brad-Point Drill Bits

Q. *Every time I try to sharpen twist drill bits, I wind up with a not-so-sharp bit that bores an oval hole. What's the trick?*

Sounds as though you're grinding the tip slightly off-center. Sharpening a twist drill bit is harder than it looks.

For a very sharp drill bit that is easy to resharpen, we suggest a different approach: Grind a conventional twist drill into a brad-point bit. It is easy to do, and you'll discover that these custom-ground bits bore quickly and leave clean holes.

To grind your own brad point, first use a bench grinder to flatten the tip of the bit; then use the corner of the wheel to cut the scalloped cutting edge. (Work slowly. If you overheat the bit, it will lose its temper and be unable to hold an edge.) Viewed from the side, the point should be slightly longer than the cutting tips.

To sharpen your homemade brad point, simply touch up the scalloped edge with sandpaper wrapped around a small dowel.

To grind your own brad point, use a bench grinder to flatten the tip (center); then cut the scalloped cutting edge (left).

SHARPENING A KNIFE

There are many different kinds of sharpening tools, but nothing is better for your knives than simple maintenance. Revive nicked or really dull knives with a wedge stone, also called a sharpening stone. Before each use, push the knife from handle to tip, across a honing rod, making alternate passes on each side. Shown below are the angles placed on knives according to their intended uses; the heftier the task, the broader the angle.

To test a knife for sharpness, hold a sheet of notebook paper in one hand and make a slice about 2 inches away from your grip. The paper should slice cleanly without tugging or tearing.

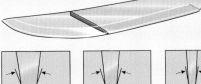

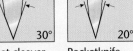

30°	20°	10°
Meat cleaver	Pocketknife	Kitchen knife

Move a sharpening stone across the blade in a spiraling motion.

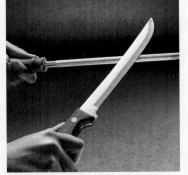

Push the knife across a steel honing rod to maintain an edge.

Sharper Spade Bits

Q. *Spade bits work well but dull quickly. Can I sharpen them myself, or am I asking too much from an inexpensive tool?*

Due in part to their simple design, spade bits are easy to sharpen. To sharpen a spade bit, use an 8-inch single-cut file to file the two straight edges. Sharpen each cutting lip to about 15°. Be careful to file each side evenly. Next, lightly touch up the two sloped edges of the point. To remove any burrs, push both faces of the bit flat across a sharpening stone.

Spade bits can be sharpened freehand. Sharpen each lip with a few light strokes.

Tools and Materials

Splinter-Free Cutting

Q. *I bought some beautiful oak plywood to build a bookcase, but I can't seem to cut a clean edge. How can I avoid tearing the veneer?*

How you cut the piece depends on the tool you're using to make the cut. Your best approach is to use a table saw equipped with a carbide blade with at least 60 teeth. Orient the plywood so that the good side is up. The higher you raise the blade, the less it will tend to tear the top veneer; however, raising the blade increases tearout on the bottom. Some professional saws have a small auxiliary blade in front of the primary blade to score the bottom veneer. You can produce this same effect with your saw by making the cut in two passes. For the first pass, raise the blade so that the teeth just score the wood. Without moving the fence, raise the blade height and finish the cut.

For circular, radial arm, and chop saws, orient the good side down. To further prevent splintering on the bottom (good) face, place a scrap of plywood beneath the workpiece. The scrap wood supports the wood fibers on the bottom and reduces tearout.

Even with these precautions, getting a smooth cut with a circular saw can be a challenge. Be sure to use a blade with at least 36 teeth. For extra insurance, cover the cut line with masking tape, then score the line through the tape with a utility knife. The tape holds down any splinters that might otherwise be lifted by the blade. When making the cut, remember to keep the blade to the waste side of the line.

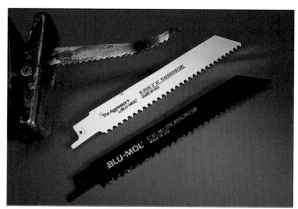

Bimetal blades cost a little more than steel blades, but they last a lot longer and have hardened teeth for cutting through nails.

Bimetal vs. Steel Blades

Q. *What is the difference between bimetal blades and steel blades?*

High-speed, high-alloy, or spring steel blades are made entirely from one kind of metal. Bimetal blades are made from one of these metals and have fused-on teeth made of special hardened metal. In use, bimetal blades have the flexibility for cutting curves and the strength for cutting through tough materials like nails or metal lath.

Bimetal blades may cost a little more than high-speed steel blades, but they will last up to three times as long. Bimetal blades are available for reciprocating saws, jigsaws, and band saws.

Cutting Threads

Q. *How can I cut threaded rod, or shorten bolts, and still keep the threads usable?*

No matter how carefully you try to cut a bolt or threaded rod, the threads will become slightly damaged. The trick is to thread a nut on before you do your cutting. Backing off the nut after you've made your cut will clean up any minor damage. For really mangled threads, bevel the cut end of the bolt or rod before removing the nut.

For cutting small machine screws and bolts, use electrician's pliers. Simply thread the long screws into the cutter and squeeze the handle. The cutter cleans up the end of the screw as you unthread it from the tool.

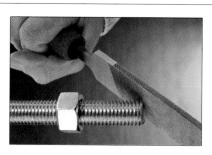

To restore the threads on a thick rod, file the damaged end; then remove the nut.

Electrician's pliers can shear small screws and bolts without damaging the threads.

Cutting a Circle

Q. *How can I cut a perfectly round circle to build a table?*

The easiest way to cut a round tabletop or any large circle or arc is to use a router as the cutting tip of a large compass. Remove the router's plastic base and use the base screws to attach a compass arm of ¼-inch plywood. Pin the arm to the circle's center with a single nail or screw. The distance from the router bit to the center point must be equal to the radius of the circle you want to cut.

Swing the router around the pivot screw to cut the circle. If necessary, make several passes, cutting a little deeper with each pass. For the final cut, support both the circle and the waste section to prevent splintering.

To cut a perfect circle, attach your router to a plywood compass arm. Using a ¼-in. straight bit, swing the router counterclockwise around the pivot point.

Cutting Through Metal

Q. *What's the best way to cut through steel?*

For cutting thin steel, like corrugated roofing, chain link fence posts, or steel studs, you can use a circular saw with either a hardened steel or an abrasive blade. Thicker steel, such as metal pipes or angle irons, can be cut with the abrasive blade or with a reciprocating saw or a hacksaw.

When cutting metal with either a hacksaw or a reciprocating saw, start the cut so that the maximum number of teeth are in contact with the metal. Starting the cut on the edge of the metal, as you would saw a piece of wood, stresses the teeth and shortens the life of the blade.

Cutting steel with a circular saw will produce a ton of sparks. Be sure to wear the proper safety equipment.

When using a hacksaw, start the cut on the flat face. Starting the cut on the edge will cause the teeth to wear or break.

Color-Coded Snips

Q. *Why do aviation snips come with different-colored handles?*

Aviation snips, also called offset snips, are spring-loaded and have compound lever action to help chew through heavy-gauge metal. Their handles are color-coded to indicate how they're designed to cut: red snips cut to the left, green snips cut to the right, and yellow snips are for straight cuts and gentle curves. The curve cutters can also cut straight.

If you are a lefty and are planning to buy one pair, start with the green-handled snips. Lefties tend to feel more comfortable cutting curves toward their right (clockwise).

You should also note that, unlike other snips, aviation snips have a top and a bottom—the curve of the blades must point upward when you cut. The handles are contoured to help you tell when you're holding the tool properly. (See Cutting Ducts, p.277.)

Tools and Materials

Table Saw Kickback

Q. *What is table saw kickback and how do I avoid it?*

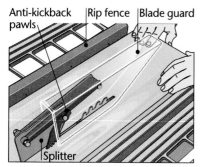

Kickback happens when the blade of a table saw throws a piece of wood toward you. This usually happens when the piece you're sawing gets trapped between the spinning blade and the fence or the blade guard.

There are a few ways to avoid kickback. First, make sure the fence is set parallel to the blade to prevent it from pinching the wood. You should always use a blade guard that has a splitter and anti-kickback pawls (see illustration, left).

Never use the fence as a guide when crosscutting (cutting at 90° to the board's length). Cut-off pieces could get stuck between the fence and the blade and be hurled at you. To prevent this, clamp a stop block to the fence. Always position yourself out of the kickback zone, which is directly behind the blade.

Also watch the condition of your wood. Twisted and bowed boards are more likely to get kicked back, so avoid cutting these with a table saw.

Never use your rip fence as a guide for crosscuts. Attaching a stop block ensures that the cutoffs don't get stuck between the blade and the fence.

Long-Bed Fence

Q. *Cutting long lengths of wood on my small saw is quite a balancing act. Do you know a better way?*

A long-bed fence is easy to build, allows you to cut long pieces accurately, and supports the cut pieces as they pass beyond the back edge of the saw. Make the fence to fit your saw. Round over the leading edge of the outfeed table so your workpiece won't get caught on it. Screw the infeed and outfeed beds to the bottom edge of the fence extension. Screw the fence section to your saw fence from the back side of the factory fence.

For cutting wide panels, use an outfeed table for additional support.

The long-bed fence supports the stock and helps keep the cut straight.

Underpowered Saw

Q. *I'm having trouble ripping lumber with my bench-top saw. No matter what I do, I wind up burning the wood and sometimes stalling the blade.*

Even when properly adjusted, some saws just don't have enough power to plow through thick stock and tough hardwoods. Here are a few tips for ripping thick stock on an underpowered saw:

■ Use a thin-kerf blade. Thin-kerf blades require less horsepower because they remove less wood. Likewise,

use a ripping blade instead of a combination blade. Ripping blades have fewer teeth, bigger gullets, and a tooth geometry designed specifically for cutting with the grain.

■ Raise the blade. A lower blade places more teeth in the kerf, which causes the blade to heat up and burn the wood. The higher you raise the blade, the fewer teeth actually in the wood and the coarser the cut.

■ Expect some burning. Despite these precautions, some woods, like oak and cherry, are notoriously tough to cut cleanly. Use a sharp hand plane to remove any burn or blade marks.

Quick Saw Test

Q. *How can I check that my blade and miter gauge are exactly square to make a simple 90° cut?*

To check that your blade is perpendicular and that your miter gauge is cutting square, try this test with a piece of scrap.

First, make a cut. Now flip one piece over, butt the cut ends together, and lay the pieces against a straightedge. There should be no gap at the joint. If there's a gap at the face of the boards, adjust the angle of the blade. A gap at the edge means you need to adjust the miter gauge.

Use this "cut and flip" test to see if your saw is cutting square before making important cuts.

A gap along the edge of the wood indicates an inaccurate miter gauge. A gap along the face points to the blade.

how is it done?

MAKING FIRST-RATE CUTS

The first requirement for getting clean, accurate cuts with your saw is making sure all its working parts are in tune. That means having the blade and the fence set accurately. Since each brand of saw is made differently, we'll show you how to check your saw for accuracy. Your owner's manual will indicate the location of the adjustment screws.

First, adjust the blade's alignment. The blade should be exactly parallel with the miter gauge slot of the table. To check this, use an adjustable square to measure the distance of the front and back of the blade. For accuracy, rotate the blade so that your measurement will be against the same tooth at both the front and the back.

Next adjust the saw fence so that when locked it's $1/32$ inch farther away at the rear of the blade than at the front of the blade. Only the leading edge of the blade does the cutting; the $1/32$-inch space prevents burning and blade marks on the cut edge. As you make a cut, be sure that the board stays tight against the fence.

To ensure square edge cuts, check the blade for exact vertical relative to the tabletop. To do this, remove the throat plate and place an adjustable square along the full flat surface of the blade.

1 *Use a square to check the alignment of the blade relative to the table. Slide the square along the miter gauge slot.*

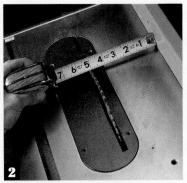

2 *Measure your fence to make sure it's parallel plus $1/32$ in. at the blade's rear. Repeat this step to check the fence lock.*

3 *Remove the throat plate to set the blade to 90°. Position the square between the carbide teeth.*

ROUTERS

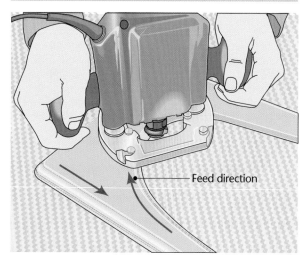

Feed direction

Right Way to Rout

Q. *I'm having a hard time controlling my router. What am I doing wrong?*

A common mistake is to move the router in the wrong direction. Viewed from above the router, a router bit rotates clockwise. You should always try to feed the wood into the spinning bit. This makes the tool easier to control, because the cutting action pulls the router against the edge. If you rout in the other direction, the bit could climb away from the wood and run out of control along the edge of your workpiece.

For example, when forming the edges of a picture frame, you would move the router counterclockwise along the outside edges and clockwise along the inside edges. If you mount your router upside-down in a table, you would feed the wood from right to left.

Fixed-Base or Plunge?

Q. *I'm ready to buy my first router. Should I buy a fixed-base or a plunge-type model?*

For hand-held operations, a plunge router is more versatile than a fixed-base router. The plunge base allows you to start cuts in the middle of a board—for example, for cutting mortises. The base also locks in place so that it can be used just like a fixed-base router. If you can afford only one tool, this is it.

If you're planning to install your router in a router table, you might be better off buying a fixed-base model. Fixed-base routers are generally easier and quicker to adjust; usually you can set the height with just a twist of the motor. With a plunge router, you'll need to reach under the table and turn a depth adjustment knob.

In terms of size and power, a 1½- to 2-horsepower router is light enough for most hand-held operations, yet has enough power to make heavier cuts. For the most versatility, look for a model with a collet that can hold both ½-inch- and ¼-inch-diameter shank bits.

No-Chip Routing

Q. *I recently ruined not one but two wall plaques while attempting to rout the edges. Is there a surefire way to eliminate chipping and splintering on the corners?*

For starters, make sure you're using a sharp bit; dull bits tend to tear the wood. Second, when removing large amounts of wood, do it in three progressively deeper passes.

Finally, on pieces of solid wood, rout the end grain first. If the corner does chip, you'll be able to remove the damage when you rout the sides.

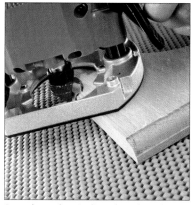

Rout the end grain first, then the sides, to prevent rough corners and splinters.

Cleaning Power Tools

Q. *How do I clean my router to prevent it from becoming damaged?*

An annual cleaning and lubricating of your router and other power tools is highly recommended. Plan the disassembly of the tool in advance. Place a clean shop rag or white towel on your workbench to help keep track of the tool's internal parts. Or use a compartment tray to hold the parts in the correct order.

Unplug the tool and remove the screws that hold it together. Gently open the tool's case, and use a gentle blast of compressed air to blow away dust and dirt. Check the condition of the motor brushes, replacing them as necessary. Some tools require lubrication at specific points, using either a lightweight grease or a light motor oil. Your owner's manual is your best guide to the cleaning, oiling, and checking that should be done. One product you might want to have on hand is aerosol electrical contact cleaner to use on all electrical connections with built-up grime.

Router Safety

A router bit spins at speeds from 10,000 to 25,000 rpm. At these speeds, a two-flute bit makes hundreds of cuts per second—enough to make a fine cut on wood or a disastrous one on your finger. Keep these rules in mind when you use a router:

■ Watch your power. Always unplug the router before changing bits. Make sure the on-off switch is off before plugging in the cord.

■ Use sharp bits. Dull bits leave burn marks and increase feed resistance, which can strain the motor and bearings and may also put you off balance.

■ Don't bottom out a bit. To ensure that the collet grips the bit evenly and securely, insert the bit all the way into the collet, then withdraw it 1/16 inch.

■ Tighten the bit in the collet. It's not unusual for a bit to work itself loose. If the collet won't hold the bit tightly, inspect the bit's shank for any burrs. You may need to replace the collet.

■ The router should be running at full speed before the bit touches the wood. This prevents the router from kicking away from the wood when it's started. When the cut is complete, keep the router on until the bit is clear of the wood; then shut it off.

■ Hold your work securely. Use a router pad or clamps for large pieces. Double-stick tape is good for holding smaller pieces.

■ Make sure that all nails and fasteners are out of the path of the router bit and that the path you walk while moving the router is clear. Check that the power cord is long enough to make an uninterrupted cut.

Making Guided Cuts

Q. *Can I use my router to cut straight lines and angles like a circular saw?*

Yes. To get a clean edge on plywood, or to clean up any rough edge, you can use a straightedge to guide the base of your router. To determine where to position the cutting guide, measure from the edge of the bit to the edge of the router base. Place the guide that distance away from your cut line.

A carbide-tipped 1/2-inch straight-cutting bit will produce a smooth, splinter-free cut on plywood or hardwood. If you need to remove more than 1/8 inch of stock, make the cut in multiple passes.

Use a straightedge to guide the router when trimming plywood or squaring a rough edge.

Measure from the edge of the bit to the outside edge of the base to determine where to position the straightedge.

what do you need? BUYING BITS

Bits come in two types: high-speed steel and carbide-tipped. Although they can cost two to three times as much as steel bits, carbide-tipped bits are your best bet because they stay sharper longer. Carbide-tipped bits will cut manufactured woods, such as plywood, particleboard, and hardboard, as well as plastics. They can also be used to cut solid wood boards. High-speed steel bits should be used only to cut solid wood.

Look for bits that feature an anti-kickback design. Anti-kickback, or safety, bits have solid bodies with just a narrow opening in front of the cutting tip. This full-body design reduces the possibility of jamming too much wood into the bit.

Two bits you should start out with are 1/4-inch- and 1/2-inch-diameter two-fluted, carbide-tipped straight-cutting bits. You'll be using these two bits for dozens of different projects, so buy the best ones you can afford. Better quality bits also have larger carbide tips so that they can be resharpened several times; you'll wind up saving money. Buy other bits only as you need them.

Tools and Materials

SANDERS

Clamp a belt sander on its side for sanding edges or curves.

Drill Press Drum Sander

Q. *I cut out a few pairs of shelf brackets with a jigsaw, and now I'm looking at a lot of tedious sanding. Is there a quick and easy way to sand out saw marks?*

A sanding drum mounted to your hand-held drill is a good, inexpensive solution for small sanding jobs. If you own a drill press, you might want to consider building a sanding table. The table maintains square edges on your work, and the vacuum port sucks up sawdust before it can become airborne.

Screw the top and bottom pieces to the sides of the box; then drill a hole in the top for the sanding drum, about ¼ inch larger than the diameter of the drum. Raise the sanding drum to expose the workpiece to fresh sandpaper.

Cleaner-Running Belts

Q. *I tried stripping a painted bench with my belt sander and succeeded in gumming up the sanding belt. How can I revive the belt?*

The fastest way to clean a caked-up belt is with a rubber abrasive cleaner (available in hardware stores). The rubber digs between the abrasive grains and pops out the caked-in gunk. It does not, however, sharpen a dull abrasive. If the belt sands slowly and tends to burn the wood after you clean it, it's time for a fresh belt.

Small Part Sanding

Q. *Belt sanders are great for removing stock fast, but the weight of the machine makes it almost impossible to sand a little bit. How can I better control this tool for finer work?*

The best way to control a belt sander is to turn it into a stationary tool. That way you can safely smooth small pieces and keep an eye on your progress.

Many sanders have a relatively flat top so that they can be held on their backs. You can also convert your belt sander into an edge sander by making a platform out of ¾-inch plywood. Shim the sander's handle so that the belt is perpendicular to the sanding table; then clamp the tool to the base. Support the workpiece on a ¾-inch-thick plywood feed platform screwed to the base platform.

Build this simple box and convert your drill into a spindle sander.

Prolong the life of your belts by cleaning off sawdust and gummy paint with a rubber belt cleaner.

Liquid Sander

Q. *What is liquid sander and how is it used?*

Contrary to what some people think, liquid sander will not sand a rough-sawn board into a smooth board. Liquid sander is a mild stripper that's used to degloss a finish when you are applying multiple coats of finish, providing adhesion for the next coat. It is sold at paint and hardware stores. (As with all products, read the label carefully before using, and make sure that there is plenty of ventilation.)

Always sand with the grain. Where pieces meet at a right angle, sand the pieces with exposed end grain last.

Sanding Frame Joints

Q. *How can I sand a frame joint without leaving cross-grain scratches?*

First, make sure that the joint is level. The best way to level a joint is with a block plane, but you can also sand the joint level by moving a sanding block in a circular motion to minimize cross-grain scratches.

To sand the frame, first sand the pieces whose ends butt into adjoining pieces. In the case of cabinet doors, these are usually the horizontal rails. Sand over the joint line—don't worry about cross-grain scratches at this point. Next sand the other pieces (stiles), taking care to remove the cross-grain scratches without adding new scratches to the first pieces.

To sand a mitered frame, hold the edge of the sanding block parallel with the joint line and sand up to the line. You might also try masking off one side of the joint while sanding the other.

Form-Fitting Sanding Block

Q. *I have a room's worth of custom-made base and crown molding to sand. What's the fastest way to finish this sanding job?*

Your choice of sanding blocks depends on what types of molding profiles you're sanding. Sanding sponges (available at hardware stores) are great for sanding gently curved pieces because they can conform to the molding. The downside to using a sponge is that it tends to round over sharp profiles.

Consider making a custom block. Glue a piece of 80-grit sandpaper to a scrap piece of the molding; then sand down a block of foam until it conforms to the profile. Stick sandpaper to the foam and you're ready to go.

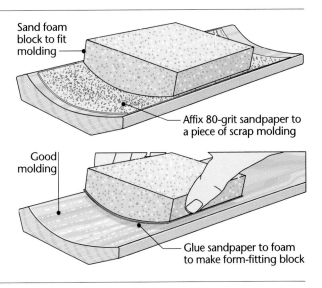

Sand foam block to fit molding

Affix 80-grit sandpaper to a piece of scrap molding

Good molding

Glue sandpaper to foam to make form-fitting block

Smoother-Running Belt Sander

Q. *My new belt sander makes a thumping noise whenever I use it. What's the problem?*

Sounds as though the problem may be your sanding belt. The drive roller on a sander is slightly convex, to keep the belt centered on the roller when it's running. The hump can deform the belt if the machine is left idle for too long, resulting in a bulge that will make a thumping noise each time it passes over the workpiece.

To avoid this problem, rotate the belt each time you use your sander so that the roller contacts different spots on the belt. If you won't be using your sander for a couple of weeks, remove the belt from the machine.

When to Stop Sanding

Q. *How do I know which sanding grits to use?*

What grit you start with depends on the condition of your surface. For example, 60- or 80-grit paper is fine for removing flaking paint or for shaping an edge, but not for general smoothing. Most lumberyard pine and plywood is smooth enough to start at 120 grit. Progress up to the finer grits, without skipping any grit steps. Each step replaces the last grit's scratches with progressively smaller ones, until they're too small to notice.

When to stop depends on your choice of finish and on the type of wood you're finishing. In general, painted surfaces need only be sanded to 100 grit; varnished surfaces should be sanded to 220 grit. If you're sanding a hardwood, like cherry or maple, and are planning to use an oil finish, you may want to sand up to 400 grit.

Tools and Materials

Bad Drill Switch

Q. *My electric drill runs fine, but I can't get it to turn off. What is wrong with it?*

Sounds as if you need to replace the drill switch, which is an easy job. Begin by unplugging the tool and brushing off any sawdust. Remove the screws that hold the drill together, and lift off the top portion of the plastic housing.

Cleaning out sawdust that is packed around the trigger might restore the switch's ability to work properly.

If sawdust isn't the problem, record the model number of the switch and order a replacement. If the new switch looks different from the one you're replacing, ask the supplier how to reconnect the wires correctly.

The trick to a switch replacement is to remove one wire at a time, attaching them to the new switch as you go. Once all the wires are reconnected, screw the drill halves back together and try it out.

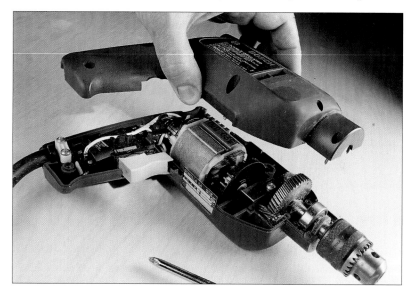

Remove the screws holding the housing together to open the drill (left). Disconnect the old switch and attach the new switch, one wire at a time.

Mark your shelf support drilling template with an up arrow to ensure that it's correctly placed on your work.

Drilling Shelf Supports

Q. *What's the best way to drill shelf support holes that line up?*

To guarantee the accurate placement and depth of shelf holes, use a ¼-inch perfboard template and a wooden stop block on your drill. To make the stop block, tighten a ¼-inch-diameter drill bit (most shelf support pegs are ¼ inch in diameter) in your drill and measure the length of the exposed bit. Subtract from this length the depth of the peg hole plus the ¼-inch thickness of the template. Cut a piece of scrap wood to this length and drill a hole through it.

Disposing of Worn-Out Batteries

Q. *My cordless drill's battery has given up the ghost. I know you're not supposed to throw the battery out with the regular trash, but how am I supposed to get rid of it?*

Nickel-cadmium batteries shouldn't be thrown out with the trash. If incinerated or dumped in a landfill, the toxic cadmium they contain can be released into the air or can leech into the soil. Nicads may also explode if they contact water or fire.

Some stores accept nicads for recycling. You can also call your sanitation department. Many towns have drop-off sites or schedule special days for dealing with problem trash.

Replace a Drill Chuck

Q. *How can I replace my old keyed chuck with a new keyless chuck?*

First open the jaws of the old chuck and look inside. Some drills have a reverse-threaded screw that secures the chuck to the drill. To remove the screw, insert a hex wrench and turn it clockwise. Once any screw is removed, place the key in the chuck and rap the key with a rubber mallet to spin the chuck counterclockwise, off the threaded shaft.

Screw the new chuck onto the shaft; then replace the screw.

Check to see if the drill has a chuck screw before you try to tap off the old chuck.

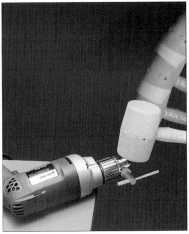

Strike the chuck key with a mallet to unscrew the old-style chuck.

Cordless Drill Battery Memory

Q. *I've heard that the rechargeable batteries in my cordless drill have memory and that I should run them down completely before recharging. Is this true?*

Contrary to what many people believe, nicad batteries don't "remember" a low charge if they're not completely drained before recharging. Manufacturers eliminated this memory effect years ago. In fact, draining a battery may shorten its life. Ideally, you should switch batteries as soon as you detect that the drill is slowing down.

You can extend a battery pack's life by following these simple steps:

■ Keep your batteries fully charged. Charged cells resist shorts better than partially discharged cells. Allow a hot battery a few minutes to cool down before charging.

■ Don't force the tool—this can cause the battery to overheat. Keep bits and cutters sharp to avoid overstressing the tool.

■ Don't expose the tool to extremely cold or hot environments (below 20° or above 110° F). Nicads perform best between 50° and 80° F.

Straight-Shooting Drill

Q. *I don't own a drill press. Do you have any tips for making perfectly vertical holes? How about horizontal ones, too?*

You don't need a drill press to drill a perfectly vertical hole. You can make this drilling guide from two pieces of ¾-inch plywood, 1½ inches high and 2 inches wide. Glue and nail the pieces together with finish nails to form a corner. To use this guide, simply run your drill bit along the inside corner.

When drilling a horizontal hole, it's tough to keep the bit aligned from side to side and perfectly horizontal at the same time. You could use the guide block, but if you're using a spade bit, you'll need a different approach. Slip a washer over the shank of the bit. If the washer slides forward or backward as you drill, you're off horizontal.

A simple guide block ensures a perfectly perpendicular hole.

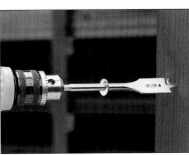

Keep the drill aligned from side to side by eye, and use the washer to indicate if you're tipping the drill up or down.

Tools and Materials

Dressing a Grinder

Q. *My bench grinder doesn't cut as quickly as it used to, and lately it's started to vibrate. How can I fix it?*

Grinding wheels are made up of hard grains held together by a bonding agent. As a wheel is used, the grains dull and fall off, exposing new sharp ones. If the dull grains don't fall off, or if metal particles stick to the wheel, the surface may become glazed. A glazed wheel will work poorly and will overheat the tools you're trying to grind. A worn wheel can also become lopsided.

A wheel dresser can clean a glazed wheel and true up a lopsided wheel. Star-wheel dressers (see photo, right) are the least expensive. Diamond-point dressers cost more but are easier to use and will last a lifetime.

To true the wheel of a grindstone, hold the dresser on the tool rest and pass it across the face of the stone.

Motors
That Run
Our Tools

THE MOTORS THAT RUN our power tools can be divided into two main categories: universal motors and induction motors. Understanding how each type works will help you take better care of the tools you already own, and help you choose the right tools for your shop in the future.

How They Work

Universal motors consist of two sets of windings that, when energized, create opposing magnetic fields. The shaft windings are connected to the contacts of the commutator in such a way that as the inner magnetic field starts to get lined up, the current is switched back to a set of windings farther back in the direction of the rotation. The alignment process repeats itself, producing continuous rotation.

Induction motors rely on a different principle of magnetic fields, namely, that when you move a wire through a field, a current will be generated. Thick conductors surround the shaft of the induction motor. A current is set up, or induced, in those conductors. That current also produces its own magnetic field,

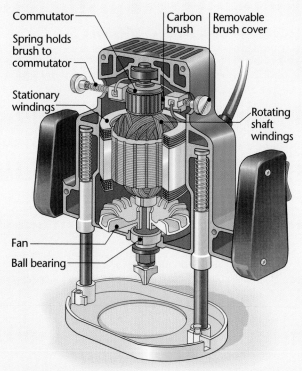

Universal Motor

Commutator — Carbon brush | Removable brush cover
Spring holds brush to commutator —
Stationary windings —
Fan —
Ball bearing —
Rotating shaft windings

which forces the shaft to turn so the field is aligned with the outer stationary field. Your house's alternating current (AC) changes back and forth from positive to negative, which keeps it constantly spinning.

Differences Between the Two Types

Universal motors behave very differently than induction motors. Each has its own place in your shop.

Keeping Your Cool

Q. *How can I prevent burning the edges when sharpening tools on a bench grinder?*

Because bench grinders are so aggressive they can easily overheat a thin cutting edge. Burning an edge destroys it's ability to stay sharp.

To prevent this from happening, first make sure that your grinder's wheels are freshly dressed—glazed wheels don't sharpen, they burn.

One way to keep a blade cool is to keep it damp. To do this, place a piece of wet sponge on the blade. As long as the sponge stays wet, the steel can't overheat.

You may want to adjust your grinding technique. Thin edges tend to build up heat quickly. If you have a lot of grinding to do, flatten the edge first, before working on the cutting angle. You might also want to stop grinding earlier and finish the edge at the whetstone.

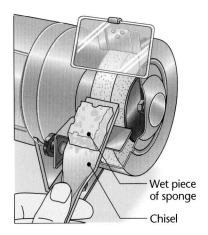

Wet piece of sponge

Chisel

Universal motors are designed to run very fast (20,000 rpm or more). This is perfect for high-speed tools like routers and circular saws. The speed of a universal motor can be varied by decreasing the voltage, which decreases the strength of the magnetic fields. The high speeds of a universal motor, coupled with the whir of the cooling fan and the rubbing of the brushes combine to produce a characteristic whining roar, which can be dangerously loud. As the carbon brushes of a universal motor wear out, the commutator can become pitted and worn from the constant sparking as the brushes break contact.

In contrast, induction motors depend on the 60-cycle-per-second frequency of household current, which means that their speed is fixed. With the standard two sets of windings, these motors run at either 3,450 or 1,725 rpm. To get other speeds, you usually have to use belts and pulleys, as on a drill press. Compared to universal motors, induction motors are almost silent. Induction motors last until the bearings wear out, making them the first choice for long-running tools, such as band saws and lathes.

Measuring Power

It seems that manufacturers try to make it difficult to compare power tools.

The power of an induction motor is measured by the horsepower it can deliver continuously, under load, without overheating. By contrast, the power of a universal motor is measured by its peak horsepower, the maximum power it delivers before it stalls out. If the motor were to deliver this power for more than an instant, it would quickly fry the motor.

Although peak horsepower can be useful for comparing motors within a category of tools, a table saw with a 1-hp induction motor will give you more power than an universal motor of the same horsepower. Some types of tools, such as table saws, jointers, and planers, are available with either universal or induction motors. Stick with induction motors; they'll give you more power, longer life, and less noise.

For tools that are not rated in horsepower, the most useful way to compare power is in amps: More amps equals more power.

Induction Motor

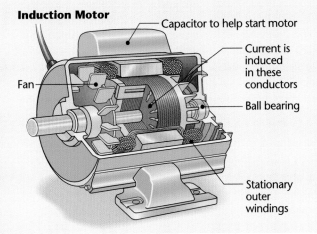

Capacitor to help start motor

Current is induced in these conductors

Fan

Ball bearing

Stationary outer windings

Tools and Materials

GLUES

Glue Stopper

Q. *I'm frustrated with the glue I use in my woodworking projects. It's hard to scrape the dried glue out of the corners, and it ruins the finish. How do I clean up excess glue?*

The best way to avoid the hassle of cleaning and scraping dried glue is to keep your finish surfaces glue-free. Here are two easy ways to do this:

■ When assembling mortise-and-tenon joints, cut a small chamfer along the edge of the mortise. The chamfer will give any excess glue a place to go and will be hidden under the shoulder of the tenon.

■ When gluing moldings or other types of surface-applied pieces of wood, use a table saw to cut a shallow kerf near the edge of the piece you're gluing down. The excess glue will get trapped in the groove instead of oozing out onto the other piece, where it can be hard to remove and can ruin your staining job.

Chamfering the edge of a mortise creates a groove to catch any glue. The tenoned piece covers the chamfered edge.

The shallow saw cut on the back of the molding (bottom corner) keeps glue from oozing out and ruining your staining job.

Clamping Glue Joints

Q. *What's the best way to use glue and clamps to get a good joint?*

Before applying glue, dry-assemble the parts. Clamping the parts together without glue tests the fit of the joints and allows you to rehearse the clamping procedure.

Once you have applied the glue according to the manufacturer's directions, reassemble the parts and apply pressure to the joints with clamps. With the exception of epoxy, contact cement, and cyanoacrylate (instant) glues, wood glues cure best under pressure. The clamping pressure forces the surfaces together,

squeezes air out of the joint, and helps the glue penetrate the wood.

When gluing up long surfaces, use several clamps to provide even clamping pressure across the entire joint. Contrary to myth, excessive pressure will not force out the glue and "starve" the joint, but it can crush the wood fibers around the joint, which will make the wood more likely to break or split.

Once the clamps are in place, clean up the squeezed-out glue. Water-base glues can be washed off the wood with a sopping-wet rag or scraped off once the glue starts to turn rubbery. Other types of glue are best sanded or scraped off when dry.

Edge-Gluing Wood

Q. *Should the edges of wood boards be rough or smooth when they are glued together?*

For the strongest possible joint, both edges should be as smooth as possible, with no perceptible gaps or voids. Additionally, the surface must be clean of any chemical contaminants (paint or other finish) that might prevent the glue from spreading and penetrating the wood.

Smooth knife-cut surfaces, such as those cut with a hand plane or on a jointer, make the best glue joints. Routed or well-sanded surfaces also glue well. Surfaces cut with an ordinary saw blade or a band saw are usually too rough to bond well.

Filling Gaps

Q. *What's the best way to conceal woodworking joints that are less than perfect?*

At one time or another, we have all tried to fill gaps with a little extra glue. Unfortunately, most glues shrink as they dry, so the gap usually reappears. In addition, most glues do not have enough strength to bridge gaps on their own.

When you need to fill a gap, use epoxy. Epoxy shrinks less than other glues, and a thick epoxy joint is as strong as, or even stronger than, the surrounding wood.

To hide an ill-fitting joint, you might also try filling the gap with small wedges or slivers of a matching wood. Choose the wedge so that its grain direction blends in with the joint. When the glue is dry, cut and sand the wedge flush.

Yellow or White Glue?

Q. *What's the difference between white and yellow wood glue?*

You can use either white or yellow glue to bond almost any porous material. The basic difference is that yellow glue is specifically formulated as a wood glue and white glue is for general purposes.

Polyvinyl resin glue (white glue) is a general-purpose adhesive made from polyvinyl acetate (PVA) resin. Aliphatic resin (yellow glue) is also made from PVA resin, but it's modified to be less runny, quicker-setting, and easier to sand than white glue.

Yellow glue is the adhesive of choice for most woodworkers, but white glue is a good choice when you need its slower set-up time—for example, when assembling a particularly complex joint.

Frozen Glue

Q. *Which glues can I keep in my unheated shop during the winter?*

The only glues that are freezeproof are polyurethane adhesives; in fact, some manufacturers suggest storing the polyurethane glues in the freezer to prevent them from absorbing moisture and curing in the bottle.

Water-base products, such as yellow and white glues, can be ruined by repeated freeze-thaw cycles. You'll know something is wrong if the glue has the consistency of cottage cheese, with the water separated and floating on top. Most yellow glues can freeze once or twice and still be usable; if you can remix the product and make it smooth again, it's usable.

Your best bet is to protect your glues from freezing in the first place.

The simplest way to do this is to store the glues indoors and take them out with you to the shop when you're ready to work.

Note that cold weather can also affect a glue's ability to cure. When any white or yellow glue dries chalky, it's an indication that the glue hasn't cured properly and the glue bond will be weak. Chalking can occur if the temperature of your shop drops below 40° F. It can also occur with wood that has been brought indoors from a cold storage room.

Cold temperatures also affect other glues. Epoxies tend to cure more slowly when it's cold. Resorcinol, a waterproof glue used for outdoor applications, won't cure in temperatures colder than 60° F.

FIVE COMMON WOOD GLUES

	YELLOW	WATER-RESISTANT YELLOW	LIQUID HIDE	POLYURETHANE	EPOXY
Assembly/ Drying time	5 min./1 hr.	5 min./1 hr.	20 min./2 hr.	20 min./2 hr. (varies widely)	5 min./1 hr.
Convenience	Widely available, easy to use, water cleanup. Nontoxic.	Widely available, easy to use, water cleanup. Nontoxic.	Found at specialty stores and in catalogs. Easy to use, water cleanup. Reversible.	Found at specialty stores and in catalogs. Easy to use, but once dry won't wash off skin.	Available at some hardware stores. Two parts must be mixed. Won't wash off skin. No clamping pressure required.
Application	Interior wood only.	Interior and exterior wood.	Interior woodwork only.	Interior and exterior wood. Bonds to most other materials.	Interior and exterior wood (and just about anything else).
Best uses	Most interior repair and woodworking projects.	Most interior woodworking and repair jobs. Also for kitchens, baths, and other damp locations.	Antique restoration projects that take a long time to assemble; for example, gluing an old chair.	Slow-assembly jobs; nonwood repairs; cosmetic gap filling (possible because polyurethane takes stain).	Structural gap filling; nonwood repairs; projects that must withstand constant moisture contact—for example, window boxes.

FINISHING WOOD

Faster Furniture Finish

Q. *Is there a way to finish furniture without having to sand and varnish over and over again?*

There is no way to completely eliminate sanding when finishing furniture. Sanding before applying a finish smooths the wood and erases tool marks and scratches. Sanding between coats of varnish knocks off any dust nibs and hardened drips of varnish, and gives each coat the necessary tooth for the subsequent one to adhere to.

If you want to make the finishing job easier, try a wiping varnish or an oil-varnish blend. Both finishes are easy to wipe on. The downside is that they are much thinner than their brush-on competition and do not provide as much protection against water and wear.

To use a wipe-on finish, sand the wood with progressively finer sandpaper, working up to 400-grit; then remove all dust with a tack cloth. Apply the finish and give it time to soak in, according to the manufacturer's instructions. Wipe off any finish that remains on the surface, and allow it to dry overnight. The following day you can scuff the piece with superfine steel wool and apply another coat. Wiping varnishes can be built up to create a higher gloss, but most oil-varnish finishes reach their maximum sheen in two or three coats. To add more shine and a little extra protection, apply a coat of wax.

Smooth Particleboard

Q. *How should I finish my new particleboard shelves so the surface will be smooth?*

Start by sanding the surface of the particleboard with 80- to 100-grit sandpaper, rounding the edges slightly. If you plan to paint the shelves, fill in rough areas of the particleboard with spackling compound or wood putty (the ends and edges tend to be the roughest and most porous parts). Sand any areas that you have filled, and remove all dust with a tack cloth.

If you are using an oil-base paint, you can get a super-smooth finish by using spray paint or a brush and wet-sanding between coats.

Refinishing an Old Table

Q. *I recently acquired an old Stickley Brothers table and would like to refinish it. Is it the stain that gives the tiger-stripe look to the wood?*

You may have a valuable antique on your hands. Check with a reputable antiques dealer to find out if its value will be reduced by altering the original finish.

The original color of your table was probably achieved by a combination of fuming, colored shellac, and possibly a varnish top coat. Fuming is a process not recommended for most do-it-yourselfers because it involves exposing the raw wood to ammonia fumes, which are extremely toxic. The tannic acid in the wood reacts with the ammonia to give the wood a rich red-brown color. The tiger-stripe effect exists because the wood was quarter-sawn rather than plain-sawn. The stain has nothing to do with it.

An easier way to get a similar-looking effect is to use an oil-base stain followed by an oil-varnish top coat. (Be sure to test the stain and finish combination before starting your piece.) Apply the top coat with a brush or cotton cloth, let it stand for 15 minutes, then wipe it dry with a clean cloth. Wait 24 hours before applying another coat for a deeper tone.

Water-Base Strippers

Q. *Do the paint strippers labeled safe that I see in home centers really work as well as the old-fashioned strippers? Are there any tricks to using them?*

Diabasic esters (DBE), commonly called safe strippers, are indeed a lot less toxic than other strippers, such as methylene chloride, and other solvents like methanol, acetone, and toluene. Compared to their competition, DBE strippers work relatively slowly. Another big difference with DBE strippers is that they contain water and must be rinsed clean with water. The water in the stripper and the rinse tends to raise the grain of the wood, which can loosen joints and lift veneer. For this reason, DBE strippers are fine for interior trim and most furniture, but aren't recommended for delicate pieces of furniture.

To use DBE strippers, follow the directions on the package and avoid using metal tools or steel wool. Use plastic scrub pads and disposable plastic tools instead. Scrape the stripper-paint sludge into a cardboard box. Once the sludge has dried out, you can throw it out with the trash.

Realize that regardless of type, all solvents are potentially dangerous. Make sure your work area is well ventilated, and wear gloves when working with the stripper.

STAINING PINE

Pine is not easy to finish; it needs to be carefully prepared even before you begin brushing on the sealers, stains, and varnishes. Following the advice here should make the job a successful one.

SANDING TIPS

Pine is a soft wood that dents and scratches easily, so begin by sanding all surfaces with 80-, 120-, then 180-grit sandpaper (in that order). You can use a finishing sander or a belt sander, but be careful not to oversand or gouge the surface, and always do your last sanding by hand, with the grain, with a sanding block.

If there's a dent that's too deep to sand out, wet the dent and cover it with a few layers of wet paper towel. After 5 minutes, press a hot iron over the towels. The iron will force steam into the wood, swelling the crushed fibers. Repeat as necessary. Before staining, wet the wood with mineral spirits or paint thinner, which will emphasize any dents or scratches you missed earlier.

STAINING OPTIONS

Pine often takes stain unevenly. One way to eliminate stain problems is not to stain at all. A clear finish, like an oil-base polyurethane, will slightly darken the wood and lightly accentuate the grain.

Using a sealer, also called conditioner or prestain, is a another good way to help avoid a blotchy stain job or grain reversal (see right). These brush-on liquids limit the absorption of stain, so you may need to buy a darker stain to get the shade you're after.

Gel stains give wood a more even, less blotchy color than many liquid stains. They are easy to apply to vertical surfaces because of their consistency, but wiping excess stain out of cracks and corners is more difficult. Gels work slightly better after a sealer has been applied.

THE CLEAR COAT

Pine takes thick brush-on polyurethane or varnish as well as any other wood. Let oil-base sealers or stains dry for at least 24 hours before you apply a water-base clear finish. If you opt for a thin finish, like a penetrating oil or wipe-on polyurethane, you may need to apply six or more coats to build up an even sheen because pine is so porous. If you use a finish other than polyurethane, seal any knots with shellac to keep them from bleeding through the finish.

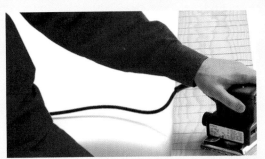

To avoid oversanding, draw pencil lines across the grain and sand just enough to remove them.

Sealers even out a finish. Use a double dose of sealer on end grain to prevent it from absorbing too much stain.

Without sealer, the lighter grain absorbs more stain than the darker grain, producing a severe grain reversal.

Gel stains are available in traditional tones and in bright primary colors like these.

Repair and Finishing

CLEAR FINISHES

Polyurethane over Oil?

Q. *I used an oil finish on some furniture and now I want to apply polyurethane. Do I need to remove the oil finish first, or can I apply polyurethane right over it?*

Assuming the oil finish has completely cured, you should be able to apply a polyurethane top coat without any problems. When working with a new oil finish, allow at least a month to be sure the finish has cured completely.

Polyurethanes have a reputation for having adhesion problems. The best way to ensure a first-rate finish is by making sure that the surface is clean, dull, and dry. To prepare the piece for finishing, first sand it lightly with 220-grit sandpaper. This scuff-sanding helps create a better mechanical bond. Next, use a tack cloth to remove any sanding dust.

You can apply the polyurethane straight from the can with a brush. For a more natural-looking protective finish, you can also cut the polyurethane 50:50 with mineral spirits and apply the mixture with a rag.

APPLYING A SMOOTH POLYURETHANE FINISH

Applying polyurethane finish is not a brush-slapping, one-afternoon job. Getting a great-looking finish isn't hard, but it involves several steps. Considering that you will be looking at the finished product for many years, it's worth taking the time to finish it right. The following steps work for both oil-base and water-base polyurethanes. However, don't thin a water-base varnish to make a sealer; use a clear sealer instead. Most people prefer the way the amber hue of oil-base polyurethanes bring out the wood color.

PREPARING THE SURFACE

To begin, sand the surface of the wood with progressively finer paper, up to 220-grit. On a newly built table, you would start with a medium (100-grit) sandpaper, then fine (150-grit), then finish with extra-fine (220-grit). Dust the surface before stepping up to the next finer grit.

When you have finished sanding, wipe the surface with a clean cloth dampened with denatured alcohol.

If you use stain, let it dry before applying any sealer or finish. (You can use any type of stain before using any type of polyurethane as a top coat.)

THE FIRST COAT

A sealer is like a clear primer. It soaks into the wood and enables later coats of finish to flow more evenly onto the surface. Some stains are self-sealing, meaning that they have a sealer built right into them. If you're using this type of stain, proceed to the next step. If you're using a stain without a built-in sealer, or just leaving your wood natural, you can use a commercial sealer or make a thinned mixture of 3 parts oil-base polyurethane and 2 parts mineral spirits.

Buy a good brush (synthetic-bristle brush for water-base products, natural-bristle for oil-base) for applying the sealer. Brush on the sealer with long strokes, and apply only enough to cover the entire surface. Catch any drips along the edges before the sealer dries. The end

1 *Use a natural-bristle brush to apply oil-base sealer. Smooth the coat with the tip of the brush to reduce brush strokes.*

2 *Cut away any drips with a razor blade after each coat has dried. Be sure not to cut too deeply into the finish.*

3 *Wet-sand the varnish with 400-grit paper after the second and third coats to remove any blemishes or dust particles.*

Toy Finish Safety

Q. *Is polyurethane a safe toy finish?*

The Food and Drug Administration (FDA) lists all the ingredients commonly used in finishes (except solvents) as safe for food contact. As long as it has cured completely, polyurethane can be used safely.

For projects that come in constant contact with food or children, consider using walnut oil or salad bowl finish. Technically, shellac is the only FDA-approved finish (it's used on candy and pills); however, it's not water-resistant.

Durable Furniture Finish

Q. *I'd like to apply a harder finish than my usual mixture of boiled linseed oil and turpentine to my furniture. Is it possible to add varnish to this mixture?*

You can make your own oil-varnish finish by adding polyurethane varnish to a turpentine-oil mixture. Adding polyurethane will improve the finish's resistance to scratches, water, and stains. If you add too much, however, you'll lose the ease of application. Start with equal portions of each; then experiment to get the best results.

grain of some types of wood can be particularly thirsty; apply several coats to the end, until the wood stops absorbing any additional finish.

THE SECOND COAT

Using polyurethane right out of the can, load the brush without wiping it along the rim of the can. This will prevent air bubbles in the brushed finish. Spread it evenly, and don't use too much at once. Overlap your strokes to get the varnish uniform. As soon as the surface is coated, lightly run the tip of the brush over it in the direction of the grain (Photo 1). Let this coat dry for about 24 hours.

FIXING UP

Once the finish is dry, you can correct any minor mistakes. Cut away any dried drips with a sharp razor blade (Photo 2), being careful not to cut through the finish and into the wood. Use 400-grit wet/dry sand-

paper mounted on a sanding block to rub out any bumps or dust specks (Photo 3). Use a little water to lubricate the paper as you sand. Be careful near the edges, where the finish will be thinnest. When the surface feels smooth, wipe it with a damp cloth to remove the sanding residue, then follow up with a dry cloth.

THE THIRD COAT AND FINAL FINISH

Brush on a third coat, sand out any imperfections, and then wait a few days to let the finish dry completely.

To remove sandpaper scratches, you'll need to rub out the finish (Photo 4). You can do this with automotive rubbing compound. Follow up with polishing compound. If the surface isn't shiny enough, wait a few days, then apply paste wax and hand-buff the surface to achieve a fine luster.

4 Rub out the finish with a damp cloth and automotive rubbing compound. For a higher gloss, use polishing compound.

5 For an even higher shine, you can apply a light coat of paste wax. Wait for the wax to haze over, then buff the surface with a clean cloth.

Repair and Finishing

FINISHING PROBLEMS

Oil-soaked rags heat up as they dry and can burst into flame. Dispose of used rags in an approved fireproof can, or hang them outside to dry before throwing out with the trash.

Spontaneous Combustion

Q. *If I leave oily rags in my shop, can they really burst into flames?*

Yes, they can. Linseed oil, a common ingredient in oil varnishes, is particularly dangerous when left to dry. This oil has a low ignition temperature and is exothermic (generates heat) as it dries. This heat ordinarily dissipates harmlessly; however, when trapped within a pile of oil-soaked rags, the heat can build up until the rags ignite.

Handle all solvent- or finish-soaked rags with caution, and never bunch them into a pile. Once you have finished using a rag, spread it out outside. When it is dry, you can safely throw it in the trash.

Milky Varnish

Q. *Why do water-base varnishes look milky when they're applied?*

The reason for the cloudy look is that light travels through the clear resin and the water on different paths. When these two solutions are mixed, the light changes direction as it passes through each particle of resin and water, causing the solution to look milky and opaque. As the water evaporates from the solution, the light waves can again travel in a straight line, so the varnish appears to turn clear as it dries.

You can observe this same effect by putting a pencil in a glass of water: The pencil appears to have a break as a result of the light changing direction as it passes from the air outside the glass to the water inside.

Shellac Won't Dry

Q. *Why won't the shellac I applied 4 months ago dry?*

Unfortunately, if it hasn't dried by now, that shellac will never dry and should be removed. Alcohol is the correct solvent to use for this job.

The shellac may have been old when you applied it. Old shellac takes longer to harden, and never gets as hard as it does when it is new. As soon as shellac is dissolved in alcohol, it begins to deteriorate. Although this process occurs slowly, you should always check the date on the can. Most canned shellac has a shelf life of 18 months to 2 years from the date stamped on the can.

To check for freshness, put a drop of shellac on a piece of glass and allow it to dry overnight. If you can push your fingernail into any part of the drop the next day, it's probably time to buy a fresh can.

Bleaching Wood

Q. *When I used water to neutralize the stripper on an oak door, the grain turned black. How can I restore the natural wood color?*

The stains you describe are formed when iron comes in contact with wood that has a a high tannin content. Oxalic acid (available at paint stores) can bleach out the stains.

Wearing goggles and gloves, mix a small quantity of the acid into 2 cups of warm water. Continue adding crystals until they no longer dissolve. Brush the solution over the entire surface, not just the stain, to avoid creating lighter spots. Repeat this process until the stains disappear.

Once the stains are gone, let the wood dry; then wash off the crystals with a well-soaked rag. To neutralize any remaining acid, wipe on a mixture consisting of 1 tablespoon baking soda and 1 cup water. Follow up with one more water rinse.

A Polyurethane Finish without Bubbles

Q. *Water-base polyurethanes seem to bubble more than oil-base polyurethanes. How can I avoid the bubbles and get the smoothest possible finish?*

Most water-base polyurethane finishes can level themselves out; simply apply the finish, then leave it alone. Try to lay on as thin a coat as possible so that the bubbles can work their way out of the finish before the surface of the finish begins to form a skin.

Make sure you use the right brush. Avoid exploded-tip or flagged brushes. The ends of these bristles are split, providing many more places where bubbles can form. Use a tapered-tip brush instead. Foam brushes are also a good choice; they tend not to make bubbles, but they don't hold that much finish. Paint pads work especially well on flat surfaces.

Avoid brushes with so-called exploded or flagged tips (top). Get a brush with tapered bristle tips (bottom) instead.

Flow on the polyurethane with a few strokes and let the finish level itself out.

Working with Water-Base Finishes

Q. *I'm interested in trying water-base polyurethanes. Are there any major differences between water- and oil-base polyurethanes that I should know about?*

Clear water-base polyurethane finishes are an excellent alternative to oil-base polyurethane finishes. They have little odor, and you can clean brushes with soap and water. Water-base finishes are quick-drying and are not flammable. These finishes are easy to use, but the techniques are different from what you may be used to. The biggest differences involve surface preparation and application.

To prepare a piece for finishing, you'll need to sand the piece and then raise the grain by dampening the surface. If you skip this step, the finish will raise the grain and it will dry very rough. When you've finished sanding, dampen the surface with a damp cloth. Let it dry; then lightly knock off any whiskers with a piece of worn 220-grit sandpaper. Never use a tack cloth or steel wool with a water-base polyurethane finish. Tack cloths leave an oily residue and steel wool leaves iron filings that can rust; both can ruin your finish. To remove any sanding dust, use a clean damp cloth.

Water-base polyurethane finishes are more sensitive to weather conditions than oil-base finishes. In general, avoid applying the finish when the humidity is high (80 percent or more), because it can prevent the water from evaporating and thus affect the curing process. You may also run into curing problems if the shop or the wood itself is too cold (less than 50° F).

Raise the grain with a damp cloth, then sand off the whiskers with 220-grit sandpaper. Avoid tack cloths and steel wool.

Paint pads are a popular tool for covering flat surfaces with water-base polyurethane. Be careful not to overwork the surface.

FURNITURE FINISH REPAIRS

Mineral spirits on a clean rag can do wonders for dirty furniture.

Dirty, Greasy Surfaces

Q. *I own an old table that I would like to refinish, but it's covered with greasy dirt and grime. What should I use to clean it?*

The easiest—and safest—way to clean greasy, gummy furniture is with mineral spirits and a clean rag. Continue rubbing the finish until the rag no longer picks up dirt; then do a final rubdown with a fresh rag. When you're done, you may discover that your piece doesn't need refinishing at all.

Wipe Away Scratches

Q. *The wood on my table appears undamaged, but the finish has a few small scratches. Is it possible to fix the scratches without refinishing?*

If there are just fine scratches in the finish, you might be able to wipe them away. Using very fine steel wool saturated with clear Danish oil, rub the area around the scratches, following the grain of the wood, until they disappear. Remember, you are trying to rub away only enough finish to eliminate the scratches, not any of the stain below the finish.

Once the scratches are rubbed out, wipe away all the Danish oil with a clean rag; then clean the entire surface with mineral spirits several times to make sure no oil is left on the furniture. Allow the surface to dry overnight; then apply a light coat of spray lacquer.

Patching Gouges

Q. *I own an antique desk that is marred by a few ugly gouges. Is there a way to repair it?*

To fill in small gouges, try colored putty. These waxy sticks are available at hardware stores. To get a good color match, buy several sticks and mix the flakes with your fingertips. Press the putty into the gouge, then scrape away any excess. Seal the patch with spray shellac; then spray on a lacquer top coat.

Touch Up Scratches

Q. *What is the best way to hide scratches in wood furniture?*

Art supply stores sell permanent-ink felt-tip and fine-tip markers in dozens of colors. When in doubt, use a color that is slightly darker than the wood.

To hide a scratch, dot the ink onto the bare wood and let it dry. To even out the color, try stroking across the scratch with the tip of the marker. Try to keep the ink off the finish.

Use very fine steel wool to rub out light scratches. Be careful not to rub through the finish.

Press the colored putty into the gouge with a small flat stick.

Use a dotting motion to fill scratches. Keep the ink off the finished wood.

PAINTING FURNITURE

Furniture that is solidly constructed and not in need of a lot of repairs can be brought to life with paint. All you need is time and patience—this is one job you don't want to rush. Plan to set aside an hour or two a day for 3 to 4 days, depending on the size of the piece of furniture you want to paint. Note that paint may not adhere well to furniture that has a plastic laminate surface.

GETTING STARTED

First clean the surface with mineral spirits. Then remove the hardware and lightly sand all the areas you intend to paint to provide a good surface for the paint to adhere to (there's no need to remove all the old paint completely). If the paint is more than 15 years old, it may contain lead; instead of sanding, use a liquid deglosser. If the old surface is stained and varnished, go ahead and sand it, but only enough to dull the surface.

FIXING AND PRIMING

If the furniture has any nicks or gouges, fill them with a wood filler. Apply the filler with a putty knife and let it dry. Use fine sandpaper to smooth any filled areas, making sure the patch feathers out with the surrounding wood. Clean off all the sanding dust with a tack cloth before you apply primer.

Always prime unpainted wood before painting; an unprimed surface requires more coats of paint and the paint won't cover as evenly. Use an oil-base primer, which goes on easily and provides the best surface for the top coats, regardless of the type of paint (oil-base or latex) you will use.

CHOOSING PAINT

For a bright, wet look, use an oil-base enamel. For a softer look, choose a latex enamel. Use a paint brush designed for the type of paint you are using, and plan to apply at least two coats of paint. It is important that you wait until the previous coat is completely dry before recoating. Some paints require sanding between coats—follow the directions on the can. Whether you sand between coats or not, wipe the surface with tack cloth after each coat has dried, to remove any lingering dust before painting again.

TIPS FOR SUCCESS

■ When you prime and paint drawers, cover only the drawer fronts and their edges; paint on the sides of the drawers will make them stick.

■ Keep the room you're working in as free of dust as possible; any dust in the air will settle on the wet painted surfaces. Mop the room before painting.

■ Let rags with oily dirt residue or ones saturated with cleaning solvents (including mineral spirits) dry outside before you throw them in the trash.

■ Use a high-quality brush designed for the finish you're using. Good brushes leave a smoother finish.

1 Use a putty knife to fill any nicks and gouges with wood filler. Use a sanding block to feather out the patches.

2 Prime the surfaces to be painted with an oil-base primer.

3 Paint the primed surfaces with an oil or latex enamel. Multiple thin coats provide a tough finish.

Repair and Finishing

Fix an Old Rocker

Q. *The crosspieces on my rocking chair keep popping out of the legs, and I can't get them to stay in place with glue. What am I doing wrong?*

The problem may be the glue joint. All of the old glue must be removed so the new glue can create a strong bond. Thoroughly scrape and sand the tenon of each rung and its socket to remove the old glue. Next test-fit the rung and socket. If it's a snug fit, apply yellow glue to the rung and socket; then use clamps to hold the joint tightly together.

If a cleaned joint feels loose, glue a wood shaving around the tenon to better fill the socket. If the joint is very loose, saw a slit in the end of the tenon and tap a small wedge partway into the slit. Then apply glue to all the parts and tap the two pieces together (see photo, below). The wedge will expand the end of the tenon, locking it in place.

This wedge trick should be done only as a last resort because it's almost impossible to undo. The size of the wedge is critical. If it is too long, you'll split the rung; if it's too thick, you may not be able to fit the two pieces together.

Adding a wedge is a good way to lock a loose tenon in place, but the fit has to be perfect to work properly.

Wobbly Table

Q. *Our kitchen table has seen a lot of use—and abuse. Lately, it has developed an unhealthy wobble. Do you know a cure for this problem?*

Most table legs (as well as many chest legs) are attached to the apron by means of a bolt that extends through an angled support block. Nine out of ten wobbly tables can be cured simply by tightening the nuts on the leg-mount bolts.

Sometimes a loose leg can crack the leg support block. Fortunately it's easy to make a replacement block. If the ends of the leg support block are cut at an angle, cut the new block the same way, using a miter box. If the threads of the leg-mount bolt have stripped out of the leg, fill the stripped hole with glue and a few

Antique Mirror

Q. *How can I replace the reflective coating on my antique mirror?*

Check the Yellow Pages under "Mirrors." You should be able to find a number of companies that will replace the silver coating on a mirror. You also might consider having a new custom-made mirror installed in your antique frame. Replacing the glass is usually less expensive than trying to repair the old mirror. Local antique dealers can help you determine how the repair will affect the value of your antique.

If you decide to keep the original glass, another option is to remove the glass from the frame and scrape off the old reflective coating using a window scraper with a single-edge razor blade. This leaves you with a plain piece of glass under which you can put a new, thin mirror.

toothpicks. When the glue has dried, drill a new hole a little less than two-thirds the diameter of the bolt and reinstall the bolt in the leg.

Replace a cracked leg support block. Make the new block from hardwood, using the old block as a pattern.

Softening Old Glue

Q. *It seems that I'll need to disassemble most of a table in order to properly repair a few loose joints. What's the best way to disassemble a good glue joint?*

Reversing a glue joint depends on what type of glue was used in the first place. You'll find that most old furniture was assembled with hide glue. In this case, you should be able to dissolve the glue with steam or by squirting alcohol into the joint.

Most of the furniture made today is assembled with PVA (yellow) glue. If this is the case with your table, you might have luck with steam or by squirting a hot mixture of vinegar and water into the joint.

If the table was assembled, or later repaired, with epoxy, try to work around the joint. You'll destroy the table before you will break the joint.

FIXING A WOBBLY CHAIR

Wooden chairs come in two basic styles. Stick chairs are made of spindles with tapered ends, called tenons, that fit into the sockets. Frame chairs are made from squarish parts and are usually held together with square tenons or dowels. Tenons that break have to be rebuilt. Broken dowels can be removed and replaced.

To fix a stick chair, start the repair by dismantling the loose parts and removing all of the glue. Label each joint with masking tape as you disassemble the piece, to help you reassemble it later. Use a small chisel or a wire brush to clean the glue out of the sockets. Tenons can be scraped with a utility knife or—if they're about ½ or ¾ inch in diameter—cleaned with a plumber's tube cleaning brush, which you can find at home centers. If you remove some wood along with the glue, wrap the undersized tenon with strips of thin fabric or wood shavings to make it fit tightly in its socket. Apply glue to both the tenon and the socket.

To rebuild a broken tenon, cut away the splintered end of the spindle; then drill a hole into the cut end and insert a dowel in the hole. Next drill a hole for the dowel in small block of wood and glue the block to the protruding dowel. Use a chisel or a rasp to shape the block so that it fits tightly into its socket.

1 Knock loose joints apart with a soft rubber mallet.

When you reassemble the chair, use liquid hide glue. Standard wood glue begins to set in about 10 minutes, but hide glue gives you about 30 minutes to put all the pieces back together. Hide glue is also reversible—in case you need to make future repairs.

1 Use a tube cleaning brush to scrub off the old glue. Wrap loose-fitting tenons with strips of thin fabric or wood to make them fit tightly.

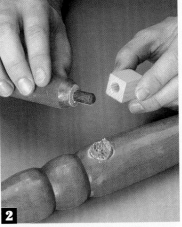

2 Rebuild a broken tenon by cutting away the splintered end, inserting a dowel, and attaching a block of wood. Shape the block to fit.

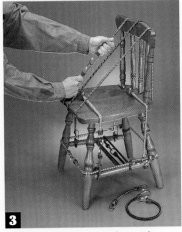

3 Hold the glue joints together under pressure until dry, using elastic tie-downs or bar clamps. Make sure all four legs touch the floor.

Paving

340 Sidewalks
342 Sidewalk and Patio Repairs
344 Driveway Repair

Decks

346 Care and Repair
350 Deck Finishes

Fences

352 Installation and Repair
355 Sheds and Outbuildings

Lawn and Garden

356 Lawns
358 Mulches
360 Planting and Pruning Trees
362 Pest Control

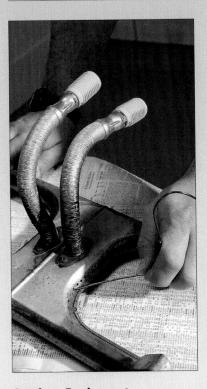

Outdoor
Do-It-Yourself

Outdoor Equipment

366 Lawn Mowers

368 Tool Repair

370 Grills

371 Snow Throwers

how is it done?

POURING A CONCRETE WALKWAY

Preparation is the key to success with concrete. Make certain all tools and materials are on site before you start. You'll need a wheelbarrow, a float, an edging tool, a grooving tool, a finish trowel, and a push broom. You can rent any tools you don't own. Also, concrete is very caustic, so be sure to wear appropriate protective gear to protect your skin and eyes. It's also nice to have a helper to mix concrete and clean up the tools while you work the concrete.

Concrete cures best at 50° to 70°F. From the time you start mixing until the concrete is ready to finish, you'll have about 3 to 5 hours. Temperature and humidity can significantly alter the working time. Hot, dry weather can cut your working time in half. Freezing conditions can ruin your project. Rain can spell real disaster—keep a roll of polyethylene plastic handy just in case.

The sidewalk shown here is built on tamped earth because it is in a warm climate not subject to frost heave. In a cold climate you may need a gravel base. You may also need to put wire mesh in the slab to control cracking. Check with your local building inspector.

Begin by installing the 2 x 4 forms. The tops of the forms should be at the height of your finished sidewalk. Secure the forms with 1-foot-long 1 x 3 stakes at the ends and every 2 feet in between. Attach the stakes to the forms with double-headed nails, making sure the tips don't extend inside the form. Don't let the stakes protrude above the form or they'll be in the way when you level the concrete. Brush used motor oil on the inside of the forms so they won't bond to the concrete.

One 60-pound bag of concrete mix will cover 1½ square feet of walkway, 4 inches thick.

Working on a sheet of plywood or in a wheelbarrow, add water to the dry concrete. To test the mix's consistency, jab the surface with your shovel; the ridges should remain clear-cut.

Starting at one end of the form, dump the concrete, then use a screed board (Photo 1) to level it off. Shuffle the screed board from side to side to level and compact the concrete. You may need to pack the corners and edges with a shovel. Fill any low spots and rescreed if necessary. When you're done, the surface should be flat and level with the top of the forms.

Immediately after screeding, smooth the surface with a float (Photo 2). The float pushes the gravel below the surface and levels small dips. Holding the float at a very slight angle so the leading edge doesn't dig in, make a series of large arcs. Don't overwork the concrete—just smooth out ripples and ridges.

While the concrete is still pliable (within the first hour after pouring), edge the slab and cut the control joints. Edging rounds and compacts the edges, making them less susceptible to chipping (and more friendly to bare feet). Before edging, cut the concrete away from the form, about 1 inch deep, with a trowel. Next push the edging tool along the form in a series of short seesaw strokes (Photo 3). Once you've completed an edge, go back and take a long, continuous swipe to smooth it out. To help the edger slide more easily, keep the blade wet.

Cut control joints every 3 feet or to match the rest of

1 Dump the concrete into the form starting at one end; then use a screed board to level the concrete, making it even with the tops of the forms.

2 Smooth the surface with a float. The float will also push the gravel below the surface and level any small dips.

the walkway. Use the screed board as a straightedge to guide the grooving tool (Photo 6). As you did with the edger, work the grooving tool in a series of short, jabbing strokes; the gravel below the surface will want to block and misdirect the grooving tool, so be firm. Smooth the cut with one final long swipe.

Use the float to remove any unwanted tool marks on the concrete. You may have to use the edging, grooving, and float tools a couple of times to get the surface flat and the edges just right.

When the surface water has disappeared and the concrete has cured hard enough so it's difficult to indent, smooth the concrete with a finish trowel held at a slight angle. Work in a series of arcs. A thick "cream," or slurry, should rise to the surface to help fill small voids and grooves. Bear down hard. To give it a broom finish—one that is more slip-resistant—wait until the concrete has hardened enough so a stiff-bristle broom leaves crisp marks.

Clean your tools as soon as you're done with them; wet concrete washes off easily, but if it dries, you'll have to chip it away. Cover the area with plastic for about 3 days to allow the concrete to cure, or harden. Secure the edges of the plastic by laying boards over them. Keep the surface moist while it cures. Let the concrete cure for a week before allowing heavy traffic on it.

Once the concrete has cured, remove the support stakes. To release the forms, you may need to tap down on them with a hammer. After you've removed the forms, fill in the space along the walkway and tamp down the dirt.

Round and compact the edges of the slab using an edging tool. Work in a series of short, jabbing motions; then make one long, continuous pass.

Use an edging tool (Photo 4) to fashion round edges. The grooving tool (Photo 5) is used to cut control joints.

Cut control joints, keeping them the same distance apart as those in the rest of the walkway. Guide the grooving tool along a straight 2 x 4.

SIDEWALKS

Estimating Concrete

Q. *This summer I plan to pour a new sidewalk in front of my house. I'm going to order the concrete by the yard from a ready-mix supplier, but I'm unsure how much I need. Can you tell me the formula for converting square feet of a certain thickness into yards of concrete?*

The trick to measuring volume is to make sure you're using the same unit of measure, such as feet, for all of your dimensions. For your slab, just measure everything in feet, including the thickness of the slab. For example, if you have a sidewalk that is 3 feet wide and 20 feet long, and you want it to be the standard 3 inches thick, use the following formula: Width (3 feet) x Length (20 feet) x Thickness (¼ foot) ÷ 27 (number of cubic feet in a cubic yard) = cubic yards (.55 in this case). For this example, you would need a little more than a half yard of concrete.

Control Joints

Q. *What does the control joint do?*

Control joints are used to try to "control" cracking. Concrete slabs expand and contract with changes in temperature and moisture. Freezing and thawing also put stress on a concrete slab. All of this movement and stress causes concrete slabs to crack. By putting in control joints at specific intervals, you're in essence building a weak spot in the slab. If the slab is going to crack, you want it to happen at the control joint. This eliminates random, unsightly cracks. Installing a control joint is no guarantee that you won't get cracking in other areas of a concrete slab, but it helps.

SIDEWALK AND PATIO REPAIRS

Raising Sunken Concrete

Q. *Our concrete sidewalk has sunk in two places. Is it best to rip it out and pour a new walk, or can I pour a thin layer of concrete over what's there?*

Pouring a thin slab over the old one is not a good idea. If you don't address the underlying problem, your new walk will sink and crack in the the same spot as the old one. Tearing out the old walk and pouring a new one is one solution, but you also have another option: hiring a mudjacker and raising the sunken area.

Companies that specialize in this procedure drill 1½- or 2-inch-diameter holes through the sunken sections, then pump a special limestone, fly ash, or cement slurry through the holes to the slab from below. When the walkway is level, the holes are patched with concrete.

This isn't a do-it-yourself job. The equipment is specialized and expensive, and requires training and a special touch to operate. The slabs must be raised gradually, commonly in ¼-inch increments. Slurry may have to be injected through each hole as many as a dozen times.

Mudjacking, also referred to as concrete raising, can cost less than demolishing old sections and pouring a new slab and the entire job can be completed in hours. Mudjacking is frequently used to relevel exterior stairways, and basement and garage floors.

This procedure is not for every situation. The concrete must be sound; a few large cracks are OK, but not a lot of little ones. There's typically a minimum service charge—often in the $200 to $300 range—so if the damaged area is very small, it may make more sense for you to break up and remove the sunken section, then pour a new section yourself.

Concrete around new houses often sinks because the backfill placed around the foundation continues to settle for several years. Rotting tree roots, water from misdirected downspouts, and frost heave can also undermine concrete. Do what you can to address the cause of the problem before making any repair, or it will probably recur.

To inject the slurry under the concrete, the mudjacker will first need to drill a series of large-diameter holes through the slab. To drill holes of this size, the pros use a percussion drill with a carbide bit. Even if you can rent this tool yourself, this job is best left to the pros.

Holes in Concrete

Q. *How can I patch a divot in a concrete driveway?*

The amount of work it takes to repair holes in concrete depends on the depth of the hole. Commercial patching compounds are fine for for shallow repairs (½ inch or less). For deeper repairs, use sand mix.

First use a cold chisel to chip away all the loose, weak concrete from in and around the hole. If the hole is deeper than ½ inch, you should also make a ⅜-inch-deep "shoulder cut" around the hole so the edges of the patch will be squared rather than tapered. Brush and blow debris out of the hole, then wet the damaged area. Soak up any standing water with a rag.

Next, prime the patch to ensure that the concrete adheres properly: Mix up a small batch of patching material to the consistency of pancake batter. Use a paintbrush to coat the repair area with the slurry.

Mix a regular batch of patching material and pack it into the hole with a wood trowel. If you want a smooth surface, glide a steel trowel across the patch. For a rougher texture, use a broom. For maximum strength, leave the patch covered with plastic for 5 days, soaking it with water each day.

To create a shoulder for a large patch, use a circular saw with a masonry blade.

Pavers Dip and Heave

Q. *Some of the pavers in the center of my patio have been pushed up by tree roots. Other pavers at the edge of the patio have begun to sink. How do I fix them?*

To raise sunken pavers, you'll need to remove them, add some coarse sand to level the base, and then wiggle them back into place.

Where the pavers have heaved, you'll need to eliminate the cause of the heaving—in this case a tree root. You shouldn't cut out the tree root

Removing the first paver is the toughest part of the job. Slip the tips of two screwdrivers along opposite ends of a paver and carefully pry it up until you can remove it by hand.

since you might damage the tree, but you can shave off some of the root if necessary. If you have a lot of major roots to contend with, check with a nursery on what you should and should not do to the plants.

The trickiest part to this repair is removing the pavers. The photo below left shows how to remove them without breaking them. To get the last few pavers to fit back in, first wiggle them in place by hand. Then lay a short length of 2 x 4 on the pavers and tap the board down until the pavers are level with the others.

Reinstall the pavers once the problem has been corrected. The last few pavers will be tight. Spread coarse sand over the area with a broom to fill the joints when you are finished.

Patio Blocks

Q. *Our 8 x 12-inch patio blocks are dirty and pitted from weather. Can they be restored?*

A few years ago, patio blocks were as common as paver bricks are today. Although they're less popular than they once were, patio blocks are still available at most home centers and landscape supply stores.

Any problems associated with these blocks are easy to fix. Because they're porous, they hold a lot of dirt and sand. Cleaning them is easy— spray the blocks with your garden

hose, scrub them with a stiff-bristle broom, and then hose them off.

If your blocks are really dirty, you can rent a power washer to blast them. The high-pressure stream of water will remove a small amount of the block's surface too. If the blocks have become pitted or grooved, just flip them over; the newly exposed surface will last as long as the side you just laid to the ground.

Cracked block can easily be removed by hand and replaced with a new one.

DRIVEWAY REPAIR

Driveway Sealers—Help or Hoax?

Q. *Does seal-coating a driveway help it last longer? And if so, how often should I apply sealant?*

Seal-coating won't mend a crumbling driveway, but it will add years to a sound driveway. If left unprotected, asphalt breaks down in sunlight and will eventually fade and become brittle. Moisture then works its way into the cracks, and in cold climates, freezes and expands to create larger cracks and upheavals. If water works its way beneath the asphalt, it can wash away the underlying soil and create dips. Seal-coating protects asphalt in much the same way that paint protects wood. It helps block water and sunlight from penetrating the asphalt's surface.

Of the two types of sealants on the market, asphalt-base types are usually better suited for residential driveways than coal tar-base products. When you apply a seal coat:

- Pull any weeds that grow through cracks, and use a stiff broom to thoroughly sweep the driveway clean.
- Pack holes with cold-mix asphalt patch. Fill cracks with pourable filler.
- Pick a dry 55°F or warmer day. Apply the sealer with a roller or special sealer applicator. Work in 100-square-foot sections.
- Keep everyone off the newly sealed driveway for 24 hours.

how is it done?

REPAIRING ASPHALT

Sealer alone will correct hairline cracks. Use filler before sealing cracks that are ⅛ to 1 inch wide. The filler will prevent moisture from working its way into the asphalt. Cracks that are wider than 1 inch should be repaired the same way you repair a hole (Photos 1 and 2).

A driveway with a lot of wide cracks or broken-up areas will require more than a simple fix. Tree roots under the asphalt, an asphalt bed that's too thin (less than 4 inches thick), and eroding edges are major problems and should be left to an asphalt contractor.

BEFORE MAKING REPAIRS

Careful preparation is the key to long-lasting repair. First apply a degreaser to all oil stains. If you don't get rid of oil stains, they'll bleed through the sealer. Scrub the areas thoroughly with a stiff-bristle brush. Next, remove any vegetation growing in cracks. Finally, sweep or hose off all dirt and loose debris. Once the water has dried, you're ready to make any necessary repairs and apply the sealer.

WATCH THE WEATHER

When you make your asphalt repairs is as important as how you make them. Select a day when the temperature is at least 55°F. The higher the temperature, the easier the sealer is to apply and the faster it dries. (Cooler days are a plus when you have a large surface to seal.) Make sure that the sealer has time to dry. If there's a chance of rain, hold off until next weekend.

1 *Fill holes with asphalt patch. If the hole is more than 1½ in. deep, fill it in layers. Add 1 in. of asphalt patch, tamp it, and then add more.*

2 *Add asphalt until it's about ½ in. above the driveway surface. Tamp with a post. Repeat until it's flush with the driveway surface.*

3 *Squeeze in crack filler until it's flush or slightly below the driveway surface. Allow it to dry completely before applying the sealer.*

4 *Apply driveway sealer every 2 to 3 yrs. Stay off the asphalt for 24 to 48 hrs. after applying sealer.*

Asphalt Over Concrete

Q. *Our concrete driveway is starting to wear and look bad. Can we apply asphalt over the old concrete?*

You can if the concrete is solid and doesn't have any large cracks that go completely through the slab. If you apply asphalt over concrete that has large cracks, the cracks may reappear on the surface within a few years. This will be more common in areas of the country where freezing causes the concrete to move.

Because you will need to install a 2- to 4-inch-thick layer of asphalt over the concrete, your resurfaced driveway may be higher than your garage floor. This could cause water to flow into the garage. Also, if your driveway is already fairly steep, adding a couple of inches may cause your car to "bottom out" on the road.

Hiring someone to break up and haul off the old driveway shouldn't cost more than a few hundred dollars and may be the best way to prevent future headaches.

Moss on Driveway

Q. *Every year, moss grows on my brick driveway and the surface gets very slippery. What can I do to get rid of the moss?*

Elbow grease and a nonmetallic brush will get rid of any unwanted moss. Use a cleaning solution consisting of 1 part household bleach and 2 parts water. Avoid getting the bleach on surrounding plants. Protect yourself by wearing gloves and goggles.

When you have finished scrubbing, rinse the brick with a hose. To slow down the return of the moss, seal the surface with a brick sealer.

Fiber–Reinforced Concrete

WHEN YOU BUY CONCRETE, your supplier may ask whether you want "fiber-reinforced" concrete. To make fiber-reinforced concrete, plastic fibers are added to the mix, typically at the rate of 1 to 2 pounds per cubic yard, or about a tenth of a percent by volume. The fibers can range in shape from simple hairlike strands to more complex twisted or netlike forms.

You may be told the fibers strengthen the concrete, thereby reducing cracks, pop-outs, and other problems, both cosmetic and structural. You may even hear claims that the fiber reinforcement eliminates the need to use wire mesh.

Research indicates that fibers improve the strength and the impact resistance of concrete. In addition, they also reduce surface shrinkage and cracking, even when the surface experiences rapid drying.

In comparing cured shrinkage (cracking caused by gradual dry-out), the research results are mixed. The studies indicate that although the fibers help, wire mesh is still the best way to prevent unwanted cracking.

Based on these test results, we recommend using wire mesh reinforcement, even with fiber-

Plastic fibers increase concrete's strength and impact resistance.

reinforced concrete. And though the fiber reinforcing does help prevent the surface cracking caused by rapid drying, these cracks can also be reduced by good techniques. These include keeping the surface of the slab damp while it cures by putting plastic over it or spraying a retarder on the surface.

Skilled installers agree that how well your concrete lasts depends not on fibers but on how well the base of the concrete is prepared, plus how well the concrete is mixed, installed, and finished. If you want the extra insurance of stronger material and protection against installation problems, fibers can provide it.

Decks

Attaching Joists at an Angle

Q. *How do I attach deck joists to my house at an angle?*

You have three options.

■ If the joists meet the ledger board at anywhere from 40° to 50°, you can use factory-made 45° joist hangers. In most cases the joist ends can remain square-cut, but angle-cutting them as shown gives the end of the joist more surface to bear down on. The holes on the 45° side of the hanger are elongated so nails can be driven in at an angle. Double hangers can be special-ordered. Always use those special stubby galvanized joist hanger nails to secure joist hangers or framing anchors. Ordinary shingle nails don't have the required strength and can shear off.

■ Squeeze blocks, cut at the same angle as the joist ends, can also be used to secure joists. A squeeze block is secured to the ledger strip with 16d galvanized nails; then the angled joist is nailed to the squeeze block. As the next squeeze block is installed, it pinches the joist. Squeeze blocks are a good way to use scrap lumber. One drawback is that water can get trapped between the ledger and the block, providing an environment for rot. To minimize this, you can use treated or rot-resistant lumber, install flashing over the joint, or position the first deck board to cover the joint between the ledger board and the blocks.

■ Bendable framing anchors can be adjusted by hand to accommodate angles ranging from 45° to 135°. To prevent metal fatigue, they should be bent only once. Place the anchors on both sides of a joist.

Use 45° joist hangers if the joists meet the ledger board at a 40° to 50° angle.

Squeeze blocks can also be used to secure joists; and they're a good way to use scrap lumber.

Bendable framing anchors can be used for angles between 45° and 135°.

Which Way Up for Deck Boards?

Q. *When I install deck boards, should the rings on the ends of the boards face up or down? I've heard it both ways.*

Here's the rule to remember: Bark side up.

To tell which side is the bark side, look at the annual growth rings on the end of the board and visualize the board inside a tree. More simply, just remember that the rings should be concave side down.

With the boards attached this way, they'll have less tendency to cup, and you'll also avoid "feathering," the splitting of a board along the annual rings that results in long, spearlike splinters. On pressure-treated wood, the chemicals sometimes penetrate better on the bark side as well. You can put the bark side down if the board has a bad knot, splits, bark pieces, or other problems, but normally the bark side should be up. To cut down on warping, use galvanized deck screws instead of nails.

Handling pressure-treated wood

■ Don't use preservative-treated wood where it would come into contact with food or drinking water.

■ Throw away leftover scrap wood in the garbage for regular collection. Don't burn it.

■ When cutting, wear eye protection and a NIOSH-approved dust mask.

■ Wash your hands before eating when working with this kind of wood.

■ Wash work clothes separately from other clothing.

PRESSURE-TREATED LUMBER

When you invest money in building a wood deck or in other projects for the yard, you expect to get many years of enjoyment out of those investments. But any wood projects you build are naturally vulnerable to the damaging effects of moisture, rot, and insects. To combat these conditions, and to ensure that the deck or fence you build lasts, you can use pressure-treated lumber.

WHAT IS PRESSURE-TREATED WOOD?

Pressure-treated wood is lumber or plywood that has been impregnated with preservatives that protect it from attack by termites and fungi that cause decay. The most common type of wood preservative used today is chromated copper arsenate (CCA). CCA is poisonous, so it's important to use treated wood as directed by the manufacturer. (See Safety Check p.346.) In addition to products that resist termites and fungi, there are pressure-treated products impregnated with water repellants that slow the rate at which moisture is absorbed and released.

You can expect pressure-treated lumber to last more than 40 years without rotting. But longevity isn't a sure bet and, you have to choose the correct level of treatment. Every board and timber should have a treatment tag or stamp fixed to it. The stamp states the concentration of preservative in the wood in pounds per cubic foot. Treatment levels are .25, which is suitable for wood used above ground, .40 for wood used in contact with the ground, and .60, which is used for wood foundations. Because the .25 level costs almost as much as .40 lumber, many retailers stock only .40 lumber, which most builders use above ground as well as in the ground. The .60 treatment level is usually available only by special order.

NOT ALL LUMBER IS TREATED EQUAL

According to the treatment standards, at least 85 percent of the sapwood of lumber up to 5 inches thick should retain the chemicals. You should see a greenish cast throughout almost all the sapwood of a freshly cut cross section. Poor preservative penetration is a tough problem to spot. Obviously you can't saw up boards while at the lumberyard to check it out. But it pays to keep an eye out for poorly treated lumber as you cut it at home. Either return lumber that clearly is not 85 percent treated, or use it in areas where it won't be as vulnerable to moisture.

Even if a piece is well treated, cutting off an end exposes vulnerable wood fiber. You can stop potential rot by coating cut ends with a brush-on preservative that contains a fungicide such as copper naphthenate.

TREATMENT RATINGS

.25 (LB./CU FT). *Rated for above-ground use. Because wood treated to the .25 level costs almost as much as .40 lumber, retailers often stock only the .40.*

.40 (LB./CU. FT.). *Rated for ground contact. This is what you find at most lumberyards and home centers.*

.60 (LB./CU. FT.). *Rated for foundations and for posts that support decks or other structures. Usually available only by special order through lumberyards.*

Decks

Preventing Deck Decay

Q. *Our deck sits under pine trees, and dropped needles and sap lodge between the deck boards. This crud looks bad and holds onto moisture that makes the deck slippery. What is the best way to remove this stuff?*

Use a dull saw—any size coarse-tooth saw will do—to either push or pull the crud out from between the boards. You'll help your deck breathe better and last longer by getting rid of this rot-promoting gunk.

You can remove any sap that has fallen onto the deck with a heavy-duty stain remover available at home centers and paint stores. Some stain/finish removers are formulated to remove oil-base clear and semi-transparent finishes, as well as buildup from repeated applications of deck sealer. Others are specially formulated to work on tough stains and dirt such as sap. You apply the stain remover with a mop or just pour it onto the surface. Wait 15 minutes, scrub it with a brush, then rinse it off. Because sap is similar to oil-base finishes, it should come off easily.

Remove pine needles from between deck boards with a coarse saw.

Quick Questions about Deck Cleaning and Sealing

Q. *How often should I clean my deck?*
You should wash it whenever dirt or mildew is visible. Generally, once or twice a year is enough.

Q. *Should I seal my deck after I clean it?*
After your deck is clean, you can apply a sealer that provides ultraviolet protection. Apply only one coat of sealer to a new or freshly cleaned deck (too much sealer will actually attract dirt). Reapply the sealer as needed. Most sealers last only 2 to 3 years.

Q. *Do I have to seal the deck after every cleaning?*
No. The protective finish you've applied will continue working for 2 or more years even if you clean it.

Q. *Do I need to strip off the sealer before I can clean my deck?*
Most sealers don't need to be removed for the cleaner to work. If there is a varnish or gummy buildup of old sealer or finish that blocks the cleaning, you should remove it by sanding, scraping, or by using the appropriate solvent for the sealer.

Clean a Deck

Q. *What's the best way to clean my deck?*

Deck cleaners are designed to clean away grime and to remove loose wood fibers on the surface of deck boards and railings. There are a variety of formulas to choose from at your home center or hardware store.

Some cleaners contain only detergents; others may contain oxalic acid or bleach or a combination of these ingredients. Unless you have mildew, moss, or berry stains, you won't need a cleaner containing bleach (sodium hypochlorite). Avoid the bleach if you can; heavy concentrations of it can damage the wood. Read the labels and choose a cleaner that best suits the discoloration or staining problems of your deck.

Before you clean the deck, replace any rotten wood. When you're ready to clean, pick a time of day when the deck is shaded. Hot sun will dry out the cleaner before it has a chance to work. Some deck cleaners can safely splash onto plants, but fragile plants, like flowers, could take a beating. Water surrounding plants to saturate the roots, then cover them. Be careful not to wet the deck when you water the plants if the product you're using must be applied to a dry surface.

Mix and apply the deck cleaner according to the manufacturer's specifications. Wear a sturdy pair of rubber gloves and safety goggles.

You don't need any fancy equipment to apply the cleaning solution. An ordinary cotton mop, a garden sprayer, or a thick-nap paint roller will do the trick. Give the deck cleaner a little time to soak into the wood. Then scrub the surface with a brush to loosen the dirt and mildew. Finally, rinse away the residue.

REPLACING DECK BOARDS

Whether you have one bad deck board to replace or many, the process is the same. Here's the strategy:

You will not need to replace an entire board if you can cut out sections where the boards cross over joists. Make replacement pieces span at least three joists. This keeps the new boards from splitting as they age. Stagger the splices so adjacent boards don't end on the same joist. Staggered splices look better and make a stronger deck. To avoid confusion, mark the replacement boards before you begin.

MATERIALS

If you want a close match between old and new deck boards, you'll have to match the species of wood. This is tricky, because weathered deck boards look alike. Remove a board, cut it with a circular saw, and smell the wood to identify the species. Pressure-treated pine has a sweet smell, cedar has an aromatic smell, and redwood a more pungent smell. Ask your lumberyard to cut a scrap from each species, and match the smell to your own board.

Since you'll be cutting replacement board of various lengths, buy the longest boards you can transport; they'll yield less waste.

The length of the fasteners depends on the thickness of your decking. Buy galvanized or stainless steel nails or screws long enough to penetrate the joists by at least 1½ inches.

You'll need a jigsaw and a circular saw, pry bar, cat's paw, angle square, sawhorses, and hammer.

INSTALLATION TIPS

Position the new boards so the growth rings cup down. The grain won't split open and collect water as readily. For a really clean cut, identify the top side of the board, flip it over, and make the cut. The bottom of the board gets a cleaner cut because circular saw teeth cut from the bottom up. When you cut a board, don't leave a knot at the end.

To get a tight joint between old and new boards, angle the jigsaw slightly when cutting out the bad board so the bevel on the remaining deck board is longer at the top.

1 Cut the bad board free with a jigsaw. Cut alongside the joist using an angle square as a guide. Angle the saw blade so the new board will butt the top edge of the old board tightly.

2 To pull nails, drive a cat's paw into the wood under the nailhead. Pull back on the handle to remove the nail.

3 Nail or screw 12-in.-long cleats to the joists to support the ends of the new board.

4 If the top edge of a joist is soft and beginning to rot, place a flashing tin on top of it and bend the edges down.

5 Flatten the tip of the nail before driving it into the board. The flattened tip reduces splitting.

Care and Repair **349**

Decks

DECK FINISHES

Treat or Not?

Q. *We just built a new cedar deck and are getting conflicting advice on whether we need to seal the wood or not.*

While cedar is naturally decay-resistant, it'll eventually rot like any other wood. Treating your cedar deck will greatly prolong its life, provided you do it correctly.

Follow these guidelines to keep your deck in good shape: Use a water-repelling wood preservative that contains a fungicide and a mildewcide (check the label).

Treating the deck only once is a waste of money. You'll need to reapply the preservative from time to time—every 1 to 3 years in most areas of the country. It's time to reapply the preservative when your deck begins to look dry and when rainwater soaks into the wood instead of beading on the surface.

Cedar will naturally weather to a silver-gray color. If you want a color other than silver-gray, use a tinted wood stain before applying the preservative. Unfortunately, no one has come up with a way to keep cedar looking the way it does when it comes from the mill. All preservatives will darken the wood a little when they're applied.

How you apply the preservative (brush, roller, or spray) is a matter of personal preference. But you need to treat the entire surface of the wood: top, sides, and bottom. Apply just enough preservative to soak the wood. The preservative shouldn't run down or puddle on the surface.

Also, don't forget that the ends of all boards (the end grain) need to be treated. This is where most moisture enters wood.

Latex or Oil Stain for Decks

Q. *Does it matter whether I use latex or oil-base stain on my deck?*

Latex stains are best suited for vertical surfaces, such as siding or trim, where water will not stand and foot traffic isn't present. Oil stains work well on horizontal as well as vertical surfaces, making them a better choice for decks. The stain has enough pigment to give the wood color, and the oil penetrates deeply and actually helps harden the surface as it dries. It won't peel or mar easily. For high-traffic areas, it's best to reapply the stain every 2 to 3 years.

If you've already applied latex, scrape or sand it off (otherwise the latex will peel), then apply a coat of oil stain.

Deck Protection

Q. *How long should I wait to seal my new redwood deck? Someone told me to wait at least a year. Is that true?*

No, it's not. A redwood or cedar deck begins to weather as soon as the deck is completed. Exposure to the elements can dry out the wood and cause premature aging. So give your deck a fighting chance by applying the sealer as soon as you're able; but never seal the deck when the wood is moist. Wait for a few days of dry weather, then start sealing.

Pressure-treated decks usually need more time to dry thoroughly. Give it at least a month after it's built to dry out; then apply a sealer.

Fuzzy Deck

Q. *Before treating my deck with a clear preservative, I washed it with a wood cleaner and rinsed it with a power washer. When the wood dried, the surface was "fuzzy." What happened?*

Scrubbing with a stiff brush may have raised the grain of the wood. Or when you rinsed your deck with the power washer, you may have used unnecessarily high pressure. You don't usually need high pressure to clean a deck; a garden hose and nozzle work just fine.

Before applying the preservative, you'll need to sand off the raised grain. Make one pass across the grain using coarse sandpaper, and one pass with the grain using medium sandpaper. To make this a little easier, buy a sanding pad that's attached to the end of a long handle, the type professional drywallers use to sand drywall joints. Pick one up at a home center and save yourself a sore back.

Knotty Problem

Q. *I'm having difficulty staining my pine deck. I've tried several stain products, but none are absorbed by the knots. Is there anything else I can do?*

Unfortunately, there's little that can be done. Knots are extremely dense, and therefore stains just don't penetrate them. If the knots occur in just a few boards, you might try replacing the boards with a higher-grade pine (the higher the grade, the fewer the knots). This would at least reduce the problem.

OUTDOOR WOOD FINISHES

There's no perfect finish that will keep wood looking natural forever. Completely opaque paints, with lots of pigment, form a film to prevent weathering but hide the color and grain of the wood. Clear penetrating finishes allow the grain and color to shine through but offer less protection against ultraviolet light, water, and other elements; the wood is more likely to fade.

Use products containing mildewcides (poisons that kill mildew) when available. Allow the siding to dry for 2 full days before applying any finish; longer for damp, shady areas.

There are three basic categories of finishes you can use to keep your wood looking natural. Each has its trade-offs.

Semi-transparent stains (this one tinted a cedar color) offer protection for up to 6 years but let only some of the wood grain show through.

SEMI-TRANSPARENT STAINS

These allow the texture, and to varying degrees the grain, of the wood to show through. Two coats of oil-base penetrating stain (apply the second coat before the first is fully dry) can last up to 5 or 6 years on rough-sawn or weathered wood (less on smooth wood). Latex-base stains—easier to apply and less likely to show lap marks—are also available, but they aren't as durable because they don't penetrate as deeply as oil-base stains.

Many companies offer semi-transparent stains in cedar and redwood tones that mimic the original color of the wood. The final appearance is a blend of the stain and the natural color of the wood over which it's applied.

Solid stains are basically thinned-down paints. They hide all the grain and most of the texture of wood, creating an unnatural look. They should never be used on decks because they're a nightmare to maintain.

TRANSLUCENT MULTICOAT FINISHES

Transluscent finishes let the wood show through, yet have sufficient body and pigment to offer protection. The best are flexible enough to stand up to the elements but may require several coats to work and can be very expensive. Check the label to make sure they're designed for exterior use and contain UV (ultraviolet) protectors or blockers.

Avoid using spar or urethane varnishes outside. They'll rapidly become brittle and peel.

Translucent multicoat finishes allow the natural richness of the wood to show through but are expensive and time-consuming to apply.

WATER REPELLENTS AND WATER-REPELLENT PRESERVATIVES

These don't form a protective film but do help prevent water staining, checking (small cracks), and they hold mildew at bay. Some repellents, both clear and tinted, contain UV blockers to inhibit weathering and create a more uniform look. Those labeled "preservative" offer better protection than plain repellents.

For best results, apply two coats of water-repellent preservative when the wood is completely dry. Follow up with additional coats every year or two on decks, every 3 or 4 years on siding and fences.

Water repellents, sealants, and preservatives help prevent water stains, checking, and mildew growth but must be applied frequently.

Fences

INSTALLATION AND REPAIR

Need a Surveyor?

Q. *I'd like to install a fence around my property, but I don't know exactly where the property corners are. Do I need to hire a surveyor?*

Probably. If you don't hire a surveyor, you could end up spending a lot of money in court when a neighbor sues you for putting up a fence on "his side." If you install a fence and it doesn't meet local zoning requirements, or if the fence is built across your neighbor's property line, your neighbor has the legal right to require you to move the fence. When you hire a surveyor, you put the responsibility for locating the property lines on him or her. Keep in mind that your new fence should be far enough back from the property line so that you can maintain it on both sides without trespassing.

If your property has straight boundaries, and if you are planning a simple, straight fence, you might be able to avoid the survey. Also, check at your county surveyor's or assessor's office to see if they have a survey of your property that you don't know about. If a Certificate of Survey exists, the surveyor probably placed "monuments" at all the property corners. Monuments are metal rods driven into the ground; if you cannot locate them easily, try using a metal detector. Once you've located the corners, mark the property line by running string between the corners.

Bury the posts for a garden arbor about 30 in. into the ground and anchor them with concrete.

Anchoring Posts

Q. *How should I anchor the 4 x 4 posts to hold up an overhead lattice on an outdoor shade arbor?*

For the type of top-heavy, open sided-arbor you are building, bury the posts about 30 inches into the ground and use concrete to anchor them. You could pack crushed gravel or sand around the posts, but concrete will provide the best anchor. Setting the posts on an above-ground pad won't give you enough stability.

In other situations, like building a deck, it is best to keep the wood above ground level to prevent decay. In the case of a deck, posts can be placed on top of concrete piers because the structure is often low to the ground and very heavy, and therefore more stable.

Wood for Fence Posts

Q. *What type of 4 x 4 posts should I use for a wooden fence: cedar, redwood, or pressure-treated wood?*

All three woods you mention are regularly used for fence posts. However, they differ significantly in appearance, price, and longevity. If your fence site has average moisture or is dry, cedar posts can be expected to last up to 27 years, while redwood posts will last about 20 years, and pressure-treated wood, indefinitely. If your fence is going into wet, marshy ground, use pressure-treated posts.

Pressure-treated wood that is used for fencing should have a retention rate (the amount of chemical that actually ends up in the wood) of at least .40. Look for a label on the wood that says "LP-22 .40." If you use redwood, be sure it's "Construction Heart" grade, which is the most rot-resistant part of the wood. Cedar posts should be cut from heartwood for the longest life. Avoid fence posts treated with creosote and pentachlorophenol; both are known carcinogens, and creosote can contaminate ground and surface water supplies. As for cost, prices vary regionally, but cedar and redwood usually cost about twice as much as pressure-treated wood.

Aside from price and longevity, the woods also look very different. Cedar and redwood weather to a dark gray unless you apply an ultraviolet blocking sealer that will preserve the original color for several years. Pressure-treated lumber has a distinctive green cast that gradually turns gray. All three woods can be stained or painted. Lumber for fencing is typically a grade lower than construction lumber, so you'll find a lot of knots, splits, and warped boards. If the wood seems too flawed, return it for a refund.

Caring for Treated Wood

Q. *I just installed a treated-wood fence around our swimming pool. How do I take care of it?*

Contrary to what some people think, weather will still affect treated wood, so it does need care. A treated fence should be allowed to air-dry for at least 2 weeks after construction. Then, to protect it, apply a water-repellent preservative sealer with a wide brush or roller. A sealer will help reduce warping, shrinking, and splintering in treated wood. Reapply the sealer every 2 years.

Rusty Fence

Q. *Is there any way to make a weathered, rusty chain-link fence look better? Can it be painted?*

This is not a fun job, but rejuvenating a rusty fence can be done. To remove the rust and corrosion, use a 2- to 3-inch-diameter wire brush chucked into a drill. Wear goggles to protect your eyes. Next, apply a base coat of rust-inhibitor sealer/primer with a long-nap roller or paint mitt. Now you can apply a top coat of aluminum paint.

how is it done? REPLACING A FENCE POST

A wobbly post does not necessarily need to be replaced, just firmed up. A post that is set directly into dirt can be supported by digging an 18-inch-deep circle around it, then filling the circle with concrete. Wobbly posts set in a thin collar of concrete can be solidified by pounding the old concrete into the ground with a sledgehammer, then pouring new concrete at least 6 inches deep over it. For minor wobbles, drive cedar shingles around the base of a post (see Straighten, Tighten, and Maintain Your Fence, p.355).

Fences that have loose or rotting posts, but are otherwise in good shape can be salvaged by installing new posts midway between the existing ones. This is a major project and the end result doesn't always look good unless the new posts are kept to the back side of the fence or can be blended somehow to look like part of the original design.

To replace just a couple of posts, pull the nails that secure the fence sections to the vertical post on each side. Swing the sections out of the way, propping their free ends on scrap boards. Next, pry the old post out of the ground, pulling at an angle so that it doesn't slip back into the hole. Finally, set the new post in the hole, then level and nail the sections back together. Pack a few inches of dirt around the base of the post; then pour in the concrete to a little above ground level.

1 Temporary support blocks

Pull the nails securing the fence sections to the bad post. Move the sections a couple of feet out of the way, supporting them with scrap boards.

Prying block | Sturdy 2 x 4 | Scrap lumber

2 *Posts embedded in concrete can weigh over 100 lb.; lever out the post with a prying block, a 2 x 4, and a pile of lumber scraps.*

Slight slope | Concrete | Tamped dirt

3 *Once you've poured the concrete to above ground level, trowel the top so water will run away from the post.*

Fences

what do you need?

THE RIGHT TOOLS FOR POSTHOLE DIGGING

Whether you're building a fence, a gate, or a deck, you'll need to start by setting one or more posts beneath the frost line. To dig beyond the reach of a shovel, you'll need a special tool.

Clamshell-style diggers can dig in all types of soil. Plunge the digger into the ground, pull the handles apart so the jaws grab a mouthful of soil, then lift the dirt from the hole. To use a hand auger, push down on the handle and twist the head into the dirt, then withdraw the tool and dump.

A power auger has a motorized shaft that literally drills itself into the soil. Periodically lift the auger out of the hole so it can spin out the dirt.

A clamshell-style digger works slowly but can be used in all types of soil.

The auger-type digger is good for sandy soil but can't handle rocks.

A power auger digs quickly but may kick back if it hits a rock.

Sagging Gate Repair

Q. *Is there an easy way to fix a sagging gate?*

To support a sagging gate, install a light cable and a steel gate turnbuckle. Attach two lag bolts to the gate—one at the top of the gate on the hinge side and the other at the bottom of the gate on the latch side. Attach the turnbuckle and cable as shown. The turnbuckle can be easily tightened at any time to make up for small changes in post movement or for additional sagging.

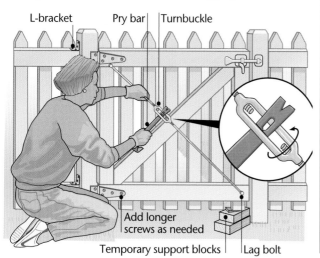

L-bracket   Pry bar   Turnbuckle

Add longer screws as needed

Temporary support blocks   Lag bolt

Installing a Flagpole

Q. *I want to install a 30-foot-tall flagpole. Do I need to set it in concrete, like a fence post? How deep should the hole be to ensure that the pole doesn't blow over in a strong wind?*

The force of the wind on a flag can exert tremendous stress on a flagpole. Unless the pole is solidly anchored to the ground, a relatively gentle breeze can be enough to uproot it.

To prevent this, you'll need to embed the bottom of the pole in a concrete foundation. Dig a hole that's at least 12 inches in diameter and 5 feet 6 inches deep. Make the bottom of the hole slightly larger in diameter than the top. Save your back and rent a power auger (around $40 for a half day).

To make the pole removable, don't set it directly into the wet concrete. Instead, install a metal pipe in the hole so its top is flush with the ground level. Pour concrete around the pipe to anchor it in place. Make sure that the inside diameter of the metal sleeve is slightly larger than the outside diameter of your flagpole.

Straighten, Tighten, and Maintain Your Fence

Q. *Our wood fence is just a couple of years old. What can we do to keep it looking good?*

Routine maintenance is the best way to add years to your fence. For starters, keep leaf piles and any other debris away from the fence; they trap moisture that promotes rot and can be a home to termites and other wood-eating critters.

Installing gravel or a row of patio block below the fence eliminates the need to trim the grass in this area and thus prevents the damage caused by weed trimmers and lawn mowers. To make a grass-free zone, dig a shallow trench and line it with black plastic before installing the rock or block.

Installing intermediate support blocks, shimming loose posts, and adding cap blocks will improve both the look and the durability of a fence. Resecure any loose pickets or cross members with galvanized screws.

Staining or painting your fence after repairs are made will not only help blend old and new wood parts but will also add an extra coat of protection against the weather.

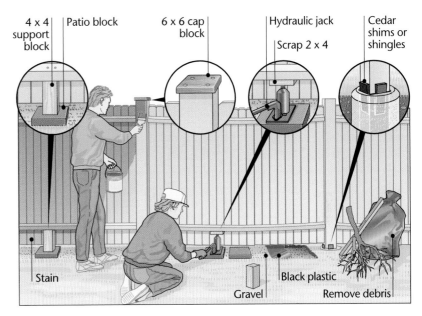

4 x 4 support block | Patio block | 6 x 6 cap block | Hydraulic jack | Scrap 2 x 4 | Cedar shims or shingles | Stain | Gravel | Black plastic | Remove debris

SHEDS AND OUTBUILDINGS

Storage Building Site Requirements

Q. *Do building codes also apply to backyard storage sheds, or can I do whatever I want?*

Although there are few building codes governing portable storage units under 100 square feet, there are local zoning requirements. The first thing you should do is check with a local building inspector or the zoning office for any local guidelines.

Obtain any building permits that are necessary in your area and check for completed size restrictions (square footage and height). Make sure the shed is located the minimum required distance from your (and your neighbor's) property lines.

From a practical standpoint, the area you decide to put your shed on should be high and dry. The better the area drains, the less likely any wood will rot. If you build a concrete foundation, bevel the top edges slightly for water to drain away. If you use a wood-base foundation, match it as precisely as possible to the floor frame. If the base foundation is wider than the floor frame, water will collect, which leads to rot and decay. Whatever kind of foundation you decide on, be sure it's level.

Work with a partner whenever you can. Positioning, holding, and securing the side walls and roof is difficult for one person. The day you choose to erect the shed should be dry and calm; an 8-foot or 10-foot wall can easily be blown over in light to moderate wind, especially when you are trying to do the job alone.

Plan for a Dog Run

Q. *I'd like to build a fenced-in dog run. Do you have layout tips?*

For starters, place the run in a shaded area or plan to provide a screen for shade. A good dog run should have a concrete floor over the entire area to keep your dog from digging and to make it easy for you to clean. A sloped floor will make it even easier to clean. Install chain link fence high enough so the dog can't jump over, or install chain link over the top of the run. A good way to keep your dog from digging under the fencing is to set the fence into the wet concrete.

Remember to include a properly sized doghouse—big enough for the animal to stand up and turn around in, but not so big that the dog won't stay warm in the winter.

Lawn and Garden

Soil Testing

Q. *We'd like to start a garden in our new yard. How can we find out if the soil's any good?*

Soil chemistry is complicated, and different plants thrive in different types of soil. You can buy a do-it-yourself soil-testing kit or send a sample to a soil-testing lab for analysis.

A good test should reveal at least four major soil conditions: pH, nitrogen, phosphorus, and potash. The pH level tells you the acidity or alkalinity of the soil. Some plants can live only within specific pH ranges. Nitrogen is especially important to lawns and leafy vegetables. Phosphorous promotes colorful flower formation and seed germination. Potash is essential for root, stalk, and stem formation.

Be sure to prepare the sample exactly as instructed by the package or lab. Since soil conditions may vary from one area to another, you may want to take several samples from around your property.

You can test your soil with a home testing kit or send samples to a lab and get a report of the results.

House-Damaging Vines

Q. *I'd love to plant some climbing vines on the side of my house but have been told the plants will damage the walls. Is this true?*

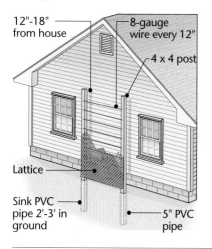

12"-18" from house

8-gauge wire every 12"

4 x 4 post

Lattice

Sink PVC pipe 2'-3' in ground

5" PVC pipe

On houses that are sided with wood, aluminum, or vinyl, the weight of vines can loosen the siding. Also, moisture accumulates underneath the vines, causing wood siding to rot. On brick houses, the vines may work their way into mortar joints. In all cases, regular exterior maintenance projects, such as painting, will be more difficult because the vines will be in the way.

On a positive note, vines shade the siding, helping to keep the house cool, and are an effective way to cover unattractive features. If you want vines but also want to protect your house, you can train them to climb a freestanding trellis placed away from the house.

Road Salt on the Lawn

Q. *How can I revive the areas on my lawn that have been damaged by road salt?*

A little road salt will delay grass growth in the spring; a lot of salt can kill the lawn. Gypsum can absorb and neutralize excessive amounts of salt. To save salt-contaminated grass, use a spreader to apply gypsum after the snow has melted and the top inch of soil has thawed. You'll need about 40 pounds of gypsum per 250 square feet of lawn.

It's important that you apply the gypsum before the new roots start feeding and growing; once the salt is drawn into the grass, it's too late.

Getting Rid of Bermuda Grass

Q. *How can I get rid of the Bermuda grass in my lawn?*

Bermuda grass is difficult to get rid of because it spreads both on top of and below the soil. To rid your lawn of Bermuda grass, you have two choices:

The first is to use a herbicide. When the grass is actively growing in the spring or summer and is not dusty or dry, spray a herbicide, like glyphosate, according to the manufacturer's instructions. Realize that some herbicides kill every plant they contact, so be careful where you spray it. As with any poison, keep this solution away from children and animals. Sprayers, buckets, and other tools used with the herbicide must not be used for any other purpose.

A chemical-free solution is to cut the grass as short as possible and then cover the area with black plastic. Periodically check the grass. When the grass turns brown, brittle, and breaks apart easily, it's dead. (This process may take a couple of weeks.) Remove the plastic and rake away the dead grass; then reseed the area.

Stripping Off Sod

Q. *What is the best way to remove a large area of grass to make room for a garden?*

If you want to reuse the sod or if you don't want to disturb the soil where you remove sod grass, there are three sod-removal methods you can choose from:

For small strips of grass, a straight-bladed shovel will do the trick. If you have less than 50 square feet of sod to remove, a sod kicker is a good choice. If you have a plantation-size area to clear, rent a sod cutter.

If you plan to reuse the sod, leave at least an inch of the dirt and root mat to hold the sod together. This mat will provide a solid base for establishing roots.

Slice through the grass with a shovel. Lay the shovel flat and push it under the sod. Roll up the sod mat.

If you need a smooth, even edge, remove the grass with a sod kicker.

Use a gas-powered sod cutter for stripping large areas. Keep rolled-up sod moist, and use it as soon as possible.

how is it done ?

LAYING SOD

Laying sod is the the best way to get a great-looking lawn fast or to do major repairs on a mature lawn. Lay sod in the early spring or late fall so that it can take root in cooler weather. Pick up the sod, or have freshly cut sod delivered, on the day you are going to lay it; sod won't last more than a couple of days. Be sure to use topsoil (not black dirt) when you lay new sod.

Once you've laid the sod, go ahead and water it—you cannot over water sod. Don't walk on it for at least 3 weeks or you might damage the root structure and slow root growth. Likewise, you shouldn't mow it for 4 to 6 weeks. When you do mow, don't cut more than one-third of the grass blade length at a time. After about 6 weeks, the sod should be established well enough for light foot traffic.

Turn under your old lawn with a gas-powered rotary tiller. Once the grass and soil are mixed, add fresh topsoil and fertilizer.

Smooth the tilled soil with a metal garden rake. Spread lawn starter fertilizer on top of the soil to stimulate rapid grass root growth.

When you lay new sod in place, make sure each new roll butts tightly against the neighboring roll to minimize seam lines. Stagger the end seams to help reduce erosion and runoff.

Lawn and Garden

MULCHES

Weed-Free Planting Beds

Q. *What works best at preventing weeds—fabric or a black plastic weed barrier?*

Weed barriers control weeds by preventing sunlight from reaching weed seeds and by inhibiting new plants from taking root. Fabric weed barriers allow some moisture and air to reach your plants' roots. Unfortunately, weed seeds can land on and grow through the top of the fabric. As the weeds grow through, the roots become tangled in the fabric and can tear the barrier when you try to pull the roots out.

Weed roots cannot penetrate black plastic, but neither can the rainwater and oxygen essential for your other plants. By punching holes in the plastic to let in water and air, you're also creating openings for weeds. Plastic is quite slippery and sheds water readily. During a rainstorm, the water can wash away any mulch on top.

For flower beds, try the fabric. Reserve the black plastic for those areas you want absolutely weed-free.

Back plastic (top) is good for directing water away from a house and for eliminating weed growth. Fabric barriers suppress weeds but also allow water and other nutrients to reach plant roots.

Mulch Benefits

Q. *What are the advantages to using mulch?*

Mulch not only adds color and texture to your landscaping, it also blocks weeds from taking root in the soil. In addition, it conserves moisture by slowing evaporation, insulates the soil, and prevents flowering bulbs from emerging too early. Mulch also protects the soil from being compacted by heavy rains, sprinklers, and foot traffic.

When you apply mulch, make a 4-inch-thick layer and thin it out to 2 inches around plants. Don't place any mulch directly against your house siding or tree trunks, as it will promote rot. Because mulch compacts, decomposes, and/or blows away, you'll need to renew it yearly.

Mulch Maintenance

Q. *I know mulch cuts down on yard and garden maintenance, but is there anything I need to do to maintain the mulch itself?*

Mulch does present a few more chores for you. In the fall, leaves need to be removed from the planting beds. Try not to remove a lot of the mulch as you rake. Shredded materials tend to stay put underneath leaves, but wood chips or hulls tend to tag along with the leaves. Clean rock beds with a leaf blower.

When you mow, direct grass clippings away from mulched areas, especially those with a weed barrier; otherwise when the clippings decompose, they can form a weed planting bed on top of the barrier.

In the spring you should renew the mulch bed with ½ inch of fresh material. During the growing season, fluff up the mulch with a pitchfork to improve air circulation.

Some mulches, such as straw and sawdust, steal nitrogen from the soil as they decompose. If your plants look yellow or stunted, try adding some high-nitrogen fertilizer.

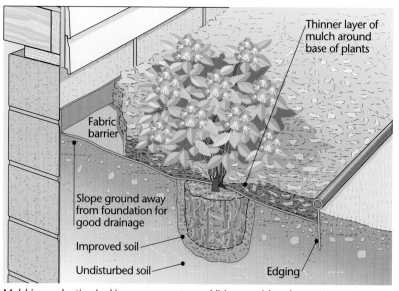

Fabric barrier

Thinner layer of mulch around base of plants

Slope ground away from foundation for good drainage

Improved soil

Undisturbed soil

Edging

Mulching a planting bed is an easy way to establish a weed-free, low-maintenance environment for your flowers and shrubs.

Types of Mulch

MULCH IS A TIME-SAVING, WATER-conserving, weed-busting magic carpet for your yard and garden. When selecting mulch, some things to consider are attractiveness, performance, and longevity.

Organic Mulches

Shredded and chipped tree and bark products are the most popular. Cedar, redwood, and hardwoods last longer and are less likely to promote mold than softwood mulch (like pine). Shredded-type mulches are less likely to blow or float away, which makes them ideal for use on sloped land and areas where water splashes from roof overhangs.

Grass clippings and leaves break down quickly, so there's no need to use a black plastic or fabric weed barrier beneath them. Grass clippings that contain fertilizer or weedkiller may harm other plants, so use them with caution. Grass and leaves may start to smell as they decompose: Experiment with them on a remote area of your yard first.

Peanut, cottonseed, and cocoa hulls make excellent mulches, especially in flower beds. Cocoa hulls smell sweet after a rain. Straw and hay are inexpensive, but be sure that they were cut before going to seed. Be aware that pine needles often make the soil more acidic and are therefore not ideal for certain plantings.

Compost is good because it also feeds nutrients to the soil. Many people spread wood chips or other mulches on top of a thin layer of compost.

Mineral Mulches

Rock adds color, texture, and variety to your landscape. Choose from plain gravel, volcanic rock, multicolored stone, and more. If you choose some type of rock mulch, know that it can overheat, crowd plants, and damage tender stems and leaves.

Cocoa bean hulls and other finely ground organic materials make excellent mulches for flower beds.

Bark and other wood products are great around ornamental bushes and shrubs.

Washed gravel, rock, and stone provide a permanent mulch in established planting beds. Always use a weed barrier beneath rock mulch beds.

Lawn and Garden

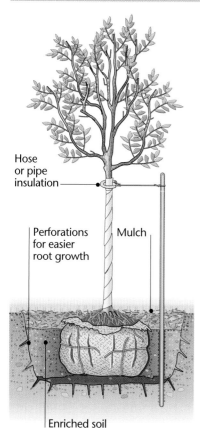

Hose
or pipe
insulation

Perforations
for easier
root growth

Mulch

Enriched soil

Tree Planting Basics

Q. *What do I need to know in order to plant a tree?*

To help your tree get off to a healthy start, dig a hole that's twice as wide as, but only a few inches deeper than, the root ball. Mix one-third peat moss or topsoil in with the soil removed from the hole. Don't over-enrich the soil or the roots won't want to grow beyond the hole. Jab the sides and bottom of the hole to provide channels for root growth.

Plant the tree so the top of the root ball is slightly above the surface. Cut all ropes holding the burlap. Fill the hole three-quarters full with enriched soil, and tamp; then cut and remove the top portion of burlap. Soak the area around the tree to settle the soil; then finish filling the hole. Surround the tree with no more than 4 inches of mulch; any deeper and the roots may grow up into the mulch rather than down into the ground.

Why Prune?

Q. *Pruning trees is extremely time-consuming. What is the point? Can't I let my trees grow naturally?*

Most people don't realize that pruning is one of the best things you can do for your trees. For starters, pruning ensures good growth when transplanting or planting a new tree. Pruning also controls the form of the tree to produce a better appearance. It keeps the tree healthy and can often even rejuvenate a tree. You will get more and better fruit if you prune your fruit trees regularly. You'll also be removing branches that endanger property or get in the way of overhead wires or nearby structures.

It's best not to neglect a tree for many years and then prune too severely. Take a few hours every year to do the job right, and your trees will be a lot stronger, healthier, and better looking. Incidentally, pruning should not significantly alter the shape of a mature tree, especially a conifer.

Cooling
with
Shade

Trellis and vines

Evergreens

LANDSCAPE SHADING blocks the sun before it hits your house. The idea is to place trees and other foliage in a way to provide shade in summer but not so much in winter. A good plan is to position low foliage on the east and west sides to block the early morning and late evening sun. Moderate-size trees block late morning and early evening sun, and tall trees closer to

Arbor and vines

N W E S

Awnings

Tall shade trees

the house cast shade over the roof during midday hours.

Trees that lose their leaves in the winter will let warming sunlight in during the colder months. In stormy areas with frequent wind, you might not want to plant trees close to your home; ask experts at your local nursery for advice.

No single plan is best for every home. The basic principles of shading should help you choose what fits your home's style, your local climate, and your budget.

Removing a Tree Limb

Q. *It doesn't make sense to hire a pro just to remove some broken and low-hanging tree limbs from my front yard. How can I safely remove the limbs myself?*

The equipment you'll need to do the job yourself depends on the size of the limbs. It's too dangerous to use a chain saw above waist height. For larger limbs, use a pruning saw or a bow saw. If you can't safely reach the limb from the ground or from a ladder safely, use a pole saw.

Most large limb removal should be done in three cuts. If the limb is longer than 10 feet or larger than 4 inches in diameter, cut off half its length first; then remove the second half. Do not coat or paint a freshly cut area; the cut will seal itself naturally.

Make the first cut about 12 in. from the trunk. Make the second cut from the top, 1 in. out from the undercut. The third cut removes the remaining piece of limb.

Remove large limbs in two or more sections; tie a rope around the cut-off section to control the speed and direction of its fall. Have a helper hold the rope.

Reach high limbs with a pole saw. Use smooth, even pulling strokes for the best results, and watch out for power lines!

Wounded Tree

Q. *An old oak tree in our yard was damaged during a storm; a large branch snapped, off leaving a gaping wound in the trunk. Can anything be done to protect the area from insects, rain, and rot?*

Trees naturally close off wounds to prevent rot and damage from spreading. Trying to help the process along might only cause additional damage. For example, packing a cavity with insulation or painting a wound will only trap moisture and promote rot. What you can do to help your tree is to prune off any remaining portions of the branch in stages, as close to the branch collar as possible without cutting into the trunk. Cut off dead limbs before they break off.

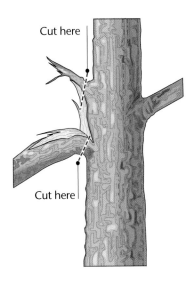

Cut here

Cut here

Cut Roots with Caution

Q. *How far can we dig around our oak trees without hurting the roots? We want to put in a concrete patio.*

Here's a good rule: Don't dig inside the "protected root zone" directly below the branches or drip line of a tree. Keep in mind that more than half of a tree's root system is in the top 12 inches of soil.

Note that aspen, elm, willow, and oak have root systems that are aggressive enough to buckle concrete; it's in your best interest to build a patio away from these trees.

Lawn and Garden

PEST CONTROL

Pigeons Be Gone

Q. *How can we get rid of the pigeons that roost on our roof?*

Pigeons love to roost in eaves, dormers, window ledges, roofs, and any place that resembles the caves and cliffs of their original wild habitat. Pigeon droppings are an unhealthy, messy nuisance and the cooing can be very annoying.

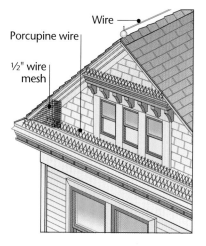

Only two methods work for getting rid of pigeons. One is to eliminate their food supply by cleaning up any pet food or spilled grains, especially around bird feeders, and by covering your garbage cans.

The other method is to physically exclude them from their roosting areas. To do this, block the openings to lofts, vents, and eaves where pigeons gather. Galvanized wire mesh is a good choice; wood, glass, and masonry will also work. Plastic or nylon netting won't last very long. If the birds are roosting on the ridge of the roof, try stringing a wire about 3 inches above the roof, to make roosting there impossible.

"Porcupine wire" has sharp stainless steel prongs that can be fastened to windowsills, ledges, roof peaks, and wherever pigeons are a problem. This wire is pretty expensive, but it offers long-term results and is unobtrusive. Look for it at a home center or farm supply store.

Mole Trouble

Q. *Is there an effective way to get rid of the mole that is tearing up my front lawn?*

You may not know it, but moles do not feed on your lawn or on flower roots; they eat the grubs, worms, and insects that live just beneath the surface of your lawn. Moles will be attracted to your yard as long as there is an abundant food supply.

An effective way to get rid of moles is to install a harpoon trap in an active mole tunnel. To determine if a tunnel is active, stomp on a raised portion of tunnel in your yard; if it's raised up the next day, it's active. Flatten the area again; then push the legs of the trap into the ground over that area of tunnel. When the mole tries to open the collapsed tunnel, the sharp tines harpoon and kill the mole. Place the trap out at night, and keep children and pets away from it!

If killing the mole is not the route you want to take, you could capture the mole and release it elsewhere, far away from your lawn. When you see the mole making a tunnel (they're more active at night), push a shovel in behind the mole's ridging path and scoop the mole up into a bucket. Wear heavy gloves even if you don't scoop the critter by hand (they have sharp teeth and claws). Sometimes compacting the soil in your yard will make moles go elsewhere.

Boring Woodpeckers

Q. *The wood siding on our house has become a favorite spot for a family of woodpeckers. What can we do to discourage them from damaging our house?*

Woodpeckers peck to find food, create a home, and send messages to other woodpeckers. If your house has cedar or fir plywood siding, they're probably drilling for bees and insects inside. Plywood siding contains voids where insects live and where woodpeckers can easily reach them.

Woodpeckers are birds of habit and like to set up home in the same place. If their home in a tree was cut down or damaged, your house might be the closest place for a suitable new home.

The first thing you should do is to repair any existing damage to deter other woodpeckers from coming to check out the food source. To get rid of the ones already there, your best bet is to use scare tactics. Hang pie tins, strips of aluminum foil, or toy whirligigs a few inches out from the siding. You can also buy bird scare balloons at garden centers.

As a last resort, you could try lightly spraying the birds with a garden hose. Don't hurt them; they're protected by federal regulations.

A bird scare balloon should keep unwanted woodpeckers from boring into your siding.

A Rodent-Free House

Q. *On occasion, we have seen and heard mice, squirrels, and bats in our attic. How do we make them leave and never come back?*

Mice, squirrels, bats, and raccoons would prefer to live in a house where it's warm and safe, just like you. When these critters show up in your home without an invitation, you need to evict them right away.

Catch a mouse as soon as you see or suspect one. Place two snap-traps side by side, because a mouse can't jump over more than one trap at a time. You can reuse a mousetrap, too. If you prefer, use a bait station and poison block. Be aware that when a mouse dies from poisoning, it crawls off and dies somewhere in your house, leaving a nasty odor for a few days afterward.

If you can be sure there are no squirrels in the attic, block off all openings so they cannot come back. If the squirrel is in the attic, use a live trap with bait (peanut butter on a cracker works well). Wear heavy gloves when you release the squirrel.

Let a pest control worker remove a raccoon from your home (often they set up camp in the chimney). Raccoons are smart and dangerous. As for bats, just open the window, close the door, and let them fly out. Bats want to get out of your house as badly as you want them to.

Here are some tips to keep rodents out of your house:
- Trim all branches 8 to 10 feet from the house so animals cannot jump from a tree to the roof.
- Install a chimney cap and secure it tightly to keep raccoons from setting up residency.
- Fix damaged screens in roof, soffit, and gable vents.
- Keep bird feeders 15 feet from the house; store birdseed and pet food in sealed containers.
- Keep the woodpile away from the house; mice can start families in it and then decide to move into your house.
- Seal around dryer vents and other gaps in the foundation and siding.

Set snap traps with the bait end against the wall. Wear gloves when you dispose of a dead mouse; then reuse the trap.

Use bait stations to poison mice. Mice eat the poison, then crawl off to die. Keep these away from children and pets.

To capture a squirrel, use a live trap. Check the cage daily and release the squirrel as soon as possible.

Snakes in the House

Q. *How can I keep garter snakes out of my house?*

Getting rid of a few garter snakes is pretty easy—just remove their homes, their food, and their favorite places to hang out. Reduce their feed supply by cutting your lawn short to control the grasshopper population. Clean up brush piles and other cool, dark places, and plug all holes in your foundation that are larger than ¼ inch to eliminate nesting sites. If you know where the snakes like to sun themselves, surround the area with flypaper strips laid end-to-end—they hate the stickiness.

By no means should you try to kill the snakes; they help take care of other pests and are protected in most states. If you really can't tolerate any more snakes around your house, build a snake fence from hardware cloth that extends 6 inches below ground. Snake fences are sometimes used around children's play areas in parts of the country with poisonous snakes.

Lawn and Garden

Ants in the Kitchen

Q. *I have ants in my kitchen that keep coming back. How can I get rid of them safely and permanently?*

Try a simple remedy first, like ant traps; or sprinkle bonemeal or powdered charcoal around the foundation to act as an ant fence. Washing your countertops, cabinets, and floor with vinegar and water will remove the scent trails ants use to lead others back to the food source.

Some people claim that bay leaves discourage ants. Put sweet and greasy foods in sealed containers, don't stack firewood against the house, and caulk small openings.

If all else fails, you'll have to find and destroy the colony. Locate the nest by following the ants. Once it's found, drill a ¼-inch hole in the wall and shoot in ant killer dust labeled for indoor use. If you can't find the nest, call in a professional exterminator.

There are plenty of ant-repelling products available, including poisonous traps and home remedies; if you can find the nest, you can usually get rid of ants at the source with poison.

Moths in the Pantry

Q. *I occasionally find little moths in the rice and flour I keep in the pantry. How do they get in there, and how can I keep them out?*

Pantry, or meal, moths get into dry food like flour, cornmeal, beans, and dried fruit. They can also get into food-based decorations and holiday ornaments, bags of birdseed, and dog food. Believe it or not, a meal moth can even penetrate unopened plastic-wrapped food.

The solution is to toss the food into the trash or to kill the bugs by putting the food in the freezer for at least 4 days or heating it in a 130°F oven for 30 minutes. Pantry moths don't carry disease, so after picking out the dead moths and larvae, the food can still be used safely if you choose to. Store your food in well-sealed glass or heavy-plastic containers.

Safe, Effective Flea Killer

Q. *Flea collars don't work on our cats as well as I wish they did. Are there are any new strategies for long-term flea annihilation?*

There is now a very promising flea killer called Program. It's an oral medication (available from veterinarians) that goes into your pet's bloodstream and gets sucked up by the pesky fleas. The fleas are left infertile, and eventually the whole population dies off. Program is completely harmless to mammals, unlike other powerful flea killers.

Although fleas seem to live on your pet, they actually live where your pets sleep and hang out. When you treat your pet for fleas, treat these areas as well. Vacuum, then wash your pet's bedding in hot water.

Persistent Bees

Q. *Bees have been building hives in the walls of my home. The exterminator hasn't been able to get rid of them. What else can I do?*

It's possible that the insecticide that the exterminator used did not kill the queen bee. As long as the queen survives, she can continue to lay eggs and produce new worker bees.

Another possibility is that the exterminator is killing the bees but not removing the combs. If the combs remain and the entrance to the nest is not sealed, new bees will take over the old nest. You may need to cut into the wall to remove the combs.

Seal up holes and cracks around the outside of your home to prevent new bees (and other insects and rodents) from getting into the walls.

Paper Wasp Invasion

Q. *What's a good way to get rid of the wasps that are chewing on my cedar deck and siding?*

The wasps are probably paper wasps, which chew on wood in order to make a paperlike substance for nest building. Unless you can find and remove their nest, the wasps might be there to stay. They can be nesting anywhere up to a mile away from your house, even underground. If you find the nest, use an aerosol wasp killer to wipe them out; do this after dark, when the wasps are inactive. Kill individual wasps as you find them. The good news is that wasps die in the winter, so these particular wasps won't be back in the spring.

Safer Insecticides

Q. *I hate to use insecticides because of their potential danger. How do I know how toxic they are? Are there safer ones available?*

Not all insecticides are equally dangerous. Some, like hydroprene and fenoxycarb, are insect growth inhibitors; they mimic an insect hormone and disturb the development of the larvae into adults. These have not been found to harm mammals. Other insecticides, like boric acid, are harmless unless they're eaten. Among synthetic insecticides, pyrethrins have a lower toxicity than chlorpyrifos or diazinon.

Federal law requires that pesticides be labeled with one of these three words: "caution," "warning," or "danger." All pesticides can be dangerous if misused or ingested by children. Those labeled "danger" have the greatest toxicity; those with "caution" labels are the least harmful.

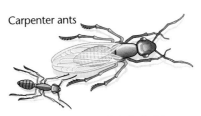

Termites

Carpenter ants

Termite or Carpenter Ant?

Q. *How can I tell the difference between a termite and a carpenter ant? How do I get rid of whatever type I have?*

Winged antlike bugs on your siding can spell trouble. A carpenter ant has a pronounced "waist," and back wings that are shorter than the front wings. If this is what you have, you can probably get rid of them yourself. Find the working ants, which are large and black, try to locate the nest, and use an insecticide labeled for carpenter ants. Then fix the moisture problem that was providing a good habitat for them.

If you think you might have termites, call a state-certified professional exterminator immediately. The inspection might cost $100, but you could be saving thousands of dollars on repairs. The exterminator's work should be guaranteed, and you should have your house inspected every couple of years after a treatment.

Sealing Out Pests

Q. *How do I keep mice and other pests from getting into my house during the winter?*

Spiders, mice, and other pests often enter homes around electrical or gas lines. Fill small gaps around utility lines with a good-quality latex caulk. Fill larger gaps with duct sealer. Look for duct sealer with the electrical supplies at a home center. To use it, just roll it into a "snake" and then press it in place.

Use duct sealer to seal off points where electrical and gas lines enter your home.

Not-So-Dear Deer

Q. *Every year, deer raid our flower and vegetable gardens. Is there a safe, humane way to keep these browsers at bay?*

Deer have a wide range of culinary tastes. It's a good idea to try to keep them out of your yard because they could be carrying the deer ticks that cause Lyme disease. An electric fence that gives them a little shock will teach them to stay away. Due to deer's leaping ability, any other type of fence must be at least 8 feet tall.

You can try surrounding your gardens with lemony- or minty-smelling foliage or with plants with sticky, hairy leaves and stems. You could also try a home brew by mixing 3 or 4 eggs in a gallon of water, then applying it to your plants with a garden sprayer. You won't notice the smell, but it will help keep deer away.

Outdoor Equipment

LAWN MOWERS

Mulch Mower Convert

Q. *Can I use a conversion kit to turn my old mower into a mulching mower?*

If you convert both your mower and your mowing habits, this kit can come close to doing as good a job of mulching as a new mulching lawn mower. Mulching cuts grass into tiny bits that decompose quickly and add nutrients to your soil. Mulching blade kits usually contain a specially designed blade and a chute blocking plate for containing the cuttings.

Since your engine will be working harder, it should be at least 5 horse-power to handle the extra load. You'll also have to cut more frequently. You should cut no more than the top one-third of the grass. Also, make sure the lawn is dry or the mower will quickly clog and stall.

A converter mulching blade kit with a chute blocking plate can mulch your grass very well if you change your mowing habits by mowing the grass more often and cutting only when the grass is dry.

Disappointing Mulch Mower

Q. *How can I get my new mulching mower to cut the lawn so that it's even and unmatted?*

Don't let the engine get bogged down by trying to cut too much grass at once. Mow only when the lawn is dry; if the grass is really long, cut it in two passes. Keep the mower blade sharp and the motor at full throttle.

The blade and deck on mulching mowers should be designed to channel the grass clippings from the outside edge of the blade toward the inside, where they get cut again. On some models, the manufacturer may have simply plugged the side discharge hole without adding any extra design features to provide a true mulching action. If this seems to be the case, see if you can return the mower for a refund.

Sharpening a Reel Mower

Q. *I bought an old reel-type lawn mower at a garage sale and have no idea how to sharpen it. Any tips?*

To sharpen a dull reel mower blade, apply valve grinding compound to each blade of the reel and then turn the reel backward so the blades sharpen themselves against the cutting bar. To turn the reel backward, remove the drive wheel and the small pinion gear behind it. Wrap the shaft in a rag, clamp the shaft with locking pliers, and rotate.

If the mower's blades are really dull, bring it to a lawn mower repair shop. You could also try a local golf course. Golf courses use gas-powered reel mowers and may be willing to sharpen yours for a small fee.

Mower Safety

Each summer, hospitals treat thousands of people who have been injured by lawn mowers. It's a good idea to read over these tips and brush up on lawn mower safety, especially if you plan to teach one of your kids to use a mower.

■ Know how to operate the equipment. Read the owner's manual and learn where all the controls are and what they do.

■ Never disable guards or other safety devices.

■ Dress properly. Wear heavy shoes, long pants, and close-fitting clothes.

■ Handle gas carefully. Store it in an approved container away from the house, flames or sparks, and children and pets. Don't smoke or fill the tank while the engine is hot or running.

■ Inspect the yard before you mow. Remove rocks, sticks, toys, and trash. Keep children and pets away.

■ Keep hands and feet away from the moving parts of the mower. Turn off the engine and disconnect the spark plug wire before attempting to unclog the mower or perform any maintenance. Turn the mower off if you need to leave it unattended, even for a minute.

■ For walk-behind mowers: Walk, don't run, and push the mower. Never pull the mower toward you; it could slip and hurt you. Don't mow wet grass. Mow across slopes, not up and down. Turn the mower off before removing a grass catcher.

SHARPENING A MOWER BLADE

It's actually quite easy to sharpen a mower blade because you don't need to get the blade razor-sharp, just sharp enough to cut cleanly instead of tearing the grass. However, if your blade has major dents in the cutting edge, it may make more sense to buy a replacement.

Before removing the blade, disconnect the spark plug. Turn the mower upside down. Wedge the blade into position with a 2 x 4. Grasp the blade with a gloved hand, and remove the bolts with a wrench. If a bolt sticks, tap the wrench with a hammer.

Inspect the blade (and the stiffener if the mower has one) for damage. Replace any damaged parts with new ones specified by the manufacturer. If the blade is bent, throw it out and get a replacement.

Secure the blade in a vise. Then use a medium-rough file to sharpen the blade along the original angle of each cutting edge, on opposing ends of the blade. File in one direction only—toward the edge. Try to remove equal amounts of metal from each edge.

To check if the blade is balanced, stick a screwdriver through the center hole and make sure the blade hangs horizontally. If the blade is not balanced, file metal off the tip of the heavy end. Don't file the newly sharpened cutting edge.

Once the blade is balanced, reinstall it, making sure that the lift wing on each end points up toward the deck of the mower. This will allow the blade to cut and discharge grass properly.

1 Wedge the blade in place with a 2 x 4 and remove bolts with a wrench.

2 Follow the original cutting angle. Draw the file toward the edge.

3 If you need to balance the blade, remove metal from the tip of the blade.

4 As you reinstall the blade, make sure the lift wings point toward the deck.

Riding Mower Maintenance

Q. *What can I do to keep my mower operating smoothly? I've had it for a few years.*

Begin with the engine. Change the oil, air filter, and spark plug. Drain any old fuel and fill the tank with fresh gas. Look for any debris under the flywheel cover and around the engine. Clean any corrosion off the terminals to the battery cable clamps with a battery terminal cleaning tool. Squirt a little oil on the throttle cable.

Now take a look at the chassis and cutting deck. Examine all belts for cracks and glazing (shiny surface), and replace them as needed. Raise the cutting deck and inspect each blade. If there is any back-and-forth movement in the spindle bearings and shafts, have it professionally repaired before you use the mower again. Clean the underside of the deck with a hose, and have the blades sharpened. Check the air pressure in the tires.

Check the safety features. The engine should not start if the transmission is in gear. The engine should also quit if you get off the seat while the blades are engaged. If either of these safety features doesn't work, have it checked immediately. The tractor should not be used until these problems are resolved.

Outdoor Equipment

TOOL REPAIR

New Handles for Old Shovels

Q. *Should I try to replace the handle on my spade-type shovel or just buy a new shovel?*

A good replacement handle for your shovel will cost just a few dollars. A replacement shovel will cost significantly more, unless you settle for a thin metal blade and a junk-wood handle. If the old blade is in good shape, it makes sense to replace the handle. Begin by using a hacksaw to cut off the head of the old rivet; then punch the old rivet out with a nail or nail set. Next use a small section of dowel to punch the broken handle from the socket.

Place the new handle in the socket, hold the tool vertically with the blade up, then rap the end of the handle down on a solid surface. This will help drive the blade and socket firmly onto the new handle. Then drill, install, and flatten the new rivet.

Cut off or drill out the old rivet; then use a piece of dowel to hammer out the broken handle.

Once the new handle is on, drill and install a new rivet. Use a ball-peen hammer to flatten the rivet.

Non-Feeding String Trimmer

Q. *Last week I used my string trimmer for the first time this season. It ran great, but the string wouldn't feed out automatically. What's the problem?*

The string advance system relies on centrifugal force to feed out the nylon line. This means that the spool must be free to turn when the head is bumped on the ground. The most likely problem is a dirty or worn spool. Here's what to do:

■ Disassemble the head assembly by unscrewing the spool retainer knob. Some units use two release clips on the sides of the head instead of a knob.

■ Remove the spool and check the amount of line on the spool. If it's more than three-quarters full, the head won't advance properly.

■ Clean all the parts, including the inside of the spool housing, with water and a stiff-bristle brush.

■ Now, install a new spool or wind new line onto the old spool. Don't twist or overlap the line as you wind it onto the spool, either of which can prevent the spool from advancing when the head is bumped.

■ Reassemble the spool and head assembly.

■ To test the unit, push in on the bump knob and pull on the line. The line should pull out about 1 inch and stop. Release the bump knob and another 1 inch of line should feed out.

If this doesn't fix the problem, you may need to replace the head, which could cost as much as a new trimmer.

SAFETY CHECK

Chipper-Shredders

The tremendous power—and appetite—of these machines makes them extremely dangerous. Read the manual, and bear these tips in mind:

■ When the instructions say to stay in the "safety zone," they mean it. Half-digested pieces of wood and debris are often kicked out through the chipper chute and shredding hopper.

■ Keep the machine on level ground, preferably a soft surface. They're noisier and more likely to move around on concrete or asphalt surfaces.

■ Watch what you feed your machine. Hidden rocks, wire, and steel stakes can dull cutters, damage drive-shafts, and harm you.

■ Never run a branch larger than what the manufacturer specifies through the chipper or shredder. And don't give the machine too much, too fast—overfeeding is the most common reason these machines bog or break down.

■ Wear goggles, a face shield, or safety glasses with side shields. Hearing protectors and gloves are other necessities.

■ Keep your arms perpendicular to the hopper and hold branches loosely, so your arms aren't pulled in.

■ Before changing the screen or cleaning out the machine, wait until the machine is completely stopped, then pull off the spark plug wire.

how is it done?

QUICK GARDEN HOSE FIXES

Don't toss out the garden hose just because one section or end is damaged. Resurrect it with easy-to-use splices and couplings.

You'll find one of at least three different types of couplings and splices at hardware stores: the clamp type, the clinch type, plus a type that's secured in place with automotive-type hose clamps. They all cost about the same, take 15 minutes to install, and can be secured using everyday hand tools.

ADDING A CLINCH FINGER COUPLING

1 To replace a damaged coupling, cut off the damaged end and insert the replacement coupling into the hose.

2 Use a hammer to lightly tap the clinch fingers until they bite into the hose.

SPLICING WITH A CLAMP COUPLING

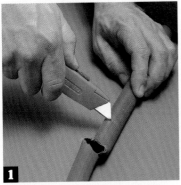

1 Cut out the damaged section with a utility knife. Keep cuts square, so the hose will squarely butt to the coupling.

2 Soak both cut ends of the hose in hot water for a minute or so to soften the material.

3 Install the splice: Push the coupling into each section of hose; then secure it in place with the external clamps.

Backflow Preventer

Q. *I applied liquid fertilizer to my lawn using a dispenser that screwed to the end of the hose. The instructions said I should use this only if my outside spigot was equipped with a backflow preventer. What is it, and how do I install one?*

Backflow, or antisiphon, devices aren't needed very often—but when they are, they're really needed. They prevent water, and any chemical in your hose, from backing up into the water system. Usually all the plumbing in your house is under positive pressure. But in the event of a huge water usage—such as when firefighters tap into a hydrant or a water main bursts—the plumbing can become negatively pressurized, sucking water out of your pipes and back into the drinking-water system. If that water contains fertilizers, it could contaminate the water in your area.

Most toilets, as well as outdoor spigots on newer homes, have built-in backflow preventers.

Attach antisiphon devices to outside spigots. Make sure the unit is designed to drain off any trapped water that could freeze, expand, and burst the spigot.

GRILLS

Cleaning Out the Grill

Q. *My gas grill is only a year old. When I tried to use it this spring, only half of the burners would light. Is it time for a replacement already?*

It sounds as if you have a clog somewhere in the venturi tube that feeds gas to your grill, or in the burner itself. (Spiders love to nest in the tubes; a small blockage can not only affect your grill's performance but also create a fire hazard.)

To clean a blocked grill, remove the burners and tubes from the gas valves. Push a venturi brush or pipe cleaner into each tube. Clean the outside of the burners with a wire brush and soapy water. Next, use a hose to flush water through the venturi tubes and burner. You can use a thick wire or pipe cleaner to clear the blocked burner ports.

Use your hose to flush out the venturi tube and burners and to identify any clogged ports.

Clean out clogged burner ports with a thick wire. Carefully inspect the burner for corrosion or split seams.

High-Temp Paint

Q. *I've been trying to repaint my barbecue grill, but nothing seems to stick. The paint keeps peeling and blistering. What should I do?*

Good prep work is the key to a long-lasting paint job. Clean the surface with a household degreaser, and if necessary, sand it clean. Next, paint the body of the grill with a high-temperature paint (sold at home centers and auto parts stores). Mask off the spots you don't want painted.

Running Out of Gas

Q. *It seems that my gas grill always runs out of fuel in the middle of a cookout. Is there an easy way to know in advance when it's time for a fill-up?*

If your grill doesn't have a built-in gauge, buy a stick-on type, available at most propane-refill stations. To activate the gauge, pour hot water on it; then watch its color. An orange gauge means empty; a yellow stripe indicates the level of fuel in the tank.

Testing the Tank

Q. *I want to be sure that my old grill is still safe to use. How can I test it for leaks?*

Any leak, no matter how small, can cause a fire where you don't want it. Inspect all gas connections by brushing the hose fittings and valves with a soap solution—1 part dish soap and 2 parts water. Watch for bubbles, which indicate leaks.

Updating your tank with a Type I adapter will make your propane grill safer and more convenient. Type I connections (supplied with most new grills) are designed to quickly disconnect the tank from the regulator in the event of a fire. They're also more convenient to use because you don't need a wrench to disconnect the tank for refueling.

To convert an old-style grill, you'll need a Type I adapter for your tank, and a replacement regulator with Type I threads.

Turn the grill on; then use a soapy water solution to check for gas leaks.

Updating your old grill with a Type I adapter will make it safer to use.

Storing a Snow Thrower

Q. *Should I drain the fuel from my two-stroke snow thrower and then run it until it quits before I put it away for the season? Or can should I add a fuel stabilizer and keep gas in the tank?*

How you store your snow thrower depends on what type of carburetor is on the engine. If yours has a diaphragm-type carburetor, which is square and boxy-looking, treat the fuel with a stabilizer and leave it in the tank. This fuel will keep the rubber diaphragm from drying out and cracking.

If your snow thrower has a float-feed style carburetor, which has a round fuel bowl on the bottom, drain the fuel.

You can dispose of the old gas by adding it to your car's gas tank. The small amount won't harm the car's engine.

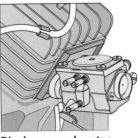

Diaphragm carburetor

Float-feed carburetor

SNOW THROWER PREP

When snow season hits, you'll want a snow thrower that you can count on. Here's how to revive your machine from its summer hibernation and make sure that it runs smoothly all winter long. If it's not too late, do all of these steps before the first snowfall.

■ Drain any leftover fuel from the tank. Old fuel turns gummy and can foul up the engine.
■ Change the engine oil in four-stroke engines (two-stroke engines use a gas and oil mixture). Consult your owner's manual for the recommended weight.
■ If your machine has rubber auger blades, check their thickness. If any are less than ¹⁄₁₆ inch thick, replace them.
■ If your snow thrower is a chain-driven type, get a spare chain master link and clip. Lubricate the chain for smoother operation.
■ Buy a few extra shear pins. If you hit a rock or good-size chunk of ice, you'll have to replace the pin. Without it, the auger won't turn.
■ Inspect the drive belts for glazing (shiny areas) and cracks.
■ If your machine has tire chains, check them for weak links or couplings. Buy a new set of chains, just in case.
■ Replace the fuel filter and air filter if they're disposable. If the air filter is foam, wash it in mild soapy water, rinse thoroughly, let dry, and then reinstall.
■ Apply wax to the auger and the inside of the discharge chute. The wax keeps the snow from sticking.

Sluggish Snow Thrower

Q. *My single-stage snow thrower won't throw snow as far as it did earlier this winter. What can I do to restore the original power?*

Most single-stage snow throwers have a fixed engine speed, so you may be able to identify a change in the machine's performance simply by listening to the engine. If the engine is running slower than it used to, the auger will also run slower. Try changing the spark plug first.

Another potential problem is the drive belt. The belt transfers power from the engine to the auger. If the belt is glazed (shiny where it rubs on the pulleys) or cracked, it's time to replace it. Check the idler pivot arm to be sure it's applying pressure to the back (flat) side of the belt.

Next, check the clearance between the auger and top of the scraper blade. Here are the proper clearances:

■ ⅛ to ¼ inch between the rubber flightings on the auger and the scraper blade
■ up to ½ inch between the rubber flightings and the housing

Adjust the flightings for the proper clearances. If they're not adjustable, you'll need to replace the flightings.

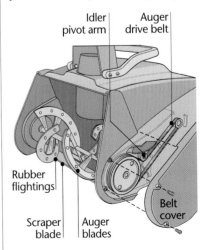

Idler pivot arm

Auger drive belt

Rubber flightings

Scraper blade

Auger blades

Belt cover

Index

A

ABS (acrylonitrile butadiene styrene) plastic pipe, 194, 200, 201
Acrylic paint, 140, 147
Adapter plug, 235
Adhesive
  removing, 223
  tile, 45, 46, 49
  See also Glue
Aerator, 215
Air
  booster fan, 281
  cleaner, 294
  filter, 279, 294
  leak, 272, 274–275, 278
  quality, 294–297
  sprayer, 31
Air conditioning
  central, 277, 280, 288–289
  cleaning, 288–289
  window, 288–289
Air-driven nail, 165
Airless sprayer, 31
Air pollution, 294–297
Al/Cu connector, 236
Alkyd paint, 33, 140
Alligator crack, 27
Aluminum
  gutter, 116
  ladder, 141, 144–145
  patio door, 128
  screen door, 120
  siding, 105, 145
  storm door, 133
  window, 124
  wiring, 236
American Society of Home Inspectors (ASHI), 180
Angle, 172, 173
Angle square, 177
Ants, 364–365
Antique(s)
  finishing, 328, 334
  mirror, 336
Antisiphon devices, 369
Aquarium heater, 202
Arbor post, 352
Argon-filled window, 126

Asbestos
  ceiling, 25
  flooring, 69
  shingles, 105, 145
Ashes, 284
ASHI. *See* American Society of Home Inspectors
Asphalt
  over concrete, 345
  repairing, 344
  shingles, 112–113
Attic
  bypasses, 274
  insulation, 268, 271
  moisture in, 299
  rodents in, 363
  storage, 186
  vapor barrier, 268, 299
  vents, 268, 271, 290–291, 292
Auger
  closet, 203
  power, 354
  snow thrower, 371
Auto-body filler, 134
Aviation snips, 276, 277, 315

B

Back-cutting joint, 99
Back draft, 286, 295
Backflow preventer, 369
Back support belt, 179
Bait station, 363
Ballast, 244, 249
Ball-style faucet, 217
Baluster, 78
Band clamp, 311
Band saw, 306
Bar clamp, 311
Bark, 346
Baseboard, 70, 73, 74
Base cabinet, 89
Basement(s)
  floor, 33, 153
  moisture in, 153, 154, 301
  remodeling, 182–185
  steel studs, 182–183
  toilet, 204
  walls, 22, 154

  waterproofing, 155
  windows, 184–185
Basket strainer, 212
Bat (animal), 363
Bathroom
  fan, 290–291
  plumbing, 194–195
  sink, 203, 215
  tile, 44, 45, 46, 48, 50–53
  See also Shower; Toilet
Bathtub
  drains, 210–211
  faucets, 214
  fiberglass, 224
  grab bar, 51
  porcelain, 222
  replacing, 224–225
  rust stains, 223
  surround, 224
Battery
  cordless drill, 322, 323
  nickel-cadmium, 322, 323
Bay window, 189
Beam(s)
  notches in, 236
  sizing, 157
  structural, 156–157, 159
  weight on, 159
Bearing wall, 158
Bees, 364
Belt sander, 320, 321
Bench grinder, 325
Bench-top table saw, 177, 316
Bench-top tools, 306
Bermuda grass, 356
Bifold door, 87
Bimetal blade, 314
Bird scare balloon, 362
Bit(s)
  carbide-tipped, 319
  drill, 313, 319
  router, 312, 319
  spade, 313
  steel, 319
Blade(s)
  bimetal versus steel, 314
  carbide-tipped, 312
  mower, 366, 367
  thin-kerf, 316

Bleaching, 332
Block plane, 177
Block(s)
  patio, 343
  sanding, 321, 335
  squeeze, 346
  stop, 322
Blown-in insulation, 266, 273
Board(s)
  cement, 46, 47
  cutting, 92, 94
  deck, 346, 348, 349
  dimensions, 161
  oriented strand, 162
  toenailing, 174
Boiler, 276
Bookcase, 98
Booster fan, 281
Bottle jack, 178
Bowed lumber, 160
Box nail, 164, 165
Brad-point drill bit, 313
Braided tube, 197
Brick(s)
  chalky, 106
  drywall and, 12
  mortar joints, 107
  painting, 146
  paint removal from, 149
  siding, 106–107
  thin, 106
  whitewashed, 142
British Thermal Units (Btu's), 278
Brush(es)
  cleaning, 37
  finishing, 330, 333
  paint, 140
  wire, 148, 337
Brush mark, 34
Btu's. See British Thermal Units
Bubble
  in joint tape, 18
  in polyurethane finish, 333
  in wallpaper, 38
Bucket, 18
Bug, in dishwasher, 258

Building code, 180, 181, 206
Building inspector, 195
Building permit, 355
Built-in ironing board, 187
Built-in shelving, 98
Bulb. *See* Light bulb
Bullnose tile, 44
Bungee cord, 311
Burn
    in carpet, 65
    in laminate, 97
Burner
    electric, 255
    gas, 370
Butt joint, 16

C

Cabinet(s)
    base, 89
    carpeting under, 98
    doors, 94
    drawers, 94
    finish, 92
    framed versus frameless, 88
    hinges, 92
    installing, 88–91
    kitchen, 36, 88–91
    metal, 36
    painting, 36
    pulls, 92
    renewing, 92–93
    repairing, 94
    stock, 88
    wall, 90–91
    wood, 36
    See also Countertop(s)
Cable
    coaxial, 232
    electrical box, 237–241, 243, 247
    nonmetallic, 242
    steel armored, 232
Canvas lining paper, 27
Cap molding, 76
Carbide-tipped bit, 319
Carbide-tipped blade, 312
Carbon filter, 220

Carbon monoxide
    detector, 295
    from furnace, 279
    preventing, 296
Carpenter ants, 365
Carpenter's pencil, 171
Carpentry
    measuring and marking, 172–173
    nailing, 174–175
    tape measures, 170–171, 176
    tools, 176–177
Carpets and carpeting
    burns, 65
    cabinets over, 98
    concrete under, 62
    glue, 60
    indentations, 65
    installing, 62–63
    pads, 62
    pet odor, 64
    seams, 62
    snags, 65
    stains, 64
    tears, 65
    thick, 65
    at threshold, 62
    wall-to-wall, 63
    wear, 64
Car roof rack, 163
Cartridge faucet, 216
Casement window, 118, 137
Casing, 70
Cathedral ceiling, 169
Cat's paw, 177
Caulk and caulking
    attic bypasses, 274
    ceramic tile, 52
    gun, 176
    joists, 271
    plumbing fixtures, 223
    technique, 274
Caustic chemical, 208
Caustic stripper, 29
CCA. *See* Chromated copper arsenate
C-clamp, 311
Cedar
    decks, 350

fence posts, 352
    odor, 76
    shakes, 114
    shingles, 103, 114
Ceiling(s)
    box, 245
    cathedral, 169
    concrete, 24
    drywall, 12, 24
    fans, 250–251
    framing, 169
    insulation, 268
    plaster, 24
    streaks on, 26
    textured, 24–25, 26
Cellulose, 266, 268, 273
Cement
    hydraulic, 154
    tile backing, 46, 47
Central air conditioning, 277, 280, 288–289
Central heating, 280
Ceramic tile
    adhesives, 45, 46
    bathroom, 44, 45, 46, 48, 50–53
    caulk, 52
    cement board under, 46, 47
    chipped, 52
    choosing, 44
    cleaning, 52
    concrete mortar bed under, 45, 46, 47
    countertops, 45, 96
    cutting, 50
    floor, 44, 46, 48, 50
    grout, 45, 52–53
    installing, 48
    installing underlayment, 46–47
    layout, 44
    over old tile, 45
    painting, 33
    planning work, 44–45
    plastic laminate and, 45
    removing paint from, 29
    replacing damaged, 53
    sliding, 49
    tools, 45

wall, 44, 48–49
Chair
    rocking, 336
    wobbly, 337
Chair rail, 70, 73
Chalk
    colors, 172
    line, 173, 177
Chemical drain cleaner, 208
Chemical paint remover.
    See Chemical stripper
Chemical stripper, 28, 29
Child safety
    balusters, 78
    buckets, 18
    lead, 196
Chime, 253
Chimney, 284, 285, 286–287
Chipper-shredder, 368
Chipping, avoiding with router, 318
Chips, repairing, 222
Chisel, 177, 312
Chopsaw, 177
Chromated copper arsenate (CCA), 347
Chrome-plated copper tube, 197
Circuit breaker, 230–231, 234
Circuit tester, 232, 233
Circular saw, 177, 312, 315, 343
Clamp
    coupling, 369
    glue joint, 326
    woodworking, 311
Clamshell-style digger, 354
Cleaning
    air conditioner, 288–289
    ceramic tile, 52
    copper roof, 115
    deck, 348
    drain, 208
    fireplace, 284
    graffiti, 149
    grill, 370
    paint, 149
    paintbrushes, 37
    pipe, 198

Index

Cleaning (continued)
  power tools, 318
  roller, paint, 37
  router, 318
  vinyl siding, 104
  wall, 26
Clear finish, 329, 330–331
Climate, 272, 273
Clinching nail, 175
Clog
  aerator, 215
  pipe, 208–209
  shower head, 219
  sink sprayer, 214
  toilet, 203
Closer (storm door), 134
Closet
  cedar, 76
  shelves, 98, 186
  space, 186
Closet auger, 203
Clothes dryer. *See* Dryer
Clothes washer.
  See Washing machine
Coaxial cable, 232
Color-coded snip, 277, 315
Color-rendering index
  (CRI), 249
Column, decorative, 188
Combustion, 332
Compact fluorescent
  lighting, 248, 249
Compost, 359
Compound(s)
  glazing, 118
  joint, 17–18, 26, 27
  pipe, 196
Compression set, 308
Compressor, 288–289
Concrete
  asphalt over, 345
  carpeting over, 62
  ceilings, 24
  fiber-reinforced, 345
  floors, 185, 273, 299
  foundations, 158
  holes in, 343
  paving, 340–343, 345
  pouring, 340–341
  reinforced, 345

  sidewalk, 341, 342
  staining, 33
  sunken, 342
  tile over, 45, 46, 47
  walkway, 340–341
  walls, 185
  white powder on, 153
  wood floor over, 56, 58
Condensation
  cures, 300–301
  interior, 298
  metal, 301
  new-house, 299
  skylight, 121
  window, 123, 300, 301
  See also Moisture
Conduction, 126
Contact lens, 31
Contractor, 180
Control joint, 341
Cope joint, 74
Copper
  gutter, 116
  pipe, 196–199
  roof, 115
  tube, 197
  wiring, 236
Cord, of wood, 282
Cordless drill, 177, 322, 323
Cork, 69
Corner(s)
  angles, 172
  baseboard, 73
  bead, 17–18
  drywall, 14, 15, 17–18, 20,
    74
  miter joints, 71, 72
  paint in, 29
  taping inside, 17
  wallpaper, 43
Cornice molding, 70
Corrugated gas connector,
  254
Countertop(s)
  ceramic tile, 45, 96
  edge, 95
  installing, 89–90
  laminate, 45, 95, 96–97
  materials, 96–97
  repairing, 95

  solid surface, 96
  stone, 97
CPVC (chlorinated
  polyvinyl chloride)
  plastic pipe, 200, 201
Crack(s)
  alligator, 27
  door, 34
  drywall, 21
  foundation, 152
  plaster, 24
  stucco, 103
Crawl space
  insulation, 270
  moisture in, 154
Creosote, 287
CRI. *See* Color-rendering
  index
Crooked studs, 160
Crown, chimney, 286–287
Crown molding, 70, 75, 76
Crystalline waterproofing
  material (CWM), 155
Cultured marble, 223
Cumulative Trauma
  Disorders, 178
Cup-and-gun sprayer, 31
Cupping, of lumber, 161
Curved wall, 15, 167
Cutting
  ducts, 277
  large circle, 315
  machine threads, 314
  metal, 315
  with router, 315, 319
  splinter-free, 314
  See also Saw
Cutting board, 92, 94
CWM. *See* Crystalline water
  proofing material
Cylinder lock, 136

D

Damper
  fireplace, 281, 285
  forced-air system, 280
Danish oil, 334
DBE. *See* Diabasic ester
Deadbolt, 133, 135, 136, 137

Dead load, 156, 159
Deadman. *See* T-brace
Deck
  boards, 346, 348, 349
  cleaning, 348
  converting to porch,
    190–191
  decay, 348
  finishes, 350–351
  "fuzzy," 350
  joists, 175, 346
  posts, 178
  sealing, 348, 350
Deer, 365
Dehumidifier, 299, 301
Dent, in metal door, 134
Detergent
  dishwasher, 208
  washing machine, 261
Diabasic ester (DBE), 328
Dielectric fitting, 196
Dimensional lumber, 160,
  161
Dimmer switch, 242, 243
Direct-vent gas fireplace,
  283
Dishwasher
  adding, 259
  bugs in, 258
  detergent, 208
  installing, 259
  stopping, 259
  sudsy, 258
  wiring, 258
Disposer, garbage, 208
Diverter valve, 218
Dog run, 355
Doorbell, 252–253
Doorknob, 84
Door(s)
  cabinet, 94
  chimes, 253
  cracks, 34
  drywall around, 15
  hollow-core, 81, 86, 137
  left-handed reverse, 80
  locks, 80, 84, 133,
    135–137
  painting edges, 35
  peephole, 137

refrigerator, 256–257
right-handed, 80
screen, 120
sliding glass, 132, 137
storm, 133, 134
sweeps, 275
trim, 49
See also Exterior door(s);
    Hinge; Interior door(s)
Dormer, 189
Double duplex outlet, 234
Double-pane window, 127
Downdraft, 286
Draft(s)
    back, 286, 295
    chimney, 286
    skylight, 121
Drain
    bathtub, 210–211
    cleaner, 208
    overflow, 212
    shower, 210
    sink, 210, 212–213
    stopper, 210–211, 212,
      213
    waste, 194
Drill
    alignment, 323
    bit, 313
    chuck, 323
    cordless, 322, 323
    press, 320, 323
    stop block, 322
    switch, 322
    variable-speed, 176
Driveway
    moss, 345
    paving, 343, 344–345
    sealers, 344
Drop-down stopper, 212
Drum sander, 320
Drum trap, 211
Dryer
    ink-stained drum, 262
    inspecting, 263
    non-spinning, 262
    venting, 262, 263
Drywall
    bending, 15
    buying, 12

ceilings, 12, 24
compound, 17–18
corners, 14, 15, 17–18, 20,
    74
cracks, 21
cutting, 14
electrical outlets and, 16
hanging, 13–14
holes in, 21
installing, 12–15
jack, 13–14
joint, 16, 20, 22
materials, 17–18, 20
moisture-resistant, 12
nails versus screws, 12,
    20
repairing, 20–21
rust stains, 14
sanding, 18–19, 26
taping, 16–19
tile backing, 47
Dry well, 154
Duct
    booster fan, 281
    heating, 276–277, 281
    insulation, 271
Duct sealer, 365
Duct tape, 276
Duplex outlet, 234
Dust
    lead paint, 27
    mask, 305
    workshop, 307
Dustless sander, 19

E

Easy Out screw extractor,
    215
"Eating an inch," 170, 171
Elastic tie-down, 163
Elastomeric paint, 146, 147
Electrical box, 237–241,
    243, 258, 271, 291
Electrical grounding. *See*
    Grounding
Electrical mast, 110
Electrical outlet. *See*
    Outlet(s)

Electrical overload, 231,
    234, 239
Electrical safety, 230,
    234–235
Electrical switch. *See*
    Switch
Electrical wiring. *See* Wires
    and wiring
Electric drill. *See* Drill
Electric fence, 365
Electrician's pliers, 314
Electric range/stove, 255
Electric screw gun, 12, 182
Electric water heater, 226
Electronic air cleaner, 294
Electrostatic filter, 279, 294
Electrostatic spray-painting,
    36
Enamel paint, 33, 148, 335
Enamel sink, 221
Encapsulated insulation,
    267
Energy efficiency
    audit, 269
    fireplace, 282, 283
    light bulb, 249
    window, 126–127
Energy Policy Act (EPACT),
    249
Engineered wood, 162
EPACT. *See* Energy Policy
    Act
Epoxy
    wood glue, 326, 327
    wood trim, repairing, 109
"European-style" cabinet, 88
Evaporator coil, 289
Exploded-tip brush, 333
Extension cord, 177, 234,
    310
Extension ladder, 144
Extension spring, 138
Exterior door(s)
    installing, 128–131
    left-handed reverse, 80
    metal, 134
    patio, 128, 132, 134
    repairing, 132–134
    replacing entry door,
      130–131

security, 135–137
steel, 133, 138, 148, 149
storm door, 133, 134
threshold gasket, 132
tips on buying, 129
weatherstripping, 132,
    275
See also Deadbolt;
    Garage door
Exterior lighting, 137
Exterior paint, 30, 140
Exterior trim, 108–109, 141
Exterior wall, 191
Exterminator, 364, 365

F

Face-frame cabinet, 88
Face shield, 305
Fan
    air booster, 281
    bathroom, 290–291
    ceiling, 250–251
Fastener, hollow-wall, 23
Faucet
    ball-style, 217
    bathroom, 215
    bathtub, 214
    cartridge, 216
    kitchen, 214, 221
    leaky, 216–217
    pressure-balancing, 218
    sand in, 215
    sink, 214, 221
    slow-flowing, 214, 215
    spout, 214
    washer, 214–217
Feathering, of board, 346
Felt, 110
Fence(s)
    electric, 365
    long-bed, 316
    maintenance, 355
    posts, 352, 353, 354
    rusty, 353
    surveyor for, 352
Ferrule, 116
Fiberboard, 72, 97, 309
Fiberglass
    air filter, 279

Index

Fiberglass (continued)
  bathtub, 224
  insulation, 267, 270, 271
  lining paper, 27
  water heater blanket, 227
Fiber-reinforced concrete, 345
Filler
  auto-body, 134
  wood, 335
  See also Insulation
Filter
  air, 279, 294
  water, 220
Finishes and finishing
  antiques, 328, 334
  brushes, 330, 333
  cabinets, 92
  clear, 329, 330–331
  concrete, 33
  decks, 350–351
  furniture, 328, 331, 334
  garage door, 149
  lacquer, 92
  oil, 330
  particleboard, 328
  peeling, 142
  pine, 329
  polyurethane, 329, 330–331, 333
  problems, 332–333
  reviving natural, 35
  semi-transparent, 351
  shellac, 331, 332
  translucent multicoat, 351
  water-base, 332, 333
  wood floor, 60–61
  See also Varnish
Fire extinguisher, 297
Fireplace(s)
  cleaning, 284
  dampers, 281, 285
  direct-vent gas, 283
  energy efficiency, 282, 283
  inserts, 283
  no-vent, 285
  smoke, 285, 286
Fire-resistant drywall, 12

Fire safety, 187, 292, 297
Fixed-base router, 318
Fixed stopper, 212
Flagged brush, 333
Flagpole, 354
Flange, 207
Flapper
  foam seal, 275
  toilet, 204, 206
Flashing, 110, 112
Flat paint, 141, 149
Flea killer, 364
Flexible corrugated gas connector, 254
Flexible plastic tube, 197
Flip-up elements (electric range), 255
Floating laminate floor, 55, 57
Floors and flooring
  basement, 33, 153
  bouncy, 168
  concrete, 185, 273, 299
  cork, 69
  dew-covered, 299
  framing, 168
  hardwood, 54, 56, 60, 61
  insulation between, 268
  joists, 156, 168
  laminate, 55
  marble, 69
  parquet, 55, 59
  slate, 69
  tile, 44, 46, 48, 50
  See also Vinyl floor; Wood floor
Floor-to-ceiling bookshelf, 98
Flue, 286, 287
Fluorescent lighting, 244, 248, 249
Flux, 198
Foam
  flapper seal, 275
  insulation, 236, 267, 270
Foil-faced insulation, 266
Folding door, 87
Forced-air system, 280
Formaldehyde foam insulation, 267

Foundation
  concrete, 158
  cracked, 152
  leaky, 152, 154
  repair, 152–153
  See also Basement(s)
Four-in-one screwdriver, 176
Frame chair, 337
Framed cabinet, 88
Frame joint, 321
Frameless cabinet, 88
Framing. *See* House framing
Framing anchor, 346
Framing square, 176
Freezer, 256–257
French patio door, 128
French pocket door, 86
Freon refrigerant, 257
Frozen glue, 327
Frozen pipe, 197
Furnace
  filter, 279
  flue liner, 287
  inspection, 279
  noisy, 280
  sizing, 278
  wasted heat, 276
Furniture
  finishing, 328, 331, 334
  indents in carpet, 65
  painting, 335
  repairing, 336–337
  See also specific types of furniture
Fuse, 230–231

G

Gable
  dormer, 189
  vent, 292
Galvanized pipe, 196
Garage door
  choosing, 138
  opener, 136, 137, 138–139
  painting, 148
  springs, 138
  steel, 138
  tune-up, 139

  varnish, 149
  wood, 138, 138
Garage fire, 292
Garbage disposal, 208
Garden
  deer in, 365
  soil, 356
Garden hose, 369
Garter snake, 363
Gas
  boiler, 276
  connector, 254
  direct-vent fireplace, 283
  grill, 370
  leak, 370
  stove, 254–255
  vent-free heater, 285
  water heater, 229
Gasket, 132
Gate, 354
GFCI. *See* Ground fault circuit interrupter
Gingerbread trim, 108
Glass
  insulated, 127
  low-E, 123, 126
  sliding door, 132
  window, 118, 123, 126, 127
Glasses, safety, 305
Glazing compound, 118
Glue
  carpet, 60
  on edges, 326
  excess, 326
  frozen, 327
  gaps, 326
  joints, 326, 336, 337
  plastic pipe, 201
  polyurethane, 327
  wood, 326, 327
  yellow versus white, 327
  See also Adhesive
Glue-down laminate, 55
Glue-laminated lumber, 157
Goggles, 305
Gouge, 334
Grab bar, 51
Graffiti, 149

Grass
  Bermuda, 356
  clippings, 359
  See also Lawn
Grease, 334
Grill, 370
Grinder, 324–325
Grit, 321
Groove-joint pliers, 176
Ground fault circuit
    interrupter (GFCI),
    232–235, 238, 240–241,
    290
Grounding
  ceiling fan, 251
  outlet, 233, 235, 238
  supply pipe, 232
  wire, 232–235, 237–241
Ground-source heat pump,
    277
Grout, 45, 52–53
Gutter(s)
  aluminum, 116
  choosing, 116
  copper, 116
  installing, 116–117
  leaks, 116
  sagging, 116
  sealant, 112, 116
  seamless, 116
  steel, 116
  vinyl, 116, 117
Gypsum, 356

H

Hacksaw, 315
Half wall, 166
Halogen lighting, 244, 248,
    249
Hammer, 176, 310
Handle
  hammer, 310
  shovel, 368
Handrail, 35, 78
Handsaw, 176, 312
Hand screw, 311
Handyman jack, 178
Hardwood
  floor, 54, 56, 60, 61

thickness, 309
Hearing protection, 304
Heat and heating
  central, 280
  chimney, 285, 286–287
  duct, 276–277, 281
  exchanger, 276
  forced-air system, 280
  furnace, 276, 278–280,
    287
  pump, 276–277
  register, 278
  thermostat, 278, 281
  wasted, 276
  woodstove, 284
  See also Fireplace(s);
    Heater
Heater
  aquarium, 202
  vent-free gas, 285
  See also Water heater
Heat gun, 28, 142
Heavy lifting, 178–179
HEPA. *See* High-efficiency
    particulate air cleaner
Herbicide, 356
High-efficiency particulate
    air cleaner (HEPA),
    294
High-gloss paint, 33, 141,
    148, 149
High-volume low-pressure
    (HVLP) sprayer, 31
Hi-lift. *See* Handyman jack
Hinge
  cabinet, 92
  door, 80, 82, 83, 84, 129
  garage door, 139
Hipped dormer, 189
Hitch knot, 162, 163
Hollow-core door, 81, 86,
    137
Hollow-wall fastener, 23
Home inspector, 180, 181
Homeowner's insurance,
    180
Horsepower, 325
Hose, 369
House framing, 160–169
  ceilings, 169

floors, 168
nails, 164–165
trim screws, 164
walls, 166–167
See also Lumber
Housepainting
  aluminum siding, 145
  ladder, 141, 144–145
  surface preparation,
    142–143
  tools, 140–141
  wood siding, 140
  See also Paint
House structure
  beams, 156–157
  bearing walls, 158
  common problems, 181
  loads, 156, 159
  settling, 156
Housewrap, 272
Humidity, 298–299, 300, 301
HVLP sprayer. *See* High-
    volume low-pressure
    (HVLP) sprayer
Hydraulic cement, 154
Hydraulic jack, 178
Hydraulic ram, 209

I

I-beam,
  joist, 236
  wood, 156, 162
Ice dam(s)
  detecting, 112
  melting, 113
  membrane, 111
  preventing, 113, 115, 116
Idler pulley, 262
Incandescent bulb, 248, 249
Induction motor, 324–325
In-floor safe, 187
Insecticide, 365
Instant water heater. *See*
    Tankless water heater
Insulated glass, 127
Insulation
  attic, 268, 271
  between-floor, 268
  blown-in, 266, 273

ceiling, 268
cellulose, 266, 268, 273
crawl space, 270
duct, 271
encapsulated, 267
fiberglass, 267, 270, 271
foam, 236, 267, 270
foil-faced, 266
glass, 127
porch, 191
recessed lighting around,
    246
settled, 273
types of, 266–267
upgrading, 268–269
wall, 266, 271, 273
window, 271
Insurance, 180
Interior door(s)
  binding, 82
  folding, 87
  frame, 83
  hinge, 80, 82, 83, 84
  installing, 80–81
  knob, 84
  latch, 83
  pocket, 86
  rattling, 85
  removing, 83
  repairing, 82–86
  sagging, 85
  self-closing, 82
Interior storm window, 122
Ironing board, 187

J

Jack
  drywall, 13–14
  handyman, 178
  hydraulic, 178
Jamb, 130–131
  extension, 124
  liner, 119
J-bead, 12
Jigsaw, 177
Joint(s)
  back-cutting, 99
  compound, 17–18, 26, 27,
    196

Joints (continued)
  control, 341
  cope, 74
  drywall, 16, 20, 22
  frame, 321
  glue, 326, 336, 337
  lead, 196
  mid-wall, 74
  miter, 71, 72
  mortar, 107
  pipe, 196
  plaster, 22
  tape, 16–19
Joist(s)
  caulking, 271
  deck, 175, 346
  floor, 156, 168
  hanger, 346
  I-beam, 236

K

Key box, 135
Kickback, table saw, 316
Kitchen
  ants in, 364
  cabinets, 36, 88–91
  sink, 210, 212, 214,
    220–221
  wood floor, 56
  work triangle, 188
  See also Countertop(s);
    specific appliances
Knife
  putty, 176, 335
  sharpening, 313
Knot, in lumber, 161
Knot, rope, 162, 163

L

Lacquer finish, 92
Ladder
  aluminum, 141, 144–145
  buying, 141
  extension, 144
  housepainting, 141,
    144–145
  roof, 111
  stepladder, 141, 145, 176

wooden, 141
Laminated veneer lumber
    (LVL), 157
Laminate(s)
  burns on, 97
  floating, 55, 57
  floor, 55, 57
  glue-down, 55
  lumber, 157
  plastic, 45, 96–97
  scratched, 95
Landscape shading, 360
Latch plate, 83, 133, 135,
    137
Latex paint, 31, 32, 33, 140,
    141, 145, 147, 148
Latex stain, 350, 351
Lathe, 306
Laundry tub, 212
Lawn
  Bermuda grass in, 356
  road salt on, 356
  sod, 357
  soil, 356
Lawn mower, 366–367
Lead
  joints, 196
  in paint, 27, 142
  safety, 27, 142, 196
  in water, 220
Leak(s)
  air, 272, 274–275, 278
  basket strainer, 212
  drain, 210, 212
  faucet, 216–217
  foundation, 152, 154
  gas grill, 370
  gutter, 116
  pipe, 199
  roof, 110, 115
  skylight, 121
  washing machine, 261
Left-handed reverse door,
    80
Level, 172, 176
Lever, 118
Lifting, 178–179
Light bulb, 242, 245,
    248–249
Lightning rod, 232

Lights and lighting
  buzzing/humming, 242,
    244, 249
  exterior, 137
  fixtures, 242, 244–245
  flickering, 230
  fluorescent, 244, 248, 249
  halogen, 244, 248, 249
  motion detector, 137, 252
  pull string, 242
  recessed, 246–247
  track, 245
  undercabinet, 244
  See also Switch
Lining paper, 27
Linseed oil, 332
Lint, 263
Liquid hide glue, 327, 337
Liquid sander, 320
Live load, 156, 159
Load-bearing wall, 158
Lock
  cylinder, 136
  deadbolt, 133, 135, 136,
    137
  strike box, 136
Lockset, 80, 84, 136
Long-bed fence, 316
Loudness, 304
Low-E glass, 123, 126
LPW. *See* Lumen per watts
Lumber
  buying, 160–161
  core, 309
  dimensional, 160, 161
  hauling, 162–163
  laminated, 157
  pressure-treated, 347
  sizes, 160
  See also Board(s)
Lumen, 248
Lumen per watts (LPW),
    249
LVL. *See* Laminated veneer
    lumber

M

Marble
  cultured, 223

floor, 69
Mask, 305
MDF. *See* Medium-density
    fiberboard
Measurement
  carpentry, 170–173
  horsepower, 325
  square footage, 180
  See also Tape measure
Medium-density fiberboard
    (MDF), 72, 309
Metal
  cabinet, 36
  condensation on, 301
  conduit, 232
  cutting, 315
  door, 134
  duct, 276, 277
  pipe, 196–199, 200
  roof, 115
Mildew, 299, 300
Mildewcide, 141, 299, 351
Mineral deposit, 196
Mineral mulch, 359
Mineral spirits, 334, 335
Mirror
  antique, 336
  hanging, 23
Miter box, 176
Miter gauge, 317
Miter joints, 71, 72, 74
Miter saw, 72, 74, 176, 177,
    306
Moisture
  in attic, 299
  in barriers, 272, 273
  in basement, 153, 154,
    301
  in crawl space, 154
  in mildew, 299, 300
  in patio door, 134
  in stucco, 146
  in wood, 308
  See also Condensation;
    Humidity
Moisture-resistant drywall,
    12
Mold, 298
Molding
  buying, 72

cap, 76
cornice, 70
crown, 70, 75, 76
picture, 71
Mole (animal), 362
Monument (surveyor's rod), 352
Mortar, 51, 107
Mortar bed, 45, 46, 47
Moss
    on driveway, 345
    on roof, 114
Moths, 364
Motion detector, 137, 252
Motor, power tool, 324–325
Mouse, 363
Mower. *See* Lawn mower
Mudjacking, 342
Mulch
    benefits of, 358
    maintenance, 358
    mineral, 359
    mower, 366
    organic, 359
Musty odor, 298

N

Nail(s)
    clinching, 175
    common, 165
    drywall, 12, 20
    finishing, 71, 174, 175
    house framing, 164–165
    popping, 20
    pulling, 174
    ridged types, 165
    roofing, 112, 113, 165
    siding, 102
    size, 164
    wood splitting, 175
Nail set, 174
National Fenestration Rating Council (NFRC), 126
National Fire Protection Association (NFPA), 284
Natural-bristle brush, 330
Net-free venting area (NFVA), 292

Newel post, 79
NFPA. *See* National Fire Protection Association
NFRC. *See* National Fenestration Rating Council
NFVA. *See* Net-free venting area
Nickel-cadmium battery, 322, 323
Noise, 304, 306
Non-bearing wall, 158, 188
No-vent fireplace, 285
No-wax vinyl floor, 69
Nuisance tripping, 246
Nylon strap, 163

O

Octopus plugs, 234
Odor(s)
    cedar, 76, 349
    musty, 298
    pet, 64
    pine, 349
    redwood, 349
    sulfur, 227
    in water, 227
Oil-base paint, 31, 33, 36, 37, 140, 142, 145, 148, 335
Oil-base polyurethane, 333
Oil finish, 330, 350, 351
Oil stain, 261
Oily rag, 332
On demand water heater. *See* Tankless water heater
Open-web joist, 156
Operator (window lever), 118
Organic mulch, 359
Oriented strand board, 162
Outbuilding, 355
Outlet(s)
    adding, 239
    drywall and, 16
    duplex, 234
    grounding, 233, 235, 238
    installing, 238
    outdoor, 238
    polarized plug, 234

screw-in, 234
taps, 234
tester, 232
wallpaper on cover, 42
Oven. *See* Stove
Overflow drain, 212
Overload, 231, 234, 239
Oxalic acid, 332

P

Paint
    acrylic, 140, 147
    additives, 36
    alkyd, 33, 140
    brushes, 140
    ceramic tiles and, 29, 33
    chemical removers, 28, 29
    cleanup, 37, 149
    in corners, 29
    elastomeric, 146, 147
    enamel, 33, 148, 335
    exterior, 30, 140
    flat, 141, 149
    high-gloss, 33, 141, 148, 149
    high-temperature, 370
    latex, 31, 32, 33, 140, 141, 145, 147, 148
    lead, 27, 142
    leftover, 37
    mix, for decorative techniques, 32
    oil-base, 31, 33, 36, 37, 140, 142, 145, 148, 335
    peeling, 27
    rollers, 140
    selecting and using, 30–31
    sprayer, 30–31
    stripping, 28–29, 142, 328
    vapor barrier, 272
    See also Housepainting; Painting
Painting
    avoiding brush marks, 34
    basement floor, 33
    brick, 146
    cabinets, 36
    ceramic tiles, 33
    contact lens and, 31

decorative techniques, 32
door edges, 35
furniture, 335
garage door, 148
masonry, 33
paneling, 34
primer, 140, 143
shingles, 141, 145
siding, 140, 145
sponge- and rag-, 32
staircase railings, 35
steel, 148
stenciling, 32
stove, 255
stucco, 146–147
trim, 34, 141
veneer, 36
over wallpaper, 27
walls, 26–27
woodwork, 34–35
See also Housepainting; Paint; Spray-painting
Palmetto bug, 258
Pane, window, 118, 124, 127
Paneling
    lighter, 76, 77
    painting, 34
    tongue-and-groove, 77
    wallpaper over, 39
    walls, 76
    warped, 76
    wood, 76–77
Pan-head screw, 182–183
Pantry, 364
Paper wasp, 365
Parquet floor, 55, 59
Particleboard
    finishing, 328
    substrate, 97
Paste activator, 40
Patio
    block, 343
    door, 128, 132, 134
    paver, 343
Paving
    concrete, 340–343, 345
    driveway, 343, 344–345
    patio, 343
    sidewalk, 341, 342

Index

Paving (continued)
    walkway, 340–341
PB (polybutylene) plastic
    pipe, 200, 201
Peeling paint, 27
Peephole, 137
Pest control, 362–365
Pesticide, 365
Pet odor, 64
Pickling, 35
Picture molding, 71
Picture window, 127
Pigeons, 362
Pilot light
    gas boiler, 276
    gas water heater, 229
Pine
    deck, 350
    finishing, 329
    odor, 349
Pipe(s)
    clamps, 311
    clogged, 208–209
    copper, 196–199
    cutting, 199, 200
    drywall and, 15
    fitting, 196, 198, 200
    frozen, 197
    galvanized, 196
    gluing, 201
    grounding, 232
    joints, 196
    lead, 196
    metal, 196–199, 200
    mineral deposits in, 197
    plastic, 194, 200–201, 225, 226, 287
Plain-sawn wood, 308
Plain-sliced face veneer, 309
Plaster
    ceiling, 24
    crack, 24
    wall, 22-23
Plastic
    laminate, 45, 96–97
    pipe, 194, 200–201, 225, 226, 287
    tube, 197
    weed barrier, 356, 358

Pleated fabric filter, 279
Pliers
    electrician's, 314
    groove-joint, 176
    slip-joint, 176
Plug
    adapter, 235
    polarized, 234
Plug-in element (electric range), 255
Plumbing
    fixtures, 222–223
    traps, 194–195, 209
    vents, 194–195, 203, 204
    water supply lines, 195, 197, 199
    See also Bathtub; Drain; Faucet; Pipe(s); Shower; Sink; Toilet; Water heater
Plunger, 176, 203, 208
Plunge router, 318
Plywood
    cutting, 307
    garage door, 148
    grades, 309
    laminate substrate, 97
    sheathing, 114
    tile backing, 47
    window surrounds, 183
Pocket door, 86
Polarized plug, 234
Pollution, 294–297
Polyester lining paper, 27
Polyurethane finish, 329, 330–331, 333
Polyurethane glue, 327
Polyvinyl acetate (PVA), 327, 336
Polyvinyl resin, 327
Pop-up stopper, 213
Porcelain
    bathtub, 222
    sink, 221, 222
Porch
    deck conversion to, 190–191
    screened, 190–191
    three-season, 191
    window, 191

Porcupine wire, 362
Post-and-beam
    construction, 169
Posthole, 354
Post(s)
    anchoring, 352
    arbor, 352
    deck, 178
    fence, 352, 353
    newel, 79
    pulling, 178
Power auger, 203
Power washer, 142, 143, 145, 146
Pressure-balancing faucet, 218
Pressure relief valve, 228
Pressure-treated wood, 346, 347, 352
Primer, 140, 143, 330, 335
Program flea killer, 364
Programmable thermostat, 278
Propane tank, 370
Pruning, 360, 361
Pry bar, 177
P-trap, 211, 213
Pull, cabinet, 92
Pump
    heat, 276–277
    radon, 297
    sump, 154
Putty knife, 176, 335
PVA. See Polyvinyl acetate
PVC (polyvinyl chloride)
    plastic pipe, 194, 200, 201, 225, 226, 287

Q-R

Quarter-sawn wood, 308
Rack, car roof, 163
Radial arm saw, 306
Radon, 297
Rag
    oily, 332
    painting with, 32, 37
    toxic, 37
Rail-style tile cutter, 50
Range. See Stove

Receptacle, electric. See Outlet(s)
Recessed lighting, 246–247
Redwood
    fence posts, 352
    odor, 349
    sealing, 350
Reel mower, 366
Refrigerator
    door, 256, 257
    moving, 257
    switch, 256
    water in, 256
Reinforced concrete, 345
Remodeling
    basement, 182–185
    deck/porch, 190–191
    design, 188–189
    heavy lifting in, 178–179
    regulations, 180–181
    storage, 186–187
Repellent, 351
Ribbed chrome tube, 197
Ridge vent, 292
Riding mower, 367
Right-handed door, 80
Ring-shank nail, 165
Road salt, 356
Rocking chair, 336
Rodents, 363
Rod saw, 50
Rolled-edge metal roof, 115
Roller
    cleaning, 37
    garage door, 139
    paint, 140
    patio door, 132
Roofs and roofing
    cedar, 114
    copper, 115
    dormers, 189
    dryer vent hood, 263
    electrical mast, 110
    felt, 110
    flashing, 110, 112
    installing, 110–111
    leaks, 110, 115
    metal, 115
    moss on, 114
    nails, 112, 113, 165

pigeons on, 362
safety, 111, 115
shakes, 114
tile, 115
vents, 291, 292–293
wood preservative on, 114
See also Gutter(s); Ice dam(s); Shingle(s)
Rope knot, 162, 163
Rotary-cut face veneer, 309
Rotogravure vinyl (rotovinyl), 66
Rough-sawn wood, 308
Rough Service bulb, 242
Router(s)
bits, 312, 319
chipping, 318
cleaning, 318
cutting, 315, 319
direction, 318
fixed-base versus plunge, 318
portable, 177
safety, 319
Rugs. *See* Carpets and carpeting
Rust
on bathtub, 223
drywall, 14
on fence, 353
stains, 27
on tools, 310

S

Safe, 187
Safe stripper. *See* Diabasic ester
Safety
asbestos, 25, 69
baluster, 78
bucket, 18
caustic chemical, 208
chipper-shredder, 368
contact lens, 31
electrical, 230, 234–235
equipment, 176–177
garage fire, 292
gear, 304–305

heavy lifting, 178
insecticide, 365
lead, 27, 142, 196
leftover paint, 37
mower, 366, 367
polyurethane, 331
pressure-treated wood, 346
roof, 111, 115
router, 319
sawing concrete wall, 185
soldering, 199
stripping, 29
tile cleaner, 52
torsion spring, 138
tree limb, 361
ventilation, 292
water heater pressure, 227
wood cutting board, 92
workshop, 304–305
Safety glasses, 305
Safety harness, 111
Salt
deposit, 153
road, 356
Sand, 215
Sandblasting, 142
Sanders and sanding
belt, 320, 321
block, 321, 335
deck, 350
drum, 320
drywall, 18–19, 26
frame joints, 321
grits, 321
liquid, 320
particleboard, 328
pine, 329
polyurethane, 330
Sandpaper, 321
Sash, 119, 123
Saw
band, 306
chop-, 177
circular, 177, 312, 315, 343
hack-, 315
hand-, 176, 312

jig-, 177
miter, 72, 74, 176, 177, 306
radial arm, 306
scroll, 306
table , 177, 306, 307, 316–317
underpowered, 316
Sawdust, 307
Scissors truss, 169
Score-and-whap method, 74
Scratches, 334
Screen door, 120
Screened porch, 190–191
Screw
door closer, 134
drywall, 12, 20
hinge, 84
pan-head, 182–183
plaster, 22
trim, 71, 79, 164
Screwdriver, 176, 312
Screw extractor, 215
Screw gun, 12, 182
Screw-in outlet, 234
Scroll saw, 306
Sealant
deck, 348, 350
driveway, 344
gutter, 112, 116
primer, 330
stucco, 146
Seamless gutter, 116
Security
exterior door, 135–137
window, 137
Sediment
filter for, 220
in water heater, 229
Semi-transparent stain, 351
Sensor, motion, 137, 252
Settling, 156
Shade, 360
Shake (lumber), 161
Shake (roofing), 114
Sharpening
chisel, 312
knife, 313
mower blade, 366, 367
screwdriver, 312

spade bit, 313
stone, 312, 313
Sheathing, roof, 114
Shed, storage, 355
Shed dormer, 189
Sheet vinyl, 66–68
Shelf
bookcase, 98
closet, 98, 186
shower, 51
support, 322
Shellac, 331, 332
Shingle(s)
asbestos, 105, 145
asphalt, 112–113
cedar, 103, 114
painting, 141, 145
repairing, 112–113
wood, 141
Shop vacuum, 177
Shovel, 368
Shower
cold, 218
diverter valve, 218
drain, 210
handle cover plate, 219
head, 218, 219
pressure-balancing faucet, 218
shelf, 51
Shutter, 108
Sidewalk, 341, 342
Siding
aluminum, 105, 145
asbestos shingle, 105
brick, 106–107
nailing, 102
painting, 145
stucco, 103
vinyl, 104
wood, 102–103, 140
Silicone, 223
Sill. *See* Windowsill
Sill plate, 152
Single-pane window, 127
Sink
bathroom, 203, 215
drain, 210, 212–213
gurgling, 203

Sink (continued)
kitchen, 210, 212, 214, 220–221
plunger, 208
sprayer, 214
stainless steel, 221
See also Faucet
Sinker nail, 165
Siphon hole, 205
Skip sheathing. *See* Spaced sheathing
Skylight, 121
Slab floor, 185, 273
Slate floor, 69
Sliding glass door, 132, 137
Slip-joint pliers, 176
Smart bulb, 249
Smell. *See* Odor(s)
Smoke, 285, 286
Snake (plumber's), 209
Snake (reptile), 363
Snap-trap, 363
Snips, aviation, 276, 277, 315
Snow thrower, 371
Sod, 357
Soffit vent, 271, 292
Soil, 356
Soil stack, 194, 203
Soldering, 196, 198–199
Solvent, 29
Solvent welding, 201
Soot, 282
Sound level, 304
Soundproofing
walls, 166
workshop, 306
Sound Transmission Class (STC), 166
Spaced sheathing, 114
Spade bit, 313
Speed Square, 173
Spigot, 369
Spike, gutter, 116
Spin-and-lock stopper, 212
Spiral-shank nail, 165
Spline, 120, 132
Split (lumber), 161
Sponge-and-rag painting, 32
Spontaneous combustion, 332

Sprayer
air, 31
paint, 30–31
sink, 214
Spray-painting
electrostatic, 36
metal cabinets, 36
walls, 30
Spray texture, 25
Spring
extension, 138
torsion, 138
Spring clamp, 311
Spring hinge, 129
Spring-metal weather-stripping, 275
Square footage, 180
Squeeze block, 346
SSD. *See* Sub-slab depressurization system
Stain
carpet, 64
dryer drum ink, 262
grease, 334
on marble, 223
rust, 27, 223
on vinyl window, 149
washing machine oil, 261
water, 60, 106, 112
Stainless steel sink, 221
Stains and staining (finishing). *See* Finshes and finishing
Stairs
baluster, 78
handrail, 35, 78
newel post, 79
squeaking, 79
Standing seam metal roof, 115
STC. *See* Sound Transmission Class
Steel
armored cable, 232
bit, 319
blade, 314
cutting, 315
door, 133, 148, 149
garage door, 138
gutter, 116

painting, 148
railing, 148
stainless, 221
studs, 182–183
wood grain over, 148
Stenciling, 32
Stepladder, 141, 145, 176
Stick chair, 337
Stock cabinet, 88
Stone
countertop, 97
foundation, 152
Stone, sharpening, 312, 313
Stop block, 322
Stopper
drain, 210–211, 212, 213
drop-down, 212
fixed, 212
pop-up, 213
spin-and-lock, 212
Storage
attic, 186
closet, 186
remodeling, 186–187
shed, 355
Storm door
closer, 134
sagging, 133
Storm window(s)
combination, 123
condensation on, 123
interior, 122
sealing, 123
tilting, 123
wood, 122
Stove
electric, 255
gas, 254–255
painting, 255
wood-burning, 284
Strap, nylon, 163
Streak, on ceiling, 26
Strike box, 136
Strike plate. *See* Latch plate
String trimmer, 368
Strippers and stripping
chemical, 28, 29
fast-acting, 29
paint, 28–29, 142, 328
water-base, 29, 328

woodwork, 28
Structure. *See* House structure
Stucco
to cover foam insulation 270
painting, 146–147
paint removal, 149
siding, 103
whitewashing, 146
Stud
steel, 182–183
wood, 160, 161, 166, 173
Sub-slab depressurization system (SSD), 297
Substrate, 97
Sulfur odor, 227
Sump ejector system, 206
Sump pump, 154
Sun-shading fabric, 120
Surface-mounted weatherstripping, 275
Surge protector, 232
Surveyor, 352
Switch
dimmer, 242, 243
drill, 322
light, 242, 243
refrigerator door, 256
three-way, 242
wallpaper on cover, 42
Synthetic-bristle brush, 330

T

Table
refinishing, 328
scratches on, 334
wobbly, 336
Table saw, 177, 306, 307, 316–317
Tankless water heater, 227
Tape
drywall, 16–18
Teflon, 196, 254
Tape measure, 170–171, 176
Tapered-tip brush, 333
Taps, electrical, 234
T-brace, 12, 13
Teflon tape, 196, 254

Temperature, 281
Tempering valve, 202
Tenon, 337
Termites, 365
Texture, ceiling, 24–25, 26
Thermogram, 273
Thermostat, 278, 281
Thin-kerf blade, 316
Thread, machine, 314
Three-way switch, 242
Threshold gasket, 132
Tie-down, 163
Tile
    roof, 115
    vinyl, 68
    See also Ceramic tile
Tile nipper, 50
Tilting window, 123
Tilt-in 2 x 4, 179
Toenailing, 174
Toilet
    basement, 204
    flanges, 207
    flapper, 204, 206
    installing, 206–207
    old, 222
    repairing, 202–205
    seat, 204
    slow-flushing, 205
    space, 206
    sweating, 202
    tank, 202, 204, 205
    tightening, 206
    trickling, 204
    unclogging, 203
    up-flush, 206
    water level, 204, 205
    wax ring, 207
Tongue-and-groove
    paneling, 77
Tool(s)
    belt, 177
    bench-top, 306
    carpentry, 176–177
    cutting, 314–315
    housepainting, 140–141
    motor, 324–325
    power, 318
    repairing, 310, 368–370
    rusty, 310

sharpening, 312–313
on wheels, 306
See also specific tools
Topsoil, 357, 360
Toxic rag, 37
Track lighting, 245
Transformer
    doorbell, 253
    See also Ballast
Translucent multicoat
    finish, 351
Trap (plumbing), 194–195,
    209, 211
Trap, rodent, 363
Tree
    limbs, 361
    planting, 360
    pruning, 360, 361
    roots, 361
Trim
    baseboard, 70, 73
    exterior, 108–109, 141
    gingerbread, 108
    installing, 72–75
    painting, 34, 141
    pickling, 35
    plaster around, 22
    repairing, 71, 109
    screw, 71, 79, 164
    types of, 70
    wood substitute, 72
    See also Molding
Trimmer, 368
Trisodium phosphate
    (TSP), 143, 145, 149,
    298, 299
Trowelable membrane, 48
Trucker's hitch knot, 162,
    163
Truss, 159, 169
TSP. *See* Trisodium
    phosphate
Tub
    laundry, 212
    See also Bathtub
Tube cutter, 199
Tuck pointing, 107
Twist (lumber), 160
Two-by-four, 160, 179

UFFI. *See* Urea formalde
    hyde foam insulation
Undercabinet lighting, 244
Universal motor, 324–325
Up-flush toilet, 206
Urea formaldehyde foam
    insulation (UFFI), 267
Utility knife, 176
U-value, 126

Valve seat, 215
Vapor barrier, 268, 272, 273,
    299
Varnish, 330, 331
    garage door, 149
    milky, 332
    pine, 329
    woodwork, 35
Veneer
    laminated lumber, 157
    painting, 36
    plywood, 309
Vent-free gas heater, 285
Vents and ventilation
    attic, 268, 271, 290–291,
        292
    chimney, 286
    dryer, 262, 263
    plumbing, 194–195, 203,
        204
    roof, 291, 292–293
    safety, 292
    soffit, 271, 292
    See also Fan
Venturi tube, 370
Vine, 356
Vinyl
    gutter, 116, 117
    jamb liner, 119
    sheet, 66–68
    siding, 104
    weatherstripping, 133
    window, 124, 149
    See also Vinyl floor
Vinyl floor
    installing, 66–67
    moisture on, 68

no-wax, 69
tile, 68
VOC's. *See* Volatile organic
    compounds
Volatile organic com-
    pounds (VOC's), 31

W–Y
Walkway, 340–341
Wallcovering.
    See Wallpaper
Wallpaper
    bubble in, 38
    choosing, 40
    corners, 43
    electrical outlets and, 42
    finishing touches, 42–43
    hanging, 40–41
    hole in, 38
    over paneling, 39
    painting, 27
    pattern matching, 43
    removing, 39
    repairing, 38
    seams, 38, 40
    sizing walls for, 39
    trimming, 42
    windows and, 42–43
Wall(s)
    basement, 22, 154
    bearing, 158
    bees in, 364
    cabinets, 90–91
    cleaning, 26
    concrete, 185
    cracks, 27
    curved, 15, 167
    exterior, 191
    fasteners, 23
    framing, 166–167
    half, 166
    hanging things on, 23
    insulation, 266, 271, 273
    non-bearing, 158, 188
    painting, 26–27
    paneling, 76
    plaster, 22–23
    sizing for paper, 39
    smoothing, 26

Index

Wall(s) (continued)
soundproof, 166
spray-painting, 30
studs, 160, 161, 166, 173, 182–183
support, 179
tiles, 44, 48–49
vapor barrier in, 273
wiring, 236, 237
See also Drywall; Wallpaper
Wall-to-wall carpeting, 63
Wane, 161
Warp, 161
Washer, 214
Washer-style faucet, 217
Washing machine
inlet valve, 260, 261
leaks, 261
oil stains from, 261
slow-filling, 260
water temperature, 261
Wasps, 365
Water
in basement, 154
filter, 220
inlet valve, 260, 261
in refrigerator, 256
repellent, 351
sandblasting with, 142
stain, 60, 106, 112
sulfur odor, 227
supply line, 195, 197, 199
See also Water heater
Water-base paint, 140
Water-base polyurethane, 333
Water-base stripper, 29, 328
Water-base varnish, 332
Water heater
buying, 226
electric, 226
fiberglass blanket, 227
gas, 229
lighting, 229
pressure, 227, 228
repairing, 228–229
sediment, 229
tankless, 227
Waterproofing, 155

Water-repellent
preservative, 351
Water-saving flapper, 206
Waterstone, 312
Watts, 248, 249
Wax ring, 207
Weatherproofing
air leaks, 274–275
concrete slab floor, 273
housewrap, 272
vapor barrier, 268, 272, 273
See also Insulation; Weatherstripping
Weatherstripping
door, 132, 275
spring-metal, 275
surface-mounted, 275
vinyl, 133
window, 123, 278
Weeds
Bermuda grass, 356
preventing, 358
Weep gap, 123
Weight, on beam, 159
Well
dry, 154
screen, 215
Wheel
grindstone, 324
tools on, 306
White glue, 327
Whitewash
brick, 142
stucco, 146
Window box, 107
Window(s)
air conditioner, 288–289
aluminum, 124
argon-filled, 126
basement, 184–185
bay, 189
casement, 118
condensation on, 123, 300, 301
drywall around, 15
energy efficiency, 126–127
glass, 118, 123, 126
insulation, 271

jamb, 119, 124
lever, 118
operator, 118
pane, 124, 127
picture, 127
porch, 191
repairing, 118–121
replacing, 124–125
sash, 119, 123
screen, 120
shutter, 108
skylight, 121
vinyl, 124, 149
visibility, 137
wallpaper and, 42–43
well, 184
wood, 122, 124
See also Storm window(s)
Windowsill, 108
Wire brush, 148, 337
Wires and wiring
aluminum, 236
connectors, 236
copper, 236
dishwasher, 258
doorbell, 252
drywall and, 15
in foam insulation, 236
grounding, 232–235, 237–241
wall, 236, 237
Wood
beams, 156, 157
bleaching, 332
for burning, 282
cabinets, 36
cord, 282
cutting board, 92, 94
engineered, 162
fence post, 352
filler, 335
garage door, 138, 139
glue, 326, 327
ladder, 141
painting, 34–35, 140
paneling, 76–77
pickling, 35
plain-sawn, 308
preservative, 114, 351
quarter-sawn, 308

rough-sawn, 308
shingles, 141
shrinkage, 77, 308
siding, 102–103, 140
splitting, 175
stripping, 28
studs, 160, 161, 166, 173
substitute, 72
treated, 346, 347, 352, 353
varnished, 35
window, 122, 124
See also Cedar; Hardwood; Lumber; Plywood; Trim; Wood floor; Woodwork
Wood floor
choosing, 54–55
concrete under, 56
finish, 60–61
hole in, 59
installing, 56–57
kitchen, 56
refinishing, 61
repairing, 58–60
solid, 54
squeaking, 59
Wood-graining kit, 148
Wood I-beam, 156, 162
Woodpecker, 362
Woodpile, 363
Woodstove, 284
Woodwork
built-ins, 98–99
painting, 34–35
staining, 35
stripping, 28
types of, 70
See also Trim
Workbench, 306
Workshop
dust, 307
noise, 304, 306
safety, 304–305
small, 306–307
soundproofing, 306
See also Tool(s)
Work triangle, 188
Yellow glue, 327, 336